HUGO GROTIUS

ANNALS OF THE WAR IN THE LOW COUNTRIES

BIBLIOTHECA LATINITATIS NOVAE

www.bln-series.eu
www.upers.kuleuven.be/en/bibliotheca-latinitatis-novae

The series *Bibliotheca Latinitatis Novae* offers Latin literature from the later Renaissance and the Early Modern period. By combining each critical Latin text with an English translation, an historical introduction, and notes, *Bibliotheca Latinitatis Novae* makes texts accessible to specialists and general readers alike.

Submissions or questions can be sent by e-mail to publish@lup.be

HUGO GROTIUS

ANNALS OF THE WAR IN THE LOW COUNTRIES

EDITED WITH TRANSLATION AND INTRODUCTION

BY

JAN WASZINK

LEUVEN UNIVERSITY PRESS

This publication has been made possible by the generous financial assistance of:
Louise Thijssen-Schoute Stichting
Hendrik Muller Fonds
Gilles Hondius Foundation
Vrijzinnige Fondsen
Stichting Fonds voor de Geld- en Effectenhandel
NWO (VENI-grant 2004-2008)
Polish National Science Centre, project no. 2019/35/B/HS1/04039

ISBN 978 94 6270 351 3
eISBN 978 94 6166 485 3
D / 2023 / 1869 / 11
NUR: 621
https://doi.org/10.11116/9789461664853

Lay-out: Crius Group
Cover design: Friedemann
Cover illustration: Portrait of Hugo Grotius. Bary, Hendrik (ca. 1640–1707) Mierevelt, Michiel van (1567 – 1641). Teylers Museum. https://picryl.com/media/portret-van-hugo-de-groot-67cbf6

GPRC
Guaranteed
Peer Reviewed
Content
www.gprc.be

CONTENTS

PREFACE vii

INTRODUCTION 1
1. Hugo Grotius' *Annales et Historiae* 1
2. The AH and the States of Holland, the Revolt and the Truce Conflicts 2
  2.1. The main setting 2
  2.2. The publication plans for the AH in 1612–13 3
  2.3. The States and History 5
  2.4. The Truce Conflicts 9
3. Hugo Grotius 13
4. Tacitism and Reason of State in the *Annales et Historiae* 20
5. The Statesman-Historian: Grotius and the historian's role in society 25
6. Controversial content and the non-publication of the AH in 1612–1613 29
7. Tacitism 34
  7.1. Tacitist content and ideas 34
  7.2. Syntax and forms of Grotius' imitation of Tacitus' literary style 44
  7.3. Compositorial aspects and narrative structure 49
    7.3.1. Is there dramatic structuring in the AH? 50
  7.4. Conclusion: Grotius' imitation of Tacitus 56
8. Some important characters in the AH 57
  8.1. William the Silent 57
  8.2. Philip II 62
  8.3. Robert Dudley, Earl of Leicester 65
9. Other aspects 67
  9.1. Grotius and the Twelve Years' Truce 67
  9.2. The AH's relationship with Grotius' other work 72
  9.3. Grotius as Historian 79
  9.4. Is there a sense of 'Netherlands' or 'Dutch' nationhood in the *Annales*? 80
10. Sources of the *Annales et Historiae* 82
11. The composition and reception of the *Annales et Historiae* 90
  11.1. Original composition and manuscripts 90
  11.2. Reception during Grotius' lifetime 93

11.3. The survival of the manuscripts 96
11.4. The printed editions of 1657–1658 99
11.5. The AH and the Vatican Index of Forbidden Books 1657–1659 102
11.6. Translations 104
11.7. Further reception, 17th–21st centuries 106
11.8. Scholarship on the text 116
12. Conclusion 117

THIS EDITION 123
1. Principles of this edition 123
1.1. Sigla 125
1.2. Neo-Latin aspects 125
2. About this translation 127

SUMMARIES OF *ANNALES* 1–5 359
Appendix 1. The extant manuscripts of the *Historiae* 367
Appendix 2. The Vatican Index reports 377
Appendix 3. Biographical epilogues on Philip II by Grotius and by Van Meteren 391
Appendix 4. The Nijmegen copy of Pompeio Giustiniani's *Bellum Belgicum* 397
Appendix 5. Pieter Feddes van Harlingen's 'Monster' print of 1619 401
Appendix 6. Sententiae and epigrams in *Annales* 1 and 2 405
Appendix 7. Book summaries by the editors of 1657 409

BIBLIOGRAPHY 415

ILLUSTRATION CREDITS 433

INDEX TO THE INTRODUCTION 435

INDEX OF NAMES TO THE TRANSLATION AND NOTES 441

PREFACE

Although Hugo Grotius counts among the great names of the western intellectual tradition this does not mean that all of his works are readily accessible (let alone in reliable editions or translations). This is particularly true with respect to Grotius' historical oeuvre, of which many are hardly aware that it was ever written in the first place. However the situation for this part of Grotius' oeuvre has slowly improved over the past few decades, and the present book aspires to be a significant step in this process. The historical chapters of *De Iure Praedae* had been accessible ever since the 1868 edition by Hamaker and the translations derived from it. The short *De Antiquitate Reipublicae Batavicae* was available in a reprinted old Dutch translation, and subsequently in an edition with new translations into Dutch and English by a group including the present editor in 1995 and 2000 (for BLN). The current edition of the *Annales* is the first since 1658 (although it still leaves the 500-page *Historiae* to be desired). An edition of Grotius' introduction to the *Historia Gotthorum* is in preparation, also for BLN. On the level of the study and interpretation of Grotius' political and legal thought, the present editor believes that the *Annales* comprise a reminder of the importance of reason-of-state thought for Grotius' thought in general; a position argued in further detail in the Introduction.

This book is indebted to the support of, and discussions with, many friends and colleagues.

When I completed the Dutch translation by the end of 2013, the decision to proceed with a Latin/English version for BLN was already made. I am greatly indebted to Cynthia Damon for editing my English translation of Grotius' Book 1 from her profound acquaintance with Tacitus' style. Martine van Ittersum, Henk Nellen and Lisa Kattenberg provided many valuable comments and additions to my introduction. Over the years I benefited from input or discussions of this project with Marc van der Poel, Daan den Hengst, Jacob Soll, Robert von Friedeburg, Geoffrey Parker, Peter Borschberg, Mark Somos, Victor Enthoven, Chris Coppens, Saul Bermejo, Randall Lesaffer, Laurens Winkel, Hans Blom, Jaap Nieuwstraten, Ingmar Vroomen, Marianne Klerk, Lies van Aelst, Kate Rudy, Jacques Bos, Liesbeth de Wreede, Hans Cools, Herman Schwedt, Anna Laskowska, Amaranth Feuth, Christoph Pieper, Wouter Kool, Hanneke de Bruin, Marc Beerens, Helmer Helmers, and Guus van Breugel. I am especially indebted to Roek Vermeulen and Manon van der Loo who read the entire translation and suggested improvements. I thank my children Johanna and Will for their interest and support, as well as my mother Vera Swelheim; and finally my father, Jan Waszink, who also read the translation, suggested improvements and never failed to support the project with his active interest and encouragement. I dedicate this book to his memory.

HVGO GROTIVS,
Reginæ Regnique Suedici Consiliarius, eorundemque ad Regem Christianissimum Legatus ordinarius. quondam Sÿndicus Roterodamensis, ejusdemque Urbis in Conventu Ordinum Hollandiæ & Westfrisiæ Delegatus.

INTRODUCTION

1.
Hugo Grotius' *Annales et Historiae*

In 1612 the young humanist and lawyer Hugo Grotius (1583–1645) finished his grand, 600-page *Annales et Historiae de rebus Belgicis* or History of the Dutch Revolt which he had worked on for more than a decade, on a commission from the States of Holland and West-Friesland. After consultation of a review committee the States appear to have shelved the publication plans, and not much is heard of the work until its eventual publication by Grotius' sons in 1657, twelve years after its author's death. Why did the States leave the work unpublished? And what does the answer to that question tell us about the nature and purposes of Grotius' text, and the context in which it was written? In the first section of this introduction (§ 1–6) this will be the leading question to approach the work.[1]

In 1601 Grotius had been commissioned by the States of Holland and West-Friesland (further: States of Holland) to write a history of the revolt in the Low Countries against the Spanish Habsburg monarchy. In 1604 the States appointed Grotius as their official historiographer, as successor to Janus Dousa who had died earlier that year. In this role Grotius composed, among other works, the *Annales et Historiae* (further: AH), a history in 23 books of the Dutch Revolt up to the Twelve Years' Truce in 1609. For us the sizeable work remains valuable and intriguing for its idiosyncratic and un-glorifying approach of the Dutch Revolt, for its specific, contemporary interpretation of that revolt, and its accomplished imitation of the Tacitean model of style. The title is a direct reference to the *Annales* and the *Historiae* by the Roman historian Cornelius Tacitus (*c.* AD 55–*c.* 115) and makes the 'Tacitist' register of Grotius' work very explicit from the outset of the book. It also plays on the work's late-humanist interests and concerns, as well as on its particular conception of historiography. This introduction will emphasise the Tacitist aspect of the AH since it seems to be of such predominant importance; but this is not to imply that approaches to the AH from the perspective of other classical authors from Grotius' immense reading would be fruitless. The purpose of an edition like this is precisely to enable such research.

Apart from its not being published in its own time, an aspect that requires clarification is the relationship with Grotius' other works from the same years.

[1] In the (few) available studies of the AH before the present editor's research, this aspect of the work has hardly been addressed.

Combining scarce data from the correspondence and the surviving parts of the AH's manuscripts (see § 11.1 below), a tentative estimate can be made that the five books of the *Annales* were composed mainly in the years 1604–1605, and the 18 books of *Historiae* between 1606 and 1612, the greater part of those possibly having been completed by 1608. This means that the AH were composed not long after the *Parallelon Rerumpublicarum* (1602), and alongside *De Iure Praedae* (written 1604–1606, but also unpublished at the time) and *De Antiquitate Reipublicae Batavicae* of 1610. These works however are all distinctly more normative, patriotic and optimistic in tone than the AH, while also less profound in terms of historical analysis. Nevertheless the AH have until recently not received too much attention in the scholarship, a relative neglect due on the one hand to the States of Holland's omission to publish the work when it was submitted to them, and to a 19th-century positivist disdain for 'literary' history on the other.

The *Annales et Historiae* were eventually published by Grotius' sons in 1657–8. This edition appeared in three formats and seems to have sold well (given the numbers currently available on the antiquarian book market), but no subsequent editions of the Latin text appeared. A French translation was published in 1662, an English one in 1665, and a Dutch one in 1681. The present volume presents an edition and translation of the first part of this voluminous work, the *Annales*, which relate the roughly three decades from *c.*1559 to 1588 in a condensed manner, by way of introduction to the longer *Historiae,* which deal with the two decades from 1588 to 1609 in eighteen books.[2]

2. The AH and the States of Holland, the Revolt and the Truce Conflicts

2.1. *The main setting*

The *Annales et Historiae* were commissioned from Grotius in November 1601 by the States of Holland and West-Friesland, the self-proclaimed sovereign assembly that acted as government of the province of Holland (the area of the present-day provinces of North and South Holland). Holland in turn was the leading province in a federal republic made up of seven nominally independent provinces, which had very recently emerged out of a rebellion against their sovereign head, the Habsburg Philip II (habitually referred to as the king of Spain, although that title was technically irrelevant in the Low Countries). The Act of Abjuration (*Acte van Verlatinghe*) of 1581 by the States-General had officially declared Philip stripped of his sovereign rights, and after several attempts to find a new sovereign head had to come to nothing, the provisional republican government had become permanent. From *c.*1590 onwards, under the joint leadership of William of Orange's son

[2] In the *Ordinum Pietas* of 1613 (§ 191) and in a letter of 1607 to N.N. (*Briefwisseling* vol. 1 p. 85 & n. 4) Grotius places the beginning of the war at 1572.

Maurice and Johan van Oldenbarnevelt, leading voice in the States of Holland, the new republic managed to successfully roll back the Spanish re-conquest of the preceding decade, at least in the North, and negotiations about a temporary Truce with its former overlord were opened in 1607. This 'Twelve Years' Truce', concluded in 1609, established the United Provinces *de facto* as an independent power. The phenomenon of a new state on the European stage, and a republic at that, was unheard of, and constituted one of the greatest political and historical marvels of the time.

In the year 1600 Prince Maurice's States army had achieved an unexpected but internationally resounding victory over a large Habsburg army at Nieuwpoort on the Flemish coast. Although the larger campaign of which this battle was a part became a failure, it boosted self-consciousness in the Northern Netherlands. The new state needed the history of its birth written down in a grand manner, and the well-connected scholarly prodigy Grotius was the obvious candidate to become its historiographer. When Janus Dousa died in 1604, Grotius succeeded him as the States' official historiographer and continued the work on the AH.

The fact that the AH was written in Latin does not indicate that Grotius and the States envisaged only a purely scholarly and/or international audience for it; Grotius' interventions in the domestic politico-religious debate in the Republic in the same years, *Ordinum Pietas* of 1613 and *De Imperio Summarum Potestatum* (composed in 1617) are also written in Latin and were clearly directed primarily at clergymen and administrators in the Republic as well as educated sections of the general public. A similar intended audience can be assumed for the *Annales et Historiae*. The imitation of Tacitus suggests a desire both to recommend the work by following an international literary fashion, and to give the contemporary history of the Low Countries the status and weight of world history, just as Tacitus' account had done for the Julio-Claudian period.

2.2. *The publication plans for the AH in 1612–13*

In 1612 Grotius submitted his history of the Revolt up to the conclusion of the Truce of 1609 to the States. As appears from their resolution, the States now appointed a committee of two city burgomasters, Paulus van Asperen from Dordrecht and Diederick Bas from Amsterdam to assess work's fitness for publication.[3] Unfortunately, neither a report by these gentlemen nor any other informa-

[3] *Resolutien van de Heeren Ridderschap, Edelen ende Steden van Hollandt ende West-Vriesland, in hare Ed. Mog. Vergaderinghe in den Hage, genomen van den 12. July in den Jare 1612*, p. 242 (4 October 1612): 'Den Heere van Oldenbarnevelt, Advocaet, vermaendt hebbende dat den Fiscael Grotius in sijne handen gelevert had de Kronijck ofte Historye, by hem beschreven; dan dat noodigh ware de selve te doen visiteren, om te letten of dienstlijck ware de selve uyt te laten gaen ofte op te houden; zyn daar toe gecommittert de Heeren Asperen ende Bas, Gecommitteerde Raden; ende met eenen aen den Fiscael gedaen hebbende de laetste ses hondert guldens van de achtien hondert guldens hem voor 't voltrecken van het voorsz. werck geaccordeert by Ordonnantie op Mierop': 'Lord Oldenbarnevelt

tion regarding their conclusions is known, but the AH remained unpublished at the time. Consequently we do not know with certainty the reasons why the book was not published in 1612–13.[4] However, over the years and in several installments the States had awarded at least 1200, perhaps even 1800 guilders to Grotius for the composition of the work.[5] Given this amount of money, and the time invested by Grotius it seems unlikely that this non-publication was incidental.[6] It seems significant that the resolution just mentioned refers explicitly to a 'need' to establish whether it is better 'to publish or to withhold the work'. The phrase also reminds us that this decision was with the States, not Grotius, which is only logical given that the work was commissioned and paid for by the States. As we shall see below, the States monitored publications related to their policies very closely.

Therefore the present editor believes that, formally or informally, a *choice* was made at this time not to publish the AH, and that this choice is rooted in the work's content and/or nature. If this is true, an explanation of this decision must be the main clue to the interpretation of the AH in relation to its immediate contemporary context, and therefore this will be our main concern in this introduction. In order to propose this joint 'explanation with interpretation-in-context' (§ 6), we shall consider in the next chapters the States' supervision of historiography,

having announced that the advocate-fiscal Grotius had delivered the Chronicle or History written by him into his hands; then that it was necessary to have it investigated in order to see whether it were beneficial to publish or to withhold it, this task has been assigned to the Lords Asperen and Bas, Counsellors. At the same time the remaining six hundred guilders of the 1800 agreed upon for completing the work have been given to the advocate-fical via an order to Mierop'. See also H. Nellen, *Hugo Grotius. A Lifelong Struggle for Peace in Church and State,* Leiden (Brill) 2015, p. 179. A fascinating detail in this respect is that in the same year 1612 Grotius and Van Asperen were competing for an appointment in the Supreme Court (Hoge Raad); an appointment won by Van Asperen; see Nellen, *Hugo Grotius* p. 148. Interestingly, Bas was also the dedicatee of the Dutch Tacitist Pieter Corneliszoon Hooft's history *Hendrik de Groote* (on Henry IV of France) in 1626. See S. Groenveld, 'Pieter Corneliszoon Hooft en de geschiedenis van zijn eigen tijd' in: id., *Hooft als historieschrijver. Twee Studies*, Weesp (Eureka) 1981, pp. 7–46, 7.

[4] It seems conceivable that this lack of recorded opinions on the AH within the States' orbit is connected with the fact that since his appointment as pensionary of Rotterdam in the spring of 1613, Grotius was himself a member of the States; which may have added to the delicacy of the book's situation if leading States members were uncomfortable with some of its contents.

[5] For further details see § 11.1.

[6] Nellen, *Hugo Grotius* pp. 179–180 examines the evidence without proposing one explanation, but suggests that the non-publication was unintentional and merely a result of Grotius' busy involvement in political business from 1613 onwards, possibly aggreviated by the difficulties following the publication of *Ordinum Pietas*. According to Nellen it is unlikely that the committee gave a negative advice because Grotius never refers to such criticism, which he would certainly have done if it had existed. Further on however he suggests that the committee may instead have made a list of remarks and improvements to the text, although for a such a document there is even less evidence that it ever existed. For comparison, Grotius' manuscript treatise *De Iure Praedae* (or *De Indis*), written to defend the Dutch East India Company's capture of the Portuguese carrack Santa Catarina in 1603, also remained unpublished, but in this case Grotius made sure one chapter was published separately as *De Mari Libero* in 1609; see further § 9.1 below.

Grotius' biography, the ideas behind his role as a scholar in the service of the government, and aspects of the AH's content, with special emphasis on its relationship to reason-of-state thought and 'Tacitism'.[7]

In any case, after 1612 Grotius by no means abandoned the project. A letter of April 1613 from Isaac Casaubonus (1559–1614) to Jacques-Auguste de Thou (on whom see § 5 below) shows that Grotius carried the manuscript with him on the embassy to England in that year (see § 3), with the apparent aim of discussing the work or its revision with fellow scholars like Casaubonus;[8] thus providing another indication that loss of urgency was not a cause of the non-publication. Grotius kept working on a revision of the text at various intervals after this period; the main revisions in the work took place around 1622 and in 1635–1637. Due however to difficulties with the publisher in 1637 and the following years,[9] the work appeared only long after his death, in 1657. The edition is a stout volume of almost 600 pages. By that time, however, it was not really a work of contemporary history any more, and the AH had to compete with Pieter Corneliszoon Hooft's similarly grand and Tacitist history of the early Revolt, which however was written in Dutch and thus more easily accessible. For a more detailed discussion of the composition and publication of the AH, see § 11 below.

2.3. *The States and History*

The States of Holland took an active approach towards scholarly publications and debates in their province, both with respect to the content of printed books and to the organisation of the scholarly community assembled in 'their' university at Leiden.[10] A clear pattern of supervision and intervention emerges. Although a full

[7] As to method, the above explanation of Grotius' possible intentions and their effects in the Dutch context of the Truce years, is based on the 'Cambridge School' approach as described in e.g. J.H. Tully, 'The pen is a mighty sword. Quentin Skinner's analysis of politics', in: *British Journal of Political Science*, vol. 13 no. 4 (1983) pp. 489–509, and J.D. BeDuhn, 'The Historical Assessment of Speech Acts: Clarifications of Austin and Skinner for the study of religions', in: *Method and Theory in the Study of Religion*, vol. 14 no. 1 (2002) pp. 84–113. My explanation then extends this approach by also taking stylistic and formal aspects of the text into account as meaningful elements for the explanation of text-in-context. Beduhn's article elaborates (among others) the impossibility of strict proof of a particular intention with respect to historical actors, which has a particular relevance in the present case where meaning is ascribed to the fact that a particular action (the publication) was *omitted*. The convincing force of explanations like the one above lies in the fact that they explain a number of documented facts (controversial content in that context, the peculiar style, the non-publication) *in conjunction*.

[8] See further in § 11.2 and note below.

[9] See J. Waszink, 'Hugo Grotius' Annales et Historiae de rebus Belgicis from the Evidence in his Correspondence, 1604–1644', in: *LIAS* 31–2 (2004), pp. 249–267.

[10] For the example of the States' handling of the debates rising from the publication of Justus Lipsius' *Politica* in 1589–1591 and the ensuing controversy with Dirck Coornhert, see Waszink, 'Introduction' to Lipsius, *Politica*, pp. 115–120.

discussion of this topic goes beyond the purposes of this introduction, some cases related to that of the AH need to be mentioned for context.

It has been noted that from around 1600 there was a notable rise of interest in the early history of the revolt.[11] The interference by the States of Holland with the historiography of the Revolt started right when the first general work in Dutch on the topic was published in their province. In 1599 they confiscated almost the entire print-run of *Memorien der Belgische ofte Nederlantsche Historie van onsen tijden*[12] ('Memoirs of the Low Countries History of our Time') by Emanuel van Meteren (1535–1612) from the printer Vennecool at Delft because parts of the book's contents displeased the regents.[13] From the subsequent censure of the work it appears that their main objections were against Van Meteren's 4-page *Staet* ('Present state') of the United Provinces supplied at the end of the narrative,[14] against Van Meteren's treatment of Count Hohenlohe, one of Maurice's most trusted (but impetuous) generals, and against the disclosure of documents relating to negotiations with the English in 1598.[15] Hohenlohe himself had also submitted a protest against the book. The States had a replacement for the *Staet* printed, which was made available to owners of the confiscated edition.

Also, it seems that Van Meteren and his printer had a disagreement about the title of the work, shortly *before* it was confiscated, and that the first title words (*Memorien der*) were first removed, then re-instated not in capital letters but in

[11] J. Pollmann, '"Brabanters do fairly resemble Spaniards after all." Memory, Propaganda and Identity in the Twelve Years' Truce', in: J. Pollmann & Andrew Spicer (eds.), *Public Opinion and Changing Identities in the Early Modern Netherlands*. Essays in Honour of Alastair Duke, Leiden (Brill) 2007, pp. 211–228.

[12] *Memorien der Belgische ofte Nederlantsche Historie, van onse tijden. Inhoudende hoe de Nederlanden aenden anderen gehecht, ende aen Spaengien ghecomen zijn* [etc], Delft 1599. The printing history of this work is extremely complicated, and German and Latin reworkings of Van Meteren's narrative (printed, it seems, without Van Meteren's approval) appeared earlier (1593) than the Dutch editions; see L. Brummel, *Twee ballingen 's lands tijdens onze opstand tegen Spanje; Hugo Blotius (1534–1608) Emanuel van Meteren (1535–1612)*, Den Haag 1972, 81 sqq. A useful list of editions is available at https://dutchrevolt.leiden.edu/dutch/geschiedschrijvers/Pages/Meteren.aspx

[13] For a discussion, see Brummel, *Twee ballingen*, 91–116 (Brummel does not seem to have been aware of the copy in Lund); C. Ridderikhoff, 'Een aristocratische geschiedenis van de Opstand: Grotius' "Annales et Historiae de rebus Belgicis". *De Zeventiende Eeuw,* 10–2 (1994), 277–291, esp. pp. 278–280. See also J. van der Steen, *Memory Wars in the Low Countries* 1566–1700, Leiden (Brill) 2015, pp. 57–61 who discusses opposition against the book from the Reformed Synod in South-Holland over the subsequent decade, and their attempt to have Van Meteren's history 'replaced' by the one that was being prepared by Paullus Merula as the States-General's official historiographer (see below). However Van der Steen seems unaware of the revision of the work in 1599 and presents the revision process as only leading to the officially approved (posthumous) edition of 1614, while leaving the intermediate supplemented editions (published with or without Van Meteren's collaboration) unmentioned.

[14] Van Meteren, *Memorien* etc. 1599, pp. 432r–433v. In the revised version of 1599 (*Historie*) the *Staet* has grown to 8 pages, 432r–[435]v (several errors in the page numbering appear within this short section). Digital copies of both the *Memorien* and the *Historien* are available on Google Books.

[15] See Brummel, *Twee ballingen*, p. 105.

small italic print. At some point the confiscated books were returned to the printer, who was only allowed to sell these outside the Republic, and subsequent re-binding and partial re-printing of this stock led to a bewildering range of slightly different copies, now under a different title, *Belgische ofte Nederlantsche Historie van onsen tijden* ('Low Countries History of our time'). This matters for our purposes because Grotius' copy as preserved in Lund UL has the intermediate variant of the title page (with *Memorien der* in small italics), indicating that he was one of the early owners of the book before it disappeared from the market.[16] A new, entirely revised version of the book was printed later in 1599 also under the same new title.[17] At the same time (February 1599) the States acted to prevent the sale of a short pamphlet, anonymously printed under a sensational title (*Book of Secrets*... etc.) containing several items of supposedly sensitive information picked from Van Meteren's *Memorien*.[18]

Van Meteren's case contains several direct links to Grotius' work. Grotius must not only have been well informed about the affair around the book; but that he was among the early owners of a copy squares with his occupations and connections in The Hague and Delft in 1599.[19] The copy now in Lund UL contains manuscript annotations in Grotius' hand. Another *Staet* of the United Provinces in Latin, by the Leiden Law professor and then official historiographer of the States-General Paullus Merula (1558–1607), would be included in Petrus Scriverius' annotated re-edition of Grotius' *De Antiquitate Reipublicae Batavicae* of 1630. Grotius' *Annals*, edited here, also conclude with a *Staet* of the Dutch Republic (5.48–68).[20]

In the year 1600 the States-General's historiographer, the same Paullus Merula just mentioned, submitted the first part of his own *Historia Belgica* on the Revolt and its causes to its commissioners. The States-General however refrained from publishing the work, apparently because it provided more detail on the legal

16 Brummel, *Twee ballingen* pp. 110–111, who describes a copy in the Provinciale Bibliotheek Friesland with this title page (and the further text entirely as in the original print-run).

17 For a quick identification, the new edition can be recognised by the fact that it misses the line *Toegheschreven den Staten, Steden ende inghesetenen der Nederlanden* near the bottom of the engraved title page. The main text was typeset again in its entirety; although the division of the text over the pages runs almost exactly parallel, there is a myriad of orthographical differences as well as textual revisions; for an impression see the notes to the fragment in appendix 3.

18 See Brummel, *Twee Ballingen*, pp. 105–108.

19 At the end of a short letter dated 13 December 1608 (*Briefwisseling* vol. 17 Supplement, no. 152A), Johan Boreel (residing in Middelburg, Zeeland, at the time) writes to Grotius in The Hague that he had 'not yet missed his copy of Van Meteren,' thus implying that the book has been borrowed by Grotius some time ago. It is not clear which title by Van Meteren he is referring to, and why and how Grotius had borrowed it. Grotius and Boreel probably lived with the same landlord, Johannes Wtenbogaert in The Hague, until their recent weddings (Boreel in June 1608, Grotius in July), so possibly the loan dated from that period?

20 Which makes it attractive to hypothesise that the new *Staet* for Van Meteren's work was also composed by Merula, given the latter's position as the States-General's historiographer (which he held since 1598).

relationship between the Low Countries and the whole of the German empire than the Generalty found it expedient to put a public spotlight on at that time.[21]

In 1611 the States-General commissioned the Leiden professors of history Johannes Meursius (1579–1639) and Dominicus Baudius (1561–1613) to write histories of the truce negotiations; their books appeared in 1612 and 1613 respectively.[22] Meursius' book met with resistance from the orthodox Calvinist audience and had to be reworked into a new book, which also covered a much longer period and came from the press in 1614.[23] Although the States wanted Meursius to continue his histories, orthodox resistance against this commission led to its cancellation in 1620. Meursius eventually moved to Denmark and became Christian IV's historiographer and professor of history at the Academy at Sorø.[24]

These cases make it clear that both the States of Holland and the States-General actively initiated, monitored and influenced publications on the recent history of the Republic. An further interesting case in this connection is Grotius' own *Ordinum Pietas* of 1613, a long scholarly treatise to justify the States' religious policy. The appearance of the book illustrates the active position that the States of Holland aspired to in the political *and* the learned debates on the religious controversy of the time.[25] The university at Leiden, instituted in 1575 by William of Orange and the States, and was never far away, both physically and mentally, from the seat of the government at The Hague. Its Law faculty was an important breeding ground for administrative officials (such as Grotius himself, see below) and both intellectually and in terms of professorial appointments there were close ties between the provincial and the city governments on the one side and the university on the other.[26] These ties achieved an acute relevance amid the tensions

[21] S. Haak, *Paullus Merula 1558–1607*, Zutphen 1901, p. 66 sqq.; see also notes 20 and 215.

[22] J. Meursius, *Rerum Belgicarum liber unus, in quo Induciarum historia,* Leiden (Elzevir) 1612; D. Baudius, *Libri tres de Induciis belli Belgici*, Leiden (Elzevir) 1613; repr. 1617, 1629 (transl. into Dutch: *Van 't bestant des Nederlantschen Oorlogs drie boecken,* Amsterdam 1616).

[23] J. Meursius, *Rerum Belgicarum libri quatuor in quibus Ferdinandi Albani sexennium belli Belgici principium,* Leiden (Elzevir), 1614.

[24] E. Haitsma Mulier, G. van der Lem and P. Knevel, *Repertorium van Geschiedschrijvers in Nederland 1500–1800,* The Hague 1990, nos. 334 and 334a. Meursius was a friend of Grotius' from their undergraduate years in Leiden in the 1590s. See Nellen, *Hugo Grotius*, pp. 41–43, 54, 58, 60–65; R. Fruin, 'Meursius' geschiedenis van het bestand', in: id., *Verspreide Geschriften* vol.VII, The Hague, 1903, pp. 449–453.

[25] For overviews, see J. Spaans, 'Public opinion or cultural celebration of concord? Politics, religion and society in competition between the chambers of rhetoric at Vlaardingen in 1616', in: J. Pollmann & Andrew Spicer (eds.), *Public Opinion and Changing Identities in the Early Modern Netherlands.* Essays in Honour of Alastair Duke, Leiden (Brill) 2007, pp. 188–209, esp. 198–202; Rabbie, 'Introduction' in: Grotius, *Ordinum Pietas* and Nellen, *Hugo Grotius*, esp. pp. 171–177, and further literature. referenced there.

[26] See among others J. Waszink, 'University and Court: the case of Leiden, 1572–1618' in B. Lindberg (ed.), *Early Modern Academic Culture*, Stockholm 2019 (Kungl. vitterhets historie och antikvitets akademien, Konferenser 97), pp. 139–160, where further literature is given.

of the Truce period. With respect to the nature of the States' involvement and interference with the academic controversy, it is important to note that after the appointment of a professor with Remonstrant (Arminian) leanings as successor to Arminius, the States took care that when his opponent Gomarus left his chair in protest and a successor had to be found, this successor was one of Gomarist (Counter-Remonstrant) convictions too, in order to maintain the balance.[27]

Another perspective relevant to the relationship between government and historiography is that of the 'Memory Culture' branch of research. Recent investigations by, among others, Judith Pollmann and Jasper van der Steen into the 17th-century reception of the history of the revolt have focused on the roles which the memory of the Revolt played in the creation of the identities and self-perceptions of the various groups in society in North and South (including 'national' identities). They also asked why and how North and South developed so fundamentally different memories and understandings of the revolt during the 17th century, and sought to explain the political uses of the memory of the revolt in that century. Whereas in the South, according to Pollmann, 'the victory over heresy took central stage', in the North 'religious pluralism prevented the emergence of a collective religious memory culture. Instead, a secular memory culture developed, which did not focus on the struggle for the true faith, but on seemingly much more modern concepts like *patria*, patriotism and liberty'. According to Van der Steen, there was a lively memory culture about the revolt in the Dutch Republic, parts of which were contested between the various groups in society. These differences figured in the debate for or against peace in the early 1600s, and especially in the Predestination controversy during the Truce period, where the question whether the revolt had been a struggle for freedom or for the true faith (*libertatis ergo* v *religionis ergo*) rose to crucial importance. By Van der Steen's definition, 'memory wars occur when political opponents use conflicting interpretations of the past to conduct their political disagreements.' Although Van der Steen does not mention the AH in this respect, the story of the AH fits this framework very well, as we will see in more detail below.[28]

2.4. *The Truce Conflicts*

The conflict with the former Habsburg overlords ended provisionally with a truce for twelve years in 1609. With the young republic's external enemy temporarily removed, a mixture of internal political and religious tensions (re-)emerged.

[27] They appointed both the counter-remonstrant Johannes Polyander van Kerckhoven (but with a more conciliatory approach than Gomarus') and the remonstrant Simon Episcopius as successors to Gomarus and Vorstius. See also W. Otterspeer, *Het bolwerk van de vrijheid. De Leidse universiteit 1575–1672*, Amsterdam 2000, pp. 248–250; Waszink, 'University and Court', p. 159.

[28] See e.g. J. Pollmann, 'Met grootvaders bloed bezegeld. Over religie en herinneringscultuur in de zeventiende-eeuwse Nederlanden' in: *De Zeventiende Eeuw* 29 (2013) pp. 154–175; eadem, 'Brabanters do fairly resemble Spaniards after all'; Van der Steen, *Memory Wars*, p. 10; 140–155; 289–292.

These tensions had been brewing in Dutch society since at least the 1580s, and were stirred up by dissatisfaction with the idea of a truce and, in particular, by a theological dispute on free will and predestination between two groups in the Dutch Protestant church, that also involved opposing views on state-church relationships. The latter dispute had become more vehement from *c.*1600 onwards (the same time that Grotius started the work on the AH). Known as the Truce Conflicts (*Bestandstwisten*) they soon generated a fundamental political confrontation regarding the relationship between Church and Government, and indeed almost a civil war.

As noted above, the Republic was a composite state consisting of nominally independent provinces that operated as a unity primarily on the levels of war and foreign policy. If this republic was not a unity politically, it was even less so with respect to ecclesiastical matters. The Catholic church had disappeared as public church, but no new common church had taken its place. The orthodox Calvinist (Reformed) church exercised a strict admission policy based on the religious 'quality' of those selected, and therefore decidedly was not (yet) a broad church. Many believers had divergent views, and for this reason regents (often rather liberal-minded themselves) supported the idea of a new public church in which dogmas were not laid down too stringently. Such an institution, however, proved difficult to establish.[29] Moreover, Catholic parishes were still functioning in many places.[30] Nor had the relation between state and church been well defined yet: the Reformed church was organized in a decentralized and presbyteral fashion and had no wish for government interference, whereas secular administrators did aspire to a certain hold of the state on the church. In ecclesiastical matters, the Republic was thus characterized by a high degree of fragmentation and difference of opinion. Another important root of the discord was the disagreement within Dutch society regarding the Truce itself; the 'war party', led by prince Maurice, had vehemently opposed the truce negotiations in 1607–1609 and pressed for a continuation of the war until all demands on the Dutch side, such as formal and definitive transfer of sovereignty, had been met (see also § 9.1 on Grotius and the Twelve Years' Truce).

Thus the government was already facing opposition from inside at a time when the Republic had barely been instituted. During the first two decades of the 17th century, the aforementioned differences of opinion on the relation between church and state and the flexibility of religious doctrine developed into a near civil war in

[29] E. Rabbie, 'Grotius' denken over kerk en staat', in: H.J.M. Nellen and J. Trapman (eds.), *De Hollandse jaren van Hugo de Groot (1583–1621): Lezingen van het colloquium ter gelegenheid van de 350-ste sterfdag van Hugo de Groot ('s-Gravenhage, 31 augustus–1 september 1995),* Hilversum (Verloren) 1996, pp. 193–206'; J. Pollmann, *Religious Choice in the Dutch Republic. The Reformation of Arnoldus Buchelius (1565–1641),* Manchester UP, 1999; B. Kaplan, *Calvinists and Libertines: Confession and Community in Utrecht, 1578–1620,* Oxford: (Clarendon Press) 1995.

[30] See L. Rogier, *Geschiedenis van het Katholicisme in Noord–Nederland in de 16e en de 17e eeuw* Amsterdam (Urbi et Orbi), 1947, vol. 1.

the Republic. The quarrel at the Theology faculty of Leiden University played a pivotal role in this from 1611 onwards. In 1618–1619, a crisis ensued in which the government fell, Van Oldenbarnevelt was eventually executed, and Grotius (who as pensionary of Rotterdam had a prominent place in the ruling government) was sentenced to lifelong imprisonment at Loevestein castle. Having escaped from his prison in 1621, Grotius mostly stayed in Paris afterwards. The fact that Grotius made his escape in a book chest is not merely an amusing, but also a significant detail in his case.

The history and interpretation of these controversies and Grotius' role in them have been discussed extensively elsewhere.[31] For our purposes we consider them as a conflict between two factions, although the ideological coherence of the factions should not be overestimated, nor the predominance of the ideological points of contention (there were many other, for instance local, conflicts and loyalties which often overshadowed the theological and/or political issues).[32] However since Grotius saw the conflict in terms of these two factions, we will adhere to this image for the present discussion. To Grotius' mind, the theological and the political quarrel were one and the same conflict, i.e. that between 'Erasmian-minded regents on one side, and intolerant Calvinist ministers on the other.'[33]

If we maintain this conception of two factions, the first group (also called the *Staatsgezinden* or *Remonstranten*) in the theological debate opposed the idea that God has from the beginning of time preordained, or predestined, every individual human being for salvation or damnation by giving him or her an inner faith, or withholding it respectively – so that faith is not the cause, but the *consequence* of election for salvation. Instead, the Remonstrants hold that God merely *knows* from eternity which choice the individual will make, so that a person's faith does cause him or her to be elected. This view of divine grace and free will was defended by Jacobus Arminius (1559–1609) at the university of Leiden, and was opposed by more orthodox Calvinist theologians such as Franciscus Gomarus (1563–1641) ever after Arminius' appointment in 1603.

As to the relation between church and state, the Remonstrants favoured giving secular authorities a certain influence on church policies (regarding the appointment of ministers, for instance). In practice this amounted to a subordination of religion to politics. Since in Holland and a number of other provinces this position was held by the States, Oldenbarnevelt *cum suis,* and the circles of citizens and

[31] E.g. J. Israel, *The Dutch Republic: Its rise, greatness, and fall, 1477–1806*, Oxford (Clarendon Press), 1995; Rabbie, 'Grotius' denken over kerk en staat'; id., *Intr.* in Grotius, *Ordinum Pietas;* Nellen, *Hugo Grotius.*

[32] S. Groenveld, *Evidente factiën in den staet: Sociaal-politieke verhoudingen in de 17e-eeuwse Republiek der Verenigde Nederlanden,* Hilversum (Verloren) 1990; Rabbie, 'Grotius' denken over kerk en staat'. The controversy from 1607–8 on whether or not to agree to the Truce, for instance, had a continued effect as well: Den Tex, *Oldenbarnevelt* vol. II *Oorlog 1588–1609*, Haarlem 1962, p. 566.

[33] Rabbie, *Intr.* in Grotius, *Ordinum Pietas*, p. 13.

regents connected to them, this group is also known as the *Staatsgezinde* faction. The interpretation of the Revolt itself played a crucial role here:[34] the *Staatsgezinde* position implied the view that the Dutch revolt against the former ruler had first and foremost been a *political* struggle, i.e. a struggle to preserve the (medieval) liberties and privileges of nobility, cities and provinces, and only in the second place a struggle for the true faith: *Haec Libertatis ergo*. For understandable reasons, in the period before and after 1610 the *Staatsgezinde* side also emphasized the legitimacy of the government in power and the citizens' duty to obey.[35]

The opposing side was that of the Counter-Remonstrants, who believe in divine predestination as outlined above. Moreover the Counter-Remonstrants strived for a much more independent position of the church from the secular authorities. Because in the final stage of the conflict the Counter-Remonstrants received the support of the Stadholder, prince Maurice, this side is also called the *Prinsgezinde* faction. They saw the Revolt primarily as a battle for the true (Reformed) faith, and its murdered leader William of Orange as *pater patriae* and a Calvinist 'martyr', to whose sacrifice eternal gratitude was owed as well as acknowledgment of the Oranges' central position. In the years around 1617 some adherents of this faction pronounced views on the Oranges' leadership in which a monarchist tendency can be recognised.[36]

[34] In 1612 the Leiden university Senate even considered a ban on discussions of this topic in academic disputations, as being too dangerous and controversial; see Dominicus Baudius' letter to Grotius of 2 July 1612 (*Briefwisseling* 1 no. 241, p. 211; see also H. Wansink, *Politieke Wetenschappen aan de Leidse Universiteit*, Utrecht 1981, pp. 89–90). Examples explicitly mentioned are the theses that religion does not belong to the essence of the state, and that religion does not justify opposition to the secular authorities. In his discussion with the Senate professor Baudius maintained that in a free country like Holland the expression of opinions on such points should not be forbidden, but he also promises them to admonish his students to not carelessly express agreement with the above positions. Also, compare the incident during the siege of Leiden (1573–1574) in which the town secretary Jan van Hout threatened using his gun against a minister who defended the *haec religionis ergo* (see G. Kalff, *Geschiedenis der Nederlandse Letterkunde*, vol. III, Groningen 1907, 417–118 and R. Bremmer, 'Het beleg en ontzet van Leiden (1574): een venster op de opstand', *Nederlands Archief voor Kerkgeschiedenis* 47 (1965): 177). A late example is Joost van den Vondel's poem of 1630, *Haec Libertatis Ergo. Papieren Geld geoffert op het autaer dan de Hollandsche Vryheyd* (in: *De werken van Vondel II*, ed. C. de Vooys Amsterdam 1929, 329–333), which shows again the central position of this difference of interpretation in the Truce Conflicts. See also L. Rogier, *Eenheid en Scheiding,* Utrecht 1968, pp. 103–108; H. Klink, *Opstand, politiek en religie bij Willem van Oranje, 1559–1568. Een thematische biografie*, Heerenveen 1997; H. van Nierop, 'De troon van Alva. Over de interpretatie van de Nederlandse Opstand' in: *Bijdragen en Mededelingen betreffende de Geschiedenis der Nederlanden 110* (1995), 205–223; J. Pollmann, *Herdenken, herinneren, vergeten. Het beleg en ontzet van Leiden in de Gouden Eeuw*, Leiden 2008; Van der Steen, *Memory wars* pp. 140–155 (and see below); C. Lenarduzzi, 'De oude geusen teghen de nieuwe geusen' in: *Holland, Historisch Tijdschrift* 43 (2011), pp. 65–81.

[35] E.g. Simon Stevin's *Het Burgherlick Leven* of 1590 (e.g. in the edition S. Stevin, *Het burgherlick leven & anhangh*, ed. by Pim den Boer; transl. [into modern Dutch] by A. Fleurkens, Amsterdam 2001.

[36] See the pamphlets quoted in Y. van Vugt and J. Waszink, 'Politiek in Hoofts Baeto: De middenweg als uitweg?' in: *Tijdschrift voor Nederlandse Taal- en Letterkunde,* 116-1(2000) pp. 2–22.

After Arminius' death in 1609, the States appointed Conradus Vorstius (1569–1622) from the High School in Burg Steinfurt as his successor (1611), a very controversial appointment as in his most recent publications Vorstius had defended views which were considered Socinian (after the Italian/Polish theologian Fausto Sozzini or Socinus (1539–1604), whose theology was considered hardly Christian by most other Christian observers of the period). In protest Gomarus quit his chair, to be succeeded by the moderate Counter-remonstrant Johannes Polyander van Kerckhoven (1568–1646). The wider (international) impact of the struggle can be seen from the fact that the English king James I weighed in as well, siding with the Counter-Remonstrants and expressing his condemnation of Vorstius as a 'pest of the churches'. Under this public and political pressure, the States relieved Vorstius of his teaching duties in 1612. Preparations for a national synod to settle the issue were started, but its agenda and timing themselves soon became part of the struggle. In several places Counter-remonstrant believers left the public church to start their own. Given their championing of a 'broad' public church, and in spite of their more liberal theological views, the *Staatsgezinde* government came to ban all preaching on predestination and discussions of founding dissident churches; bans which Counter-remonstrants (who outnumbered the Remonstrants in most regions) felt were only maintained against them. Tensions mounted, and in July 1617, Maurice chose the Counter-remonstrant side by publicly joining their service in the Kloosterkerk in The Hague. In August the (Remonstrant-dominated) States of Holland issued the *Scherpe Resolutie* which enabled city councils in the province to hire their own militias (the *waardgelders*) to maintain order – thus *de facto* creating a fighting force not under the command of the Stadtholder. Maurice responded by having Oldenbarnevelt and his closest collaborators, including Grotius, arrested on accusations of treason. Oldenbarnevelt was executed in 1619; Grotius was sent to the imprisonment in Loevestein Castle for life.

The National Synod was eventually held in Dordt (Dordrecht) in 1618–1619 and secured the victory of the Counter-remonstrants over 'Arminianism'. After that time, only Counter-remonstrant (orthodox) worship was allowed in the public space. Remonstrant worship (and that of other Christian denominations) had to take place in so-called *schuilkerken* ('hidden churches'), which on the outside were not recognisable as churches. Thus the Dutch Republic knew a degree of religious freedom, but certainly no complete freedom.

3. Hugo Grotius

Hugo Grotius was born in the city of Delft in 1583 into a well-connected patrician family that had served in the city government for at least two generations when Hugo was born. Both his father (Jan) and paternal grandfather (Hugo) combined activities in trade (for example in wood) with property investments and a role in the local civic government. Hugo's father Jan de Groot (1554–1640) served as one of Delft's burgomasters from 1591–1595 and as town secretary afterwards. Both men also had an interest in humanism, and the family played a role in the expansion of the new university in Leiden. Jan had been the institution's third registered student in 1576; his elder brother Cornelis (1544–1610) was appointed as professor of Law in 1575. Jan served the university as curator from 1594 to 1601 and maintained personal contacts with people like Justus Lipsius, Janus Dousa and Simon Stevin, the innovative mathematician and engineer who served prince Maurice's military operations and played a central in the institution of the Engineering School in Leiden (Nederduytsche Mathematique).

Hugo's capacity for learning was clear from an early age. As the pace of a pupil's progress through Holland's school system was defined not by age but by progress and ability, there was no standard age to finish school. Hugo finished the Latin School at Delft at the very forward age of 11 and matriculated at the university of Leiden on 3 August 1594. The promising pupil was welcomed there by Janus Dousa, one of his father's connections, with a poem written for the occasion. He lived in the house of his uncle and aunt Cornelis and Geertruyt Uytteneng, but since neither his parents nor his uncle and aunt could look after him as much as was required given Hugo's age, a tutor was appointed in the person Jacobus Lassonius, a former schoolmaster from Harderwijk who would soon, through his contacts with the De Groot family, move on to become rector at the Latin school at Delft. Hugo was then lodged with the professor of Theology Franciscus Junius (1545–1602), who would have a pervasive influence on his religious and social thought.

Hugo must have followed the standard propaedeutic curriculum in the Artes and remained active in the humanities not only throughout his time in Leiden but throughout his life. After the propaedeutic stage, a student would choose his main subject, that is, Law, Theology or Medicine. In Grotius' case this must have been Law, and his contacts with the Law faculty are plainly in evidence. Nevertheless little real information as to his fulfillment of the Law curriculum appears available, other than that he apparently qualified for a promotion in Law in Orléans during the journey in 1598 (see below). The two disputations known by Grotius are on topics in Aristotelian logic. Of the professors whose influence can be established, apart from Junius, Bonaventura Vulcanius' classes in Greek, are important and most of all Joseph Scaliger's scholarly gatherings in his private lodgings on the Breestraat.

Joseph Scaliger (1540–1609) was not a regular professor but could select his own students whom he taught in a private setting in his spacious lodgings on the Breestraat. Grotius was admitted to this company, together with others like Johannes Meursius and Daniel Heinsius (who is said to have been Scaliger's star pupil). The so-called 'late humanism' represented by Scaliger and especially his predecessor Justus Lipsius dominated the interests and approaches in Leiden' s Arts faculty during Grotius' years of study.[37] Late humanism gave a particular promi-

[37] On the intellectual relationship between Lipsius and Grotius, see J. Waszink, 'Lipsius and Grotius: Tacitism' in: *History of European Ideas,* 39–2 (2013), pp. 151–168, and § 7.1 below.

nence to the study of history, combining it with the naturalist, or 'realist', tendencies of the time which were also present in such varied fields as astronomy, physics, medicine (e.g. in anatomy and botany), politics and law. A few more words about this late humanism and its relation to the study of history are in order (and see also § 9.2 on Grotius as historian and § 11.7 on the reception of the AH).

By the middle of the 16th century, a new approach to history arose next to existing applications of historical information. Anthony Grafton[38] has described this change in terms of the rise of the genre of *artes historicae* (methods of studying history), and of a move away by some historians from a traditional focus on rhetoric and exemplarity, or the *production* of historical accounts, towards the *reading* of historical sources, their interpretation and understanding, and the hermeneutics of that process. As a result, historical research, aimed at understanding the phenomena of the (past) world, rose to prominence. 'The ars historica formed part of a much larger effort to master and use the floods of information pouring into Europe from travelers, navigators and missionaries [...].'[39] According to Grafton, the university of Leiden, especially through the influence of Lipsius and Scaliger, was one of the most vibrant centres of this development.[40] The rise of late humanism and the realism that it embodied forms an integral part of it.

The influence of this realism, and its manifestation as 'reason of state' in the study of history and politics, is one of the major influences on Grotius' thought – not only his scholarly thought but also his stance in the actual politics of the province of Holland in the 1610s. In contrast to the earlier humanist historiography with its stress on exemplarity, these late humanist writers brought a far more critical and sceptical approach from their reading of history to their consideration of politics. They rejected the idea of an inherent connection between virtue and success, thus proposing a fundamentally different and controversial view of the relationship between ethics and politics.[41] The 'secularising' tendencies (in the sense of: the opposite force to confessionalisation) which can be perceived in Grotius' life and works must also be viewed in this connection.[42]

In 1598, 15-year-old Grotius was included in the company surrounding a States embassy to the French court, which was led by Oldenbarnevelt and Justinus van Nassau. The experiences in this journey became an important event in Grotius' early life. During the journey he was formally presented to King Henry IV, who reportedly greeted him as 'le miracle d'Hollande.' While in the town of Orléans

[38] A. Grafton, *What was History? The Art of History in Early Modern Europe*, Cambridge UP, 2007

[39] Grafton, *What was History*, p. 200.

[40] Grafton, *What was History*, p. 193 and id., *Athenae Batavae. The Research Imperative at Leiden, 1575–1650*, Leiden (Primavera Pers) 2003.

[41] As for example expressed in the strongly sceptical opening chapter of *Politica* book 4; see Waszink in Intr. to J. Lipsius, *Politica, pp.* 81, 207; id., 'Lipsius and Grotius: Tacitism'; id., 'Henry Savile's Tacitus and the English role on the Continent: Leicester, Hotman, Lipsius', in: *History of European Ideas*, vol. 42.3 (2016), 303–319, pp. 11–12.

[42] See further in § 4.

Grotius registered at the University and passed the examination for a doctorate degree in Law.[43] After his return in Holland he settled as an independent advocate in The Hague. He moved into lodgings in the house of the liberal (later Remonstrant) court minister Johannes Wtenbogaert (1557–1644), who was a near-neighbour of Oldenbarnevelt, and who was regarded for some time as a possible successor to Arminius at Leiden. Thus Grotius came to live very near to Johan van Oldenbarnevelt too. At the same time, Grotius continued his literary pursuits and earned a name for himself with scholarly and literary work: around 1600 he published a play, poetry and two editions of classical texts.[44] In 1607 Grotius was appointed advocaat-fiscaal (comparable to a modern public prosecutor, a.o. in fiscal cases brought before the court).

In this first decade of the 17th century the States government employed the young lawyer regularly as a scholar and 'spokesman'. At first Grotius fulfilled this role in the background. In 1604 he received a request through a former fellow lodger at The Hague, Jan ten Grotenhuys (1573–1646), to write a legal treatise in support of the Amsterdam Admiralty's ruling that the seizure of the valuable Portuguese carrack Santa Catarina in the Straits of Malacca in early 1603 had been legitimate. The precise objectives and intended audience of this text (*De Iure Praedae*: 'The Law of Prize and Booty') are not entirely clear, but it marked the beginning of Grotius' long-lasting involvement with the VOC.[45] Even more importantly, the treatise provides an innovative and systematic theory of natural rights to justify warfare and prize-taking in specific cases (*in casu* to justify Dutch actions against other Europeans in the East). The application of natural rights to the rules of warfare would eventually be carried further in his epoch-making *De Iure Belli ac Pacis* (DIB) of 1625. For more on Grotius' activity in this role see § 9.1 below on Grotius and the Twelve Years' Truce.

In 1610 Grotius' public role as the States' learned spokesman became more prominent when he published his *De Antiquitate Reipublicae Batavicae* ('The Antiquity of the Dutch Republic'). In this treatise, addressed to a European audience, he

[43] Attendance of the Law school in Orléans by students from the Low Countries was an established tradition, dating from times when there were no universities in the Low Countries. After the foundation of the universities in Louvain (1425) and Leiden (1575) however academic peregrination to Orléans persisted for a long time, as supplement to the curriculum at home. Grotius' uncle Cornelis had also been a student at Orléans. See J. van Kuyk, 'Lijst van Nederlanders, studenten te Orléans (1441–1602)', in: *Bijdragen en Mededeelingen van het Historisch Genootschap* vol. 34 (1913) pp. 293–349.

[44] Grotius' first scholarly editions were those of Martianus Capella's *Satyricon* and Aratus' *Syntagma Arateorum*. The play is *Sacra in quibus Adamus Exul* (1601), later followed by *Christus Patiens* (1608). For the poetry, see the multi-volume edition *De dichtwerken van Hugo Grotius*, ed. B.L. Meulenbroek e.a., Grotius Instituut Amsterdam, & Koninklijke Nederlandse Akademie van Wetenschappen, Assen, (Van Gorcum) 1970 and later.

[45] See also § 9.2 below. See further M.J. van Ittersum, *Profit and Principle: Hugo Grotius, Natural Rights Theories and the Rise of Dutch Power in the East Indies, 1595–1615*, Leiden 2006, especially Intr. and pp. 24–25, 125–188.

defended the legitimacy and maturity of the Republic, whose existence had been formalised by the Truce.[46] This work – a brief historical discourse on Holland's form of government since the Roman period – is both a cleverly constructed plea for the legitimacy of the revolt and for the acknowledgment of Holland and the Republic as full-bodied actors on stage of European politics. Towards its Dutch audience, it appears also as a call for unity and harmony within the Republic. Furthermore Grotius presented himself as the learned champion of Dutch interests with the publication of one chapter from *De Iure Praedae* as *Mare liberum* ('The Free Sea') in 1609.[47]

Around the same time he completed the AH and submitted it to the States of Holland (1612), Grotius composed a treatise entitled *Meletius* arguing that the beliefs which all Christians held in common (and even Jews and other believers), were more important than the issues dividing them. Although its focus on the Christian religion sets the *Meletius* clearly apart from the spirit and purposes of the AH, in their conception of religion the two works show obvious similarities.[48] Around 1615, when the Truce Conflicts had made acute questions of religious policy and the position of minorities, he would also turn to the issue from the perspective of the position of Jewish inhabitants in Dutch society. He drafted a policy paper that has come down us as the 'Remonstrance regarding the rules to be introduced with respect to Jews in Holland and Westfriesland.'[49] In Grotius'

[46] H. Grotius, *The Antiquity of the Batavian Republic*, ed. J. Waszink et al., Assen 2000 (Bibliotheca Latinitatis Novae).

[47] A separately published chapter from the longer, but unpublished treatise *De Iure Praedae*.

[48] See the edition by G.H.M Posthumus Meyjes: *Hugo Grotius, Meletius sive de iis quae inter Christianos conveniunt Epistola*, Leiden Brill 1988. *Meletius* was not published in Grotius' own time. As we shall discuss below in § 4, the *Annales* consistently present a negative view of organised religion, i.e. as a force for chaos in society, and only view religion as a positive thing where it concerns individual piety and constancy. This squares with Meletius' almost exclusive focus on faith as a set of (rational) beliefs, knowledge and attitudes in the individual rather than on the societal role of religion. The view that ethics rather than the Christian revelation was the essence of philosophy (see Posthumus Meyjes p. 35) has the same 'secularising' implications that are central to the *Annales*. Also, some textual similarities appear, such as the brief histories of developments in Christianity in *Annales* 1.22–23 and *Meletius* § 2.

[49] *Remonstrantie nopende de ordre dije in de landen van Hollandt ende Westvrieslandt dijent gestelt op de Joden*. See the editions by J. Meijer, Amsterdam 1949, and the new one by D. Kromhout and A. Offenberg, *Hugo Grotius' Remonstrantie of 1615. Facsimile, Transliteration, Modern Translations and Analysis, written by David Kromhout and Adri Offenberg*, Leiden (Brill) 2019; W.J.M. van Eysinga, 'De Groots Jodenreglement' in *Mededelingen der Koninklijke Nederlandse Academie van Wetenschappen* afd. Letterkunde NR vol. 13.1 (1950) or in id., *Sparsa Collecta*, Leiden (Sijthof) 1958, pp. 423–429; cp. also the review by J. Spaans in *Grotiana* 41-1 (2020), 246–250. The States had commisioned Grotius (representing Rotterdam) and Adriaen Pauw (Amsterdam) to submit proposals for a regulation regarding the Jews. Pauw's proposals are probably preserved as the *Ordonnantie* on the topic which was in Grotius' archive with the *Remonstrantie*. It would appear that the States passed a regulation made on the basis of both proposals on 12 December 1619 (when Grotius was already in prison). For the discussion, see Meijer pp. 9, 95–98 and Eysinga note 1.

view this matter should be regulated by the secular government. With respect to religious policy as such, the piece recognises that in a country where there is such religious diversity already, some minorities may be led further astray by the example of Judaism. However, toleration is owed to the Jews for a whole range of reasons: shared human nature, hospitality to strangers, the antiquity and dignity of Judaism, and because toleration opens the road for Jews to convert to Christianity. Further, given that there are several confessions in Dutch society anyway, the presence of Judaism poses no threat to orthodox Christian confessions since it is the most different religion from those. And finally, toleration also brings practical advantages with it, while many Roman emperors have also extended toleration to Judaism.[50]

That Grotius was perceived as a scholar even in his years of legal and political service can be concluded, for instance, from the letter in which the Leiden mathematician Willebrord Snellius (1580–1626) dedicated his *De Re Nummaria* (on ancient numismatics) to Grotius in 1613. Although dedicating books to people of political influence was common practice and such dedications are always full of hackneyed laudations, Snellius' remark that Grotius combined a knowledge of jurisprudence with knowledge of other arts more than was usual for his time, seems so free of exaggeration that the fact that the combination is so explicitly noted seems significant in this case.[51]

An important caesura in Grotius' activity as scholarly spokesman lies in the year 1613, in which his *Ordinum Pietas* appeared, and in which the AH would probably have appeared if the States had proceeded with its publication. In that year, he had been appointed pensionary[52] of the city of Rotterdam. In this quality he also occupied a seat in the States' assembly, and was thus becoming a prominent member of the ruling administration. Until that moment, he had not overtly chosen sides and had presented himself as a neutral observer and possible mediator in the conflict. *Ordinum Pietas* however stands out as an explicit and undisguised defence of the States' policy. This turnabout was resented by the Counter-remonstrants, and cost Grotius his respect and trustworthiness in their eyes. Grotius also drafted a *Tolerance Resolution* in 1614 which the Counter-remonstrants perceived as an attempt to submit the churches to the complete control of the States, in

[50] For all of the Remonstrantie's arguments, see the Remonstrantie and the discussion by Meijer.

[51] Grotius, *Briefwisseling* vol. 17 no. 250A (p. 101): 'Ad te autem, vir consultissime, βιβλίδιον hoc, tanquam ad iudicem suum mittitur. Nam cum tu praeter huius aevi consuetudinem iuris scientiam cum reliquarum artium cognitione coniunxeris, in quibus doctrina et ingenio praeter reliquos excellis neque illarum sis expers quae inter has primum olim tenebant locum, quarum rudes a limine suae academiae arcebat Plato, quemnam alium fuerat aequius me huius rei capere arbitrum quam eum qui horum iudex aequissimus iuxta et peritissimus esse posset?' The reference to Grotius' mathematical knowledge aims at his edition of Aratus' astronomical works, for instance, and his Latin translation of Stevin's book on maritime navigation.

[52] Legal advisor.

organisational as well as doctrinal matters.[53] He further propounds and defends the States government's position in his correspondence, in a preserved political oration from 1616,[54] and in a treatise on the secular authorities' rights in ecclesiastical matters (*De Imperio summarum potestatum circa sacra,* 1617).

Also in 1613 Grotius took part in the embassy to King James, the main subject of which was British and Dutch trade in the East. His role as a scholar was obvious already insofar as *Mare Liberum* was an important starting point for Dutch-English discussions and negotiations regarding the rules of competition in the East-Asian trade. Apart from that, Grotius tried to win the support of several English political and ecclesiastical leaders for the Remonstrant positions concerning predestination and the relation between church and government. If we are to believe the English opponents of the Remonstrants, he exposed himself in the process as a pedant and an actual ignoramus regarding the matter itself (and we cannot go back in time to form our own judgment of Grotius' appearance on that stage). Behind the scenes he tried to induce the king to side with the Remonstrants, acting as the learned envoy by surveying the history of the predestination debate with the king, in an attempt to make him see the orthodox Calvinists' error.[55] Grotius initially thought that his mission had succeeded. However, the king's advisors as well as the contents of Grotius' own *Ordinum Pietas* soon made the king change his mind, and the affair led James to feel that Grotius had misled him.[56]

[53] F. Sierhuis, *The Literature of the Arminian Controversy. Religion, Politics and the Stage in the Dutch Republic,* Oxford UP 2015, pp. 76–77 and passim, where more can be found about Grotius' case for limited toleration and the surrounding debate.

[54] *Oratie vanden hoogh-gheleerden voortreffelycken Meester Hugo de Groot, Raet ende pensionaris der Stadt Rotterdam ghedaen inde vergaderinghe der 36. Raden der Stadt Amsterdam* (Enkhuizen 1622). Knuttel 2250. See also Israel, *Dutch Republic,* p. 430 and Waszink, 'Lipsius and Grotius' pp. 13–14.

[55] An account of this conversation (which took place on 15 May 1613 and lasted about two hours) has been preserved: see E. Rabbie, 'Grotius, James I and the Ius Circa Sacra' in: *Grotiana* NS, vol. 24–26 (2003–4), pp. 25–39; and id., Intr. to Grotius, *Ordinum Pietas.*

[56] On the role of *Ordinum Pietas* here, see E. Rabbie, 'An Illegal Manuscript Copy of Hugo Grotius' Ordinum Hollandiae Ac Westfrisiae Pietas (1613)', in: *Nederlands Archief voor Kerkgeschiedenis,* vol. 74.2, (1994), pp. 162–172.

4.
Tacitism and Reason of State in the *Annales et Historiae*[57]

Until recently the scholarly literature on the AH had little to offer on the Tacitist aspect of the text,[58] in spite of the fact that the imitation of Tacitus is among the most conspicuous features of the work. In this section we will concentrate on reason-of-state and Tacitist aspects with a direct bearing on the political interpretation of the *Annales*. A longer discussion of the AH's Tacitism (regarding both content and style) is included further below (§ 7).

In essence the idea of reason of state centres on the notion that politics have a logic of their own, independent from the rules contained in ethics, law or religion. Thus reason of state challenges widely shared and cherished assumptions regarding the moral nature of politics, such as the idea that civil life and the pursuit of a common purpose imply the active employment of virtues such as justice, loyalty, wisdom, courage, mildness, modesty etc; the idea of an inherent connection between moral virtue and success; as well as (certainly for the great majority of citizens in the 16th and 17th centuries) the importance of religious observance, the idea of a divine 'supervision' of human affairs, and the notion that the first duty of a government is the protection of the true faith.

The term *ragion di stato* was first coined by Francesco Guicciardini in the *Dialogo del reggimento di Firenze* of 1525 as a more neutral expression of the idea that the *ratio* of a given action by a ruler may be explained not by its ethical but by its political logic.[59] This alternative understanding of politics was notoriously launched into the European political debate in the 16th century in an extreme form by Niccolò Machiavelli's *Il Principe,* which first appeared in print in 1532 and soon made the author's name synonymous with unscrupulous power politics and cruel irreligious tyranny. For Machiavelli, successful politics are about the preservation or extension of power, a goal to which in many cases the actual exercise

[57] The literature on reason of state is vast, but for an introduction the following works might be helpful: P. Burke, 'Tacitism, scepticism, and reason of state', in: J. Burns & M. Goldie (eds.), *The Cambridge History of Political Thought 1450–1700*, Cambridge UP 1991, pp. 479–498; F. Meinecke, *Die Idee der Staatsräson in der Neueren Geschichte*, Munich and Berlin (R. Oldenbourg) 1925; J. Soll, 'The reception of The Prince 1513–1700, or why we understand Machiavelli the way we do', in: *Social Research: An International Quarterly*, Vol. 81/1 (2014), pp. 31–60; M. Stolleis *Arcana imperii und Ratio status: Bemerkungen zur politischen Theorie des frühen 17. Jahrhunderts*, Göttingen (Vandenhoeck & Ruprecht) 1980; R. Tuck, *Philosophy and Government 1572–1651,* Cambridge UP 1993; M. Viroli, *From Politics to Reason of State. The Acquisition and Transformation of the Language of Politics 1250–1600*, Cambridge UP 1992, Ideas in Context 22; J. Waszink, 'Introduction' in: J. Lipsius, *Politica. Six books of Politics or Political Instruction*. Ed. with translation and introduction by Jan Waszink, Assen (Van Gorcum) 2004.

[58] With the exception of the little-noticed article by A. Droetto, 'Il Tacitismo nella storiografia Groziana' in: id., *Studi Groziani*, Torino 1968, pp. 101–151 (Pubblicazioni dell' Istituto di scienze politiche dell' Università di Torino, vol. 18).

[59] R. Descendre, 'Ragion di Stato', in: *Enciclopedia machiavelliana*, vol. II, Istituto della Enciclopedia italiana fondata da Giovanni Treccani, pp. 382–384, 2014.

of the above virtues will be an obstacle rather than a precondition for success – although the prince must be very careful to uphold an *image* of virtuousness in the eyes of his subjects. In the subsequent century however several authors attempted to 'tame' these ideas in order to make the realism embodied in reason-of-state thought a usable tool and register for regular (i.e. ethical) political practice and counsel, and for public debate.

In this process, Tacitus' *Annals* and *Histories* played an important, and in most aspects independent role, which by the end of the 16th century had even earned Tacitus a reputation of being *the* author on political realism (*magister in politicis*[60]). Tacitus was a relatively new author among the Latin classics, as most surviving parts of his works had only re-emerged in the 15th century, with one part (*Annals* book 1–6) only as late as 1508. This re-discovery led to a rise of interest in Tacitus, and the first 'complete' printed edition in 1515.[61] However Tacitus stood apart from the main body of classical literature because the *Histories* and *Annals* went against received preferences and were not regarded as models fit for imitation, neither on a level of style nor of content.

For early modern readers, the Tacitist style had two main features: first, the literary style proper, in terms of syntax, choice of words, etc. and, second, Tacitean content, that is, Tacitus' particular view of politics, human psychology and social relations. As to the style itself, this is marked by brevity of diction (*brevitas*), designed 'ruggedness', asymmetries and incongruities, many *sententiae* (which present political wisdom and insight in short pithy sayings), and the general difficulty of the text which results from the sum of these characteristics. With respect to content, readers found many of the core notions of reason-of-state thought already well-developed in Tacitus' texts, and many valuable (sceptical) insights into the nature of man and his politics. Characteristic of Tacitus are the concern with 'is' rather than 'ought', a pessimistic view of man (highlighting his self-interested and disorderly nature, and the deficiency of his moral motivation), and a non-religious view of history and politics. It is important to note that style and content cannot be separated here: in many cases the special style is used to convey messages 'between the lines' to the attentive reader, while these are not made very explicit on a literal level. This is one of the features that lend the text its enduring fascination as literature.

For some, Tacitus' works may have provided a cover or substitute for the expression of Machiavellian ideas, but in general his works functioned in a different and independent role. As a source for reason-of-state ideas, on the one hand Tacitus is more implicit than Machiavelli, while on the other hand he is richer, more moderate, and often explicitly or implicitly moral. Thus, unlike the extreme positions of *Il Principe*, Tacitus' works provided at least a more acceptable starting point for a

60 See the early-modern judgments of Tacitus in § 7.1 below.
61 By Philippus Beroaldus, Rome, 1515; the central part of the *Annals* (books 5–10) is still missing.

wider debate on political realism and for the construction of a 'morally sound' reason of state that takes on board the realism, scepticism and secularism which many felt was so urgently required in the European politics of the 16th century, while avoiding the moral vacuum of *Il Principe*. Nevertheless, this realist (as in non-moralist, non-religious) analysis of history and politics would remain controversial for a long time to come. It is crucial to note this paradox of Tacitism: at this time Tacitism was in many ways a fringe phenomenon, popular with an educated elite minority, and influential as a result, while it remained unacceptable to and rejected by majorities everywhere at the same time.

It is possible to view the history of Tacitism as equivalent to the early history of secularisation of social and political thought in Europe. The recent re-emergence of the idea of 'secularisation' for the period around 1600 has also led to a new debate on the merits of this view.[62] In favour of the 'secularising' interpretation, it should be noted that it is crucial first and foremost to avoid black-and-white schematisations: secularisation is a *process* through various shades of grey, and a fluctuating process at that, sometimes even going in reverse, which continues up to the present day, rather than a stable 'development' (in the 20th-century historiographical sense of that word) leading up to a fixed 'modern' outcome. In the early-modern context under discussion here, the idea that politics and religion should be separated, led in practice to an effort to *reduce* the hold of religion on politics, which is one step, however imperfect, in a secularising process.

The interest in Tacitus received a particular boost from the activity of Justus Lipsius, who published a new edition of the surviving works during his brief tenure at the university of Jena in 1574. Lipsius then expanded his range of 'Tacitist' works during his memorable professorship at Leiden: a philological and historical commentary on Tacitus' works in 1581, and his abundantly Tacitist 'handbook for princes' *Politicorum sive Civilis doctrina* in 1589. Although Lipsius had already left

[62] See J. Waszink, 'A *nouveau agenda de recherche: Origins of Secularisation, Tacitism*', in: C. Secretan and D. Antoine-Mahut (eds.), *Les Pays-Bas aux XVIIe et XVIIIe siècles. Nouveaux regards*, Paris, 2015, pp. 217–238 (based on a research proposal first submitted to the Dutch NWO in 2009), and the far more solid and elaborate discussion in the introduction of Mark Somos' *Secularisation and the Leiden Circle,* Leiden (Brill) 2011, esp. pp. 1–6. I broadly agree with Somos' terms and approach. The term secularisation enjoys a bad reputation in more recent scholarship because of its central role in an older historical teleology which held that the modern, 'developed' western society of the late 19th and 20th century was the best and necessary outcome of history, and would eventually prevail worldwide. The (justified) critique of this use of secularisation within the modernisation paradigm led some scholars to reject the secularising tendencies in Western history altogether. However, even without an underlying or necessary tendency towards secularism, it makes sense to study *particular* secularising authors, groups, currents, contexts etc. and their influence on the course of history. According to Somos, secularisation is a meandering *process* (not a fact) that may even go into reverse in particular places and times, while some 'secularising thinkers were deeply religious,' their works and actions may have produced unintended effects (Intr., p. 4), and 'the motivation behind the process of secularisation was not atheism but pacifism' (p. 5), all of which are important qualifications to understand this view of secularisation (cp. Sierhuis, *Literature of the Arminian Controversy* p. 63 n. 52).

Leiden when Grotius matriculated, the interest in his type of scholarship was very much alive there, and Lipsius still figured in the personal and scholarly networks around the university (Grotius exchanged a few letters with the older scholar who was also an acquaintance of his father). The correspondence of the Leiden professor Dominicus Baudius notes the high interest in Tacitus among students and scholars in Leiden precisely in the years around 1605, the same time as Grotius' greatest activity on the AH.[63]

That Grotius knew Lipsius' *Politica* and Tacitus commentary can be established beyond doubt.[64] In October 1606, at the height of his work on the AH, he also received a copy of Janus Gruterus' Tacitus edition.[65] Moreover, while he was revising the AH again for publication around 1637 Grotius was also working on a set of textual notes and emendations to Tacitus' main works (see § 11.2). The AH's title loudly professes the link with Tacitus' main works. Even a brief inspection of the style reveals Grotius' attempt to imitate that of the ancient master – an imitation which has earned him both praise and criticism (such as by Jerôme Bignon, Stefano Gradić and Pierre Bayle, see § 11.5 and § 11.7 below).[66] With respect to Tacitist content, two main features of the narrative in the *Annales* stand out:

1. Grotius' sceptical and pessimistic approach of the revolt: he continuously stresses the lack of order, solidarity, dedication and discipline among the Dutch, the selfishness and short-sightedness among the nobility and the provinces, etc. The *Annales* convey no sense of patriotism or heroism regarding the hardships of the towns under siege, the perseverance of persecuted protestants, or the glory of the struggle for liberty against tyranny. And it is no different on the Spanish side: next to (sometimes) Philip's political craftiness, Grotius emphasises his arrogance

[63] See J.D.M. Cornelissen, 'Hooft en Tacitus. Bijdrage tot de kennis van de vaderlandse geschiedenis in de eerste helft der zeventiende eeuw' (orig. 1938), repr. in: id., *De Eendracht van het Land*, eds. E. Haitsma Mulier and A. Janssen, Amsterdam (Bataafse Leeuw) 1987, pp. 65–66; P. Grootens, *Dominicus Baudius. Een levensschets uit het Leidse humanistenmilieu 1561–1613*, Nijmegen and Utrecht 1942, pp. 132–133; see also § 11.1. Arnaldo Momigliano noted Lipsius' contempt in 1605 for the crowds gathering around Tacitus; Momigliano, 'The first political commentary on Tacitus' in: *The Journal of Roman Studies* Vol. 37 (1947), pp. 91–101, 92.

[64] As appears from his unpublished tract *De Bello ob libertatem eligendo* (written *c.*1608, manuscript now kept in Leiden UL, BPL 922); see in § 9.1 on Grotius and the Twelve Years' Truce. See further C. Damon, ' "Tritus in eo lector": Grotius' emendations to the text of Tacitus', in: *Grotiana* 29 (2008), pp. 133–148. Another indication is the quote from Seneca Maior in *De Iure Praedae* fol. 31v (ch.7; p. 111 in the edition by Van Ittersum): *Necessitas* enim *magnum imbecillitatis humanae patrocinium, omnem legem frangit.* which appears in this form in Lipsius, *Politica* 4.14, i.e. with the crucial *omnem legem frangit* printed in italics as if part of the original quote, which it is not. With thanks for this observation to Bene Colenbrander; see his forthcoming article on reason of state in DIP.

[65] *C. Cornelii Taciti opera quae exstant. Ex recognitione Iani Gruteri,* Frankfurt 1607; see Grotius, *Briefwisseling* vol. 1 ep. 86, 1 Nov. 1606 to G. Lingelsheim, pp. 72–73 & note 1. Gruterus had previously published *Discursus politici ad Tacitum* (Heidelberg 1605).

[66] For a modern reappraisal, see D. den Hengst, 'Naturalis sermonis pulchritudo?' in: *Grotiana* 29 (2008), pp. 77–84.

and inflexibility, as well as the religious dogmatism, arrogance, greed, cruelty and resentment among the Spaniards in the Low Countries.

2. The logic of the story is political before anything else; the motivation of decisions is political in nature, and events are either caused by political circumstances, or the result of chance or human failure. There is very little by way of heroic portraits of individuals that inspire imitation. Even the portrait of William of Orange balances his dedication to the cause and virtuous inspiration with a clear awareness of his political self-interest and astuteness, and (in many cases) simply his bad luck. Religion is basically written out of the story. Not only does Grotius consistently present religious institutions in a negative light, but the revolutionaries' religious motivation as well, insofar he discusses it at all: it is seen as a source of intolerance, conflict, and social disruption. For example *Annales* 1.55:

> ... There was not much distance between [Lutheranism] and another [doctrine], distinguished by the talent of Zwingli especially and Calvin's, and which would have united with that of Augsburg a long time ago if in religious matters it weren't an established fact that everything leans more to stubbornness than concord;

or see Grotius' thoroughly negative image of the ardent Calvinism represented by John of Hembyze in 3.14 and 4.25–32, or the followers of the earl of Leicester in 5.14-15 (see also § 8.3 below).

Religious motivation in the political leadership (on both sides) is presented as feigned and/or a cover for underlying political purposes. For example, Grotius presents Philip II in a Machiavellian light by presenting his submission to the pope as feigned and serving political purposes (1.31):

> As the real reason [behind his religious policies] it can be conjectured that Philip had decided to let the pope's authority work for him in many matters. (...) Now Philip had turned the Pope into his instrument by showing docility, and the most trusted people around him by largesse; and this seemed to provide abundant warranty and pretext.

This type of analysis is not limited to the Spanish side, but appears on the friendly side too, see the quotes on William the Silent and Elizabeth I to which we shall return in § 6.

Historical causation too appears almost entirely without divine or religious aspect. The few times a notion of divine will or providence appears in the narrative, its purpose seems rather to complicate or deny the idea of a divine agenda behind the events than to assert it. See for example Ann. 2.25 on the capture of the town of Den Briel in 1572 by the unruly 'Sea-Beggars' where Grotius asserts the history of this war showed that human logic is worthless in understanding divine providence: 'It has pleased the Almighty's Providence in the Netherlands war almost invariably to deceive human planning and confidence in such a way that great hopes and a happy outcome were never together in the same place.' More on this in § 7.3.1 on dramatic structuring.

Thus, Grotius appears to be actively resisting (pseudo-)religious interpretations of the revolt and the idea of a divine plan behind the events. This resistance however was no reason not occasionally to play with the idea in his narrative, if only to make it clear that he is rejecting such readings altogether. This rejection squares entirely with the Tacitean, secular interpretation of politics, and the sceptical element in that strand of thought.[67] And in turn this *realpolitische* reading of the Revolt squares with Grotius' *Staatsgezinde* parti-pris in the political and intellectual controversies of the Truce period and beyond.[68]

5.
The Statesman-Historian: Grotius and the historian's role in society

In the AH scholarly and political concerns of the tense period of the Truce controversies intertwine in a striking and intense way – all the more striking because Grotius followed a path very much his own (and ultimately unsuccessful). We have seen that both the States of Holland and the States-General took an active stance with respect to the historiography about the revolt, and that the memory of the revolt was a contested item in the early decades of the 17th century. As we shall see, Grotius attempted to employ his knowledge of literature, especially that of Tacitus, the political author *par excellence,* to exert a conciliatory influence on the quarrels in the Republic, by demonstrating what he saw was the true character of the Revolt. The reason-of-state-related problem of consolidating the government's position in a context of increasing opposition occupied Grotius' thought intensely. The fact that his attempt to help restore concord and unity was first and foremost a scholarly one characterises the world of thought that had produced him. In the AH he presents himself as a political insider and historian at the same time, who

[67] For a fascinating illustration of the type of religious political reasoning of the period that Grotius' position would be a critique of, see e.g. the passages from one of Philip's letters to the Duke of Alva quote in G. Parker, *The Imprudent King. A New Life of Philip II*, Yale UP 2014, p. 368. Philip argues that, although Alva has convincingly demonstrated that an attack on England to overthrow queen Elizabeth is not feasible in practice, his belief in God's support of the plan is to strong that he will carry it through nevertheless.

[68] Cp. also M. Somos, 'Enter Secularisation: Heinsius' *De Tragoediae constitutione*' in: *History of European Ideas*, vol. 36–1 (2010), pp. 19–38. It makes perfect sense to read the above account of the AH in the context of the secularising tendencies in the Leiden circle, of which Grotius' was a central part, as sketched by Somos. In such an approach the AH would be the work secularising the interpretation of the Revolt, in a way complementary to Heinsius' secularisations of tragedy and Bible criticism.

hopes to build bridges between the warring factions by presenting the truth of a solid historical analysis of the previous history of the Revolt.[69]

Remarks on the AH project in Grotius' correspondence tell us some important things about his views of the historian's role in politics.[70] To him, this role is something very specific. First, a remark on the selection of facts to be presented refers to an important dichotomy in historiography as seen by the humanists: that between sources of facts, chronicles (the 'lower' form of historiography) on the one hand, and the 'higher' historiography that is based on it, on the other: i.e. the historiography that produces narratives with a literary and philosophical aspect, in which moral judgments are passed, praise and blame are meted out, and insight into the deeper truths of history is presented. Thus the selection and combination of the available material, the development of explanation and vision, and the phrasing of the Revolt's story in Tacitus' style (which, as we shall see, actually presupposes a particular type of judgment and 'insight') belong to the higher historian's task. This division of tasks in historiography too stems from antiquity.[71]

The higher genre of historiography was supposed to be useful to the individual and to society in various ways. In the first place, there was the general formative and intellectual benefit that could be ascribed to historiography as a part of the *studia humanitatis*. Secondly, there was the exemplary use of great men and their deeds: this function of historiography drives the mechanism by which virtue receives its reward in the form of glory and, moreover, those living in the present are inspired to imitate past greatness, to the benefit of all. Vice versa, the bad also receive their punishment in the form of dishonour and by serving as negative examples. In the third place, history was seen as a useful record, as the memory of humankind from which one could, among other things, gain wisdom to act upon in the present.[72] In the second and third forms of use, for instance in political deliberation and laudatory, vituperative or deliberative texts (published or not), references to the past may be more or less politically motivated and biased. Judging from Grotius' statements, this political motivation is a significant factor in the case of the AH.

[69] The same has been said of Grotius' theological oeuvre: see Israel, *Dutch Republic*, p. 580, with reference to H.J. de Jonge, 'The Study of the New Testament' in: *Leiden University in the Seventeenth Century*, pp. 65–110.

[70] For a more extensive account, see J. Waszink, 'Tacitism in Holland: Hugo Grotius' Annales et Historiae de rebus Belgicis' in: Rhoda Schnur (ed.), *Acta Conventus Neo-Latini Bonnensis: Proceedings of the 12th International Congress of Neo-Latin Studies* (Bonn 2003). Medieval & Renaissance Texts & Studies vol. 315, 2006. For Grotius' correspondence regarding the AH, see Waszink, 'Grotius' AH in his correspondence'.

[71] In precisely this sense the histories by Grotius and Hooft have been contrasted with the 'annalistic approach' by e.g. Emanuel Van Meteren, Pieter Bor and Everhard van Reyd; see A. Janssen, 'A 'Trias Historica' on the Revolt of the Netherlands: Emanuel van Meteren, Pieter Bor and Everhard van Reyd as Exponents of Contemporary Historiography' in A.C. Duke and C.A. Tamse (eds.), *Clio's Mirror, Historiography in Britain and the Netherlands*, Zutphen 1985, pp. 9–30, p. 10.

[72] For the 'exemplary and 'deliberative' use of history, see e.g. Lipsius, *Politica* § I.9.

It is important to keep in mind that humanist historiography is almost invariably politically driven. This is a consequence of one of the essential characteristics of the humanist movement: its strong engagement with practical ethics, life and society. The classical Roman view that a gentleman has a duty to make himself useful to the *res publica*, as especially promoted by Cicero, exercised a great influence on all humanists from the fourteenth century onward. Around 1600 Grotius speaks of his duties in The Hague in similar Ciceronian terms.[73] To Grotius, a politically motivated use of historiography as part of the fulfilment of his duties to society, was not only legitimate, but was the most desirable use of history.

When speaking about the usefulness (*fructus*) of the AH, Grotius makes a direct connection between the Leicester period and the Truce controversies. In a 1614 letter to Jean Hotman de Villiers (1552–1636), Leicester's former secretary who had provided him with information for the AH, Grotius emphasises the use that the material sent to him would have in the present circumstances through the AH. It appears that in his view he would serve the public peace and the *Staatsgezinde* cause alike by spreading his interpretation of the Revolt.[74] In an earlier letter to the Heidelberg councillor Georg Lingelsheim (*c.*1556–1636) he had made an explicit connection between the troubles of the Leicester period (1585–1587) and those of the Truce years, and the importance of historical understanding in this respect.[75]

73 E.g. *Briefwisseling* vol. I, ep. 49 (25 January 1604, to Lingelsheim), 'ego quidem paene totus in foro sum', ('I am almost entirely absorbed by advocacy').

74 See Grotius, *Briefwisseling* vol. 1, ep. 389 (Dec. 1614, to Jean Hotman de Villiers).

75 *Briefwisseling* vol. I, ep. 304 (mid-November 1613), pp. 281–282: 'Cum viri boni de capite ac fortunis periclitarentur pro publica libertate adversus Licestrium decertantes, ministri quam diligentissime poterant promotum ibant externam dominationem. Haec quam vera sint, quam cogitatu necessaria, difficile est iis persuadere, qui a nobis absunt longius, cum plerique etiam nostrum, qui rem publicam non nisi extrinsecus spectant, vix satis ista intelligant. Tu vero etiam ad edendam historiam me hortaris, cum videas quam mihi noceat tam exigui libelli fortis libertas. Eadem quae hic de ministris scribuntur, ibi taceri sine flagitio non poterunt. Veritas et lex historiae id exigunt: patefacienda sunt omnium et bene et male facta. Quomodo igitur illa, de quibus modo tractabam, Flandrica, item Licestriana tempora tractabo? (...) Vivimus place seculo indigno, quo scribatur historia. Thuanus Romanam censuram patitur: sed sunt etiam extra Romam censores, quibus si idem potentiam dares, quod habet Romanum sacerdotium, non multo ea moderatius uterentur.', 'When the good men were risking their lives and fortunes for the sake of public freedom in their fight against Leicester, the [Calvinist] clergy went out to push for the establishment of a foreign domination with all the energy they had. But however true this is, and however necessary to contemplate, it is difficult to persuade others of it who live far away, since most of them, even among ourselves, who observe our commonwealth only from an outside perspective, do not sufficiently understand these things. However, you stimulate me to publish this history, although you see how much the unrestrained expression of this little book is harming me. The things written on the clergy in these letters cannot then be hushed over without wrongdoing. Truth and the law of historiography demand it: all deeds, good and evil, must be brough to light. But how will I narrate the matters just discussed, the Flanders campaign and similarly the Leicester period? (...) Without doubt we live in an age unworthy to have its history written. De Thou is undergoing Roman censorship; but there are censors outside Rome as well, who would use that power which the Roman priesthood has, if it were given to them, with not much greater moderation'; see also § 8.3 below.

During the years in which he wrote the AH, Grotius communicated his thoughts on historiography in correspondences with men like Lingelsheim and the great French politician and historian Jacques-Auguste de Thou (1553–1617). These letters make it clear that it was Grotius' ambition to become a statesman-and-contemporary historian after the ideal image he cherished of De Thou.[76] However, Grotius takes the traditional humanist 'uses' of history[77] a significant step further.

The classical *topos* held that an Achilles needs a Homer in order to gain fame with posterity. When Grotius, a pensionary and a States member, writes to De Thou that he wants to help overcome the Truce controversies by means of his historical writings, Achilles (the statesman) and Homer (the historian) merge into one and the same person. His inside knowledge of the *res*, the actual events and their backgrounds, combined with his insight into the true motives and causations, inform and define not only his historical work, but also steer the events themselves. For his own work on the Revolt and the birth of the Republic he chose Tacitus as a model: the political and psychological *acumen* of the Tacitean historian works both on the political stage and in the historical work. Thus, in this ideal, the Tacitean statesman-historian occupies a pivotal place in politics and society: through his person and work, the events and (contemporary) historiography influence *each other*.

For Grotius historiography is no longer merely a related activity for the educated councillor, with or without political implications, but a direct instrument for ruling in the hands of the government itself. Crucial to the working of this instrument is the statesman-historian's sharp perception of the *real* historical motives and causes. As we will see in § 7.1 many commentators of the period made a direct connection between Tacitus' historical works and *civilis prudentia* (statesmanship, political prudence with a real application in the present. Thus the (Tacitean) *acumen* or *iudicium*, the keen and pungently expressed insight into the true motives and psychological state of man and his politics, belongs to the core of Grotius' ambitions both as a politician and a historian: the combination of *inside* knowledge and Tacitean *insight* imposes that if any history of the Revolt is to be seen as its real history, it is this one. At least, this seems to have been Grotius' ambition in choosing the Tacitean model. In 1614 and 1615 however, about two years after the work was left unpublished, we find him writing that he had lacked knowledge and judgement when writing the AH, and expressing dissatisfaction with the work as it is.[78]

To Grotius, his older contemporary De Thou came close to this ideal. It is clear from their correspondence that at the time Grotius sought to be such a statesman-historian himself. He repeatedly compares himself to De Thou and

[76] See Waszink, 'Grotius' AH in his correspondence' and id., 'Tacitism in Holland'. For Grotius' admiration for De Thou see also § 11.2 and note.

[77] E.g. intellectual *fructus*; the creation of *gloria* and of *exempla* to the living; the provision of guidance in political deliberations.

[78] See Grotius, *Briefwisseling* 1 ep. 315 of 5 Febr. 1614 and ep. 409 of 5 June 1615 (both to J.A. de Thou).

complains about his own uneducated compatriots.[79] Besides the AH, *Ordinum Pietas* too can be regarded as a product of an author with this ideal; which makes it only natural that Grotius sent a copy of the book to De Thou. This bold ideal is characteristic of the high ambitions and expectations which Grotius fostered in his 'Holland years'. Tacitean *acumen* belongs to the core of his ambitions on *both* the political and the historiographical level.

6.
Controversial content and the non-publication of the AH in 1612–1613

With respect to our opening question why the AH were not published in 1612 or 1613, the above puts us in a position to propose an answer.

By the early 1600s, the States' government in Holland had become a stable, if not to say normal governing body, while the Revolt had turned into a more or less regular foreign war. Rather than the rightfulness and glory of the rebellion against a tyrant and his servants, it was now in the interest of the States, as rulers, to stress the need for public obedience and civic order.[80] This development was also stimulated by the Truce Conflicts, as the rise of these troubles involved the risk that those disaffected with the States' religious policies would turn rebellious once again, referring to their perceived duty to protect the true faith. This may help explain why Grotius, who was writing directly at the request of the States of Holland and stood in close contact with their leader, Johan van Oldenbarnevelt, does so little to glorify the early years of the rebellion. In 'deconstructing' the glory of the original resistance, Grotius thus seems to be speaking in harmony with the ideological needs of the progressively stabilising republican government.

Reason of state figures in several forms in the AH, and some of those, such as the description (or speculation) about hidden motives, may help explain the difficulties the AH experienced when the work was submitted for publication. For even if the author of the narrative does possess the proper source-material to base his claims on (which can only rarely be the case), making them public involves many risks. The *Annales* contain several claims which might offend the orthodox readership, inside and outside the Republic, by presenting their pursuits and institutions in a negative light (see the quotes given earlier).

However, even more risky it was to press thoroughly *Staatsgezinde* interpretations of the religious policies of Elizabeth and even William the Silent himself, the revered *pater patriae* of the Dutch Republic who, according to the Calvinists in the Dutch Republic, had given his life for the sake of the true faith, and who figured,

[79] E.g. *Briefwisseling*, vol. I, ep. 128 (1608), 169 (1609), 409 (1615); the complaint in ep. 22 (1601).

[80] For a related argument see Simon Stevin's *Burgherlick Leven*, which dismisses the issue of a ruling government's legitimacy altogether, on the grounds that such a question would lead to a *regressio ad infinitum*, as every government came into being at the cost of a previous one.

with his descendants, more or less as their own *defensor fidei*.[81] In Grotius' description however Orange is presented as using religion as a mere instrument to secure short-terms political objectives; a suggestion which, in the political and religious sentiments of that time, amounts to an accusation of Machiavellian atheism. See the following passage on the unsuccessful peace negotiations of 1579 (in 3.25):

> While the siege [of Maastricht] continued, the Emperor, to whom as we said the attempt to arrange peace was entrusted, sent an embassy to Cologne; the Spanish sent the Duke of Terranova to that place with mandates from the king, and from the Low Countries' side, the Duke of Aarschot and others came. William of Orange however, who had never doubted that any peace with the king would result in danger to him, since the Low Countries were then divided and he himself right in the middle between all these parties, and was therefore hated, feared not without reason that he would be surrendered to foreign and domestic enemies alike. On the other hand, to turn away from the negotiations and the German referees, was difficult and damaging to his reputation. *More in the dark, to achieve the same, he took care that the religious issue would be insisted upon, and other things which no one expected the king to agree with* [italics mine]. Otherwise it is credible that fairly reasonable peace conditions could have been obtained at that time, if some individuals had not with private agreements subverted the public peace.

Similarly, about Elizabeth: (5.7, 1585, during the Anglo-Dutch negotiations on military aid from Britain):

> But the wise woman foresaw the accusation of having pilfered someone else's dominion: and avoided the involvement of her own fame and fortune by such a close tie in doubtful circumstances. It seemed wiser to have secret bases of support spread over the Low Countries, and, while keeping moderate forces there, and sending forces over every now and then to destroy the American colonies, to exhaust the Spaniard, until he would turn his thoughts to peace and remove the hated troops. However, she promised help, testifying her promise in writing, in which she referred to the custom of princes to relieve the oppressed, to the old friendly alliances between Britain and the Low Countries, together with a condemnation of Spanish crimes. At the same time, *she pretended to act for the sake of religion* [italics by the editor], the security of which she demonstrated, by referring to the events in France and Scotland, to be entrusted to her without any desire for another one's possessions.[82]

[81] For some pamphlets from the period which express this view of the Princes of Orange, see Y. van Vugt and J.H. Waszink, 'De Middenweg als uitweg? Politiek in Hoofts Baeto', *Tijdschrift voor Nederlandse Taal- en Letterkunde* 116 (2000): 2–22.

[82] As to the question of Grotius' documentary sources for his claims, see § 10. More on Elizabeth in the long biographical epilogue after her death in 1603 (at the opening of *Historiae* book 12),

In keeping with the Tacitist register, both quotations display no tone of accusation, just one of cool, disengaged description. Grotius' general point appears to be the *observation* (without explicit judgment) that politicians do things for political (or perhaps for legal) reasons, not for religious ones.[83] However, to a reader not introduced to the particular sentiments connected with the Tacitean style and conception of man and morality, passages like these can hardly fail to produce the impression that Grotius is accusing William the Silent of a very impious use of the faith for short-term and self-interested political ends. Taking into account Grotius' pronouncements on the role of his work in the Truce Conflicts, it seems that he hoped his 'Tacitist' revelations about William the Silent and others might convince the Calvinist opponents of the States' government that Orange had primarily been driven by political motives, more particularly the defence of the ancient liberties, rather than that of the true faith. This should then reconcile them to the conclusion that the true origin and nature of the Revolt, and consequently of the Dutch republic, had to be sought at political rather than the religious level: and that therefore the States' party's drive for the submission of religion to politics was justified, that the Calvinist demands for a strong and independent church were unjustified, and that obedience was owed to the States.

Style plays a crucial role here.[84] The way key 'characters' are credited with thoughts and motives like the above, would have made them look Machiavellian to many. In ordinary (literary) language, depictions like the two just discussed would have been highly controversial, and would either have looked like an attack on the character in question, or would have made Grotius and/or his commissioners look like Machiavellians. To neutralise them in this respect, while preserving the *purport* of Grotius' politico-historical analysis (i.e. that in reality moral ideals and religion submit to political needs), the Tacitist style would indeed be

where Grotius a.o. praises her tolerant religious policies. The combination of the two passages thus provides another confirmation of the connection in Grotius' mind between reason of state and religious toleration.

[83] Grotius stresses a similar point in a letter to Georg Lingelsheim in 1617 (after the publication of his *De Imperio Summarum Potestatum* which provoked a debate about precisely this issue); see *Briefwisseling* vol. 1 ep. 529 (p. 582): 'Regina Angliae, cum olim legati nostrae reipublicae causam belli in religionis veritate collocarent, dixit: Arbitratam se pro legibus pugnari ab iis, quibus credita esset legum tutela, si aliter se res haberet, neque se neque principem ullum se immixturum causae iniustae et principibus formidabili. Abbothus [=R. Abbot in *De Antichristo*] .... obiectionem Belgicorum armorum solvit eo, quod non privata pro religione, sed publica pro legibus fuerint, [..]' ('At one point, when representatives of our Republic based the righteousness of their war on religious truth, the queen of England said that in her opinion those to whom the protection of the laws is entrusted, fight for the laws, and that even it were different, nor she nor any other prince would get involved in a cause both unjust and fearful to princes. R. Abbot [...] solved the objection to [taking part in] the Low Countries war by pointing out that it was not a private war for the sake of religion, but a public one for the sake of the laws.)' See also ibid. ep. 552, p. 602 to Vossius, 'armorum iustitiam petant a religione.'

[84] For a fuller discussion, see Waszink, 'Tacitism in Holland'.

a very suitable instrument. In a Tacitean world, *all* human political behaviour is morally defective, so that from this (relativistic) perspective, Grotius' view of the early Revolt appears as observation and analysis of fact, disentangled from moral judgement. The literary style thus works as a permanent reminder to the reader of Grotius' application of this particular (non-)moral perspective, and should enable him to say things about e.g. William or Elizabeth which otherwise would have been too controversial.

For this mechanism to work however, recognition and understanding of the Tacitean perspective by the reader is essential, and here the shoe pinches. The States might have feared that accounts of the Prince and the Revolt like the one just quoted would only offend and deepen the rift of the Truce Conflicts instead of bringing reconciliation. The '*Politique*' approach to religious policy, as well as reason of state in general were still controversial categories and could very easily provoke accusations of Machiavellism, atheism and tyranny.[85] Moreover, by publishing this view of the Revolt officially as *their* view, they would even run the risk of tainting their own rule with the same odour of Machiavellism that could so easily be read in these descriptions. For by referring to it while justifying their own regime, they would almost necessarily imply their agreement with it. It seems no coincidence that the States' resolution quoted above (note 2) mentions a need to investigate whether it would be 'wiser to publish or to withhold the work'. Also, if the dating of the *Annales*' composition to the years 1602–1605 is correct, the ongoing polarisation in Dutch society, especially from 1611 onwards, may help explain why views that were merely unvarnished around 1604 would be deemed too risky for print by 1612–1613.[86]

That such fears were justified can be demonstrated by some of the public responses to government policies from the Truce period. Two satirical prints from a few years later charge precisely these incriminations of political deceit and atheist abuse of religion against the policies of Oldenbarnevelt and the States of Holland. One is an adaptation of the well-known Breugel image 'Big fish eat little fish', with added names re-framing the image for the context of the Truce Conflicts; the other is a print by Pieter Feddes van Harlingen (1586–*c.*1623) with a long satirical poem attacking Johan van Oldenbarnevelt's politics (see appendix 5).[87]

Obviously this type of response was not the only one around; there are also many other, and more moderate voices from the public which stress the crucial

[85] For a discussion of the difficult position of reason-of-state thought around 1600, see M. Viroli, *From Politics to Reason of State,* Cambridge 1992, p. 252, and Waszink, 'Introduction' ch. 2 and 4 in: J. Lipsius, *Politica*.

[86] Cp. also '*quam mihi noceat tam exigui libelli fortis libertas*' in note 74.

[87] For further discussion of these prints, see J. Waszink, 'Oldenbarnevelt and Fishes. Satirical Prints from the 12-Years Truce', in: *History of European Ideas* vol. 46.7 (2020), pp. 903–915. Further H. Helmers, 'Angstcultuur en complotdenken tijdens het Bestand', *Tijdschrift voor Geschiedenis*, vol. 134-2 (2021), pp. 230–253.

importance of concord and dialogue.[88] But however that be, the Feddes poem and print reflect the deeply conflicted and polarised state of the public debate in the United Provinces in the later 1610s. Insults, accusations and incriminations are towered upon the leading men of the *Staatsgezinde* party in Holland; not just on Oldenbarnevelt's head but on Wtenbogaert, Grotius, Moersbergen, Hoogerbeets, Leedenberg and Van Toor as well. Nor is there any attempt or willingness, not even satirically, to understand the perspective of the others or a sense of a need to present evidence for the poem's outrageous claims. The text is seething with words invoking the orthodox perception of the *Staatsgezinde* religious policy as deceptive, immoral, tyrannical, Machiavellian: *loos, deurtrapt, arg, list, listich, listigheyt, bedwang, 'secreten van het land', Tyranny, twist, 'schijn van Godsdienst', beveynsd, regiersucht, hovaerdy* [false, rogue, evil, ruse, cunning, slyness, force, 'secrets of State', tyranny, discord, 'semblance of religion', dissembled, lust for power, conceit]. The link between the two images is the use of a big fish to represent tyranny, with an added dimension of Machiavellism, deceit and foul play in the Feddes image. In summary, the poem's main polemical points are:

- Oldenbarnevelt is a secret agent of the Spaniards, conspiring to bring about the downfall of the Dutch Republic and re-conquest by Spain;
- The Twelve Years' Truce of 1609 is part of a secret Spanish plan to reconquer the Dutch Republic;
- The religious controversy and near-fatal discord of the 1610s were deliberately engineered by Oldenbarnevelt as the instrument to achieve the above;
- Oldenbarnevelt is a master of political deceit, cunning, manipulation and tyranny;
- Remonstrant theology is a false 'new doctrine' introduced in order to sow discord
- one fish 'eating' another means: subjugate, make one's instrument.

Thus the Feddes poem and image confirm that the type of reason state-logic and 'Machiavellism' at play in the AH were indeed highly sensitive items in the intellectual context in which Grotius was writing, and that consequently the AH, if published, could have contributed to this negative image of the States' policies. The fear of this damaging effect seems likely to have helped persuade the States to refrain from publishing this work.[89]

[88] See the plays of 1616 discussed by Spaans, 'Public opinion or cultural celebration of concord' and e.g. Hooft's *Baeto* (see Van Vugt & Waszink, 'De middenweg als uitweg' and lit. referred to there).

[89] It is interesting here to note two documents kept in the Municipal library in Rotterdam, stemming from the Remonstrant church archives, *Apologia Remonstrant*[ium] *verbis praecipue Taciti conscripta. Juny 1620* ('An Apology of the Remonstrants, written primarily in words from Tacitus. June 1620') and *Pro Contraremonstrantibus Apologia verbis Taciti praecipue conscripta* ('An Apology for the Counterremonstrants, written primarily in words from Tacitus'), which indicate that in Remonstrant circles

For balance, some idea of the wilder suspicions entertained on the opposite side among the *Staatsgezinden* regarding their opponents' motives, may be derived from Grotius' own reminiscences in conversation with Guy Patin in the 1640s. Grotius there claims (1) that Maurice hated Oldenbarnevelt because the Truce had robbed him (Maurice) of the occasion to conduct a war; and (2) that Maurice had ambitions to become German emperor through the protestant revolt in Bohemia (1618–1619), and then to obtain monarchical control of the Republic, a design Oldenbarnevelt allegedly set out to prevent.[90]

With respect to the memory-culture perspective on the early-17th century memory and historiography on the revolt (see § 2.3, end), the present discussion of Grotius' AH confirms very clearly how much the interpretation of the Revolt (i.e. the *libertatis/religionis ergo* controversy) mattered in the polarised politics of the Truce period. However the story of the AH enriches the picture of both this 'memory war' and the 'secular memory culture' in the North with several dimensions, such as the intimate connections of the *libertatis/religionis* controversy with the ongoing debates everywhere in Europe on reason of state, Machiavellism and political ethics, and the submission of religion to politics (or their separation); the government (States of Holland)'s direct involvement with and supervision of the historiography on the Revolt; the view that the seeds of the Truce troubles had been sown by Leicester and his partisans in the 1580s; and the *Staatsgezinde* side's distrust of *all* organised and dogmatic religion.

7. Tacitism

The implications of the Tacitist nature of the AH for its position in the political context of the Truce period have been discussed above in § 4. In this chapter we will investigate the Tacitism in the work as such. For perspicuity we shall distinguish Tacitist content and ideas from the literary 'style' proper, although these aspects are intimately connected, as we have seen above, and must not be separated when we read the *Annales* in their historical context.

7.1. *Tacitist content and ideas*

The word *Tacitism* was coined by Giuseppe Toffanin in 1921 and is nowadays used to refer to a range of moral, political, historiographical and critical discourses in

the Tacitist angle on contemporary politics remained alive after the crisis of 1617–1618; Rotterdam, Gemeentebibliotheek, MSS. Remonstrants-Gereformeerde Gemeente, 417a and 417b. These mss. are not in Grotius' hand, nor are the assembled quotations used in Grotius' *Apologeticus* of 1622, all indications that someone else than Grotius is the author. However the item 'cuncta et privata vulnera reip[ublicae] malis operire statuerunt' (Tac. *Hist.* I.53.2) is recognisable in Grotius, *Annales* 1.20 'Multi publica mala suis remedium, aut obtegumentum quaerebant'.

[90] See Patin, 'Grotiana' p. 79 in Pintard (ed.), *La Mothe le Vayer, Gassendi, Guy Patin*.

Europe from the mid-16th to the eighteenth century, that took their chief inspiration from the works of the Roman historian Cornelius Tacitus (*c.* AD 55–115).[91] Tacitus' *Annals* and *Histories* describe the disintegration of Roman political society after the decline of the Republic had led to the establishment of the Principate. These works are marked by a keen eye for 'true' causes and motivations of people (notably self-interest) and the paradoxes of power. Tacitus conveys moral judgement mostly implicitly and looks at things as they really *are* (according to him), rather than the way they *should* be. This disenchanted, undisguising realism is complemented by a particular literary style that is marked by short and irregular forms, intentional asymmetry and unusual choice of words, as well as a fondness for sceptical, almost proverbial observations (*sententiae*). Similarly, for Tacitus the causes of historical events reside on the level of either human action (politics, intrigue, bravery, error, etc) or that of chance, rather than on that of some kind of divine oversight or an inherent connection between virtue and good fortune.[92]

As already noted the Tacitean character of the AH is made very explicit already by the title alone, and no less by the work's unusual literary style itself.[93] This observation, however, calls for a closer study of that imitation, as perceptions of style and taste are both personal and historical in nature. What are the actual qualities and characteristics of Grotius' imitation of Tacitus? For indeed, modern readers of the AH will miss in Grotius' work many conspicuous (and attractive) features of Tacitus' prose that we see today, such as the intense involvement with individual character and psychology, and narrative development in the longer lines of the 'story'.[94] Thus at the core of this chapter is a question that belongs as much to Conceptual history (*Begriffsgeschichte*) as it does to philology proper: What was 'Tacitism' and 'Tacitean' for an author from the late 16th and early 17th century? A comparison of Grotius' imitation of Tacitus' style and approach with the modern view of those, even if such a comparison has to deal with a few theoretical tangles, will also tell us something about the specific qualities and characteristics of the early-modern perception of Tacitus, and thus about Tacitism itself.

91 G. Toffanin, *Machiavelli e il 'Tacitismo'. La Politica storica al tempo della Controriforma*, Padova: Angelo Draghi, 1921 (repr. Napoli: Guida Editori, 1972). The literature on Tacitism is extensive, esp. on individual authors and contexts. For overviews see, P. Burke, 'Tacitism, Scepticism and Reason of State'; id., 'Tacitism' in T. Dorey (ed.), *Tacitus*, London (Routledge) 1969, pp. 149–171; M. van der Poel and J. Waszink, 'Tacitismus' in: *Historisches Wörterbuch der Rhetorik*, ed. G. Ueding, vol. 9, Tübingen: Max Niemeyer Verlag, col. 1113–1123.

92 See e.g. R. Mellor, *Tacitus*, New York (Routledge) 1994 pp. 63–67, 87–112; or e.g R. Syme, *Tacitus*, Oxford 1958 vol. 1 § 30 'The sceptical historian' (p. 397–407) and vol. 2 § XLI (pp. 547–565) 'Doctrines and government'.

93 In a letter to Georg Lingelsheim of 1 November 1606 (i.e. at the height of the work on the AH) Grotius calls himself 'infelix imitator' of Tacitus. *Briefwisseling* vol. 1 ep. 86 pp. 72–73.

94 See e.g. the questions posed by Marc van der Poel in 'Tacitean Elements in Grotius' narrative of the Capture of Breda (1590) by Stadtholder Maurice, Count of Nassau (*Historiae*, book 2)', in: *Grotiana* 30 (2009), pp. 207–246.

Although Tacitus' modern reception starts in the mid-15th century, his works did not come out of the shadow of Livian and Ciceronian moral and stylistic ideals before the last quarter of the 16th century. By that time the *Annals* and *Histories* became recognised as a pessimistic, but highly appealing account of human greatness and weakness and their roles in history. As civil and religious wars broke up the old political order in Europe, the Tacitist approach gained influence as a way of looking at contemporary events, while his prose style met with a new appreciation, first with scholars in history and politics, then with a wider audience (though Tacitism never became a 'popular' phenomenon). This new interest in Tacitus reflected crucial changes in the conception of politics – that is, a shift from politics as an activity centred on civic or princely virtue and participation, towards one mainly determined by interest and the preservation of power.

The most influential Tacitist and Tacitus-scholar in this period was undoubtedly the South-Netherlander Justus Lipsius (1547–1606),[95] whose works and teaching created the intellectual context in which Grotius chose Tacitus as the model for his historical narrative of the Low Countries' revolt. Lipsius' presentation and interpretation of Tacitus' works was to have a lasting influence on early modern historical and political thought. In the dedication to the Emperor Maximilian of his famous edition of Tacitus' works of 1574 Lipsius gives the following characterisation of this author:[96]

> A sharp writer, my God, and a sagacious one; and whose being circulated among men was never more useful than in our time and circumstances. He does not discuss the victories of Hannibal, terrible to the Romans, nor the beautiful death of Lucretia, or the prophesies of soothsayers, or Etruscan portents or other things which serve more to delight the reader than to instruct him; but here everyone can inform himself about the courts of princes, their inner lives, their plans, commands, and deeds, and, in most things the similarity with our own time being evident, his mind can grasp the truth that similar causes lead to similar outcomes. Under the Tyranny you will find flattery and accusations, evils not unknown to our own time; everything dishonest, nothing straightforward, and confidence not even safe with one's own friends; repeated accusations of lèse-majesté, the only crime of those who were without crime; murder after murder of great men; and a peace more cruel than any war.

[95] For the place of Lipsius' Latin style, see e.g. M. Fumaroli, *L'âge de l'éloquence: rhétorique et 'res literaria' de la Renaissance au seuil de l'époque classique*, Geneva 1980; J. Jansen, *Brevitas. Beschouwingen over de beknoptheid van vorm en stijl in de renaissance*, Hilversum (Verloren) 1995, esp. vol. 1 pp. 179–195 (and passim); Waszink, 'Introduction' to Lipsius, *Politica;* T. Deneire, 'The Philology of Justus Lipsius' Prose Style', Wiener Studien vol. 125 (2012), pp. 189–262.

[96] Also published as *Iusti Lipsi Epistolae* 1, 74 07 00M. Translation from *Politica*, ed. Waszink.

In the *Notae* appended to Lipsius' *Politica* of 1589, we find the following:[97]

> Then the Latin [historians], of whom the leading one in my view is Cornelius Tacitus. Before Livy? you will ask. Not with respect to eloquence or other [stylistic] virtues, but with respect to the things we are dealing with now, i.e. the marks of prudence and good judgement [*prudentiae et iudicii notis*]. Who tells more truthfully than he, or more briefly? Who teaches more in telling? Which moral topic is there which he does not touch upon? Which emotion that he does not reveal? He is an amazing writer in every respect, and one who thoroughly treats even that which he does not treat. Nor is it just History, but as it were a garden and nursery of instructions. Just as people who colour clothing with needle-work ingeniously add gemstones without disturbing or detracting from the form of the garment, just so Tacitus inserts Sententiae all over, without in any way losing or damaging the line of the narrative. Still he seems rugged and obscure to some. Is that his fault or their own? For I admit his writing is sharp and penetrating: and such must be those who read him. Therefore I recommend him more to the Counsellors of Princes, than to the Princes themselves; and let them employ him as a guide to both their Wisdom and Prudence alike.

Lipsius had taught in Leiden until three years before Grotius' own arrival at that university, and his memory appears to have been very much alive in the university during Grotius' undergraduate years. Jan de Groot had been among Lipsius' students and acquaintances in the 1570s, had remained in contact with him and had once taken the young Hugo specifically to Leiden to visit the great scholar (although Grotius later confessed he did not remember the occasion[98]). Grotius and Lipsius exchanged a few polite, but mutually appreciative letters in 1600 and 1601, after the publication of Grotius' Aratus edition and the *Adamus Exul* respectively.[99] After Lipsius' death in 1606 (at the time when Grotius was writing the AH), Grotius joined in the chorus of voices that insisted on Leiden's share

97 *Nota* to *Politica* I.9 (published separately in 1589).

98 In a conversation recorded by Guy Patin (1601–1672), French doctor and man of letters, whose notes and letters preserve a wealth of information on the scholarly world of his age. His notes from conversation(s) with Grotius are published as 'Grotiana' in: R. Pintard, *La Mothe le Vayer, Gassendi, Guy Patin. Études de bibliographie et de critique suivies de textes inédits de Guy Patin*, Paris (Boivin), 1943. See also Nellen, *Hugo Grotius*, pp. 18, 22, 30, 40, 56–58.

99 *Briefwisseling* vol. 1, ep. 17, 18, 25, 28. On the intellectual relationship between Lipsius and Grotius, see J. Waszink, 'Lipsius and Grotius: Tacitism'; A. Eyffinger, 'Justus Lipsius and Hugo Grotius: Two views on Society' in *Lipsius in Leiden*, ed. by K. Enenkel and C. Heesakkers (Voorthuizen) Florivallis, 1997; and id., 'Amoena gravitate morum spectabilis – Justus Lipsius and Hugo Grotius' in *The world of Justus Lipsius: A contribution towards his intellectual biography*, ed. by M. Laureys, Proceedings of a colloquium in the Belgian Historical Institute in Rome, 22–24 May 1997, Brussels (Belgisch Historisch Instituut te Rome), 1998, pp. 297–328.

in Lipsius' fame, calling him *Lipsius noster*. That Grotius knew Lipsius' notes on Tacitus appears abundantly from his own.[100]

Furthermore, Grotius and Lipsius shared some basic assumptions regarding religious policy and reason of state in the controversies of their time, to which readings of Tacitus were of crucial importance. Thus, Lipsius and Grotius are related as readers of Tacitus, and Lipsius' comments on Tacitus can serve to give us an idea of the perception of Tacitus' works that must roughly have been shared by Grotius.

Tacitus' special capacity for historical truth, as perceived at this time, is further illustrated by Traiano Boccalini's satire *Ragguagli di Parnasso,* ('News from Parnassus', 1612), where Livy and Tacitus are contrasted as embodying beauty of style and historical truth respectively. Other authors in Grotius' environment expressed similar ideas, which can be seen for example in Daniel Heinsius' (1580–1655) *Orationes* on Tacitus,[101] and in Gerardus Johannes Vossius' (1577–1649) *De historicis Latinis* (1627).[102] Here we also find recorded some of the doubts that were voiced against Tacitus' style:

> Tacitus' style is brighter and richer in the *Histories*; more sober in the *Annals*. And at the same time it is grave and eloquent in both. (...) And what to think of that which [Alciatus] and Aemilius Ferretus say, that is, that Tacitus doesn't write proper Latin? How foolish! And what lack of taste! For who does not see how elegant, polished and finished Tacitus' style is? And even so, still greater praise to this writer is that nothing that is more sagacious than he can even be thought of. (...[that the emperor Tacitus cultivated the historian, may be explained by his belief in family ties]) But what else to make of the fact that no other historian was read equally eagerly by Cosimo de Medici, duke of Tuscany, a man, if ever one was, of unsurpassed insight in statesmanship, and obviously born to rule.

Similar judgments appear in many other places in Europe at the time.[103]

[100] See Damon, 'Tritus in eo lector'.

[101] *Danieli Heinsii Orationum Editio Nova*, Leiden 1627. See e.g. *Oratio XIV De secunda et postrema Romanorum aetate* etc. after a brief outline of Roman history from the first Punic war to the early Principate, Heinsius expands (p. 190): '[In the early Principate] Videbitis ubique aulicas patriciasque artes et insidias occultas: nihil liquidum, sincerum nihil, nihil sui simile aut unius formae. (...) Haec ita docet, ita eruit ac detegit, ita ob oculos ponit Tacitus, ut in animis Principum atque in pectoribus vixisse et eorum cogitationes perlustrasse videatur. Nihil illum latuit aut fugit. (...) Nihil illo gravius, compressius, castigatius, prudentius', etc. On the style: 'Sententiae abruptae, circumdictiones intercisae, verba paucis usitata, et erepta Graecis (...).' In *Oratio XVI Post absolutum primum librum Annalium Taciti olim habita* Heinsius writes (p. 210): 'Caii Cornelii Taciti (...) quem prudentiae civilis ducem ac magistrum unicum esse arbitramur. (...) Cornelius hic noster, ita veritatis rationem habuit, ut usum quoque adjungat: rerum successus examinet [...]', etc.

[102] pp. 146–147.

[103] See e.g. J.-M. Philo, 'Elizabeth I's Translation of Tacitus: Lambeth Palace Library, MS 683' in: *Review of English Studies*, New Series (2019) pp. 1–30, esp. pp. 3–5; and B. Irish, 'The Literary Afterlife of the Essex Circle: Fulke Greville, Tacitus, and BL Additional MS 18638' in: *Modern Philology*

However it is important to keep in mind here that this enthusiasm for Tacitus lived among certain (educated) elites, and was not, at least at this stage, a mainstream phenomenon. This can be read for example from Giovanni Botero's scathing remarks in the preface to his 1589 *Ragion di Stato* on the then-current fashion in royal courts for continuously quoting Machiavelli and Tacitus because of their insights in the techniques of power preservation.[104] For the majority of educators, clergy and others, the 'Ciceronian' approach to both ethics and Latin style remained the norm; the popularity of the Tacitist model remained relatively limited throughout.[105] This can be observed for example in the learned Isaac Casaubonus' preface to his edition of Polybius, where the nefariousness of the examples presented by Tacitus is emphasised – although Casaubonus also makes it clear that the deficiency is not Tacitus' fault, but of the age he describes, while he generally endorses Lipsius' views of Tacitus' sharpsightedness.[106]

The specific nature of Grotius' Tacitism becomes clear when we compare it with that other grand history of the Dutch revolt, the *Nederlandse Historien* by Pieter Corneliszoon Hooft, which is also written in imitation of Tacitus' style, but in the Dutch language. In Hooft's account, the early revolt appears as a heroic struggle between the courageous defenders of Dutch liberty and Protestant faith on the one hand, and the powerful, efficient and no less virtuous defenders of the Spanish imperial might on the other. When we compare Grotius' account, we find a thoroughly disenchanted and pessimistic view of both parties at war. With some simplification one could say that Grotius presents Dutch successes more as

112 (2014) pp. 271–285, esp. pp. 276–279, quoting Thomas Wilson's adaptation of a passage in Trajano Boccalini's *Ragguagli di Parnasso* where Tacitus is referred to as '*that Father of humaine Prudence, and Inventer of moderne policie*' whose works however '*out of divine providence were lost and exterminated for the benefitt of the world.*' See also the quotes collected by Amelot de la Houssaie in *Tacite avec des notes politiques et historiques, premiere partie,* Introduction ('Discours Critique'), pp. Lii–Lx.

[104] G. Botero, *Della Ragion di Stato libri dieci*, first version, Venezia 1589, preface, opening: 'Questi anni adietro [...] mi è convenuto far varii viaggi [...] nelle corti di re e di prencipi grandi, [...]: dove, tra l'altre cose da me osservate, mi ha recato somma meraviglia il sentire tutto il dì mentovare ragione di Stato, et in cotal materia citare ora Nicolò Machiavelli, ora Cornelio Tacito; quello, perché dà precetti appartenenti al governo et al reggimento de' popoli, questo, perché esprime vivamente l'arti usate da Tiberio Cesare, e per conseguire e per conservarsi nell'imperio di Roma.'

[105] See e.g. Fumaroli, *L'âge de l'éloquence*; J. Jansen, Imitatio. *Literaire navolging* (imitatio auctorum) *in de Europese letterkunde van de renaissance (1500–1700)*, Hilversum (Verloren) 2008, p. 86.

[106] See the preface to the Polybius edition of 1609: 'Tacitus[...] magni et accerrimi vir ingenii, novae cuiusdam, gravis, concisae et sententiosae eloquentiae genere eximie praeditus; si a Fortuna non esset destitutus, quae dignam ei tanta facultate materiam negavit; quemvis e principibus sive Romanorum sive etiam Graecorum historicorum videtur potuisse provocare. [...] Cornelius Tacitus Tiberios, Caligulas, Claudios, Nerones, Vitellios, non homines, sed humanae naturae prodigia nobis narrat [etc...]. Tacitum igitur facile nos quidem excusamus: illos excusari non posse iudicamus, qui unicum hunc historicum omnibus aliis anteponunt: unum Tacitum politicis hominibus assidue terendum pronuntiant [...]. Quid enim Principi, praesertim iuveni, lectione illorum Annalium esse queat pernitiosius? [..]', quoted from: Isaac Casaubon, *Polibio*, ed. G.F. Brussich, Palermo (Salerno editore) 1991, pp. 174–178. On Casaubonus and Grotius' AH, see § 11.2 and note 245.

the consequence of yet another oversight on the Spanish side, than as the fruit of virtue and discipline on the Dutch part. He continuously stresses the disorderly, self-interested and undisciplined nature of the Dutch effort, as well as the faltering military and political organisation on the Habsburg side. In this respect Grotius' imitation comes closer to the spirit of Tacitus' example than Hooft's.[107]

The above passages from Lipsius, Heinsius and Vossius provide us with a relatively clear-cut list of what Grotius' age would have seen as the main characteristics of the Tacitist register: *iudicium*, brevity, irregularity and difficulty, many *sententiae;* revelation (of hidden motives). We shall now look at the way these re-appear in Grotius' imitation.

'Judgment'

The Tacitean mode of writing involves a particular relationship between text and (perceived) historical truth for which we shall here use *iudicium* as a general term, in accordance with the terms from the above fragment from Lipsius. In this view of Tacitus, truth, perceptiveness and revelation appear as the central terms in that relationship: Tacitus' strength was felt to reside in his capacity for fact *and* judgement, that is, for a truth that transcends mere factual truth and offers insight into the real and deeper causes of events and into human nature in particular. Consequently, the discussion of *iudicium* as a Tacitean feature of Grotius' AH is a complex one that involves several sub-topics, and it is here that form and content meet and merge in a way crucial to the entire phenomenon of Tacitism. 'Sharp' for example is said of both the Tacitean style in the narrower sense of the word, and of Tacitus' content. Ronald Mellor's observation on Tacitus that 'while the use of the first person is rare, the reader is always aware of the author's critical, astringent personality conveyed through his style'[108] is also wholly applicable to Grotius' stylistic intentions and ideals.

Thus Tacitean political *iudicium* and sharpness belong to the core of Grotius' ambitions as statesman-historian (see § 5 above), and their expressions litter the AH (including many *sententiae)*, many of which also breathe the spirit of reason of state. In that sense the examples below are a continuation of those given in § 4 above on the backgrounds of William the Silent's and Elizabeth's religious policies. *Iudicium* may appear in several different forms or objects it refers to, such as (1) generalising characterological statements about groups or people involved in the conflict (the Dutch, the Spanish, the Dutch nobility, William the Silent, Philip II); (2) analysis of the general course of events, or the (possibly secret) motivations of chief agents at specific moments in the narrative; and (3) insights into the general nature of human politics, such as the role of self-interest or its secular nature. See the following examples:

[107] See § 11.2.

[108] R. Mellor, *Tacitus*, p. 126, with ref. to L. Storoni-Mazzolani, *Empire without End* (New York: Harcourt, 1976), p. 144.

1. Character:
Ann. 2.15 (1568): failing solidarity among the Dutch, esp. when it comes to contributing money:

> Orange himself made debts as well for this expedition, partly by pawning possessions of his relatives, while some small amounts were given by Lowlanders abroad who had no choice but to return home, or people at home with a secret desire for liberty. In most cases however these contributions were promised but postponed until the actual effectuation.

Ann. 2.22 (1570); the Dutch take action only when their private interests are threatened:

> Now their anger taught the oppressed the love of arms and gave them proof that no unity is so strong as that created by shared self-interest. Only then did this nation, which had looked on almost unmoved as its citizens were burned, its leaders killed, its laws, religion and constitution snatched away, make a common decision to take revenge for what had passed and forestall what was still coming.

Ann. 3.30 (1579); in William the Silent there was no harshness, but he had a fine sense of how to use people and occasions:[109]

> For every kind of cruelty was alien to him, but at the same time he knew how to use an occasion prudently, and, with the objective of bringing other people's efforts in line with those of himself, he sowed early in order to pluck the benefits in the long term.[110]

2. Analysis of courses of events or political decisions:

Ann. 2.55 (1575); sheer luck and superstition on the Spanish side:

> Next Requesens' men [...] reached the island both by ship and wading through the waters, while it remains unclear whether it was their courage more or their luck which let them do this. In their own descriptions it is the latter cause, which they relate in the fashion of old miracle tales, describing how the sea was lit up before them by heavenly torches as they went.

Ann. 2.66 (1576, after the Pacification of Ghent). The evil of religious fanaticism:

> In this entire history this was the only time one could have confidence in the Netherlands cause, if at least together with the weaponry, the internal hatred would be put down. However, when I look at it more closely, I see as the surest root of evil the competing ambitions of the nobility, and a vice in the

[109] For more on Grotius' image of William, see § 8.1 below.

[110] As to Grotius' *iudicium*, note how the purport of the lines would change if *but* was simply *and*: '... nam erat ille ab omni truculentia alienus, *sed* qui dato casu sapienter uteretur, aptandisque sibi hominum studiis in longum iaceret olim profutura.'

population which resembles it, the impatient love of their own religion, which will never acquiesce in agreements or the present situation. As long as these exist, there will always be party strife and instruments to use against liberty.

Ann. 2.14–15 (*c.*1568); the German Emperor tries to intervene on behalf of the Dutch, but leaves off for the sake of peace and because of private relationships:

This polemic touched the emperor Maximilian deeply. (...) He sent his brother Charles to Spain to deliver the message in his own name and that of the other German princes that it was not thought to be in the general interest to act too severely against the Netherlanders. Philip however, with ill-concealed anger, had the reply sent back that he could handle his own work, and that he knew which was the time for mildness and which for severity towards a people who had spurned God and would soon find out how to spurn their prince. (...) Of his own accord however the Emperor was keen on preserving peace, and soon moreover bound to Spain by new ties; and therefore he did not move.

Ann. 2.40 (1572, political motives for William the Silent to promote the accession of new towns' representations to the States of Holland):

Orange assumed the power of a prince while renouncing the title; he appointed magistrates, issued laws, administered military and naval affairs and most public business; and did all this together with a chosen council, or, in questions of greater importance, as president of a meeting of the States. This large number of gatherings served not only to create an image of popular support, but also to bind as many as possible to the cause. Whereas in earlier days six towns in Holland met (Dordrecht, Haarlem, Delft, Leiden, Amsterdam, and Gouda, together with the nobility), to deliberate upon most of the public business, Orange introduced no fewer than twelve smaller towns, which would doubtlessly be loyal to him, as they thanked their right to vote to his assistance.

Secrecy and hidden strategies

From the historian's sharp *iudicium* with respect to character, causes, and reason of state follows Tacitus' cherished capacity for revelation of hidden facts and motivations (cp. Lipsius' *interior vita* and Heinsius' discussion above). Grotius very frequently presents hidden or inner motivations of chief characters in his story, though he never explains what his privileged access (if any) to the information was. Reason-of-state thinking can often be recognised by the use of phrases like *tanquam...revera*; *specie...revera*; *dissimulare*; *praetendere*; *quasi* with subjunctive; words like *obtentus*; *arcana imperii* or *imperii artes* and other formulations which point at secrecy and deception. The examples of the hidden political intentions behind William's and Elizabeth's religious policies as discussed above in § 6 are a case point here again. Another example is Ann. 2.57 (1576):

France was ruled in these years by Henry, Charles' brother, who foresaw Spain's deceitful intentions and considered that these should be dealt with by equal measures. He fostered relations with all those looking to destroy that power, but only within the limits of secret assistance, and in this displayed an unforgettable subtlety of nearly criminal scheming. Thus he convened with the king that the Nassau party's collectors in Calais, a city in France, would sell their license to navigate the adjacent seas (...).

A special category are insinuations, which can approach the quality of Tacitus' own descriptions of character, e.g. about Philip II and his son (Ann. 2.8):

The story told about the king's son Carlos himself is even more spectacular and more darksome. It was an established fact that the successor to so many crowns was put in custody, either because his young age, ripe enough to assume power, aroused suspicions that he cared too much for the Lowlanders, as if they weren't his father's province; or because one and the same crime carried him and his step-mother away to their ends. In any case, his death came soon, and it remains unknown for which reasons father persisted in his wrath until he had killed his son.[111]

Note Grotius' skill here in combining material from the Dutch revolt with Tacitean echoes to a striking effect, heightening the sense of doom esp. by *in filii necem durasset* as adapted from the ominous Tiberian prelude in Tac. Ann. 1.6.

As to the sources and authority of such claims, see § 10 below.

3. The prominent role of self-interest in politics, or further remarks regarding the secular nature of history and politics, Ann. 1.20:

Many sought a remedy for their own in public troubles, or at least a cover: they turned disagreement into disturbances that would lead to the rise of factions, according to whatever represented a man's greatest hope or despair.

or Ann. 1.28:

Only the city of Antwerp, whose sophisticated mixture of liberty and obedience had brought her to the peak of prosperity, dared to complain that the Germans and Britons (a significant portion of her trade), were being put to flight by the severity of the edict. As a result they were granted that foreigners be treated a little more loosely, and that the part of the edict which prescribed that the sales and wills of offenders were rescinded, even before a trial – a great disturbance to trade – would be without force in their city.

[111] In this particular case the source of the claim seems quite obvious, i.e. William of Orange's *Apology* of 1580 (see reff. in § 10); *Apologie* ed. Wansink 1969 (English), pp. 45–45; or *Apologie* ed. M. Mees-Verwey 1942 (Dutch), p. 47.

Ann. 1.25, submission of religion to politics:

> I find that the sagest of princes established remedies against people of divergent religion in proportion to the magnitude of their error and the number of offenders.

Historiae 1 (p. 117) on the Pope's promise of impunity to whoever would capture queen Elizabeth for him:

> As reward for this crime he added impunity for all crimes, even before God, and other such absurdities, which would certainly have carried force in primitive centuries but today are awarded only for show, and received in show.[112]

7.2. *Syntax and forms of Grotius' imitation of Tacitus' literary style*[113]

a. Brevity

We have seen brevity mentioned by Lipsius, Heinsius and Vossius as a major characteristic of Tacitus' prose, and indeed Grotius strives to imitate it with great energy, especially in the *Annales*. No reader will overlook the dense and concise nature of Grotius' language, even if his sentences, with many sub-clauses, can be very long from full stop to full stop. Brevity is achieved in two ways: by formulations designed for shortness, pressing a maximum of information into a minimum of words, and, at a more general level, through a rigorous selection of topics and a radical reduction of the number of historical 'items' discussed. A numerical comparison of the words/narrated time ratio confirms that in Grotius' *Annales* brevity is pushed to a maximum, not only in comparison with historians of Grotius' age, but also with Tacitus himself (for example: Tacitus' *Annals* has about twice as many words/year as Grotius': Pieter Bor's *Van de Nederlandse oorlogen en beroerten*[114] about 70 times as many).

At the concrete level of paragraphs and sentences, the brevity of the *Annales* is best demonstrated by an example. Here too rigorous selection is the chief process,

[112] 'Praemium addidit sceleri scelerum impunitatem, etiam apud Deum: atque alia id genus ludibria, quae rudibus seculis haud invalida nunc tantum in speciem dantur, in speciem accipiuntur.'

[113] For more details and examples to the discussion below, see J. Waszink, 'Shifting Tacitisms. Style and Composition in Grotius' Annales' in: *Grotiana* 29 (2008), p. 85–132. On Tacitus' syntax and style, see A. Draeger, *Syntax und Stil des Tacitus,* Leipzig 1882; repr. Amsterdam, 1967; *The Annals of Tacitus*, ed. with intr. and notes by H. Furneaux (2nd edn), Oxford 1896–1907, vol. I, pp. 38–74; E. Löfstedt, 'The Style of Tacitus', in: id., *Roman Literary Portraits,* Oxford 1958, pp. 157–180; id. 'Stilgeschichtliche Gesichtspunkte' in: id., *Syntactica. Studien und Beiträge zur historischen Syntax des Lateins*, 2 vols, Lund 1933–1942, 2.11; B.-R. Voss, *Die pointierte Stil des Tacitus,* Münster 1963; R. Martin, *Tacitus,* London 1981, ch. 10 (pp. 214–235). An earlier study of Grotius' Tacitean style is available in J.C.G. Boot, 'Hugo Grotius et Cornelius Tacitus', in: Verslagen & Mededelingen van de Koninklijke Academie van Wetenschappen afd. Letterkunde, 2e reeks, 12 (1883), 333–362.

[114] P. Bor, *Vande Nederlantsche oorloghen, beroerten ende borgerlijcke oneenicheyden, gheduerende den gouvernemente vanden hertoghe van Alba inde selve landen,* Utrecht (S. de Roy) 1601.

dense formulation its completion. The lengthy and crucial siege of the town of Leiden and its lifting, which lasted in all from the autumn of 1573, with an intermission, to the autumn of 1574, is dealt with by Grotius in just seven lines (Ann. 2.53):[115]

> While this was happening, the siege of Leiden, inaugurated somewhat earlier, continued for a long time. It brought everything into peril, as the Spanish had taken hold of the heart of Holland, and there was no force to resist them except God's help and a stubborn hatred of the faithless tyranny, which at this time was so great that the story is told of a sailor who ripped the heart from a Spanish soldier's corpse and tore it to pieces with his teeth. And thus, exhausted by war and disease, having gone through all extremities of famine and a long anticipation vested in an exchange of messages through birds, as at Modena, Leiden was saved by the destruction of dykes to open the rivers' walls, and the entry of sea onto land; the moon's full circle drove up the waters, with miraculous help of the winds. And even a collapse of the walls, the worst of evils for a town, then became an instrument of salvation, for it put the image of a sortie into the enemy's ear and threw him into panic.

The departure of the besieger and the intermission in the siege, the battle on the distant plains of the Mokerhei, and the unexpected return of the Spanish (to find even their trenches undemolished) are not mentioned at all[116]; the protracted starvation and misery of the town that followed, as well as the many stories connected with the perilous and near-failed inundations of the surrounding region in order to rescue the town (which had become celebrated stories of the Revolt) are all compressed into a few elements of a minimum of words each. The reference to the moon deepens the darkness in which the entire scene is set, and the brevity itself adds a tone of solemnity. By virtue of this concentration of force, Grotius' cold depiction conveys an image of despair and cruelty which brings out the message of *Annales* book 2 with particular force: that between Philip and his Low Countries subjects a real and bitter war was now going on. However, this extreme brevity also positions the *Annales* not as a 'complete' history of the period, but as *a version* of it, interesting primarily for its literary and/or political approach, or for those readers who only want a general overview of the events and developments (e.g. a foreign audience).

[115] See for comparison Van Meteren's account of this siege, which comprises about 6000 words. On Grotius and Van Meteren see § 2,3 above.

[116] The battle on the Mokerheide is mentioned earlier, implicitly, at p. 43. The phrase 'ut Hollandia hostem detraheret' creates the link with the events in Holland, but only for a reader already familiar with the events in question.

With respect to syntax, brevity is often achieved by imitation of characteristically Tacitean syntax, such as the compression of sub-clauses into either absolute ablatives or appositions, as in Ann. 3.43:

> Sed rudem belli, et incompositam multitudinem missus ab Arausionensi Hohenloius, *commissis aliquot praeliis*, disiecit. Frisii quoque, *suspecta praefecti fide*, arces, quae remanserant, aggressi, in tempore solo aequavere: et Transisalanorum gentem ad defectionem sollicitatam, nutantemque discordiis, *missis praesidiis* restituit Arausionensis. ('This untrained and unorganised mob however was dispersed in a handful of battles by Hohenlohe, who was sent by Orange. The Frisians too, from distrust of their Stadtholder's loyalty, attacked the castles which remained in his control and levelled them to the ground. By sending garrisons Orange restored the loyalty of the people of Overijssel, who had been tempted to defect and were close to doing so due to an internal conflict.')

b. *Sententiae*

The *sententiae*, as already mentioned, are another very prominent feature of the AH. As with brevity, their presence is intensified compared to Tacitus' works. With respect to numbers, Grotius' *Annales* contain more than twice as many *sententiae* in comparable lengths of text.[117] By way of sample, a list of the *sententiae* and epigrams in books 1 and 2 is given in Appendix 6 (without claims to exhaustiveness). Not surprisingly, some of these contain formulations borrowed from or inspired by Tacitus'.

According to Quintilian's definition, a *sententia* is 'an utterance of general application, which can be deserving of praise even beyond the particular circumstances to which it refers. Sometimes it refers merely to things, as in the sentence: "There is nothing that wins the affections of the people more than goodness of heart"; or it may have a personal reference, as in the following utterance of Domitius Afer: "The prince who would know all, must needs ignore much".'[118] Cynthia Damon gives a more streamlined definition: 'a more elaborate figure of speech [than the metaphor], that provides a generalizing and elevating effect'. Related but different is the epigram: 'an expression of conspicuous verbal neatness'.

Grotius shows himself a particularly inventive creator of *sententiae*, and wrote more than a few memorable ones that would not have looked out of place in

[117] Tacitus *Historiae* book 1 has 53 *sententiae* in *c.*20.000 words (ratio of roughly 1 : 400). Books 1–2 of Grotius' *Annales* have *c.*90 sententiae in *c.*17.000 words (1 : 188). See the counts in Tacitus, *Histories* 1, ed. & comm. by Cynthia Damon, Cambridge UP, 2003, p. 15, and Appendix 6 below.

[118] Inst. 8.5.3 'Est autem haec uox uniuersalis, quae etiam citra complexum causae possit esse laudabilis, interim ad rem tantum relata, ut "nihil est tam populare quam bonitas": interim ad personam, quale est Afri Domiti: "princeps qui uult omnia scire necesse habet multa ignoscere." ' Translation adapted from that by H.E. Butler: Quintilian, *Institutio Oratoria*, Loeb Classical Library, Cambridge MA (Harvard UP) 1920–1922.

Tacitus' original. Just as in Tacitus' case, commentators often see a connection between *sententiae* and 'insight' (or the appearance of it). In Cynthia Damon's words: 'a modern scholar, more concerned with tone than type, ascribes to Tacitus' many *sententiae* the impression that the historian gives of being "master of all he surveys".'[119] The *sententiae* are a particularly Tacitean manifestation of Grotius' political and historical *iudicium*, and, just as in Tacitus, a mark of the elevated style. The *sententiae* (and brevity) serve to enhance the impact of Grotius' relation on the reader, to enhance the impression of truth of Grotius' argument and views, and to strengthen the idea that he reveals an important, deeper truth – Grotius' 'rhetoric of exposure'.[120] His *sententiae* primarily expose

– flaws in the Netherlands national character;
– Philip II's pride and mismanagement of the situation;
– the unorderly nature of the original revolt;
– reason of state (in general).

In the *Annales* Grotius shows himself a faithful disciple of Quintilian in that his *sententiae* often appear at the end of a sub-topic or content item in the narration. They round off, with a kind of punch-line, a unit which in a modern edition would become a paragraph. With respect to the structure of the text, these punch-lines, by their very conspicuousness, accentuate the divisions between sub-topics in the text. Often a new sub-topic or chronological item starts after a *sententia*. By virtue of the sententious punch-lines, the narrative, over the length of several 'paragraphs', thus becomes a succession of punches that hammer home Grotius' Tacitean, disenchanted vision of the first phase of the Netherlands conflict. In connection with his stress on the need for obedience to the States' government (which his negative interpretation of the Revolt as chaos and mutiny seems to serve), the *sententiae* thus appear as a kind of literary whip of Grotius' political authority and purposes, i.e. as a direct political tool employed in a specific historical context.

In a few places (notably 1.29 and 2.14) Grotius gives a particular literary emphasis to his point by piling *sententiae* on top of each other, and indeed these places concern primary elements of his analysis of the revolt: the destructive force of orthodox religious attitudes, and Philip II's arrogance.

c. Rugged and difficult style

Lipsius and Vossius further note, as we saw, that Tacitus' difficult style makes him unpopular or too difficult for some readers. Naturally Grotius imitated this aspect too. He employs many devices to disturb smoothness, symmetry, regularity and

[119] Damon, commentary to Tac. Hist. 1, p. 15; the quote is from P. Sinclair, *Tacitus the Sententious Historian. A sociology of rhetoric in Annales 1–6,* Pennsylvania State UP 1995, p. 147.

[120] Mellor, *Tacitus*, p. 126: [Tacitus'] 'rhetorics of exposure, in which acute political diagnosis reveals the hidden truths of the Empire'; cp. Damon, comm. to Tac. Hist. 1, p. 15.

ease of reading in the text, and sometimes this spills over into outright obscurity (for example: ruggedness resulting from brevity, Ann. 2.18: 'Iam vero in religiones inquisitio, acta Synodi Tridentinae, novi antistites, excusata hactenus aut repudiata, *parato qui cogeret*, velut sponte recipiebantur (...)'; deliberate irregularity, Ann. 2.23: 'Negarunt *Danus et Sueo,* metu adversus validiorem certandi; nec *Angliae regina* ausa (...)'; less transparent grammar: Ann. 3.31 '...quo *a Belgis recepto,* captivus ipse...' (for 'having been *captured back by...*'). Although not specifically Tacitean, the use of the absolute ablative without substantive could perhaps also be brought under this heading, e.g. Ann. 1.52 *dissimulato.*[121]

d. Other

Some other recognisably Tacitean stylistic devices are the use of euphemism (e.g. Ann. 2.14 'in Belgas durius consuli', and Ann. 4.5 'res arctas urbi facturus'); unusual wording for familiar concepts (e.g. Ann. 2.24 'Caspar Coliniacus, dux novatae religionis praecipuus', 'the reformed religion'); overuse of dative, e.g. Ann. 4.4 'At alii hoc potius indignari, quod *Gallicae potentiae* seorsim manciparentur.'

Tacitus' favourite combination of *spes* (hope) and *metus* (fear) is often imitated by Grotius (e.g. Ann. 1.52 'addendam fiduciam securitatis ne poenae metus in spem belli transiret...': See also expressions like Ann. 2.25 'odio et formidine' and Ann. 5.6 'per metum et imprudentiam').

Grotius naturally also included some specific expressions borrowed from Tacitus (Ann. 1.34 'Isque praecipuus dies Philippo sollicitatae liberatis fuit' (derived from Tac. Hist. 4.4 'isque praecipuus illi dies magnae offensae initium et magnae gloriae fuit'); Ann. 4.34 '[gaudii signa] erubuit permittere' from Tac. Ann. 6.23.4 'consultusque Caesar an sepeliri sineret, non erubuit permittere'. This type of more literal imitation seems to be relatively rare, and is always employed in a very independent and creative way. Grotius never copies phrases or sentences literally or in full. For example, Tac. Ann. 5.3 'et publica mala singulis in occasionem gratiae trahuntur' is echoed in Grotius Ann. 1.20 'multi publica mala suis remedium, aut obtegumentum quaerebant.' Moreover, of the borrowed expressions, many come from other classical authors (e.g. Horace, Pliny, Quintilian,[122] but also legal language such as 'cautiones...hoc titulo inscriptae' appears, Ann. 3.1).[123] Thus, from the perspective of borrowed expressions, although Tacitus prevails, the AH appears as a rich mixture of influences that reflects Grotius' wide reading in ancient literature.[124]

[121] Cp. H. Menge, *Repetitorium der lateinischen Syntax und Stilistik*, 17. Auflage, Darmstadt 1979, § 444, where this type of usage is identified primarily with the historians.

[122] e.g. Ann. 2 p. 49 *causantibus* 'speaking' (Livy, Quintilian); p. 51 *elatior* 'over-bold' (Pliny Jr., Seneca, Quintilian, Aulus Gellius, Columella).

[123] For more legal language see § 7.5 below.

[124] See also Boot, 'Grotius et Tacitus' and Den Hengst, 'Naturalis Sermonis Pulchritudo'.

Thus it appears that Grotius' imitation of the Tacitean prose style omits none of the characteristics of Tacitus' prose that we find in the contemporary literary and scholarly criticism on Tacitus. We have also found textual echoes, borrowed expressions and poetical colouring (which all seem to have been recognised in Tacitus at the time). Thus Grotius' *Annales* emerge as a highly accomplished imitation of the Tacitean style by early 17th-century standards, in which he has successfully translated key elements of Tacitus' approach to the Dutch context of the Revolt, both with respect to literary style and to historical and political interpretation.

7.3. Compositorial aspects and narrative structure

This however does not yet satisfy all questions. If we want to obtain a view of Grotius as a reader of Tacitus rather than of the contemporary criticism on Tacitus, and investigate the nature of his imitation, we need to go beyond that criticism and compare Grotius' text with the model itself. But this complicates our question, because in doing so we are comparing Tacitus with early-modern readings of Tacitus and present-day ones at the same time. It stands out for example that classicists today read Tacitus primarily as literature, rather than history, and that the scholarship on Tacitus focuses more on e.g. the influence on him of classical tragedy than on reason of state. First therefore a bit more on this 'literary' turn.

Classical scholarship on Tacitus in the past two centuries has identified a range of Tacitean narrative techniques, such as 'foreshadowing' and 'dramatic structuring', which reside in the structure and longer lines of the narratives, and which create narrative development. As I have argued elsewhere,[125] the humanist fascination for quotable *sententiae* may have been a dominant factor that diverted the attention of readers in Lipsius' and Grotius' time *away* from the structure of and the longer lines in the narrative. The modern novel uses similar narrative techniques which did not exist when Grotius composed the AH, while our familiarity with the novel may have enhanced our sensitivity for such techniques in historic prose such as that of Tacitus. This may help explain why the early-modern sources give us every reason to believe that even a careful reader of Tacitus like Justus Lipsius was unaware for example of the moral condemnation of the Julio-Claudian dynasty that is expressed implicitly but unmistakeably – for us – in the narrative development in Tacitus' *Annales*. Although this is straightforward, if we next want to judge Grotius as a reader and emulator of Tacitus, we are attempting a comparison that is impossible to perform properly, since we lack a fixed point of reference. We cannot compare what Grotius is doing to what Tacitus did, because we have no real access to what Tacitus did, only our perception and reconstruction of it from his text. From his imitation, we can derive an idea of how Grotius viewed Tacitus, but our own view, although it builds on a longer tradition, is not necessarily more privileged than his. We cannot know for example if Grotius overlooked things in the original, if we

[125] Waszink, 'Introduction' to Lipsius, *Politica*, § 5.5.

overlook them too. And even if the prominence of literary features such as narrative development seems obvious to us, we cannot be certain how (un)prominent or important they were to Tacitus and/or readers of the 2nd century. Since the research is unlikely ever to reach a point where 'the truth' is known, all conclusions must be incomplete and provisional, and the only useful question we can ask when judging Grotius as emulator of Tacitus, is: which qualities that we find prominent in Tacitus, were studied and imitated by Grotius and contemporaries? Grotius' imitation suggests quite clearly for example that narrative development (and its implications, as indicated above), as well as an interest in the individual character and psychology of chief agents in the 'story', were not. Therefore in the remaining part of this chapter we shall look at a feature of Tacitus' prose that plays a central role in modern discussions of Tacitus' style and that rewards closer scrutiny in Grotius' imitation: that of the imitation of classical tragedy, especially dramatic structuring.

7.3.1. Is there dramatic structuring in the AH?

Modern study and interpretation of Tacitus (and other classical historians, notably Sallust) since the early nineteenth century has shown that their histories, as literary narratives, were deeply influenced by ancient poetry and especially tragedy. This influence has been pointed out in their works with respect to, for example, narrative structure, thematic choices, conceptualisation and characterisation of *personae* and events, as well as vocabulary and style: the way historical figures are characterised (and turned into 'characters' in a 'story') may remind the reader of those in tragedies, and regularly the order and logic of events seems to allude to tragic story models. Though scholars have remarked upon the poetic and/or dramatic character of Tacitus historical works from the early nineteenth century onwards, the systematic and wide-spread study of this side of Tacitus' works did not take off before the 1950s.[126] Conversely, in most present-day interpretations, issues of reason of state and political analysis (and thus of Tacitus as a major text in political theory) have moved more out of the centre of attention to make place for study of Tacitus' literary and narrative techniques. Tacitus-interpretations in Grotius' time display no awareness of this aspect of Tacitus' text, which, indeed, requires an approach of his text as literature – and one influenced by the study of the (fictional) novel – that was simply not available by 1600.[127] This alone seems sufficient reason to not expect signs of dramatic structuring in Grotius' AH.

[126] F. Santoro L'Hoir, *Tragedy, Rhetoric, and the Historiography of Tacitus' Annales* (Ann Arbor: University of Michigan Press, 2006), pp. 1–3 and footnotes.; A.D. Leeman, 'De functie van de dramatisering bij Tacitus', *Lampas*, 7 (1974), 368–377, and P.S. Everts, *De Tacitea historiae conscribendae ratione* (Utrecht doctoral dissertation; Kerkrade, 1926), p. 20, who refers to an article by F. Süvern of 1822–1823 as the starting point of this approach.

[127] To see the spectacular gap between present-day and early-modern readings of Tacitus, it is instructive to compare the literary analysis to which Tacitus is subjected for example in Santoro L'Hoir's study (note 126) with the historical and political approach by Lipsius, Grotius and

However, caution is in order. Some connections between Tacitus and tragedy were already made in Grotius' time, especially in the realm of literary imitation and the *Nachleben* of classical themes and stories. Parts of Tacitus' narratives became subject-matter for tragedies, notably events from Nero's reign such as the marriage with Poppea and the death of Seneca (although the flowering of this imitation seems to lie more towards the middle of the 17th century).[128] The stage author Ben Johnson figures prominently among the British Tacitists, and the concept of a court and its intrigues appears in many tragedies. Moreover, we know of at least one other instance where Grotius displays a philological awareness that was to become general knowledge only centuries later, i.e. his understanding of Pindar's metrical technique (as noted by Chris Sicking[129]). During the composition of the AH, Grotius also wrote two tragedies after the Senecan model (*Adamus Exul* and *Christus Patiens*, published in 1601 and 1608). The division of the *Annales* into five books might speculatively be read as a reference to Senecan tragedy, and the final part contains two main events that could potentially be constructed, by an author so inclined, as a *peripeteia*, i.e. the assassination of William the Silent and the failure of the second experiment with a 'monarch' invited from abroad – both crucial moments in the process towards the birth of the Republic as a political reality and the accession of Maurice as military commander, which in turn led to the military breakthrough of the Republic in the 1590s. The story of William the Silent and his assassination was staged as drama several times in the period around 1600 (not by Grotius, but among others by his close friend Daniel Heinsius).[130] Thus a conscious imitation of tragic forms and language within an imitation of Tacitus seems more than a theoretical possibility for Grotius' time, and we do have reason to perform a closer search for tragic elements in the *Annales*. Then what are we looking for?

contemporaries. For the moderns, Tacitus is literature, not history, and their chief concerns are his models and the (conscious or subconscious) literary influences from the preceding literary history. Reason of state and political analysis play no role in their assessment of Tacitus' purposes.

[128] e.g. Monteverdi's opera *L'incoronazione di Poppea* was first staged in 1642.

[129] C.M.J. Sicking, 'Inleiding', in *Bataafs Athene. Een bloemlezing van klassiek Griekse poëzie van de hand van Leidse humanisten van de zestiende tot en met de twintigste eeuw*, ed. Collegium Classicum cui nomen M.F., (Leiden, 1993), pp. xv–xvi.

[130] Toussaint Sailly (Salius), *Nassovius*, 1589; Caspar Ens, *Princeps Auriacus sive libertas defensa*, 1599, Daniel Heinsius, *Auriacus sive libertas saucia*, 1602; Jacob Duym, *Het Moordadich Stuck van Balthasar Gerards begaen aen den Doorluchtigen Prince van Oraignen 1584*, 1606. More plays on the theme would be written in the 17th, 18th, 19th and 20th centuries. See also B. Vermaseren, 'Humanistische drama's over de moord op de vader des vaderlands', in: *Tijdschrift voor Nederlandse Taal- en Letterkunde*, vol. 68 (1951), pp. 31–67. For an epic application of the theme, see Georgius Benedicti Werteloo, *De rebus gestis illustrissimi principis Guilielmi* (Leiden: J. Paets, 1586; modern edition in: G. Benedicti, *De Krijgsdaden van Willem van Oranje*, ed. Collegium Classicum c.n. E.D.E.P.O.L., Leiden 1990.

On the basis of Leeman's discussion,[131] four characteristics of tragic dramatisation[132] can be discerned:

- presentation of the course of events as a broken continuum, into which suspense is brought by means of a contrast between rise and decline (or the other way round) to a degree over and beyond that warranted by the diversity of actual fact;
- (exaggerated) concentration of the narrative on one or a few protagonists;
- stimulation of emotional involvement of the reader to a degree beyond what is required for teaching or edifying purposes;
- the events and experiences in the narrative acquire a symbolic significance, a general validity, such as in *exempla* of man's subordination to fate.

We should remain aware however that the structural model of 'rise – breaking point – decline' is one of the most basic narrative structures, common to all genres of writing, so that we must be careful not to fall into *Hineininterpretierung* or labelling any such breaking point as a *peripeteia*. There must be good additional reasons why the breaking point in question should be seen as a 'tragic' one, i.e. specifically tragic language, pathos, etc. On the level of the actual text therefore, we should look for

- tragic terms and concepts, such as fate, pride, blindness, *miasma*, heavenly wrath;
- adaptations in the chronological order of events, so that the episode comes to be centred on one or a few protagonists and comes to contain a *peripeteia*.[133]
- an increased level of pathos or emotional involvement.

A search for dramatic structuring gives different results when applied to the *Annales* than when applied to the AH as a whole.

In the *Annales* the five books can be said to have a more or less clear-cut theme each:

1. *Previous history of the conflict* (–1567).
2. *Tyranny and War.* From Alva's arrival to Don Juan's (1567–1577).
3. *Struggle and Experiment.* Shifting tides of battle, the Pacification of 1576, weakness of the Dutch unity; political experiments (from Don Juan to the invitation to Anjou and Parma's arrival, 1577–1581).
4. *The Revolt hard-pressed.* Failure of the Anjou experiment. Parma's advances from the south. Assassination of William the Silent. Search for a new ally (1581–1584).
5. *The rebuff of the monarchical quest.* England as new ally. Loss of Antwerp. Leicester and his prolonged struggle with the States. Parma's further advances. Maurice's first successes. (1584–1588).

131 Leeman, 'Functie van de dramatisering', passim.

132 As opposed to rhetorical dramatisation; see Leeman, 'Functie van de dramatisering'.

133 See Leeman, 'Functie van de dramatisering', pp. 370–372 who discusses the changed chronology in Tac. Ann. 1.1–5 as an example.

Over the whole of these five books, a gradual movement 'downwards' can indeed be discerned: the gradual, but inexorable crumbling away of the territory and safety of the Revolt, and the equally gradual and inevitable crumbling away of the perspective of a restoration of the old political order in its proper form (i.e. a good, constitutional monarchy). A recurrent theme is the failing unity and solidarity among the Dutch towns and regions. Less often but frequently mentioned issues are the ambition, *luxuria* and jealousy of the nobility, and the intolerant and intractable attitude of Protestant hard-liners. But are these developments and issues presented as tragic?

To start with the first of the phenomena quoted above, tragic concepts and vocabulary are more or less absent from the *Annales*. Paradoxically this seems mostly due to precisely its (Tacitean) affinity with reason of state, that is with disenchanted, realistic and secular approaches to politics and history.[134] Divine involvement or even interest in the course of events, typical for tragedy, are hardly ever brought into Grotius' narrative. One of the rare places were heavenly influence is alluded to can serve to demonstrate this point, for the sentiment here is distinctly disenchanted and non-tragic, if not actually anti-tragic. It appears right before the account of how the Sea-Beggars captured the town of Den Briel, more or less by chance, the event that re-launched the war and would consequently acquire a status as one of the founding moments of the Republic (Ann. 2.25, 1572):

> At that point in time however the Almighty's Providence decided to employ this lot as her helpers: in the history of the Low Countries war it has pleased her almost invariably to deceive human planning and confidence in such a way that great hopes and a happy outcome were never together in the same place.

Further indications of conscious dramatic structuring or conceptualisation are also lacking. The two moments indicated above, which could potentially be stylised as *peripetiae*, have not received such treatment. Although both are certainly crucial breaking points in the narrative (William's assassination for the *Annales,* the failure of the monarchical experiments for the AH as a whole), pathos as well as tragic language and concepts are lacking, so that interpretation of these moments as tragic *peripetiae* is impossible. Elsewhere too in the *Annales* there is little, if any, pathos or enhanced emotional involvement. Horror and cruelty are not depicted, and hardly any attention is paid to character or passions of individual protagonists. On the contrary, the *Annales* are characterised by a cool and distanced approach of events, and a tone of euphemism. There are some adaptations in chronology (see the footnotes to *Annales* book 2) but these do not appear to be geared towards a 'tragic' effect.

[134] See also Lipsius' characterisation above of Tacitus' works as serious, useful, political discussion rather than interesting stories which 'serve more to delight the reader than to instruct him'.

If we look at the structure of the AH as a whole however, a different picture arises. Apart from introductory pre-history in book 1, the main narrative of the rebellion covers the 42 years from 1567 to 1609, divided into two parts of roughly equal length, (21 years): the *Annales* from 1567 to 1588 and the *Historiae* from 1588 to 1609. The *Annales* cover their portion, the way 'downwards', as outlined above, in a framework of intense brevity in just five books. The *Historiae* give more space to their material and cover their 21 years in 18 books, in an annalistic year-by-year format from book 4 (1595) onwards.[135] This part describes the way 'up' from the crisis of the year of Leicester's return to England and the Armada, through the military and organisational renewal under Maurice and Oldenbarnevelt and its successes, to the eventual *de facto* recognition of the Republic as an independent state at the Twelve Years' Truce of 1609. This pattern resembles the first of the tragic criteria listed earlier: 'presentation of the course of events as a broken continuum, into which suspense is brought by means of a contrast between rise and decline or the other way round', but does it also fulfil the part that makes it specifically tragic, that is: '...to a degree over and beyond that warranted by the diversity of actual fact'? It stands out with this respect that the opening passage of the chronological narrative of the *Historiae* does play with a 'tragic' stylistic register:

> Annus agebatur Christiano nomini post mille quingentos octuagesimus et octavus, quem ultimum rebus humanis Mathematici edixerant: seu vana ars est, et intra nostram credulitatem, futura invadere: sive error iste non recte fatorum magnitudinem interpretantium; ac pars coelestium minarum fuerit classis ingens, quae pari spe atque ira Hispanis, dum pax cum Turca et Gallia, in semet armata festinabatur.
> ('The fifteen hundred and eighty-eighth year to Christ's name was on its course down, foresaid by the astrological calculators to become the last year of humankind – whether accessing the future be a futile skill, and one that doesn't reach beyond our credulity; or that prediction an error from human miscalculation of Fate's magnitude, and part of Heavens' threats a colossal fleet: which the Spanish, from great hopes as much as from great anger, now that there was peace both with the Turks and France, hastened to completion, equipped with arms against themselves.')

This sentence resumes the narrative after the central breaking point, and introduces the spectacular story of the Armada. The placement of the Netherlands struggle in a cosmic perspective is deliberately tragic in tone and the crucial, central place at which it happens suggests quite strongly that the idea of presenting the Revolt's history in a tragic framework has indeed occurred to Grotius. But the idea only: for the passage actually mocks those who interpret the events within

[135] As in the first six books of Tacitus' *Annals*.

this cosmic perspective. It should be kept in mind here that belief in the significance of astrological signs was perfectly common at this time, also in academic circles, and that Grotius thus seems to distantiate himself (again) from some commonly held perceptions of his own time.[136] The purport of his sentence is related to that of the previous quoted passage and suggests that, although the idea of applying a tragic colouring has occurred to Grotius, he is in fact actively resisting such interpretations and presentations of the Revolt.[137] This however did not deter him from occasionally playing with the idea in his literary realisation of the narrative, if only to make it clear that he dismisses such readings altogether. This dismissal fits well with Grotius' Tacitean, that is: *secular* interpretation of politics. In other words, he seems to be resisting the religious perspective applied for example in the above-mentioned stage-plays on William's assassination, most of which present William as a kind of protestant martyr, for this tragic perspective conflicts with Grotius' *realpolitische* reading of the Revolt and the corresponding qualification of the image of William the Silent.

Thus the conclusions from this investigation include some interesting paradoxes. Grotius cannot reasonably be believed to have imitated Tacitus' dramatic structuring since that way of reading Tacitus was simply unavailable in his time. Nevertheless the search for dramatic structuring in the AH produced a few useful insights into the text. Grotius must have been perfectly well aware that the Revolt (and stories from it) could be perceived and presented in forms alluding to classical tragedy. The idea of putting in a 'tragic', 'cosmic' or 'divinely-steered' perspective has occurred to him occasionally, and he permitted the idea to enter his text, but only in order to show his reluctance regarding such interpretations of the events, and to make way for his own political, secular, and indeed (to him) truly *Tacitean* understanding of that history. This can in turn be connected with the *Staatsgezinde* position in the Truce Conflicts, for it removes the religious perspective from the political realm and its history. As, moreover, the tragic perspective is important to modern readings of Tacitus, the above also serves as another illustration of the wide gap between modern and early-modern readings of Tacitus.[138]

In connection with this a short note on character development. Closer study of individual character, another chief element of Tacitus' *Annals* and *Histories* in modern interpretations (and perhaps under influence again from the modern novel), is similarly lacking in Grotius' *Annales*. Lipsius' 'inner lives' [*interior vita*] must refer to

[136] See e.g. E. Jorink, *Reading the Book of Nature in the Dutch Golden Age, 1575–1715*, Leiden 2010, p. 107–179; M. Bass, 'Introduction' in: *Insect Artifice. Nature and Art in the Dutch Revolt,* Princeton UP 2019, p. 2 and n.8, who points at the attempt by Bonaventura Vulcanius (Grotius' professor of Greek in Leiden) 'to make sense of the revolt through signs and portents [that] was as unscholarly as it was aligned with popular sentiments'.

[137] See also § 4 above on the secular and reason-of-state-type view of historical causation.

[138] For the secularising approach to tragedy by Grotius' friend and contemporary Daniel Heinsius, see Somos, 'Enter Secularisation'.

private thoughts and interior motives of the protagonists, that is, to invisible political considerations, confined to particular moments, rather than to their individual psychology or even character development. The fact that it is indeed the first, not the second of these that we find in Grotius' imitation, is another symptom of the divide between 16th- and 17th-century readings of Tacitus and modern ones.

7.4. *Conclusion: Grotius' imitation of Tacitus*

This section begun with an investigation into what the concept of Tacitism (and 'Tacitean', 'Tacitist') comprised and alluded to in Grotius' time, and how Grotius realised those in his imitation of Tacitus' political historiography. Literary criticism contemporary with Grotius identified a set of characteristics of Tacitus' historiography and prose style: brevity, difficulty, ruggedness, *sententiae,* revelation, *iudicium,* practical value for present political actors. These features are all easy to recognise in Grotius' *Annales,* so that it follows that the style of the *Annales* is Tacitean in every respect by 16th- and 17th-century standards (while brevity and the use of *sententiae* are even intensified in comparison with Tacitus).

Compared with modern readings of Tacitus, Grotius' imitation appears to miss some characteristics of Tacitus' prose which are nowadays considered as chief qualities of that prose, such as narrative development, study of individual character development and application of tragic story models. With respect to this last issue, the AH nevertheless rewards a closer examination, which shows that there is no real trace of dramatic structuring beyond the construction of rather elementary and universal story lines, let alone a conscious imitation of Tacitus' dramatic structuring as studied today. However, Grotius does occasionally play with tragic concepts and style but does so primarily, it seems, in order precisely to *dismiss* 'tragic' interpretations of the Revolt and the religious perspective these would bring in. Such tragic readings of the conflict would actually conflict with a Tacitean approach as it was understood in Grotius' age, which was felt to carry a disenchanted, secular political realism as its chief mark. Thus it appears possible to connect this dismissal of a tragic perspective with the *Staatsgezinde* parti-pris of the AH.

Thus, in Grotius' imitation, Tacitus' style is characterised by a particular syntax and verbal style, as well as by his significance as a political historical author, not by his narrative, dramatic, and other more structural literary qualities and techniques that have moved to the centre of attention in modern scholarship. Modern scholarship on the other hand tends to focus on those rather than on Tacitus' political analysis and the (sometimes controversial) political ideas that can be derived from his works. If however we use these modern views of Tacitus as a basic guide to what Tacitism was, the boundaries and contrasts between Tacitism and its early-modern intellectual context might appear more blurred than they actually were. For the late 16th and early 17th centuries, the Lipsian Tacitism which Grotius represents comprised a moral relativism that was offensive to many and therefore prone to stir up controversy. Looking at early-modern Tacitism from a basis of modern readings of Tacitus, these tensions might become overlooked, since these modern interpretations generally do not take on board the moral and political 'sting' that Tacitus had for his early-modern readers, while they do discern a tragic (divine, cosmic) perspective in his works.

The argument developed so far also has potentially significant implications for the interpretation of the relationship between Neo-Stoicism and Tacitism. It suggests that these currents many not be as closely related or intellectually 'friendly' phenomena in the way they are often seen today.[139] Given the ethically controversial aspect of Tacitist thought, it was not easy to reconcile with Neo-Stoicism's underlying agenda of universality, reconciliation and the transcending of confessional partialities. A general study of Tacitism as a controversial current in his own time, however, with an investigation of these points of tension, has yet to be written.

8. Some important characters in the AH

8.1. *William the Silent*

The picture that Grotius presents of William the Silent is appreciating without idealising the person or the statesman. Grotius attempts to give a realistic image of William's achievements and his merits for the revolutionary commonwealth; an altogether positive image which emphasises William's unwavering dedication to the Netherlandish cause, his personal sacrifices and his popularity with the people; but which at the same time does not obscure his stratagems, failures, bad luck and occasional reason-of-state behaviour from sight. In § 6 above we have seen the passage in which William is credited with feigned religious zeal at the Cologne peace negotiations in 1579 designed to serve his personal political goals. From within the Tacitean world-view and discourse in which the *Annales* are written, where politics are not necessarily a moral enterprise, such things could be said without necessarily implying an accusation of 'Machiavellism'; this mode of speech allows for a non-judging, 'ethically neutral' analysis of how power politics and its agents operate in actual reality.[140] A few other places re-confirm Grotius'

[139] E.g. P. Burke, 'Tacitism, scepticism, and reason of state', p. 492; P.N. Miller, *Peiresc's Europe. Learning and Virtue in the Seventeenth Century*, New Haven and London: Yale UP, 2000, p. 12–13; J. Papy, 'Lipsius' (Neo-) Stoicism: constancy between Christian faith and Stoic virtue', in: H. Blom and L. Winkel (eds.), *Grotius and the Stoa*, Assen: Van Gorcum, 2004 (*Grotiana* NS vol. 22/23).

[140] On William of Orange see also Klink, *Opstand, politiek en religie bij Willem van Oranje,* and E. Haitsma Mulier, 'Willem van Oranje in de historiografie van de zeventiende eeuw' in: id. & A. Jansen (eds), *Willem van Oranje in de historie 1584–1984. Vier eeuwen beeldvorming en geschiedschrijving*, Utrecht 1984, p. 36–37 which discusses the picture of William the Silent in the AH, focusing entirely on Grotius' praise for William (schrewd, constant, moderating influence on the hostilities, collaboration with the States, defence of the Liberties, well-versed in politics, political approach of religious strife; unifier of the resistance against the king). Although Haitsma Mulier recognises that Grotius always

view that William wasn't fighting for the sake of Calvinism, such as the reminder that William harboured no principled aversion of Catholicism in book 1.44:

> This at least is clear, that [Orange, Egmond and Horne] had not left the Roman faith, and that the man who was the leader of their plans permitted no religious change in his own province of Orange.

and the conspicuous *tamen* ('however') in 2.11:

> He did not hide the fact that he had left the Roman church since he had learned about a better one. 'However,' he declared, 'I am taking up arms for the public sake and in order to drive servitude from the country'

which expresses Grotius' belief that for William the revolt was not about religious but political freedom.

A similar point (though not explicitly attributed to William) is the strictly practical, not principled motivation for barring Catholics from public office in 1573 (2.42):

> ...and for the followers of that confession it became very difficult to obtain high office, not because of any law, but from prudence, to make sure neither loathing of dissenters nor greater chances of mercy would induce them to separate their own from the public cause.

William is introduced into the narrative in Ann. 1.18 in the following terms:

> The first of these in energy, grace and skill was William, Prince of Orange [... who] had learned to rule in military commands and important embassies. In addition he carried the brilliance of an ancient family, [...] a magnanimous spirit good at keeping its own counsel,[141] plus a mind that matched it and was ready for any fortune however great. No human being had cruelty and greed more alien. His understanding of even the most remote topics gave him a position of strength, and he had a reliable memory for everything. Among his subjects his power rested on many inducements [...].

William's aversion of cruelty and tyranny is a recurring theme, e.g. in 1.45 where he voices his aversion of tyrannical machinations in the context of the belief that there was a secret alliance against Protestantism between Philip and the king of

'translates' the religious issue into political terms, he presents Grotius' image of William as plain and uncomplicated moral praise.

[141] *celans sui*, Grotius' rendering of *De Zwijger* ('The Silent'), and possibly an echo of Tac. Ann. 4.1.3 *sui obtegens*, applied there to Tiberius (!).

France (which is said to have been accidentally disclosed to the young William during a hunting party[142]): '… "and already by that time" [William] would keep asserting, "I was scared by plans that were being concealed".'

Grotius presents this aversion of autocracy not just as a personal and political quality but also as a political advantage and tool: 'With his skills in the art of governing, and his characteristic mildness which endeared him even to his enemies, he brought the troubles to rest […]' (2.39, summer of 1572). Soon Grotius makes another connection, linking aversion of autocracy not just with political dexterity but with constitutional scruples as well (2.40):

> Orange assumed the power of a prince while renouncing the title; he appointed magistrates, issued laws, administered military and naval affairs and most public business; and did all this together with a chosen council, or, in questions of greater importance, as president of a meeting of the States. This large number of gatherings served not only to create an image of popular support, but also to bind as many as possible to the cause. Whereas in earlier days six towns in Holland met (Dordrecht, Haarlem, Delft, Leiden, Amsterdam, and Gouda, together with the nobility), to deliberate upon most of the public business, Orange introduced no fewer than twelve smaller towns, which would doubtlessly be loyal to him, as they thanked their right to vote to his assistance.

And similarly in 2.71:

> Orange however enjoyed great fame in all towns and villages in the Low Countries as the founder of liberty, and, being an expert in the personal conduct which incites people's support, he strengthened his power by the goodwill he won by pretending to reject it. Given moreover his mildness and prudence, and the fact that his keen-witted investigations and intercepted letters had shown that he and his family would be the first target of Don Juan's scheming, then all the others, when the ties of the treaty would be resolved, he achieved such popularity that the people of Brabant summoned him to the dignity of the stadtholderate.

However, this advantage and his popularity also worked against him as they roused jealousy in others. In spite of Oranje's efforts for the commonwealth, he ends up in conflict with several of the other nobles:

> This however was more than Aarschot, […] and several others could bear, that is, that the supreme power was moving in Orange's way, who was seen as having

[142] A story taken from William of Orange's own *Apology* of 1580; see Eng. ed. Wansink p. 61–63; Dutch ed. Mees-Verwey p. 60–62.

> only a few equals in birth, and none in experience and authority. Therefore, as they were aware that he far surpassed them in popularity, and because they feared that once in power he would use the faith for his own purposes, they looked for ways to obscure his fame by the glittering of an even greater name. (ibid.).

After an uprising against the clergy in Antwerp, William is accused of instigating it (3.30, 1579):

> A threatening mob [the Calvinist populace] rose against the clergy who were in the midst of the sacred adorations. Even Orange could not stop this plebs of his from violently throwing the priesthood out of the city gates; his enemies however interpreted this as if things had happened at his instigation which he had only been unable to forbid. For every kind of cruelty was alien to him, but at the same time he knew how to use an occasion prudently, and, with the objective of bringing other people's efforts in line with those of himself, he sowed early in order to pluck the benefits in the long term.

Nevertheless, Grotius does not hide that it was not only jealous fellow nobles who disliked Orange's government (3.30):

> But however this be, the events in Antwerp brought a good part of the population, who had now lost their regular worship, to turning their prayers against the new commonwealth, because they expected a milder slavery from the king's rule; a handful of noblemen even jumped upon this occasion to defect to the Spanish.

A decade later some find that even the Earl of Leicester compared favourably with Orange (5.11, 1585):

> There were even people who rated [Leicester] higher than William of Orange, in the expectation that from now on so many fewer individual favours would be granted as it would be easier for Leicester to keep a straight course [...].

In William's biographical epilogue after the assassination Grotius depicts him as a prince with a true moral motivation for the well-being and ancient rights of the people in the Low Countries, and a willingness to sacrifice much of his own for it (4.34–35, 1584):

> Then however the danger mounting from all sides received a new impulse from William's death, at a time most unfavourable for the Low Countries [...] Seen from his own perspective it is hard to maintain that his death came too early, given the rising tide of trouble among which he was snatched away from

> the country to which he had so intimately tied his own fortune. For after his decease, the Low Countries ran into serious trouble as a result of the internal discord and the never-ending row of enemy victories, until the day the commonwealth and in a way the Prince himself revived in the person of his son. [...].
> While he was dying his only words were to God: 'Have mercy on this people.' Among the people who knew him in his final years there was no doubt that the vicissitudes of fortune which he had experienced from his earliest childhood over the fifty years of his life [...] and suffered from the wrath and the violence of the mighty, the calumny of his fellow noblemen, and often even the attacks of the people, invested him with endurance in the face of human hardship as well as the deepest piety [...].

Thus William is presented as a politician with a strong moral inspiration and dedication to the common cause of the provinces, but also with his own political agenda, and with great skills in building personal loyalties as well as in creating an *image* of indifference to power which seems designed to work for that same purpose (such as 'assumed the power of a prince while renouncing the title' above). These and other references to the conscious manipulation of appearances allude to Machiavelli's prince, and the suggestion thus created is reinforced by the passage quoted earlier on feigned religious motivation. Consequently one might also find that Grotius' repeated references to William's popularity with the crowds have a Machiavellian flavour, and ask whether Grotius isn't perhaps hinting that in certain aspects William resembles the Machiavellian prince of a newly acquired dominion.[143] On the other hand, there are many other aspects of Grotius' portrait which set William very clearly and explicitly apart from the Machiavellian prince, such as his unquestionable moral indignation at the Spanish cruelty and tyranny, the fact that he did not turn the arms that he controlled against the liberty of the Low Countries but precisely and only to defend it; and, ironically perhaps, his lack of control and effectiveness.[144]

[143] Machiavelli, *Il Principe* esp. ch. 6, 15, 19. In pro-Spanish propaganda William is regularly depicted as a Machiavellian, see P. Geurts, *De Nederlandse Opstand in de Pamfletten 1566–1584*, 1956/ Utrecht 1978, 269–270. William's 'Machiavellian' image received some attention in the scholarship: G. Wells, 'The unlikely Machiavellian: William of Orange and the Princely Virtues' in: Ph. Mack & M. Jacob (eds), *Politics and Culture in Early Modern Europe. Essays in honour of H.G. Koenigsberger*, Cambridge 1987, 85–94; E. Haitsma Mulier, *Het Nederlandse gezicht van Machiavelli*, Hilversum 1989, 8 and id., 'Willem van Oranje in de historiografie', 45–46. For the reception of Machiavelli in the Low Countries in general in this period, see A. Clerici, 'Trust, Heresy and Rebellion: Reactions to Machiavelli in the early Dutch Revolt' in: L. Kontler and M. Somos (eds), *Trust and Happiness in the History of European Political Thought*, Leiden, Brill, 2018, p. 257–280.

[144] For another late-humanist (and Tacitist) portrait of a morally inspired, but ultimately ineffective hero see Henry Savile's picture of Julius Vindex (which, ironically, may allude to Robert Dudley); see D. Womersley, 'Sir Henry Savile's Translation of Tacitus and the Political Interpretation of Elizabethan Texts', in: *The Review of English Studies*, 42, no. 167 (1991), 313–342; and Waszink, 'Henry Savile's Tacitus'.

It is important to note here for context that while Grotius was writing the AH, the image of William of Orange was going through profound changes. As we have just seen, at the time of his death in 1584 his figure was not uncontroversial, and met with both praise and scorn from observers in the provinces. The construction of the magnificent triumphal grave monument in the New Church in Delft, designed by the great architect and sculptor Hendrick de Keyser (1565–1621), was only commissioned a generation later in 1609 (the actual construction lasted from 1614 to 1623).[145] During the Truce Conflicts, two divergent images of the prince developed: on the *Staatsgezinde* side (by e.g. Johannes Meursius) Orange was depicted as a champion of Dutch unity and mediator between parties, while his constitutional scruples (evident from his consistent consultation with the States) were highlighted. On the Counter-remonstrant side, his significance for the cause of Dutch Calvinism was highlighted (by e.g. Willem Baudartius), while glorifications of William often seem subservient to those of his son Maurice.[146] Against this backdrop Grotius' picture of William the politician obviously belongs under the *Staatsgezinde* perception.

8.2. *Philip II*

The main figure on the Spanish side is obviously King Philip II. Grotius' image of the king and his policies must be constructed from his various utterances on the matter; in the *Annales* there is no main or overarching discussion of the king as such. In *Annals* 1.15 Philip is introduced into the narrative:

> Philip, his youth spent amidst courts and flattery, clothed himself in response with austere gravity, parsimony of words, and avoidance of the crowd. Brought up in Spanish ways, he was addressed in no other tongue. When his father had been compelled to settle his old age in private retirement, they hastened to put Philip in charge, whose ancestral lust for power, not yet chastened by experience, could hardly tolerate limit or measure. Nor is there any doubt but that he believed that the best instruments of his rule were the Spaniards' faith and virtue. How great a passion enters the hearts and minds of kings for abolishing the laws which curb the force of power, we find testified by striking ruins of princes, or peoples, old and new. This same zeal in Philip the peoples of Spain themselves came to feel later.

[145] De Keyser also designed the bronze statue of Erasmus which was placed in Rotterdam in 1622, its creation having been initiated by Grotius; see Nellen, *Hugo Grotius* p. 446. It is now the oldest existing bronze statue in the Netherlands.

[146] See A. Janssen, 'Prins Willem van Oranje in het oordeel van tijdgenoten' and Haitsma Mulier, 'Willem van Oranje in de historiografie', p. 9–31 and 32–62.

A general evaluation of Philip's reign follows at his death in 1598 (*Historiae* book 7, pp. 330–332; see Appendix 3). This discussion is as interesting for what it says as for what it does not say. After a relation of the king's death (Grotius details a disgusting illness) the usual biographical epilogue in the style of the classical historians follows. After mentioning his physical appearance, Grotius describes Philip as seemingly pleasant in person but less clever than his father, which deficit he compensated by energy and a strong work ethic. Grotius then presents the core of his analysis of Philip's reign, which has three main themes: reason of state, religious policy, and war (thus also implicitly confirming that these are indeed Grotius' chief concerns as a historian). As already announced with heavy emphasis in *Annals* 1.15, Grotius regards lust for power as Philip's chief motivation. According to the epilogue, in spite of his personal kindness, Philip was merciless when it concerned his hold on power (*dominium*), and disregarded the effects of this on his reputation. He knew where to put his money (with the result that he had emperors and popes at his disposal); understood the *arcana regnorum* (stock phrase for reason of state); was unaffected by prosperity and adversity alike (mixing in a hint of Stoicism); was a great dissimulator, fostering scores of anger and resentment under a quiet appearance (adding a reminiscence of Tacitus' Tiberius); was immodest in his expectations; as eager for domination as the most extreme princes known from Antiquity; very fanatic in the *external* aspects of religion; and with respect to the techniques (*artes*) of ruling, no better or worse than other princes of his time.[147] Philip waged wars from his youth onwards, but he never took part in person, except in the French war when he was young. He won and lost territories, of those the losses of Golette,[148] Tunis and Holland being particularly shameful.

Grotius then concludes by summarising two judgments which he says circulated of Philip's reign. First that of the more sensible people (*prudentiores*), who point out that Philip's time was different from his father's and that great virtue and good fortune no longer met in the same men; but that Philip's competitors and adversaries were women, children or cowards (thus providing an excuse for a lack of glory in Philip's reign?). Secondly the judgments of 'others', and those inspired by partisanship against Philip, which castigate him for the cruelty applied in restoring order in Spain and the Low Countries, the cruelty caused in France[149] and other misfortunes, and employ his gruesome end as proof, by presenting it as punishment for his cruelty and hostility to the true faith and liberty, although – Grotius concludes – we know that many great minds have perished by the same illness.[150]

[147] '... circa imperii artes principum exemplo excusatus', Hist. 7, p. 331.

[148] Goleta (Golette) is a strategic fortress on the Bay of Tunis, near the site of ancient Carthage. Spain lost Tunis and Goleta in 1574 to the Ottoman ruler Selim II, the confrontation being a 'second front' that was hampered by Spain's involvement in the Netherlands, while conversely the struggle reduced pressure on the Dutch. Via Charles IX of France William of Orange maintained contact with Selim II for some time; see G. Parker, *The General Crisis of the 17th Century*, London 1978, p. 61.

[149] By supporting the Catholic League, e.g. *Annals* 4.8.

[150] For a modern assessment of Philip's character (including many of the traits noted by Grotius), see esp. 'Epilogue' in Parker, *The Imprudent King*.

In this account the usual Low Countries complaints about Philip's reign are in curious positions. That of failing to be a 'father to his people' and protect their interests (the main point of e.g. the *Act of Abjuration*) is simply omitted, while those of cruelty and the persecution of Protestantism are rendered more or less irrelevant by putting them in the mouth of allegedly less judicious and partisan observers. It stands out moreover that in this epilogue Grotius judges Philip without applying a particular Low Countries perspective, and that he leaves the problems of arrogance and inflexibility out of consideration, although he has frequently brought it up in his narrative (see e.g. *Annals* 1.31 on the response to the heresies, 1.53 to the Petition of Nobles and 2.14 on a reply to the Emperor).

Issues mentioned in the narrative which do return in the epilogue include fostering suspicions and resentment in silence, such as in Philip's treatment of the States in *Annals* 1.16 and 1.34, or in that of the duke of Parma in *Historiae* 2, pp. 168–170 (1592). For Philip's tendency to deal with everything himself, see *Annals* 1.53 (although here the epilogue is not completely consistent with Grotius' earlier narrative); for cruelty, see e.g. 2.8 on the deaths of Montigny, Elisabeth and Don Carlos, and 2.29 & 2.32 on that of other Spaniards. Also, while Philip's reported dexterity with money and reason of state, as well as the concern with *outward* religion contribute to an image of a Machiavellian ruler, that image is seriously complicated by the added remark that Philip disregarded the negative effects of his attachment to power on his public image. The epilogue comes without a serious evaluation of Philip's religious policy (although the *Annales* provide plenty of material for it, see e.g. Philip's clever employment of papal authority and the response to heresies and cruelty in 1.31, 1.53, 2.8, 2.14 as above).

Taking into account that Philip's policies were that which the Revolt was ultimately directed against, and Grotius' own descriptions of them, his final evaluation comes across as mild and curiously defensive, and may well have contributed to the reputation of impartiality that the AH enjoyed. In effect, to present Philip as a flawed Machiavellian is comparable in several ways to the way in which William of Orange is presented (see above).

But however that be, with respect to Grotius' view of Philip's administrative policies the AH allows for a more detailed investigation. Recent historical research has drawn attention to the politics of the 'agglomerate polities' or 'dynastic agglomerates' of the early-modern period and their difficulties,[151] and this perspective provides a useful angle on Grotius' text. Grotius appears well aware of the fact that the Spanish empire was such an agglomerate polity[152] and that, moreover, the Revolt took place within the European and global context of the Spanish empire. Many circumstances elsewhere on the globe had a decisive influence on

[151] See e.g. R. von Friedeburg and J. Morrill,'Introduction' in: *Monarchy Transformed. Princes and their Elites in early modern Western Europe*, Cambridge UP 2017, p. 1–14 and esp. J. Morrill, 'Dynasties, Realms, Peoples and State Formation 1500–1720', ibid. p. 17–20.

[152] *Annals* 2.1, *disiecta dominatio.*

the Revolt. Grotius includes overviews of the general political situation in Europe twice in the *Historiae*, i.e. in book 7 right before his relation of Philip's death and in book 15 right before the arrival of the Archduke's delegates which would lead to the Truce of of 1609.

If we sum up the chief aspects and focuses of Grotius' analysis of the problems of Philip's agglomerate polity, as arising from the *Annales*, a fairly coherent set of issues arises. Philip's chief problem in Grotius' view appears to be the problem of acceptation and legitimacy. By ignoring the local customs, rights and interests of his various dispersed territories, Philip lost the trust of his remote subjects in the Low Countries. They came to view his person and his rule as inimical to them and illegitimate in terms of their received constitutional laws and customs.

A second serious problem that appears is Philip's choice and use of representatives and intermediaries, such as governors, military commanders, ambassadors etc. Their mismanagement of the situation, or the king's mismanagement of his intermediaries, seriously reduce his chances of success. There is an inconsistency here with Grotius' picture of Philip in the epilogue, where 'dealing with everything himself' is presented as a mark of Philip's approach. Obviously this shouldn't be taken literally, but in the narrative in the *Annales* Philip is acting via intermediaries all the time, and his difficulties in getting this right is one of the hallmark issues of his reign.

Thirdly, the conflicting and contradictory demands of international (or even global) politics;

Finally, the problem of controlling armies, and the connected issue of raising financial resources (which is not so much, at least in Grotius' picture, a problem of financial *management*: Grotius depicts the Spanish Habsburg empire as (at times) unable to afford the war rather than incapable of organising the payments).

8.3. *Robert Dudley, Earl of Leicester*

An important character in the final book of the *Annales* is Robert Dudley, Earl of Leicester (1532–1588), Elizabeth's commander in the Low Countries for the military aid she sent in 1585. Leicester's puritan tendencies gave him a large following among the orthodox Calvinists in the Low Countries who relied on him for a correction to the all-too-lenient religious policies of the States and the town regents, as they saw them. As noted above (§ 5 and note 75) Grotius viewed the Leicester period in the 1580s as the first episode in the long story of the partisanships within Dutch society that would eventually culminate in the events of 1618–1619. Not surprisingly Grotius depicts the Earl in a thoroughly negative light (while he remains appreciative of Elizabeth's wisdom). The reason-of-state element in Elizabeth's approach has been discussed already (§ 6).

Leicester is introduced in the narrative in 5.9 and the tone is set immediately: 'The command of the English force was given to Robert, Earl of Leicester, an outstanding forger of virtues, who hid the unpopular and unfortunate arrogance of the house of Dudley under very friendly manners.' The next paragraph sketches the atmosphere of flattery and rashness surrounding his arrival in the Netherlands: 'At his arrival in the United Provinces he was greeted by the people's enthusiasm and flattery by the elites [... and supreme power was] granted, before they had obtained any experience of his talent and character, to a foreigner who wasn't of unreproached behaviour at home,' and in spite of Elizabeth's disagreement with this appointment. This setting is then further elaborated in terms of flattery, vanity, stubbornness, credulity and the earl's ignorance of Dutch politics (a reminder of Philip's deficiencies), while Grotius discredits those supporting Leicester as a faction only motivated by desperation and desire for revolution. Leicester and his party proceed by bringing false accusations against the States and by introducing a ban on trade with the enemy as well some other countries which would miss its desired effects but undermine the financial basis of the revolt nevertheless. The joint Anglo-Dutch military effort suffers defeats and some small successes; several of the senior English officers meet with serious distrust. Widely shared protests against these developments are presented by the States to Leicester, who then launches an attempt to have the States and magistrates removed from the effective government, using religion as the instrument to create division (5.27): 'First, for the sake of the appearance of piety and in order to set himself clearly apart from others, he allied himself with the interpreters of Scripture, the only ones in our age to which the masses pay heed', and: 'He assigned most of the business of government not to the magistracy but to people with some kind of religious function, or to popular officers who, even when they acted from the best of intentions, lacked the relevant knowledge and experience', thus creating precisely the inverse relationship between church and state of that which the States government were trying to achieve in Grotius' time. Soon however the popularity of the States plunges and Leicester makes a name for himself as protector of the faith, while his treatment of potentially competing authorities has Machiavellian traits: '[...] These intentions had Leicester's full support, as it was his aim to weaken the powers that came closest to his.' Having thus secured a firm position for himself, he returned to England for some time to secure Elizabeth's favour as well; outwardly however he claims his ill-treatment by the States as the reason for his departure and adds a threat that he will not return if this does not change (5.30). This leads to a popular movement that actually produced an unconditional offer of sovereignty to Elizabeth,[153] only to be refused by her again. Meanwhile the war effort was halted

[153] An offer of sovereignty *sonder eenighe conditie* ('without any restriction') is recorded to have been made to Elizabeth, via Leicester, by pressure groups of civilians within the province of Utrecht in June 1586; the movement was backed by some city councils but not by the magistrate, who, in reaction, sent a polite letter to Elizabeth reaffirming their *conformiteyt ende goede affectie* ('compliance and good-willing affection') while avoiding the word sovereignty; see Pieter Bor, *Nederlantsche oorloghen, beroerten, ende borgerlijcke oneenicheyden*, vol. 3.1 (Amsterdam: Basson and Colyn, [1626]), book 21, fol. 31 r–v.

for lack of a commander, since Leicester had reserved that for himself before his departure. Complaints about this remained unanswered because in England all eyes were on the plot involving Mary Stuart.

Then two high-ranking English officers, Stanley and York, hand over the towns under their protection (Zutphen and Deventer) to the Spaniard. This act of treason finally turns popular sentiment in favour of the States (5.33). The ban on foreign trade is mitigated. Parma's siege of Sluis in Zeeland prompts Leicester's return, in vain, as well as the subsequent surprise expedition to Flanders. Leicester blames this failure on the States, thus re-invigorating the nearly buried tensions from the recent past. The Spanish however use the moment of their success to draw Elizabeth to a new round of peace negotiations; the States on their part resist such ideas and point out that their revenues are large enough again to continue the war. Leicester then appears to be attacking the very authority of the States and accusing them of disobedience; against which the States publish a constitutional defence of their authority. Leicester however, disappointed by the lack of effective support for his rule now resorts to an attempted coup to secure his supremacy, which is discovered before it gains popular support. Leicester leaves for England, where he continues to influence the politics of the provinces but dies within a year, perhaps through poison (5.39). Grotius' concluding characterisation of Leicester as 'a danger bigger than any other which had threatened [the Dutch] commonwealth' seems best explained by assuming that he saw his role in the Low Countries as the main cause of the partisanships within Dutch society that manifested themselves from the early 1600s onwards.[154] At the same time this picture of the Puritan contribution to the history of the Republic may well have been another reason why the States decided in 1612/1613, given their already complicated relationship with James I, to refrain from publishing the AH.

9.
Other aspects

9.1. *Grotius and the Twelve Years' Truce*[155]

The Twelve Years' Truce was the most momentous political development during Grotius' early political career, and serves as the narrative conclusion of the entire AH. In a comparable way to the end of the *Annales*, where he halts the narrative for a general overview of the administrative structure and workings of the Republic, Grotius inserts an overview of the general situation in Europe near the end of *Histories* book 15 (pp. 496–500), right before introducing the first sign of the future Truce, i.e. the Portuguese entreaties to Philip III to seek peace with the Dutch,

[154] See the quote discussed above (§ 5 and note 75) from *Briefwisseling* vol. 1, no. 304 to Lingelsheim, Nov. 1613.

[155] See also Nellen, *Hugo Grotius*, esp. p. 102–106; Van Ittersum, *Profit and Principle*, 197–244; 325, 351; an important letter is *Briefwisseling* vol. 1 ep. 100 (p. 85) of 21 April 1607.

because their Asian trade is suffering from the war (p. 500). In Grotius' rendering this plea is then seconded by the general Spinola, who is said to fear the loss of his military advances built up in the preceding years (p. 501).[156] Early in book 16 (pp. 506–508) the theme of the Asian trade is taken up again by discussing the institution of the Dutch East India Company and the debates regarding its role in Dutch policies and interests on a global scale (including the Americas). This account then continues seamlessly into a summary of the heated debate within the republic on whether to seek peace or continue the war with the king, and the proposal from the Archdukes to initiate negotiations (p. 509). Thus in Grotius' account the Truce arises out of both the European and the global dimensions of the Republic's politics and trade.[157]

An account of the peace negotiations themselves then fills most of books 16 and 17, and centres on a number of issues: the meandering process of the negotiations themselves with the Archdukes and Spain; the internal disagreement within the Dutch Republic whether to negotiate, or to continue fighting, and whether to seek a truce or a permanent peace; the impact of the talks on the relationships with France, England and Germany (see also below); the respective demands by Spain and the Republic as to the future of the VOC and the Asian trade; the impact on the relationship between Spain and England. At the end of book 17 Grotius introduces the theological disagreement that would lead up to the Truce Conflicts in the republic, and provides some more developments regarding the VOC. The short book 18 mentions the province of Zeeland's acquiescence in the proceedings[158] and the proclamation of the Truce.

The (unexpected) arrival of the Archdukes' delegates is also marked in Grotius' correspondence in a letter of 21 April 1607; the accompanying cease-fire came into force not more than three days later, on the 24th of April 1607.[159] As close confidant of Oldenbarnevelt Grotius was not only well-informed but also actively, if indirectly, involved in the background.[160]

[156] A few pages before this point Grotius would later insert a long digression on the Dutch exploits in the far east (p. 492–494); it appears from the ms Papenbroeck 9.2 that this passage was not in the first version of the text; see Appendix 1 below.

[157] On the relationship between Dutch Revolt and the VOC's Asian trade see also IPC chapter 11.

[158] In 1648 the province would again oppose the termination of the war and refrain from ratifying the final peace settlement as part of the general peace treaty of Westphalia (although the signature of Zeeland's representative, Johan de Knuyt (1587–1654) does appear on the treaty). This omission came to the surface in 1993 and was a news item that year, see https://www.trouw.nl/nieuws/zeeland-wil-vrede-met-spanje~bc15acb8/ and https://www.omroepzeeland.nl/nieuws/104486/Hoe-de-oorlog-met-Spanje-die-nooit-eindigde-nu-toch-afgelopen-is.

[159] *Briefwisseling* vol. I ep. 100 to N.N. of 21 April 1607; see also W. van Eysinga, 'Eene onuitgegeven Nota van De Groot', *in: Mededelingen van de K.N.A.W. afd Letterkunde,* Nieuwe Reeks vol. 18 (1955), p. 235–252; reprinted in: id., *Sparsa Collecta*, p. 488–504.

[160] Cp. Van Ittersum, *Profit and Principle*, p. 325, 357; followed by M. van Oosterhout, *Hugo Grotius' Occasional Poetry (1609–1645),* PhD Nijmegen 2009, p. 290–293, who refer to the documents mentioned here but also repeat Grotius' own claim made during the interrogations after his arrest in 1618 that he was not involved in the truce negotiations.

While the negotiations were developing, the choice between war and peace split both the population and the ruling elites in the Republic. What about the religious issue? Could the VOC's Asian trade activities be continued, and what about potential Dutch prospects in the Americas? And most importantly, could the former sovereign be relied upon to keep faith with respect to the Republic's liberty and sovereignty in the future?[161] The Northerners were acutely awake to the possibility that peace or peace talks might be a cover for a strategy aimed at re-conquest in the long run, a suspicion being talked of at least since the publication of Justus Lipsius' infamous *Sent-Brief* of 1595.[162] While Oldenbarnevelt and a large part of the commercial elites came to favour peace or at least a truce, Maurice and the orthodox Calvinists favoured a continuation of the war until the transfer of sovereignty and the position of the Protestant faith were absolutely secured. These disagreements continued after 1609 and became more acute as the expiration of the Truce approached. As a result, popular suspicions of a conspiracy between Dutch ruling elites and the Spanish court arose and aggravated the internal tensions during the years of the Truce; incriminations of this sort would keep appearing for the entire period up to 1618.[163] Moreover there was a perception on the orthodox Calvinist side that on the level of European politics, the Oldenbarnevelt government was not doing enough to support the cause of Protestantism abroad.[164]

[161] See again *Briefwisseling* vol. I ep. 100, where Grotius appears to summarise the Dutch view of things: '[nos] qui satis norunt hostem nisi commodi sui causa nihil facturum', ('[we] who know well that the enemy will only act if it serves his own advantage'). Also, Grotius seems well aware of the possibility of an outbreak of internal conflict within the Republic; '... eam rem [...] quae in corpore parum cohaerente magnis morbis viam aperit', ('this issue [...] which opens the road towards serious afflictions in a community barely holding together').

[162] See Waszink, Intr. to Lipsius, *Politica*, p. 127; N. Mout, 'Justus Lipsius between war and peace. His public letter on Spanish foreign policy and the respective merits of war, peace or truce (1595)', in J. Pollmann & A. Spicer (eds.), *Public Opinion and Changing Identities in the Early Modern Netherlands*, Leiden – Boston, 2007, pp. 142–162. Grotius mentions the re-publication of the letter in 1608 and summarises it deftly in *Historiae* book 17, p. 545. See also in § 6 above on the Pieter Feddes print.

[163] Such as *Pracktyke van den Spaenschen Raedt, dat is: clare vertooninghe dat den Raedt door I. Lipsium, Er. Puteanum ende F. Campanellam gegeven om de vereenighde Nederlanden wederom te brengen onder t gebiet van den Coninck van Spaengjen* etc (1618), and François van Aerssen's *Provisioneele Openinghe van verscheyden saecken*; see also Nellen, *Hugo Grotius* p. 279–280; Den Tex, *Oldenbarnevelt* vol. III, *Het bestand 1609–1619,* Haarlem 1966, p. 565–570, 588–589 and Lenarduzzi, 'oude geusen teghen de nieuwe geusen' p. 75–78; F. Sierhuis, *The Literature of the Arminian Controversy. Religion, Politics and the Stage in the Dutch Republic,* Oxford UP 2015; J. Waszink, 'Oldenbarnevelt and Fishes'. For (unconvincing) evidence for an actual information leak to Spain, see J. Poelhekke, *Het verraad van de pistoletten?,* Amsterdam/London, 1975. A closer look at the details of the intelligence provided by this agent indicates that he did not actually have access to inside information from the Republic's leadership (with thanks to Prof. Dr. H. Nellen).

[164] For an overview, see H. Helmers, 'Foreign News in Times of Domestic Crisis: the Truce Conflicts, the Thirty Years' War and the Rise of the Dutch Newspaper' in: A. Wilkinson and G. Kemp (eds.), *Negotiating Conflict and Controversy in the Early Modern Book World,* Leiden 2019, p. 253–268.

In the context of the peace negotiations however Grotius was an important advisor and 'ghost-writer' in the background. We know of (at least) four documents he wrote in this role, falling in two subject groups which neatly reflect the drift of his discussion of the genesis of the truce in *Historiae* 15 and 16 as outlined above. The draft treatises *Observationes Iuridicae contra Pacem*[165] and *De bello ob libertatem eligendo,*[166] both preserved among his working papers currently in Leiden UL, concern the legal and political aspects of the proposed truce. Two other pieces concern the future and interests of the VOC: a *Memorandum* for the VOC directors, which came to serve as their position in the peace negotiations and is now in the Dutch National Archives in The Hague,[167] and his renowned *Mare Liberum* (a re-worked version of chapter 12 of the above-mentioned draft treatise *De Iure Praedae)* which was published anonymously in 1609 to counter Spanish-Portuguese claims to exclusive access to Asian and American markets and peoples.[168]

In the *Observationes Iuridicae* Grotius considers whether the recognition of the Republic's sovereignty by the Archdukes of the Southern Netherlands would be a hard legal guarantee that the Republic's independence would be respected by Spain in the future. The entire argument is geared towards demonstrating that this is not the case: according to Grotius, as vassals of the king of Spain the Archdukes were not in the constitutional position to grant sovereignty to the Republic, and no document to that effect issued by them would keep Spain from reclaiming sovereignty over the North in the future if it pleased to do so. Moreover the Catholic thinking on keeping faith with peoples deemed heretic, or the validity of acts by heretic administrators, was such that such a move would logically be supported by Papal authority.[169]

Van Eysinga places the truce negotiations in the context of the very competitive French-Spanish relations at the time, both of which monarchies had interests at stake by a Dutch-Spanish agreement. The Archdukes' willingness to negotiate with the Dutch as 'free men' seems prompted by the rising prospect of a

[165] Leiden UL, BPL 922.I.d; not in Grotius' handwriting. The title *Observationes* etc. is a 19th-century one not on the document but inscribed on the folder that contains it; following Eysinga's article of 1955 the piece is often quoted in the scholarship as *Onuitgegeven Nota* ('Unpublished Memorandum'); see Van Eysinga, 'Eene onuitgegeven nota'. See also Tuck, *Philosophy and Government,* p. 156; Van Ittersum, *Profit and Principle*, pp. 194–217.

[166] Leiden UL, BPL 922.I.c, in Grotius' own hand.

[167] As discussed by Van Ittersum, *Profit and Principle* p. 217–244.

[168] See Van Ittersum, *Profit and Principle* and Nellen, *Hugo Grotius*, p. 107–109; in November 1608 the Zeeland chamber of the VOC, via the mediation of Grotius' friend Johan Boreel, asked Grotius to compose a treatise on the freedom of navigation. Grotius complied with the specific aim of serving the company's interests in the negotiations, while by March 1609 Oldenbarnevelt came to ask for a delay in the publication, precisely to avoid upsetting the other party. The Truce was signed on 9 April 1609 before *Mare Liberum* could have any real influence on it.

[169] Cp. also A. Clerici, 'Trust, Heresy and Rebellion: Reactions to Machiavelli in the early Dutch Revolt' in: L. Kontler and M. Somos (eds), *Trust and Happiness in the History of European Political Thought*, Leiden (Brill) 2018, pp. 257–280.

closer alliance between the French and Dutch, that would leave the Southern Netherlands enclosed by French-controlled territory. On the opposite side the possibility of recognition of Dutch independence by the Habsburgs would rob the French king of the prospect of extending his influence over the Northern Netherlands, a prospect which prompted French diplomacy to try regain a hold on developments in The Hague and secure a continuation of the war.[170] Van Eysinga argues convincingly that in this puzzle of competing political relations, the outcome of the peace negotiations was uncertain until the very last moment and Van Oldenbarnevelt needed to have an explanation to the public ready in case the negotiations would fail. Grotius' text served as the basis of a Dutch version, possibly composed by Grotius too, which is preserved in drafts as *Memorie van Oldenbarnevelt,* the surviving copy of which is actually in Oldenbarnevelt's hand. The text has a very limited force of proof regarding Grotius' personal preference for war or peace – he wrote it on request and either for internal use, or for a situation that might very well never occur.[171]

The other draft treatise kept in Leiden carries the working title *De Bello ob Libertatem eligendo*, and is probably datable to around 1608.[172] Departing from one of Cicero's letters to Atticus,[173] it presents a philosophical deliberation, in a fairly standard humanist dialectical fashion, as to whether the wise man should strive to overthrow a tyrant suppressing his country at any cost, even if that puts the survival of the country at risk, or whether that decision should depend on the circumstances. Grotius' references at the outset to *prudentia* as his criterium, and to his ideal reader as a *vir politicus* suggest an affinity with a Lipsian realm of thought[174] and prefigures his mixed conclusion that however important freedom is, life and

[170] Amsterdam UL, special collections, IIIC2, fol. 50–65 (on 1607), fol. 66–75 (on 1608) and fol. 76–83(on 1609) together are a bundle of autographs notes by Grotius on the negotiations with the French. There is a title on fol. 50 *negotiations du president Jeannin* and on the back leaf *Negotiations du president Jeannin 1607 1608 1609.* The papers seems intended for private use; the handwriting is dense and not easy to read (and now partly faded).

[171] Van Eysinga supposes that the paper also reflects Grotius' own opinion (because he saw the war against Spain as legitimate and necessary). Den Tex (*Oldenbarnevelt* vol. II p. 564) is at a loss about the document. Van Ittersum (*Profit and Principle,* 197ff.) points out that Grotius also expresses concern elsewhere about the unclear situation after the temporary ceasefire of 1607, and considers the paper as having been written for Oldenbarnevelt (which could support Van Eysinga's view), but suspects that it served Oldenbarnevelt more to familiarise himself with counterarguments, to be able to neutralise them better. But perhaps VOC interests are involved as well? For further discussion see Van Ittersum, *Profit and Principle* ch. 4–5.

[172] An edition of this treatise by A. den Haan and J. Waszink will appear in *Grotiana* in the future. This brief discussion leans on preparatory work by Den Haan under the supervision of Waszink.

[173] Cicero, Att. IX Ep. 4.

[174] The beginning of the argument in *De Bello* connects implicitly but unmistakably with the discussion on tyranny in Lipsius, *Politica* 6.5; further into the treatise, Grotius copies an incorrect source reference to Tacitus from *Politica* 6.5.4 (fol. 295r: '[...] quibus ut Tacitus loquitur, sola obsequii gloria relicta est', which is from Tacitus *Annals* 6.8, not *Annals* 4).

virtue are greater goods; that war is not such an evil that to avoid it would justify accepting servitude, but that nevertheless war should only be risked if a positive outcome is probable. Therefore the wise politician should weigh all circumstances and decide accordingly.

Like with the *Observationes* the purpose of the piece is unclear; a comparable purpose is imaginable – perhaps with Oldenbarnevelt as the *vir politicus*? – but certainly not a given. *De Bello* may just be a private tool by Grotius to help him sort out his thoughts on the question for or against the Truce. As discussed above (§ 6 and App. 4), 'prudential' thinking in Lipsius' manner did not necessarily have a good reputation in the public sphere in the Republic. With that respect the realm of thought represented in *De Bello* resembles that of the *Annales* (and the reasons for not developing it into a publication, if that was ever on the cards, may overlap with the reasons the AH was not published at the time). If this is true, *De Bello* might perhaps be seen as representing Grotius' own thoughts on the question for or against the Truce.

Thus, judging by the draft documents in Leiden, it would be possible to see Grotius both as a moderate supporter of Oldenbarnevelt's peace policy and as a moderate adherent of the war party; or perhaps as an educated mortal still in the process of making up his mind. Around and after the conclusion of the Truce Grotius wrote four poems celebrating but also questioning this event, which were eventually published in his *Poemata Collecta* edition of 1617.[175] The *Ode pro Induciis* for example expresses worries about the reliability of the treaty, while the *Apologus* presents a fable invoking Machiavelli's famous figure of the lion and the fox to present a vision of the Truce as a strategy of deceit that leads to the ruin of an innocent people.[176]

9.2. *The AH's relationship with Grotius' other works*

The view of Grotius' life as a unified moral quest for peace and justice has lost ground in modern scholarship. Awareness of Grotius' role(s) as spokesman for particular interests, and of the specific political and discursive contexts of individual works has gradually achieved greater prominence. However a consideration of his historical works as a group reveals a tension between two approaches to reason of state which both seem fundamental to Grotius' thinking.[177] This bipolarity reflects what is perhaps the most crucial issue at stake in the methodological debates on history and politics of his time; that is, the opposition between legal

[175] For this poetry, see the edition, discussion and commentary by Van Oosterhout, *Hugo Grotius' Occasional Poetry*, section H (p. 287–334).

[176] H2 *Ode pro Induciis,* p. 296–298), H3 *Apologus*, p. 299–304.

[177] Compare also the related debate between readers of Grotius such as Richard Tuck who emphasise the role self-interest in Grotius' 'system', and those who focus on Grotius' assertion of a principle of sociability; a summary of this discussion in C. Brooke, 'Grotius, Stoicism and 'Oikeiosis', in: *Grotiana* 29.1 (2008), 25–50, at 25–31.

normativity, moral optimism (and often, but not always, religious orthodoxy) on the one hand, and scepticism, moral pessimism and reason of state on the other. Thus the 'Lipsian' or even 'Machiavellian' aspects of the AH render the question of the AH's place within Grotius' oeuvre especially urgent. In this section we will compare the *Parallelon Rerumpublicarum* of *c.*1600, the then-unpublished *De Iure Praedae* of 1604–1606, *De Antiquitate* of 1610, *De Iure Belli ac Pacis* of 1625 the *Historia Gotthorum* of *c.*1637 (published 1655), and the two treatises on the origins of the inhabitants of the Americas.

The *Parallelon Rerumpublicarum* is often grouped with Grotius' historical works. It was written around the turn of the 17th century and was never brought to the press by Grotius, although it is very likely that at the time it circulated in manuscript in Grotius' circle of acquaintances. It appears that by 1605 Grotius had lost interest in having it printed.[178] The text has not been preserved in full; only the third book survives and was first published by Johan Meerman in 1801–1803.[179] Although the *Annales* and the *Parallelon* must thus have been in preparation simultaneously or at least almost simultaneously, the two works could hardly be further apart in substance and temperament. The *Parallelon*'s highly optimistic and patriotic character is entirely different from the sceptical, critical and pessimistic tone of the *Annales*.

The *Parallelon* compares aspects of Athenian, Roman and Dutch cultures and societies respectively, demonstrating in each case the superiority of the culture and society in the Dutch Republic. It makes a strong connection between the virtuousness of a society and its historical success. It reflects a wide knowledge of classical history and refers frequently to the Batavian Myth. For the argument of the *Parallelon* its rhetorical brilliance seems to carry greater weight than an any attempt at serious historical investigation. Arthur Eyffinger argues that the work should be read as a critical analysis of and warning against rising moral defects in Dutch society around 1600 resulting from the success of the Revolt, i.e. especially *luxuria* and lack of unity. If this is true, the work for our purposes provides another case of 'exemplary' usage of the past for moral purposes in the present, with a very strong rhetorical aspect as the means to secure the desired effect. It seems plausible to connect this too with teaching practices at the university of Leiden, where the rhetorical aspect of the teaching of ethics was of overwhelming importance rather than, for example, Aristotelian philosophical analysis of ethics.[180]

[178] A. Eyffinger, 'Het Parallelon Rerumpublicarum van Hugo de Groot' in: Z. von Martels, P. Steenbakkers & A. Vanderjagt, *Limae Labor et Mora. Opstellen voor Fokke Akkerman ter gelegenheid van zijn zeventigste verjaardag,* Leende 2000, p. 127–144; p. 132.

[179] *Hugonis Grotii, Batavi, Parallelon rerumpublicarum liber tertius: De moribus ingenioque populorum Atheniensium, Romanorum, Batavorum. Vergelijking der gemeenebesten door Hugo de Groot. Derde boek: Over de zeden en den inborst der Athenienseren, Romeinen en Hollanderen,* Haarlem (Loosjes) 1801–1803.

[180] Compare Wansink, *Politieke Wetenschappen*, passim and J. Waszink, 'Dominicus Baudius' teaching of ethics in Leiden,' paper presented at the conference *Teaching Ethics at Early Modern Universities, 1500–1700*, Warsaw 14–15 June 2018 (forthcoming).

The (then-)unpublished tract *De Republica Emendanda*, probably written around 1600, uses historical information taken from Scripture to propose a re-organisation of the political organisation of the Dutch Republic on the basis of the ancient *respublica Hebraeorum*.[181]

9.2.1. *De Iure Praedae Commentarius* and *De Antiquitate Reipublicae Batavicae* (1604–1610)

These two treatises present, among others, very similar constitutional justifications of the revolt against Philip II and will be here be discussed together; the argument could also be extended to the unpublished *Theses XI* and *Theses LVI*.[182] Grotius' then-unpublished treatise *De Iure Praedae Commentarius* (IPC) was written in 1604–1606 at the request of the directors of the Dutch East India Company (VOC). Except for one chapter which was published separately as *De Mari Libero* in 1609 it remained in manuscript until the later 19th century. Its aim is to defend the capture of the Portuguese carrack Santa Catarina by a VOC captain in 1603. Part of Grotius' argument in justification of that taking is an extensive reference to the war between the Dutch and the Spanish empire, of which Portugal was a part since 1580. An account of the legitimacy of the Dutch Revolt thus also corroborates Grotius' argument in IPC.[183] In this historical section of the work (chapters 11–14) Grotius presents essentially the same constitutional legitimisation of the Dutch Revolt that returns in a more developed form in *De Antiquitate*.

On a different and more implicit level however, it seems possible to argue that in one sense IPC is also indebted to reason-of-state thinking. Since the legality of the capture was dubious at best by the rules of existing positive law around 1600, IPC provides a justification of it beyond the letter of the law (just as reason of state may legitimise action not legitimised by ethics, law or religion): there is an affinity, or even an overlap between the *realism* of reason of state and the *naturalism* of Grotius' system of natural law. On the other hand, in IPC's argumentation normativity remains paramount, whereas in reason-of-state arguments this is not usually the case. In any case Grotius provided his justification in terms of an

[181] A. Eyffinger, P. de Boer, J. de Schmidt and L. van Holk, 'De Republica Emendanda: a juvenile tract by Hugo Grotius on the emendation of the Dutch polity' in *Grotiana* NS vol. 5 (1984); provides an edition of the Latin text and English translation.

[182] See P. Borschberg, '"Commentarius in Theses XI". Ein unveröffentlichtes Kurzwerk von Hugo Grotius' in: *Zeitschrift der Savigny-Stiftung für Rechtsgeschichte* vol. 109 (1992), 450–474 and id, 'Grotius, the Social Contract and Political Resistance. A study of the Unpublished Theses LVI' in: *IILJ Working Paper* 2006/7

[183] On DIP, see esp. Ittersum, *Profit and Principle*; ead., Intr. to Grotius, *Law of Prize and Booty*, and lit. given there. An online critical edition of the ms. of DIP with Grotius' variants by the present editor is available at http://arkyves.org/view/DeIurePraedae.

alternative concept of law which lent itself to (subsequent) elaboration into a new legal system.[184]

De Antiquitate Reipublicae Batavicae appeared in 1610 after the conclusion of the 12-year Truce in 1609 and presents a constitutional legitimation of the Revolt against Habsburg domination, based on available knowledge of the political practices of the Batavians from Roman times and the medieval 'ancient constitutions' of the provinces in the Low Countries (especially Holland and Brabant). The aim is to show that ever since Roman/Batavian times, sovereign power in the Low Countries was only delegated to the executive by a representative council which remained, essentially, the actual sovereign and could impose rules on the executive; and that these representative sovereign councils are the provincial States of medieval and later times. Thus it follows that the deposition of Philip II by the collective provincial States cooperating in the States-General was legitimate since the prince had broken the rules of their agreement; and that the Republic's form of government is legitimate in both the constitutional and the historical sense, as it amounted in fact to the restoration of a form of government which had existed for 1700 years. *De Antiquitate*'s tone is optimistic, patriotic and constitutional. A chief mark of Grotius' reasoning is the 'constitutional optimism' which it expresses: the well-being of all is secured if the magistrates and social elites stand up to defend the rules and liberties laid down in the age-old Privileges of the provinces, towns and nobility against rulers eager for domination. This is a very different register from the wary Tacitist scepticism of the AH, although Grotius must have worked on both texts simultaneously. The detailed description of ancient Lower Germany in *Historiae* 7 might well be a reflection of the Grotius' work on *De Antiquitate*;[185] in which case it might indicate a date for the composition of that passage of 1609–1610. For a more detailed discussion of DA, see the edition in BLN and the literature given there.

9.2.2. *De Iure Belli ac Pacis* (1625)

As noted above a bipolarity can be perceived within Grotius' oeuvre between legal normativity and moral optimism on the one hand, and scepticism, moral pessimism and reason of state on the other. This bipolarity becomes particularly intriguing if we regard *De Iure Belli ac Pacis* (DIB) as Grotius' chief work, as a major part of the Grotius scholarship since the 19th century does. With respect to

[184] Similarly, it may be significant that in these same years Grotius also wrote an argument entitled *De Aequitate* discussing the notion that a strict a application of laws is insufficient to always produce justice, but should be corrected by roughly what is now called 'reasonableness and fairness'. *De Aequitate* however does not apply the idea to public law and/or politics, but only to private and penal law. The manuscript is preserved in Leiden UL as BPL 921 (dated 'before 1615') and has been printed several times, in an edited version by Nicolaus Blancardus, as appendix to editions of *De Iure Belli ac Pacis* (e.g. that by Leers in The Hague, 1680).

[185] Edition 1658, p. 337–341.

Grotius' oeuvre in general, this approach made a connection between the legal and constitutional optimism of the earlier DA (and some other works) and the well-known programmatic rejection of 'Carneades' in the Prolegomena to *DIB* (§ 3–6). This led to a vision of one Grotian 'system' of human reason and sociability that leaves little room for the sceptical and realist understanding of politics, society and history expressed in the *Annales*. Some readers on the other hand have emphasised the role of self-interest in Grotius' system, including DIB, and have accordingly presented a picture of a much more sceptical and realist thinker.

But however that be, over the past decades Grotius scholars generally have become more clearly aware of both Grotius' role as a spokesman for particular interests, and of the specific political and discursive contexts of each of his individual works. Building on this awareness the results of the present enquiry suggest that we might simply accept the above-mentioned bipolarity as a given: as a mark of a human oeuvre produced under changing circumstances over the course of almost 50 years; but especially as one that reflects Grotius' own questions and doubts regarding the problem of ethics and reason of state that figured so prominently in the intellectual debates of his generation.

Although this is not the place for an analysis of DIB, some brief remarks on the role of Grotius' historical thought in DIB are in order. The influence of reason-of-state thought can be perceived in Grotius' ideas on natural law and the reasoning in IPC and DIB; not only in the central foundational role of self-interest Grotius' theory of natural rights, but also in the extensive use of historical data and examples in the exposition of the argument in DIB. And finally actual expressions of reason-of-state ethics are included in the DIB, such as the reasoning with respect to pre-emptive strike in 2.1.17.[186]

9.2.3. *Historia Gotthorum* (1637)

This work is a compilation of ancient and early medieval written source information on the Gothic people as inhabitants of the territory of Sweden, composed by

[186] 'But I can by no means approve of what some authors have advanced, that by the law of nations it is permitted to take up arms to reduce the growing power of a prince or state, which if too much augmented, may possibly injure us. I grant, that in deliberating whether a war ought to be undertaken or not, that consideration may enter, not as a justifying reason, but as a motive of interest. *So that where we have any other just cause for making war, it may for this reason too be thought prudently undertaken* [italics mine]. And this is all that the authors before cited do in effect say; but to pretend to have a right to injure another, merely from a possibility that he may injure me, is repugnant to all the justice in the world: For such is the condition of the present life, that we can never be in perfect security. It is not in the way of force, but in the protection of Providence, and in innocent precautions, that we are to seek for relief against uncertain fear' (translation from the 1738 Morrice/ Barbeyrac edition re-edited by Richard Tuck; Grotius, *The Rights of War and Peace* ed. with intr. by Richard Tuck, 3 vols., Indianapolis, 2005); see further J. Waszink, 'Grotius as Historian' in R. Lesaffer & J. Nijman (eds.), *The Cambridge Companion to Hugo Grotius,* Cambridge UP 2021.

Grotius when he was in the service of the Swedish crown as their ambassador in Paris (1634–1644). The work's main argument is concentrated in the introduction, and presents a 'Gothic Myth' to boost Swedish international prestige in the present. Apart from the fact that both works could be seen as (proto-)'national' histories, the AH and HG hardly lend themselves to instructive comparisons, since the themes of rebellion, religious policy, reason of state and the composition of contemporary history are not prominent in the HG.

The recent characterisation of the *Historia Gotthorum* as a work in the antiquarian tradition[187] has been criticised as questionable if one takes the concern with physical objects and data as a defining mark of antiquarianism, for indeed the HG shows little use of such information to confront the written record with.

9.2.4. *De Origine Gentium Americanarum* (1641–1643)

Towards the end of his life Grotius wrote two treatises on the history of the peoples inhabiting the Americas, entitled *De Origine Gentium Americanarum* (1641) and *De Origine Gentium Americanarum dissertatio altera* (1643)[188] which provide a fascinating opportunity to observe his reflexes as a historian, not least because of the contrast with his approach in the AH. In the first *Dissertatio* Grotius presents himself as raising the question of the origins of the original inhabitants of the Americas for the first time. Characteristically he begins by turning to classical history, and throughout the two treatises a leading theme is the drive to harmonise and connect recent discoveries and observations from the New World with classical, biblical and medieval history and language from the Old world. This however does not exclude a critical approach to Scripture and the classics, but, characteristically for the humanist, there is less interest in information outside the circle of written ancient sources, and when Grotius does consult such other sources, his use of them looks haphazard and selective. Grotius proposes that the original inhabitants of North-America arrived in that continent via Greenland from Norway; those of middle America (e.g. Yucatan, Mexico) from Aethiopia, and that those of South-America originally came from South-east Asia via the (largely hypothetical) 'Southland' beyond Strait Magelhaes which we now know to be a wide sea and Antarctica.[189]

[187] See L. Janssen, *Hugo Grotius, antiquarianism and the Gothic myth. A critical study of the ideological dimension and methodological foundation of the Historia Gotthorum* (1655), PhD Leuven 2016; and the forthcoming edition of Grotius' foreword to the HG in Bibliotheca Latinitatis Novae.

[188] See Nellen, *Hugo Grotius* p. 684–690 and lit. in the notes there. Futher esp. C. Laes and T. Van Houdt, 'Over Goten Germanen en Indianen: de controverse Grotius-De Laet', in: *De Zeventiende Eeuw* vol. 25:1 (2009) 120–136 and B. Schmidt, 'Space, time, travel: Hugo de Groot, Johannes de Laet, and the advancement of geographic learning', in: *Lias* 25 (1998), 177–199.

[189] Nellen (*Hugo Grotius*, p. 687–688) simplifies Grotius' view to one holding that 'the peoples of the Americas (...) had arrived from Norway (via Greenland), parts of Africa and the Far East.'

Grotius' views on the matter were immediately attacked by Johannes the Laet (1581–1649), who was recognised as a leading specialist on the Americas.[190] He was one of the directors of the Dutch West India Company (WIC) and author of a 'Yearly Report' on the progress of the WIC in the period 1621–1636.[191] De Laet was also a passionate Counter-remonstrant and had sat on the Synod of Dordt in 1618–19. Their confrontation centred on method, Grotius being accused by De Laet of ignoring the most recent observations and reports by sailors who had actually visited the Southern hemisphere. Following remarks by De Laet himself, several modern authors interpret the controversy as an instance of the *querelle des anciens et des modernes*, i.e. between (old-fashioned) humanist scholarship and (progressive) empirical research.[192] However it could be argued in Grotius' defence that the fact that he did use contemporary descriptions, eye-witness accounts and maps demonstrates his awareness of the dangers involved in his usual humanist approach.[193] At his time of writing, the 'Southland', which plays a central role in the controversy, still appeared on world maps as '*Terra Australis Incognita*' or '*Magellanica*'. Thus at least Grotius' geography was potentially plausible and founded on recent empirical documentation as it was available when he wrote.[194] Fascinatingly the Southland begins to disappear from the maps precisely *after* 1640.

The scholarship on this controversy further observes that we do not know why Grotius wrote these treatises.[195] Nellen and others suppose that Grotius was trying to show that all inhabitants of the Americas descend from known territories in the Old World, with the intention of saving the biblical world-view that all humans are descendants of Adam and Eve. Against Grotius' view, that of De Laet would allow for the possibility of a kind of 'polygenetism.' It seems highly unlikely however that this was the issue at stake. First, De Laet departed from the hypothesis that a migration from the Old World to the New had happened via a passage at the east end of the Eurasian continent (that had not yet been discovered in their time): thus his theory in no way conflicts with the possibility of a common descent from Adam. Conversely, Grotius' 'Southland' hypothesis regarding the origins of the populations of South-America complicates a 'monogenetic' explanation rather than supporting it. Moreover, this supposed intention of Grotius' to save the literal truth of the

[190] Ioannis de Laet Antuerpiani, *Notae ad dissertationem Hugonis Grotii De Origine Gentium Americanarum: et Observationes aliquot ad meliorem indaginem difficillimae illius Quaestionis,* Amsterdam (Elzevier), 1643.

[191] Published as *Iaerlyck Verhael van de verrichtinghen der geoctroyeerde West-Indische Compagnie* in Leiden in 1644.

[192] Esp. Schmidt, 'Time, Space, Travel', 195–198; followed by Nellen, *Hugo Grotius,* 688.

[193] See Grotius' defence of his method in the reply to the critics in the *Dissertatio altera*, pp. 6–7.

[194] See R. Shirley, *The Mapping of the World. Early Printed World Maps 1472–1700,* London, 1983, Holland Press Cartographica series vol. 9, pp. 350–400.

[195] Van Houdt & Laes, 'Goten, Germanen, Indianen', 123–125; Nellen, *Hugo Grotius,* 684 and D. van Miert & H. Nellen, 'Media en tolerantie in de Republiek der Letteren. De discussie over Isaac de la Peyrère (*c.*1596–1676) en zijn pre-Adamitae' in: *De Zeventiende Eeuw* 30 (2014), pp. 3–19.

biblical account is never made explicit, and it is unsupported by the free and secularising approach to Scripture which we find him displaying elsewhere. Finally it remains unexplained why Grotius would find a pamphlet (and a sketchy one at that with provisional conclusions) the best format to contribute to this type of scholarly debate. This format might point at a political purpose, perhaps connected with Grotius' role as Swedish ambassador, but unfortunately the contemporary political map of Scandinavia fails to provide explanations as well (esp. given Grotius' emphasis on the supposed Norwegian origins of the peoples of North-America).[196]

9.3. *Grotius as Historian*[197]

In a discussion of Grotius' main historical work an assessment of the author as historian is in order, and many aspects of this historical thinking have already emerged in this introduction: (1) the polarity between constitutionalism and patriotism on the one hand, and reason of state and scepticism on the other; (2) Grotius' secularising reading of history; (3) the close correlation between scholarship and politics; (4) Grotius' approach to historical sources and his (weak) relation to contemporary developments in Antiquarianism; and (5) the important role of historical perspectives in his other works such as *De Jure Belli ac Pacis*. His use of sources specifically for the AH (6) will be discussed below in section 10.

Although for Grotius, history was always subservient to political ends and this led him to creative over-interpretation of sources in some cases, this does not mean he has not contributed to the discipline as such or to its methods. For him, the progress of the historical discipline lay in the movement towards secularism and realism/naturalism, not so much in the antiquarian direction. In his correspondence of the 1630s, Grotius includes the AH among his main achievements and expresses an expectation that the work will earn him lasting fame with posterity. The chief methodological thrust of the AH is an attempt at analysis of the true logic behind human history; i.e. of the real causes, motives and effects, regardless of the demands of moral exemplarity and religious teleology. Obviously this separation runs parallel to the rise of reason of state in politics itself and the gradual 'emancipation' of politics from the demands of ethics and religion; as Grotius' ideas on the statesman-historian show, politics and the writing of history were

[196] During the 17th century, Sweden and Denmark-Norway were regularly in and out of war. The Second Treaty of Brömsebro in 1645 awarded three Norwegian provinces to Sweden but this occurred too late to help explain Grotius' text of 1641. Sweden's most important activity in the Americas at the time seems to be foundation in 1638 of a colony on the Delaware. In cooperation with Dutch and German stakeholders Sweden founded New Sweden and brought settlers to expand it in the subsequent period. After 1648 there was competition with Dutch attempts to settle in the area, which led to a Dutch take-over in 1654. The Swedish settlements however remained in place as an 'independent' Swedish nation until they came under English rule in 1681; see P.S. Craig, 'Chronology of Colonial Swedes on the Delaware 1638–1713' in: *Swedish Colonial News*, Volume 2, Number 5 (2001).

[197] For a more elaborate discussion see Waszink, 'Grotius as Historian'.

intimately connected activities. The postponed publication of the AH until 1657 however robbed Grotius of a good part of his actual influence on the field, for by that time, the secular and realist view of history and politics was no longer as controversial as it had been in the period around 1610. Nevertheless, the work's quality of realist analysis ensured that it enjoyed a reputation as 'the' work on the Dutch Revolt from its publication up to some point in the eighteenth century. These conclusions apply to the *interpretation* of the historical record.

On the other hand, it is also obvious that with respect to the *creation* of the historical record, the censorious judgment of Grotius by the Dutch historian Robert Fruin (1823–1899, an admirer of Ranke; see also § 11.7)[198] makes sense. Grotius' approach to his task is not that of a critical historical researcher in the 'modern' sense of the word, but that of the (Late-) humanist. Although he uses a wide array of sources, these are limited to written materials: composed historical narratives – ancient, medieval and modern ones –, documentary sources such as letters, diaries, treaties, decrees, laws or pamphlets, as well as etymological and linguistic evidence. Grotius displays only limited interest in information outside these realms, and never really adopts the innovations of the antiquarian branch of scholarship. The antiquarian notes to *De Antiquitate* were written and added not by himself but by Petrus Scriverius.

With respect to Grotius' awareness of the contemporary developments in historiography, as brought up by his treatises on *De Origine Gentium Americanarum*, it seems that, although his use of new empirical evidence appears less limited than some of the scholarship suggests, in the end he was insufficiently aware of the *pace* at which the new knowledge was changing and expanding. One might suspect that it was precisely this new phenomenon of permanently *changing* facts that he was insufficiently awake to.

9.4. *Is there a sense of 'Netherlands' or 'Dutch' nationhood in the* Annales?

Texts like the AH and *De Antiquitate* may be searched for early-modern precursors of nineteenth- and twentieth-century ideas of nationhood.[199] Is there any sense of a 'Netherlands' or 'Dutch' nationhood in the *Annales*? An investigation[200]

[198] 'History, as understood by Grotius, belonged to the sphere of philology; its main aspect was form, and this had to be modelled on the examples from Antiquity. In-depth and extensive research, [and] critical evaluation of transmitted information was less important. This is why Grotius considered himself fit to write history, and was seen as such by others.' R. Fruin, *Verspreide Geschriften* vol. III, edd. P. Blok, P. Muller and S. Muller Fz., The Hague 1901, pp. 405–406; see also H. Muller, *De Groots Annales et Historiae*, PhD Utrecht 1919, pp. 159–161.

[199] For the debate and more literature, see L. Jensen, 'Introduction' in: ead. (ed.), *The Roots of Nationalism. National Identity Formation in Early Modern Europe, 1600–1815,* Amsterdam 2016.

[200] For a fuller discussion with respect to DA and AH, see J. Waszink, 'The Low Countries: constitution, nationhood and character according to Hugo Grotius', in: Jensen, *The Roots of Nationalism*, pp. 135–152.

shows that in Grotius' mind, the logical unity of a people, a specified territory, and a political organisation existed, and did so at the level of the province (e.g. Holland, Brabant; i.e. *not* a unit like the nineteenth-century nation state), and that moreover this entity is the bearer of sovereignty. The Latin words for a people are often *natio* if used in the formal constitutional sense and *gens* if in a wider sense. These words apply to the provincial unit in most cases, although *gens Belgica* is found for the inhabitants of Low Countries as a whole. *Belga* and *Belgicus* are the regular words for 'Lowlander' and 'Low Countries'; *Batavus* and *Batavia* for Hollander and Holland (which is also sometimes found in the wider sense of the 'Dutch Republic'). However the usage of these words is by no means consistent; the Synod of Dordt for example, which assembled all the provinces in the North, is called 'national' also at the time itself.[201]

Accordingly, the more formally constitutional argument in *De Antiquitate Reipublicae Batavicae* focuses on the province of Holland and the legitimacy of its sovereignty. The *Annales* on the other hand do not display this exclusive focus on Holland. Grotius describes a shared Low Countries history and character or culture that apply to all 17 provinces (with the possible exception of the Walloons and the Luxemburgers, who are described as partly different in character); which means that the provincial unit of people, territory, and government does not also 'own' its cultural identity, but is part of a much larger cultural and linguistic space. On a more speculative note, however, it seems possible to distinguish another sub-group in Grotius' perception (apart from the Francophone South) consisting of Holland, Zeeland, Flanders and Brabant, which attract most of his interest and concern.[202] This would automatically create a third regional subgroup consisting of the North and East, probably including the former bishopric of Utrecht. With these three parts the geographical make-up of the Low Countries in Grotius' mind does not even remotely resemble that of the modern nation states of the Netherlands and Belgium. Note Grotius' regret at the separation of North and South as expressed in Ann. 2.66, 4.25 and 5.1.

For a comparison with a different but contemporary text dealing with the same concepts, one might compare the image of the Dutch presented in John Barclay's *Icon Animorum* of 1614.[203] Barclay's discussion of the Low Countries' character shows, first, that national character is defined only as a subcategory to the chronological ages of mankind, but is nevertheless important, given the space devoted to

201 E.g. by the English ambassador Dudley Carlton in *The speech of Sir Dudley Carlton* [...] *Touching the discord and troubles of the church and policie, caused by the schismatic doctrine of Arminius*, London 1618, pp. 5–6.

202 For example the failed Spanish siege of Steenwijk in 1580–1581 and the potentially very consequential loss of the town in 1582 are mentioned only in passing. P.C. Hooft devotes ample attention to it in his *Nederlandsche Historien* of 1642 (see also §§ 7.1 and 11.2).

203 John Barclay, *Icon Animorum or the Mirror of Minds.* Translated by Thomas May (1631), ed. M. Riley, Leuven 2013, Bibliotheca Latinitatis Novae, pp. 130–152.

it in the book. With respect to the Low Countries' character and the then-current stereotypes of it, the foreigner Barclay's description in many ways confirms that by Grotius (e.g. rejection of autocracy, drinking, urbanisation, trade and industry) and indeed applies this character to the Low Countries as a whole, not to individual provinces. He distinguishes only between the political cultures of North and South, which difference was by then well established. Thus, in the eyes of observers both at home and abroad, the Low Countries were a recognisable whole at the level of their cultural identity. At the constitutional level and that of practical politics, the Hollander Grotius perceived them as a collection of separate entities, which could cooperate but often failed to do so, and among which a regional grouping might be discerned without any resemblance to the map of the present-day nation states. While the roots of the idea of a national identity may be found in early-modern historiographical texts like those of Grotius and Barclay, the concept underwent profound transformations in the centuries since their time.

10. Sources of the *Annales et Historiae*

The question as to Grotius' sources for the AH is a complicated one and partly impossible to answer. Grotius witnessed a substantial part of the described period (especially that described in the *Historiae*) himself, and knew the years before his own conscious observation not only from written histories and documentary sources, but also from first- and second-hand stories and experiences from (older) contemporaries. With this respect Corrie Ridderikhoff has already pointed at his father Jan de Groot's involvement in the creation of the AH – although on balance it appears unlikely that his actual involvement in the composition of the text went very deep.[204] But however that be, Grotius' understanding of the period was not only informed by (written) sources still available to us, but also by a (no longer accessible) mixture of several kinds of unwritten information, i.e. experiences, relations and perceptions from his own and contemporaries, oral transmission, and collective memory.

This distinction is particularly important in the case of the AH because, as noted above, the AH is not a factual account centring on evidence and documents, but first and foremost an interpretation of the period and a literary presentation of it. It is significant that the text provides no source-references, although Grotius habitually provides them in many other works.[205] Therefore the question how and why Grotius arrived at his particular interpretation of the early phase of the revolt is not so much a question regarding his sources of information (however relevant

[204] See § 11.1.

[205] E.g. *De Antiquitate* and the ms. of *De Iure Praedae* (BPL 917 in Leiden UBL). In the AH on the other hand neither the printed text nor the preserves mss. of the *Historiae* contain Grotius' usual source-references in the margin.

this may be from a scholarly point of view), but primarily a question regarding the genesis of his own individual position in terms of political agenda, personal character, talents and interests, scholarly concerns etc., plus collective factors such as education, social and religious background and the collective memory of his age. Consequently your answer to this question will depend on your own views on the relationships between these factors and a historical subject's historical and political opinions.

However this leaves unaffected that we remain curious as to Grotius' sources of information and material, and that some of them can be identified. In any case it is important to heed the warning formulated by Martine van Ittersum with respect to *De Iure Praedae* and *De Iure Belli ac Pacis*, in the case of the AH too, i.e. that we should investigate which sources Grotius *actually* used, and how he used them, instead of making sweeping assumptions as to his familiarity with all the preceding literature.[206] The AH itself as well as related documents (such as his correspondence) identify some of the work's sources. We shall distinguish these into a few groups.

Printed general histories of the Revolt were a very new phenomenon when Grotius started composing the AH, but he evidently used the ones that were available in his time, the most important of which are the works by Emmanuel van Meteren (the first of such works, 1593/1599 and later, see above § 2.3), and that by Pieter Bor (1595 and later). He has demonstrably worked through Van Meteren's *Memorien* as appears from the manuscript notes in his own copy now kept in Lund UL.[207] A third prominent early history of the Revolt, that by Everard van Reyd (1550–1602), may have been consulted by Grotius in manuscript, since the work was only first published posthumously in 1626, and he praises the author by name in the *Historiae*.[208]

206 M. van Ittersum, 'The Working Methods of Hugo Grotius: Which Sources Did He Use and How Did He Use Them In His Early Writings on Natural Law Theory', in: P. du Plessis & J. Cairns, *Reassessing Legal Humanism and its Claims*, Edinburgh University Press 2016 pp. 154–193.

207 See the discussion in § 2.3 above. Grotius' own copy is now in Lund UL, Hs.-avd. fol. utl. hist. nederl; bar code 799251620. There are underlinings in the text, keywords and noted events in the margins, and notes on the flyleaves in Grotius' hand. One of those reads 'dicmael iet lang, daerna te pas gekomen' ('often a bit long-winded, but useful later on') suggesting that Grotius spent quite a bit of time with the book.

208 *Historiae* 14 (1605) p. 458, mistakenly referred to as Franciscus Rhedanus: 'Prodiit per eosdem dies et Francisci Rhedani, viri doctissimi, et in Republica cum honore versati, deque eadem etiam res gestas patrio sermone scribendo bene meriti, liber, sed scriptore mortuo ab amicis vulgatus, qui vetera novaque, et Austriacae domus, et Hispanorum malefacta referens, et quam infida principum in populos foedera, praesertim quos Pontifex periurii religione exsolveret, par periculum Reformatis et Romanensibus ostentabat: nec alium quam vincendo exitum: desperatas hominum vias Deo patescere'. Grotius refers to Van Reyd's *Trouhertige vermaninge aen het vereenichde Nederlandt, om niet te luysteren na eenighe versierde vreed-articulen, nu onlangs wtgegaan ende ghestroyt*, s.l., 1605 (pamphlet, Knuttel 1300–1302, Tiele 544–546; 'Faithful admonition to the united Netherlands not to listen to

A detailed investigation of Grotius' relation of the *Turfschip van Breda* story (*Historiae* 2) has demonstrated that Grotius takes much of his factual information from these works, but abbreviates it considerably and does not represent all details correctly.[209] A similar pattern arises from a comparison of Grotius' biographical epilogue of Philip II with that in Van Meteren (see Appendix 3), which shows that not only facts but several of his main observations are actually adapted from Van Meteren as well. In fact Grotius makes this quite explicit; his epilogue refers to judgments of Philip by other observers which he has consulted (*prudentiores* and others); from which it follows that he counts Van Meteren among the better interpreters of the Revolt's history, even though there is no explicit reference to this important source.

Bor's histories were indispensable anyway as a documentary source; the volumes which were published in 1601 and 1603 moreover contain gratulatory poems by Grotius in the prefatory matter, which indicates that he would have had Bor's works at his disposal while he was working on the AH. Even a brief comparison between Bor's works and the AH brings out the different characters of both works very clearly: whereas Bor keeps close to the causes and motives named by the various agents in the sources and documents, which he often quotes in full or at least at great length, Grotius' project on the other hand is to reveal the 'true' or hidden causes and motives in a concise and cogent presentation. Where Bor's focus is on documentation, Grotius' is on judgment and interpretation.

Secondly, Grotius has often used primary texts which played a role in the events themselves: for example well-known ones such as William of Orange's pamphlets, Philip II's *Ban* against Orange, the *Act of Abjuration*, and of course William's *Apology* of 1580.[210] *Annals* 2.11 for example summarises William's *Waerschowinghe* of 1568 in a way that may serve to illustrate Grotius' working process: rigorous selection and reduction of the pamphlet's content to a small number of key thoughts, which are then rephrased in a manner and style that fits those of Grotius' text (a very different approach from e.g. Pieter Bor's abundant quoting and documenting). In a similar way lesser-known texts can be recognised, such as the pamphlets recognisable as sources in *Ann.* 3.47–3.51, 4.12–14, and 4.27 including the *Corte Verclaeringe* ('Short Declaration') by the city government of Antwerp, which appears to be a source of Grotius' relation of the French Fury of 1583 in 4.12; and of course the texts of treaties such as the Pacification of Ghent of 1576, the Union of Utrecht of 1579, and letters between the king and his representatives in the Low Countries, the provinces or the towns. In many cases the contents of such letters were published and

the beautiful articles of peace recently circulated'). He is also praised in Grotius' papers preserved in Amsterdam UL, ms IIIC3 fol. 263 (229). See further A. Janssen, 'Trias Historica'.

209 See M. van der Poel, 'Tacitean Elements in Grotius' narrative of the Capture of Breda'.

210 'Waerschowinghe' in: *Prins Willem van Oranje, Geschriften van 1568,* ed. M. Schenk, Amsterdam (Wereldbibliotheek) 1933, pp. 117–128; *The Apologie of Prince William of Orange against the proclamation of the king of Spaine*, ed. H. Wansink, Leiden 1969; or *Apologie ofte Verantwoordinge van den Prince van Orangien*, ed. M. Mees-Verwey, Santpoort 1942; see also Geurts, *Opstand in de pamfletten, pp.* 102–108.

had an influence on the course of events. These are only a few examples; many of these documents were available to Grotius via Bor's lavishly documented histories.

Next, in his capacity as advocate-fiscal, as official historiographer, and as a well-connected participant in regent circles, his network gave Grotius access to documents not available to most others. As advisor to the VOC, he had direct access to information about their exploits in the east, and for the composition of *De Iure Praedae*, the VOC had provided him in 1604 with reports on the interactions with the Portuguese. These papers must also have contributed to the passages on the Dutch Asian trade mentioned above (see § 9.1).[211] In the later half of 1614 Grotius asked Jean Hotman de Villiers, who acted as secretary to the Earl of Leicester in the 1580s, for documents relating to Leicester's period of command in the Low Countries.[212] Amsterdam University Library keeps a number of folders with various collected papers from Grotius' possession, which include notes and copies relating to the politics described in the AH, such as the military English assistance to the Dutch in 1585,[213] Leicester's powers, and the Anglo-French alliance of 1596 (to which the Dutch would also accede to make a triple alliance), as discussed in *Historiae* book 5.[214] In 1610 Grotius and Cornelis van der Myle were delegated by the States-General to inspect the collection of books and documents collected by Paullus Merula for his *Historia Belgica*, which collection was subsequently acquired by the Generalty.[215] It is only reasonable to assume that Grotius had his eyes open at that occasion for documents that would be useful to him as well. Further, Grotius repeatedly suggests that he has 'hidden' information, sometimes with reference to the source (e.g. an intercepted letter[216]), but often without, however much one would wish to have a source for that particular statement.[217]

211 See Van Ittersum, *Profit and Principle,* Intr., p. lvi and id., 'The working methods of Grotius' pp. 159–160 and note 8.

212 See Waszink, 'Grotius' AH in his correspondence', 256.

213 Amsterdam UL, IIIC2, nrs. 96a *Articles du Traitte et accord....entre les deputez de la Ma.te de la Reine d'Angleterre et ceux des estats generaux pour le secours de la ville d'Anvers;* dated 2.8.1585 (old style); 96b *Projet ou forme de traitte sur laide durant la guerre*; 97 *Cum nuper tractatus habitus esset* etc; 98 *Elisabetha dei gratia Angliae, Franciae et Hiberniae Regina Fidei Defensor* etc; 102 *Ordines Generales confederatarum Provinciarum in Belgio omnibus* etc.

214 *Historiae* 5 p. 263; in Amsterdam UL, IIIC2, no. 104 gives a copy of the Anglo-French treaty; no. 99 of the Anglo-French-Dutch treaty.

215 Haak, *Paullus Merula*, pp. 75–77. Merula had finished the *Historia Belgica* in 1604 but the mss. got lost before it was printed. Unfortunately the whereabouts of the books and papers acquired by the States-General are unknown as well, and it does not appear that any subsequent historian working for the States-General ever used them. A catalogue of all the documents he used (many of which he returned to their owners) was drawn up by Merula himself and has survived as Leiden UL, BPL 731. On Merula see also notes 9 and 17.

216 See e.g. Don Juan's 'true' thoughts in *Annals* 3.22.

217 Other examples are Philip's hidden intentions behind the agreements made on his departure from the Low Countries in 1559, (Ann. 1.34); Don Juan's secret orders (2.67); Philip's secret treaty with Lorraine (4.49); Leicester's secret deliberations (5.13).

The latter is particularly true for Grotius' controversial claims regarding the intentions behind William of Orange's and Elizabeth's the religious policies, as discussed earlier (§ 6). Are we looking at Grotius' own interpretation of their intentions here or did he actually have evidence to document his claims?[218] With respect to William's stance during the peace negotiations at Cologne (*Ann.* 3.25), the following can be said. In September 1579 Orange advised the provinces newly united in the Union of Utrecht not to accept the king's peace conditions, because this would soon lead to a renewed prohibition of Protestant worship. This advice however is not situated in the peace negotiations, nor an indication of any kind of 'double agenda' on William's part, let alone of a *feigned* religious motivation. A search for other possible sources for Grotius' claim has so far produced little result. If this claim is not of Grotius' own making but based on other documents or literature, one would perhaps expect it most in a history or pamphlet produced by one of Orange's adversaries, given the Machiavellian element that Grotius' interpretation contains. And indeed two passages in Catholic publications seem to approach Grotius' view somewhat, i.e. the claim by the Antwerp chronicler Adriaan van Meerbeeck (1563–*c.* 1630) in his *Chroniicke* of 1620 that William deliberately led the negotiations to fail by making unrealistic territorial, political and religious demands; and secondly the accusation made by Philip in the 1580 *Ban* against William of Orange of having wilfully undermined the peace talks by forging the Union of Utrecht while the negotiations were running. But even these texts do not suggest that William did this out of disguised self-interest or counterfeited religious zeal (– even apart from the question whether Grotius would let his image of William of Orange be shaped by such 'enemy' sources).[219] Therefore, for the time

[218] See also the documents in note 213 above and cp. § 6. The elements of the old ties between England and the Low Countries, Spanish cruelty and the rescue of the true faith appear in various wordings in these documents (esp. 97 and 98, and also, from the Dutch side, in 102); but I have not found references to 'the recent events in France and Scotland' here.

[219] *Ban ende edict by vorme van proscriptie, vuytggaen ende ghedecreteerd by ... de Coninck, tegens Wilhelm van Oraignyen* etc., 's Hertogenbosch 1580 (Pamphlet Knuttel 527), p. Bii; Van Meerbeeck, *Chroniicke van de gantsche werelt, ende sonderlinghe van de seventhien Nederlanden*, Antwerpen 1620, p. 538; B. Vermaseren, *De katholieke Nederlandse geschiedschrijving in de 16e en 17e eeuw over de opstand*, Leeuwarden 1981, pp. 246–263, m.n. 258; Grotius requests a copy in *Briefwisseling* vol. 2, ep. 681, pp. 126–127.

I have compared the accounts of the Cologne negotiations in the following works: Aggaeus van Albada, *Acten van den vredehandel, gheschiet te Colen*, Leiden 1580; Van Meteren, *Belgische ofte Nederlantsche Historie*, Delft 1599 fol. 151v–157v, and a later revised edition (The Hague 1614) fol. 168–171; Van Reyd, *Historie der Nederlandtscher Oorlogen*, ed. Leeuwarden 1650, p. 23; Bor, *Vervolgh der Nederlandtsche oorloghen*, vol. 2, Leiden 1621, book 13, fol. 104-r-111v en 139v–155r. Haraeus, *Annales Ducum seu Principum Brabantiae totusque Belgii*, Antwerpen 1623, pp. 294–298; Bentivoglio, *Della Guerra di Fiandra*, ed. Livorno 1831 vol. 3, pp. 674–679; Strada, *De Bello Belgico decas secunda*, Rome 1648, pp. 84–114. For an overview of the development of the talks, see V. Soen, *Vredehandel*, Amsterdam UP 2012, pp. 139–143; K. Swart, *Willem van Oranje en de Nederlandse Opstand 1572–1584*, ed. by A. Duke et al., Den Haag 1994, pp. 177–182. With respect to William of Orange's personal position, some histories on the side of the Revolt relate how representatives from the king in Cologne made failed

being we must conclude that the above image of William's stance during the 1579 peace talks indeed originates with Grotius himself.

In any case Grotius did consult several authors on the Revolt from the Catholic world. It appears however that in most cases this happened after his departure from Holland, when he was revising the AH. Most of the publications in question appeared after 1613, that is, after Grotius' original completion of the AH. It seems that the composition of *Grollae Obsidio* in 1628 was the occasion to read up on Catholic accounts of the Revolt; by the end of July we find Grotius referring to a map in Pompeio Giustiniani's history (see below). In October 1628 Grotius reports to his brother Willem he is reading Italian, Spanish and Low Countries authors on the Revolt, and comparing their accounts with his; unfortunately no further names are mentioned.[220] In 1629 he is said to have extensively praised the *Historia Belgica* by the South-Netherlands historian Nicolaus Burgundius (which appeared in that year) to the humanist Jean Dupuys (1591–1656);[221] and also Florentius van der Haer's *De Initiis Tumultuum Belgicorum* of 1587.[222]

In a letter of April 1635 Grotius bestows praise on the *Relationi* on the Netherlands by the cardinal Guido Bentivoglio (1579–1644) and the *Istoria delle guerre della Germania Inferiore* by Ieronimo Conestaggio (1540–1611), but is also

attempts with promises of personal gain and exemptions to persuade Orange to abandon the Revolt. Van Meteren (ed. 1614), Haraeus and Strada ascribe the failure of the negotiations to extreme lingering by the United Provinces; according to Strada this started when the prospect of an agreement became possible, but precisely this caused suspicions on both sides (this part of Strada's work however appeared only after Grotius'death). Bor provides a more detailed description of how the king's delegates present a peace proposal in July, which is insufficient in the eyes of the Dutch delegates but is sent to the provinces nevertheless, while the delegates simultaneously request a truce for two months, which is rejected. Also, the royal delegation tries to undermine the position of the Dutch delegates in Cologne by writing directly to the States-General without consulting them – a move which also undermines the unity among the provinces. The provinces convene a general meeting in Antwerp in late October, but the resulting counter-proposal arrives in Cologne only by late November, when the king's delegates have left and continuation of the talks is no longer possible. Nevertheless the proposal from July remains valid and is accepted by some towns (e.g. 's Hertogenbosch). Finally Bor discusses a number of pamphlets on the breakdown of the peace negotiations (152r–155r).

220 *Briefwisseling* vol. 3 ep. 1325, p. 391.

221 Vermaseren, *Katholieke geschiedschrijving* p. 145 n. 88. Grotius had been in contact with Burgundius since 1621–1622, see *Briefwisseling* vol. 2, ep. 699 pp. 146–147, and vol. 17, ep. 713a pp. 191–192. *Briefwisseling* vol. 5, ep. 2057 pp. 423–424 refers to a Philippus Burgundius who is said to have written against William of Orange; this does not seem to refer to Nicolaus Burgundius, but it is not clear to whom it does. On Burgundius' Tacitism, there is now M. Laureys, 'Sine amore, sine odio partium': Nicolaus Burgundius' *Historia Belgica* (1629) and his Tacitean quest for an Appropriate past' in: K. Enenkel and K. Ottenheym (eds.), *The Quest for an Appropriate Past in Literature, Art and Architecture*, Leiden (Brill) 2018, Intersections vol 60, pp. 397–417.

222 See Muller, *De Groots Annales et Historiae*, p. 114. This is very indirect information: the poet Joost van den Vondel is said to have written this in a letter to the poet and historian Pieter Corneliszoon Hooft in 1631.

very critical of the Spanish partiality of Bentivoglio's *Guerra di Fiandra.*[223] It is in this period that he sets out on the final revision of the AH which would put the work in the form in which it was printed. In a letter of October 1635 Grotius refers to Famiano Strada's (1572–1649) *De Bello Belgico* and that author's hostility to William of Orange.[224]

Of minor importance, but interesting because of an accidental discovery is the *Bellum Belgicum* by Pompeio Giustiniani (1569–1616), a captain from Parma's army who served in the Low Countries from 1587–1609. A Latin translation of his *Delle Guerre di Fiandra* appeared in 1611, after Grotius must have completed most of the AH.[225] During the Spanish campaign in Guelders and Overijssel in 1606 (in which Giustiniani took part) the town of Grol (modern Groenlo) was conquered by Spinola, and for this reason Grotius turned to Giustiniani's work in 1628. He mentions 'Iustinianus' twice in the *Historiae*,[226] and he refers to his published work in a letter written in July 1628 during the composition of *Grollae Obsidio,* remarking that he will use a map from Giustiniani's history.[227] During the research for the present edition I found a copy of the *Bellum Belgicum* in the Radboud University library (Nijmegen, NL) which contains manuscript notes that are almost certainly in Grotius' hand.[228] One of the flyleaves at the back gives a list of noted places in the text, and at these places themselves there are underlinings much like the ones in the Lund copy of Van Meteren's *Memorien.* The notes on the flyleaves are given in Appendix 4. As the *Bellum Belgicum* can only have reached Grotius after all or most the AH had been completed, any influence it may have had on the AH must be recorded as changes in the preserved manuscripts now in Leiden and Paris. The obvious assumption would be that when Grotius consulted the work in connection with the *Grollae Obsidio* in 1628, he also found pieces of information which he expected to be useful for his (then dormant) project of reworking the AH, and that he made notes of them on the flyleaf at the end. A comparison of these notes with the corresponding places in the narrative of the *Historiae* produces a small

223 *Briefwisseling* vol. 5, ep. 2057, p. 423.

224 *Briefwisseling* vol. 6, ep. 2307, p. 272; Strada, *De Bello Belgico decas prima*, Rome 1632. The *decas secunda* on the period 1578–1590 appeared only in 1647, after Grotius' death. On Grotius' image of William of Orange see § 8.1.

225 Pompeio Giustiniani, *Delle guerre di Fiandra libri VI*, Antwerp 1609. The translation, probably by Giuseppe Gamurini, appeared in Cologne in 1611.

226 In his accounts of 1604 and 1606; book 13 p. 460 and book 15 pp. 482–484 (ed. 1657).

227 *Briefwisseling* vol. 3, ep. 1292, p. 354 & n. 4.

228 Radboud Universiteit Library, Nijmegen, sign. 80 C37. The flyleaves indicate that the copy was once owned by the Catholic polemicist B.H. Klönne (1834–1921, who worked on Grotius' later relations with the Catholic world) but unfortunately no further details regarding its provenance are known. See B.H. Klönne, 'Leonardus Marius en Hugo de Groot' in: *De Katholiek. Godsdienstig, geschied- en letterkundig maandschrift*, no. 95 (1889), 337–350 en Id, 'Nogmaals Leonardus Marius en Hugo de Groot' in: ibid. no. 96 (1889), 220–225. I thank Prof. Dr. Henk Nellen for his advice on this; he agreed that the identification of the hand as Grotius' is convincing.

number of minor changes which do however provide plausible grounds to suspect a connection.

In the relation of the death of Federico Spinola Grotius added *haud uno vulnere confectus* ('swept away by not just one wound') to his manuscript, which might very well be a highly compressed summary of Giustiniani's colourful account of Federico's last action.[229] To *Bellum Belgicum* p. 109 the flyleaf notes *Spinola proficiscitur in Hispanias* ('Spinola departs for Spain'), referring to Spinola's temporary absence from the Low Countries from late 1605 to somewhere in 1606, which absence is unmentioned in the AH but which the author may therefore have found useful to note for his future reworking of the text. A third of these notes (three out of nine) concern statements of financial amounts relating to the Spanish operation, a topic which Grotius is clearly interested in, although he does not explore it to great depth. A few further manuscript additions to the account of the operations in Guelders and Overijssel in 1606 may also derive from Grotius' consultation of Giustiniani's work, although they do not correspond to a note in the Nijmegen copy of *Bellum Belgicum*. Further, the *Historiae* ms shows four small marginal additions to the account of the campaign (on fol. 87v–88v), all written in a similar hand and in a somewhat browner ink than the (almost black) original text on these pages, two of which may well be inspired by Giustiniani's text (BB pp. 120–122).[230]

Finally, there are a few topics in the *Historiae* for which Grotius did not have to rely on other sources, but which he knew from first-hand or from his own active involvement: his discussion of the Dutch trade expansion in the Far East, the competition and conflicts with the Portuguese in that area, and the peace negotiations between the Republic and Spain from 1607.[231] Hopefully the present edition will stimulate further research into Grotius' sources for his history of the Dutch revolt.

[229] *Historiae* book 12, ed. 1657, 8o p. 438 and Leiden UL, ms. Papenbroek 9.2 fol. 52v; Federico was the great general Ambrogio Spinola's brother; cp. BB p. 26.

[230] See Hist. 15, pp. 483–484 & ms Pap. 9.2, fol. 88r: 'ita in Frisiam aditum quae intercedunt palustria plus solito humentia abstulerant' ('thus the entrance to Friesland was blocked by the marshes in between which were even wetter than usual') may be an addition inspired by Giustiniani's repeated references to the difficulties the Spanish troops experienced from the marshes and high water levels; ibid., 'praecipue simulata peti Daventria Mauritium in se traxerat resembles Giustiniani's Ipse (i.e. Spinola) [...] quo pedites per stagnantes campos transirent, die nocteque ita stringentes ex latere Daventriam (quo Mauritium occupatum in eius tuitione teneret) persequutus'. On the other hand, the addition 'in octo haud amplius,] plura simul agitans, Frisiaeque, sed magis [Velaviae intentus' (fol. 87v / p. 483) and the change to 'nunc insulae in modum redegit' from 'nunc insulam fecit', as well as the mere corrections or clarifications of names (*Ridbergius, Transamasiani Comitis* instead of *Ridbergius Emdani Comitis*, p. 483; the addition of 'quem nunc Vectim vocant', (river Vecht); *Warnerus Dubosius* for Warnerus Lignanus; and *Gravewarta* for *Scenquianis a castris* (Schenkenschans), p. 484) look unconnected with the *Bellum Belgicum*.

[231] The value of his account as a source for that history was recognised for example by John Lothrop Motley in the *History of the United Netherlands* 1584–1609, The Hague 1867, vol. 4, chapter 40 (esp. pp. 98–104).

II. The composition and reception of the *Annales et Historiae*

Given the long half-century that the work remained in manuscript, the composition and reception of the AH overlap. Therefore they are here presented as one narrative.

II.1. *Original composition and manuscripts*

At the end of 1601 the States awarded Grotius a commission to write a history of the revolt and a subsidy.[232] From Grotius' correspondence and the preserved manuscripts a rough indication of the time(s) of composition of the AH can be derived. Many of Grotius' early letters however seem to be lost, and this affects the precision of our picture of the progress of his work around the turn of the century. The extant manuscripts show that the original working title of the entire work was *Hugonis Grotii Commentarii de rebus Belgicis.*

Grotius includes announcements of the *Parallelon* and the work on the AH in the front- and endmatter of *Adamus Exsul* in 1601.[233] In 1603 the States awarded

[232] The Hague, National Archive, 3.01.04.01 *Inventaris van het archief van de Staten van Holland en West-Friesland, 1572–1795*: Resolutien 1601–1605, fol. 14v (8 nov. 1601), or the printed *Resolutien van de Heeren Staten van Holland en Westvriesland* 1601 (available online via Google books), 8 november 1601, p. 448: 'By den Heer Advocaat voorgedraagen zynde de groote apparentie, die schynt te weesen in Hugo de Groot de Jonge, om geëmployeerd te worden in het schryven van de Historien en saaken van de beroerte deser Landen, soo verre men om sijnen geest daartoe meer te verwekken, hem eenig subsidie van penningen deede, tot een proef en besoek, op verseekeringe van iet goeds onlangs van hem te moogen sien; de Gecommitteerde Raaden hebben verstaan dat hem Ordonnanie van drie honderd ponden van xl. [40] grooten verleent sal worden, op vaste hoop dat hy het stuk van de Historische beschryvinge sal by de hand neemen en daar in voort gaan, sulks dat men onlangs daar van iets sal moogen sien, of in het ligt laaten komen', ('It being proposed to the Lord Advocate to employ the great talent, that appears to be present in Hugo Grotius to write the account of the history and events of the troubles in this country, and since in order to further encourage his mind towards this task a certain amount in subsidy was given to him, in order to receive a sample and an appearance [i.e. in the council meeting] as assurance that something good by him would be shown; has the Executive Council learned that an order of 300 pounds of 40 groats shall be awarded to him, in the solid expectation that he will set out to compose the historial description and continue to do so, in such a way that in the foreseeable future some result of it will be shown or be published.')

[233] *Sacra in quibus Adamus Exul tragoedia* etc., The Hague (Albert Henrici) 1601, page Aiii, in the dedication to Henry king of France: 'Quantum mihi a Iuris studiis, Historiis et arte civili otii datum est...', ('Whatever time I have left from the study of Law, from history, and from politics, [I can spend on poetry])'. At the end of the book Grotius lists his publication plans for the future, including (p. 55): '...Ad Civilem scientiam spectant, nostratis Reipublicae cum aliis olim nobilibus, sucessuumque inter se comparatio; et alia, ut spero, ad historiam eorum quae in mea patria meo aevo, aut circiter illud accidere', ('With respect to civil affairs, a comparison of our Republic with other great republics of the past, and their respective successes; and another, I hope, concerning the history of the events in my country in and around my own time').

him a second subsidy,[234] apparently in order to keep the work going in spite of Jan de Groot's departure from Holland (the province) in that year.[235] It has been argued on the basis of this resolution that the entire text is in fact a collaborative effort by Hugo and his father. The documents however do not provide real evidence for a much larger role of Jan de Groot than copying out finished books, collecting documentation and similar supportive tasks.[236] The aim of the second subsidy was precisely that Hugo would continue the work *without* his father, and no large portions of the text seem to have been finished by that time. Given however that the resolution implies that Jan de Groot took an active interest in the project and encouraged it, background discussions between Hugo and his father may certainly have contributed to the content of the narrative, especially during earlier stages of the work in 1602–1603. A more extensive discussion appears only in a letter of early in 1604, and indicates that the plan was still at a very incipient stage.[237] In the course of the year however a large enough portion of the work became fit to be shown to others. In October Grotius' friend Jan ten Grotenhuys writes

[234] The States' *Resolutien* record payments to Grotius in relation to the AH at three moments: when he receives the commission in 1601, of 300 guilders (see above); a second grant of 300 guilders on 8 January 1603 (see note below), and the 'final installment of 600 out of 1800' when the result was submitted in 1612 (see § 2.2) – which would however add up to 1200 guilders, not the 1800 which is mentioned in the resolution of 1612. In 1610 Grotius had also received 300 guilders for his *De Antiquitate Reipublicae Batavicae* (see the edition by Waszink e.a., 'Introduction', p. 6 n.10); perhaps this payment and another are included in this count to 1800?

[235] (printed) *Resolutien van de Heeren Ridderschap, Edelen ende Steden van Hollandt ende West-Vriesland etc.*, 1603 p. (5), 8 January 1603: 'Voorgedragen zijnde dat Hugo Grotius mits 't verloop ende verminderinge sijns Vaders Jan de Groots saecken, lichtelijcken soude laten steecken t Werck by hem in handen genomen, daer in hy alreede seer veel gevordert hadde, ten ware hy extraordinaire daer toe gesubsidieert ende ge–encourageert ware: Is geresolveert, dat men den selven Hugo Grotio met noch eens drie hondert ponden van veertig grooten by Ordonnantie op den Ontfanger Mierop sal subsidieren, ten eynde hy sijn aengeboden Werck tot eere en dienste van den Lande voorts voltrecke', ('It being proposed that Hugo Grotius, given the developments and adversity in his father Jan de Groot's business, could easily abandon the work he has taken upon himself, and in which he has already made much progress, if he won't be uncommonly subsidised and encouraged; the decision was made that the same Hugo Grotius will be subsidised with another 300 pounds of 40 groats via an order to the receiver Mierop, to ensure that he further continue the work offered by him, towards the country's honour and service').

[236] Ridderikhoff, 'Aristocratische geschiedenis' pp. 280–285 and cp. Waszink, 'Grotius' AH in his correspondence', 253–254. In the surviving mss, one book of the *Histories* is copied out in Jan's hand (see app. 1). The surviving ms of the *Parallelon Rerumpublicarum* (in Meermanno Museum, The Hague) is also in his hand.

[237] *Briefwisseling* 1, ep. 48, 25 January 1604. Grotius writes to Lingelsheim in Heidelberg that he is spending his leisure hours writing *historiae*, adding that he has already reached the present 'infelicissima tempora', and a general outline of the work which indicates that the period up to 1588 will be dealt with in two books (for confirmation of this, see App. 1). The latter statement shows that the caesura between *Annales* and *Historiae* was already in his mind, but the eventual form of the *Annales* was still far away. The claim that he has already reached the present looks like mere bluff; even the year 1600 is only in book 10 of the eventual *Historiae*.

back expressing his praise for the section of the *Commentarius historiae* which Ten Grotenhuys had read, as well as his wish to read the preceding part.[238] It appears that at this stage the first part of the work (later entitled *Annales*) was conceived as consisting of two books, not five. Watermarks in the paper of the ms. Papenbroeck 9.1 (the first section of the *Historiae*), which also appear in some dated letters, suggest a possible dating of that part around 1606. This suggests that the *Annales* would have been completed before that time, leading to a tentative period of composition of the *Annales* of roughly 1602–1605, with the bulk in 1604–1605. A general confirmation of this picture is provided by Grotius' letter of 6 August 1608 to his father,[239] in which he refers to finished copies of the part eventually entitled *Annales* which are then stored away in his parents' home in Delft, suggesting that they had been lying finished for some time. The same letter shows that the books of the *Annales* were copied out by various people; except by Hugo himself also by Jan de Groot and by the servant Johannes. Since there is mentioning of two copies of *Annals* book 5, one in Hugo's hand and one in Johannes', one would be inclined to think that the one in Grotius' hand was the draft text, and that by Johannes the fair copy.

Grotius submitted the completed manuscript to the States of Holland in 1612, upon which the examination followed as discussed in § 2.2 above, as well as a payment of another 600 guilders, but no publication. Grotius kept the manuscript with him for reconsideration, as remarks in the correspondence show. The letters contain no indications that more than one fair copy was made (although this is certainly possible). In all likelihood this was the manuscript now preserved in three parts in Leiden and Paris, which thus provide us with the original 'fair copy' of the *Historiae* (but with textual modifications added later).[240] As discussed above, the work would remain unpublished at this time. Grotius kept the manuscript with him for publication, if possible, at some later point.

The correspondence indicates that he had the manuscript(s) sent to him in France[241] and worked on the text in 1622 and 1635–1637. The part of the manuscript which is now Papenbroeck 9.1 in Leiden UL was interleaved at some

[238] *Briefwisseling* 1, ep. 53, 15 Oct. 1604.

[239] *Briefwisseling* vol. 1, ep. 141, p. 124.

[240] Leiden UL, ms. Papenbroek 9.1 and 9.2, and Paris BN ms. *Fonds Latin* 17796. See Appendix 1. It seems that the individual cahiers are the fair copies that were made of the consecutive parts when Grotius had finished them and that were eventually bound into three volumes. The fact that one book is not in Grotius' hand seems to confirms these are fair copies not the 'rough' first orignals produced in the actual writing process. There is no reason to assume much time elapsed between the composition of the draft books and that of their respective fair copies. If this is indeed the copy delivered to Oldenbarnevelt, the present manuscript Papenbroeck 9.2 was finished not later than 1612. On the events following the submission, see § 2.2 above.

[241] *Briefwisseling* vol. 2, no. 720 (16 Feb. 1622) and 744 (14 April 1622) to Nicolaes van Reigersberch. The controversial quality of the work is stressed in ep. 707 of 23 Nov. 1621 to Reigersberch (p. 156).

point with extra white pages to create space for additional sections of text.[242] The pages of the manuscripts of the *Historiae* display many (but unevenly distributed) larger and smaller additions and changes to the text. At least one major inserted passage invokes the polemics of the Truce period by presenting a short history of the debate on free will and predestination in the Christian church.[243] Another expands the account of the Dutch exploits in Southeast Asia by adding a brief history of the contacts between that region and Europe, but including Chinese, Arab and Persian aspects of that history.[244]

The correspondence shows that Grotius had a new fair copy made in 1637, and in 1638 sent his son Pieter to Holland with this copy with a view to having it printed. This again did not actually come about at that time, as no satisfactory agreement with the publisher (Blaeu in Amsterdam) could be reached. The new manuscript copy of 1637, which must be the link between the surviving manuscripts and the printed edition, is now lost. It must have been used as the printer's copy in 1657 and was either discarded after use, as was common practice at the time, or perhaps went lost in the fire in Blaeu's printing shops that Brandt-Cattenburg refers to – see Appendix 1).

11.2. *Reception during Grotius' lifetime*

References to the AH in letters, dedications and, more recently, academic scholarship allow for an outline of the reception of the AH since its composition.[245] After Grotius completed the manuscript in 1612/13, it took 45 years for the work to appear in print, so there is no immediate contemporary reception of the work in the regular sense of the word. Nevertheless, the work did not remain entirely unknown during this period, as appears primarily from Grotius' correspondence. The work was seen by at least his study friend Daniel Heinsius, his friend and housemate in The Hague, Jan ten Grotenhuys, and by Isaac Casaubonus (whom Grotius met during the embassy to London in 1613).[246] Heinsius and Casaubonus

242 See appendix 1.

243 Hist. 17 pp. 553–554 (see app. 1, under ms Papenbroek 9.2, book 17, insert 1).

244 Hist. 15 pp. 492–494 (see app. 1, ms Papenbroek 9.2, book 15). The inserted piece concludes by describing in brief how the Dutch entered the competition with the Portuguese on the island of Tidore by joining one side in an internal struggle for succession which involved partiality for or against the Portuguese.

245 For an overview, see Waszink, 'Grotius' AH in his correspondence'.

246 Letter from Casaubonus in London to J.A. de Thou, see *Isaaci Causauboni Epistolae, quotquot reperiri potuerunt* etc., The Hague (Theodorus Maire), 1638, no. 303, pp. 359–360: 'Nolo nescias, vidisse me hic Hugonem Grotium, virum probitatis et doctrinae admirandae. Multus mihi cum eo fuit et quotidie est sermo de tua dignitate, teque ille, uti par est, et amat et suspicit. Scripsit Historiarum libros XXI. de rebus gestis in patria ab annis circiter L. Pauca adhuc legi, sed quae valde mihi sunt probata. Sunt aliae virtutes illius, propter quas pluris etiam illum facio. Nam de hodiernis contentionibus in negotio religionis et docte et pie iudicat, et in veneratione antiquitatis cum iis sentit, qui optime sentiunt', ('I want you to know that I saw Hugo Grotius here, a

praised the AH in letters and publications, with the result that the work's existence became known within the scholarly world. In a 1613 dedicatory letter to Grotius, Daniel Heinsius writes: 'As if in spare time from your many occupations, you have written the definitive History of our country. Those who will later read it, will be stunned at how, while preserving Tacitus' splendour and sovereign majesty, things can be said with even greater beauty.'[247]

After Grotius' escape from imprisonment and re-location to France, and judging by the correspondence, the main significance of the AH for him shifts from its usefulness in the context of the Truce Conflicts to that connected with his own self-justification. The aspect of usefulness to Dutch society now recedes into the background. He includes the work in his 'shortlist' of works for which he expects to achieve fame with posterity.[248] He worked on the AH again at least in two periods, around 1622 and in 1635–1637. In roughly the same years (1635–1640) Grotius worked on a set of textual notes and emendations to Tacitus, meaning that he was immersed in his model of style at the same time as revising the AH.[249] The learned Jérôme Bignon (1589–1656) is said to have studied the AH when it was in manuscript and to have advised Grotius against the Tacitist style, although a letter by Guy Patin speaks of Bignon's great enthusiasm for the work (see § 11.3).[250] In 1637 or '38 a new fair copy was prepared for the printer (see § 11.1). By this

man of admirable goodness and learning. We talked a lot, and still do every day, about your greatness, and he loves and admires you, as you deserve. He wrote a History in 21 books about the war in his country in the last ca. 50 years. So far I have read a small portion of it, which however pleased me very much. And he has other qualities as well which gave me a high opinion of him. For with respect to the current religious controversies his judgment is both pious and learned, and in his admiration for [the Christian church of late] Antiquity he shares the judgment of the best'). Grotius' journey to Engeland in 1613 lasted from 25 March to 31 May; see Nellen, *Hugo Grotius*, pp. 151, 162.

[247] Of his *Peplus Graecorum Epigrammatum* (epigrams on the Greek philosophers), Leiden 1613. See also Grotius, *Briefwisseling* 1, p. 222 (ep. 247). The judgment of the AH is quoted with approval in the *Bibliothèque Choisie de M. Colomies,* La Rochelle (Pierre Savouret) 1682, p. 25; which is in turn referred to by Pierre Bayle, *Dictionnaire* (see § 11.7).

[248] For this project, see also M. van Ittersum, *The Working Papers of Hugo Grotius: How a Process of Transmission, Dispersal and Loss Shaped a Jurist's Legacy to the Modern World, 1604–1864* (forthcoming), chapters 2 ('Knowledge Production and Records Management in Early Modern Europe: The Case of Hugo Grotius') and 4 ('Creating a (Definitive) Corpus of Writings').

[249] These notes were published in 1640 as an appendix to a new edition of Lipsius' Tacitus: *C. Corn. Tacitus ex I. Lipsii recensione cum not. et Emend. H. Grotii*, Leiden, Elzevir 1640; TMD 515 (p. 194); see notes and literature given there.

[250] J. Bignon was The King's Sollicitor in the Supreme Court of Audience at Paris, with whom Grotius stood in contact in the 1630s and to whom he dedicated *De veritate religionis Christianae.* His judgment of the AH is recorded by Johann Heinrich Boeckler (1611–1672) in the preface of his *In Hugonis Grotii ius belli et pacis Commentatio*, (p. 30 in the ed. Strassbourg 1704), and referenced by Pierre Bayle in the *Dictionnaire.* Unfortunately Boeckler gives no source for his information (and no letters between Grotius and Boeckler are known).

time it was Grotius' plan to dedicate the book to queen Christina of Sweden.[251] All through this period Grotius shows himself very nervous about the danger of disclosure of the text, from fear that his opponents, if they get to know about the work, will prevent its publication. Therefore he demands complete secrecy from all those involved. In 1641 Grotius rejects the request by the poet and historian Pieter Corneliszoon Hooft (1581–1647) to see the work for this reason. At the time Hooft was working on his own Tacitist history of the Revolt (in Dutch, the *Nederlandse Historien*, first published in 1642) – a decision which thus prevented a direct connection between two chief products of Dutch Tacitism.[252] The points of resemblance between Hooft's history and his own did not escape Grotius: he refers more than once to the lukewarm reception Hooft's work enjoyed at publication.[253] He also keeps asking his contacts in Holland to inform him which elements of the AH might offend impartial readers (which connects with the

[251] The dedication is printed as ep. 3402 (early 1638), *Briefwisseling* vol. 9, ed. B.L. Meulenbroek, The Hague 1973, pp. 1–2. A rough summary is: 'To Queen Christina. Your abilities allow me to address you in Latin. There is no doubt that of all books, history books are the most useful to rulers. Whereas Swedish history would be the most suitable history to offer to you, other nations too provide books which will give you instruction how to protect allies and overcome your enemies, and in the arts of war and peace. Postponing a history of the achievements of your father Gustavus to a different time, [I present here] the history of the Dutch war which has drawn the attention of all prudent observers, so that they all desire to be informed about it, and histories of it have provided glory to cardinals and commanders form France, Spain and Italy. For what was more remarkable than the defence of their freedom by the Dutch (whose love of trade and quiet people assumed would render them indolent) against the Spanish world empire? By fighting, making treaties with kings and a truce with their enemies they turned the tables on Spain and attacked it even in the far east and the new world, which seemed only discovered in order to impose slavery on the old world. No war provides more or better teaching on sea-battles and sieges. To write this history I was not motivated by competition with the best historians of our time, esp. Italians, but because as a Dutchman and public office holder I had access to the original documents and the actual people who had conducted the war, a knowledge which must be passed on to future generations. And also I wanted to sing the praise of prince Maurice, who knew well of my admiration for him, before he decided to choose sides against the legitimate power States of Holland. However, while ruling a kingdom and a free nation are different things, this history is well-dedicated to you since in Sweden traditionally as well as under your rule, freedom and kingship are in perfect harmony; the change which some imprudent people tried to introduce in Sweden 40 years ago led to investigations into peoples' minds and to similar fires as the peaceful Dutch felt they had to extinguish by war. Then moreover the nation which is the subject of this book feels an ardent love for your majesty; and let it be added that a large part of that story is Elizabeth I, whose qualities I see reflected in you; and we pray for your good fortune, only to be completed with a husband and offspring which will rule noble Sweden as long as the sun lasts.' Brandt & Cattenburg, *Historie* p. 34 mention this dedication and quote from it; see § 11.7.

[252] *Briefwisseling* vol. 12, ep. 5097, p. 159 (11 March 1641); ep. 5111, p. 178; ep. 5290, p. 417; Grotius' reaction after reading Hooft's history in ep. 5303, p. 433 (3 August 1641). On the relationship between Hooft's *Baeto* and Grotius' *De Antiquitate*, see Van Vugt & Waszink, 'De Middenweg als uitweg'.

[253] See also Jansen, *Imitatio*, pp. 88–90.

above insistence on secrecy), so that he might still change them. This is important because it should remind us that we cannot be sure that the text of the AH as we have it was definitive in Grotius' eyes. The talks, via his proxies, with the publisher Blaeu regarding the publication project of his key works proceed very slowly, and by the time of Grotius' death in 1645 the AH are still unpublished.

11.3. *The survival of the manuscripts*

Four years after Grotius'death, in 1649 the French poet and literary critic Jean Chapelain (1595–1674) writes to his Dutch erudite friend Nicolas Heinsius (1620–1681, son of Daniel) that Madame Grotius prefers to have the work in printed in Leiden rather than in Paris. The edition of the AH is mentioned frequently in their correspondence in the subsequent years, showing that the edition project was followed with eager interest by scholars in France.[254] In 1648 the French scholar Claude Sarrau (Sarravius, 1588–1653) had expressed worries about the survival of the manuscript of the AH, and makes an attempt to buy it for 2000 *livres* from Grotius' widow, who however refuses the offer.[255] Given the fact that the new fair copy had been carried over to Holland in order to be printed, Sarravius' offer must refer to the original manuscript(s) now preserved in Leiden and Paris.

From 1649 onwards another French scholar and former acquaintance of Grotius, Guy Patin, mentions the imminent publication of the AH several times in his correspondence, confirming once again that the project enjoyed the active interest of French scholarly circles. In 1652 Patin writes to his friend and learned medic Charles Spon (1609–1684) that Grotius' history is being printed in Holland, and that Adriaan Vlacq (1600–1667)[256] had purchased 'the manuscript' for a considerable sum. Vlacq, who stood in contact with the Grotius family since 1640 and also, at least for some time, with the publisher Blaeu, apparently played some role as intermediary or agent in the project of publishing Grotius' main works.[257] Did

[254] J. Chapelain, *Les Lettres authentiques à Nicolas Heinsius (1649–1672). Une amitié érudite entre France et Hollande*, ed. by B. Bray, Paris (Champion) 2005, p. 34 and passim (via index); with thanks to Henk Nellen.

[255] Claudius Sarravius to Claudius Salmasius, letters of 29 Sept. 1645 and 16 Oct. 1648, in *Claudii Saravii senatoris Parisiensis epistolae,* Orange 1654; also included in *Marquardi Gudii … Claudii Sarravii … epistolae*, Utrecht 1697, ep. 138, p. 143 & ep. 184, p. 189; see also C. Brandt & A. van Cattenburgh, *Historie van het leven des heeren Huig de Groot* etc., Dordrecht & Amsterdam 1732, p. 422 and Grotius, *De Imperio summarum potestatum circa sacra*, ed. H.J. van Dam, Leiden 2001 vol. 1, p. 90 note 5.

[256] A mathematician, printer and bookseller then based in The Hague, who was also accused of business wrongdoings and later of plagiarism. On his biography, see Van Dam, 'Introduction' in Grotius, *De Imperio*, pp. 87–91.

[257] See the online edition *Correspondance complète et autres écrits de Guy Patin*, ed. by L. Capron, https://www.biusante.parisdescartes.fr/patin/, esp. the letter to Charles Spon, no. 207 of 16 Nov. 1649: '(…) le libraire hollandais nommé Vlacq (…) combien que l'on imprime encore ici un livre de M. Grotius pour lui, qui est le reste de ses commentaires sur le Nouveau Testament, et principalement sur l'Apocalypse; et d'autant que le volume ne peut être gros, ils ont dessein de l'augmenter du

Grotius' sons entrust the new copy of the AH brought to Holland in 1638 to him? Or perhaps another copy from that copy? Did Vlacq actually become the owner of the new copy (in spite of Grotius' orders of secrecy regarding the AH until the work would actually have been printed)? But however that be, Patin must be confusing the two manuscripts that existed at that time (or he was not aware that there were two) when he continues that '*ce manuscript*' had been given in loan to Jérôme Bignon by Grotius' widow ever since the death of her husband, and that Bignon noted the work's strong similarity to Tacitus.[258] This cannot but refer to the original manuscript, not to the new copy of 1638.

Later we find two of the three parts of the original manuscript of the *Historiae* (without the *Annales*) in the collection of the cardinal Guillaume Dubois (1656–1723) whose immense library was auctioned in The Hague in 1725.[259] How these two parts had ended up in Dubois' library is not known precisely, but it is probably relevant that Dubois' library included that of the abbot Jean-Paul Bignon (1662–1743), great re-organiser of the royal library and a grandson of Jérôme Bignon.[260] Guy Patin's information from 1652 that Jérôme Bignon had held the manuscript

traité du même auteur *De Veritate religionis Christianae, cum notis*, tel qu'il fut ici imprimé l'an 1640, in-12. Et après que cela sera achevé (...), il m'a dit qu'il imprimera son *Histoire de Hollande* en latin, in-fo, que l'on dit être une fort belle pièce; au moins je l'ai ouï dire à un témoin oculaire, qui est un des plus habiles hommes du monde, à qui la veuve de l'auteur l'a donné à voir, savoir à M. Le Bignon, avocat général au Parlement, qui a été un des grands amis de feu M. Grotius, mais qui est extrêmement capable d'en bien juger.'

[258] *Correspondance complète Guy Patin* no. 288, 5–7 June 1652: 'J'apprends que l'on imprime en Hollande un beau livre et bien curieux, savoir l'histoire de feu M. Grotius, *de bello Belgico*. C'est un in-f dont le marchand nommé Vlacq, que M. Ravaud connaît bien, a acheté la copie manuscrite 200 pistoles. M. Bignon, avocat général au Parlement, qui est le plus savant homme du monde, m'a plusieurs fois loué ce manuscrit qu'il a lu tout entier, que Mme Grotius lui a prêté depuis la mort de son mari qui était son intime ami; il dit qu'il n'a point vu de livre qui approchât si près de Tacite', https://www.biusante.parisdescartes.fr/patin/; with thanks to Henk Nellen and Martine van Ittersum for the reference. A *pistole* is a gold coin worth approximately 10 *livres* – meaning that 200 *pistoles* would amount to same sum that Sarravius had offered to Maria for the original manuscript (?).

[259] *Bibliotheca Duboisiana,* The Hague 1725, vol. 1, p. 407: "*no. 4146. Hug. Grotii annales et historiae de rebus Belgicis. 2 vol. Ms.*" The auction of no. 4146 is scheduled for [Wednesday] 3 October 1725. In the Leiden UL copy (sign. 750 E4.1) there is a ms. note:' 5-: ', which may mean 'hammer price 5 guilders'. A ms. copy of Grotius' *De Imperio Summarum Potestatum* was sold at the same auction (with thanks to Martine van Ittersum for this information). Dubois' library was very extensive; the catalogue comprises seven volumes and 17.060 items. The auction lasted from 27 August through to 19 October (the schedule of auction days has the weekdays wrong from 30 September onwards: Saturday 29 September is followed by Monday 30). Brandt & Cattenburgh, *Historie* (of which the first edition appeared in 1727), p. 422 records that Gerard van Papenbroeck showed his recent acquisition to Adriaan van Cattenburgh.

[260] J. Clarke, 'Abbe Jean-Paul Bignon 'Moderator of the Academies and Royal Librarian', in: *French Historical Studies,* Vol. 8, No. 2 (1973), p. 213–235. Jean-Paul Bignon sold his own book collection when he was charged with the re-organisation of the royal collections in 1718; it was subsequently bought by Dubois. See H.J. van Dam, 'Introduction' in Grotius, *De Imperio, pp.* 48–66, and R. Kerviler, 'Les Bignons: Grand Maitres de la Bibliothèque du Roi', in: *Le bibliophile français* 6 (1872)

in loan from Grotius' widow might be the crucial clue here: Bignon may very well still have had the manuscript in his possession when Patin was writing to Spon. Maria had moved back to Holland and died only one year later (and Jérôme himself in 1656). Had he eventually become the owner, perhaps after a payment? In any case at the Dubois auction in 1725 the two parts of the AH manuscript were bought by the Dutch collector Gerard van Papenbroeck (1673–1743), who left them to Leiden University Library at his death (see Appendix 1).

The third part, which was not included in that auction, is currently preserved in the Bibliothèque Nationale in Paris. It is not known with certainty how and when the Paris volume became separated from the parts now in Leiden, or whether Dubois or a Bignon played any role in this, but the fact that several members of the Bignon family served as royal librarians may well be part of the explanation. The part now in Paris carries as ex-libris a coat of arms which appears to belong to François-Michel de Verthamon (1657–1738), marquis de Breau, president of the Grand Conseil du Roi and a bibliophile who enriched the Grand Conseil with its own library (which was unfortunately lost in the fire in the Palais in 1763).[261] It is probably on the basis of the rubber stamps in the manuscript (see Appendix 1), that the 19th-century catalogue of the manuscripts in the BN by Léopold Delisle states that the manuscript came from the *archives de l'Empereur,* which would imply that it arrived in the BN only after 1800.[262] But however this be, the three volumes together are the complete and original manuscript of the *Historiae* from 1612, with Grotius' changes to the text from the 1620s and '30s added on the pages.

The new fair copy mentioned in § 11.1, made in 1637 and sent to Holland in 1638, must be the actual link between the manuscripts surviving now and the printed editions, but it is now lost. This manuscript must have been the printer's copy and was either discarded after use or perhaps lost in the fire in Blaeu's printing shops that Brandt-Cattenburg refers to (see Appendix 1). In 1640 Grotius asked his brother Willem in The Hague to remove this and other manuscripts from his (Hugo's) son Pieter's possession and keep them with himself.[263] On the possibility that the bookseller Adriaan Vlacq bought this manuscript (or newer copy?) in 1652, see above. On the printing see § 11.4 below.

It is possible that Johannes Gronovius (1611–1671, professor of rhetoric at the Athenaeum Illustre in Deventer, later professor of Greek and librarian in Leiden (and a personal acquaintance of Grotius' since they had met in Hamburg in 1633)

esp. pp. 326–327. With thanks to Martine van Ittersum for pointing at this connection; see also her *Working Papers of Hugo Grotius*.

[261] Incidently or not, Verthamon married a granddaughter of Jérôme Bignon, Marie Anne Françoise Bignon (1650–1720), daughter of Thierry Bignon (1632–1697).

[262] At the same time it indicates in error that the manuscript contains only *Historiae* book 5 and 6, not 7; L. Delisle, *Inventaire des manuscrits de Notre-Dame et d'autres fonds conservés à la Bibliotheque Nationale sous les numeros 16719–18613 du Fonds Latin,* Paris 1871, p. 68, no. 17796; and see Appendix 1 below.

[263] See Waszink, 'AH from the evidence in the correspondence', pp. 264–265.

was somehow involved in or consulted about the eventual publication in the 1650s. In a letter to Nicolas Heinsius written early in 1658, right after the appearance of the printed edition, Gronovius writes that he had read the greater part of the work before publication, but he does not indicate when this happened. His formulation however seems to suggest that he saw the manuscript (or perhaps the proofs?) only in the period when the work was actually being prepared for publication (as we would also expect, given Grotius' unwillingness in the 1630s and 40s to share the work with anyone).[264]

An unanswered question is why is there no surviving ms. of the *Annales*. Did this part circulate in France together with the manuscripts of the *Historiae*, as discussed above? Were the (probably four) volumes of the original manuscript sold separately, or divided upon inheritance between branches of a family? Did the *Annales* once also belong to Verthamon and was it burned in the above-mentioned fire in the Palais in 1763, with the *Historiae* manuscript now in Paris surviving because of some coincidence (e.g. being borrowed by someone)? Did it ever belong to the *archives de l'Empereur*, as referenced by Delisle? Is there a theoretical possibility that the *Annales* manuscript will still re-surface somewhere someday? An entirely different explanation however could be that between 1612 and 1637 Grotius made so few changes in the *Annales* that he felt no need to have a new copy made in 1637. It might be noted with this respect that Grotius also made very few changes to the original text of book 16, which is extant in his father's hand in ms. Papenbroeck 9.2 (see App. 1). If that is the case the original copy of the *Annales* could potentially have been used as the printer's copy in 1657 and have been subsequently discarded.[265] If this is true, the printed text of the *Annales* is also that of 1612–1613.

11.4. *The printed editions of 1657–1658*

In 1657 Grotius' sons Pieter and Cornelis eventually saw the work through the press at Blaeu's in Amsterdam under the title *Hugonis Grotii Annales et historiae de rebus Belgicis.* As noted above, Guy Patin's correspondence indicates that Adriaan Vlacq, who was in close contact with Blaeu, figured as intermediary at the background of the edition project of Grotius' main works including the AH. Given

[264] P. Burman, *Sylloges Epistolarum* vol. III, Leiden 1725, ep. 314 p. 382, 14 January 1658 to Nicolas Heinsius 'Grotii historiam maiorem partem legi nondum editam, eoque patientius desiderium fero. Nomen viri faciet [...]' (see also § 11.7 on the 17th-century reception).

[265] On one of fly-leaves of Papenbroeck 9.1, Gerard van Papenbroeck has written that the ms of Hist. 5–7 (which he missed, being the part now in Paris) may have been lost in the fire in Blaeu's printing shop together with the *Annales* ms. (see appendix 1). Obviously this is guesswork; Papenbroeck's remark fails to explain why the two parts which he possessed, did survive and suggests that he did not realise that at least the *Historiae* had been typeset from a newly made fair copy. However if the *Annales* were in fact typeset from the original manuscript, Van Papenbroeck' s guess may in fact be true for the *Annales* manuscript.

the loss of the *Annales* manuscript(s) as described above, the Blaeu editions are our only witness for the Latin text of *Annales*. For about a century, the AH now became a relatively well-known and widely respected work on the Dutch revolt throughout Europe, with translations into French, English and Dutch.

The first edition (TMD 741) appeared in the last weeks of 1657[266] in an attractive large format (small folio), with front matter containing a dedication to the States of Holland and West-Friesland by Pieter and Cornelis, an address to the reader, printers' *privilegia*, and an engraved portrait of the author by Willem Delff (based on the painted one by Van Miereveld). The dedication to queen Christina (see § 11.2) has not been used. The new dedication re-states, in very standard humanist terms, the importance of history for rulers and connects this theme with the miraculous outcome of the Dutch revolt, as it was witnessed by all of Europe and turned the tables on the Spanish world empire. This dedication conveys no sign of Grotius' Tacitism but adheres to an optimistic humanist vocabulary of *libertas, patria* and *gloria*. It concludes by re-stating Grotius' intentions in writing the work in terms of the usefulness for posterity and the Dutch Republic, only just mentioning his life as an exile, but otherwise glossing it over, and thus re-affirming the work's (and the editors') dedication to the States of Holland. Further research might reveal whether the publication was meant to play a role in the political controversies of the first Stadtholderless era, in which at least Pieter de Groot was involved.[267] The next item, 'To the Reader', is apparently written by the publisher, Blaeu.[268] It does mention the special style and sings the praise of the author and this work in particular, which emulates if not surpasses the works by the classical historians: any reader who loves the Republic should be grateful to God not only for the success of the Republic but also for Grotius who, unlike others, delivered on his promise to relate the truth without submitting to fear, favour or partiality. It concludes by affirming the publisher's commitment to the continuing edition of Grotius' works.

The pages of the main text carry marginalia which provide the year and a running summary of the narrative. Each book is preceded by a summary based roughly (but not exactly) on these marginalia. These marginalia and summaries do not appear in the extant manuscripts and must have been supplied by the editors, Pieter and Cornelis de Groot (the summaries are included in Appendix 7). A comparison of a section of the *Historiae* shows that the text provided conforms in detail with the final version as apparent from the manuscripts kept in Leiden. The present editor's use of the Blaeu editions for this new edition confirmed the high

266 Nicolas Heinsius in Amsterdam informs Gronovius in Deventer of the appearance of the book in a letter of 24 December 1657, see Burman, *Sylloges Epistolarum* vol. III, ep. 311, p. 378: 'Prodiit tandem eximium opus historiae Grotianae: nec dubito eius iam tibi copiam esse factam.'

267 See e.g. I. Vroomen, *Taal van de Republiek. Het gebruik van vaderlandretoriek in Nederlandse pamfletten, 1618–1672*, PhD Erasmus University Rotterdam 2012, e.g. pp. 175, 181 and elsewhere.

268 And made explicit in the Dutch translation of 1681 (see 11.6 below); Ter Meulen-Diermanse, *Bibliographie*, p. 337.

quality of the effort by Grotius' sons and Blaeu's typesetters and correctors; the number of printing errors and difficulties is very low indeed.

A near-identical new edition appeared very soon after the first, in 1658 (TMD 742), with the addition of a dedicatory poem (*Scazon*) after the dedication and the full text of the Imperial privilege in place of an abbreviation. That TMD 741 and 742 are entirely separate editions has been demonstrated by the book historian and antiquarian bookseller by Bob de Graaf, by showing that the type-setting was re-done in its entirety.[269] The copies of TMD 741 all contain a list of errata which have been duly corrected in the main text in TMD 742.[270] Comparison of multiple copies of TMD 741 shows that there are at least three versions of the list of errata, containing 75, 34 and 11 corrections respectively. 7 errors on the shortest list do not appear in the other lists, suggesting that errors were found and corrected during the production of the print-run, and the errata list modified accordingly.[271] The present editor has seen no copies of TMD 742 with a list of errata.

In 1658 two smaller editions appeared: one in octavo format (TMD 743), with identical front matter to TMD 742, except for a very different portrait of Grotius (and a different inscription under it; this is the portrait reproduced in the present edition). There is no list of *errata*, while the distribution of the text over 567 pages is almost identical to that of the folio editions. The presentation of the text, with the marginalia and summaries, is also identical to the folio editions. This seems to indicate that TMD 743 was typeset from a copy of TMD 742, not from the manuscript. This suspicion seems confirmed by the fact that the 1657 editions can be used to correct problems in TMD 743, but never the other way round.[272] However in several sections TMD 743 appears to have a slightly reworked punctuation compared to 741–742. Another, and simpler edition appeared in the same year in duodecimo-format (TMD 744), without portrait and without the year and summary

[269] See B. de Graaf, 'Grotius' *Annales et Historiae de rebus Belgicis*. De beide uitgaven van 1657 nader beschouwd' in: *Van pen tot laser. Opstellen aangeboden aan Ernst Braches,* Amsterdam 1996.

[270] With the exception of p. 109 line 16 (§ 5.54) *consilium* > *Concilium*, which has not made it to TMD 742 or the editions of 1658.

[271] A fact not mentioned by De Graaf. For the longest list, see the copy in Österreichische Nationalbibliotek 62.R.17; for the 'middle' one Amsterdam UL, OTM: OG 80–91; for the shortest list, see e.g. Leiden UL, 1196 A26 (all accessible via Google Books). There may be more versions of the list in other copies. However the very close ties between all four editions appear for example from the (rare) remaining typos. For example *imperantum* for *imperantium* in 1.25 (p. 10 line 10) appears in all four editions (while correct *-ium* in 1.9, 1.10 and 2.12); 1.56 *mandaciis* (*mendaciis,* p. 22 line 15), 2.36 *posito* (*positu*, p. 39 line 6) and 5.12 *accesre* (*accessere*, p. 95 line 17) all appear in *both* editions of 1657, but are corrected in those of 1658; and similarly the dubious *caetus* in 1.56 in both folio editions and the 12o of 1658, reads *coetus* in the octavo 1658 only. The 1658 octavo has a reworked, and sometimes easier, punctuation in several places. It also introduces a small number of new printing errors, four of which were noted by Peerlkamp and Boot; see § 11.8 below.

[272] On p. 90 (§ 4.49, *imminutionem / immunitionem*) the reading in the folio editions of 1657 is wrong and the 8o of 1658 correct, but the correction is obvious enough to have been performed without access to the manuscript.

marginalia provided in the other editions. Moreover, this edition gives a less reliable text and includes a *Corrigenda* section listing more than 350 items.

11.5. *The AH and the Vatican* Index of Forbidden Books *1657–1659*[273]

In response to the editions of the AH in 1657 and 1658, the Vatican *Index of Forbidden Books*[274] looked into the work in 1659, in order to establish the admissibility of its image of the Dutch revolt and the Catholic faith from a Catholic point of view.[275] Research by the present editor produced two censure reports on the AH for the Vatican Index and some surrounding data; translations of these reports are given in Appendix 2.[276]

That the Vatican investigation had taken place had been more widely known since the Nijmegen cultural historian J.D.M. Cornelissen published a 17th-century summary of a censure report on the AH by the Roman Index in 1928.[277] By publishing the only known documents on the censure and subsequent prohibition of the AH by the Vatican in 1659, Cornelissen made an important addition to the doctoral dissertation on the AH by H.C.A. Muller of 1919, in which the condemnation of the work was not even mentioned. Cornelissen also used the article to point again at the arguments that can and have been adduced, both during Grotius' lifetime and afterwards, in favour of the view that Grotius would have tended towards Catholicism later in his life.[278] The Congregation for the Index of Forbidden Books

[273] I thank dr H. Schwedt (Limburg, Germany) for providing me with data on the *consultores* of the Index, Dr J. De Landtsheer for her valuable remarks to my transcriptions and translations, and Prof. dr. L. Winkel and Prof. dr. C. Coppens for their help with the search for Arata's legal sources. For more on the Index and the *consultores*, see esp. T. Lagatz & S. Schratz (eds.), *Censor Censorum. Gesammelte Aufsätze von Herman H. Schwedt. Festschrift zum 70. Geburtstag*, Paderborn 2006 and H. Schwedt, *Die römische Inquisition. Kardinäle und Konsultoren 1601 bis 1700*, Freiburg 2017.

[274] A. Cifres, 'Das historische Archiv der Kongregation für die Glaubenslehre in Rom', in: *Historische Zeitschrift* 268 (1999), pp. 97–106; P. Godman, *The Saint as Censor. Robert Bellarmine between Inquisition and Index*, Leiden, 2000; U. Baldini, 'Una fonte poco utilizzata per la storia intellettuale: le "censurae librorum" e "opinionum" nell' antica Compagnia di Jesu' in: *Jahrbuch des italienisch-deutschen Instituts in Trient* 11 (1985) 19–68; P.F. Grendler, 'Printing and Censorship', in: C. Schmitt & Q. Skinner (eds.), *The Cambridge History of Renaissance Philosophy*, Cambridge UP 1988 pp. 25–54.

[275] For a comparable case see the investigation into Lipsius' *Politica* by the *consultores* Laelius Peregrinus and Marcus Petilius in J. Lipsius, *Six Books of Politics or Political Instruction*, ed. J. Waszink, Assen, 2004, Bibliotheca Latinitatis Novae, pp. 712–714 and 716–720.

[276] For the full editions, introduction and notes, see J. Waszink, 'New documents on the prohibition of Grotius' Annales et Historiae by the Roman Index' in: *Grotiana*, 24–25, (2003–2004), 77–139. This paragraph is a summary of my conclusions.

[277] Cornelissen occupied the post of the Dutch institute in Rome's historian from 1923 until 1930. See H. Cools and H. de Valk, *Institutum Neerlandicum MCMIV–MMIV*. Honderd jaar Nederlands Instituut te Rome, Hilversum, 2004, 51–52.

[278] Ever since his escape from prison, Catholic attempts to draw Grotius over to their side had been going on, as appears from a letter from Johannes Wtenbogaert, who does however not doubt Grotius' constancy in the face of such attempts (ep. 990, *Briefwisseling* vol. 2 pp. 456–457, 9 July 1625;

(*Sancta Congregatio Indicis*, further referred to as SCI) reviewed the AH in 1658–1659, and published a decree by which it was prohibited on 16 September 1659.

The archives of the Congregation for the Doctrine of the Faith in the Sant' Uffizio, which contain those of the Index, were opened for research in 1998. The papers relating to the AH investigated by the present author in February 2004 produced a number of hitherto unknown documents, including two full censure reports (not summaries) on the AH, as well as additional information which together enable a full reconstruction of the 'trial' of the AH by the Roman Index. The first report was written by Stefano Gradić (1613–1683), a *consultor* originally from Dubrovnik (Ragusa) in Croatia, diplomat and prefect of the Vatican Library; the second report by Giovanni Battista Arata (1621–1696) a clergyman from the order of the Theatines. These documents fundamentally change the picture of the events which led to the prohibition of the AH, and they especially change the picture of the reasons for prohibition. Most importantly, it appears that it was *not* Cornelissen's document that provided the grounds for the prohibition of the AH. Cornelissen's findings are evidently a summary and discussion of the first report by Gradić, which (as appears from the original) does not even ask for a prohibition, but for inclusion in the Index *donec corrigatur* ('until the work gets improved'). It was the second report by Arata that led to the prohibition.

Cornelissen's documents, however, do have an independent value in themselves, and a fascinating one, in that the *Iudicium* provides additional considerations that are not present in the report(s) themselves. These considerations must be a direct reflection, or even a summary of the discussion between the cardinals in the meeting following the first report on 24 March 1659, for example the reference to the relationship between the AH and Lipsius' thought on religious policy (the report brings Lipsius into the discussion, but with respect to a very different part of his oeuvre). For these documents, see Cornelissen's article. In addition to the reports, the minutes of the meetings of the cardinals available in the *Diarii* of the SCI's *secretario* supplement the data available to Cornelissen. Although this was apparently missed by Cornelissen's informer(s), a second source in the Vatican Library, a miscellany manuscript in the *Vaticana Latina* fund, contains a second complete copy of Gradić's report as also preserved in the SCI archives (i.e. the very report of which Cornelissen's document is a summary).

The logic of events becomes clear when we put the evidence from Cornelissen's documents and the newly found reports together. Upon hearing Gradić's report, the cardinals were interested most in the eleven points summed up in Cornelissen's summary, and which they developed further in their subsequent discussion, as reflected in the *Iudicium*. The cardinals (who had not seen the text with its particular literary approach itself) apparently found that Gradić's mild judgement was

Brandt & Cattenburg, *Historie*, pp. 324 sqq; and Nellen, *Hugo Grotius* 323, 334, 418–419). For the later attempts, see Klönne, 'Leonardus Marius en Hugo de Groot' and id, 'Nogmaals Leonardus Marius en Hugo de Groot'.

insufficiently supported by the content of his censure. They therefore ordered a re-censure (instead of prohibiting the work straight away). Whether Arata's judgement was somehow steered by this opinion among the cardinals, or whether there were special reasons for assigning the re-censure of the work to him after Ferdinando Ughello apparently appeared unavailable for the task, remains unclear. The newly found material does not clarify this either.

The first report by Gradić turns out to be generally sympathetic to the AH, and sophisticated, if very critical, in its assessment. Gradić seems to have enjoyed reading the AH; it becomes clear that he appreciates Grotius' attempt to imitate the Tacitean style, although he is not convinced of its success (see § 11.7 below), and that he has read the work from a perspective beyond party affiliations. He formulates a mixed judgment on the work's content: on the one hand he points at a number of passages and remarks which the Roman Catholic Church cannot accept, but on the other he concludes that these do not justify a complete ban of the work given its many other qualities (among which he includes, indeed, the elegant style). His advice therefore is a ban *donec corrigatur*.

The minutes and the existence of the second report suggest that the cardinals in the Index meeting found Gradić's conclusions too mild given the problems he had identified, for they ordered a second report, which was written by Joannes Arata. This consultor shows himself very annoyed at the (for him) strongly anti-Catholic content of the book and calls for an outright ban. His report is almost aggressively critical and much less sophisticated than Gradić's; it displays no sense of the relativity of the Church's position in the religious constellation of the reformation period, nor any sensitivity for the Tacitean linguistic 'game' that is played in the AH – see e.g. Arata's objections to the use of the word *secta* for parts of the Catholic Church: his report displays no awareness of the fact that similar disdainful language is applied to *all* parties in the narrative. Moreover, the report is characterised by an ostentatious display of scholarship which is not always clearly relevant to the assessment of the AH. The cardinals however based their decision on Arata's report, and in their meeting of 16 September 1659 issued the verdict that placed the AH on the Vatican *Index of Forbidden Books*.

A copy now preserved in the Universidad Complutense in Madrid carries a 17th- or 18th-century inscription between the lines of the title on the title page *autoris damnati opus vero permissum* ('by a banned author, but this work is permitted').[279]

11.6. *Translations*

The AH was translated into English, French and Dutch. A French translation emerged in 1662 from the Blaeu presses in Amsterdam under the title *Annales et Histoires des troubles du Pays-Bas, par Hugo Grotius* (TMD 746; and again in 1672,

[279] See Hathi Trust, https://hdl.handle.net/2027/ucm.5320299842

TMD 747). The edition is of very similar appearance to the Latin quarto editions of 1657. The identity of the translator is not revealed in the book. It also includes a translation of the indexes. In the portrait of Grotius, the poem and decorative elements are identical to that in 1657, but the face has been re-drawn to a somewhat younger-looking, but less characteristic appearance with a different beard.

An inaccurate English translation by 'T.M.' (Thomas Manley) was published by Twyford in London in 1665: *Hugo Grotius, De Rebus Belgicis: or, The Annals, and history of the Low-Countrey-Warrs*[280] (TMD 748).

The Dordrecht schoolmaster Joan Goris published a Dutch translation in Amsterdam in 1681 under the title *Hugo de Groots Nederlandtsche Jaerboeken en Historien, sedert het jaar* MDLV *tot het jaer* MDCIX, *met de belegering der stadt Grol* [...] *Alsook het Tractaet van de Batavische nu Hollandtsche republiek en de Vrije Zeevaert* [...] *alles vertaelt door Joan Goris* (TMD 749). It appeared in a beautiful and grand folio edition which also includes an index of names and subjects to the AH, Dutch translations of *Grollae obsidio, De Antiquitate* and *Mare Liberum,* and a series of engravings. Although Goris' translation is generally accurate and reliable, he made no attempt to render the Tacitist style into Dutch. An excerpt from Goris' translation of *Historiae* book 1 was re-published in 1963 in a paperback collection of excerpts from old Dutch historians.[281]

This translation is embellished with almost 50 images of several kinds and makers. An allegorical frontispice and a portrait of Grotius by A. vander Wenne[282] (after the well-known portrait by Van Mierevelt), are followed by a series of portraits of prominent figures in the narrative. These are probably based on older portraits and engraved by Andries Vaillant (although only three carry a signature).[283] The portraits are alternated with a series of very accomplished engravings depicting scenes from the war. Some of these are by Jan Luyken (1649–1712), some others by C. Decker,[284] and some carry no signature. All of the images derive from a collection of images which the publisher had made with a view to using them in a range of publications on Dutch history. The images and comparable ones, in various different stages of development, appear in editions of works by Pieter Bor,

[280] See TMD 748 (p. 341) and notes; the translationis also available from University Microfilms International; Early English Books 868:8. On the deficiencies in Manley's translation see also Muller, *De Groots Annales et Historiae* pp. 143–146.

[281] H. Wansink and C.B. Wels (eds.), *Zeven pijlen, negen pennen. Negen Nederlandse historici over de vaderlandsche geschiedenis,* Zeist (W. de Haan N.V.), 1963 pp. 107–118.

[282] Very little is known about this engraver.

[283] Andries Vaillant (1655–1693), half-brother and pupil of the engraver Wallerrant Vaillant. See C. Kramm, *De levens en werken der Hollandsche en Vlaamsche kunstschilders, beeldhouwers, graveurs en bouwmeesters van den vroegsten tot op onzen tijd,* vol 5, Amsterdam 1861, pp. 1665–1666; reff. to further lit. in Hollstein, *Dutch and Flemisch Etchings and Engravings* vol. 11, p. 118.

[284] Of Coenraat Decker it is known that he was originally from Nürnberg, where he was born around the middle of the 17th century, and that he was a pupil of Romein de Hooghe. He lived in Delft. See Van der Aa, *Biographisch Woordenboek*, vol 4, p. 78.

Pieter Corneliszoon Hooft, and Jean Le Clerc by the same publisher.[285] Some of these images are included in this book; see List of Illustrations p. 433.

11.7. *Further reception, 17th–21st centuries*

After the eventual publication in 1657 and 1658, the AH were a fairly well-known book throughout Europe for at least half a century. A very frequent topic in discussions of the work is whether the imitation of Tacitus' style was successful; as we have seen, both judgments appear (while imitating that style was not always regarded as a good thing in itself).

Right after the appearance of the book this fact is also discussed in the correspondences of Nicolas Heinsius with both Jean Chapelain and Johannes Gronovius. Chapelain writes from Paris, already on the 18th of January 1658, that he has a copy of the book which he judges important although he has doubts about the twisted style and would have liked it more if Grotius had included more reflection on politics.[286] With both correspondents Heinsius also discusses his idea of continuing the narrative onwards from 1609 where Grotius broke off, and adds (to Gronovius) that he may obtain the access to information necessary for such an endeavour if he is given a secretarial role in the service of the States-General. Gronovius points at the expected partisan objections to the work, at home as well as abroad.[287] Guy

[285] On the Dutch history project by this publisher, see J. de Waard, *Portretten van Marnix van St Aldegonde,* Deventer 1988, p. 45. For information on the images by Jan Luyken, see P. van Eeghen & J. van der Kellen, *Het werk van Jan en Casper Luyken,* Amsterdam 1905. Of these 16 images by Jan Luyken, 9 were published earlier in the edition of Pieter Bor's *Oorsprongk, begin, en vervolgh der Nederlandsche Oorlogen* by the same publisher in 1679. The other 7 first appeared alongside Goris' translation of Grotius, and again in the same year with Bor, vol. 3. The engraving depicting William of Orange' s assassination (no. 6) follows a design by Romeyn de Hooghe, executed again by Jan Luyken.

[286] Chapelain, *Lettres Authentiques*, pp. 218–219; '… un Ouvrage grave entre tous ceux des derniers temps tant pour le style que pour la tissure et des plus prochants des bons Anciens en l'un et en l'autre surtout de Tacite dont il me semble avoir affecté l'imitation par préférence à tous, et je ne sais s'il en est fort louable, pouvant par la flexibilité de sa plume si bien imiter Tite Live ou Cesar, sans s'engager dans ces expressions entortillées, courtes et obscures qui sont particulières à Tacite, sa matière qui est toute de guerre ou peu s'en faut ne lui donnant guère moyen d'ailleurs de faire les réflexions politiques aussi fréquentes que Tacite les a faites en celles du règne paisible de Tibere et de Neron, et dont le Cabinet faisait le sujet le plus considérable.'

[287] Chapelain, *Lettres Authentiques*, pp. 222, 236, 240, 296, etc; and the letters published in P. Burmannus, *Sylloges Epistolarum* vol. 3 no's 311, 314, 315, pp. 378–385.

Gronovius in ep. 314 p. 382: 'Grotii historiam maiorem partem legi nondum editam, eoque patientius desiderium fero. Nomen viri faciet, ut appetatur etiam a barbaris et amicis, quos nosti, nostris, qui nolunt stilo sollicitudinem adesse. Secus quid ibi, quod aut isti intelligant, aut hi intelligere malint quam reprehendere? Facinus illud Amazonicum quis non detestetur? Sane et me iamdudum pudet tam falsa ominatum fuisse. Non poteram tamen excutere misericordiam, et veniebat in mentem illius Tulliani: 2. ad Att. ep 21 Ut Apelles si Venerem, aut si Protogenes Ialysum illum suum caeno oblitum videret. Scis caetera. Et flagitia utcumque excusari poterant: in sceleribus quid faciemus? Nimirum satis exsultavit et illusit soccis: cothurnos indueret, oportebat, quorum exitus eo magis

Patin (one of Grotius' former acquaintances in Paris) appears to have experienced more difficulties in obtaining a copy than Chapelain, for he refers repeatedly to copies being sent to him, as well as to his great expectations regarding the book. Ironically however in April 1658 we find Patin cancelling his order, apparently after inspecting a copy, as he instructs his contact in the Netherlands to remove the book from the package being prepared for him because he has found out that the work contains no index of names. In June he seems to receive a copy after all, either as a gift or as part of the order just mentioned. In August he writes to Charles Spon that he finds the work less outspoken than Strada but more learned and more like Tacitus.[288] In 1663 Hermann Conring praises the AH in his joint edition of Gaspar Schoppius' *Paedia Politices* and Gabriel Naudé's *Bibliographie Politique*, and in the 1675 *Thesaurus Rerumpublicarum,* commending once again Grotius' *iudicium,* his freedom from partisanship, and his successful imitation of Tacitus. Interestingly Conring notes a stylistic difference between the *Annales* and the *Historiae*, labelling the *Annales* more Tacitean and therefore less perspicuous.[289]

horresco, quia inevitabiles videntur, et exempli interest, ut sint. Noster quoque exulceratur dolor, quo allevari debebat, quod non una illa nobis decoxit. Quod ego minore interdum, tu ingenti cummaxime mercede experiris. Atque id eo indignius, quo nobilius et majore animo iniuriam fers, quum et patriae ignoscis, et strenua ex literis solatia petis.' [etc?]

Heinsius replies to this in ep. 315 (p. 383): 'De Historia Grotiana recte iudicas. Fortassis audebo aliquando in eadem palaestra desudare: scis enim annos propemodum quinquaginta nobis per τὴν μακαρίτην reliquos esse, quos annos ille intactos reliquerit, a tempore induciarum. Sed aditus pateat oportet ad arcaniora reipublicae scrinia hoc tentaturo, et patebit mihi fortassis. Narro enim tibi ex collegio Ordinum Generalium nonnullos esse, qui me monuerint, Patres in eo esse, ut sibi addicant aliquem Romani sermonis non ignarum, cuius opera in literis Latinis ad Principes exteros exarandis utantur imposterum. Urgent rem prae caeteris Legatus Gallicus et Petrus Grotius; ex Ordinibus autem Gentius et Amerongius heroes, quorum hic totus mihi militat, etiam in privata causa, oblato nuper testimonio, quo adfirmet virum nobilem ex cognatis suis se praesente fassum esse, pudicitiam Lucretiae nostrae sibi quoque substratam fuisse non semel. Sed haec in sinum tuum. Certum enim mihi fixumque est nil ambire. Slingelandus ex legatione Suecica nuper rem quoque promovendam suscepit apud Ordines Hollandiae, quibus idem debere curae esse contendit.'

[288] *Correspondance complète de Guy Patin,* lettres lat.99, 26-4-1658 to J. Antonides van der Linden; no. 528, 18-6-1658 to C. Spon; no. lat.103, 26-7-1658 to J. Antonides van der Linden; no 533, 13-8-1658 to C. Spon.

[289] H. Conring (ed), *Gasparis Scioppii Paedia Politices et Gabrielis Naudaei Bibliographia Politica ut et ejusdem argumenti alia. Nova editio reliquis omnibus multum emendatior,* Helmstedt 1663, foreword, p. 10; and id., *Thesaurus Rerumpublicarum* Pars 1, Geneva 1675, p. 121: 'Dum vero hi duo [i.e. Nicolaus Burgundius and Famiano Strada] favent Hispaniae, hinc eorum fides interdum claudicat, omnes vero superat meo quidem Iudicio, Hugo Grotius, si quis velit integritatem Iudicii aestimare: Hic depositis omnibus affectibus unice sectatus est veritatem, ea Eloquentia et nervosa brevitate, ut eum Tacito optime mereatur comparari. Felicissime imitatus est Tacitum Grotius. Interim nemo temere ex Grotio historiam discere poterit, qui plane rerum Belgicarum non habet aliquam notitiam. Obscurus enim aeque est ac Tacitus, hinc qui iam praelibarunt Historiam belli Belgici, eum possunt facile assequi. Tribus enim verbis interdum totam historiam aliquam habet'.

Ibid., Pars 3, p. 161: 'Accuratissime omnium motus omnes ab initio ad pactas inducias peregregie conscripsit Hugo Grotius. Observandum tamen est hunc in primis libris esse obscuriorem,

Gisbertus Voetius refers to Grotius' account of the execution of Egmond and Horne in his *Politicae Ecclesiasticae pars secunda* of 1669.[290] The Radboud University Library, Nijmegen preserves a copy of the AH with 17th-century manuscript notes reiterating Conring's praise.[291] The English historian Edward Hyde, Lord Clarendon, expressed a judgement in 1667 which implies that for him, Grotius failed to pierce into the subtleties of actual political decision-making (a judgement which does concern the Tacitean quality of the work).[292] The French critic Jean-Baptiste Denys, writing in the 1670s, refers (dismissively) to the great praise that several others bestowed on Grotius' histories: 'Nous ne dirons point, comme ont fait quelques autres, qu'il passe les Sallustes, les Tite-Lives, les Tacites, et les Polybes (...)'.[293] In his 1672 *Synopsis* or overview of the history of Brabant, the South-Netherlands lawyer and historian Hubert Loyens (1599–1684) includes material from Grotius' AH without mentioning Grotius' name.[294]

affectatione styli Taciti; et hinc factus est obscurior: in reliquis libris satis est perspicuus: eius tamen historia facit ad cognitionem Rerum Belgicarum; et ad Prudentiam Politicam prodesse potest, et ad eloquentiam; ita ut illum omnibus aliis praeferam.'

[290] *G. Voetius, Politicae Ecclesiasticae pars secunda,* Amsterdam (Janssonius a Waesberge), 1669, p. 170. Voetius refers to Grotius more often in the work, but mostly to the *Ordinum Pietas*.

[291] Nijmegen UL, shelfmark 9 d 16, AH, ed. 1658 (120). Notes on flyleaf in 17th-century handwriting: 'Herm. Conring. Thes[aurus] Rerump[ublicarum] P.III p. 161. Accuratissime omnium...' [etc., see preceding note] et Pars 1 p. 121: 'Dum v[ero] hi duo favent Hispaniae, ...' [etc., see preceding note].

[292] Edward Hyde (Lord Clarendon), *A Collection of Several Tracts,* London (Woodward & Peele) 1727, pp. 167–204, esp. 181. See also P. Seaward, 'Clarendon, Tacitism, and the Civil Wars of Europe', in: *Huntington Library Quarterly* 68 (2005), pp. 289–311 (with thanks to Jacob Soll).

[293] *Recoeuil des Mémoires et conferences sur les arts & les sciences, presentées à Monseigneur Le Dauphin pendant l'Année M.DC. LXXII par Jean Baptiste Denis conseiller, et Medecin ordinaire du Roy, qui y continuë Le journal des Sçavans,* Amsterdam (Le Grand) 1673, septième mémoire, 11 april 1672; p. 96.

[294] *Brevis et succincta synopsis rerum maxime memorabilium bello et pace gestarum ab serenissimis Lotharingiae, Brabantiae, et Limburgi Ducibus* etc., Brussels 1672, see e.g. p. 567. Hubert Loyens (1599–1684) was a lawyer, historian and Royal Secretary of the Council of Brabant (Fruytier in *Nieuw Nederlandsch Biografisch Woordenboek* vol. 6 pp. 971–973). His *Synopsis* constructs an account of the history of the counts of Brabant from the 13th to the 17th century by excerpting other works of history. In the prefatory letter to the reader, Loyens describes his method by referring to the cento format of Lipsius' *Politica* (preliminaries, unnumbered, 11th page): 'Facio quod ante me Clarissimus Iustus Lipsius a se factum memorat. Lapides atque ligna ab aliis accepi, tamen exstructio mea est: architectus ego sum, licet materiam varie undique conduxi.' (Lipsius, *Politica*, Nota to 1.1, p. 722). Unlike Lipsius however Loyens is less open as to which sources he constructed the book from. Van der Aa, *Biographisch Woordenboek der Nederlanden* vol. 11 pp. 668–669 identifies Haraeus as an important source; there must be many more. With this respect it may be noteworthy that the dedicatory letter to the cardinal Giacomo Rospigliosi places the book firmly in a Catholic ecclesiastical universe, and that it carries an approbation of the Catholic book censor Matthaeus Middegaels, while Grotius' AH had been placed on the *Index* in 1659 (see above). This raises the question whether perhaps more of Loyens' sources were less acceptable in the Catholic world of his day, and not listing them a strategic choice. The preliminary material however also includes a gratulatory letter from Dirk Graswinckel in Leiden. For an idea of Loyens' process, cp. Grotius (Hist. 15, p. 487, 1606) 'Movit Batavos famosi oppidi [Rijnberk] iactura, quae posthac belli ac fortuna reputantes, si nec exercitu contra iretur, nec munimenta nisi

The Jansenist philosopher Antoine Arnauld (1612–1694) presents the Index's prohibition of the AH and *De Iure Belli ac Pacis* as an example of his thesis that book prohibitions by the Catholic church may be mistaken.[295] After praising *DIB* as a work of great wisdom, moderation and scholarship, that contains nothing on religion, and therefore nothing to offend the church, Arnauld concludes that *DIB* was only prohibited because its author happened to be Protestant at the time of writing, and continues that all of the above applies to the AH as well, and that the Church should not distrust its children so much as to keep them from reading any non-Catholic authors, especially if they display such moderation as Grotius does. Arnauld opens his chapter by repeating the assertion that at the end of his life Grotius had decided to convert to Catholicism. Unfortunately Arnauld thus only discusses the works in terms of the confessional controversy, and does not give any details on his reading of the contents of the works.

Most of the critical voices confirm the likeness between Tacitus' and Grotius' styles, but not always in a positive sense. We have already noted the critical judgement of the 'twisted, short and obscure' expression by Jean Chapelain. In his *Dictionnaire*[296] Pierre Bayle speaks negatively about Tacitus' style and criticises Grotius for imitating it, referring to the Strasbourg scholar and follower of Lipsius, Johannes Boeckler, and to Jérôme Bignon who expressed similar judgements. Bignon is said to have read the AH in manuscript and to have tried to persuade Grotius to change the style.[297] The *consultor* of the Vatican *Index of Forbidden Books*,

breve in tempus subsisterent' with Loyens, p. 567: 'Deditae Rhynberkae fama Batavos haud mediocriter commovit, dum belli fortunam et suas vires reputantes, quid deinde futurum, si porro cum victore exercitu ingruat hostis, ex aliis coniecturam faciunt'. Grotius' sentence (ibid., p. 489) 'Cognito per exploratores quae pars castrorum leviter nec nisi palis firmata, illac, longiore quamvis et per palustria impedito itinere, ostentat aciem' is copied by Loyens in its entirety.

[295] In the *Difficultés proposées a M. Steyaert,* Cologne 1692 (here quoted from vol. 9 of the *Oeuvres de Antoine Arnauld*, Paris 1777, pp. 299–301).

[296] P. Bayle, *Dictionnaire historique et critique,* Rotterdam (Leers) 1697, s.v. Grotius, note (P).

[297] See also § 11.2 above; Bignon probably played a role in the survivial of the manuscript of Grotius' *Historiae.* Bayle refers to Boeckler's *In Hugonis Grotii ius belli et pacis Commentatio* (p. 30 in the ed. Strassbourg 1704), where it says (without further source ref.): 'Satis constat, virum nostri saeculi summum, omnisque doctrinae et auctorem et censorem gravissimum, Hieronymum Bignonium, cum ineditas adhuc Grotii Historias et Annales legisset, non probasse brevitatem orationis, obscuritati obnoxiam, in illo genere scripturae, quod a perspicua venustate potissimam commendationem caperet; peneque Grotio persuasisse, ut rescriberet. Sed invito genio, qui format fere orationem, vix suscipi feliciter alquid videmus: et in historia, facilitas erudita optari, gravitas non inepta ferri debet. Quae in hoc quidem opere plus rationis habere videtur.', ('It is sufficiently established that one of the greatest men of our time, Jérôme Bignon, that most significant author and critic of every kind of scholarship, when he had read Grotius' Histories and Annals, disapproved of the work's brevity, as suffering from obscurity in a genre that earns its greatest praise precisely from elegant transparency; and that he had almost succeeded in pesuading Grotius to rewrite it. However we see that almost nothing can be undertaken successfully if our natural inclination, which molds the text so to speak into form, does not cooperate: and in historiography, a learned easiness of style is desired, but gravity, as long as it's fitting, must be tolerated').

Stefano Gradić, who wrote the report discussed in § 11.5 above, commented however that Grotius had affected, but not actually achieved the Tacitean style:

> In the argumentation of this book he sets out to equal the renown for novelty achieved by other authors by the merit of his eloquence, studiously and quite successfully emulating the greatness of Sallust's style, and the brevity and tense dignity of Cornelius Tacitus. However, he did not attain to the fruit he hoped his laborious effort would bear: for indeed, since the sparkling expression is kept up neither evenly nor in all parts, he seems more to have affected, than to have actually achieved it, and he either unwisely postponed or proudly neglected to relieve, by work of the file, the aspired brevity from the usual trouble of obscurity.[298]

The pseudonymous *Parrhasiana, or pensées diverses sur des matières de critique, d'histoire, de morale et de politique* (Amsterdam 1699, by Jean Le Clerc) praises Grotius' objectivity in the AH, but again disapproves of the Tacitean style, presenting both Tacitus' and Grotius' styles as examples of a misguided desire for uncommonness for its own sake, with obscurity as the result.[299] In his *Mémoires pour servir à l'histoire de la République des Provinces-Unies et des Pays-Bas (...) donnés avec de Notes Politiques, Historiques et Critiques par Amelot de la Houssaye,* the French scholar Louis Aubery du Maurier (1609–1687) often refers to Grotius as a source, and not only to the AH but also other works such as the poetry. Aubery du Maurier had maintained a frequent correspondence with Grotius and includes a life of Grotius in this work.[300]

From the late 17th to the early 19th century, the AH enjoyed a solid reputation as a work of history.[301] In his *History of the Reformation*, Geeraert Brandt (1626–1685) praises Grotius' impartiality and undaunted truthfulness, connecting these with some Tacitean phrases on the eventual inexorability of historical truth. His formulation reflects an assumption that Grotius wrote the work after, not before, the escalation of the Truce Conflicts.[302] In their biography of Grotius first pub-

[298] See Waszink, 'New documents', p. 87.

[299] Grafton, *What was History?*, part 1 discusses the enlightenment-age debate on the direction historiography should take between the 'modern' Le Clerc and the 'classical' Jacobus Perizonius.

[300] First published in 1680; I have seen the edition from London, 1754: L. Aubery du Maurier & Amelot de La Houssaye, *Mémoires pour servir à l'histoire de la République des Provinces-Unies et des Pays-Bas: Contenant les vies des Princes d'Orange, de Barneveld, d'Aersens & de Grotius,* Lonson 1754. A reference to *Annales* 2.28 in vol. 1 p. 75 ('Pacheco... Grotius dit qu'il etoit Savoyard'; a reference to a poem by Grotius on the battle of Newport in vol. II p. 37 ('pars haud temnenda triumphi...').

[301] See also § 3 on Grotius' intellectual formation and § 9.2 on Grotius as historian.

[302] G. Brandt, *Historie der Reformatie en andere kerkelyke geschiedenissen in en omtrent de Nederlanden* vol. 1, Amsterdam 1671, 'Voor-Reden aen den Leser', pp. 2–3: [Even onpartijdig] 'droeg sich bij onsen tijde die wijdtberoemde Hollander, Hugo de Groot die in sijne Historie niemants lof, in 't stuk des krijgshandels, hooger opsette, als des geenen, die hem, soo hij meende in 't burgerlijk bestier op het allermeest' *hadt verongelijkt* [italics mine]; tot een klaer bewijs, dat geen besonder leedt op sijn gemoedt hechtte, noch sijn pen in 't schrijven van 't geen hij der waerheit, den vaderlande, en den geenen die 't hadt verdedigt,

lished in 1727, Caspar Brandt and Adriaan van Cattenburgh praise the AH extensively as a successful emulation of Tacitus and Thucydides. Their lengthy praise of the work (which includes a long quote from the unused dedication to Christina of Sweden) puts particular emphasis on Grotius' judgment, style, impartiality and unwavering truthfulness.[303] The historian Frans van Mieris (1689–1763) urges his fellow historians to follow the examples of Grotius, Hooft and Brandt.[304] His colleague Jan Wagenaar (1709–1773) presents Grotius as one of his main sources (together with Hooft) and makes special mention of Grotius' discussion of the Truce negotiations.[305] Amsterdam UL preserves a copy of the AH once owned by the classicist and historian Petrus Burmannus II (1713–1778, professor at the Athenaeum Illustre) with notes on the flyleaves showing that he had read a good part of the reactions to the AH above, and providing a few emendations to the text.[306] In his biography of Nicolas Heinsius, Burman mentions Heinsius'

schuldig was, wederhouden kon. Doch die sich selve weleer best queten voor de waerheit, verdienden veeltijds den grootsten haet bij de boosen en nijdigen. D' onschuldige waerheit baerde haet. De snoodtste menschen wierden tegen de waerheit en der selver Schrijvers gaende, met naemen als se welspraeken van d' onderdrukte deugt, ten smaedt der Tijrannij. D' oprechtigheit en vrijheit in t schrijven verwekte vervolging tegen de getuigen der waerheit. Derhalven schreven sommige veel liever oude, dan nieuwe of versche geschiedenissen en wist de wereltwijse Tacitus wel aen te wijsen, hoe gevaerlijk het was, dat een Historieschrijver verscheide dingen van al te nabij wilde melden. De waerheit wierdt echter vergeefs door 't geweldt der Tijrannen bestreden. Al deedt men de Historie van Cremutius, ten gevalle van Tiberius, verbranden, se wierdt niet te min onder de handt behouden, daer na uitgegeven, en des te graeger gelesen. "Daerom lust het mij," seit de selve Tacitus, "te meer te lacchen met de domheit der geenen, die sich diets maeken, dat se met hunne tegenwoordige maght ook de geheugenis der navolgende eeuwen konnen uitblussen. Want in 't tegendeel, als de vernuften gestraft worden dan groeit hunne authoriteit." 'On Brandts' history, see also P. Burke, 'The Politics of Reformation History: Burnet and Brandt', in: Duke & Tamse (eds.), *Clio's Mirror*, pp. 73–85, mentioning Brandt's reference in his preface to reason-of-state historians Thucydides, Polybius and Tacitus (p. 75); and S. Groenveld 'Pieter Corneliszoon Hooft in de Geschiedschrijving' in: *Hooft als historieschrijver*, pp. 60–92, 62.

303 *Historie* pp. 34–35; see above § 11.2. Brandt & Cattenburg's rendering in Dutch shows some differences with the original printed in the *Briefwisseling*; in their version Grotius informs the queen that he did not write the AH in order to compete with other (mostly Italian) historians, but out of pure love of his country, and that his public office had given him access to the best sources; while however a very important motive was to praise prince Maurice whom he had always held in high esteem, and who had also acknowledged his (Grotius') merits; even when his conscience had forced him to hold a different view of the country's interests than the prince.

304 *Verhandeling over het zaamenstellen en beoevenen der Historien* etc., 1757; see Groenveld, 'Hooft in de Geschiedschrijving', 64.

305 'Voorrede' in: *Vaderlandsche Historie vervattende de geschiedenissen der nu vereenigde Nederlanden* etc., vol. 6 (orig. 1752), pp. V–X in ed. Amsterdam 1792; see also Groenveld, 'Hooft in de Geschiedschrijving', 59–64; Janssen, 'Grotius als Geschichtsschreiber', pp. 164–167; Muller, *De Groots Annales et Historiae*, chapter 5. Wagenaar relates Grotius' imprisonment in book 39 of the *Vaderlandsche Historie* (vol. 10, 1754, pp. 241 sqq.).

306 A copy of the second folio edition of 1657 (TMD 742); shelf-mark UBA, OTM KF62-4241. The copy also carries an ex-libris of P.A. Pijnappel. see also § 11.8 'Scholarship on the text'. On Burman, see also Janssen, 'Trias', p. 11.

aforementioned plan to write a sequel to the AH.[307] Tilburg UL preserves a manuscript set of lecture notes on Dutch historians taken from Burman's teaching by one M. Romswinckel (and dated to 1779, although this is after Burman's death). The notes echo the then-conventional praise of Grotius' objectivity and understanding of *arcana,* and they defend Grotius' imitation of Tacitus against critical voices like Bignon's. Interestingly Burman makes a point of Casaubonus' reference to the work in 1613 (that is, to the fact that the AH are a work of Grotius' younger years not of the mature scholar. However Burman does not apply this insight to his assessment of the AH's impartiality).[308] Thus 17th- and 18th-century historians valued Grotius' impartiality and his (Tacitean) judgement regarding the true causes and motives of events.[309]

The turning point seems to come with the views expressed by the great historian Robert Fruin (1823–1899) who wrote extensively on Grotius, but very little on the AH or Grotius' other historical works. Fruin refers to the AH only a few times and very briefly. His judgment on Grotius as a historian shows that Fruin saw him primarily as a humanist, that is, a literary scholar, who produces a literary rendition of a period of history, rather than a critical historical investigation in the sense of the term which it had for Fruin, who was an admirer of Leopold von Ranke's 'historical positivism'.[310] The wider tendency among late-19th century scholars to conclude that the early-modern interest in and imitation of Tacitus was only concerned with *form* was already noted and criticised by the Nijmegen

[307] Petrus Burmannus II, *Nicolai Heinsii Dan. Fil. Adversariorum libri IV* etc, Harlingen 1742, pp. 39–40.

[308] Tilburg university library, ms. KHS D91, P. Burmannus & M. Romswinckel, *Aantekeningen*, pp. 7–10; see also Janssen, 'Trias Historica', p. 11 & n. 17.

[309] The AH's contemporary reputation is further confirmed by book titles such as *Histoire de Hollande depuis la treve de 1609, ou finit Grotius jusqu'a notre tems. Par M. de la Neuville*, Paris 1702. For the 18th- and 19th-century reception of the AH's type of historiography, one might consult the discussion of the reception of P.C. Hooft's *Nederlandsche Historiën* in Groenveld, 'Hooft in de Geschiedschrijving'.

[310] 'De historie, zoals De Groot ze opvatte, behoorde ook tot den kring der philologie; de vorm was hoofdzaak, en deze moest naar de modellen der oudheid worden nagebootst; diepe en uitvoerige nasporingen, strenge kritiek bij het aannemen van overleveringen kwamen minder te pas. Vandaar dat De Groot zich reeds in zijne jeugd voor het geschiedschrijven berekend hield, en door anderen ervoor berekend werd geacht', ('History, as understood by Grotius, belonged to the sphere of philology; its main aspect was form, and this had to be modelled on the examples from Antiquity. In-depth and extensive research, [and] critical evaluation of transmitted information was less important. This is why Grotius from an early age considered himself fit to write history, and was seen as such by others.') Fruin, *Verzamelde Geschriften iii*, pp. 405–406; see also Muller, *De Groots Annales et Historiae*, pp. 159–161. Judith Pollmann provides an interesting discussion of Fruin's 19th-century judgement of Grotius in 'Hij had geen oog op zijn tijd. Robert Fruins gebruik van egodocumenten als bron voor de cultuurgeschiedenis' In: P. Herman & H. te Velde (eds.), *Het vaderlandse verleden. Robert Fruin en de Nederlandse geschiedschrijving,* Amsterdam (Bert Bakker) pp. 60–81. She shows that in general Fruin did appreciate the value of information on how people in the past perceived and experienced their own time. See also Grotius as Historian in § 9.2 above and § 10 on the sources of the AH.

cultural historian J.D.M. Cornelissen in his studies of P.C. Hooft's emulation of Tacitus.[311] As I hope to have shown in this introduction however Grotius does display critical historical judgment according to the newest standards of his own time, that is, the sceptical and reason-of-state-guided inquiry into the actual causes and human motivations behind past events. For Fruin however, it seems this was no more than ill-documented guesswork. Given Fruin's influence his judgment has undoubtedly contributed to the relative obscurity of the AH since the 19th century, in addition to the fact that in the 19th century Grotius was 'canonised' as foundational thinker of the then-emerging system of international law. This development put his juridical oeuvre at the foreground and made the author primarily a jurist in the public perception. The American historian John Lothrop Motley (1814–1877), author of two extensive histories on the Revolt which celebrate the Dutch 'protestant' struggle for liberty, quotes from a range of historians of Grotius' time (including Bor, Van Meteren, Hooft, Strada, De Thou) but very rarely from Grotius, except in vol. 4 of the *United Netherlands*, where the AH appear in the notes very frequently.[312]

In agreement however with Fruin's view that form was the chief aspect of Grotius' historical work, 19th-century classicists spent a good deal of attention on Grotius' stylistic ability in Latin, long before the study of Neo-Latin arose as a discipline, but at a time when classicists (no longer humanists) in the Netherlands, aspired, with some success, to revive the glory days of Low Countries philology in the 16th-18th centuries by building a strong and deep culture of ability in Latin and Greek in schools and universities. A conspicuous example of this culture is the *Certamen Hoeufftianum,* a competition in Latin verse composition held since 1845.[313] In 1843 C. Abbing, director of the gymnasium (Latin school) in the town of Hoorn, published a study of the Latin styles of Grotius and his contemporary Italian historian of the revolt, Famiano Strada (see also § 10 above). The book is basically an anthology of prose passages from Grotius' and Strada's histories.[314] In 1883 the Latinist J.C. Boot published a detailed study of Grotius' imitation of Tacitus' Latin, which he labels as very successful. Boot's study also builds on

311 J.D.M. Cornelissen, 'Hooft en Tacitus', esp. pp. 53–56.

312 This neglect of precisely Grotius from the 17th century historians may be found surprising given Motley's enthusiasm for the 'constitutional' view of the rebellion as expressed primarily by Grotius in *De Antiquitate* and related works; e.g. Motley, *Rise*, vol. 1 p. 75: 'By any reasonable construction of history, Philip was an unscrupulous usurper, who was attempting to convert himself from a duke of Brabant and a Count of Holland into an absolute king. It was William who was maintaining, Philip who was destroying', etc. See J.L. Motley, *The Rise of the Dutch Republic. A History.* [first printed 1856] London (Routledge), no year, 3 vols.; id., *History of the United Netherlands from the death of William the Silent to the Twelve Years' Truce – 1609*, (4vols), edition ofThe Hague 1867. See also above (§ 10, end) on the account of the Dutch exploits in Java and Malaysia and the confrontation with the Portuguese.

313 Named after the poet and lawyer Jacob Hendrik Hoeufft, 1756–1843.

314 C.A. Abbing, *Hugonis Grotii et Famiani Stradae Latinititas. Loca selecta e Grotii Annalibus et Stradae, De Bello Belgico, Decadibus*, Hoorn 1843.

the notes on the AH left by an older Leiden Latinist, Petrus Hofman Peerlkamp (1786–1865). Boot provides a list of emendations to the Latin text (combining his own and Peerlkamp's emendations) which was extended in turn by H. Muller in his 1919 PhD on the AH (see further § 11.8 below on the scholarship on the text).

In the 20th century scholarly interest in the AH was very limited. In 1911 the Swiss historian Eduard Fueter (1876–1928) expressed a positive judgment because he found Grotius a perceptive and objective searcher for true causes.[315] In his PhD thesis on the AH of 1919 H.C.A. Muller praises the work as a Latin work of art, and with respect to its historiographical merits, speaks positively about Grotius' analysis of causes and consequences, his character portraits and his objectivity regarding both the Spanish and his (eventual) opponent Prince Maurice; although, as already noted, the latter judgment only makes sense if one assumes that the AH was mainly written in or after 1618, which is not the case. However in Muller's time the systematic publication of Grotius' correspondence had not even started, so that he did not have the easy means of access to this rich source of contextual data and information that we have now. The cultural historian J.D.M. Cornelissen, already mentioned, was inspired by Guiseppe Toffanin's conceptualisation of Tacitism in 1921 to look at Dutch literature from this perspective, especially the *Nederlandse Historiën* by P.C. Hooft.[316] From these very diligent studies it transpires that for Cornelissen, Tacitism and the early-modern debate on reason of state must be placed in the context of the (then-prevailing) paradigm of the rise of the nation state; he does not connect them with the themes of church-government relations, secularisation and religious wars. In 1928 Cornelissen also published the information he found on the Roman Index's treatment of the AH, as discussed in § 11.5.[317] In 1950 the Italian intellectual historian Antonio Droetto published an article on the AH which has remained relatively unknown, on the Tacitism in Grotius' historical works. In his view Grotius' purely political interpretation of history was responsible for the fact that the work was not published at the time of composition, because such views were repulsive to some members of the States of Holland.[318] In 1963 a small portion of Joan Goris' translation of *Historiae* 1 appeared in a paperback collection of ancient Dutch historians from the 17th and 18th centuries.[319]

The debate was only resumed in the 1970s and on a very limited scale. The 1973 PhD thesis *Hugo Grotius Historian* by the American historian Jordy Bell, and an article by the Dutch historian Eco Haitsma Mulier of 1985 present fairly similar

[315] E. Fueter, *Geschichte der Neueren Historiographie*, München 1911, pp. 244–245. Fueter is also aware that the AH's relative neglect of the religious issue is connected with Grotius' own views regarding state, religion and orthodoxy.

[316] Toffanin, *Machiavelli e il Tacitismo*.

[317] In his (still relevant) article of 1938, 'Hooft en Tacitus', Cornelissen refers repeatedly to Grotius but not to the AH.

[318] Droetto, 'Il Tacitismo nella storiografia Groziana', p. 118.

[319] See § 11.6 above.

images of Grotius as a historian.[320] Both authors look at the AH primarily from the perspective of the humanist historiography of Grotius' time and the preceding period, and, like Fruin, consider form to be its central aspect. Both Bell and Haitsma Mulier conclude that the AH were composed entirely in accordance with the humanist, rhetorical pattern of historical writing, and were therefore old-fashioned already at their time of composition, and not innovative. The connection with early-modern Tacitism (which represents a break with several key aspects of traditional humanist historiography) is hardly made by these authors. Bell concludes unconvincingly that Tacitus was not an important model for the AH, and for Haitsma Mulier it is not clear that Tacitus' thought about power and ethics occupies a central place in the AH. It was probably this that led both authors to conclude that it is hard to discover any leading themes or concerns in the AH.[321] In the context of the commemorations of Grotius' 400th birthday in 1983 some articles devote limited attention to the AH.[322]

The first time the composition of the text is put in a detailed historical context (personal as well as political) is in a 1994 article by Cornelia Ridderikhoff, which also recognises the value of the information contained in the correspondence for the interpretation of the work's content. Henk Nellen's great biography of Grotius (2007) provides many further details from the correspondence regarding the composition of the AH, and puts it in the context of Grotius' life. However the Tacitist and reason-of-state aspect of the work, Grotius' intentions in writing this sceptical account of the Revolt, its significance in the context of the Truce Conflicts, the work's controversial character, the question as to *why* he chose the Tacitean register for the work, as well as its value as a source for the historiography and intellectual history of the Truce period are not discussed in the above scholarship. The research undertaken by the present editor has been an attempt to provide answers to these questions in order to arrive at a more precise interpretation of the AH.[323] The discussion of the AH in Nellen's recent shorter biography of Grotius (2021) mostly agrees with the research on which the present edition is based, while adding valuable detail in some places.[324]

320 J. Bell, *Hugo Grotius Historian* (Ph. D. diss., Columbia Univ., 1973); E. Haitsma Mulier, 'Grotius, Hooft and the Writing of History in the Dutch Republic' in: A.C. Duke and C.A. Tamse eds., *Clio's Mirror* (Britain and the Netherlands 8, 1985), 55–72. On the changing image of Grotius in the 20th century, see e.g. H. Nellen, 'Het Leidse haylichje'. Hugo Grotius in de twintigste eeuw', in: *Jaarboek van de Maatschappij der Nederlandse Letterkunde* 1995, pp. 37–58.

321 'It is remarkable that in fact no single theme clearly emerges,' according to Haitsma Mulier, 'Grotius, Hooft', p. 61

322 C.L. Heesakkers, 'Grotius als geschiedsschrijver' in: *Het Delfts Orakel. Hugo de Groot*, Delft 1983, 103–110; A. Janssen, 'Grotius als Geschichtsschreiber', in: *The World of Hugo Grotius*, Amsterdam 1984, 161–178.

323 As part of this research project a symposium took place at the Radboud University Nijmegen in 2007 in which various aspects of form and content of the work were discussed in connection; the papers from this meeting are edited in *Grotiana* 29 (2008) and 30 (2009).

324 H. Nellen, *Geen vredestichter is zonder tegensprekers. Hugo de Groot; geleerde, staatsman, verguisd verzoener*, Amsterdam (Polak & Van Gennep) 2021, pp. 69–73 and n. 45–56, esp. 45.

11.8. *Scholarship on the text*

There is not much previous scholarship on the text of the AH.

The notes preserved in the copy owned by Petrus Burmannus II (1713–1778) have already been mentioned.[325] On three flyleaves at the end there are 7 proposed corrections to proper names; one of these concerns the *Annales*, i.e. the (justified) correction of 'Iohannes Montiniacus' to Florentius in § 1.52.

In the 19th and early 20th century three scholars devoted attention to the Latin text, i.e. the classicists Petrus Hofman Peerlkamp (1786–1865) and Johan Cornelis Gerard Boot (1811–1901)[326] provided critical remarks and proposed a number of emendations in the text; they were followed by the historian H.C.A. Muller in a Ph.D. of 1919.

The Leiden latinist Petrus Hofman Peerlkamp left an 8o copy of the AH (now in Leiden UL) with manuscript notes on flyleaves and in the margins, the bulk of which concern *Annales* book 1 and 2.[327] These include a number of proposed emendations to the text. As a classicist, Hofman Peerlkamp is known for his method of 'subjective criticism', in which the critic could reject whatever in his opinion did not meet the standards of what the classical author under consideration should have written. Peerlkamp himself for example declared spurious the greater part of Horace's *Odes*.[328] But however that be, the 6 emendations Peerlkamp proposes for Grotius' *Annales* are generally careful, small-scale, and palaeographically convincing corrections. However some of them seem unnecessary, and evidently proceed more from a judgement of taste than from philological necessity (e.g. *invisi* for *inviti* 2.9).

Peerlkamp's corrections were published by J.C.G. Boot in an article in 1883, and supplemented by Boot's own remarks to the text. Together, Boot and Peerlkamp propose 29 emendations to the most widely available text, that of the 8o edition of 1658. Boot also consulted one of the folio editions of 1657. Twenty-three of their proposed corrections concern the text of the *Annales;* of these readings, four had in fact already been printed in the editions of 1657. With respect to the corrections proposed by Boot, the same can be said as about Peerlkamp's: they are small-scale and carefully considered proposals, but often unnecessary. In the present edition, only two proposals from Peerlkamp and two from Boot have been accepted into the main text. Of the remaining fifteen proposals, some are given in

[325] See § 11.7; Amsterdam UL, OTM KF62-4241. A copy is on Google Books: https://books.google.nl/books?id=AcVkAAAAcAAJ&printsec=frontcover&hl=nl#v=onepage&q&f=false

[326] A silhouette portrait of J.C.G. Boot is preserved in the image collection of the Walloon Church in Leiden UL, no. BWB 413. A lithographic portrait of Hofman Peerlkamp by Leendert Springer can be found at https://rkd.nl/explore/images/167496.

[327] Leiden UL, coll. Maatschappij Nederlandsche Letterkunde (KL), 1499 D 34.

[328] L. Müller, *Geschichte der klassischen Philologie in den Niederlanden,* Leipzig 1869, and J.E. Sandys, *History of Classical Scholarship*, vol. 3, Cambridge 1908, p. 276.

the a.c. as alternatives but the present editor does not believe they can be regarded as intended by Grotius.

Two examples of redundant corrections will illustrate the critical assumptions and practices of Peerlkamp's and Boot's age. In Ann. 1.11 in the line 'Castellani regnari amant aliquanto, quam nonnullae Hispanorum gentes, addictius' Peerlkamp proposes to change the last word to *adductius*, because the phrase echoes that in Tacitus, *Germania* 43.6. The wording in Tacitus however was only corrected to *adductius* in Peerlkamp's own time. In Grotius' time all Tacitus editions read *addictius;* the other form was simply not available and cannot possibly be the one intended by Grotius. Peerlkamp's suggestion is anachronistic and distorts Grotius' reading of the classical texts as they were in his time. Grotius quotes the passage again in *De Antiquitate* 1.4, in the same form. Similarly in 1.38 Peerlkamp and Boot propose to correct *Leodicensi* to *Leodiensi*, probably because the latter seems more frequent; however the former certainly exists in other early-modern sources and is not wrong. The emendation proposal is hypercorrect and suppresses historical variation; it reflects 19th-century ideals of consistency rather than Grotius' actual writing.

12. Conclusion

The *Annales et Historiae de rebus Belgicis,* written for the greater part, it seems, in the years 1604–1608, are at the nexus of all of Grotius' activities in his years of service to the government of Holland: his roles as spokesman and counsellor in the Oldenbarnevelt government amid the peace negotiations in 1607–1609 and the subsequent tensions of the Truce period; his thinking on reason of state and religious policy, as well as his gradual re-thinking of political ethics as apparent in his later thinking on natural law; his ambitions in the literature and historiography of the late-humanist circles centring on the university at Leiden; and his background role in support of the VOC. The work should remind current scholars of the central importance of reason-of-state ideas for Grotius' thought in general. Grotius' correspondence around the AH suggests that he saw himself as combining the roles of historian and statesman: the deeper insight of the (Tacitean) historian informs the statesman's decisions in the present, while the statesman's inside knowledge of affairs enables him to write the true history of his own time. The work was finished (in a first version) in 1612 but not published at that time by its commissioners, the States of Holland. Grotius revised it for publication in the 1620s and '30s, but eventually it was only published posthumously by his sons in 1657. While Grotius was working on the AH, the work became known within his circle of acquaintances and expected with anticipation. These great expectations seem eventually to have been co-responsible for the work's survival after its author himself failed twice, for very different reasons, to see the work through the press during his lifetime.

Both the idiosyncratic literary style of the work and its sceptical, secularising content place it firmly in the then-vibrant genre of Tacitism. The Roman historian Cornelius Tacitus was seen, especially since the times of Justus Lipsius, as the '*magister in politicis*', that is, the main authority among the Classics regarding the true rules and mechanics of politics without the veil of moralism, religion and exemplarity. Moreover, and attractively for the humanists, in Tacitus such thinking was partly expressed in handy examples and *sententiae* ready for re-application in contemporary argument. The Tacitist mode of political literature thus includes a *taste* for realism; for cool, strictly factual analysis of political processes and human behaviour, which covers both the domain of literature and that of guidance in actual practical politics. This orientation also characterises Grotius' idea of the tasks of history as a discipline.

Thus Grotius' *Annales* present an image of the first decades of the Revolt in which the role of religion is reduced to minimum or, as to organised religion, even to a negative one, i.e. as a source of chaos, division and strife in society; they present a pessimistic view of the solidarity within the Low Countries, of the political naivety of the Dutch population, and of the discipline and public spirit of the Dutch nobility; and they contain none of the glorification of the struggle of the Dutch towns and nobility against the Spanish oppression expressed in many other writings on the Revolt. Even in the case of the notable exception to this, Grotius' admiring portrait of William of Orange, stratagems, calculation and *Realpolitik* are not lacking.

Grotius uses the Tacitean sceptical and 'disenchanted' register as a tool to present some policies of key figures on both sides (not only William of Orange, but also Elizabeth and Philip II) as instances of *Realpolitik* without including the negative ethical implications such an image would carry in other registers. As to whether it was a political or a religious struggle, the memory of the revolt was highly contested, and Grotius appears to be implicitly weaponising a *Staatsgezinde* interpretation. The present editor concludes that the image Grotius presents should be understood in the context of the disagreements over church-government relations in the Republic in the first decades of the 17th century, i.e. that they are presented in order to corroborate the *Staatsgezinde* view that religion played at best a secondary role in the genesis of the Dutch Republic, that consequently the churches should submit to the secular governments, and that the citizens should obey the States government and its policies.

However, in presenting this picture of the early Revolt, Grotius may well have overstretched his Tacitean instrument, and have miscalculated the potential opposition his account would provoke in readers who did not know, or share the taste for, Tacitism and its assumptions regarding man and religion, politics and history. The publication histories of several other historical works in the same period show that both the States of Holland and the States-General took a very active and directive role in the publication of narratives about Holland and the Republic. The AH were no exception, and after the work had (presumably) been reviewed by the committee of two appointed for the purpose, its publication plans have apparently been shelved, although no exact information survives as to what happened. The difficult position of reason of state and *politique* religious policy in the public eye (especially the orthodox Calvinist majority), together with their emerging perception of the Oldenbarnevelt government precisely as 'Machiavellian' might help explain the omission of the States to publish the work in the already tense atmosphere of 1613.

After the non-publication Grotius kept the manuscript with him and worked on it again during his subsequent careers after his escape from prison, notably around 1622 and in 1635–1637. Negotiations with Blaeu about its publication, as part of a wider attempt at a 'collected main works' publication by that publisher, did not lead to a printed edition of the work within Grotius' lifetime; however Grotius' sons Pieter and Cornelis eventually saw the work through the press at Blaeu's in 1657–1658 (in folio, octavo and duodecimo editions). Translation were published in French (1662), English (1665) and Dutch (1681).

After its publication the AH soon achieved a solid reputation as an authoritative history on the Dutch Revolt. This seems due both to Grotius' relative impartiality and the successful imitation of Tacitus' model of historical analysis. The Tacitean style of the work had a mixed reception; on the one hand all critics agree that Grotius delivered a close imitation of Tacitus' original style, an accomplishment which was admired by some, but rejected by others together with the Tacitean style as such, as being too uncouth and liable to obscurity. The work was investigated twice by the Vatican Congregation for the Index in 1658–1659 and put on the *Index of Forbidden Books* because of some disparaging remarks on Catholicism that the second investigator objected to. References in other historical literature testify to its continuing standing during the 18th century. The rise of positivist historiography in the 19th century meant the end of the AH's esteem as a work of historiography, and reduced it to a model of Latin literary style interesting for a specialised and numerically limited audience.

With respect to this style, we have considered what the concept of Tacitism (and 'Tacitean', 'Tacitist') comprised and alluded to in Grotius' time, and how Grotius realised these features in his imitation of Tacitus' political historiography. Literary criticism contemporary with Grotius identified a set of characteristics of Tacitus' historiography and prose style: brevity, difficulty, ruggedness, *sententiae,* revelation, *iudicium,* practical value for present political actors. These features are all easy to recognise in Grotius' *Annales*, so that it follows that the style of the *Annales* is Tacitean in every respect by 16th- and 17th-century standards. However this image of Tacitus' literary style differs sharply from modern readings which emphasise precisely the bigger compositorial and 'dramatic' structures, and the longer lines in Tacitus' narrative, in ways comparable to the workings of modern prose fiction such as the novel (a genre which only first began to develop in Grotius' time). In more recent Tacitus criticism the elements of reason of state, political acumen and historical truth have receded into the background. With this respect

Grotius' *Annales* provide a fascinating demonstration of the wide gap between modern and early-modern readings of a classical author.

With respect to the historical material the AH are based on a variety of sources. Grotius used a (mostly) identifiable range of printed histories of the Revolt from both the Protestant and the Catholic side; a variety of documentary sources to which he had access either directly in his role(s) close to the Oldenbarnevelt government, or indirectly via contacts in his expanding network; as well as oral information as it circulated in his family or generally. However, and perhaps even primarily, his own judgment and analysis of the chief agents' motivations appears as a major force in the formation of his narrative. His main aim was to analyse and to interpret, rather than to document, as appears also from the absence of source references to the text, which Grotius does include in many other works.

An analysis of Grotius' picture of the some of the main characters the narrative of the Revolt shows not only his deep immersion in reason-of-state thinking (applied to both sides in the war) and his relative impartiality (evidenced by the cool or even admiring depictions of Philip II and Alexander Farnese, duke of Parma), but also his veneration for William of Orange and his loathing of militant Protestantism (as embodied by the Earl of Leicester and his Dutch entourage).

As to the AH's place among Grotius' wider oeuvre a complicated and intriguing picture emerges. On the one hand it is obvious that in its scepticism and focus on reason of state, the *Annales* clearly stand apart from the normativity and legal optimism embodied in the contemporaneous *De Iure Praedae* and *De Antiquitate Reipublicae Batavicae,* and the later *De Iure Belli ac Pacis*. However at the same time there are also important similarities and connections with these works. The sceptical attitude in the *Annales*, with its un-glorifying take on the Revolt, is never explicitly extended to affect the constitutional argument for the Revolt, thereby avoiding a direct clash with the purport of *De Antiquitate*. The reason-of-state-based realism in the AH seems to spring from the same (late-humanist) naturalism as the natural rights-argument on which IPC and DIB are based, and some elements of reason-of-state thinking can actually be pointed at in DIB. In that sense the AH are a reminder of the importance of reason of state for Grotius' thought in general, including DIB, and of the relative neglect of this topic in the Grotius scholarship. But however this be, the range of various different arguments about the same or very similar topics that the circle of Grotius' works contains, means that each of his works should be interpreted in its own historical or discursive context, and that we should be wary of sweeping characterisations pretending to describe Grotius' oeuvre as a whole.

It is noteworthy that Grotius, as a scholar and humanist (or if one prefers: rhetorician) when applying his scholarly instruments to questions of government and lawmaking, repeatedly preferred new and unconventional arguments and means of persuasion to tried and familiar ones. In this respect he deviated from the usual pattern in classical and humanist rhetoric, in which a preference for well-established forms of argumentation and presentation can certainly be distinguished. In fact this reduced Grotius' chances of realizing his objectives, and without doubt it contributed to the outcome of the AH not being published in its own time.[329]

The AH also reflect the various ways Grotius was involved in the genesis of the Twelve Years' Truce between the Republic and the house of Habsburg. His role as a spokesman-in-the-background of potential government statements to the outside world enabled him to obtain an informed judgment of the negotiation process. He witnessed the progress of the negotiations directly and is aware of the various interests (Dutch, Spanish, French. English, German) competing around that process; he has a detailed view of the place of the Low Countries war in both a European and a global perspective, and of the competing interests with respect to the Spanish, Portuguese and (nascent) Dutch commercial empires. With respect to the war or peace debate within the Republic, it is possible to see Grotius both as a moderate supporter of Oldenbarnevelt's peace policy and as a moderate adherent of the war party.

It is possible to discern a picture of Dutch 'nationhood' in the text, albeit of a very different appearance than the present-day Dutch national identity. The *natio* for Grotius is what we call the province (i.e. Holland, Brabant, etc) which is also the bearer of sovereignty, but not the owner of its cultural identity, for that seems placed at the level of the *gens* Belgica, i.e. all of the Low Countries together. Only the Walloons seem set apart from this group on account of their different language, as well as Luxemburg. As to the territory of this *gens*, one might observe that Grotius' text displays a focus of interest on the West and South (Holland, Zeeland, Brabant, Flanders) rather than on the East and the North – which might suggest a division in his mind of the Low Countries into three parts, West and South, North and East, and the Walloon area.

[329] A comparable observation has been made about the argumentation in *De Iure praedae*; see M. Somos, 'Secularization in *De iure praedae*: from Bible Criticism to International Law', in: *Grotiana* 26–28 (2005–2007), pp. 147–191.

THIS EDITION

I.
Principles of this edition

This text in principle follows the second edition of 1657 (TMD 742), as this edition constitutes our most reliable witness of the now-lost manuscript (see § II.4). In the absence of the *Annales* manuscript, the aim of the present edition is to present the most accomplished text by Grotius' sons, with the remaining textual issues resolved or at least addressed. Obvious printing errors have been silently corrected (for examples see § II.4 and notes above). On the manuscript sources of the text, see § II.1–II.3. The text of the 1658 octavo edition (TMD 743) has been used as a second reference; its significant variants are given in the apparatus and in some cases its punctuation has been preferred over that of 1657 (see below). The duodecimo edition of 1658 (TMD 744) has been considered unreliable given the large number of printing errors it contains, and has not been used.

A curious case is the consistent misapplication of *impiger* with negation in 1.5 and 1.37. It looks as if the author was confused about the negation already included in the word and put one too many in his text. The fact that the exact same issue appears twice indicates that we are not looking at a printing or editing error but at Grotius' intended text. I have therefore opted to accept the text as it stands, but print the word in italics to indicate the problem, and given the (probably) intended meaning in the translation. In 5.65 the word is used correctly. A similar pattern of two near-identical errors appears in 1.52 and 1.62 where the names Iohannes Montiniacus and Carolus Arscotius are used, but where Florentius Montiniacus and Philippus Arscotius would have been correct. It stands out that in both cases the wrong first name appears again later in the same line, raising the possibility of assuming an haplographic type of error (either by Grotius or the copyist) to solve the problem. In both cases the text has been left as it is, but printed in italics, as above.

Although Grotius' 'Tacitist' Latin in the AH is not easy, the difficulties are not in the spelling or punctuation, and interventions have therefore been reduced to a minimum. There are no accents on the Latin. A division of the text into paragraphs has been introduced by the present editor. Since the critical apparatus is small anyway, some of Peerlkamp's, Boot's and Muller's proposals have been included in the apparatus even if they have not been accepted into the main text. As to punctuation, given the fact that Grotius sometimes discusses flaws in the punctuation of his printed works,[1] and that the 1658 octavo edition shows that its editors made an effort to rework the punctuation, the original punctuation has been treated as part of the text and not modernised. Punctuation variants from the 1658 octavo edition have been admitted into the main text when the present editor judged this appropriate; for completeness such decisions have been recorded in the apparatus (even though the impact on the meaning of the text is generally small).

Apart from the two standard modifications given below, spelling has been left as it is in TMD 742, as it poses no problems for the reader even though it is sometimes inconsistent. Only where inconsistencies might affect the understanding of proper names have they been resolved.

- All *j* have been removed in favour of *i*, in line with Grotius' writing practice in the preserved manuscripts;
- *u*/*v* usage is adapted to modern practice (e.g. Ceurii instead of Cevrii 1.12).

Capitalisation in the 1657 and 1658 editions is inconsistent; e.g. *Rex* and *rex* both appear, and idem for *senatus, comes, princeps, senatus, praefecta, pontifex,* while no system is apparent. Since this inconsistency may be obtrusive to a modern reader and the lower-case examples are far more frequent, all instances have here been put in that form. *Ordines* however, in the meaning of 'the States', is almost consistently capitalised in the 1657 edition and this has been maintained. The Blaeu editions are almost consistent[2] in beginning each sentence with a capital, which is different from Grotius' actual writing practice in the *Historiae* manuscripts and other preserved mss. such as *De Iure Praedae*. In the mss. new sentences within one unit of thought frequently open without capital. In the absence of a manuscript of the *Annales* however this feature cannot be restored; therefore the sentence capitalisation of the 1657–1658 editions, which agrees with modern practice, is followed and the few anomalies are normalised.

Interventions not taken from the 1657–1658 editions:

- 1.12 irridere > irrisere
- 1.56 sententiae, > sententiae
- 2.2 securitas, intranti > securitas; intranti
- 2.19 rerum > reorum (Peerlkamp)
- 2.26 partibus > portibus
- 2.53 inter quas > inter quae (Boot)
- 2.65 eiusve > eiusne (Peerlkamp)
- 3.10 illos > ipsos
- 3.19 feroce > feroci
- 3.41 Sillesii > Sellesii (cp. 3.3)

[1] E.g. *Briefwisseling* vol. 2, no. 1012 (26 Sept. 1625 to Willem de Groot, on *De Antiquitate*).

[2] Exceptions are *intranti* in § 2.1 and the sentences beginning *an non*... and *ita et*... in § 5.43, p. 105.

- 5.4 ultra > intra (Boot)
- 5.70 pretia > pretia [et]

Problematic, but unchanged places:
- 1.5 impigre
- 1.37 impiger
- 1.52 Iohannes /Florentius: original kept in main text, correction in a.c.
- 1.62 Carolus /Philippus: original kept in main text, correction in a.c.

1.1. Sigla

1657: TMD 741 and TMD 742, or the folio editions of 1657
1657a: TMD 741 (the first edition of 1657)
1657b: TMD 742 (the second edition of 1657)
1658: 1658 octavo edition, TMD 743
italics: a reading which is apparently intended by Grotius and grammatically correct, but problematic in terms of content, see explanation in apparatus.
[...] square brackets: word(s) added by the editor
Burmannus: notes in Burman's copy, Amsterdam UL, KF 62-4241.
Peerlkamp: reading poposed in P. Hofman Peerlkamp's copy in Leiden UL, 1499 D34
Boot: reading proposed by J.C. Boot in the article 'Hugo Grotius et Cornelius Tacitus'
Muller: reading proposed in Muller, *De Groots Annales et Historiae*, pp. 191–194.
scripsimus: reading proposed by the present editor
del(evit): removed by ...

In comparison with the Dutch edition of this translation of 2014 (*Kroniek*), the paragraph separations have been changed in 3.9, 3.30, 5.13 and 5.22 so as to harmonise sentence and paragraph endings in all cases.

1.2. Neo-Latin aspects

In addition to the discussion of Grotius' Latin style in § 7, the following remarks on Grotius' use of Latin can be added:

Spelling

unquam, nunquam, quanquam, quicquid
praelium
concio
promtus, ademtio, contemtus, consumtus, diremtus
poena, poenitentiam, foemina (consistent), *foecundus, coetus*
sylva, hyems, lachryma, hybernare

queis and *quibus*
oportuna and *opportunus* (once, 2.4), *oppidum*
nuntius and *nuncius* (2.31/5.19, inconsistent)
solicitatus and *sollicitudine* (inconsistent)

Influence or borrowings from legal Latin
[*ita*] *ut* as in 'id est', 'meaning that' 4.2, 4.17
cautum 1.28, 1.39, 3.9 *cautio* 3.1
subsessores 1.39
responsa 1.39
libellos 1.39
crimen cuiusquam inscribere 1.41, cp. Codex 9.35.11
eo nomine 2.18
dolus 2.62
alienare 2.65
res soli 2.65
pignoratio 2.23
novae tabulae 2.60
foeneratores
aestimatores
evictiones 2.65
rata [*iudicia, acta*] 2.65, 3.35
hoc titulo inscriptis 3.1
mancipare 3.18, 4.4
imminutio 4.49
pignus obligatum 5.8
reatus 5.23
contra quam 5.24 for 'contrary to', 'in contravention of' (usage from Justinian's *Digests*)

Other syntactical observations
- *probabiliori venia* 2.42 as absolute ablative
- unwarranted use of the historical infinitive in e.g. 1.38, 2.40
- 2.25 *audacissimus quisque extorres et metuentes* and 3.10 *maximus quisque dissident*: quisque + superlative and verb in the plural; rare in classical Latin for masc. and fem., according to Lewis & Short.

2.
About this translation

The translation has been made on the basis of the octavo Latin edition of 1658 and my Dutch translation of 2014 (Grotius, *Kroniek*). Goris' Dutch translation of 1681 has been consulted sometimes for clarifications of the Latin. The 17th-century English and French translations (see § 11.6 above) have not been used. My early draft version of book 1 was revised by Cynthia Damon who suggested many improvements, for which I am extremely grateful. The final revision was done by me, as well as the translations of books 2–5.

For place names in the Low Countries which may have even three variants (i.e. Dutch, French or Anglicised) I have generally followed the forms used in Israel, *Dutch Republic,* unless there was a good reason to use a different form. Clarification appears in a note where this was deemed useful.

With respect to personal names, the form more usual in English has been adopted; Maurice for Maurits, etc. In the case of William of Orange (1534–1584), which name in English is also often used for his great-grandson William (1650–1702, king of England and Scotland from 1689–1702; or 'Willem III' in Dutch), the form *Orange* has been retained since Grotius' Latin consistently uses *Arausionensis*, and the use of an alternative like William the Silent would stray too far from the original.

HUGO GROTIUS

ANNALES DE REBUS BELGICIS

EDITED BY JAN WASZINK

HUGONIS GROTII

ANNALIUM BELGICORUM

Liber Primus

1 Bellum scribere institui, nostris temporibus nobilissimum, quod sociale haud immerito dixeris; dum Hispani Belgaeque, sueti iisdem imperiis populi, et iisdem saepe in armis victores, inter se concurrunt: quanquam et civilis in speciem transiit, inventis domi partibus, sub principis et legum nomine. Regendi, seu pugnandi, **(2)** artes spectamus, nulla foecundior exemplorum materies; nec unquam tam iniqua contentione tamdiu acriterque certatum. Iacta multo ante hostilitatis semina mireris, et, postquam auxit, vim et fraudes potentiorum, infirmorum desperationem, nova foedera, et intus iterum dissidia, externas denique gratias infoeliciter quaesitas. Quibus accessere reliquum in tempus oppidorum et castellorum expugnationes, infesti exercitus, nonnunquam et praelia, maris cursus, longa obsidia, nullum belli genus sine insigni documento.

2 Sed haec palam visitata ex quo firmatae res partium, et cuncta in vim verterunt, facilius assequar, quae et ipse propiora habeo, et alii non item praecepere. Priora belli secretis incerta, casibus turbida, claros scriptores iam habent; etiam Latino sermone. Sed quando sine his ne illa quidem satis intelligas, haud incongruens reor, tumultuum causas, et quae initio abusque intercessere, supra repetere; ut brevi inspectu, quid cuique consilii cum eventu comparetur. Est sane ea rerum gestarum magnitudo, ut peregrina etiam ingenia in scribendi curam adverterit: sed hoc nos magis adversus patriam ingrati, posterorum commodis invidi tenemur; si, quae tanto propius datum cognoscere, exactiori memoria fraudamus. Nam et nostratium plerique scriptores vanis rumoribus et incompertis, ut quaeque partium studio vulgabantur, credulitatem legentium decepere: tum si cui vera noscendi cupido, aut occasio fuit, contentus et hic velut diurna componere. Mihi populi motus, et rebus praesidentium meditamenta, et unde provecta dominatio, ubi desierit, aperire animus.

3 Quae gentes Rheni insulam et utrinque adsita, ad fretum usque Morinorum et Amasium flumen, colunt; hinc ad Germaniam, inde ad Belgicam veterem pertinent. Sed Germanica plerisque origo, et lingua: unde una cura belli et libertatis; donec commercia et suas artes Romani invexere, socii, aut victores. Mansit tamen armorum laus, sub auxiliis interim, et per rebellionem, exercita virtute. Post, ubi

HUGO GROTIUS

ANNALS OF THE WAR IN THE LOW COUNTRIES

Book 1

1 I have set out to describe a war, the most celebrated of our time, which could be called a 'War of the Allies'[1] for good reasons, insofar as the Spanish and the Dutch fell upon each other,[2] peoples habituated to being under the same rulers, and often victorious in the same campaigns. Yet the war also took the form of a civil war once rival parties had emerged internally in the name of the prince and of the laws. Whether it is the art of ruling[3] or of fighting one is considering, **(2)** no richer source of models for imitation can be found: nor has so unequal a conflict ever continued for so long, and with such intensity. You will marvel at the seeds of hostility, sown long before, and, after the hostility matured, at the violence and deviousness of the powerful, the desperation of the weak, the unprecedented alliances and the renewal of internal division, and finally at the inauspicious search for foreign favours. To these accrued at other times captures of towns and strongholds, hostile armies, frequent battles, sea voyages, long sieges—no type of warfare remaining without a remarkable instance.

2 This history, which is easy to access from the time when sides were taken and everything converged on violence, I shall quite easily do justice to; for I have witnessed it myself from closer by, and others for their part have not related the events in quite the same way. The earlier phases of the war—uncertain with secrets, confused with random incidents—have already found distinguished authors, in Latin even. But since without these you would achieve no decent grasp of the subsequent episodes, I think it not unsuitable to start by recounting the causes of the uprisings and the occurrences from the very beginning, so that everybody's plans can be compared with their outcome. The importance of these events is manifestly such as to draw even foreign talents to the task of writing; which would make us the more guilty of ingratitude to our country, and of unconcern for the interests of posterity, if we deprive the events which we have been granted to know from so much closer at hand of a more exact recording. For even in our own day many writers have fooled the credulity of their readers with empty rumours and unsubstantiated reports spread around with partisan zeal, and even those with the desire or opportunity to know the truth have been content to write a kind of day-to-day reports. My intention is to reveal the stirrings of the people, the designs of those in charge, whence tyranny advanced, and where it left off.

3 The peoples living on the island in the Rhine and the adjoining areas on both banks, from there to the Channel and up to the river Ems, belong to the ancient Germania on the one side and to ancient Belgica on the other. The origin of most is German, as is their tongue. As a result, their sole concern is war and freedom. Until the Romans introduced trade and its accompanying arts, they were either allies to Rome or victorious over it. They nevertheless retained their distinction in arms, their courage now being exercised in

plurimae nationes, velut signo dato, orbem Romanum irrupere, omnis hic tractus in ius Francorum concessit; donec scissa potentia, pars penes Galliae dominos, pars penes imperatores Germanos adhaeresceret. Utrique autem, praeter civitates sacrorum reverentia dicatas episcopis, cum primum Christianorum nomen invalesceret, quod longius ipsi aberant, praefectos dedere; qui regerent, tuerentur, comitum, ducum, aut simili vocabulo. **(3)** Duces ad bellum missi vocabantur, quibus comites attributi rationes procurabant, iudiciis praesidebant.

4 Sed hi atque illi, sua virtute, provincialium studiis, regum socordia, vix credibile est, brevi quantum rem[1] auxerint. Iam primum cunctis benefaciendo, sibi auctoritatem, et potentiam comparare; nec in bello audacia maior, quam pace religio et aequitas erant. His artibus muniti, pro praefectura perpetuam atque haereditariam ditionem obtinuere; quod eo facilius concessum est, quia ingruentibus bellis pericula cuncta promptius adituri erant, si res suas defenderent. Ea enim tempestate, maria et littora pene omnia Danorum et Normannorum classibus obsidebantur. Non multo post, metu aut gratia exempto clientelae, aut fracta vi maioris dominatus, etsi imaginem retinebant, summum, sed legitimum, imperium populi benevolentia stabilivere.

5 Secreti principibus agri, vectigalia modica; sed tamen ad dignitatem sustinendam satis: nam avaritia, luxus, et quae alia mala haud ita pridem invaluere, procul habebantur. Sola imperitandi libido aderat, antiquissimum malum. Hinc inter se, aut cum finitimis, perpetuo bellarunt; suo, non externo, milite: nam pro tutandis finibus certatim omnes excubabant; si ultra principem duceret gloriae cupiditas, ne tum quidem *impigre*[2] sequebantur, spe laudis et praemiorum.

6 Nobilitati a victoribus agri clientelares dabantur, oppidanis immunitas, sua iura, leges, magistratus, munimenta libertatis: nec ante accepti in imperium successores, quam munera haec, quibus data erant, iureiurando affirmassent. Penes utrumque ordinem, nobilium et oppidanae plebis, reipublicae cura antiquitus fuit; quibusdam in locis accessit tertius, sacerdotum. Hi legationibus, ubi necesse erat, coibant: hi maximis de rebus consulebantur; nec nisi cunctis volentibus indicere tributa, statum, qui erat, rerum mutare, ne nummi quidem pretium novare, fas erat. Adeo cavebatur, etiam cum boni principes essent, ne malis fieri liceret. Munera publica nobilissimus et optimus quisque, civium ex numero, administrabant; peregrini aula, curia, honoribus arcebantur.

7 His moribus, atque hac republica diu aequo iure agitatum est. Inde paulatim exortae seditiones florentes et divites populos attriverunt; donec per multas victorias, affinitates, pactiones, plurimae gentes in Burgundionum ditionem concessere. Qui orti domo regnatrice, pugnaces, callidi, conari plurimum posse, primorum discordiis armare **(4)** potentiam, his minari, dare illis, polliceri.

[1] rem *1657, 1658* *del. Peerlkamp*

[2] impigre *1657, 1658* pigre *vel* haud impigre *Boot (cf. 1.37, et Intr., Principles of this edition; vide et* impiger *5.65)*

Rome's auxiliary forces, and in a revolt.[4] After this period, when a great many nations, as if at a signal given, burst into the Roman empire, this entire tract came under the control of the Franks, until, with that power split asunder, part of it adhered to the rulers of France, part to the German Emperors. In each part, however (except for the cities made over to bishops out of reverence for things sacred in the time when Christianity first began to gain strength), these lords, since they resided too far away themselves, put governors in charge to rule and defend, with the title of assistant (count),[5] commander (duke), or other such terms. **(3)** Those sent for warfare were called dukes; counts assigned to these handled accounts and presided over courts.

4 However, it is scarcely credible how much dukes as well as counts extended their possessions in short order, owing to their own talent, the favor of the inhabitants, the passivity of the kings. At the beginning they procured for themselves authority and power by serving the benefit of all. But great as their audacity in war was, in peacetime their piety and equity equaled it. Fortified by these skills, they obtained perpetual and hereditary rule in place of their deputed powers. This was the more readily ceded to them because with wars threatening they would confront every danger more promptly if they were defending their own holdings. For in these turbulent times almost every ocean and shore was under attack from fleets of Danes and Normans. Not much later, when fear or gratitude among the Emperor's clientele had evaporated, or because the power of his greater dominion had been broken, they obtained a lasting, but legitimate, hold of the supreme power, with the approval of the people—although outwardly they preserved the appearance of the Emperor's dominion.

5 These princes had their own farmland, and taxation was moderate but sufficient for supporting their dignity. For greed, extravagance, and what other evils have grown up in recent times were kept at a distance. Their only passion was for command, a most ancient evil. As a result they were continually at war with one another or with their neighbours, using soldiers of their own, not foreign-born. For they all vied in vigilance over the integrity of their territory. But even when occasionally greed for glory led a prince beyond his own borders, they followed *actively*, out of hope for distinction and rewards.

6 To the nobility lands were given in loan by the victors, to townsfolk immunities, rights of their own, laws, and magistrates: all bulwarks of freedom.[6] Successors were not confirmed in power until they confirmed these donations by oath to whom they were given. Of old, the care for the common good resided with the two estates of nobility and townsfolk; in some places a third estate complemented these, that of the clergy. These States assembled by representatives when need required it and took counsel concerning the most weighty affairs. To impose financial exactions, or change the organisation of the government, or even to update the value of mere coins, except by unanimous consent, was forbidden. As diligently did they take care, even when their princes were good, that they not be given a chance to become evil. The most noble and virtuous of the citizens handled public responsibilities; foreigners were kept out of the court, the senate, and public offices.

7 By these customs and in this form of government affairs were long conducted equitably. Subsequently conflict, having arisen gradually, wore down these flourishing and wealthy nations, until a long series of victories, marriage alliances, treaties brought most of them into the control of the Burgundians. These, sprung from a royal house, warlike, crafty, tried for the greatest power, armed **(4)** their domination by sowing discord among the nobility, threatened some, benefited others, brandished promises.

8 Ita brevi cuncta eo vergere, ubi poena et merces erant; promptumque promiscuae licentiae vim destruere, egregio iuris ordine, Francicum ad instar. Nam et suus cuique nationi senatus, et pluribus commune iudicium Machliniae imponitur; quo facilius unius civitatis speciem acciperent. Abducti ab armis et coetibus populi. Institutum et collegium aureae pellis nomine, quo adscitos undique, qui genere illustres et meritis spectabantur, decus sibi ac praesidium principes circumdedere. Ius populi inter has artes Ordines tuebantur, quos cunctis ex nationibus commune in concilium acciri, depletum bellis aerarium, aut quae alia necessitas, saepe flagitabant. Eo missi fortia saepe pro republica, et, quod addebat audaciam, ut mandata loquebantur. Neque vero arces, aut pace miles, nisi pauca praesidia finibus extremis et Gallorum mobilitate suspectis: simul adversus subita trium millium equitatus, flos ipse nobilitatis, quos popularium clarissimi regebant. At nulla classis, cum privatarum navium copia, etiam improvisos ad usus, sufficeret.

9 Transfuso hoc fortunae cumulo in Austriacam familiam, quanquam accessione Hispaniae vis increvit, mitia imperantium ingenia potentiam temperando auxere; qua arte libertas, magis etiam quam vi, expugnatur. Nam in cogentes resistendo crescit ferocia, comitati et mansuetudini ultro subitur; donec corruptis licentia moribus, concedi solita imperantur; ex obsequio servitium fit. Interea abstentae ab armis plebi opificia et negotiandi commoda ostentantur, augendorum vectigalium, et ut innoxii atque florentes privati cura publicum exuerent.

10 Maximum incrementum Hispanica coniunctio attulit. Sed iam tum prudentiores, cum opes imperantium nimium praevalescerent, Hispanorum e moribus, quos bellorum commilitio inspexerant, ac sua diversitate, mutationem reipublicae formidine quadam augurabantur. Nam dum finitimae gentes pari origine, studiis iisdem accreverunt, facile tum fraterno iure inter se agebant. Hispanis Belgisque diversa pleraque, et quibus conveniunt acrius colliduntur. Bellica virtute cunctis a saeculis utrique insignes; nisi quod hi desueverant, illi per Italicas et transmarinas expeditiones longa disciplina et praemiis excitabantur. Sed Belgae attenti sane, et quaestus studio laborum tolerantes, pacem ideo et commercia expetunt; non tamen ut iniurias ferant. Alieni nulla gens abstinentior; sua fortiter defendunt. Inde una orbis **(5)** regione creberrimae urbes, munitaeque ad mare primum et amnes, passim postea, convenarum et sobolis multitudine. Ita post depulsam septentrionis rabiem, octo per saecula mansere, externis armis invicti et indirepti.

8 Thus in short order everything bent toward profit and punishment, which offered the occasion to destroy the force of widespread licence by an excellent legal system, modeled on that of France. To each province was assigned its own council, and a common lawcourt was placed at Mechelen in order that the provinces might the more easily acquire the form of a single state. The populace was made to leave weapons and mobbing aside. A company was established called that of the Golden Fleece with which the princes clothed men drawn from everywhere who were considered illustrious in birth and distinguished for services, to be an honour and bulwark to themselves.[7] The rights of the common man amidst these tactics were guarded by the States.[8] Often, a treasury depleted by war or some other pressing need required these to be summoned from all provinces to a common assembly. The emissaries often had to pronounce brave words in defence of the common interest and (which added to their boldness) without deviating from their mandates. However, there were no citadels, or soldiers in peacetime, except for a few garrisons at the country's outer edge, suspect area because of the stirrings of the French. At the same time there was a cavalry of three thousand to cope with sudden eventualities, the very flower of the nobility, commanded by the most distinguished of their own countrymen.[9] There was no fleet, since the supply of private ships was sufficient even for unforeseen requirements.

9 When this storehouse of good fortune had passed into Habsburg hands, and although the power of this house grew by the accession of Spain, the mild character of its rulers increased their control through moderation, since this is the art that overcomes liberty, even more effectively than violence will. For resistance against compulsion makes vehemence flare up; to friendship and gentleness it willingly submits, until the time when licence undermines decency, and things that used to be granted are imposed by command; then compliance turns into servitude. Meanwhile the fruits of industry and commerce—matters that increased revenues—were held available to a populace kept away from arms; all in order that this folk, as harmless men prosperous in the care for their own, would leave politics alone.

10 The conjunction with Spain brought a huge growth. But already at that time men with better insight predicted, with a certain amount of fear (since the rulers' resources had grown enormously) a change in the political system. This they based on the customs of the Spanish, which they had studied during their service with them in wars, and on their differences with themselves. For so long as neighbouring peoples with equivalent origins and identical wishes merge, they interact easily and in fraternal relationships. Between Spaniards and the Netherlanders however most things are different, and they collide the more sharply in those matters which they have in common. Both peoples had in all ages been distinguished for martial valour; except that the latter had lost the habit of it, while the former were kept vigorous by continuous discipline and rewards through campaigns in Italy and across the Ocean. But the Dutch, frugal indeed and willing to suffer hard labour in their zeal for profit, with this in view seek peace and trade, but not so much as to put up with injury. No people is more abstinent with respect to others' possessions; their own they defend stoutly. Consequently in their little corner of the world **(5)** there are cities exceedingly numerous and strengthened, originally near the sea and the rivers; later everywhere, strengthened by a multitude of newcomers and progeny. And thus, after the furies from the North[10] had been driven off, they survived for eight centuries unconquered by foreign arms and unplundered.

11 At Hispaniae, postquam sub diversis victoribus multum de eorum moribus traxerat, tandem ad Gothos possessio rediit; quos, ex quo originis sedisque miscuerant ingenia, nobis prisci novique auctores describunt, animi adversus labores et pericula invicti, dubium gloriae an opum avidiores, usque ad aliorum contemtum superbos, sacrorum quidem venerabundos, et beneficiis haud infidos, sed ultione adeo flagrantes et victoria efferos, ut in hostem nihil turpe sit, nihil illicitum. Adversa haec Belgis, genti innocenter callidae; caeterum Germaniam inter et Galliam, ut positu loci, ita moribus temperatae; non extra amborum vitia, non sine virtutibus. Haud facile fallas, haud temere insultes. Nec divinorum cultu Hispanis olim cessisse indicio est, quod unanimes, ex quo Christum semel induerant, non Normannorum armis adacti, ut professionem mutarent; non ullo infecti damnato antehac errore, tantum pietati impenderunt, ut necesse fuerit sacrorum ministris possidendi modum praescribere. In universum utrisque insitum colere principes, et admirari: sed Belgae leges supra putant, quo obtentu saepe turbatum. Castellani regnari amant aliquanto, quam nonnullae Hispanorum gentes, addictius; et tamen, quantamcumque usurpant ipsi libertatem, in aliis non ferunt. Maximum hinc periculum, quod veluti in duo imperia divisa principum sollicitudine, nec Belgae gratia superiorem ferre quenquam poterant, nec Hispani parem.

12 Cunctis sane populis, qui dominandi libidine aguntur, ubi prima successerint, proximum, socias nationes suas sub leges trahere, praefectos et iudices dare, imponere tributa, ut communium virium penes ipsos usus et arbitrium sit. Ita tum Hispani, soliti Italiam regere, Americam perpopulari, in Belgas, qui principum successione velut aequo foedere coierant, ius idem, aut causam belli quaerebant. Neque exciderant animo Adriani Florentii, qui mox pontifex Romanus, sancti quidem et probi, sed Batavi tamen, invidiosa per Hispaniam auctoritas; Croïaci fastus, et Ceurii rapaces manus, quos penes cuncta sacerdotiorum, honorumque venalia: queis vix per arma vitatis, repposituri vicem haud inique sibi videbantur. Assentando igitur validiores irrisere[3] vanam imperii imaginem, ubi **(6)** magistratus populi esset beneficium, ubi vix tenuem ad res magnas pecuniam principes eblandirentur. Frustra sane trans mare Oceanum et trans mare Tyrrhenum terminos ferri, si dominis apud suos serviendum sit.

13 Nec tamen illos flexere, quos in Belgica eductos patriae caritas, et nota gentis modestia, devinxerant. Quanquam Carolus imperator de vertendo statu, componendisque in regnum civitatibus serio consultavit: praesertim ex quo Flandriam Atrebatesque, ab omni Francorum iure liberatos, victoriae Ticinensis habuerat pretium. Sed diversis moribus, institutis, legibus deterritus est; nec tollere audebat. Enimvero provincias Hispanorum facere adeo noluit, ut contra saepe testatus sit, si illorum superbia cum harum gentium patientia committeretur, periculum ingens

[3] validiores irrisere *scripsimus* validiores irridere *1657, 1658* validioribus irridere *Peerlkamp, Boot*

11 Possession of Spain, after under various conquerors it had drawn much from their customs, at length returned to the Goths. Ancient and recent writers describe those to us as of undaunted spirit in the face of trials and dangers, ever since they mixed their character of origin with that of their dwellings; eager—uncertain whether more for glory than for wealth, so arrogant as to be contemptuous of others, respectful however of things sacred and fairly loyal in return for benefits, but so passionate for revenge and wild in victory that against an enemy nothing is shameful, nothing forbidden. With the Lowlanders, this is all just the other way round: they are a people of innocent craftiness and furthermore in customs, as in position, a blend of Germany and France: not free of the faults of both, not without their virtues. You will neither easily fool, nor rashly insult them. That they have never been second to the Spanish in religious devotion appears from the fact that ever from the time they adopted Christianity, they have collectively resisted the pressure of Norman violence to change their creed. Not infected by any condemned error until our times, they attached so much value to their faith that it was necessary to prescribe a limit to the possessions of ministers of the gospel. Generally for both peoples honouring and admiring princes was innate. But the Dutch think laws superior, under which pretext there was often disorder. The people of Castile love to be ruled even a bit more strictly than the other peoples of Spain, and yet the liberty that they demand for themselves, however great or small it be, they do not tolerate in others. Hence a very great danger, with the attention of princes divided as if over two realms: the Dutch were not able to tolerate anyone superior in influence, nor the Spaniards any equal.

12 For all peoples that are moved by a desire for dominance, when the first steps have succeeded, the next is to draw allies under their own laws, to impose governors and judges, to require tribute, in order that the use of and authority over the combined resources should be in their own control. Thus the Spaniards at that time—accustomed to rule Italy, to plunder America—sought the same right, or else an excuse for war, with respect to the people in the Low Countries. These however, through the continuous succession of their princes, had merged with them as if by a treaty on equal footing. Nor had they forgotten the influence, resented all over Spain, of Adrian Florenszoon,[11] soon to become pope and a holy honest man, but a Dutchman nonetheless; or the arrogance of Croy and the rapacious hands in the house of Chièvres,[12] from whom all offices in church and state were available for sale. When these men had with difficulty, and violence, been gotten out of the way, the Spaniards felt they had every right to seek retaliation. Flattering the rulers, therefore, the more powerful men made mock of the empty appearance of an empire in which **(6)** the magistracy was a gift of the people, and where the princes could barely coax out a slender sum for great pursuits. There was no advantage, they said, in boundaries being extended across the Atlantic and across the Tyrrhenian Sea, if the masters had to be slaves at home.

13 These voices did not, however, sway those whom, having been brought up in the Low Countries, a fondness for the country and the remarkable moderation of its people had bound with affectionate ties. And yet Charles V seriously discussed changing the constitution and a transformation of the provinces to a kingdom, most notably from the time when he had obtained Flanders and Artois, freed from all French claims, as a prize of his victory at Pavia.[13] But he was deterred by the difference in customs, institutions, and laws. Nor did he dare abolish these. He was so unwilling to make the provinces over to Spain that he often asserted that if the arrogance of the latter be mingled with the tolerance of the former a huge danger threatened—which was also a censure of his son, who, with a character after

imminere: increpito et filio, qui inter Hispanos nutrita indole, oportunitates harum regionum, ingenia populorum non perinde nosset, aut etiam contemneret.

14 Ipse aequus virtutum iudex partitorque honorum, eundem omnibus populis principem agebat; haud diuturna passus, quae novo regno usurpata Hispani querebantur. Belgas vero praesens, si res ferret, aut per proximas necessitudines, curans. Ei, qui principis vices tuebatur, triplex consiliantium classis aderat: uni consessui permissum belli pacisque regimen; alteri legum cura, aequitatis temperatio, et in publicis nationum controversiis iudicandi potestas; tertio aerarii et principis opes, ac necessitates. Primum illum coetum ex nobilissimis Belgarum componi solitum, rerum quoque tractandarum magnitudine eminentem, Senatum proprio nomine dicemus.

15 At Philippus inter regna et adulantes acta iuventute, ad haec induta gravitate austera, parsimonia verborum, turbae fuga, formatus Hispanorum ad mores, ne sermone quidem alio adibatur. Pertracto igitur patre, ut privato otio senectam conderet, illum rebus imponere festinant; cui avita dominandi cupido, nondum experimentis repressa, haud facile finem aut modum patiebatur. Neque vero dubium est, quin pulcherrimum imperii instrumentum Hispanorum fidem ac virtutem crediderit. Quanta regiis ingeniis cupido incedat subruendi leges, quae vim potentiae infringunt, insignes principum, aut populorum, ruinae vetera ac nova documenta extant. Idem Philippi studium quidam postea et Hispanorum populi sensere. Sed Belgae (ita descriptas ante gentes ex maiore sui parte nominabo) fracti quidem iam ut **(7)** parerent, sed violenti imperii ne tum quidem patientes, eo maiore cum usu frenum accepturi erant, quod egregiae hinc occasiones in proxima regna terra marique sperabantur.

16 Nec irarum semina aberant. Nam cum Gallicum bellum, domestico certamine quam populi ex usu, Philippus suscepisset, concessa post cunctationes et ambages a communi Ordinum indictio, quasi negare licuisset, praescripta insuper lege, ut ipsi quaestores tributo darent, apud insuetum vel modicae libertati in crimen trahebatur. Ex eo conventus Ordinum, velut coitionem interpretatus, districte inhibuit. Nec dubitabant Hispani offensam accendere, obtritis legibus viam ad honores, pars et in rapinas affectantes. Prudentes ergo quanti esset usus principes possidere, quorum praesentia ante subnixi Belgae non se modo, sed et Hispaniam saepe rexerant; firmata pace Gallicana, iter Philippo in Hispaniam, ceu potiora imperii, persuadent: tum quia turbas in eo regno et Turcam mari valescentem metuebat, tum ut Americae thesauris propius incubaret.

17 Etiam eo tempore nobilitas magnifica, dignitate eximia, sed attritis opibus erat; suo luxu, an principum dolo, qui specie honorum praestantissimum quemque sumptibus exhauserant.

his Spanish upbringing, was not as familiar with the potential of the provinces and the talents of their people, or even expressed contempt.

14 Charles himself, fair in his judgement of virtues and the distribution of offices, acted as prince in identical ways towards all his peoples. He did not let the practices endure which the Spanish complained had only started at the beginning of his reign.[14] To the Lowlanders he showed his care in person, if affairs permitted, or through his closest relatives. Whoever governed in his stead was assisted by three classes of councillors. To one gathering was entrusted the control of war and peace. To a second, concern for the laws, the preservation of equity, and the power of adjudication in controversies between provinces. To the third council were entrusted the funds of the treasury, the prince's possessions, and public expenditure.[15] That first assembly, drawn as custom requires from the highest nobility in the Low Countries, and distinguished for the greatness of its task, we will by its proper name call the Council of State.

15 Philip, his youth spent amidst courts and flattery, clothed himself in response with austere gravity, parsimony of words, and avoidance of the crowd. Brought up in Spanish ways, he was addressed in no other tongue. When his father had been compelled to settle his old age in private retirement, they hastened to put Philip in charge, whose ancestral lust for power, not yet chastened by experience, could hardly tolerate limit or measure. Nor is there any doubt but that he believed that the best instruments of his rule were the Spaniards' faith and virtue. How great a passion enters the hearts and minds of kings for abolishing the laws which curb the force of power, we find testified by striking ruins of princes, or peoples, old and new. This same zeal in Philip the peoples of Spain themselves came to feel later. As for the Netherlanders (thus I shall term the nations described earlier, from their most significant part[16]), previously broken **(7)** to obedience but not even then tolerant of rule by force: they were the more ready to accept the harness since they anticipated outstanding trade opportunities over land and sea from it in the nearby realms.

16 But the seeds of anger had been sown indeed. For when Philip had undertaken war with France owing to dynastic competition rather than for the common good, an impost that was granted by the joint States meetings after delays and evasions—as if a negative answer would have been possible—and to which they had added the condition that the States themselves should provide the men who would collect the revenue, this was taken as a crime by a man unaccustomed even to moderate freedom. He strictly prohibited assemblies of the States henceforth, counting them conspiracies. Nor did the Spaniards hesitate to fan the anger by trampling on the laws and setting their own course for office, some even for plunder. Understanding therefore how important it was to have the princes under their control, whose presence had enabled the Netherlanders in the past to rule not only themselves but often Spain as well, they urged Philip, when the peace with France was firm, to make the journey to Spain, as being more important part of his realm; both because he was concerned about popular uprisings there and the Turk growing strong by sea, and in order that he might lie closer to treasure from America.)

17 At that time the nobility was still magnificent, of the utmost dignity, but with resources worn thin by their own luxuriousness or by scheming of their rulers, who with a pretext of honours had drained the most distinguished men dry with expenses.

1.18. *Portrait of William of Orange* (no signature)

1.33. *Portrait of Margareth of Parma* (no signature)

18 Industria, comitate, solertia anteibat alios Wilhelmus, successione Cabelloniae domus princeps Arausionensium in provincia Gallica; sed origo illi a Nassavia, Germanica gente, quae olim Austriacis aemula imperii certamine, deinde in victricis familiae clientelam concessit. Prima hic ab infantia segregatus a patre, qui Germanicam religionem profitebatur, alumnus aulae, intima apud Carolum admissione, belli ductu et maximis legationibus addidicerat regimen: aderat antiqua gentis claritudo, possessiones per Belgicam amplissimae, animus ingens et celans sui, par animi magnitudini consilium, et quantaevis fortunae capax; crudelitas et avaritia nullo ab ingenio longius abfuere: validus rerum etiam remotissimarum indagine, fidaque rerum omnium memoria; apud subiectos multis illecebris potens: praefecturam habebat Hollandos cum Zelandis et Traiecto. Ea autem potestas et iuris et armorum, intra datos fines, curam complectitur.

19 At Lamoralius, Egmondae comes, Flandriam et Atrebates regens, apertior ingenii, et militariter ferox, multum rebus suis, multum famae credebat; egregiis ad Quintini fanum et Gravelingam de Gallo victoriis laudem et gratiam meritus, nisi nimium imputasset. Hi duo **(8)** caeteros gloria et munere anteibant. Nam Brabantia proprio rectori non paret, communis imperii sedes; caeterae praefecturae infra sunt. Maris imperium, quod per se splendidum est, Mommorantius illustrabat, Hornae comes, inclita Gallorum stirpe.

20 Hos viros tantos atque tales amoliri Hispanis necesse erat, antequam Belgicae potirentur; idque eo facilius factu videbatur, quia dum dignitati student, et cum Hispanorum fastu concertant, magnam rei familiaris iacturam fecerant: itidemque primores reliqui, neutiquam pari opulentia; minorum autem gentium plerique luxu, aut inopi militia, etiam fidem consumpserant. Quibus illi angustiis non ex spe inimicorum continuo de potentia deiecti sunt; sed industriam et vigilantiam intendere, ut quovis modo dignitatem tuerentur: multi publica mala suis remedium, aut obtegumentum quaerebant; parata dissidiis turba, et, ut cuique plurimum spei aut desperationis erat, in partes transgressura.

21 Sternebant Hispanorum audaciae gradum Belgarum inter se procerum certamina, et discors studiis nobilitas; dum pars Arausionensem, et quos iam diximus, alii domus diversas, sectantur. At plebi odium belli, malorum tolerantia, amor quietis, honorum fuga, studium omne circa mercaturam et convivia erat; ut quaererent pecuniam, prodigerentque. Sed hominem caedi et cruciari ob qualemcunque Dei cultum, etiam quibus ea crudelitas formidini non erat, miserabantur. Diu tamen inter gemitus et lacrymas dolor stetit, antequam rectorum artibus eliceretur. De eius rei, quoniam armis causam apud aliquos, apud alios speciem dedit, origine altius disseram.

22 Christianam religionem, sola quondam simplicitate venerandam, mox aggregati diversae philosophiae professores, suae quisque doctrinae placitis, tum Iudaei, Graeci, alii, patriis caeremoniis instruxere; quo maiestatem sacrorum, haud frustra

18 The first of these in energy, grace and skill was William, prince of Orange in France from his succession in the house of Châlon. But he was born in the German house of Nassau, a formerly rival family to the Habsburgs in the contest for empire, which had finally accepted the patronage of the victor's household. From an early age William lived separate from his father, who professed the Lutheran faith. Brought up at court, with intimate access to Charles, he had learned to rule in military commands and important embassies. In addition he carried the brilliance of an ancient family, ample property throughout the Low Countries, a magnanimous spirit good at keeping its own counsel,[17] plus a mind that matched it and was ready for any fortune however great. No human being had cruelty and greed more alien. His understanding of even the most remote topics put him in a position of strength, and he had a reliable memory for everything. Among his subjects his power rested on many inducements: he was stadtholder to the Hollanders together with Zeeland and Utrecht. His authority involved oversight of the judiciary and the military, and was confined within clear boundaries.

19 Lamoral, on the other hand, count of Egmond, ruler of Flanders and Artois, was more open of character and a spirited soldier; he derived much confidence from his achievements and much from his reputation. He would have earned praise and glory for his outstanding victories over the French king at St. Quentin and Gravelines,[18] if he hadn't boasted about it too much himself.[19] These two **(8)** men outstripped the others in glory and office. For Brabant, being the seat of the general government, is not placed under its own governor; the remaining stadtholderships are lower in rank. The naval command, an office splendid in itself, shared in the glory of its holder, Montmorency count of Horne, a nobleman from a distinguished French family.[20]

20 Such great men as these the Spaniards would have to remove first if they were to take control of the Low Countries, and this seemed the more easily feasible since, while they were vying for standing and competing with Spanish arrogance, they had inflicted heavy losses on their family wealth. And so had the rest of the leading men, though from entirely unequal wealth. From the lesser families many had exhausted even their creditworthiness through luxury or on shabby soldiering. In these straits they were not, as their enemies hoped, thrown from power straight away, but rather applied their industry and effort to protecting their standing by any means whatsoever. Many sought a remedy for their own in public troubles, or at least a cover: they turned disagreement into disturbances that would lead to the rise of factions, according to whatever represented one's greatest hope or despair.

21 The competition among the Dutch noblemen paved the way for Spanish boldness, and the nobility was divided in its aims, some following Orange and the men we have mentioned, others different houses. Among the populace there was just loathing of war, endurance of evil, a love of calm, evasion of offices, and an exclusive passion for trade and conviviality, to make money and waste it again. But that a man should be killed and tortured for his faith, whatever it be, was resented even by those who did not fear this cruelty for themselves. Grief long remained between groans and tears, until riot leaders' arts coaxed it out. On the origin of this matter, since it provided some people with a reason for fighting, others with a pretext, I will report in some depth.

22 Once upon a time the Christian faith was admirable for its unique simplicity. Soon a variety of teachers of different philosophical schools, —Jews, Greeks, others—outfitted it with precepts from their own doctrines and ancestral rituals, in order that they might turn

repertam, meliores ad usus verterent. Sed haec libera diu, et privato singulorum, aut ecclesiarum, arbitrio sumpta, paulatim aucto usu, docentium facundia, conciliorum suffragiis in legem ac necessitatem mutata; subnascente temporum barbarie, perque coecas disputandi ambages facile defendebantur. Atque interim Romani episcopi maximae semper auctoritatis, amotis Asiae Aegyptique urbibus, et aemulatrice Byzantio, regnum quoddam sacrorum, sibique summam imperii, Cardinales assessores, inde longam potestatum seriem stabiliverunt; detrectante nemine, quia **(9)** pleraeque Europae gentes mores Christianos missis Roma formatoribus acceperant. Hinc Latini passim ritus, et in sacris sermo. At illi, postquam divina sui iuris fecerant, nova edere decreta, vetera interpretari, sacros libros vulgi manibus excutere, perniciosum dictantes, si rei maximae iudicium indocta curiositas acciperet. Ita promptum cuncta suos ad honores et quaestum componere; sacerdotumque licentia eo vitiorum deventum est, ut remediis opus et ipsi faterentur.

23 Sed subita litterarum luce, quae novo vulgandi reperto saeculorum caliginem dispulerat, exstiterunt, qui caeteris cum artibus purgare religionem polliciti, res cunctas sacrarum ad litterarum testimonia revocarent. Gratum id populis, qui sumtuum et iniuriarum pertaesi, simul gaudebant, quod non anxia formidine coecove obsequio, sed fiducia maiore, ac paucioribus praeceptis sperare coelum iubebantur. Ne principibus quidem nolentibus erat infringi sacerdotum potentiam, quae iam et regale fastigium sibi subiecerat. Sed ubi conspectum est, non haerere manum vulneribus, ingenia turbida intercurrere, quae nihil quietum paterentur; publice impetranda privatim sumi, iamque inter ipsos discordiam, nec esse qui iudicio componeret; quamque non facilis convelli illa tot saeculorum compages, displicuit incomposita rerum facies, ut ad coercendos plebis animos non idem valitura.

24 Iamque resuscitata Hussi per Germaniam, Wiclefi per Britanniam, Valdensium per Galliam placita, inde in Belgicam transmota, conventu incolarum, contactu externi militis, commerciis denique vulgabantur. Caeterum plurimas impias atque nefarias sectas inducta semel mutandi licentia invexit. Nec aliam fuisse terram id genus monstrorum per haec tempora Belgica feraciorem, facile crediderit, siquis probrosas in Christum Davidis Delphici, et seditiosas Ioannis Bucoldi Lugdunensis sententias penetraverit. Quorum Batavus uterque, caelestis afflatus simulatione, vitreorum ille pictor, vitam haud inopem sectamque sibi superstitem paravit: vestium concinnator alter, regnum apud Monasterienses, et bellum, quanquam infoelici exitu, molitus est.

25 Sapientissimos ego principum comperio in diversos religionum, pro magnitudine erroris, pro numero peccantium, remedia constituisse. Ubi vires aequaverant, geminae interdum sectae in publicum accipiebantur, acri legum custodia, nequid eo obtentu turbarent. Alias, quos auditos imperator et **(10)** concilium damnaverant, eiecti templis, aut, siqua suspicio gravior, etiam privatis coetibus arcebantur. Nec illos plane damnaveris, qui prava et moribus noxia docentes exilio, aut honorum

religion's majesty, invented for good reasons, to better uses. But for a long time these ceremonies remained free, being adopted according to the private decision of individuals or churches. Gradually however, as they came into more widespread use, the eloquence of teachers and council decisions changed them into laws and necessities. This was easily justified in times of rising barbarism and impermeable labyrinths of disputation. Meanwhile the bishops of Rome, who had obtained a lasting supremacy once the cities of Asia and Egypt were lost along with Rome's rival Byzantium, established a virtual dominion over religion, with overall control for themselves, cardinals as associates, and thence a long series of connected authorities. None objected, since **(9)** most European peoples had learned Christian practices from teachers sent from Rome. Hence Latin rites everywhere, and Latin as religion's tongue. These Romans however made everything religious their province, issued new decrees, ruled anew on established matters, took Scripture from the hands of the common people, declaring it pernicious if untaught curiosity should form judgments about the most important matter of all. Thus it was easy to arrange everything for their own authority and profit; and priestly licence descended to such a degree of vice that they themselves admitted the need for remedies.

23 However, in the sudden light of letters, which with the new method of publication dispelled the fog of centuries, there stood forth men who, promising to purify religion along with the other arts, referred all matters to the testimony of Scripture. This pleased the people, who, sick of the expenditures and the abuses, rejoiced likewise that they were enjoined to hope for heaven no longer via anxious fear or blind obedience but with greater confidence and fewer rules. Nor was it against the princes' wishes to break the power of the priests, as it had submitted even royal eminence to itself. But soon it became clear that this helping hand would not stop at healing wounds, that "disruptive types are getting involved who will leave nothing quiet", that "matters of public importance are taken up privately", and that already "there is discord among the innovators themselves, and no one to settle it with a judgement"; and it was realised how difficult it would be to tear apart the framework that had existed for so many centuries. Then the disorderly state of affairs began to disappeal, as being not equally effective at restraining the movements among the populace.[21]

24 By this time the teachings of Hus were resuscitated in Germany, of Wyclif in Britain, of the Waldenses in France; transferred thence to the Low Countries, these creeds were spread at popular gatherings, through contact with foreign soldiers, and finally by trade. Once introduced, the licence to experiment brought in many impious and sinful sects. Nor did any other land in those times produce more of this sort of monstrosity than the Low Countries, as anyone would easily believe who got to the bottom of the shameful and seditious opinions about Christ held by David of Delft and Jan Bucholt of Leiden. Both Hollanders, the one, a painter of glass windows under a pretense of divine inspiration, earned himself a comfortable living and a sect that survived him; the other, who repaired clothing, achieved a kingship at Münster and a war, albeit with an unfortunate outcome.

25 I find that the sagest of princes established remedies against people of divergent religion in proportion to the magnitude of their error and the number of offenders. Where they were of equal strength, sometimes official recognition was given to two sects, under the strict eye of the law, lest under cover of religion they cause upheaval. Elsewhere, after being heard by the Emperor **(10)** and a council they were ejected from the churches or even, if there was a heavier suspicion, prevented from gathering in private. Nor should one

facultatumque ademtione mulctaverunt; donec paulatim melioribus assuescerent. Sed penes magistratus id iudicium, qui tali cognitione non suas iniurias exsequebantur. Sacerdotibus permissum, imprudentia devios corrigere, et sacrorum participatione arcere. Tum vero legitimus cognoscendi ordo, facta arguebantur, cogitata impune erant. Sed in sanguinem saevire eorum, quos Dei communis et imperantium reverentia teneret, episcopis inhumanum, nec principibus tutum videbatur.

26 At Romani pontifices, sensim eo egressi, ut ius solertia partum terrore munirent; quae principes, formidini suae nimium faventes, in perduellionis reos dura atque acerba constituerant, eadem voluere in eos, qui decretis suis obluctarentur, ut Deo rebelles, usurpari. Nec tantum episcopis iniunctum suam ditionem lustrare, sed et, quae res initium cepit ferme ante hos annos quadringentos, mos ipsis, quo visum insuper mittere quaesitores amplissima potestate. Hi adsessores sibi pro arbitrio adsciscere, quosvis, quacunque in potestate constitutos, sacramento interrogare. Ea arte non domuum modo, sed et animorum arcana penetrantur, cum ut quisque periurii metuens, ita se maxime prodat. Quanquam et alias latere vix possunt, quibus ante divum simulacra, panemque sacratum in templo, aut ubi publice circumfertur, procumbere religio est. Suspicio ad carcerem, indicium leve ad torquendum satis. Nec saltem testes audire reo, aut refellere, concessum; quasi testibus ipsis ac veritati inde periculum foret. Iudicibus profanis permissum, duntaxat sacerdotali sententia damnatos punire, quorum multi suppliciorum saevitia, velut pietate, certabant. Alii, qui providerent istum iudicandi ordinem non odiis tantum, sed et avaritiae, patere; quippe cum bona fisco cederent, nec sine quaestu delaturae exercerentur,[4] eripi sibi notionem non ferebant.

27 Sed omnium acerrime per Hispaniam quaestiones habitae, electis ei ministerio monachis e Dominici familia, veteri instituto adversus Hebraeos et Mauros, qui, coacti a regibus Christianos ritus subire, ad eiuratos errores furtim relabebantur. Quod primo haud ingratum barbaricarum gentium odio, inde promiscue cunctis incubuit, mira indagandi sagacitate: custoditi quippe sermones, etiam **(11)** silentium, fallaces amicitiae, et a latere accusator; ut iam facile appareret neminem esse tam innocentem, qui illis invitis posset salutem et dignitatem tueri. Quod non ad invidiam auctum, sed ex vero tradi, haud diffitebuntur, qui audierint in Hispania, et per omnem fere Italiam, gravissimos motus, eius inquisitionis causa, ab hominibus Romanae ecclesiae addictis, quin ipsa in urbe Roma, excitatos.

28 In Belgica de religione primus omnium Carolus edixit, postquam auditum in Wormatiensi Germaniae conventu Lutherum damnaverat. A mulctis ad sanguinem ventum est, ob iudicum lenitatem repetitae septies, et intentae leges. Cautum inter caetera, ne qui libri, nisi Lovaniensibus magistris laudati, in vulgus exirent,

[4] patere; quippe… eripi *1657* patere, (quippe … exercerentur,) eripi *1658*

condemn those outright who punished the teachers of doctrines depraved or harmful to morality with exile or deprivation of office and power until, gradually, they re-accustomed themselves to better ways. But in any case the judgement resided with the magistrates,[22] who in such an investigation were not prosecuting injuries to themselves. Entrusted to priests was the correction of those who went astray out of ignorance or banning them from participation in religious services. In those years the investigation procedure was still subject to laws—deeds were accused, thoughts were not punished. And to vent one's rage on the blood of men restrained by a common reverence for God and princes alike seemed to bishops inhumane, to princes not even safe.

26 But the popes of Rome gradually descended to protecting rights acquired by cunning, with instruments of terror. And they wanted the same harsh and cruel measures that princes, yielding too far to their own fear, had established against men accused of treason, to be used against those who resisted their decrees, as rebels against God. Not only was it enjoined upon bishops to travel around their own territory but it was also their custom to send, in addition, inquisitors with the broadest powers to wherever they deemed necessary—a practice that took its beginning roughly four hundred years ago.[23] These men chose "assessors" as they saw fit and investigated under oath men located anywhere and of whichever dignity. By this means they penetrate the secrets not only of houses but even of people's thoughts, for people expose themselves just as unmistakably as they fear perjury (although even elsewhere it is scarcely possible to hide for those who have scruples about throwing themselves down in front of images of the gods, or the consecrated bread in a temple, or where it was carried about in public.) Suspicion sent one to prison, a shred of evidence was enough for torture. It was not even granted to a defendant to hear or refute witnesses, as if that would produce danger to the witnesses themselves or to truth. It was entrusted to secular judges to punish people merely convicted by an ecclesiastical verdict. Many judges vied in the savagery of their punishments, as if this was a contest in piety. Others, who saw that that sort of trial opened the way not just to hatred but also to greed (since, although goods were confiscated to the public treasury, denunciations were not made without profit), did not tolerate having the inquiry snatched away from them.

27 In Spain the inquisitions were held most harshly of all, with monks chosen for that service from the Dominican order, the long-standing institution against the Hebrews and the Muslims, who, compelled by the kings to enter the Christian faith, secretly slipped back to their forsworn errors. This institution was welcomed at first because of the hatred of the barbarian peoples, but eventually weighed on everyone alike, with its amazing keenness in investigation. Conversations were monitored, even the **(11)** silence, friendships were false, and your accuser always by your side. So that it became easily apparent that no one was so innocent as to be able to protect his safety and standing when the inquisitors were opposed. That this has not been exaggerated for hatred, but is put down in accordance with the truth, they will readily confirm, who have heard that in Spain and throughout Italy the most serious uprisings were aroused by men belonging to the Roman church, and indeed in the city of Rome itself, because of this inquisition.

28 In the Low Countries Charles was the first to issue an edict about religion, after he had condemned Luther in a hearing at the Diet of Worms in Germany.[24] Fines were followed by bloodshed, and to forestall the mildness of judges the laws were repeated seven times and strengthened. Forbidden, among other things, was the publication of books except those

eorundem ad praescriptionem iuventus institueretur. Qui de litteris divinis dissertassent, privatis coetibus sacrorum causa interfuissent, in viros gladius, in foeminas sub terram defossio statuitur, publicatis bonis, ita tamen, si prius culpam agnoscerent: nam in pervicaces flammis vindicabatur. Etiam si qui falsae opinionis deprehensi, caetera insontes, resipiscerent, ab omni dignitate arcebantur. Qui hospitio iuvissent, et qui non indicassent, nocentum poenis suppositi; contra, excitandis delatoribus impunitas, et praemia. Multa in suspectos et profugos acria, saeviora in relapsos; territique poenis iudices, ne specie miserationis leges inflecterent, etiam inquisitoribus, quos Caesar mandatis instruxerat, auxilio esse iubebantur. Sola Antverpiensium civitas, quam egregie cum obsequio temperata libertas ad summas opes evexerat, ausa conqueri Germanos ac Britannos, bonam commercii sui partem, ista edicti severitate fugari, obtinuit, ut advenae paulo laxius haberentur, et ne sua in urbe valeret pars illa edicti, qua alienationes et testamenta delinquentium, etiam ante iudicium, rescindebantur, ingens mercaturae turbamentum.

29 Ea iura dictata ab ingenio alias non immiti, quo minus miremur, vis religionis facit, dissentientis impatiens; quae, cum molliendis foederandisque animis valere deberet, facta est, humanae imbecillitatis vitio, acerbissima odiorum materia. Ad hoc, plerisque tum principibus infixum, unum reipublicae corpus una religione velut spiritu contineri, sacrisque, ut humanis legibus, ita optime constare rationem, si multitudini non reddatur. Quo facilius Caesari, post Germanica exempla, persuasum, proculcata sacerdotum reverentia ne ipsi quidem mansurum **(12)** obsequium brevique poena opprimi posse virus, quod alimentum haberet licentiam. Sed contra eventus fuit, effecto ut perirent multi, plures succrescerent.

30 Ea nimirum, quae corpore exercemus, mortis et cruciatuum metu, vi atque imperio obnoxia sunt; verum animus, ut est liber et immortalis, si quid per se arripuit, non ferro, non igne eviceris: quin ipsa invitant pericula, beatumque et gloriosum habetur, extra sceleris conscientiam crudelia atque invisa perpeti; cui rei documento sunt et veteres Christianorum res, et haec tempora. Nam post carnificata hominum non minus centum millia, ex quo tentatum an posset incendium hoc sanguine restingui, tanta multitudo per Belgicam insurrexerat, ut publica interdum supplicia, quoties insignior reus, aut atrociores cruciatus, seditione impedirentur.

31 Atque haec moverant Hungariae reginam, quae fratris Caroli iussu Belgicae praesidebat, ipsum in Germania adhuc haerentem coram accedere, et edocere, in quantam stragem processissent illa, quae remedia dicebantur. Queis Philippus nihil territus, patri coepta instantius urgebat, asperatis edictis, aliaque remedia moliendo, quae vetustescens malum opprimerent. Causa, supra communes alias, haec proprie[5] coniectari potest, quod ipse pontificis Romani auctoritate ad res multas uti statuerat. Nam cum is regna dono dare, ius, fas, aequum ex usu temperare, consensu tot gentium obtineret; dum ipsum obsequio, proximum quemque largitionibus

[5] poprie *1657, 1658* propria *Peerlkamp, Boot*

approved by the theologians at Louvain; the young were to be trained in accordance with their precepts. For those who had spoken on Scripture, or taken part in private gatherings for the sake of religion, the sword was the statutory punishment if male, if female burial alive. And property was confiscated. Only thus, however, if they first acknowledged guilt. For the recalcitrant, punishment came in flames. Even if people apprehended for wrongful ideas, but otherwise guiltless, changed their thinking they were banned from every office. Those who had provided shelter, or who had not laid evidence, suffered the punishments of the guilty. On the other hand, impunity served to stir up denouncers, as well as rewards. Much harshness against suspects and fugitives, more cruelty still against those who relapsed. Judges were threatened with penalties lest they bend the laws under the guise of mercy; they were even ordered to "assist" the inquisitors whom the emperor had sent with instructions. Only the city of Antwerp, whose sophisticated mixture of liberty and obedience had brought her to the peak of prosperity, dared to complain that the Germans and Britons (a significant portion of her trade), were being put to flight by the severity of the edict. As a result they were granted that foreigners be treated a little more loosely, and that the part of the edict which prescribed that the sales and wills of offenders were rescinded, even before a trial—a great disturbance to trade—would be without force in their city.

29 That these laws were dictated by a nature not otherwise cruel, becomes less surprising if we consider the force of religion, intolerant of disagreement; and which, although it should have served to soften and unite souls, by the fault of human weakness became the bitterest substance of hatred. In addition, it was a given for most princes at that time that a single body of a state was held together by a single religion as by a soul, and that with respect to religious laws, as to human laws, the account is best balanced if not rendered to the multitude.[25] Whereby the emperor was the more easily persuaded, after the experiences in Germany, that if reverence for priests were trampled, neither would obedience to himself last **(12),** and that by a quick punishment the seed could be suppressed which had licence for its food. But the outcome was, to the contrary, that when many perished, more grew up.

30 For our physical actions are subject to force and power, because we fear death and torture. But the mind, as it is free and immortal, you cannot defeat once it has grasped something of its own accord; not by the sword, not by fire. Indeed the very dangers entice, and it is considered blessed and glorious to suffer cruelty and hostility without consciousness of guilt. As proof of this serve both the ancient history of Christianity and the present times. For after the butchery of not fewer than a hundred thousand men, since the first attempts to see if this fire could be extinguished by blood, so great a multitude arose throughout the Low Countries that from time to time public executions, whenever the defendant was more notable than usual or the tortures more cruel, were prevented by sedition.

31 These things had moved the queen of Hungary,[26] who was regent of the Low Countries by the order of her brother Charles, to go to him in person (while he was taking his time on a stay in Germany) and to inform him what great damage was being caused by the measures which were called remedies. Not at all terrified by these facts, Philip pressed on the more insistently with his father's projects: there came more forceful edicts, and he attempted other remedies meant to suppress the maturing evil. As the real reason, above other more obvious ones, it can be conjectured that he had decided to let the pope's authority work for him in many matters. For by the agreement of so many peoples the latter possessed the power to give kingdoms as a gift, and to establish fairness, human and divine right in accordance with

suum faceret, fiduciae atque obtentus in hoc abunde videbatur. Tum vero suis ipse paternisque experimentis didicerat, quam grave esset illam potentiam habere adversam, a qua veniam etiam bello victores precantur.

32 Is erat rerum status, hi populi mores, cum Philippi regis discessu de summa praefectura certatum est. Non erant infra hanc spem Arausionensis et Egmondus, sed omissus uterque hoc obtentu, ne, praelato altero, perpetuis simultatibus distraherent rempublicam. Tum inter foeminas ambigebatur, Christiernam, cui maritus fuerat Franciscus Lotharingiae dux, avunculus Carolus Caesar; et Margaritam, quae ipsi Carolo extra coniugium nata, Alexandro primum Medicaeo, inde Octavio Farnesio Parmensium duci nupserat. In Christiernam promota Arausionensis et Belgarum studia, sed contra tendebant Ferdinandus Alvares Toletanus Albae dux, et Antonius Perenottus Granvella Atrebatum antistes; quos patri individuos **(13)** quondam rerumque maximarum ministros eodem honore Philippus amplectebatur. Albanus Hispanorum genere inter primos, multis in locis summus armorum arbiter, insignes Caesari victorias, sibi inclitum nomen paraverat. Perenotti pater Nicolaus Burgundus, quanto ortu humili, tanto obsequiis promptior, pervigili industria, artes aulae, consiliorum arcana, sigillum Caesaris adeptus, functusque per annos viginti, eadem filio reliquerat.

33 Sed ut Albani ferum ac superbum, ita subdolum Perenotti ingenium; dum principis magnitudini studeret nihil ultra pensi habentis, totidem gentes, quot utrumque novere, incusant; praecipue Germani, qui Landgravii vincula non aliis imputantes, amborum potentiam inter praecipuas belli causas praetulere. Horum ubi in sententiam de Margarita Belgicae praeficienda itum est, quamvis haud aberant speciosae consilio causae, sanguinis qualiscunque vinculum, et fidei obses maritus, in urbe Hispanis arcem tenentibus obnoxia; offensos procerum animos abitus regis, non minus ipsis suspectus, quam plebi tristis, accendit.

34 Isque praecipuus dies Philippo sollicitatae libertatis, aut Belgis contumaciae in principem fuit. Nam cum discessurus Hispanorum supra ter mille praesidium vellet relinquere, tanquam tuendo adversus Gallos limiti; revera ut auctam bellis externo contactu religionum licentiam suo arbitrio compesceret; Arausionensis et Egmondus, quos leniendae invidiae cohortibus rectores destinabat, detrectavere munus ut inimicum legibus: et in ipso abitu principem rogavit Ordinum conventus, quos tantum ad valedicendum convocaverat, amoliri vellet invisum militem, addito monitu, ne ad Belgas regendos, aliis quam Belgarum consiliis uteretur. Conditum inde odium hoc implacabilius, quod ingruentem dominationem, et imperii artes intellexisse videbantur. Sed palam assensus; nam et Gomesium Figueroam Hispanum Feriae comitem, pridem in id destinatum, senatui Belgico miscere abstinuit. Alebat iram dissimulando, et iam tunc vindictam animo versabat.

his own interest. Now Philip had turned the pope into his instrument by showing docility, and the most trusted people around him by largesse; and this seemed to provide abundant warranty and pretext. Moreover, Philip had learned by his own and his father's experiences, how difficult a thing it was to be the opponent of a power from which even the winners of wars sought forgiveness.

32 This was the state of affairs, and the character of the population, when at king Philip's departure the supreme governorship became the object of competition. Orange and Egmond were worthy enough to hope for this position, but each was passed over lest, so the excuse went, if one got preference, they would tear the country apart with perpetual quarrels. Then there was hesitation between two women, Christina, whose husband was Francis, duke of Lorraine, and whose uncle the emperor Charles; and Margaret, illegitimate daughter of Charles himself, married first to Alexander de' Medici, thence to Ottavio Farnese, duke of Parma.[27] The support of Orange and the people of the Lowlands was roused for Christina, but pulling the opposite way were Fernando Alvares de Toledo, duke of Alva, and Antoine Perrenot de Granvelle, bishop of Arras.[28] These men, his father's inseparable **(13)** ministers in the most weighty affairs, Philip embraced with the same honour. Alva, born from the highest nobility in Spain, had carried chief military responsibilities in many places, and had provided the emperor with notable victories, himself with a famous name. Granvelle's father Nicolaus, a Burgundian, the more ready with flatteries as his birth was low, by sleepless industry had acquired the arts of the court, the secrets of counsel, the Emperor's seal, and after twenty years of service had left all of these to his son.

33 While Alva's nature was fierce and proud, that of Granvelle was crafty. While he was busy promoting the greatness of the prince who cared only about his greatness, as many nations complained as had made the acquaintance of either of them, especially the Germans, who, not crediting the chains of the Landgrave [of Hessen][29] to any others, held up the powers of these men as particular causes of that war.[30] When the opinion of the two men that Margaret was to be placed in charge of the Seventeen Provinces had won the day, although well-ringing reasons for the plan were not lacking—bonds of blood with whomever, and a husband surety for her loyalty in a city subservient to a Spanish garrison[31]—the already hostile spirits of the nobles were set alight by the king's departure, that was as suspect in their eyes as it was sad to the populace.

34 This particular day for Philip became the day of liberty provoked, for the Netherlanders of defiance towards their prince. For while planning his departure he wanted to leave a garrison of more than 3000 Spaniards, as if to protect the border against the French, but in fact to repress according to his own will the religious licence that had grown up during the wars owing to the contacts with foreigners. Orange and Egmond, whom he intended as leaders for these units in order to alleviate the hostile reaction, refused the task as contrary to the laws. And at the actual departure, an assembly of the States-General, which he had summoned solely to bid him farewell, asked the prince whether he would remove the hated soldiers, adding the warning to use none but Low Countries' advice for ruling the Low Countries. Thus [the king's] hatred was stored up the more implacable as they seemed to have understood the impending tyranny and the techniques domination. But openly there was assent. Indeed he even refrained from adding the Spaniard Gomez Figueroa, count of Feria, to the Netherlandish Council of State, though he had been intended for it. He nourished his anger by hiding it, and was already then turning over revenge in his mind.

Et ille quidem, dum alienos per fines ire dedignatur, mari vectus, amissa classe, vix saeva inter pericula incolumis portum Gallaecum attigit. Miles aliquanto post mansit, immodestus et gravis, donec ad Gerbim (Menynx est veterum) in Turcas male pugnato, ut Belgae interpretabantur, non suam in gratiam, sed in remedium cladis abductus est.

35 Interim Belgicae **(14)** moderamen, vocabulo penes Margaritam, vi penes Granvellam fuit, in quo industria, vigilantia, ambitio, luxus, avaritia, bona malaque omnia excellebant. Nec ipsi tamen plus in sua prudentia subsidii, quam in aliorum omnium ignavia fuit; qui luxu marcentes tempora transmiserant praesentis potentiae, cui olim adultae non sine periculo occurreretur. Is igitur callidus illigare principem conscientia secretorum, et clientes erigens, legationum intima, litterarum notas, et quae per exploratores noscebantur, in se traxerat. Hornano veteres cum illo inimicitiae, primum per Lalaenium, quem sororis Hornani maritum male obitae legationis crimine ille asperserat: deinde, quod Geldriae praefecturam valde ambitam Hornanus, illo intercedente, non obtinuerat. Arausionensi adhuc non alienum se tulerat, subsidium in eo dignitati suae sperans, sed, qui mos ambitionis, hactenus, ne nimium insurgeret. Quam ob causam, cum creandi Antverpiae essent magistratus, illius absentiam captarat.

36 At Arausionensis, qui nihil minus ferre posset, quam inanem honoris speciem, unumque hominem peregrinum et ignobilem, non sine sua atque aliorum contumelia, rerum omnium potiri, Egmondum, qui forte tum iniuriam se a Granvella accepisse iudicabat, ostentata sibi, nec praestita, Hesdini praefectura, et Trullensi abbatia, quam Egmondus agnato petebat, per illum intercepta, verbis exstimulans, plures inde aurei velleris sodales, collegas suos (nam hi eo tempore saepius coibant a Margarita exciti, ut super muniendis finibus sententiam promerent) traduxit in partes, velut ad ipsos non minus id dedecus pertineret, quorum consiliis principes res olim feliciter maximas expedissent.

37 Post quae, tres illi proceres vitare Antonii congressus, ubi in senatu pariter adsederant, manifesti discordiae. *Nec impiger*[6] Antonius, intendere vires adversum potentes et in vulgum gratiosos: adiungere sibi beneficiis homines industrios: inter quos erant Carolus Barlamontius et Viglius Zuichemus, pars et ipsi senatus: adhoc, ille rei quaestoriae summus curator, hic Friso haud magna domo, sed clarus rerum multarum peritia, consessus iuridici princeps erat. Qui cum secreto inter se commearent, et arcana componerent, exulceratum suspicionibus odium ad publica factionis insignia erupit.

38 Iam ante abitum Philippus, quo sacra rectius ordinaret, a Paulo Quarto Romano pontifice obtinuerat, ut suae per Belgicam regiones **(15)** externorum antistitum curae eximerentur. Nam Agrippinensium et Remorum archiepiscopi, quae olim principes, ista Germaniae inferioris, haec Galliae Belgicae civitates fuerant, ex veteri divisione nihil ferme praeter nomen usurpabant. Igitur horum recisa iurisdictione, simul Leodicensi, Tauriennensi, Osnaburgensi, Monasteriensi, Paterbornensi

[6] Nec impiger *1657, 1658* nec piger *vel* sed impiger *Boot (vide et 1.5, et Intr., Principles of this edition)*

Disdaining to pass through another man's territory, he was conveyed by sea and, with his fleet lost, barely reached a Galician port safely through terrible dangers. A certain amount of soldiery remained thereafter, demanding and oppressive, until after a military reverse against the Turks at Djerba (the ancient Menynx[32]) it was taken away, as the Dutch viewed it, not as a favour to themselves but as a remedy for the disaster.

35 Meanwhile, control of the Low Countries **(14)** belonged in name to Margaret, in reality to Granvelle, in whom were remarkable industry, alacrity, ambition, luxury, greed, and every other virtue and vice. However he was not helped as much by his own sagacity as by the passivity of everyone else: lethargic for luxury, they had let slip the moment of his rise to power—which once matured, is risky to oppose. Granvelle therefore, clever as he was at obliging the prince by sharing secrets and positioning dependents, had drawn to himself the inner business of embassies, all correspondences, and the knowledge gained from informers. With Horne he had a long-standing enmity, first on account of Lalaing (married to Horne's sister[33]) whom he had besmirched by charging him with a failed embassy, and subsequently in that because of Granvelle's interference Horne had failed to obtain the stadtholdership of Guelders which he had vigorously solicited. Up to now Granvelle had made sure not to alienate Orange, hoping to find in him a support for his own position, but, as is the nature of ambition, only so long as Orange did not rise too high. For this reason, when the magistrates of Antwerp were to be elected, he made clever use of Orange's absence.

36 Orange could have put up with anything better than this empty show of honour, and the fact that one man, a foreigner and no nobleman, should control everything to his own disgrace and that of others. He spoke rousingly to Egmond, who by chance deemed that he had just then suffered injury from Granvelle, the governorship of Hesdin having been offered to him and not delivered, and the abbacy of Truel, which Egmond wanted for a relative, having been intercepted by Granvelle. Next Orange drew into his party more members of the Golden Fleece, who were his colleagues (for at that time they were meeting more frequently at Margaret's behest to give advice on border fortification), on the grounds that the disgrace pertained no less to them, for in the past the princes used to conduct the most weighty affairs according to their counsel.

37 After this, these three noblemen avoided contact with Granvelle when they sat together in the Council of State, to make their disaffection manifest. Nor was Granvelle *slow* to employ all his forces against these powerful men who were esteemed by the populace. He joined active men to himself by favors, among them Charles de Berlaymont and Viglius van Zwichem,[34] themselves members of the Council of State. The first was also in charge of the public revenue, the other, from a modest Frisian house but famous for his skill in many things, head of the Legal Council.[35] When these men began to meet in secret and develop hidden plans, the hatred that was fed by suspicions burst forth into open manifestations of dissension.

38 Already before his departure, in order to achieve a better organisation of the faith, Philip had obtained from pope Paul IV that his territories in the Low Countries **(15)** be removed from the charge of foreign bishops. For the archbishops of Cologne and Reims (the capital cities of Germania Inferior and Gallia Belgica respectively)[36] retained practically nothing but the name from this old grouping. Therefore with their jurisdiction cut back, and at the same time the bishops of Liège, Thérouanne,[37] Osnabrück, Münster, and Paderborn stripped of part of their oversight, three bishoprics of the top rank[38] were proclaimed in

episcopis parte suae inspectionis exutis, intra Burgundicas ditiones superioris gradus tres, Machliniae, Traiecti Batavorum, et Cameraci, antistites renuntiantur: hos infra alii complures, quorum in finibus Brabantiae sedes Antverpia, et Silvaducis, Geldriae Rurimunda, Flandriae Gandavum, Ipra, Brugae, Hollandiae Harlemum, Middelburgum Zelandiae, Transisalanorum Daventria, Atrebatum quoque urbs cum Fano Audomari, inde Namurcum, Groninga, Tornacum, urbes regioni suae cognomines. Vetus quidem hoc, nec raro pontificibus usurpatum ob populorum incrementa, et quo sacra hoc facilius curarentur, novas ponere antistitum sedes, demto onere, quo alii gravabantur: captamque olim principibus Austriacis curam Carolus alia agitans intermiserat.

39 Sed causae tum repetendi consilii paene omnibus invisae: unam, quo plures essent ac propiores, qui in mores sacerdotum et deviam plebem inquirerent, ipsi auctores palam praetulerant, questi gliscere mala neglectu aut dissimulatione curantium: altera Granvellae artibus imputabatur, qui et pontificium Machliniense, et cardinalem dignitatem Roma acceperat: plerisque futurum augurantibus, ut, quando in Ordinum Belgicorum consessu sacerdotes antiquitus ius suffragii praerogativum habent, ipse eius numeri princeps, quique alii eius opera allecti (nam regi ius episcopos nominandi, sibi retento probandi iure, pontifices concesserant) tacito cum Hispanis foedere opprimerent libertatem. Cum reditus episcopis ex monasticis possessionibus addicerentur, primi se huic instituto obiecere abbates, cuius ordinis eo tempore liberrimae voces erant, non admissuri opum et potentiae subsessores. Socii his Brabanti per libellos commendare principi leges, queis cautum, ne invita plebe et nobilitate sacerdotia augerentur. Accessere multa ius profitentium responsa, irreligiosum convelli pias liberalitates, et suprema morientium iudicia et donata verti, in quod non ipsi dederant. Et veterum antistitum nonnulli, praesertim Leodiensis, circumventum Romanum pontificem **(16)** clamitantes, ius suum pertinaciter persequebantur. Aliae igitur urbes novos antistites non accepere, et, qui admissi erant, invisi omnibus, nec sine ludibriis agebant.

40 Consentiente Belgarum in Granvellam odio, commodissimum suis publicisque rebus proceres iudicabant, Ordinum Belgicae conventus haberi. Igitur quoties de aerarii paupertate (nam et pediti et equiti mercedes multae debebantur, et retentari apud exteros ob publica debita mercatores coeperant, et exitura iam erant promissa in novem annos tributa,) aut de seditionum metu querelae inciderant, laudare morem vetustum, de quo nunquam male sentirent boni principes. Quid autem nunc mirum complorata omnia, quando unicum cunctis malis remedium deterrima assentatio eriperet? Regerebat adversa factio, parum ipsos dissimulare quo tenderent odiis in hominem plusquam vellent Regis studiosum: egregios scilicet Philippi ministros principis potestati aemulam quaerere alteram. At quos eos fore, quibus novato rerum statu cuncta obedirent? Abbates nimirum privati commodi causa offensos, nobilitatem ipsis obnoxiam, caeteros profanorum rituum contactu ancipites, Ordinum specie.

Burgundian territory: Mechelen, Utrecht, and Cambrai[39]; subordinate to these, many others, among which, in the territory of Brabant, the seats of Antwerp and Den Bosch; in Guelders, Roermond; in Flanders, Ghent, Ypres, Bruges; in Holland, Haarlem; Middelburg in Zeeland; in Overijssel, Deventer; and also the city of Arras with St. Omar, and then Namur, Groningen, Tournai as cities that share the name of their region.[40] To establish new bishoprics, thereby removing burdens which weighed down on others, was an old practice, repeatedly used by the popes on account of population growth, and in order that religion be looked after the more easily. This project, once initiated by the Habsburg princes, had been interrupted by Charles, who was occupied otherwise.

39 But the reasons for reactivating the plan now were abhorred by almost everyone. One reason, the wish to have more men inquiring into the behavior of the priests and the heretical populace, and to have them closer on those, was made public by the authors of the plan themselves, who complained that evils were growing because of neglect or concealment by those in charge. Another reason was imputed to the ploys of Granvelle, who had received from Rome both the archbishopric of Mechelen and the rank of cardinal. Several observers, auguring the future, predicted that since in meetings of the Low Countries' States-General the clergy had from time immemorial the right to vote first, Granvelle himself, leader of that group, would oppress liberty by a secret treaty with the Spaniards, assisted by those chosen in by his effort—for the popes had conceded to the king the right of nominating bishops, keeping only the right of approving them. Since the revenues from monastic possessions were to be allocated to the bishops, the first to oppose themselves to this project were the abbots. At this time their ranks assumed an exceeding freedom of speech, and they were not going to admit underminers of their wealth and power. Their allies in Brabant reminded the prince in written requests of the laws, which forbade to increase the number of priesthoods against the will of the populace and the nobility. On top of this there were many statements by lawyers: "it is irreligious to relocate religious donations" or "to convert the final decisions and gifts of the dying to purposes for which they have not given them." Even some of the former bishops, especially Liège, defended their rights tenaciously, **(16)** shouting "the Pope is being circumvented!" Thus some cities did not accept bishops, and those who were admitted found themselves hated by all and the object of ridicule.

40 With the Lowlanders united in their hatred of Granvelle, the nobles deemed it most in the public interest and in their own that an assembly of the States-General be held. Therefore they praised this ancient custom which no good princes had ever disapproved of, as often as complaints arose about the poverty of the treasury (for much money was owed to infantry and cavalry; merchants had begun to be retained in foreign lands because of public debt, and the revenue promised for the next nine years was now about to run out), or about the fear of sedition. "Why is it so surprising", they said, "that there are complaints about everything, if the foulest flattery is snatching away the single remedy for all evils?" Their opposing faction retaliated: "it is you who are not concealing very well where you are headed in your hatred for a man more zealous of the king's interest than you desire: and you are verily proving yourselves excellent ministers of king Philip's power in seeking a second power as rival to his. Now who would the men be whom everything obeyed under a new political arrangement? The abbots of course, hurt in their private benefits, a nobility that is subservient to them, and the rest who are unreliable owing to their contact with profane rites—and the lot of them assembled under the label of 'Estates'!"

41 Ita modestiam hinc et obsequium, providentiam inde periculorum et avita iura, virtutum vocabula, simulantes, pro sua quisque magnitudine certabant. Etiam litteras tres iidem, quos diximus, ad regem componere ausi, pernegabant exitium publicum averti posse, ni Perenottus odiosa potentia dimoveretur; petita et sibi senatorii muneris vacatione, caeterum pro ipsius imperio, sororis dignitate, Romanae religionis tutela, large pollicentes. Acceptoque Philippi responso, benigno in ipsos, sed insolitum sibi, ministros nisi diiudicata causa depellere, quare si reditus suus exspectari non posset, cuius spem faciebat, velle se alicuius ipsorum adventu propius de re omni cognoscere. Instant iterum: nec enim se in crimen cuiusquam inscribere, sed quod officii sui crederent, eius principem simpliciter monuisse. At quam non falso, imminens inde periculum se tacentibus loqui: quanquam et ita se natos meritosque, ut non minus fidei litteris suis, quam verbis sperarent, nunc quidem maxime, cum rectorum absentiam praefecturae cuiusque vix ferant.

42 (1566) Permovere haec regem, ut tempori cederet, secretaque Granvellae, quem et praefecta ipsa gravari coeperat, partim ut inspectorem, partim ut odii publici contage sibi noxium, mandata abscedendi in **(17)** Burgundiam daret: sed ipse vitam suam petitam inimicorum insidiis, eo digredi vitandi periculi causabatur. Denique Belgas in universum metu reditus sui sollicitos, paucos eius spe sibi addictos, tenuit; donec longius Romam, sponte an iussus, abiit. Tum illi, qui emanserant hactenus, Margaritae precibus in senatum revocati, quo se omnibus probarent, summam incipiunt diligentiam rebus advertere; aliorum non magnus usus. Regis quoque, offensas dissimulantis, laudes et gratiae in ipsos eo quaesitiores, quo magis volebat mali sensum avertere:

43 planeque pro victoribus agentes, rationes publicas et ad leges pertinentia in se traxerant; senatus aientes summum esse arbitrium, eique consessus alios ministerium et obsequium debere. Sed quae paucorum dominatum comitantur vitia, ea et tum brevi adoleverunt: fisci neglectus, validas inter discordias remissa iuris auctoritas, flagitia inulta, honores pro beneficiis dati, sive omnium gratias captantibus multa ambitiose facienda fuere, seu mala nunquam vitata semper famam potentium onerant.

44 Minus et de religione dissimulabant, facilius eam persuaderi, quam cogi posse; comperto tandem alimenta morbi facta, quae remedia crederentur: quod populari aurae dederint, an suo ipsi ingenio a saevitia alieno, aut etiam quod sub inquisitionis tegumento latere servitutem, et fortissimo cuique periculum suspicarentur, in medio relinquam. Hoc quidem constat, et ipsos a Romanis caeremoniis non discessisse, et, qui horum consiliorum princeps erat, in sua Arausionensi ditione nihil passum in sacris immutari. Haec super, aliisque gravibus de causis, missus in Hispaniam Egmondus regiae voluntatis explorator, honore, donis, quantis ante nemo, excipitur, multaque Philippus de suo in Belgas affectu testatus, et eos quo

41 Thus all were fighting for their own power and influence, some simulating moderation and obedience, others awareness of dangers and care for the ancestral laws; all synonymous with virtue. The same three men even dared to direct a letter to the king denying that public disaster could be averted unless Antoine Perrenot be stripped of his detested power. They also requested exemption for themselves from their duties in the Council of State, and made broad promises about the king's rule, his sister's standing, and protection for the Roman Catholic religion. They got a response from Philip, benign towards themselves but saying "it is not my habit to remove ministers without hearing the case against them, and therefore, if it is not possible to await my return" (of which he made it seem that there was a hope) "I want to investigate the whole matter more closely by a visit from one of you". They replied immediately: "we are not writing to press charges against anyone, but because we believe it our duty simply to warn our prince for this man. However, the imminent danger is speaking most eloquently for itself, even if we remain silent. And yet such is our birth and service that we hope there to be no less credibility in our letters than in our words, especially now, when each of our provinces will scarcely tolerate the absence of its ruler."[41]

42 These words moved the king to yield to circumstances and to give secret orders to Granvelle for withdrawal into **(17)** Burgundy, now that even the regent had begun to object to him, in part because of his scrutiny of her, in part because she feared he would harm herself by infection with public hatred. Granvelle himself however provided the explanation that his life was threatened by the treachery of his enemies, and that he was leaving for the place mentioned to avoid danger.[42] In the end he kept the Netherlanders as a whole unsettled with fear of his return, a few devoted to him with hope of it, until he went still farther away, to Rome, either voluntarily or as ordered. Now the men who had so far stayed away were summoned back into the Council of State at Margaret's request, in order that they might win approval from all, and began to attend to affairs very diligently. The services of others were not much used. From the king, too, hiding his hurt, they received praise and thanks, all the more elaborate as he wanted to avert any awareness of evil with them.[43]

43 Bearing themselves openly as victors[44] they drew public expenditure and legal affairs to them, saying that the highest decision-making power belonged to the Council of State, and that other assemblies owed it assistance and obedience. But the flaws that accompany the rule of a few then matured in short order: neglect of the treasury, the authority of the law weakened through serious disagreements, crimes unavenged, offices given in return for favors, either because these men seeking everyone's support had to be ambitious about their great many tasks, or because these inevitable evils always burden the reputation of powerful men.

44 With respect to religion they were readier to accept that it is more open to persuasion than to force. It had finally been acknowledged that the measures which had been thought remedies had in fact become food for the disease. I leave it unresolved whether they made these concessions to popular whim, or from their own nature (to which cruelty was alien), or even because they suspected servitude was waiting under the cloak of the Inquisition, and thence danger for the bravest. This at least is clear, that they themselves had not left the Roman faith, and that the man who was the leader of their plans permitted no religious change in his own province of Orange. On these matters, and for other weighty reasons, Egmond was sent to Spain to investigate the king's wishes and was received with honour and gifts such as no one had been given before.[45] Philip gave many declarations of his affection for the Lowlanders and

minus reviseret Turcico se bello distineri: spem quoque nonnullam fecerat, posse de sententia antistitum edicta hactenus temperari, ne sectarum licentia aut poenis, aut impunitate excitaretur; reipsa totus in duriora concesserat.

45 Nam cum primum in Hispaniam advectus multos illic reperisset, et Isidoriani coenobii praecipuos, de recepta doctrina ac ritibus sequius sentire, viros ingenio, foeminas sanguine nobiles flammari iussisse non contentus, ut laeta oculis usurparat: quo terrore compressis dissidiis, eundem in Belgica exitum putabat sibi iudicum socordia invideri. Quin hoc ipso tempore missa Baionam uxore Elisabetha, **(18)** Caroli Gallorum regis sorore, unaque Albano, quo et Carolus, et mater Medicaea ad colloquium convenerant, exscindendis sacrorum novatoribus mutuam opem arcanis pactionibus firmaverat. Simile foedus post pacem Cameracensem Henrico et Philippo initum, idque sibi in Gallica legatione, cum forte venatu decurreret, imprudentia Henrici regis apertum, Arausionensis saepe asseruit; testatus iam tum consilia se metuisse, quae celabantur. Vix rediens Egmondus spem vanam attulerat, cum secutae regis litterae, iudicia laesorum sacrorum per inquisitores, additis e numero iudicum adsessoribus, immisericorditer exerceri imperantes, et, quanquam Viglio et cum eo nonnullis dissuadentibus, statim vulgatae omnium animos movere: nec segnius Synodi Tridentinae placita publicari.

46 Eo in conventu nihil eorum in doctrina aut ritibus emendatum, quorum causa totae nationes a Romana ecclesia desciverant: tantum in sacerdotum mores instituta censura, hos ipsos offendebat, nec illis medebatur. Erat sane corruptissima in Belgica eorum vita, qui sacro ministerio electi, nihil eius praeter nomen et reditus obtinebant: nec alii acrius decretorum evulgationi intercessere. Paritum quibusdam in locis, sed adscripta exceptione, in quam Philippus adsenserat, ne quid iuri cuiusquam derogaretur, quod ob patrocinia in ecclesias, et iurisdictionum terminos, additum. Ulterius Brabantorum vox libera processit, quorum urbes, mox et ipse eius nationis senatus, haud reticuere, irrepentem altius indies inquirendi morem patriis suis legibus adversari, quibus iudicia ordinarentur, et quae sacerdotalem notionem certis finibus includerent. Horum inde constantiam secuti alii.

47 Sed praecipue vulgus terribili rumore Hispanicam inquisitionem differebat, cuius quanquam manifesta apud regem auctoritas, ususque in regnis omnibus, et exemplum, ut salutare, Galliis commendatum, nomen tamen in Belgica anxie vitabatur. Fuere qui ad regem eo tempore perscriberent summam eius disciplinae, quae haereseos vocabulo male audiebat; ne tam profanam, atque intestabilem crederet, quam procul, et ab infestis fingeretur. Per Arausionensis industriam acciti et qui moderata suaderent, gnari antiquorum, Georgius Cassander, et Franciscus Balduinus Atrebas. Huius quidem et oratio exstat haud inelegans, ad usum impetrandum validae iam, sed inturbidae religionis. Id commerciorum, id pacis interesse: **(19)** an et Iudaeis illos inferiores, quibus emendam rituum impunitatem Pontifex ipse concederet.

said he was being kept from coming to them in person by the war against the Turks; he even gave them some hope that, according to the bishops' wishes, the existing placards [on heresy] could be mitigated in order that the licence of the sects not be stirred up by either punishments or impunity. In reality however he was fully resolved to resort to harsher measures.

45 For as soon as he had reached Spain he found that many men there, especially in the convent of Saint Isidore,[46] had dissenting opinions about received doctrine and rites. Not being content with merely having ordered men noble in talent and women of noble blood to be burned, he had witnessed it as if it were a happy spectacle. And since this terror had suppressed the dissent, he thought that the same outcome in the Low Countries was being denied him by the passivity of the judges. At this very time he sent his wife Elisabeth, **(18)** sister of the French king Charles, and Alva with her, to Bayonne,[47] whither both Charles and his mother Catharina de' Medici had come for talks, and promised by secret agreements mutual aid for destroying the religious innovators. Orange often asserted that a similar treaty had been initiated after the peace of Cateau-Cambrésis by Henry and Philip, and that this was revealed to him during an embassy to France by the imprudence of king Henry, when by chance he was out hunting. "And already by that time" he would keep asserting "I was scared by plans that were being concealed."[48] No sooner had Egmond, on his return, brought empty hope, than letters followed from the king ordering the investigations of injuries to religion to be carried out without pity by the Inquisition, with 'assessors' being added from among the [ordinary] judges.[49] They were published immediately, in spite of Viglius' and some others' arguments against this, and turned everyone to panic. The resolutions of the Council of Trent were to be made public with equal speed.

46 In that meeting none of the shortcomings in doctrine or ritual had been emended for which so many nations had dissociated themselves from the Roman church. Only a censure had been instituted against the behavior of priests which offended the men without curing the problem. To be sure, in the Low Countries the life of those chosen for a sacred ministry had become exceedingly corrupt; except the name and the revenue they took no holiness from it. No others tried more vigorously to prevent the publication of the resolutions. In some place the resolutions were obeyed, but with the exception, to which Philip had assented, that no one's rights should be diminished, which had been granted for the protection of churches and departmental boundaries. The free voice of the people of Brabant[50] went a step further, as the cities in that province, and soon their Council itself,[51] did not fail to point out that the methods of inquiry that were creeping in more deeply from day to day were contrary to their ancestral laws which governed the procedure of trials, and which kept priestly inquiry within fixed limits. This example of constancy was then followed by others.

47 But it was the populace especially which, with a frightful uproar, delayed the Spanish Inquisition. This name was anxiously avoided in the Low Countries, in spite of its manifest authority with the king, while it had been used in all kingdoms, and the positive example of its application given by France. There were people at that time who wrote to the king to tell him the essence of that teaching "which is unjustly termed heresy, nor should you believe it to be so profane and so detestable as it is imagined from afar and by enemies." Through the effort of Orange councilors were admitted who would urge a moderate line, men knowledgeable about antiquity: George Cassander[52] and Francis Baudouin of Arras[53]. Of the latter a speech exists, a very elegant one, on the usefulness of establishing a strong but imperturbable religion. This was advantageous (he said) to trade, to peace: **(19)** "or are those others even inferior to the Jews, to whom the pope himself had permitted the purchase of impunity for their rites?"

48 Quae postquam irrita fuere, pars poenae metu, alii rerum novarum cupientes, sermones ambiguos iactare, libellos proponere, tentamenta vulgi. Germanos religionis vindices ex bello ius aequum retinere; eiectam rursum Britannia Latinam superstitionem, eiectam eandem apud Danos et Sueonas: ne in Gallia quidem caedes inultas, salutem palam armis aut pace defendi. Unos se libertatis medios et expertes saevientium ingenia alere ferendo: quasi vero res ulla arctius populum obsequio, quam principem aequis imperiis alligaret. Utendum hac inclinatione animorum rati proceres, qui in sua sententia ipsos se a rege damnatos interpretabantur; quidam et matrimoniis illigati foeminarum externae, ut gentis, ita religionis, Arausionensis Saxonico, Nienario Hornanus, suspectos se regi inde etiam credito, quod novam senatus potentiam, quam ipsi introductum ibant, rex improbaverat.

49 Quo causam suam cum vulgi studiis sociarent, diligentius instituunt pacem religionum, si publicam non possent, at domesticam procurare, malorum metum hoc magis attollentes, quanto caeteri iniquius contemnebant. Obtendunt huic rei turbas civiles, partim et ipsi faciunt: seu flecti posse regem, seu ultra quidam speravere, non defuturos rebus novis adiutores invidia magnitudinis Hispanicae. A senatu ergo digressi, velut provisis motibus, quibus sanandis impares forent, modo per nuptiarum solemnia, modo epularum specie convivia miscentes, alios aut sanguinis, aut studiorum, vinculo aggregavere; id quo pertineret brevi erupit.

50 Nam postquam perspectum plurimos eadem velle, longe principem et militem, rem summam penes foeminam, Ordines et civitatum rectores dissuadere crudelitatem, interim perpeti, multi genere nobiles, caeterum regiminis exsortes, inter quos erant Romanae religionis nonnulli, contra inquisitionem foedus pepigere, verba dictante Marnixio, quo inter se promisere auxilium, siquis eo nomine periclitaretur; ac ne lateret quo subsidio niterentur, inter duces eius societatis eminebat Ludovicus Nassavius Arausionensis frater, a Romanis sacris palam dissentiens: unde haud difficile intellectu, vera capita occultari adhuc, in tempore eruptura, atque interim praetentantibus repositam in illorum auctoritate fiduciam, adversus acres aliorum sententias, qui nascentem coitionem armis opprimi **(20)** volebant. Aderant Ludovico Herenbergensis, et Culemburgicus comes, et Henricus Brederodius, antiquo genere Hollandiae principum, et vulgi applausibus, qui, ni alia adsint, vana et incerta sunt, in spes nimias erectus.

51 Hi, quadringentis foederatorum comitantibus, die Nonarum Aprilium inermes in curiam Bruxellensem venere, ubi tum et Arausionensis aliique, vix a Margarita ut redirent exorati, consederant. Preces (ita enim vocabant) hae fuere: ut edicta super religione a rege de Ordinum Belgicorum sententia mutarentur, interim quiescerent: quorum cum alterum praefecta se commendaturam regi promitteret, alterum suae potestatis negaret, non aliud impetratum, quam ut iudices et quaesitores

48 When these attempts had come to nothing, some people from fear of punishment, others desirous of revolution, tossed out ambiguous words, put out pamphlets, to see if they could stir up the mob, containing things like: "The German defenders of the faith retained equal rights from their struggle" and "The Latin superstition has been ejected from Britain again[54], ejected likewise from Denmark and Sweden; not even in France has slaughter remained unavenged, indeed salvation was protected openly in war and peace." Or "We alone, with liberty established everywhere around us, and being unfamiliar with the nature of cruel men, are feeding it by tolerating it. As if anything exists that would bind a people more strictly to obedience than a prince to equitable rule." The nobles thought that this state of mind was to be taken advantage of, since in their view the king's choices meant that he had already condemned them; some of them were bound by matrimony to the foreign religion of their wives, as to their country—Orange to a Saxon, to a lady of Neuenahr Horne.[55] And further they believed that the king suspected them because he disapproved of the new power of the Council of State, which they were introducing.

49 In order that they might join their own cause to the enthusiasm of the mob, they began more zealously to work towards a religious peace, if not a public peace then at least behind the front door—calling attention to the risk of troubles all the more as others trivialised it unduly. They used the civil disturbances as an argument to this end; indeed they created some of them, either hoping that they could change the king's mind, some for even more than that, namely, that supporters for revolution would not be lacking, given the dislike for Spain's magnitude. Thus they walked out of the Council of State[56], as if expecting uprisings they were unable to remedy, and, gathering in parties (at times for wedding rituals, at others with a pretext of banqueting) they joined other men to themselves by the bond of blood or cause; and soon it became evident where this was headed.

50 For after it had become clear that the majority wanted the same things—prince and army at a distance, supreme authority in the hands of a woman, the States and city rulers to discourage cruelty, and at times to suffer it—a large group of men noble in birth but without a share in rule, among whom were many of the Roman faith, made a confederation against the Inquisition, with Marnix authoring the oath in which they promised assistance to one another if someone should come in danger on this account.[57] And in order not to conceal the support on which they were relying, Louis of Nassau, Orange's brother, who had openly dissociated himself from the Roman rites, stood out among the leaders of that society. Whence it is not difficult to understand that the real heads of the movement were still lying hidden, but would burst forth in time; and that in the mean time the confidence of these fore-runners rested on the authority of those provisional leaders—against the harsh judgments of others, who **(20)** wanted the nascent conspiracy to be crushed by arms. On Louis' side were the counts of Herenberg[58] and Culemborg,[59] and Henry of Brederode,[60] who was aroused to excessive hopes by his ancient descent from the counts of Holland, and the applause of the crowd which in the absence of other things, is empty and unreliable.

51 These men, in company with four hundred of their allies, on the fifth of April came unarmed into the Town Hall at Brussels, where then Orange and others were gathered, recently begged by Margaret to return. Their Petition (for so they called it[61]) comprised this: that the king's edicts on religion be changed in accordance with the judgment of the States-General of the Low Countries, and in the interim be suspended. As the regent promised that she would recommend the former of these to the king but denied that the latter

iuberentur cognitionem prudentia temperare. Tunc primum auditum est illud non minus postea nobilitatum, quam Protestantes et Hugonoti, Gueusiorum nomen, quo cum ambesas fortunas foederatis alii exprobrarent, ipsi in honorem traxere, parum fausti nominis appellatione professi, fidem sibi in regem ad mendicitatem usque constituram.

52 Sed his visis atque auditis, varie per Belgicam et Hispaniam consultabatur. Qui circa Margaritam erant, foederatorum nobilium postulata alii ut aequa probabant, alii ut necessaria: addendam fiduciam securitatis ne poenae metus in spem belli transiret, haud dissimulato ex ipsis primoribus esse, qui graviora in se regis consilia suspectarent: et haec si negarentur, ipsos, quorum sub imperio fortissimae nationes erant, et turmae populares, praecipuum belli robur, pro legum saevitia ferrum non educturos, quo cives scilicet alter alterius manu cadentes, Hispanis usui et oblectamento cederent. Ad regem aliae post alias litterae, postremo frater Hornani *Iohannes*[7] Montiniacus, et Iohannes Marchio Bergarum ad Zomam venere, laeti honore legationis, ut prioribus se purgarent, venturis eximerentur.

53 Ipse rex, turbatus atrocioribus indies nuntiis, cum primis Hispanorum, et qui senatores Belgae aderant, saepe et secum deliberabat. Non placebat transmissa a senatu Belgico moderandarum legum forma, quae prava docentes sacrorum administros, conventuum receptores, et qui publicos oculos exemplo violassent, laqueo aut ense puniebat: indicta caeteris errorum detestatione, aut fuga: quia maior ipsi dignitatis quam periculi cura, ne minis coactus, quae nollet, largiri videretur: unde etiam siquid violentiae cedendum foret, suum nomen pactionibus illigari **(21)** vetuit. Hactenus tamen indultum, ut bene firmata episcoporum auctoritate, quorum esset munus siquid usquam turbidum scrutari, extra ordinem alii Pontificis mandato non ultra inquirerent. Veniam citra discrimen dari, et nisi discussa coniuratione, praefractius[8] quam illa ferebant tempora, olimque multo maiora concessurus, abnuebat: clementiam tamen et adventum suum pollicitus. Ordinum autem haberi conventus, quanquam fidissimae civitates orabant, suadentibus Belgarum cunctis, annisa et sorore, quae aliter retineri posse imperium desperabat, pernegare haud destitit, arma potius sumi imperans, et solvi Germanis auctoramenta, quo paratior miles haberetur: adiecto nec dubitare se, quam toties expertus esset pater Belgarum procerum fidem, eandem sibi paterna decreta exsequenti non defuturam: quippe sententiis dissidere fas cuique, sed mox iudicium principi, subditis obsequium relinqui.

54 At contra illi, ne vis ulla pararetur facile effecere, aerarii penuriam obtendentes, et siquid moveretur, foederatos nobiles bellum ante capturos, externis societatibus undique se offerentibus, quod ut in terrorem adauctum, ita a vero trahebatur. Nam

[7] *recte* Florentius Iohannes *1657, 1658 correxit Burmannus (cf. Carolus Arscotius 1.62 & vide Intr., Principles of this edition)*

[8] dari, et .... praefractius *1658* dari, et, ... praefractius, *1657*

was in her power, nothing was obtained other than that the judges and Inquisitors would be ordered to moderate the trials in prudence. Then for the first time was heard the name—no less famous than "Protestants" and "Huguenots" later—of "Gueux"[62] which, while others used it to criticise the confederates for their exhausted fortunes, the men themselves adopted as a title of honour, declaring that with a name of so little good omen, their loyalty to the king even unto poverty would be firmly established.

52 These things being seen and heard however, different plans were made in the Low Countries and Spain. Of Margaret's entourage, some approved the demands of the confederate nobles as equitable, others as necessary: arguing that the nobles should have confidence in their security lest fear of punishment turn into hope for war; it having been scarcely concealed that even some of the higher nobles suspected the king's intentions for them to be severe. Moreover, they added: " if these demands are denied, we ourselves, who have the most stout-hearted nations under our command and citizen forces,[63] a particular strength in war, have no plans to draw the sword to support the severity of the laws, for such slaughtering of citizens by citizens would only serve the profit and enjoyment of the Spaniards." To the king went letter after letter and finally the brother of Horne, *Jean* de Montigny, and John marquis of Bergen op Zoom as well, delighted by the honour of the embassy, in order that they might clear themselves of past events and exempt themselves from those to come.[64]

53 The king, disturbed by news worse day by day, was in frequent deliberation with the Spanish leaders, with the Dutch councillors present there, and with himself. Not to his pleasure was the plan transmitted from the Low Countries Council of State for easing the laws—it punished by rope or sword ministers of religion whose teachings were crooked, those who hosted congregations, and those who had violated the rules in public. Forswearing of errors was required of the rest, or else, flight. The king opposed this plan because he was more concerned for his dignity than for the danger itself: he didn't want to seem forced by threats to grant what he didn't want. Accordingly he even forbade, in case something had to be conceded to the violence, to affix his name **(21)** to the agreement. However he made a concession to this extent, that since the authority of the bishops, (whose task it was to investigate whichever disturbances) was well established, there would be no extraordinary inquisitors with a mandate from the pope looking deeper into matters. He rejected granting a pardon without distinction, and without elimination of the conspiracy, thus acting more bluntly than the circumstances could bear, and although he would later make much greater concessions. Nevertheless he promised clemency and a visit. He did not, however, cease to refuse an assembly of the States-General, although the most loyal cities besought it, at the urging of all of the Low Countries, and they received support from his own sister too, who did not see how control could be retained in any other way. Instead, he ordered her rather to take up arms, and pay their wages to the Germans, in order that the military be the more ready. He added that he was confident that the loyalty of the Netherlandish nobles, which his father had so often experienced, would not fail himself as he carried out his father's decisions. For everyone was entitled to have a dissident opinion, but in the end, to decide was the prince's, to obey the subjects' task.

54 In response however his advisors, using the poverty of the treasury as an excuse, easily brought it about that no force was being readied. They added that if any such move were made, the confederate nobles would take up war first, now that external alliances were offering themselves on all sides—an argument that, although exaggerated to produce terror,

vicinorum nonnulli eadem de sacris, aut non longe diversa sentientes, quo domi validiores ipsi agerent, contra Philippi contumaciam arma et opes ostentabant.

55 Eorum, qui Pontificis Romani imperia abnuebant, tria per Belgicam erant genera. Anabaptistarum credulitas, quae Frisiam proximaque insederat, non magnopere formidanda ob infinitas inter se discordias, et quia magistratus atque arma abdicant. At ea professio, cui ab Augustano conventu et Luthero doctore nomen est, Germanorum principum amicitia, et quadam iuris imagine fovebatur: nam quia Belgas suos Carolus Caesar Germanico foederi adscripserat, pars quoque antiquitus eius imperii maiestatem observarat, erant qui dicerent, pacem quoque religionum eo pertinere: facili quanquam responso, Belgas, etsi tributorum et immunitatum participes, Germaniae tamen leges, et conventuum decreta iam a multis retro saeculis non agnoscere. Non multum ab hac institutione discrepat altera, Zuinglii prae caeteris et Calvini ingenio illustrata, et cum Augustana iamdudum coalitura, nisi in religionibus compertum foret, esse omnia pertinaciae quam concordiae proniora. Hanc pars Helvetiorum et aliquanta Germaniae probarat, et hoc uno clarissima Geneva **(22)** Allobrogum: eadem in Anglia regnabat, paucis retentis ex antiquo ritibus. Sed potissimum magnae per Galliam eius vires, animum sectatoribus indiderant; nec eos caeteri numero aequabant.

56 (1567) Ergo hi atque alii ius novum, quod proponebatur, non minus acerbum, quam Philippus remissum, iudicabant: hoc etiam arguentes, quod loco postulati Ordinum universorum conventus, seorsim nationum sententiae[9] exquirebantur, nec omnium, nec prisco more, ab his facto initio, quibus et dignitatis minus erat, et libertatis. Quos ad motus, dum praefecta alios regis iussus, et militem, aut conducendo militi pecuniam exspectat, sperans posse periculum prolatando finiri, contra ecce e vulgo, qui flammas ferrumque timuerant hactenus, territare incipiunt, prorumpunt e latebris in apertum, conciones et sacra celebrant novo ritu, velut convincendis palam mendaciis, quibus arcani coetus infamabantur: acciti et exsules qui religionis crimine solum verterant, quibus non pauci, durioris vitae pertaesi, monasteriorum desertores aggregabantur. Apparet formidabilis multitudo et quantum nec ipsi crediderant, qui frequentiam faciebant. Licentia firmat audaciam, aut ubi vis metuitur, incedunt armati. His omnibus in tutelam receptis foederati nobiles, fama quoque supra verum crescente, muniebantur.

57 Nec multo post, incertis auctoribus orta vilissimae plebis seditio, nec fures aberant, per oppida et agros templa involat, affliguntur solo dona arae et simulacra divum: quales olim saepe motus Iudaeorum, nec dissimilis Graeciam tempestas Iconomachorum pervaserat: quin ne saevitiae quidem in sacerdotes et religiosos temperabatur, eadem in libros et sepulchra rabie motuque tam repentino, ut tanquam ex condicto Belgicam omnem eodem tempore incenderet; vix paucis

[9] sententiae *scripsimus* sententiae, *1657, 1658*

had a basis in truth. For some of the neighbors, having the same religious views, or views not much different, made a show of their arms and resources in response to Philip's intransigence, in order to stand stronger at home themselves.

55 In the Low Countries those who refused the commands of the pope consisted of three groups. The Anabaptists' credulity, which had taken root in Friesland and the nearby areas, was not greatly to be feared on account of their infinite internal quarrels, and because they forswore magistrates and arms. But the faith that got its name from the Diet of Augsburg[65] and from its teacher, Luther, was supported by the friendship of German princes and by a certain appearance of legitimacy. For because Charles V had assigned his Netherlands subjects to the German federation, and also because part had from time immemorial upheld the majesty of his rule, some maintained that the religious peace [of Augsburg] applied in these regions as well, an argument to which there is an easy response, namely, that the Netherlanders, although they shared the taxes and exemptions of the German empire, had from many centuries back not acknowledged Germany's laws or the Reichtag's decrees There was not much distance between this doctrine and another, distinguished by the talent of Zwingli especially and Calvin's, and which would have united with that of Augsburg a long time ago if in religious matters it weren't an established fact that everything leans more to stubbornness than concord. This doctrine had been accepted by part of the Swiss and bits of Germany, as well as Geneva, famous **(22)** for this fact alone. The same doctrine held sway in England, with a few rituals retained from the past. But its followers drew their most powerful encouragement from its great strength in France; nor did the rest equal the French in number.

56 Therefore these groups and others deemed the new law that was being proposed no less harsh than Philip deemed it lax. They also protested against the fact that, in place of the requested full assembly of the States-General, the opinions of the provinces were being sought separately, not all together, nor in the old way, but beginning from the provinces of lower dignity and fewer privileges. While the regent was waiting for other commands from the king with respect to these problems, and for soldiers, or the money to hire them, (she hoped that the danger could be ended by delaying) lo! there suddenly appeared men from the populace, who had up till this moment feared flames and the sword, but now started a campaign of terror. They burst into the open from their hideouts, holding sermons and ceremonies following the new rites, as if in order to openly refute the lies by which their secret gatherings used to be defamed.[66] Their numbers were reinforced by exiles who had changed soil because of religious charges, and to these mustered not a few deserters from the monasteries, tired of that harsh way of life. A formidable multitude appeared, of a magnitude that even those who caused the crowds could scarcely believe. Licence reinforces their boldness, and where violence is feared, they go in arms. By taking all these men into their protection the confederate nobles fortify their position, helped by the fact that the fame of events outgrows its reality.

57 Soon thereafter, a mob (its instigators are unknown) sprung from the lowest segment of the populace, thieves included, and burst into churches in towns and countryside, dashed to the ground altar gifts and images of saints; uprisings as they often happened in the past with the Jews, and not much different from the storm of iconoclasts that overran Greece.[67] They did not even stop at cruelty towards priests and those in holy orders, the same fury was directed at libraries and tombs, and with so sudden a movement that the flame kindled everywhere in Seventeen Provinces simultaneously as if by agreement. In only very few

1.57. *Iconoclastic Fury* by Jan Luyken (E&K 51)

2.3. *Portrait of the Duke of Alva* (no signature)

in locis auctoritate, aut armis magistratuum valentioribus: nisi quod Atrebates, Haenovii, Lucemburgenses, quique his proximi, fidem in Romanam ecclesiam regemque, ab ea contage integram tenuere. Nonnullis in locis magistratus, ne plebs licentiae adsuesceret, occupaverant amovere imagines; quibus officium iactantibus facete Viglius dixit, eos cum ratione insaniisse. Multa e sacro rapta ut redderentur, ipsi haud egentis ad odium nova infamia religionis doctores perpulere.

58 Tanta rerum perturbatione Margarita vehementius exterrita, non tam regis iam poterat e longinquo omnia audientis sero **(23)** plerumque ob gliscens periculum imperio, quam tempori, et procerum consiliis obsequi. Nam et foederati nobiles, et plebs concitata, non aliis arbitris agi secum patiebantur. Reluctata igitur diu, tandem eo pertrahitur, ut nobilibus promittat gesta hactenus fraudi non fore. Illi vicissim quamdiu maneret securitas, foederi renuntiavere. Veniae nomen et Romanae religionis addita primum conditio, aspernantibus remissa. Plebi, dum noxa et armis abstineret, quibus in locis conciones sacrae institutionis causa ad id tempus habebantur, permissae in posterum: cessantibus edictis, donec rex et Ordines propius statuissent. Statim diversa in loca abiere, qui vim prohibentes, affirmarent pactione, quod vis extorserat.

59 Inprimis Arausionensis missus Antverpiam seditione ancipiti flagrantem, vicecomitis gentilitium nomen ea in urbe obtinens, flectebat in se validissimam civitatem: ubi non in agris, ut alibi, verum ipsa intra moenia, praeter conciones, admissos etiam ritus novos, non ita, necessitatem praeferens excusavit, ut offensam praefectae effugeret. Idem cum aliis tum Hornano acciderat, cui et ex Hispania frater iram regis implacabilem nuntiabat. Sed magis angebant deprehensae ad Margaritam litterae, quibus ministri secretorum ipsos crimini et exitio destinabant. Igitur in medium consulturi Tenerimundam convenere, versis in Egmondum oculis, belli peritum, gratumque militibus. At ille promissis delinitus, an officii memor, negabat se principi quidvis paranti obsequio defuturum: sed mitigandum consiliis animum, prioremque necessitatem purgandam in posterum fide. Imprudens, magna et regibus adversa cum periculo incipi; ubi prima processerint, durando salutem et praemia sperari, sin remiseris, instare ultionem.

60 Plus Arausionensis habebat consilii, qui videns fallere coepta, regem per litteras, ut pateretur se deponere honores, otiumque et Germaniae suae secretum orabat. Cui Philippus callide respondit, et, quae fraus plurimum valet, specie simplicitatis. Nam obsecratum, ne se desereret rebus turbidis, cum maxime usus operae esset, hortabatur, ut fratrem suspectum novandi tantisper a se abdicaret, dum cuncta considerent. Sed ille superior dolis, urgebat nihilominus missionem, atque interim regressus in praefecturas, saevitiam vetans, etiam proviso ne earum regionum munimenta milite

places did the magistrates have authority or effective military power, except that those of Artois, Hainaut, Luxemburg, and the areas close by kept their loyalty to the Roman church and to the king clear of this infection. In some places the magistrates, lest the populace grow accustomed to this licence, had gotten in first to remove the images—when they boasted of their commitment to duty, Viglius[68] wittily said that they had deliberately gone mad. Restitution of many of the objects that had been taken from sacred places was forced by the preachers themselves of the religion that hardly needed new infamy to foster hatred.

58 Margaret was deeply terrified by such a troubled state of affairs. She could only, given the growing threat to control, defer more to circumstances and the plans of the higher nobility than to the plans of the king, **(23)** who heard everything from a distance and, in most cases, too late. For neither the confederate nobles nor the aroused populace were prepared to have any other arbiters deal with them. Therefore after resisting for a long time she was driven to promise the nobles that they would come to no harm for things done in the past. In return they offered to give up their confederation so long as they remained secure. The term 'pardon' and a condition of [loyalty to] the Roman faith were added at first but abandoned under pressure of the parties. To the populace, provided they refrain from damage and arms, permission for gatherings for religious instruction was granted in the same places where they had previously been taking place.[69] Meanwhile the edicts were in abeyance until the king and the States-General made more specific decisions. Envoys departed immediately for the various places, who were to prohibit violence and affirm by agreement what violence had extorted.

59 First and foremost Orange was sent to Antwerp, a town blazing with hazardous sedition,[70] and got that extremely strong city, where he held position of viscount[71], on his side. He permitted the sermons not only in the countryside, as elsewhere, but inside the city walls, and not just these but even the new worship as well, but not in such a way, although he presented necessity as an excuse, as to avoid angering the regent.[72] The same thing befell others, including Horne, whose brother announced him all the way from Spain the king's implacable anger. However they were more worried by intercepted letters to Margaret, in which secret counsellors[73] destined them for accusation and execution. Therefore, to take joint counsel they met in Dendermonde,[74] with eyes turned to Egmond, a man experienced in war and favoured by the soldiers. Egmond however, either soothed by promises or mindful of his duty, said: "I will not fail in obedience to my prince whatever he might be planning—no, we must gentle Philip's mind by advice, and justify our previous emergency actions by loyalty in the future." He did not perceive that great exploits against royal authority are begun with danger: where the first steps have succeeded, safety and rewards can be hoped for from perseverance; but if you let up, punishment awaits.

60 Orange, who saw that these attempts were doomed, had more sense and begged the king by letter that he allow him to shed his offices and seek a quiet life in obscurity in his native Germany Philip sent a crafty reply, with that which makes deceit particularly effective: the appearance of guilelessness. For after a plea not to desert him in troubled times, when his help was most urgently needed, he urged him to disown a brother suspected of revolution, at least until everything settled down. But Orange, superior to such tricks, kept urging his release none the less, and withdrew meanwhile into his stadtholderships. There he forbade cruelty, and after even providing that the defence works of those regions not be garrisoned, he

insiderentur, populos fortes et ipso soli ingenio validos libertatis dulcedine **(24)** excitabat. Scripto quoque suum ad Regem consilium complexus est, ubi docebat, nisi hae saltem religiones permitterentur, quas vicina imperia necessario recepissent, anceps ipsi discrimen, utique exhaustis populis opibusque damnosam victoriam fore. At Hornanus suos se in penates speciemque privati condiderat.

61 His disiectis, facile praefecta, quae[10] conspecto quo res erupisset, ad damnata prius Viglii consilia se receperat, nobilium et populi plebisque infimae nexus perrumpere, rescissis quae ipsa aut per alios pepigerat: primum cavillando, mox apertius, ut metu expressa, et quasi priores alii fidem exuissent. Nam cum in sacrilegos, quique ultra verba ad ritus publicos, aut ad arma processerant, secretis iudicum mandatis, animadverteretur, caeteri, quasi causa dispares, nec inter se religionum concordes, vim dissociavere. Nec minus foederati nobiles, spe aut metu diversi, rem communem prodebant. Nam subeunte paulatim factorum conscientia, fuere qui ad contraria provoluti, veniam pararent: alii cogi tributa et cohortes, ut privatis insolita dissuadent: alii, dum singula singuli conantur, omnibus excidunt. Et iam ipsa, ad tutandam vim imperii, praeter Germanum militem, quem Ericus Brunovix ducebat, alium conscribi et Walonibus iusserat. Id Belgarum populis nomen est, qui Francis contermini, Gallici sermonis usu et ferociore ad arma ingenio caeteris distinguuntur.

62 At quo duces fidos internosceret, verbis conceptis cogebat iurare, hostes sibi futuros quoscunque rex designasset citra exceptionem ullam: id sacramentum dixere Egmondus, *Carolus*[11] Arscotius, e Croiorum gente turbis prioribus impermixtus, Carolus Barlaemontius eiusque fratres; comites, Petrus Mansfeldius Lucemburgi praeses, Geldriae Megemus, Frisiorum Arembergius, et qui apud Haenovios Bergensis Marchionis locum tuebatur Norcarma. Statimque factis comprobavere: Egmondus, in Flandria eos disturbando, in quorum tutelam consenserat; Norcarma Valentinianis imperia detrectantibus obsidio ad deditionem redactis, acriterque punitis; quo exemplo maximae urbes, positis turbis, iussa praesidia accepere: caeteri manus temere coortas caedibus vastantes. Soli Arausionensis et Hoochstratanus negarunt vetus se iusiurandum, quo principi ac legibus tenerentur, alio mutaturos, adiecitque ille esse sibi uxorem eorum e numero, qui istud per iusiurandum exitio destinarentur.

63 Quae dum geruntur, **(25)** Hispani tam felicem occasionem, ut quaesita videri possit, non segniter tractavere. Ac primum manente periculo ferme consentiebatur, vultum numenque principis ad comprimendas partes immane quantum valitura: fidissimis Belgarum monentibus, si alius mitteretur, plus odii, minus obsequii fore. Nam et Carolum patrem, cum una Gandavi civitas turbaret, nihil cunctatum Galliam, paene adhuc bellum spirantem, transcurrere. Sed morae nectebantur, quod iter tutissimum disputando, dum suspecta Gallia inermi, et exercitui iter

[10] quae *1658* quae, *1657*

[11] *recte* Philippus *(cf. Iohannes Montiniacus 1.52 & vide Intr., Principles of this edition)*

aroused nations brave and strong from the character of their native soil[75] with the sweet call of liberty. **(24)** He put his advice to the king in writing too, in which he explained to him that unless at least those religions were permitted that neighboring kingdoms had admitted out of necessity, there would be critical danger to the king himself, while a victory would be ruinous in any case because of the toll it would take from the populace and the country's resources. Horne, on the other hand, had hidden himself at home under guise of private citizenship.

61 With these men disappeared from the scene, it was an easy matter for the regent, who had seen whence the trouble had burst forth and pulled back to the formerly condemned plans of Viglius, to shatter the bonds of the nobles and the people and the lowest crowd. She recalled pledges she had made herself or had pledged through others: at first evasively, soon more openly, on the grounds that they had been forced on her by fear, and as if the others had been the first to break their word. For when secret instructions came from the judges to punish the sacrilegists, and those as well who had gone beyond mere words and proceeded to public worship or taken up arms, the others dissociated their struggle, as if they were fighting for a different cause, and were not of the same religion. No less did the confederate nobles, hope or fear having driven them apart, betray the common cause. For as they gradually became conscious of what they had done, some turned to the opposite side and tried for a pardon. Others argued against the collection of taxes or troops, as something inappropriate for private citizens. Still others, each trying something different for himself, deserted everybody. And now the regent herself, in order to protect the power of her rule, ordered to enlist more soldiers, in addition to the German troops led by Erik of Brunswick, soldiers from the Walloons this time; which name applies to a number of regions in the Low Countries which share a border with France and are distinct from the rest by their use of the French language and a more warlike character.

62 In order to distinguish which commanders were loyal, she forced them to take a solemn oath that whoever the king designated, would be their enemies without any exception.[76] This oath was taken by Egmond, *Charles* of Aarschot (from the house of Croy, so far uninvolved in the disturbances[77]), Charles de Berlaymont and his brothers, counts Peter of Mansfeld, stadtholder of Luxemburg, Megemus (stadtholder of Guelders), Aremberg of the Frisians, and Noircarmes, regent for the marquis of Bergen in Hainaut. And they immediately proved themselves by deeds: Egmond by dislodging those in Flanders whose protection he had agreed to, Noircarmes by forcing Valenciennes, which had refused his orders, into surrender by a siege and punishing it harshly. This example brought the greatest cities to putting their mobs down and accepting the ordered garrisons; the others to a blood-soaked destruction of the roaming bands that had risen up arbitrarily.[78] Only Orange and Hoogstraten stated that they would not change the old oath which tied them to the prince and the laws for a new one; the former added that his wife was among those whom that oath marked out for destruction.

63 While these things were taking place **(25)**, the Spanish were not sluggish to use an occasion so happy that it seemed provoked. And first, while the danger remained, there was a general agreement that the presence and majesty of the prince would be wonderfully effective for repressing faction, and the most loyal of the Lowlanders advised that if another were sent the result would be more hatred, less obedience. For even his father Charles, when the city of Ghent revolted on its own, had crossed France without delay, though it was still practically blazing with war [against him]. But one delay followed another while they were

haud datura, et quo minus classe iretur, oceani terrent pericula, nec satis certus in Zelandiam exscensus, ignoto quousque Angli vel Arausionensis auderent. Igitur, quasi mari alio Ligustica ora, inde Germania peteretur, tentari prius Caesaris animum placuit.

64 Erat is Ferdinandi filius Maximilianus, qui consultus de re Belgica, ni quid Philippus temporibus largiretur, significabat periculum haud abfore, propter Augustanae professionis principes, Belgarum clarissimis per varias necessitudines illigatos: sin leniora probarentur, pacificatorem se offerebat: quae parum grate accepta: velut Augustus Saxo elector dictasset, qui Caesaris amicitia potens,[12] Arausionensi per fratris sui filiam iungebatur. Missae tamen ad Margaritam litterae venturum Regem vulgabant, nec sine exercitu: id quippe regiae maiestati, etiam apud exteros decorum, et aut brevi terrore quieturos motus, aut siquid restaret, adfuturum non accipiendis sed dandis legibus.

65 Paulatim apparebat Hispanos, securitate non contentos, ultioni prospicere, quo Regis iram sua in commoda traherent: oblato subigendos ad Belgas colore, perduellionis omnes teneri, quod aut ipsi res novas coeptassent, aut talia ausos non repulissent. Sunt qui addant iam ante Philippo a Romano pontifice factam gratiam iurisiurandi, quo imperium iniens legibus se obstrinxerat, ut quomodo America et Italiae plurima, ita Belgae regnarentur. Praecipua Albano consiliorum fides, qui non novus saeviendi auctor, credi voluit, nisi tam foedum rebellandi exemplum non minus insigni poena corrigeretur, defecturas omni a parte nationes, cum pleraque non tam vis praesens, quam metus contineret. Neque omittendum Philippo aptissimum perdomandae Belgicae tempus, dum regna circumiecta fidam ipsi pacem servant, aut siquid suspectum, domi inquies. Ita victi qui mitiora suadebant, ipso etiam Carolo filio operam **(26)** suam pacandis regendisque Belgis offerente, frustra adeo, ut id inter suspicionum in ipsum conceptarum alimenta fuerit. Tandem erumpit, retento Rege, velut maiores ob curas, aut ne periculo misceretur, Albanum summa cum potestate mitti; nec dubium qualibus mandatis, hominem bello semper et sanguine exercitum:

66 quem cum in Italiam transvectum Neapoli, Sicilia, Sardinia, Mediolano veteres Hispanorum cohortes, addito equitatu, adducere nuntii attulere, Arausionensis non ultra opperiendum ratus, Nassaviam petit fratri possessam; digrediens magna prosequentium multitudine palam testatur, nihil se moturum, nisi prior laederetur. Absentis vice tutari praefecturas iussus a Margarita Maximilianus comes Bossuvius. Brederodius cum et sua muniret, Traiectoque Rheni insuper et Amstelodamo, opulentissimis urbibus, immineret, fovente conatus primos Arausionensi per dissimulationem, aut tacita ope, mox armis pellitur. Egmondus et minores alii, quorum aut animus aut fortuna exsilium non tolerabat, spe vivendi inducti sunt ut perirent. At nobiles plerique et plebs multa, Hispanorum formidine, pars reducta supplicia

[12] potens, *1658* potens *1657*

disputing which route would be safest, with France unsafe if he went unarmed, and unlikely to give passage to an army; while the dangers of the sea deterred him from going with a fleet and a landing in Zeeland was insufficiently certain, as it was uncertain how far the English or Orange would dare to go. Therefore it was decided, as if the journey would go by another sea to the Ligurian coast and thence to Germany, to test the mind of the emperor first.

64 This was Ferdinand's son Maximilian, who, consulted about the Netherlands question, indicated that there would certainly be danger unless Philip conceded significantly to the circumstances, on account of the various close connections between leaders of the Augsburg confession and the highest circles in the Low Countries. If however a milder approach was adopted, he offered himself as a peacemaker. Which proposal was greeted with no enthusiasm, as if it had been dictated by August, elector of Saxony, a man powerful in the emperor's friendship and connected to Orange through his niece. A letter to Margaret nevertheless announced that the king was about to come, and not without an army. For this was consonant with the majesty of the king, seemly even among foreign peoples, and uprisings would either die out from terror in short order, of, if anything remained, the army would be present nor for receiving but for prescribing the law.

65 Gradually it became apparent that the Spaniards were not content with the restoration of order but were looking for revenge, to turn the king's anger to their own advantage. They came up with the following pretext to subjugate the Netherlanders, that they were all guilty of treason because they had either undertaken rebellion themselves or had failed to stop those who had dared it. Some add to this that the pope had already given Philip leave from the oath whereby he had bound himself to the laws upon entering office, with the result that he could rule the Low Countries as he ruled America or most of Italy. Particular trust was placed in the counsel of Alva, who, no newcomer as a perpetrator of cruelty, wished it to be believed that nations on all sides would defect if so foul an example of rebellion was not corrected by a most distinctive punishment, since most subjects are controlled less by actual violence than by the fear of it. Also, Philip should not pass up this most suitable occasion for taming the Low Countries, while the surrounding kingdoms were faithfully keeping peace with him, or else, if suspect, had trouble had home. In this way the men who urged milder approaches were overcome, among whom was no one less than Philip's son Don Carlos, who offered **(26)** his assistance for pacifying and ruling the Lowlanders.[79] This was so much in vain that it even fed the suspicions which had risen against himself. At length the outcome was that the king would stay at home as if for more important matters, or to avoid involvement in danger, and that Alva was sent with supreme powers. Nor was there any doubt about the nature of these mandates, given to a man trained all his life in war and bloodshed.

66 When the news arrived that he had crossed into Italy, and was leading regiments of Spanish veterans from Naples, Sicily, Sardinia, Milan, and extra cavalry, Orange decided that he should wait no longer and went to the castle of Nassau, then in the possession of his brother.[80] As he left he declared in the presence of a great multitude of followers that he would make no move unless he were first injured. Maximilian, count of Bossu,[81] was ordered by Margaret to take charge of his stadtholderates in his place. When Brederode was strengthening his own holdings, and threatened Utrecht and even Amsterdam as well, both extremely wealthy cities (which attempts were originally supported by Orange by looking the other way or with secret aid), he was soon driven off by violence of arms. Egmond and some other lesser nobles, whose spirit or fortune could not bear exile, were drawn to their

metuens, nec de religione parata discedere, in Germaniae proxima Angliamque et longinquiora dilabuntur: cum eodem tempore praefecta alio edicto fugere cogeret, alio vetaret. Caeterum sponte egressis qui praesentia gravabantur, compositisque rebus egregio astu foeminae, alta pax erat, et quod fere convenit, si nil ultra concupitum foret, facile mansura. **(27)**

deaths by the hope of living. But most of the nobles and many from the populace, for fear of the Spaniards (some feared a return of punishments and were not prepared to abandon their faith) dispersed into the nearest parts of Germany and England and more distant places still. Indeed the regent was at the same time forcing them to flee by one edict, forbidding it by another. For the rest, when those who were oppressed by the present conditions had left of their own volition, and the situation had been settled by this lady's remarkable cleverness, there was a deep peace, and, it is generally agreed, a peace that would easily have lasted, had nothing further been desired. **(27)**

Liber Secundus

1 (1568) Sed Albanus morbo suo nonnihil, et ob hyemantes maxime Alpes, tardatus, tandem itinere, et sterili multum et laborioso, transita Sabaudia Burgundiam attigit, eiusque loci delectu auxit agmen, quod ille maius octo hominum millibus admirabili disciplina continebat. Monstrata tunc via Hispanis tanto terrarum spatio, Lucemburgum usque impediri nunquam postea potuit, haud imprudente Philippo quos sibi principes ad continuandam vim disiectae dominationis adscisceret. Eodemque tempore in Gallia, velut ex condicto, in bellum erumpebatur, contractis a Rege Helvetiorum cohortibus, in speciem quasi finibus metueret, Albani exercitu extrema radente; reipsa contra vindices invisae religionis.

2 Belgarum mira aut formido, aut securitas;[13] intranti nemo obstitit. Quin festo concursu excipitur dux belli missus in gentem pacatam. Id enim initio potestatis vocabulum usurpabat: donec Margarita, vani honoris imaginem pertaesa et credita muliebri languore regimen corrupisse, eoque magis, quia Albanum cum exercitu mitti, literis accuratis futurique praesagis dissuaserat, abitu suo summam illi praefecturam patefecit: nullo iam dubitante, quam non ex legibus gesturus foret magistratum, ad quem salvis legibus pervenire non potuerat, cauto antiquitus, nequis nisi Belga aut principum e sanguine id munus fungeretur.

3 Primum saevituri imperii documentum fuit Egmondus et Hornanus, dolo in curiam acciti, vinctique; rogantes ut ex aurei velleris privilegio a collegis iudicarentur, non hoc modo non impetrant, sed extra Brabantiam custodiendi ablegantur, contra iura e plebe infimo cuique concessa. Inde primis Belgicae urbibus immissa praesidia Hispanorum, qui ferme soli retenti, cum alii milites tantum extra ordinem ad pericula usurparentur. Ipse Belgarum nobilium equitatus, admixtis Hispanis, ductore Arembergio, in Galliam missus, ut praesenti auxilio foedus regi Carolo probaret. Coeptae interim et arces strui exarmatis civibus, et, quod gravissimum erat, ministrandos ad sumtus subactis.

4 Quae postquam nullo vetante processerant, iudices ferme duodecim, Hispani (**29**) pars magna, caeteri, quod genus non minus inclemens perspectum est, Hispanis servientes, iubentur his qui motarum nuper rerum affines culpae essent, irrogare supplicia, reiectis ad quos patrio more iurisdictio pertinebat. Id maximum potentiae praesidium, iudiciorum potiri: cumq ue laesis sacris maiestas accederet, tam suspecta bonis principibus criminatio quam tyrannis opportuna, ut quae reos omni legum auxilio exuat, et pene sola nominis atrocitate convincat.

[13] securitas; intranti *scripsimus* securitas, intranti *1657, 1658*

Book 2

(p. 28)

1 Alva's approach however was delayed, a bit by his own illness and a lot by the winter in the Alps; after a difficult and lonely journey through Savoy he finally reached Burgundy. A troop recruitment from that area enlarged his train, which, being over eight thousand men in size, the man kept in check admirably. Now that the Spaniards had been shown the way through such a long series of countries, all future opportunities to stop him were lost as far as Luxemburg, as Philip possessed a clear sense which leaders he should employ to preserve the force of his disconnected empire.[1] At that time, as if by agreement, war broke out in France, after the king had hired Swiss regiments. This in appearance he did out of fear over the integrity of his realm, as Alva's army brushed along its borders; in reality to use them against the defenders of the resented confession.

2 The Lowlanders lived in amazing fear or unconcern; at Alva's arrival no resistance was offered. What is more, the warlord sent out to a province at peace was greeted by cheering crowds. That title (that is, the title of duke[2]) he used at the beginning of his command, until Margaret by her own departure opened the way to the stadtholderate for him, tired as she was of the empty appearance of her office and because, as it was believed, feminine languor had undermined her reign; but most of all because she had, in elaborate letters with predictions of the consequences, argued against sending Alva with an army. No one had any doubts how far Alva would go in ignoring the law while fulfilling this office, to which he could not even be admitted without infringement of the laws, since of old it was stated that it could be held only by Lowlanders or persons of royal blood.

3 The first sign of the approaching terror were Egmond and Horne, summoned by a stratagem[3] to the see of the Council of State, and arrested.[4] Their request to be tried by their peers, in accordance with the privileges of the Order of the Golden Fleece, was not only not honoured, but they were even removed to a prison away from Brabant, in contravention of the rights granted to even the lowliest from the populace. Next, Spanish garrisons were placed in the most important towns in the Low Countries; these soldiers were virtually the only ones kept in service, as others were only used against dangers outside the regular order of things.[5] The very cavalry of the Netherlands nobility was expanded by the addition of Spaniards and sent off to France under the command of Aremberg, in order to confirm the treaty with king Charles with actual support. Meanwhile citadels were being constructed after the citizenship had been disarmed and (which was the worst of it), forced to contribute to the costs.

4 After these steps had been taken without anyone objecting, a group of circa twelve judges[6]—most of them Spaniards, **(29)** the others being men subservient to Spain, a race found to be of no lesser cruelty—were ordered to demand the death penalty against all who were guilty of any connection with the recent upheavals; the judges to whom this jurisdiction belonged by tradition were excluded. Control of the lawcourts is a very important pillar of power—especially when accusations of sacrilege are supplemented with some of lese-majesty, an accusation as suspect with good princes as it is welcome to tyrants, since it robs its defendants of all legal support, and virtually condemns them by the sole horror of the term alone.

5 Stipatae[14] reis custodiae, innumeri mortales necati: ubique una species ut captae civitatis. Quippe non arma tantum huc trahebantur, sed pro motu habita aliorum quies, et infausta consilia, quaesitique honores et recusati: praecipua nobilium strage et qui auctoritate aut opibus valuerant, quorum mortes in securitatem, fortunae in fiscum et praedam Hispanis cedebant: non dissimulante quid peteret Albano, cum voce aspera suique ingenii, pauca salmonum piscium capita multis ranunculorum millibus praestare iactans, novo more veterem exprimeret sententiam, quae, sublatis e republica primoribus, munire regnum docet.

6 Egmondo et Hornano obiecta omnia, quae post Granvellana odia ad id tempus intercesserant, ingesta suspicione Arausionensi et ipsis constitutum, partita inter se Belgica regem armis excludere. Hi duo viri omnium confessione eminentissimi, nec minus factis quam stirpe illustres, Bruxellae post sacra Romano ritu peracta, loco publico cervices carnifici praebuere; capita aliquamdiu suffixa palis, Belgarum in oculis atrox spectaculum: et quanquam circumfusa arma vocibus ac prope vultibus imminebant, altius animis omnium miseratio, fortiorum etiam ultio insedit, cum incredibilis turbae osculis et fletu sepulchra celebrarentur, alii vero et comas promitterent, priscum in morem obligato oris habitu, quem non mutarent, nisi vindicato tam nobili sanguine. Arausionensis cum pluribus aliis edicto citatus, et quia poenam absens illuserat, versa in fiscum bona, filiusque Lovanio, ubi honestis artibus innutriebatur, in Hispaniam et captivitatem avectus est.

7 Stragibus et fuga magna vastitas fit. Pauci, quibus nec exsilium egestas sua concesserat, cum armis in sylvas abditi, ubi multa de sacerdotibus praeda victitarent, grassantes in se magistratus pari poena coercuere, donec maioribus Albani copiis excuterentur. Ita et ad Mosam Rhenumque coortae passim exiguae manus, coniurataeque in ducis necem primis (**30**) conatibus succubuerunt.

8 Mitiora a Rege quam ab Albano sperari atroces ex Hispania nuntii non ferebant: ubi affectus publico supplicio Montiniacus, quem missum eo retulimus, fas gentium sanctumque inter hostes legationis nomen frustra pro se fore speravit, negato subditis cum principe tale iuris commercium intercedere. Marchio Bergensis similem exitum oportuna morte praevenit, non sine dati veneni rumore, sed et huius memoria Albano faciente damnata est. De ipso Regis filio Carolo maior fama et obscurior: tot illum regnorum haeredem in custodiam datum constabat, seu suspicionem incitaverat matura imperio iuventa, quasi nimium Belgas, nec ut paternos curaret; sive idem crimen ipsum, et novercam abstulit: mox sane interiit, incertum quibus causis patris ira in filii necem durasset.

[14] convincat. Stipatae *1657, 1658* convincat, stipatae *Peerlkamp*

5 The prisons were packed with the accused; countless humans were killed. The same sight everywhere, as of plunder after a siege. For not only recourse to arms was used as a grounds for accusation, but in others their lack of movement was interpreted as rebellion, or unfortunate advice, or offices sought or precisely refused. The destruction was greatest among the nobility and those who had been prominent in power or wealth, and whose deaths contributed to the safety of the Spaniards, whose possessions to their revenues and booty. Alva made no secret of his intentions when he boasted by a harsh remark, which characterises him perfectly, that a couple of salmon heads are preferable to many thousands of frog heads.[7] Thus he gave a new expression to the ancient wisdom that a king strengthens his position by eliminating the leading people in his state.

6 Egmond and Horne were blamed for everything which had passed from the time of the loathed Granvelle up to that time, including the suspicion that with William of Orange they had decided to divide the Low Countries among themselves and throw the king out by force. These two men were in everyone's conviction the most eminent men in the Low Countries, as magnificent by their own deeds as by their descent. They offered their necks to the headsman on a square in Brussels after a service in the Roman fashion. Their heads remained on poles for some time, to serve as horrible spectacle to the Netherlanders. Incredible crowds visited their graves, crying and kissing, and although the army, which stood around in large numbers, kept a close eye on every word and almost every face, compassion seized everyone's heart, and with the brave, the decision to take revenge as well. Others even pledged their hair, following an ancient custom which puts an obligation on their facial growth, that is, to leave it untouched until such noble blood be avenged. The possessions of Orange, who was summoned by proclamation with many others to appear in court, fell to the treasury, also because he evaded punishment by being absent. His son was abducted from Louvain, where he was being educated in the Liberal Arts, to captivity in Spain.[8]

7 Carnage and flight produced one large wasteland. The few whose poverty did not even admit exile, kept hiding in arms in the forests, where rich booty looted from the clergy provided for their living.[9] They managed to keep the magistrate, who raged against them, in check with equal violence, until they were outnumbered by Alva's forces and driven out. Similarly small bands arose in many places along the rivers Meuse and Rhine, who had sworn to kill the duke and perished **(30)** at their first attempts.

8 Gruesome reports from Spain gave no reason to expect a milder attitude from the king than from Alva. For in Spain the baron de Montigny, whom we related above was sent there,[10] was submitted to public execution. He expected the sacred law of nations, and the title of envoy, inviolable even between parties at war, to work for him; but in vain, as Philip's subjects were denied such legal intercourse with their prince. The marquis of Bergen forestalled a similar end by a timely death, not without giving occasion to rumours of poison. However this be, on his memory too a *damnatio memoria* was imposed by Alva's doing. The story told about the king's son Carlos himself is even more spectacular and more darksome. It was an established fact that the successor to so many crowns was put in custody, either because his young age, ripe enough to assume power, aroused suspicions that he cared too much for the Lowlanders, as if they weren't his father's province;[11] or because one and the same crime carried him and his step-mother away to their ends. In any case, his death came soon, and it remains unknown for which reasons father persisted in his wrath until he had killed his son.

9 Arausionensem sponte ad arma non festinaturum, quod mallet Hispano ruendi in omnes, donec consilia cuncta patescerent, et oppressis coalescendi copiam dare, addita spe, fore ut in Regem aliis subinde bellis implicitum tutior daretur occasio, exsules impellebant, qui ubique inviti[15] et inopes patriae fortuna procul premebantur.

10 Pars horum Ludovici Nassavii ductum secuti in Frisiam irruunt. Hi interemto Arembergio, quem prudentius cunctantem militum ardor et convitia in praelium impulerant, disiectisque eius copiis, victores, cum descituras civitates frustra exspectarent, et iam deficiens stipendium disciplinam solvisset, Albani superventu concisi, amisso etiam in priore pugna Adolpho Arausionensis ac Ludovici fratre, alterno hostium et suo sanguine bellum imbuerunt.

11 Hoc rerum cursu pertractus Arausionensis, ut iusto imperio et robore partes refoveret, ius causasque armorum libris evulgat, obiecta sibi crimina, simulque iudicem refutans, nec dissimulato meliora se edoctum a Romana ecclesia transiisse: sumere tamen arma communi pro salute, et dipellendo patriae servitio testabatur, id civis, id viri optimatis officium: de Philippo honorifice, cuius bonitatem ab Hispanorum consiliis obsideri, nec desperandum, quin aliquando fidam gentem iuratasque leges respiceret: interim eius erroribus, ex lege Brabantica, principatus obsequium non deberi.

12 Postremum, quod ad ius causae plurimum facere videtur, ita se habet. Brabanti ut pleraque cautius caeteris libertati suae prospexere, ita contra fraudem imperantium, qui obtentu publici boni conventiones non (**31**) metuunt rescindere, illud quoque proprium pacisci solent, ut, principe leges violante, ipsi fidei et obsequii vinculo liberentur, donec demantur iniuriae. Idque maiorum exemplis firmatur, qui olim impotentia, aut assentantium dolis abreptos principes, ac maxime Iohannem eius nominis secundum ad meliora traxerant vi aut fortibus decretis; haud ante pace facta, quam iisdem staturos se principes spopondissent. Arausionensis, quanquam in Germania natus, clarissimas per Brabantiam iurisdictiones haereditarias obtinebat, quarum dominis mos antiquus procerum dignitatem asscribit: eo tum ille iure, non usum modo legum, sed et tutelam ad se praecipue pertinere contendebat.

13 Caeterum praetereundum non est, ab aliis quoque Belgarum nationibus idem ius moribus usurpatum: Maximiliani insuper Austriaci Mariaeque Burgundicae placita praeferri, quae ipsas Brabantis individuas eadem legum sanctione aequaverint. Illud constat, qui postea Carolo imperatore principe accesserunt, populos, Frisios, Traiectinos, Geldros, multa pactos propria, illud commune, ne a Brabantia atque Hollandia divellerentur.

[15] inviti *1657, 1658* invisi *Peerlkamp*

9 Exiles [from the Low Countries] stirred up William of Orange, who of his own accord would not take up arms too quickly and preferred giving the Spanish occasion to rage against all, until the full extent of their plans had become clear, and the oppressed to unite among themselves. Moreover he hoped that a safer opportunity would be provided against a king who would soon be involved in other wars. The exiles however, scattered against their will and penniless, suffered far from home from their motherland's misfortunes.

10 Part of these exiles invaded Friesland following Louis of Nassau's lead. They inaugurated the war with a toast of their enemies' blood, then of their own. First Aremberg perished, who by himself was wise enough to wait, but was driven into battle by the belligerence and reproaches of his soldiers. Having dispelled Aremberg's troops, the exiles, now the victors, counted in vain on the defection of cities and soon the absence of pay eroded their discipline, until they were butchered at Alva's sudden appearance. Adolph, brother of William and Louis of Orange, had even been killed in the first battle.[12]

11 This course of events caused Orange to strengthen his side with force and a legitimation of his power. He issued publications[13] stating the rightfulness and the causes of the fighting, in which he also refuted the crimes of which he was accused and the legitimacy of the judge. He did not hide the fact that he had left the Roman church since he had learned about a better one.[14] "However,"[15] he declared, "I am taking up arms for the public sake and in order to drive servitude from the country: that is my duty as a citizen and a nobleman." About Philip he spoke respectfully: "his goodness is being blocked by the counsel of the Spaniards. There is no reason to lose hope that one day he will come to care for a loyal nation and the laws he has sworn to uphold. Until that time however, on account of Brabant's law,[16] normal obedience to the monarch is not owed to Philip's errors."

12 Of this last element, which contributes greatly to the justice of his cause, the explanation is as follows.[17] In general the Brabantines have watched their liberties better than the other provinces. For in their covenants they include as a condition which they are entitled to, that if and when the prince acts in violation of the laws, the Brabantines are exempt from their duty to loyalty and obedience until the injustice be removed. They did this as a precaution against deceit by their rulers, who do not shrink back from cancelling **(31)** meetings of the Estates under the pretext of protecting the common good. Its wisdom is confirmed by the experiences of previous generations who used force or bold decrees to drag their princes back to better ways when they were carried away by their own weakness or the tricks of flatterers—count John II being the most notable example. They did not conclude peace before the princes would promise to keep themselves to these decrees. Orange, although born in Germany, possessed some very illustrious hereditary lands in Brabant, and ancient custom placed the lords of these among the highest nobility. On the basis of these rights Orange claimed that not merely an invocation of these laws pertained to him especially, but their protection as well.

13 Furthermore it should not be forgotten that practice had expanded the same rights to the other Low Countries provinces as well, and that on top of that decrees by Maximilian of Habsburg and Mary of Burgundy are available which put the other provinces, which are indissolubly linked to Brabant, in the same position by confirming the same laws. It is an undisputed fact that the nations which joined during the time when the Emperor Charles was prince,[18] i.e. the Frisians, Utrecht, Guelderland, have agreed many separate conditions with the Emperor, but all share this condition, that they will not be separated from Brabant and Holland.

14 His disceptationibus permotus Caesar Maximilianus, simulque Arausionensis casum miserens tantis honoribus tantisque divitiis subito exturbati, (nec enim illo ingenio mitius ullum regnis contigit) Carolum fratrem in Hispaniam misit, qui suo et principum Germanorum nomine nuntiaret, non videri e bono publico in Belgas durius consuli. Sed male dissimulata iracundia, Philippus referri iussit: sua sibi curae, cui nota ut clementiae, ita severitatis tempora, in eos qui spreto Deo, mox et principem spernere didicissent: ipsos facturos rectius tutiusque, si rerum alienarum arbitrio abstinerent.

15 Erant, qui differrent inferiora Germaniae per vim dominantium corpori suo avulsa, nunc bello redditum iri. Sed Caesar sponte pacis studiosus, mox et nova affinitate Hispaniae illigatus, quievit. Pauci Germanorum, pietatis respectu, aut regnorum invidia, et Albani nimium ibi noti odio, Arausionensem pecunia ac milite iuvabant, forte et moti suspicionibus, quasi Albanus nobiles ad Rhenum Amasiumque urbes, ob religionem et Belgarum effugia, regio imperio adiecturus, inde caeteris immineret. Simul ad expeditionem ipsius Arausionensis fides et propinquorum pignoribus devincta, datum et nonnihil a Belgis quibus peregre morantibus necessitas redeundi, aut tacita domi vota libertatis: (**32**) sed pleraque polliciti in eventum distulere.

16 Coacta igitur ipso ductante sex equitum millia, peditum quatuordecim, e Germania maxime, ubi ingens hominum multitudo praesenti aere inescata, futuri improvida, nullo partium studio, cuivis conducenti facilis, pars et e Belgica et Galliis. Has copias, cum improviso Mosae transitu primam praelii occasionem non rapuissent, exin facile Albanus debellavit, egregio usus victoriae genere non pugnando: felix id sibi etiam in Italia quondam adversus Guisium expertus. Itaque haesit usque per totos tres et viginti dies euntium tergis, tam provide positis proxime hostem castris, ut nunquam cum illius desperatione certare cogeretur. Repertus tum color iniquitatis in perpetuum duraturae, ut bellum utrique pacatis e regionibus alerent, cum dato aut negato transitu per Cliviam aut Leodium, pars semper altera rapinis se aut etiam incendiis vindicaret.

17 Sed tanta moles exercitus nullis urbibus recepta, nullo adiuta commeatu, brevi diffluxit, fame rerumque omnium, stipendii maxime, penuria: cuius vix tenues reliquias Arausionensis in Galliam trahens, eo spes suas transtulit: ibique immixtus aliquamdiu bello alieno et simili causae (nam et Albanus regi auxilia miserat) pace mox inita deceptus fuit, et in deceptos pars insidiarum.

18 (1569) Depulso exercitu, quo non dubie exhaustae vires Nassavianae erant, ut cautus periculis, ita nimius successu Albanus in eos se populos victorem ferens, quos hostes nondum senserat, quaesiti armis imperii gloriam affectabat. Eoque nomine, sacrato ense a pontifice Romano donatus, super deditam[16] scriptis rei

[16] deditam *1657, 1658* diditam *Boot*

14 This polemic touched the emperor Maximilian deeply. He also regretted Orange's fall, which suddenly drove the latter out of such splendid office and wealth—no kingdom ever befell a milder prince than Maximilian. He sent his brother Charles to Spain to deliver the message in his own name and that of the other German princes that it was not thought to be in the general interest to act too severely against the Netherlanders. Philip however, with ill-concealed anger, had the reply sent back that he could handle his own work, and that he knew which was the time for mildness and which for severity towards a people who had spurned God and would soon find out how to spurn their prince. And lastly that the senders should do better and safer if they would refrain from judging another man's business.

15 Now there were some who spread the news that Lower Germany, which by the force of its rulers had broken away from the body of the Empire, would return to it as a result of the war. Of his own accord however the Emperor was keen on preserving peace, and soon moreover bound to Spain by new ties; and therefore he did not move. A small number of Germans, for the sake of the faith or from loathing of kings, and hatred of Alva who was all too well known over there, sent support to Orange in money or soldiers. Possibly they were also motivated by suspicions whether Alva wasn't planning to annex the great cities on the Rhine and Ems for his king's realm (because of the faith and their importance for refugees from the Low Countries) and next to pose a threat to the others. Orange himself made debts as well for this expedition, partly by pawning possessions of his relatives, while some small amounts were given by Lowlanders abroad who had no choice but to return home, or people at home with a secret desire for liberty. **(32)** In most cases however these contributions were promised but postponed until the actual effectuation.

16 Thus six thousand cavalry, fourteen thousand infantry were brought together under Orange's own command, coming mostly from Germany, where an endless multitude, lured by the ready pay, unaware of what was awaiting them, and without any partiality, were easily available for whichever crimp; part of them however came from the Low Countries and France. These forces crossed the Meuse unexpectedly[19] but did not seize the first opportunity to give battle; then Alva easily overcame them by an exquisite strategy for victory, that is, not fighting. That this strategy was a good one he had found out once in Italy against De Guise.[20] Thus he stuck to the tail of the travelling army for a full twenty-three days, cleverly placing his own encampments in such places, close to the enemy, that there would never be necessity to fight against a desperate opponent. In this time another pretence for perpetual wrongdoing was invented in the practice that both sides fed their campaigns from regions at peace, and according to whether access via Cleves or Liège was given or denied, the other side would take revenge by irruptions or outright pillage.

17 An army that size however was not given access to any towns nor supported with any provisions. It fell apart in short order for starvation and lack of everything, especially wages; Orange could only just drag the scanty remains to France and put his hopes on her. In France he remained caught up for some time in another people's war for a similar cause (for Alva had also sent help to the French king); but ended up deceived by the peace that was soon concluded, and in the eyes of the deceived became part of the machinations.

18 When this army had been driven away (which had to have exhausted the Nassau resources) Alva, as careful as he had been among dangers, just so excessive in success, comported himself as victor towards a people whose enmity he had not yet felt. He appropriated the glory of a victory achieved on the battlefield and on those grounds received a blessed

2.18. *Statue of Alva in Antwerp*
(from P.C. Hooft, *Nederlandse Historien* vol. 1, Amsterdam 1703)

2.26. *Capture of Den Briel*
(anonymous, possibly by Jan Luyken, E&K 52)

famam, in arce, quam perfectissimi operis Antverpiae imposuerat, coercendae plebi, nulli praeter id usui, quod situs ipse testatur ab amne aversus, statuam sibi ponit, multo verborum honore, quod extincta seditione, rebellibus pulsis, iustitia culta, provinciis pacem firmasset. Multaque eo tempore utilia non minus quam speciosa, de moneta ac mercatura, de criminum persecutione, et libris non temere in vulgus edendis constituit, solo auctoris odio peritura. Iam vero in religiones inquisitio, acta Synodi Tridentinae, novi antistites, excusata hactenus aut repudiata, parato qui cogeret, velut sponte recipiebantur, provectis eo usque odiis, ut a Protestantibus Christiano ritu tincti, contra veterum instituta, retingerentur.

19 Nec minus perduellionis novum tribunal calebat super vetera crimina additis, quos nuper Arausionensis prospera (**33**) sperasse, aut indoluisse adversis,[17] suspicio erat. Quae tamen dum fiunt, clementiae quoque fama velut honestandae victoriae quaerebatur, proposito Regis edicto, priorum temporum culpam fatentibus ignoscentis: sed excepti ad poenam sacrorum doctores atque administri, quique eos hospitio iuvissent, et quorum scelere violata templorum religio, quique arma gesserant, aut honores, aut in nobilium coitionem adsenserant; immensum reorum[18] agmen. Oppidorum quoque et universitatum iura, et quae privatis fiscus debebat, Regis arbitrio servata.

20 Cum iam non metus, non pudor retineret, ultima Hispanorum commenta patuere, quibus effecturos se iactaverant, ut provincialium sumtu imperii onera, et, si necesse foret, bellum quoque administraretur. Iubet Albanus totius census in praesens centesimam pendi: quod ipsum grave, quia rite rogari solitum ab armato imperabatur; nec sacerdotes exceperat: deinde vicesimam soli, decimam caeterarum rerum venalium in singulas alienationes, Hispanis ita pendi asserens, quo magis aequum Belgas parere, damnatos legibus, subactos armis, nec aliter veniae compotes. Facile intellectum hoc vectigali negotiationes, artesque connexas multorum fuga iam labefactatas perverti, prima populi alimenta. Nam mercimonia, multis solita ministeriis distrahi, si tantum onus in pretii partem accresceret, non erant inventura emptorem, cum possent alibi vilius constare.

21 Si quibus obloquendi audacia, statim immisso milite exquisitissimis iniuriis vexandi tradebantur. Quin et nationum et urbium quaedam contumaciores, raro more, maiestatis interrogabantur, obiectis quae contra edicta regia pepigerant, fierive permiserant. Et quanquam privatorum furores a causa communi, necessitatem

[17] adversis, *1658* adversis *1657*
[18] reorum *Peerlkamp* rerum *1657, 1658*

sword from the pope. He erected a statue in his own honour with an inscription at the foot preserving the glory of his achievements in the splendidly constructed citadel which he placed in Antwerp in order to control the populace, and for no other purpose, as its placement proves, directed away from the river; an inscription, that is, with many glorious phrases stating that he secured peace in the provinces by putting down the rebellion, scattering the rebels and promoting justice.[21] In this time he also instituted many rules which were no less useful than magnificent, governing coinage and trade, the prosecution of crimes, and control of the spread of books, which were to disappear again only because of the hatred of their initiator. Now the religious Inquisition, the decrees of the Council of Trent, and the new bishoprics, which up to now all had excused themselves from, or refused outright, were accepted, now the man to force them through was ready. Meanwhile the hatred had risen to such a point that people baptised by Protestants by Christian ritual, were re-baptised, in contravention of ancient Christian rules.

19 The new court for high treason was no less active in the prosecution of past crimes, which now included those who were suspected of having hoped for success **(33)** for Orange in recent times or having grieved over his misfortune. While all this was being done however, a reputation for mildness was sought too, as if to clothe the victory in an appearance of decency. A royal decree was published with a pardon for those who confessed their guilt in the past years.[22] Exempted from this however, to bring them to punishment, were religious teachers and its ministers, those who had provided shelter, those whose crimes had violated the sanctity of the houses of worship, those who had been in arms or in office, or had given their approval in the meetings of the nobles—an innumerable host of defendants. What to do with the privileges of towns and corporations,[23] and the treasury's debts to private parties, was left to the king's decision.

20 When no fear or decency withheld them any longer, the ultimate ambitions of the Spanish became clear, in which they boasted that they would accomplish that the government's expenses would be paid by the inhabitants of the provinces, and if necessary even those of the war. Alva decreed that one percent of the total taxation had to be paid straight away—a shocking thing because here was commanded with the threat of force something that had always been dressed up in a careful request; while not even the clergy was exempt from this. Next there came taxes of one-twentieth on real estate and one-tenth on all other sales, and this at every single transfer. Alva claimed that in this way taxes were collected in Spain, and that therefore it was only reasonable that the Lowlanders would submit to the same system, since they had been condemned by law, defeated by arms, and had no other rights to mercy. It is easy to understand that because of these imposts, trade and the connected crafts, which were already in crisis because so many had fled, were ruined which are the people's main source of subsistence. Because commodities, which habitually pass through many servient hands would not find a buyer if so much is added to the price, because in that case they are available cheaper elsewhere.

21 Whoever had the courage to raise his voice had his life made difficult immediately by the military and the most carefully devised injuries. What's more, the more insolent of the provinces and towns were submitted, most unusually, to interrogations on suspicion of lese-majesty; held against them were agreements which they had made in contravention of royal decrees, or had allowed others to make. And although they worked hard to separate the madness of individuals from the common cause, and necessity from mischief, the

a maleficio segregarent, lata sententia, legibus omnique consilio publico exuebantur; regendae in posterum eo iure, quo principi placuisset. Nec ad Regem provocasse quibusdam impunitum fuit: et magistratuum preces mulcta coërcitae, quam ipsi de suo dependerent: quibus exemplis territi caeteri, certa pecuniae summa infinitum onus redimere conabantur. Nondum infensum Belgarum vitiis Deum tot mala satiabant: sed quasi iactandae terrae viris opibusque florentissimae, hominum crudelitas et avaritia non sufficerent, Oceanus, quanta vix unquam eluvie littora perrumpens, stragem praesentem attulit, futuram indicavit. Hoc enim illud erat tempus, cuius exiguo fine (**34**) ultima servitus et summa libertas discreta, per utrumque nomen pares clades et miserias continuarunt.

22 (1570) Iam ira oppressis armorum libidinem suggerens documento erat, nullam esse tam firmam concordiam, quam quae privatae rei vinculo continetur. Gens illa, quae cives flammari, occidi rectores, eripi leges, religionem, rempublicam, viderat pene immota, tum primum consensit priora ulcisci, imminentia arcere. Atque adeo Bruxella in urbe, quamvis praesens Albanus et ingenti praesidio minax decimam exigeret, officinas et tabernas quisque suas clausere, vel capitis periculo aspernati confessionem servitutis. Iam patibula, iam carnifices parati erant in contumaces, cum nuntiati, quos mox narrabimus, per Hollandiam motus manum iniecere saevitiae.

23 (1571) Crescens populorum indignatio animum Arausionensi restituerat, quanquam afflicta fide, ut iterum belli fortunam experiretur; dum partem Philippi virium Turca in se trahit, et ipsa Hispania a Maurorum motu vixdum satis quieverat;[19] dansque arma et ducem, viam dissidio aperiret. Misit igitur idoneos ad principes omnes, qui se religionis instauratores profitebantur, oratum societatem, aut clandestina auxilia in causam communem. Negarunt Danus et Sueo, metu adversus validiorem certandi; nec Angliae regina ausa turbare vicinam magnitudinem, quanquam ipsam Romanus pontifex devotam praedae exposuerat, et Albanus ob retentas in Anglia mercatorum Genuensium pecunias, in usum praesentem et sub reddendi fide, exorto certamine et ad pignorationes usque provecto, pridem suspectus erat causam belli in divitem insulam quaerere;[20] ac nuper cum in eius regni Septentrionalibus turbaretur, miserat qui portus explorarent, quique se duces, si res processisset, praeberent; et Scotorum reginae conatus adversus Elisabetham haud dubie foverat:[21] quibus ad tempus dissimulatis, eo usque Hispano obtemperatum est, ut Nassaviani omni effugio exuerentur, iussi intra certum diem Angliae finibus excedere.

24 At in Gallia, qui ritus Latinos aspernabantur, ut paci fiderent in admissiones gratiamque Regis adaequati, quo prodessent Arausionensi eadem sentienti, Burgundicis odiis recentia aggerebant; super motam tunc primum in conventu Tridentino de loco inter reges principe controversiam, infamato Philippo veneni in uxorem Elisabetham: cui ultionem deberi, neque minus Gallis, quos in Florida

[19] quieverat; *1658* quieverat, *1657*
[20] quaerere; *1658* quaerere, *1657*
[21] foverat: *1658* foverat; *1657*

verdict was that they lost their rights and access to political decision-making; in the future they were to be ruled according to whichever laws the prince decided. Nor did the fact that some appealed to the king go unpunished; petitions by the magistrates were punished by fines which they had to pay from their own pockets. Which example then terrified the others, who tried to buy off an unlimited burden by paying a specified amount of money. Still however these evils were not enough to satisfy God's anger at the sins in the Low Countries; but as if human cruelty and avarice were not enough to overthrow a country flourishing with people and wealth, the sea fell down on the shores with a deluge as hardly ever seen before, bringing destruction in the present and announcing more for the future. For this was a time when ultimate servitude and ultimate liberty were separated only by a thin line, **(34)** and under both headings stringed together equal miseries and disasters.

22 Now their anger taught the oppressed the love of arms and gave them proof that no unity is so strong as that created by shared self-interest. Only then did this nation, which had looked on almost unmoved as its citizens were burned, its leaders killed, its laws, religion and constitution snatched away, make a common decision to take revenge for what had passed and forestall what was still coming. Thus in the city of Brussels itself, in spite of Alva's menacing presence with a huge garrison and collection of the Tenth Penny, everyone closed their workshops and inns, in open protest against servitude, even at the risk of capital punishment. Soon gallows and executioners were ready for the obstinate when news of the turmoil in Holland, which we shall relate below, put an end to this savagery.

23 The growing indignation in the provinces had restored Orange's courage, though not with full confidence, to try his luck in war once again, and open the road to division by providing an army as well as a commander—as long as the Turk engaged a part of Philip's forces and even Spain could hardly consider itself safe from the progress of the Moors. Therefore he sent suitable men to all princes who declared themselves restorers of the Faith, in order to ask for an alliance, or secret help towards the common cause. Dane and Swede said no, for fear of having to fight a stronger party, nor did the Queen of England dare provoke the great power nearby, although the Roman Pontiff had declared her own person legitimate booty and Alva had already been suspected of looking for a grounds for war against the prosperous island, because of money belonging to Genovese merchants but retained in England. These funds were retained for immediate use and under pledge of return, but all the same the case had led to a lawsuit and confiscations.[24] Recently, when there were disturbances in the North of that kingdom, he had sent men to investigate the situation of the ports, and to present themselves as leaders in case the troubles might advance to a new level. Nor was there any doubt that the queen of the Scots had supported attempts against Elizabeth.[25] She however pretended for the time being that all this had not happened, and accommodated Spanish wishes insofar that Orange's followers were robbed of all hiding places and given orders to leave England before a certain date.

24 In France however, those in rejection of the Latin rite had been granted access to the king's environment and favour in order that they would come to trust the religious peace. With a view to serving Orange's interests, their co-religionist, they heaped up recent grievances against the house of Burgundy in front of the king. They pointed at the controversy which had then just come up in the Council of Trent as to who was the first in rank among kings—in which connection Philip was accused of having poisoned his wife Elisabeth—and they pointed out that revenge was owed to her, nor any less to the French who had

Americae provincia Hispani (**35**) obtruncaverant. Quae rex Carolus pronis auribus accipiens, credi voluit credidisse altera hac illecebra, super pactas Navarraeo sororis nuptias, suspectos sibi circumscripturus. Egregia consilii species, obviam eundum potentiae vicinis imminenti, et Gallicis ingeniis bello opus, ut pacem servarent. Iactabatur velut arcanum, eoque intentius, fracto foedere, quod captivo regi Caesar Carolus expresserat in Francici nominis dehonestamentum, restitui veterem Galliarum limitem Rhenoque tenus imperium ferri: quae ultra sunt, dicto excepisse sibi Arausionensem praemium operae. Missae ad eum pecuniae, et perlata consilia Ludovico internuntio, quem Caspar Coliniacus, dux novatae religionis praecipuus, ad Regis colloquium perduxerat. Classis quoque regia Oceano Aquitanico instructa, venditae palam in urbe Rupella praedae ex Hispanorum navibus, legati Hispanici inanes querelae, fidem dolo auxerant.

25 Interim Arausionensis tam validae societatis fama fruens, per legatos aut literas Belgarum exsulibus patriam, domi oppressis libertatem promittit: et plurimis civitatum rectoribus persuadet discidium, Albani odio et formidine. Sic studiis populorum et armis fretus vim maritimam adiunxerat. Nam audacissimus quisque Belgica extorres, et inops exilium metuentes, in naves se coniecerant, aliasque complures obvias per vim nacti, aucto numero, praedabundi Oceano[22] et per oram maritimam vagabantur. In hanc multitudinem Arausionensis, quanquam ius et regimen aberant, speciem imperii retinebat, distributis per codicillos potestatibus. Toti maritimo officio praepositus Wilhelmus comes Markius, Lumeius cognomento: animi ferox, idque illi unum pro virtute erat, et comitum plerisque consilium, aut animus, non nisi in praedam. His tunc ministris uti supremae providentiae visum, cui fere placuit Belgicis in rebus ita humanam fiduciam et consilia illudere, ut nunquam simul essent spes magna et bonus eventus.

26 (1572) Viginti quatuor modica navigia, initium belli in potentiam toto orbe praecipuam, edicto eiecta Anglicanis portibus[23] in Westfrisiam ferebantur, tentandae fortunae: sed, vento adversante, rerum necessariarum penuria impulit in maximam insularum, Vornae vocantur, quae Mosae ostia continent: ubi oppidum Brilam classiarii repentino terrore inter trepidantes, aut volentes, invasere; neque tunc mansuram sedem, sed ad paucos dies stationem decreverant. Exoraverunt prudentiores et loci oportunitas, ut (**36**) victoriam retinerent: adeo cunctis praeter opinionem evenientibus, ut Maximiliano Bossuvio duce (is tum Hollandiae praeerat) Hispanorum cohors ingressa insulam, velut subito pavore lymphata profugerit, nemine contra ire auso, tantum quia naves ipsorum oppidani incenderant.

[22] Oceano *1658* oceano *1657*

[23] portibus *scripsimus* partibus *1657* partibus, *1658*

been cut to pieces **(35)** by the Spanish in Florida, a district in America. King Charles listened to all of it with great eagerness, for he wanted them to believe that he believed it: he did not trust them and was planning to entrap them by that other bait of the intended marriage of his sister with Navarre. Thus he called it an excellent piece of advice, that there was no choice but to march against a power that posed a threat to its neighbours, and that the French character required a war to remain at peace. Repeatedly the intelligence was dropped, as if it were a secret (and therefore with all the more emphasis), that the treaty would be broken which the Emperor Charles, to the detriment of the prestige of France, had extorted from king [Francis I] when the latter was held in captivity. The ancient borders of Gaul would be restored and the realm would be extended up to the Rhine. And it was said that Orange had stipulated the area beyond as reward for his labour. Money was sent off to Orange, and the plans were delivered to him by Louis[26] who had been introduced to the consultations with the king by Caspar de Coligny, the most important leader of the reshaped confession. Also, a fully equipped royal fleet in the Atlantic Ocean, the sale, out in the open, of booty from Spanish ships in La Rochelle, fruitless complaints by the Spanish legate; it all served to give credibility to the deceit.

25 Meanwhile the spreading news of such a strong alliance brought benefits to Orange. His letters and messengers promised return to the Lowlanders in exile, and liberty to the oppressed at home; thus he induced many town governments to defect, from hate and fear of Alva. Leaning in this way on the popular support in the provinces and their willingness to fight, Orange had attached a naval force to his means. For the most daring refugees from the Low Countries, driven also by fear of a penniless exile, had flocked together in ships, and extended their number by forcefully seizing several others which they met underway. Eager for prey they roamed the ocean and the coastal regions. Orange preserved an image of command over this crowd since he had handed out letters containing appointments, although legitimacy and governance were lacking. The head of his maritime organisation was William, count of Marck, nick-named Lumey: a man of savage character, which was the only sense in which he could be called brave. Most of his fellows possessed reason and courage only in view of booty.[27] At that point in time however the Almighty's Providence[28] decided to employ this lot as her helpers: in the Low Countries war it has pleased her almost invariably to deceive human planning and confidence in such a way that great hopes and a happy outcome were never together in the same place.[29]

26 Twenty-four modest ships were the beginning of a war against the foremost power on earth: expelled from the ports of Britain by the edict mentioned before, they sailed towards West-Friesland to try their fortune. However, adverse winds and a lack of essential supplies drove them to the biggest of the islands of Voorne, as they are called, which are situated in the Meuse estuary. Here the sailors captured the town of Briel, causing sudden panic among its trembling (or thankful) citizens. At that point their plan was not to make the occupation permanent, but to stay only for a few days. However the wiser among them and the strategic location persuaded them to keep hold of their victory **(36)**; while simultaneously everything else came out beyond expectation, such as that a Spanish regiment under command of Maximilian of Bossu (then stadtholder of Holland), which had arrived on the island, took to flight as if they were out of their minds by sudden panic, and nobody dared to prevent it—and everything only because the townspeople had set fire to their ships.

27 In reditu Bossuvius transitum Roterodamo postulavit, quod, experti praesidiorum mala, concesserunt, ea lege, ut exiguae manus, aliisque dimissis, aliae ingrederentur. Sed contra pacta confertim irrumpit miles; fit magna oppidanorum caedes. Ea perfidia commotos Hollandorum animos ita impulit, ut sponte plerique, pars aut plebis motu adacta, aut vicinorum armis, aut commercii denique necessitate exsulibus admissis studium aperirent. Nam arces Albanus hic nullas struxerat, gentis simplicitate tutum se credens, quae plus caeteris quieverat hactenus, tanto validius eruptura. Quin et Hispani pars ante abducti, ut Traiectum Batavorum militaribus flagitiis punirent, quod ea civitas sacrorum fiducia, vectigalibus imperatis acrius restitisset: et eos, qui Roterodami consederant, Albanus ad primos tumultus nuntios, vanissimo metu, ne illic obsiderentur, exemerat.

28 Secuti Hollandiae oppidum Flissingani, quos surgentis arcis aspectus et praesidium adventans commoverat; Pacieco Allobroge, operum Albanicorum peritissimo curatore, ad supplicium rapto, in causam descendunt. Inde et alii Hispanos per Zelandiam exclusere, affluentibus quotidie auxiliis e Galliae et Britanniae regnis, quibus ex rebus novis spes licentiae erat. Geldriam et Transisalana Wilhelmus comes Herembergensis affinitate Arausionensi iunctus, magisque hoc nomine quam sua vi nixus, Frisiam Nederwormterus, et mox Scandenburgus incursant, validis urbibus admissi, optima civium voluntate. Nuntiato hoc motu populorum, non multum Arausionensis laetabatur, minore casu praeventum se querens, nec adultum satis consensum. Incondito adhuc corpori, primam reipublicae speciem indidere coeuntes Dordrechtum Hollandi nobiles aliquot, et praecipuarum urbium legati. Miserat eo et Arausionensis, quem Hollandiae Ordines, absentem quamvis, rectorem sibi, utpote accepta a principe praefectura, nec ullo legitimo iudicio ablata, simulque contra Albani dominationem belli ducem profitebantur.

29 Pugnae interea terra marique: pedestribus praeliis vincebat Hispanus rudes et incompositos: pelago inferior in hoc genitis. Egregiae hac in parte **(37)** Zelandorum victoriae, qui inopiam publicam navalibus praedis solabantur. Et forte Medinicaelius, iampridem dictus Albano successor, ut poenitentiae exorabilior, capta classe, qua ex Hispania advenerat, vix ipse elapsus, recusavit imperium; ne tanto rerum discrimine alieno se dedecori immisceret. Nec Albanus tamen periculis mitigari, aut agnoscere hostes et iura armorum: sed ubi quos nactus, ut in rebelles maiestatis iudicia exercere. Unde ultio, et apud adversas partes eadem in captivos feritas nullo discrimine; donec, quae olim inimicas gentes, illos quoque docuit mutua necessitas, parcere sanguini in summam belli nihil profuturo: ita terrestrium armorum inducta commercia, maris possessionem Nassaviani saeviendo retinuere.

27 During this retreat Bossu demanded passage through Rotterdam, which the citizens, from experience with the evils of garrisons, allowed him under the condition that they would come in small bands, one entering after another had left. In spite of this agreement however Joe Snuffy threw himself into the town in one thick crowd, and a big massacre of townspeople followed.[30] This show of faithlessness caused such a shock in Holland that people chose sides and admitted refugees; which most people did of their own accord, a part only in reaction to the stirrings of the populace or their neighbours' armament, or finally from commercial necessity. For in this region Alva had built no castles, assuming that the province's rusticity would keep him safe, since they had so far moved less than the others—only to break out more valiantly in the present. A part of the Spanish forces had even recently been removed, in order to punish the city of Utrecht with armed excesses because that city, from confidence in its religious importance, had too decidedly resisted the imposed taxation. Moreover, at the first news of the troubles Alva had removed his troops located in Rotterdam because of a ridiculous fear that they might come under siege in that place.

28 The example of this town in Holland was followed by those of Vlissingen, stirred into action by the sight of the castle that arose in their town and the approaching garrison. They dragged the Savoyard Pacheco, Alva's most experienced building master, to the block and joined the Revolt. Next other towns in Zeeland too locked the Spanish out of their gates, while auxiliary troops from the kingdoms of France and England were streaming in every day, hoping the revolution would give them occasion for excesses. Guelders and Overijssel were invaded by William count of 's Heerenberg, a relative of Orange (who relied more on the esteem emanating from this than his own strength); Friesland first by the lord of Nederwormter and soon by Schouwenburg. Strong towns let them in, with full support of the citizens. At the news of this popular movement Orange rejoiced but little, complaining that Fortune was blocking his way with a minor crumb of luck, as their unity was not yet ripe. The as yet unsettled whole was given the first appearance of a commonwealth by a handful of nobles and delegates of the most important towns, who assembled in Dordrecht. Orange too sent his representative to that meeting; the States of Holland declared him, although he was absent, their governor; for the stadtholderate had been given to him by the prince, and not taken away by any legitimate decree. At the same time they made him the leader of their war against Alva's tyranny.

29 Meanwhile the fighting continued on land and sea. On land the Spaniard defeated his badly trained and disorganised enemy; at sea he had no chance against a people born in the waves. Of special importance in this respect **(37)** were the victories of the Zeelanders, who relieved the treasury's emptiness with booty taken from ships. And sure enough the duke of Medina Coeli (appointed some time before as Alva's successor, as being more sensitive to repentance), refused the office, after the fleet which brought him from Spain, was seized, and he had only just escaped himself: when so much was at stake, he did not want to become part of another man's discomfiture. And still Alva's problems did not bring him to a milder approach, nor did he acknowledge that this was a war, or the rights of war. No, when men fell into his hands, he had them sentenced as rebels against the crown. Which in turn led to revenge, and with both parties to identical beastliness against prisoners without any distinction; until mutual emergency taught them, just like ancient nations at war, to spare innocent blood that would not contribute to the war.[31] In this way the exchange of forces was introduced on land, but at sea the Nassau men preserved their hegemony by cruelty.[32]

30 Coalescendi spatium Hollandis ac Zelandis datum est, dum illis omissis, quin et parte praesidiorum abducta, Montem Haenoviae urbem Albanus obsidio premit, captam a Ludovico Nassavio astu militari, cuius in vicinia amissas simul Valentinianas Hispani ex arce receperant. E Gallia liberando Nassavio, qui Montem tuebatur, auxilium advenit quingenti equites, pedites quinquies mille, non prohibente Carolo, quod ut taciti foederis argumentum accipiebatur: pariterque ex Germania Arausionensis procedebat exercitus, maior etiam quam priori expeditione. Potuisse magno terrore bellum circumferri credibile, nisi incautiores Gallos explorato itinere Hispani intercepissent. Dux ipse agminis Ienlisius, aliique nobiles in potestatem venere; pro quorum incolumitate per legatum rex Carolus acriter contendens, ultimum fabulae actum imposuit.

31 Nam subito Arausionensem atrox percellit nuntius fraudium Gallicarum, intelligitque Navarraei et Condaei vincula: primo Coliniaci sanguine foederatam Guisiorum potentiam, inde toto regno ius factum caedibus, contraque exosae religionis sectatores armata vulgi furentis odia: huc pacem, huc funestas nuptias, totque illa delinimenta, suam quoque societatem cecidisse: spe igitur prope unica deiectus, cum et stipendia cohortibus quibusdam promissa rex Galliae abrumperet, talique consiliorum exitu satis Philippo purgatus amicitiam integraret, dimittere exercitum cogitur, et vix evitata seditione, quod reliquum fortunae erat, in Hollandiam abit; suorum ipse laborum irritus, extra spem ultro oblatis usurus.

32 Secuta Montis deditio: usurpatumque ius victoriae in Machliniam, aliasque urbes, quae transeuntem Arausionensem stipendio, aut (**38**) frumento iuverant. Inde prolata formidine, quae Frisiae aut circa Isalam occupata diximus, non sine ducum ignavia, praesidiis deseruntur. Capta et Zutphania a Friderico Albani filio, dum deditio paratur, ubi in oppidanos post tormenta et stupra saevitum caedibus, nulla aetatis, nulla sexus reverentia. Post Narda Hollandiae oppidum vastatur simili feritate, dirutaque moenia antiquo ultionis exemplo. Haec Hispani aliis quoque bellis haud insolita sibi ad celerem victoriam profutura credebant, cum contra homines re nulla magis quam clementia vinci assuefeceris. Auxit caeteris impetum et constantiam, quod, sublata fide et spe veniae, graviora pacis mala, quam belli metuebant: ea desperatione in spem quoque elati fortius in medium consuluere, nec ulla omnino urbs dedita est postea, quae non extrema tolerasset.

33 Congruens arbitror cunctas nascentis reipublicae partes simul recensere, quando ea tempestate initia iacta sunt belli et libertatis, quae tum nemo mortalium tantum in tempus exitura iudicabat. Persistiterant soli in armis Hollandi et Zelandi, quarum gentium situm veteraque et recentia nomina, ut per totum opus intelligantur, exponam.

30 Now the Hollanders and Zeelanders were given the occasion to unite, as Alva ignored them for a while and even removed part of the garrisons, while he besieged the city of Mons in Hainaut. This city had been captured by Louis of Nassau by a military stratagem, and nearby Valenciennes at the same time, although the Spaniards had already reconquered the latter from its citadel. From France there arrived an auxiliary force of five hundred cavalry and five thousand footmen to relieve Louis, who was defending Bergen: the fact that Charles did nothing to prevent this was read as proof of the silent alliance. Simultaneously an army of Orange was approaching from Germany, even bigger than that of the earlier expedition. It is likely that a war could have been launched with huge terror if the Spanish had not intercepted the careless French on a reconnaissance mission. Genlis, the leader of that army and other noblemen were taken prisoner; king Charles furiously strove to get them free unharmed, and brought the stage-play of the alliance to its conclusion.

31 Thus Orange was hit all of a sudden by the terrible news of the French deceit, and learned that Navarre and Cond were locked in chains; that first the alliance with the mighty Guises had been inaugurated with Coligny's blood, and next justice was implemented throughout the kingdom with slaughter; that the hatred of a raving populace against the followers of the loathed confession had been equipped with arms: and that of the peace, the fatal wedding, of all those flattering words, and even his own alliance, this was the objective and result. Having thus robbed Orange of his sole basis of hope, the French king also cut off the wages for certain regiments, which he had promised, and renewed his friendship with Philip—providing the plans with such an outcome had sufficiently cleared his name. Orange was forced to disband his army, and could only just keep it from falling into rebellion (this was all Fortune let him have). He left for Holland, his plan being to employ whatever was offered spontaneously and unlooked for, now that his own efforts had left him empty-handed.

32 This was followed by the surrender of Mons, while Mechelen and other towns which had supported Orange's army train with wages **(38)** or food, fell victim to the conqueror. This brought the fear back again, and the places in Friesland and on the river IJssel which we said had been occupied, were abandoned by their garrisons, partly due to their commanders' faintheartedness. Zutphen was taken by Don Fadrique, Alva's son, while its surrender was being prepared; after torture and rape, frenzied slaughter was unleashed against the citizens of this place, without any distinction as to age or sex. After this the town of Naarden in Holland was destroyed with similar beastliness, and its walls taken down after ancient examples of vengeance. The Spaniards believed that this treatment, entirely normal for them in other wars as well, would contribute to a quick victory, while to the contrary nothing works better than mildness to reconcile people with their defeat. In the other towns this strengthened fervor and resolve because, now that the hope and confidence in clemency were lost, they feared greater evil from peace than from war. This despair however also gave them new hope and made them serve their common cause with greater energy, and no town was surrendered ever after, which had not gone through the worst of trials.

33 It seems useful to discuss all the parts of this nascent republic here straight away, since at this point the fundaments were laid for a freedom and a war, which at the time no mortal thought would last so long. Only Holland and Zeeland now persisted in the war; I shall relate the ancient and the recent geography of these nations, in order to make them clear for all the rest of this work.[33]

2.32. *Massacre at Naerden 1573* by Jan Luyken (E&K54)

2.45. *Siege of Haarlem* by E. Decker

34 Antiquis temporibus nobilissima fuit Batavorum insula, Germanis Gallisque media, positu ad ducendum transmittendumque bellum oportunissimo. Nomen habitatoribus et origo a Cattis. Romana societate, extra dilectus, caetera sui iuris egere; equitandi, nandi peritia, fide, virtute auxiliarium honoratissimi: nec minus clari eo bello, quo sub initia Vespasiani, Civili duce, Gallias ad libertatem excitarunt. Post quae tempora, modo Franci, modo Saxones, tandem et Angli his partibus sedere. Sunt qui Slavos et Varnos adiiciant.

35 Eam insulam Rhenus in Vahalim et sui nominis alveum distinctus, et duobus maxime capitibus in Oceanum influens, amplectitur. Dextrum Lugduno non procul exibat, olim etiam tenue, post, vi tempestatis sabulo obstructum, aquas in Leccam vertit. Sinistro Mosae mixtus Vahalis ostio tenus ripis continebatur. Hodie, antequam eo perveniat, varias insulas interfusus, ob crebra diluvia in maris speciem transiit. Tertium Rheno ostium, quod a dextro longius in Septentriones abit, Drusus aperuit. Nam in Isalam flumen perductus amnis opere militari, inde se immergens in lacus, quibus Frisiorum nationes duae distinebantur, arctatusque apud Flevum insulam, hoc eodem accepto nomine in Oceanum effluebat. Caeterum et haec (**39**) facies locorum ita mutata est, ut non emitti fluvius, sed contra mare terras irrupisse, et angusto primum ingressu laxare mox se in spatium ingentis sinus videatur.

36 Principium igitur agri Batavi vetus in parte nomen retinens Geldriae accensetur, cuius ditio latius patens Isala et Mosa amnibus fere terminatur. Vicina huic Transisalana, a positu[24] dicta, latus Frisiis maioribus ad Amasium usque excurrentibus, tergum aliis Germaniae populis obvertit. Sed Mosae Brabantia longo tractu praetenditur. Infra Geldriam, quo Velavia dicitur, Traiectum est, cum propinquis aliquot oppidis, insessum episcoporum dominatu, quorum et Transisalana erat; quae primus omnium Carolus Caesar suae ditioni adiunxit. Inde iam Hollandia frequentissime urbibus et vicis habitatur, duobusque angulis in Vahalim et sinum, quem diximus, excurrens, sensim aquis utrimque recedentibus, diffusum littus Oceano obiicit: cuius Septentrionalia, pars olim Frisiorum, partim armis, partim pactionibus adiecta Hollandiae, quia Transflevanis in Occidentem obiacent, Westfrisiae vocabulum tenuere.

37 Ager omnis Hollandiae multis amnium brachiis lacubusque, et fossis manu ductis interscissus, pascuis quam segete felicior: piscaturam et navigationem amnes et mare nulli gentium largius praestant. Zelandia huic contigua omnis in insulas sparsa Mosae et Scaldis ostiis ambitur; retro Brabantiae quoque annexa et Honta, Scaldis alveo, divisa a Flandris, qui apud exteras gentes toti Belgicae nomen dare

[24] positu *1658* posito *1657*

34 In ancient times the Island of the Batavians was world-famous. It was located between the provinces in Germany and Gaul at a very strategic place for the supply and transfer of the necessities for war. The inhabitants derived their name and descent from the Chatti. Within their alliance with the Romans, except the levies of troops, they were master of their own affairs. Given their skill in riding and swimming and their courage they were the most esteemed among the auxiliary troops. No lesser fame they derived from the war by which, under the command of Claudius Civilis, they stirred the lands of Gaul to fight for their freedom at the beginning ofVespasian's reign. After this period it was at some point the Franks, at another Saxons, and eventually Angli as well who settled in this region. According to some we should add Slavs and Warni to this list.

35 The river Rhine has two arms, one of the same name and one called Waal; most of its water reaches the sea via these two mouths which embrace the island. The right-hand one of these mouths terminates not far from Leiden, and was tiny already ages ago; in later times the force of a storm blocked it with sand, and now it turns its waters into the river Lek. Near the left-hand mouth, the Waal becomes mixed with the river Meuse,[34] and formerly used to stay within its banks. Today, it flows between several islands before it reaches that area, and assumes the look of a sea because of the frequent floodings. Drusus opened a third mouth for the Rhine, which turns from the left-hand mouth and continues towards the North. For this waterway was extended towards the river IJssel by military labour, and next poured itself into the lakes which separated the two tribes of the Frisians.[35] After this it narrowed down again near the island called Vlieland, and flowed into the ocean[36] carrying that same name [Vlie]. Otherwise the appearance **(39)** of this territory has changed so much that it looks not as if the river is flowing into the sea, but contrarily the sea has broken into the land, and entering through a small passageway, soon broadens out over the space of a very wide bay.

36 The front part[37] then of the Batavian territory has partly kept its ancient name[38] and is considered a part of Guelders, which rules a wide area roughly delineated by the rivers Meuse and IJssel. Next to this is Over-IJssel, named after its location, which has one side towards Greater Friesland[39] (which runs all the way to the river Ems), and its back towards the other peoples of Germany. Brabant however covers a long stretch along the river Meuse. Below the part of Guelders which is called Veluwe lies Utrecht, with a handful of neighbouring towns, seat of the rule of the bishops who also held Overijssel; the emperor Charles was the very first to add these lands to his realm. Next is Holland which is very densely populated with towns and villages and which has two corners running towards the Waal and the bay which we mentioned before. Since on both sides the waters retreat only gradually, Holland maintains a diffuse coastline towards the ocean. Holland's northern section, once part of Friesland, was added to Holland partly by wars and partly by treaties; as it lies west of the [Frisian] lands on the other side of the Vlie, it still carries the name West-Friesland.

37 The province of Holland is cut through everywhere by river arms, lakes and man-made canals; it is more fertile of cattle than harvests, while the rivers and the sea provide no nation with greater scope for fishing and sailing. Its neighbour is Zeeland, which consists entirely of a collection of islands and is circumscribed by the river mouths of Meuse and Scheldt. At the rear it is also connected with Brabant while the Hont, one of the Scheldt's streams, separates it from Flanders, the region whose merits achieved that all of the Low Countries are known abroad under this name. The territory of Flanders stretches out along the sea all

meruerunt. Horum tractus secundum mare urbem usque Caletum freto imminentem se explicans eam Belgicae partem attingit, quae nunc sub Francorum est imperio.

38 Hollandiae et Zelandiae insessores olim Danos de suis vocabula indidisse, quibusdam coniectura est; sed ego vetera monumenta persequens reperio hoc commune cunctis insulis esse nomen, illud proprium olim regioni haud magnae, Lugduno non procul, silvis horridae, credo; nam id nomen sonat. Id constat, ex Septentrione populos, cum saepe incendiis, caedibus, rapinis grassarentur, causam dedisse in commune consulendi, legendique aut accipiendi principes, comitum vocabulo; qui Francorum primo, post imperatorum Germaniae maiestatem ita observarunt, ut legibus non subderentur. Quae prima illis domus fuerit, ut fere antiqua, incertum: vulgo recepta opinio, ex Aquitania missos. Sed indigenas fuisse, qui multo arctius quondam eo in loco, unde Hollandiae (**40**) fluxerat nomen, imperantes, paulatim creverint, argumentis non caret. Per muliebres successiones ad Haenovios, Boioaros, Burgundiones, Austriacos, descensum est; quorum e genere rex Philippus secundus in comitum ordine tricesimus primus numeratur.

39 Sed hoc tempore belli difficultas solique calamitas inde, quod communibus coeptis Hollandiae Amstelodamum, Zelandiae Middelburgum deerant, florentissimae urbes, mole sua immotae, et quia defixior in illas Albani cura, addictos sibi praefecerat, imposito et milite. Contra muniebat Hollandiam socia partium Bommeliensis, Geldrici iuris insula, Vahali ac Mosa amplectentibus. Nihil istis rebus tam necessarium quam Arausionensis adventus fuit. Is peritus regendi artium, turbata omnia recomposuit, vimque alias haud diuturnam ratione fovit, et propria lenitate, quae ipsum hostibus quoque commendabat. Nam Markius, dum pro absente imperium Hollandiae administrat, saevitia in sacerdotes et nullo non immodestiae genere infamaverat nascentem libertatem: ferum per se ingenium accendentibus Gallis, qui sueti licentiae et sanguini, mala quae domi fugerant, alienis in armis ulciscebantur. Eam ob rem, et quia parere non didicerat, iussu Arausionensis captus mox, accusatusque est; quominus puniretur tempora obstabant.

40 Ac Arausionensis remisso principis nomine vim amplectens, honores mandare, edere constitutiones, rem militarem et maritimam et pleraque reipublicae tractare cum dilecto concilio: aut excitis Ordinibus praesidens, siquid maius incideret. Crebri autem conventus, praeter speciem popularitatis, in hoc proderant, ut quamplurimi partibus illigarentur, cumque antea sex Hollandiae urbes una cum nobilitate de rebus plerisque consulerent, Dordrechtum, Harlemum, Delphi, Lugdunum, Amstelodamum, Gouda, Arausionensis minores adusque duodecim admisit; non dubie fidas ei, cuius ope ius suffragii acceperant. Sed nec ratione carebat, consiliorum factas participes, quo introspecta onera facilius tolerarent. Nomina earum sunt et ordo, in Austrina parte Roterodamum, Gornichemum, Scidamum, Schoonhovia,

the way to the town of Calais, which overlooks the strait, and there touches that part of the Low Countries which is nowadays under French rule.

38 There are people who suspect that at some point long ago Danish occupants of Holland and Zeeland have instituted these names from their language; but if I search through ancient documents I find that the latter name was common for all the islands, and I believe that the name Holland once belonged to a small area not far from Leiden, rugged with woods; for this is what the name denotes.[40] In any case, it is certain that peoples from the North, in that era when they roamed about time and again, burning, killing, raping, provided the reason to act in defence of the common good and elect or accept princes, whom they called counts.[41] These lords first acknowledged the highness of the French, later that of the German Emperors in that sense that they did not submit to their laws. We do not know of which house the first counts were, as often with things from a far-removed past; it is widely believed that they were sent from Aquitaine. However there is no shortage of evidence that they were of local origin and once ruled in the much smaller area from which the name Holland **(40)** derived, and steadily grew to greater power. Via matrilineal succession their power subsequently came to the houses of Hainaut, Bavaria, Burgundy, Habsburg; the last of which gave birth to king Philip II: he is the thirty-first in the line of counts.

39 In this period[42] however it was an obstacle in the war and a disaster for the country that Amsterdam in Holland and Middelburg in Zeeland (very wealthy cities and unshakeable because of their sheer size) had not joined the common cause. Since Alva was particularly protective of these cites, he had put men at their head who were dependent on him, and had added garrisons. On the other side Holland was strengthened by the accession of the Bommelerwaard as ally, an island formally part of Guelders, which is contained within the waters of Waal and Meuse. Nothing was more necessary in this situation than the arrival of Orange. With his skills in the art of governing, and his characteristic mildness which endeared him even to his enemies, he brought the troubles to rest and bolstered the impetus of the endeavour by bringing system to it, while otherwise it would not have lasted for long. This was needed because Lumey, count of Marck had ruled Holland in Orange's absence and stained the reputation of the new-born freedom by cruelty against Catholic priests and every other imaginable kind of excess. Not a man with a quiet nature of his own, this was inflamed further by the French, who were used to bloodshed and debauchery, and seeking revenge in foreign wars for evils suffered at home. For this reason, and because he had never learned to obey, Lumey was soon arrested by order of Orange, and indicted. The circumstances however prevented his actual punishment.

40 Orange assumed the power of a prince while renouncing the title; he appointed magistrates, issued laws, administered military and naval affairs and most public business; and did all this together with a chosen council, or, in questions of greater importance, as president of a meeting of the States. This large number of gatherings served not only to create an image of popular support, but also to bind as many as possible to the cause. Whereas in earlier days six towns in Holland met (Dordrecht, Haarlem, Delft, Leiden, Amsterdam, and Gouda, together with the nobility), to deliberate upon most of the public business, Orange introduced no fewer than twelve smaller towns, which would doubtlessly be loyal to him, as they thanked their right to vote to his assistance. Another reason adduced was that they were given a share in the deliberations in order to have them more easily accept a financial burden which they had been consulted about. The names of these towns and their order, are

et in insula Mosae, Brila: ad Septentriones, Alcmaria, Horna, Enchusa, ibidemque in aquoso recessu, qui Waterlandia dicitur, Edamum, et Monachodamum, nec longe Medemelaca et Purmerenda. In eorum qui defugerant locum alios subrogatos iudiciis rationibusque publicis imposuit: magna penuria (**41**) hominum, qui ea munera cuperent, aut mererentur, cum plerique virium aestimatione, seu religio accedebat, eximerent se turbidis, et intutis.

41 Caeterum ne nulla subnixi societate temere invidiam defectionis susciperent, rebus omnibus contra Philippi iussa nomen Philippi praetendebatur. Nec exemplum deerat ipsis quoque ab Hispanis, qui, digresso in Germaniam Carolo, tributis ultra modum vexati regios praefectos oppugnaverant. Religionis causam primi talibus coeptis sociaverant Smalcaldico foedere Germani: post quos Galli proceres plurimis etiam scriptis disseruerant, non peccare in fas obsequii minores potestates, quae, invito quamvis principe, divina ac publica iura vitamque innocentium, si necesse foret, armis defenderent. Nassavianos hoc sublevabat, quod sumptis in Albanum armis, remoto rege, conspectui parcebatur: diriore illorum necessitate, qui pro regum suorum magnitudine paratos se occumbere dicentes, contra eosdem instruere infestas acies, inferre signa cogebantur.

42 At Romanae caeremoniae eiectae templis, et qui eius sententiae erant haud facile ad magna munera admittebantur, non lege ulla, sed prudentia, ne, infensi dissentientibus et probabiliori venia, causam suam a publica disiungerent. Recepta publice disciplina, quae Genevae, et in Palatinatu Germaniae passimque alibi docebatur: hoc tamen interest, quod eiusdem religionis alii diversas minus tolerant: quippe non in hoc tantum ordinatas a Deo civitates ac magistratus dictantes, ut a corporibus et possessionibus iniuriae abessent, sed ut, quo more ipse iussisset, eo in commune coleretur; cuius officii negligentes multos poenam, aliorum impietati debitam, in se accersisse.

43 Contra istae nationes non modo nulla auxilia repudianda iudicabant, sed sponte etiam omnes de religione leges inquisitionis nomine detestabantur; ac proinde disputabant, neminem volentem errare, aut nolentem credere, sed veram de sacris rebus sententiam a Deo humanis mentibus insinuari: nec gratam ipsi pietatem, quae non sponte procederet: pravas autem opiniones compertum, non tam vi atque imperio humano, quam spatiis temporum debellari. Hoc obtentu non tantum publica sacra impune contemnebantur, sed absurdi interdum et impii sermones crescebant inter mala libertatis.

44 (1573) In publicos usus versa eo tempore agri et vectigalia principis, sacerdotum, monasteriorum; nec non eorum fortunae qui apud hostes degebant; (**42**) et maritimae praedae. Tunc tot illa tributorum nomina in capita et possessiones, tum mutui vocabulo exactiones inventae sunt, et in eas res quas usus consumit monstrata onera, quae cum bello in immensum augerentur. Tanto flagrabant odio

in the southern part Rotterdam, Gorinchem, Schiedam, Schoonhoven, and on the island in the Meuse, Briel. To the north Alkmaar, Hoorn, Enkhuizen, and in that aqueous corner which is called Waterland, Edam and Monnikendam, and not far from them Medemblik and Purmerend. Orange had other magistrates elected in place of those who had abandoned their post, and put them at the head of jurisdiction and public finances. There was a great lack of people **(41)** who desired such offices or were capable of them, since most excused themselves considering their abilities, or because of their religion, from involvement in such a chaotic and unsafe endeavour.

41 Furthermore in order to avoid the odium of being rebels, without having any alliance to rely upon, all decisions in contravention of Philip's orders were labeled with Philip's name. Precedents of this were available even from the Spanish themselves, who, when the Emperor Charles had left for Germany, had opposed the king's viceroys as they were burdened by excessive taxation. Germans in the Schmalkaldic League were the first to connect this approach with the fight for the faith; later, French nobles issued many writings arguing that lower magistrates do not break their duty to obedience if they employ armed force to defend divine and public law and the lives of innocent people, regardless of the prince s resistance to this. The Nassau party perceived this as an excuse, in the sense that in the king's absence arms were taken up against Alva, and formalities respected thus aggravating the moral predicament of those who had declared themselves prepared to die for the greatness of their kings, but were now forced to prepare an accursed war against them and depart for battle.

42 Unstoppably however the Roman faith was thrown out of the churches, and for the followers of that confession it became very difficult to obtain high office, not because of any law, but from prudence, to make sure neither loathing of dissenters nor greater chances of mercy would induce them to separate their own from the public cause. The creed which is preached in Geneva, the German Palatinate and in many other places was accepted as the public religion. With this difference however that others of the same conviction are less tolerant of different persuasions. For these [others] maintain that societies and governments have been instituted by God not only in order to fend off wrongdoings from our bodies and possessions, but also that He be venerated in that community in the manner commanded by Him. And that by neglecting this duty many have brought punishment over themselves, due to the impiety of others.

43 Contrarily the peoples over here did not only not consider any help objectionable, but also of their own accord they had an aversion of all laws concerning religion, which they saw as forms of inquisition. Thus they argued that no one's beliefs are willingly erroneous, nor that any one believes against their will; but that God implants a true opinion concerning the sacred in the minds of men, that He does not care for piety which does not present itself, and that experience shows that false beliefs are combated better with patience than violence and human commands. Under this veil the official religion was disparaged unpunishedly; and moreover ridiculous and abominable sermons regularly rose up among the evils of liberty.

44 In this time the lands and incomes of the king, the clergy and the monasteries were allotted to the treasury, plus the wealth of those who were dwelling in he enemy territory**(42)**, as well as booty taken at sea. All those many names for the taxation of persons and possessions were invented in this time, as well as levies under the label of loans; and charges on the necessities of everyday life were instituted which grew to monstrous levels, together with

dominatus, omnia dabant ne decimam darent. Nova quoque reperta ratio ex hoste lucrandi, permissu vendito, ut commeatus aliaeque merces transportarentur; manetque mos utilis privatim et publice, vetitus saepe, semper retentus. Etiam pro navium deductione merces aliquid pendebant, cum onerarias bellicae ad secura maris prosequerentur. His ita constitutis, summa nihilominus difficultas nummaria erat, quod Rheni Traiecto prius et Amstelodamo, tunc et per Nardam (id enim ex Geldria iter est) in Hollandorum agros Hispanus irrumperet. Res plurimae civium opera, non externis et conductis copiis gerebantur. Sic quoque militantibus alimenta vix suppetebant. Non manipularis obsequio promptus, non ducibus imperandi artes; id unum salutare, quod communis cum hoste expugnandarum urbium imperitia erat. Inde in longum tractae obsidiones et summa vis, hostium famem opperiri, multis edocti cladibus, et alterno sanguine bellum artem fecerunt. Gravis error Albani fuit, quod Zelandiae non statim incubuit, dum res incompositae; sed terrebat mare belli talis inexpertum.

45 Septem menses circa Harlemum Hollandiae urbem haesit Hispanorum exercitus, multis interim millibus per arma et aspernam hyemem absumptis. Id tempus animos statumque rerum firmavit, et quanquam longa vi, post serum atque infoelix auxilium, obsessi in saevas hostium manus venere, pars magna suspensi mersique: visi tamen sunt vinci posse, qui tam lente vicerant; et ne successus continuarent dum recens consternatio, ipsorum discordia obstitit, stipendiis non solutis; quod perpetuum illis partibus malum, sub opulentissimo rege. Harlemensium suppliciis incensa iterum pertinacia, et Alcmaria vergentis in aquilonem Hollandiae oppidum, prima Hispani impetum fregit, invicta oppugnatione; atque alia subinde miseriae solatia, oppressa a Nassavianis Geertrudisberga, Hollandiae in Brabantiam prominentis oppidum, et ipse captus cum classe Bossuvius, dum maris sinum terramque Westfrisiam bello incursat. Eius classis praetoriae Inquisitionis nomen Hispani fecerant, causam belli superbe exprobrantes.

46 (1574) Albanum, cum non tam senectuti quam famae (**43**) sollicitus, quietem iamdudum oraret, tandem Philippus revocat, violentia eius parum procedere conspiciens, et quominus aliae artes felicius tentarentur, odium ipsius obstiturum, neque auditus, dum filium sibi successorem parat, paternarum ut actionum, ita odii participem. Quinque annis paulo amplius imperium administraverat: eo temporis spatio iactare solitus, octodecim hominum millia carnificis se ministerio sustulisse. Acta eius, praesertim de decima, Rege nec laudare palam, nec rescindere auso; mansit ipse in aula incolumis honoratusque: donec aliquot post annis, cum filio, qui nobilem virginem stupro circumvenerat, coniectus in vincula est, nec ante solutus, quam bellum Lusitanicum periti ducis necessitatem fecisset.

the war. However, such was the hate of the tyranny, that they gave everything to escape giving a tenth.[43] Also a new system for making a profit from the enemy was invented, that is, the sale of permissions to transfer provisions and other commodities. This remains a lucrative arrangement for both private and public purses to this very day—banned many times but always retained. Further, commerce paid a certain amount for the escortation of ships when men-of-war accompanied freighters to the safe routes at sea. Although these practices had established themselves, there was still a huge shortage of money because from Utrecht and Amsterdam, and subsequently via Naarden (for this is the path from Guelders), the Spaniard broke into the fields of Holland. Most of the warfare was carried out using civilians instead of foreign and mercenary troops, which also meant that foods supplies for the military were hardly sufficient. The lower ranks lacked the readiness to obey, the officers the skill of commanding: their sole salvation was that the enemy suffered from the same lack of experience in conquering towns. As a result town sieges were endless and the violence extreme; only a series of defeats taught them to await the enemy's starvation, and bloodshed on both sides trained them in the techniques of this war. Alva made a serious mistake when he did not concentrate on Zeeland straight away, as long as things were unsettled there: being without experience in this type of warfare, he was deterred by the sea.

45 Seven months on end the Spanish army stuck around the town of Haarlem in Holland; many thousands of lives were lost in this siege due to fighting and the severity of the winter. This length of time strengthened the rebels' determination and their organisation, and although after protracted violence and a late and unsuccessful attempt at relief, the besieged fell into their enemy's cruel hands, and many of them were hanged or drowned, it became visible nevertheless that victory was possible over an enemy who had needed so much time to win. Disagreement among the Spaniards themselves prevented their successes from continuing along with the terror they had just caused because the soldiers' wages were not paid—the everlasting evil in these parts of the realm, even under the wealthiest king in the world.[44] The murder of Haarlem's citizens re-fuelled the resolve, and Alkmaar, a town towards the north of Holland, became the first to break the Spaniard's push by not breaking down under the siege. This was followed by other events of consolation in distress, the Nassau attack on the town of Geertruidenberg (situated where Holland spreads forward to Brabant), and the capture of Bossu together with his fleet, during his invasion of the sea-bay and the land of West-Friesland. The Spaniards had called the flagship of that fleet Inquisition, in haughty display of the very cause of the war.[45]

46 At last Philip called Alva back, who had been asking for rest for a long time, not so much from worries about his own age **(43)**, as about his reputation. Philip finally realised that Alva's cruelty produced no sufficient progress, and that the hatred against his person meant that other artifices could not be attempted with more success. Nor did Alva get a hearing while he groomed his son to become his successor, as this man shared in the hatred for his father as much as in his actions. Alva's governorship has lasted for five years and a little more; he had often boasted that in that stretch of time he handed over eighteen thousand people to the headsman. The king dared neither openly to praise his administrative acts (especially those concerning the Tenth Penny), nor reverse them. Alva himself lived at the court, in unaffected safety and prestige, until, a few years later, he and his son, who had lecherously oppressed a noble daughter, were thrown in prison; and he was not released until the Portuguese war dictated the need for an experienced commander.

2.47. *Portrait of Don Luis de Requesens* (no signature)

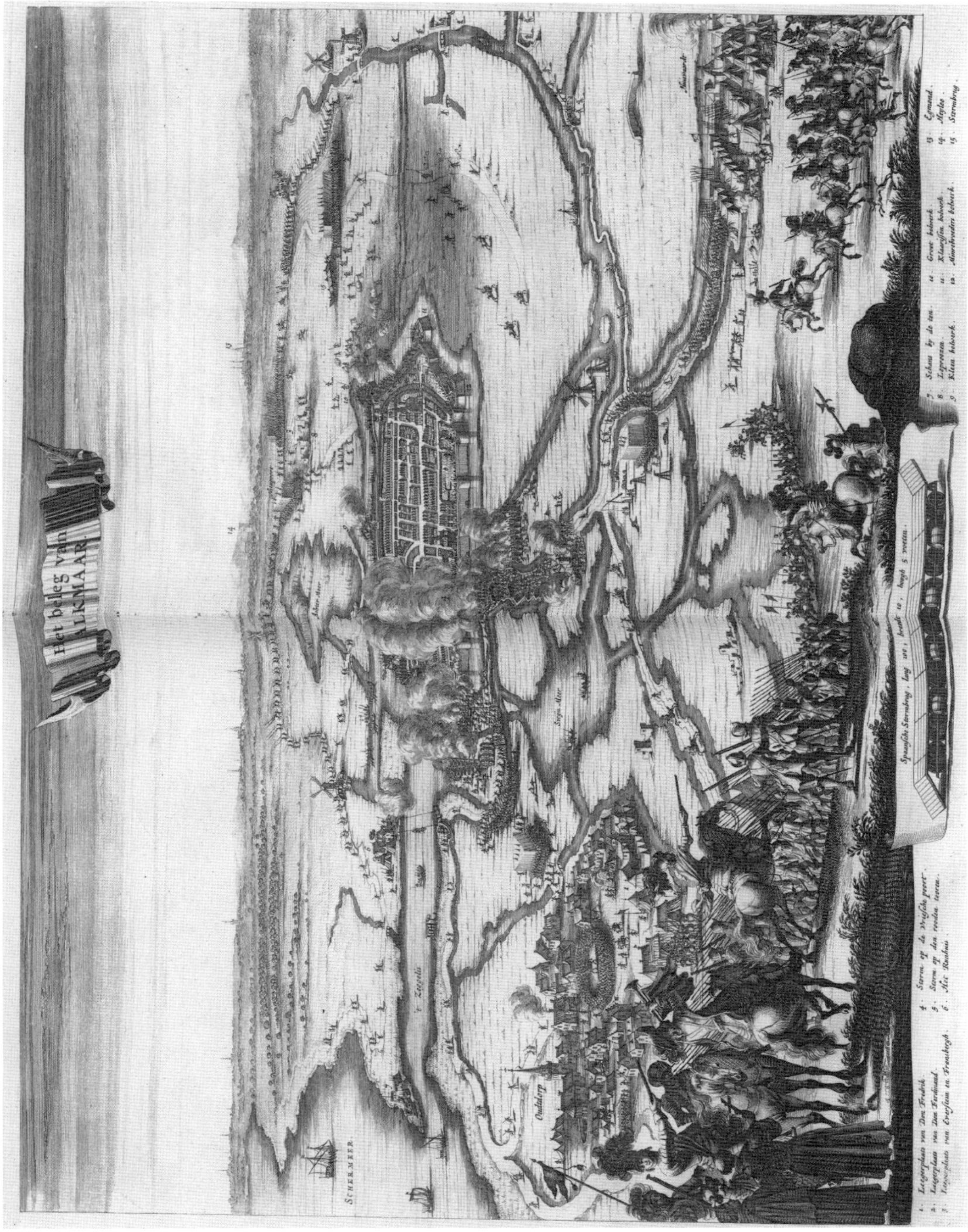

2.50. *Siege of Alkmaar* (no signature)

47 Successor regendae Belgicae Ludovicus Zuninga Requesenius mittitur, qui diversos dolis et laxiore venia irretiret, largitor et comis plusquam Hispanis solitum, peritia Albano impar: haud egenus tamen bellicae laudis, pars magna scilicet illustris ad Echinades victoriae; sed Granatae etiam, cum inquisitiones vix toleraret, perdomitae prae se famam ferens, violataeque ibi in suos et hostes fidei. Ad captandam Belgarum gratiam primum censuit, Albani statuam amoliri.

48 Hoc tempore Middelburgum diuturna fame, quae tamen haud multo minus obsessores, quam obsessos afflixerat, et devicta gravibus praeliis Hispanorum classe, Zelandis accessit, attritasque opes refecit. Sed Ludovicus Nassavius, cum copiis quas fratri adducebat, ut Hollandia hostem detraheret, prope Noviomagum caeditur, immodestia militis, qui cum strictis mucronibus hostis instaret, aera ducem flagitabat. Is finis fuit duci ingenio manuque inter laudatissimos, fratri ipsius Henrico, Christophoro praeterea Palatini principis filio.

49 Transiit in victorem exercitum, quo victi ceciderant, malum: coeperuntque et ipsi exigere praefectos, et postulare debitum sanguini pretium. Incubuit in Antverpiam is furor, urbem Brabantiae rebus tranquillis beatissimam: nimirum commercia et quae inde proveniunt opes, vota sunt pacis; ubi bellum semel omnia permisit, nihil tutius est paupertate. Per vim et minas extorta sunt Antverpiensibus quadringenta millia florenorum, sponte creditum Requesenii, quia vetuerat repugnari, at mox impunitatem sanxit, velut gaudens expressam quovis modo pecuniam, quam a volentibus nunquam impetrasset. Nam dum illarum partium Ordines, nisi edicto decima tolleretur, (**44**) tributa in bellum abnuunt, pervicacia Regis aut praefecti evenerat, ut se utroque frustrarentur.

50 (1575) Quo maior autem Hispanis quam caeteris gentibus praemiorum aviditas est, hoc notabilius tumultuantur, et providentia quadam, nec ut regi desinant. Sic tacito ducum foedere in rapinas itur, quae apud militem merces, apud populum necessitas vocatur. Neque istae tum primum artes, sed iam olim aliis Hispanorum bellis erupere. Haec iniuria studia nationum Arausionensi vehementer conciliavit, quodque, proxime secuto colloquio, postulata eius cum omnium votis congruere.

51 Nam capto Aldegondio (is et ingenio et eruditione plurimum, et apud Arausionensem auctoritate valebat) coram, inde per litteras coeptum agi de concordia, Campigniaco adiuvante, cui domesticum cum fratre Granvella certamen, et, quale inter propinquos, odium erat. Ad ultimum legati utrimque Bredam convenere, quo Caesar Suartseburgium Arausionensis affinem miserat, partibus conciliatorem. Arausionensis, et qui ab eo regebantur, haec dederant mandata: rebelles se et irreligiosos ab adversariis immerito aestimari: constare enim sibi in Deum et principem officii rationem; nec ulla in Philippum sumta esse arma; unam pacis

47 As successor in the government of the Netherlands Luis de Requesens y Zuiga was dispatched, to re-encapsulate the dissenters by artifice and easier pardon. He was more generous and friendly than usual for Spaniards, and not Alva's equal in experience, though not completely devoid of martial glory. This was mostly due to the famous victory at the Echinades,[46] although his reputation also comprised the reduction of Granada to obedience, when it refused to accept the Inquisition, and of broken faith towards friend and foe at that occasion. His first decision to obtain the good will of the Lowlanders was to remove the statue of Alva.

48 In this time Middelburg went over to the Zealanders, after a long famine (which however hit the besiegers not much less than the besieged), and the defeat of a Spanish fleet after heavy fighting. This restored the exhausted finances. On the other hand Louis of Nassau was killed near Nijmegen,[47] together with the troops which he was bringing in for his brother in order to draw the enemy away from Holland. This defeat was due to the shameless behaviour of the soldiers themselves, who demanded their money from the commander while the enemy was approaching with their swords drawn. This was the end of a commander whose talent and deeds had earned the highest praise, of his brother Henry, and of Christopher, son of the prince of the Palatinate.

49 The evil which had brought down the defeated, passed on to the victor: his troops too began to drive out their superiors and demand the reward due to the blood they had shed. This frenzy turned towards Antwerp, the most blessed city in Brabant in times of tranquility. Obviously however trade and the wealth it produces are the desires of peace: once war has cancelled all rules, there is nothing safer than poverty. With the help of threats and force, four hundred thousand florins were extorted from the citizens, with the active consent of Requesens, as it is believed, because he had forbidden resistance, but soon issued impunity [for the soldiers]—as if he was glad to have the money squeezed out by whichever means, which he would never have obtained with the citizens' cooperation. For as long as the States of those provinces refused **(44)** to contribute to the cost of war if the Tenth Penny wasn't officially abolished, the stubbornness of the king, or that of Requesens, only resulted in both sources of income not coming in.

50 However as greedier as Spaniards are for rewards than other nations, so much more vehement are their mutinies; which happens even partly by design, but not to such extent that they defect from their kings.[48] Thus with the tacit agreement of their officers they went out for robbery, which the soldiery call wages, the population panic. Nor was this the first time they used these methods, but similar things happened in the past in other wars fought by the Spanish. These crimes gave a strong boost to the sympathy in the provinces for Orange and secured that, at the meeting which followed soon, his demands coincided with everybody's prayers.

51 For after Marnix of Saint-Aldegonde had been taken prisoner (a man with great influence because of his talent and erudition, and great authority with Orange), talks were opened about reconciliation, first in person, then via letters. This was done with the help of the Lord of Champagny,[49] who fostered a private feud with Granvelle, his brother—they hated each other the way close relatives can. In the end, representatives from both sides came to Breda. The Emperor sent the count of Schwarzburg[50] to that place, a relative of Orange, to establish peace between the warring parties. Orange and those who acted by his orders instructed their men with the following demands: We are looked upon as rebels and heretics by our adversaries undeservedly: for we too accept the logic of our duties towards God and the prince. Nor have we ever taken up arms against Philip. There is but one obstacle to peace: the foreign domination. If the Spanish soldiers are removed, we will submit

moram, exteram dominationem. Si Hispanus miles amoveretur, quod ad religionem caeteraque pertineret, Ordinum totius Belgicae iudicio se fore contentos.

52 Responsum est, non recte illos facere, quod defensionem prae poenitentia elegissent; dari tamen impunitatem, dummodo religionis turbatores intra praestitutum tempus patria excederent: quippe iniquum, tanto regi de religione statuendi arbitrium detrahi, quod minimi in Germania principes usurparent. Caetera ita Regem concessurum, si prius urbes arcesque et machinae cum navibus traderentur. Displicuere conditiones ut armis saeviores; orataeque induciae, ut per annos aliquot liberi essent ritus sacrorum, armis absisteretur: ne id quidem obtentum; sed, successibus aliquot elatior, traxit pacificationem Requesenius, ut belli incuriosos interea vi supervaderet. Nam eo tempore, quo de concordia agebatur, arma Hispanica validissimos conatus habuere: qui partim prosperi improvisa celeritate, alibi admirabili constantia refringebantur. Nam transgressas in Westfrisiam cohortes regias, passim deprehensas locorum imperitia, agrestes cecidere.

53 Durabat inter haec aliquanto ante coepta Lugduni obsidio, qua cuncta nutabant, **(45)** intima Hollandiae insidentibus Hispanis, nec ullis contra viribus, nisi in divina ope, et pertinaci odio infidae dominationis, quod hac tempestate tantum fuit, ut repertus sit nauta, qui evulsum Hispano militi cor morsibus scinderet. Itaque morbis belloque consumtos, et nihil non experta fame, post longae spei commercia, ad Mutinense exemplum avibus internuntiis, perfossi aggeres, aperta amnium septa et terris immissum mare, attollente fluctus pleno Lunae orbe, ad hoc ventis mire obsecundantibus, servaverunt: quin et moenium ruina, ultimum urbibus malum, tunc fuit salutare, obiecta auribus eruptionis imagine, quae hostem decepit et terruit. Lugduno discedens miles, captumque trahens ducem Baldesium, cum Traiectum Batavorum, suarum partium urbem, specie seditionis praedae destinaret, ab oppugnatione depulsus est. Tentavit Hispanus et sinisteriora Hollandiae, secundum Mosam et Leccam, irrumpere, captis oppidis prope ripas, inter quae[25] Veteres Aquae (ita oppidum dicitur) nobilis saevitia victoris: nec ante reprimi potuit, quam ad confluentes usque pervaserat, quo loco vicus est Crimpa nomine.

54 Eadem tempestate Petrus Melendes Cantaber, Floridae victor, sed insigni in Gallos perfidia, apud suos etiam infamis, cum res Americanas Batavicis parum sapienter compararet, Brilam se aliosque portus obsequio redditurum iactabat, et iam parata classe missa in Angliam legatio, quae littus et hospitium, si eo venti adigerent, oraret impetraretque. Sed subita morbi lues nautas disiecit, et dux ipse edoctus pollicitationis vanitatem, pudore ut creditum, aut metu, vitam finiit; coactique Hispani, oppressis vi Batavorum quae ad Antverpiam excubabant navibus, et mox nova rerum sequentium facie, terrorem maritimum multos in annos differre.

[25] quae *Boot* quas *1657, 1658*

ourselves to the judgment of the States-General of all the Netherlands with respect to the religious issue and the other ones.

52 In response to this there came: "You did wrong by choosing to defend yourselves instead of being ashamed of yourselves. Nevertheless impunity will be granted provided the religious trouble-makers will have left the country before a stated time. For it would be unfair to deny to a king of such rank the power to choose the religion—a power which even the smallest princes in Germany possess.[51] The other demands will be granted as they are, if first the towns and castles, the war equipment and the ships will be handed over." These conditions were rejected, as being worse than war, and a truce was asked for, meaning that for some years the exercise of religion would be free, and armed force would be refrained from. However even this was not obtained: but Requesens, encouraged by a handful of successes, spun out the negotiations, with an intention in the meantime to bring a population averse from war back under the yoke by force. For while these peace negotiations were running, the Spanish army made a few very competent attempts, part of which were successful thanks to their unexpected swiftness, others rebuffed with admirable determination: peasants in West-Friesland finished off some royal regiments which had crossed over, and were scattered and entrapped due to their unfamiliarity with the region.

53 While this was happening, the siege of Leiden, inaugurated somewhat earlier, continued for a long time. It brought everything into peril, as the Spanish had taken hold of the heart **(45)** of Holland, and there was no force to resist them except God's help and a stubborn hatred of the faithless tyranny, which at this time was so great that the story is told of a sailor who ripped the heart from a Spanish soldier's corpse and tore it to pieces with his teeth. And thus, exhausted by war and disease, having gone through all extremities of famine and a long anticipation vested in an exchange of messages through birds, as at Modena,[52] Leiden was saved by the destruction of dykes to open the rivers' walls, and the entry of sea onto land; the moon's full circle drove up the waters, with miraculous help of the winds. And even a collapse of the walls, the worst of evils for a town, then became an instrument of salvation, for it put the image of a sortie into the enemy's ear and threw him into panic. The army retreating from Leiden drew its commander, Valdes, with it as a prisoner; it destined Utrecht (a city on its own side) for plundering, under the guise of a mutiny,[53] but the attack was beaten off. The Spaniard also attempted a raid into the left part of the province of Holland, along the rivers Meuse and Lek, after seizing the smaller towns on the banks. Among these Oude Water (this is what the town is called) achieved fame by the cruelty of its conqueror; who could not be stopped before he had reached as far as the confluence of Meuse and Lek, at the spot where the village of Krimpen is.

54 In this same period Pedro Melendez (a Basque and the conqueror of Florida, but ill-reputed even with his own side because of an amazing act of faithlessness towards the French) unwisely compared the operation in the Americas with that in Holland, and boasted that he would bring Den Briel and other ports back to obedience. A fleet was already prepared, and an embassy sent to England to ask permission to seek shelter on its shores, in case the winds would drive them thither; which was obtained. A sudden epidemic however swept away the sailors; the commander realized the vanity of his promises, and the disgrace, as it is believed, or fear, drove him to put an end to his life. When next the ships which were awaiting their turn near Antwerp, were set upon by attacks from Holland, and soon thereafter, the war situation came to look completely different, the Spanish were forced to postpone their attack via sea for many years to come.

2.53. *Lifting of the siege of Leiden* (no signature)

2.73. *Portrait of Mathias of Austria* (no signature)

55 Post haec Scaldiam Zelandorum insulam, in Hollandiae confinio, ita nominatam ab amne laevum latus alluente, vadis et classe ingrediuntur Requeseniani, dubium audacia maiore an felicitate; quam ipsi illustrantes, compositis in veterum auditionum speciem miraculis, mare sibi ingredientibus coelestes faces praeluxisse referunt. Hic expugnato portu Bomenedae, qui locus non magno praesidio fortiter defendebatur, Zyrixaeam, insulae caput, novem mensium obsidione accipiunt in potestatem.

56 (1576) Huic maximo malo, quia duarum nationum societas medio hoste turbabatur, cum iam et pecuniae et vires defecissent, alterum non levius (**46**) accessit, quod principum amicitiae frustra ambiebantur, metu potentiae Hispanicae, an quod exemplum displicebat. Angliae enim regina, quanquam sacra communia, Oceani imperium, et ipsi ab Hollandis principibus ductum genus ostentabantur, foedus, et oblatum alteris mandatis summum imperium abnuebat: pecuniae tamen nonnihil interdum suppeditabatur; sed quod intempestive repetitum in maius incommodum verteret.

57 Galliam tum Henricus habebat Caroli frater, qui Hispani dolos praesentiens, et pari arte grassandum ratus, eius vim destruentibus studebat, sed arcanum intra subsidium, haud reticenda commenti fere piratici subtilitate: qua cum Rege convenerat, ut Caleti, Gallica urbe, quaestores Nassaviani vicini maris navigandi licentiam venderent; nulla non gentium parata redimere iniurias: nam hactenus sive ad hostes ibant, a Batavis in praedam, sive alio, tamen ad disquisitiones et damnosas alieno sub iudice lites trahebantur. Iuris simulacrum adhibebatur frequens negotiantibus aversi periculi pactio, qua incertus eventus certa mercede in alium transferri solet. Idque unum tributum haud impar fuerat magnis belli impensis, nisi navalis turba, indomita legibus, ad veterem licentiam et propria a rapinis commoda recurrisset.

58 Rem undique desperatam restituit improvisa felicitas, cum subita peste extincto Requesenio ad senatum regiarum partium administratio translata est. Id gratum populis, et servandis quae tenebantur, pacandis quae defecerant, censuerat Ioachimus Hopperus Frisius, cui tum in Hispania agenti auctoritas increverat, ex quo improbata ipsi consilia male cesserant, ita ut sapientis nomen homo Belga ab Hispanis adeptus esset.

59 Sed nemo est hominum ita sapiens, ut eum nunquam fortuna fallat. Clandestinis iam dudum artibus Brabantorum animos Arausionensis sibi conciliabat, demonstrando, nihil se quod privatim utile esset desiderare. At illi ultro etiam, dum Requesenius armis occupatur, aut lenitatem simulat, quantum remiserat dominatio, tantum contra insurgere: et ipse praefectus parum provide ad coeptantes militum tumultus arma rapere agrestes iusserat, quod illic initium fuit libertatis.

55 Next Requesens' men landed on the island of Schouwen in Zeeland, on Holland's borders and named after the river Scheldt which passes by its left flank. They reached the island both by ship and wading through the waters, while it remains unclear whether it was their courage more or their luck which let them do this. In their own descriptions it is the latter cause, which they relate in the fashion of old miracle tales, describing how the sea was lit up before them by heavenly torches as they went.[54] On the island they conquered the port of Bommenee, which was courageously defended by its limited garrison, and brought Zierikzee, the island's capital in their power after a siege of nine months. Thus the alliance of two nations was disturbed by the enemy who placed himself in between them, right at a time when money and energy were running out.[55]

56 This frightening evil however was joined by another, no less worrying one **(46)** in that the campaign for princely associations turned out to be in vain, whether this be from fear of the power of Spain, or because they had no wish to set such an example. The Queen of England for example rejected the idea of an alliance and the supreme power offered to her for the second time, although the community of religion and her own descent from the counts of Holland were pointed out to her, as well as the offer of supremacy at sea. To the finances however some assistance was provided every now and then; except that by badly timed reclaiming she turned this into a greater hindrance than a help.

57 France was ruled in these years by Henry, Charles' brother, who foresaw Spain's deceitful intentions and considered that these should be dealt with by equal measures. He fostered relations with all those looking to destroy that power, but only within the limits of secret assistance, and in this displayed an unforgettable subtlety of nearly criminal scheming. Thus he convened with the king that the Nassau party's collectors[56] in Calais, a city in France, would sell their license to navigate the adjacent seas, as no nation is ever unhappy to buy off injury. For until that time, when they were travelling to the enemy, they were considered prey by the Hollanders; when to other destinations, they would still be submitted to searches and damaging lawsuits before foreign judges. To obtain an appearance of legitimacy, a form of contract against risk was employed which is frequent among tradespeople, by which an uncertain outcome is transferred on another in exchange for a certain payment.[57] This single payment would have been quite sufficient to meet the huge expenses for the war, if the unruly mob of sailors, which is insensitive to legislation, had not fallen back into its traditional anarchy and the acquisition of goods by plunder.

58 This situation, hopeless in every way, was saved by an unexpected stroke of luck, when Requesens was killed by a sudden illness,[58] and the government of the loyal provinces transferred to the Council of State. This was very welcome news with the inhabitants of the provinces, and in the judgment of Joachim Hoppers,[59] the Frisian, would serve to retain what was held, and win back the rebellious parts. Hoppers resided in Spain at that time and enjoyed a growing authority there, since plans which he had advised against had ended in failure, to such effect even that the Spanish had bestowed the nickname The Wise on this Lowlander.

59 No mortal however is so wise he is never deceived by Fortune. Orange had been employing covert stratagems for some time to win the Brabantines over to his side, by showing that it wasn't profit for himself that he was looking for. However, while Requesens was kept busy by the war or pretending mildness, the Brabantines, just as far as he relaxed control, stood up against him of their own accord. In fact the stadtholder himself, when the army mutinies began, had imprudently ordered the agrarian population to arm themselves—which in that

Iamque oblita sub Albano nomina, ius Ordinum et Leges[26] omnium vocibus celebrari. Flandri quoque ingenium recepere, gens inquies, et ne olim quidem principum satis patiens, cum tantum principes essent. Hi petenti tributa Requesenio, quo magis necessario (**47**) exigebantur, hoc confidentius negaverant.

60 Sed in senatu Hispani erant aliquot, caeteri Belgae, a quibus sperabat Arausionensis impetrari posse, ut eadem defensae patriae praemia, quam proditae mallent. Id curantis consilium casus adiuvit. Bellum enim hoc mirum in modum, quanquam validas, Hispaniae opes afflixerat, in tantum Rege obaerato, ut novarum tabularum beneficio, possessiones suas eripuerit foeneratoribus. Et forte Turca (quae potentia crevit semper Christianorum discordiis) dum Philippi robur in Belgas versum comperit, occupata Tunetensi provincia, caeteris Africae, quae Hispani tenebant, terra marique imminebat.

61 Factum per has difficultates, ut stipendiorum dies aliquammulti praeterfluerent Hispanis per Belgicam militantibus, qui recepto iam more obsequium exuentes licentiae praemia captabant. Bruxella rapinae destinabatur, imperii sedes, ni plebs veterum memor, et in arma recentis periculi magnitudine consternata, advertisset magistratus, et quibus creditae leges. Hi senatum, quem rebus Belgicae praepositum diximus, perpulere, ut improbum militem hostem patriae et principis iudicaret; quod palam concessum; clam seditio foveri credebatur, paucorum consiliis, quorum opes in externa dominatione sitae erant.

62 Sed cum, eiectis ducibus, coniuratae cohortes Alostum, Flandriae eius, quae iam olim non Francico, ut caetera, sed Germanico imperio adhaesit, oppidum irrupissent, atque inde late circumsita popularentur, nullo ultore, primores aliquot Brabantiae nullo publico consilio, sed Antverpiensis exempli memoria et metu, misere qui senatum, hoc est reipublicae caput, in curia et sedibus suis comprehenderent. Mox, ne sine legitima potestate iaceret regimen, suspiciosos et innoxios discrevere, detentis quorum dolo aut socordia effectum volebant ne contra Hispanorum iniurias vis pararetur: quin et proprio delectu habito, pellectoque in partes quantum erat indigenae militis, foedus cum Flandris aliisque civitatibus iunxere, ut in hostem communem. Nec recentia modo quietis publicae turbamenta, sed Albanicorum temporum scelera, decimas, disquisitiones, insontium supplicia, quaesitum bello quod pace habebatur, suarum quisque cladium memoria edictis obiectabant.

63 Nec iam res ad eos qui imperium detrectaverant, sed ad omnem Hispanicam nationem visa pertinere. Quare excitis copiis eius gentis, quae tum Hollandia exiere non (**48**) rediturae, ducem se dedit Roda, pars ante senatus, et tunc ad cohortes transgressus ius omne imperii ad se trahens: velut in unum recidente collegio. Addidit se et Germanus miles, spe licentiae: atque ita iuncti Traiectum

[26] Ordinum et Leges *1658* Ordinum et leges *1657*

region became the first step towards liberty. Soon words forgotten under Alva, such as 'the States' and 'laws' were on everybody's lips. The Flemish too rediscovered their true nature, a turbulent nation, intolerant of their own princes already long ago, at a time when these were only princes.[60] When Requesens demanded financial contributions from them, they refused them with the more self-confidence the more compellingly **(47)** he demanded them.

60 On the Council of State however was a handful of Spaniards; the other members were Lowlanders. Orange hoped these could be moved to prefer the same rewards from defending their country rather than from betraying it. This plan by the assiduous prince was helped by chance. For the war had eroded the Spanish financial reserves, however strong they were, to an astonishing degree; the king had incurred so many debts[61] that with the help of a debt redemption[62] he had robbed his creditors of their possessions. Now at that time the Turk (whose power could grow because of the everlasting quarrels between Christians), when he became aware that Philip's power was directed towards the Low Countries, occupied the province of Tunis and began threatening by land and sea the other parts of Africa held by Spain.

61 A result of these difficulties was that the Spanish soldiers encamped in the Low Countries missed many days of wages. These soldiers laid off their obedience and made for the rewards of licentiousness in the usual way.[63] They selected Brussels, seat of the Imperial power, for plundering, if the population (well aware the past and alarmed to arm themselves by the enormity of the recent nightmares) had not warned the magistrate and the protectors of the law. These in turn forced the Council of State, who as related before were in charge of the Low Countries, to label the offending soldiers as enemies of prince and country. This was even decreed publicly,[64] but it was believed that the rebellion was secretly supported, at the advice of some whose financial interests were vested in the foreign domination.

62 However when the conspiring regiments had shed off their commanders, they forced their way into the town of Aalst (in that part of Flanders which once belonged to the German empire, not to France like the rest) and went plundering a wide area around, without any vindication being undertaken against it. Now a few leading men in Brabant, without any official decision, but driven by fear and the recent example of Antwerp,[65] sent agents to have the members of the Council of State—that is: the government—arrested in the council room or in their own homes.[66] Soon they separated the guiltless from the suspected members, in order not to leave the executive deprived of its lawful power, and kept those men in custody whose malice or sloth had been aimed at ensuring that no armed response was set up against the Spanish crimes. They even organized their own levy of troops and lured whatever native soldiery was available over to their side, then concluded a treaty with towns in Flanders and elsewhere as if against a common foreign enemy. In their proclamations they accused [the Council of State] not only of the recent disruptions of public peace, but also of the crimes of Alva's time, the Tenth Penny, the prosecutions, the executions of innocent people, and of the attempt to secure by war what was already held in peace—each according to his own memory of his misfortunes.

63 By now the conflict seemed not just to pertain to those who had given the royal government a bad name, but to the entire Spanish nation. For this reason the troops of that nation were put in motion and left Holland, never **(48)** to return. At their head Geronimo de Roda[67] placed himself, formerly a member of the council of State, who now joined the regiments and drew the entire power of the government towards himself: as if the entire body consisted only of one man. They were joined by the German militiamen, hoping for

ad Mosam, egregiam urbem, diripuere: nec multo post in ipsam Antverpiam ex arce effusi, defensoribus exturbatis, aliquot per dies, caede oppidanorum, aedium incendio, ingenti praeda iram atque avaritiam satiarunt.

64 Quas inter clades Belgae, quibus in novo et rudi milite non satis praesidii adversus tot veteranos, tot arces erat, et longum, movere exteros principes, proximis viribus ultroque oblatis ab Arausionensi uti constituunt; conscii plerique paribus se apud Regem criminibus teneri, quae aut simul avertenda, aut simul luenda essent.

65 Ergo resumpta pacis colloquia, quae Bredae intermissa erant, et, ut inter cives, contra vim peregrinam, facile consensum est, cautumque, oblitterata offensionum memoria, nequis super religione interrogaretur, neu rata essent iudicia, quae eius rei ante facta erant: sed damnatis et res soli in fiscum versae restituerentur, aut, si alienatae essent, dati aestimatores alteri rem, alteri pretium addicendo possessionibus et evictionibus modum ponerent: ut, quos in posterum ritus recipi placeret, et de restituendis quae Hollandi Zelandique Regi propria bello detinebant, et quam isti pecuniam constituerant ob duas Arausionensis expeditiones, eiusne[27] debiti portionem caeterae nationes in se transcribi paterentur, post liberatam externis armis rempublicam, totius Belgicae concilium iudicaret. Interea refoverentur commercia, pars utraque praesenti iurisdictione et receptis iam sacris uteretur: nec liceret Hollandis eorumque sociis extra suos fines quicquam in religionis causa immutare, data tamen Arausionensi potestate cum urbibus ad suam praefecturam pertinentibus paciscendi. In has leges pax facta Gandavi inter Nassavianas gentes, et Brabantos, Flandros, Atrebates, Haenovios, aliasque nationes, praeter Lucemburgios, quorum rectores Hispanico nomini privatim obnoxii, et populis ipse antiquitus fidei in principes retinentissimus: sed Frisii accessere, et obtinentem praefectum vinxerunt Casparum Roblesium, gente Lusitanum.

66 Deiectis passim arcibus servitus exuta, et quia insessa Hispanis Antverpia commerciis nationum intercedebat aperti iuxta Scaldis aggeres, ut per mersa naves tuto vectarentur. Foedus post initum Bruxellae, et belli societas adversus (**49**) Hispanos firmata iuramento sacerdotum, nobilitatis et plebis: adsentit et senatus. Fuitque id unum omnino tempus, quo de rebus Belgicis bene sperare licuit, si cum armis et odia ponerentur. Sed mihi haec altius repetenti certissima malorum origo videtur procerum aemulatrix ambitio, et huic non dissimile populi vitium abruptus suae religionis amor, nunquam se intra foedera, nunquam praesentem intra sortem tenens: haec dum manent, nec partes unquam desunt, nec instrumenta in libertatem.

[27] eiusne *Peerlkamp* eiusve *1657, 1658*

excesses. In this combination they ravaged the splendid city of Maastricht;[68] and a little while later, rushing out into Antwerp from the castle (after chasing out its defenders), they satisfied their anger and greed with the slaughter of citizens, setting fire to buildings and an enormous amount of spoils.[69]

64 Among these misfortunes the Lowlanders were faced with the fact that their new and untrained armies provided insufficient defence against such numbers of veterans and castles, and that it took them too long to move foreign princes to come to their support. They decided to employ the means that were near at hand and those offered spontaneously by William of Orange; being well aware that the king held them all responsible for equal trespasses which they could only dispel, or pay for collectively.

65 Thus the peace talks were resumed which had been broken off at Breda, and a consensus was reached without difficulty, as by citizens among each other against a foreign threat. It was agreed that the memory of past offences was hereby annulled; that no one would be interrogated on account of his faith; and that judicial decisions from the past regarding this issue would be invalid; but that the convicted would even be restored in the ownership of their real estate in cases where it had been handed over to the treasury, or, if it was sold, that surveyors were to be appointed who would limit the number of seizures and evictions by assigning the object to the one party, an amount of money to the other. Furthermore it was decided that once the country would be freed of the foreign armies, a meeting of all the provinces in the Low Countries would decide which religion would be adopted for the future; about the restitution of property belonging to the king which Holland en Zeeland kept in possession during the war; and with respect to the funds which these provinces had set apart for Orange's two invasions, whether the other provinces would let a portion of this debt be transferred to them. Meanwhile trade would be revived, and both parts of the country would remain under the government existing at that time, and in the religion which they had. Nor would it allowed for the Hollanders and their allies to make any change with respect to the faith outside their own borders, although Orange was granted the power to conclude treaties with the cities within the area of his governorship. In order to ratify these conditions, a peace was concluded at Ghent[70] between the provinces of the Nassau party on the one side, and Brabant, Flanders, Artois, Hainaut on the other, as well as the other provinces except Luxemburg, where the leadership were too dependent personally on the house of Spain, and the people traditionally extremely persistent in loyalty to their princes. The Frisians on the other hand did join the Pacification, and they defeated their current stadtholder, Caspar de Robles, a Portuguese by origin.[71]

66 Servitude was shed everywhere by the destruction of castles, and since the occupation of Antwerp by the Spaniards obstructed trade between the provinces, the dykes along the river Scheldt were opened in to order to give the ships safe traffic routes over the flooded fields. Next a treaty was concluded at Brussels,[72] and the war alliance against **(49)** Spain was affirmed with an oath by the clergy, the nobility and the populace; which was endorsed even by the Council of State. In this entire history this was the only time one could have confidence in the Netherlands cause, if at least together with the weaponry, the internal hatred would be put down.[73] However, when I look at it more closely, I see as the surest root of evil the competing ambitions of the nobility, and a vice in the population which resembles it, the impatient love of their own religion, which will never acquiesce in agreements or the present situation. As long as these exist, there will always be party strife and instruments to use against liberty.

67 Itaque rex Philippus perlatis ad se conditionibus, edoctus quanto omnium studio probarentur, et patere externas amicitias, siquid in suos durius consuleret, cedendum tempori existimavit, editaque lege, qua pacta confirmarentur, clam interea statuit occasiones opperiri distrahendae societatis.[28] At Arausionensis filium, cui ex pactis libertas debebatur, ut paternarum actionum obsidem retinebat. Rectorem autem Belgicae misit Iohannem Austriacum, imperatori Carolo extra coniugium genitum, ut iuvenem ingenio acrem, clarum navali in Turcas praelio, et Pontificis gratia florentem, rerum maiorum meditamentis avelleret: et ut specimen esset servandarum in posterum legum, tam propinquus sanguis in regimen missus. Mandata hic pacis servandae praeferebat, secreto iussus Rodae consilia sequi, quem Hispanicae seditionis ductorem fuisse narravimus; sed non satis occultabat credita sibi odia, impatientia aetatis, et simul literis interceptis intima consiliorum intelligebantur.

68 Quae considerans Arausionensis, intentusque ne tam ferentem fortunam extrema corrumperent, auctor erat Belgis, ut, expenso, quantum apud Philippum peccassent iniussa pace, manifestum irae praefectum, sed adhuc inermem et in finibus agentem, bello opprimerent. Id alii primariae nobilitatis Arausionensi non satis aequi, veteri offensione, aut invidia recenti, inhibuere: plerique rerum turbine, quam consilio immixti partibus, reverentia principis continebant arma intra se tuendi necessitatem. Ita, pace facta in oppido Lucemburgiorum, cui Marsa nomen, concessa Austriaco praefectura, si prius Hispanum militem, deinde exteros omnes dimitteret:[29] Hollandis, et qui earum fuerant partium, multa nequicquam contra causantibus.

69 (1577) Tum autem incredibili gaudio metus omnibus abscesserat, cum Hispanorum exercitus ex pacto urbibus discederet: quanquam cruenta secum spolia, et decem annorum (**50**) rapinas trahens, atque ultro iactans, intra sex menses proximos occisa a se Belgarum triginta millia, imbellis haud dubie turbae, cum suorum supra sexaginta amissos intra idem tempus negent: nec tamen digressi longe, apud Mediolanum, quidam etiam citerius, detinebantur, dum illos parato bello Iohannes revocaret, qui summis honoribus in regimen acceptus, sed morae omnis iuveniliter impatiens, aditus interea Belgicae insidebat, brevique erupit, occupato Namurco, et aliquot oppidis ad eum limitem. Germanicas etiam cohortes, quae stipendiis nec dum solutis in Belgica manserant, ad urbium deditionem sollicitabat, eratque illis promta perfidia, sed iners animus, et ad poenitentiam facilitas eadem, si minis aut pollicitationibus tentarentur.

[28] societatis *1657* Societatis *1658*
[29] dimitteret: *1658* dimitteret. *1657*

67 When the articles of the treaty had been communicated to Philip, and he was told how much they enjoyed everybody's support, while foreign affiliations were being opened up to the Lowlanders, he decided to yield to the situation. He issued a decree which endorsed the agreements, and meanwhile decided to look out in secret for opportunities to drive the alliance apart. In any case he kept Orange's son, who should be given his freedom according to the treaty, in detention to serve as a hostage for his father's doings. As governor of the Low Countries, Philip now[74] sent Don Juan of Habsburg, an illegitimate son of the emperor Charles, with the intention of keeping this young man of passionate nature, who was made famous by the naval battle against the Ottomans[75] and glittered in the pope's favour, away from the contemplation of even greater pursuits. By sending such a close relative[76] to lead the government he also aimed at presenting a clear token that from now on the laws would be strictly maintained. For the public eye Don Juan displayed his commission to uphold the conditions of the Pacification; in secret he had received orders to follow Jeronimo de Roda's advice, the man who as we have related had been the leader of a Spanish rebellion. However Don Juan did not enough to conceal the feelings of hatred that were attributed to him, a result of the vehemence of his age, while at the same time intercepted letters revealed the inner details of his plans.

68 Contemplating these circumstances and determined not to have fortune's benevolent mood spoiled at the last moment, Orange urged the Netherlanders to consider how much they had offended Philip by their self-constructed Pacification, and to use force to oppose their governor, whom they had caught in his wrath, while he was still without army and outside the borders. The other members of the highest nobility have not been fair to Orange in their obstruction of this plan, either from offence taken in the past or jealousy in the present. Most of them had become involved with the rebel side in the whirlwind of events rather than by a proper plan, and went no further in their armed exploits than what was necessary for their self-defence. Thus, a peace was concluded in the little town of Marche in Luxemburg.[77] Although Holland and those which were on her side pled extensively against it, without success, Don Juan was given permission to hold the governorship if he would first send away the Spanish soldiers, and next the entire foreign soldiery.

69 However, when in accordance with the treaty the Spanish army left the cities, the fear had gone too, to everyone's unspeakable joy, in spite of the fact that they dragged blood-stained trophies with them (**50**), and the spoils of a decade of plundering. Moreover their wanton boasts were heard that in the last six months they had murdered thirty thousand Lowlanders, a harmless crowd without any doubt, while their own losses in this period, as they claimed, did not go beyond sixty. However these armies were not removed far, and were kept near Milan, some even closer to us, until Don Juan had prepared the war and would call them back. Don Juan was installed in power with the highest honours, but as he was intolerant of any delay in an adolescent fashion, he kept his position on the boundaries to the Low Countries and, suddenly broke out, capturing Namur and a few other towns near that part of the border. He also tried to seduce the German regiments, which had stayed behind in the Low Countries as their wages had not yet been paid, to surrender these cities: but although their disloyalty was ready to oblige him, their spirit was lame, and they were equally susceptible to repentance when tried by threats or promises of reward.

70 Hac ratione pleraque Brabantia servata est, tradente in Ordinum potestatem milite non praesidia tantum, sed ipsos duces. Ordinum nomine utuntur nationum ad commune concilium legati, ad quos post senatus regii vim fractam pleraque reipublicae devenerant. Neque dum bellum erat: sed accusabant Ordines Iohannem apud Regem aliosque principes non obscure violatae pacis: ille rursus Arausionensem criminabatur, contra foederis leges novos ritus stabilire in urbibus, quas paciscendo imperio suo adiunxerat.

71 At is apud omnes Belgicae civitates ingenti fama libertatis auctor ferebatur, egregiusque morum, quibus studia hominum elici solent, potentiam quasi remitteret, gratia muniebat: lenitate denique et prudentia, et quia acri pervestigatione literisque interceptis demonstraverat, Austriaci insidiis se primum et suos, deinde foederis nexi resoluto caeteros peti, tantum favorem est consecutus, ut ad praefecti dignitatem a Brabantis evocaretur. Id Arscotius, qui eo tempore Flandriae erat praepositus, Lalaenius, Campiniacus, aliique nonnulli permoleste tulerunt: quippe rerum summam ad Arausionensem vergere, cui genere paucos, peritia et auctoritate parem neminem haberi. Igitur quoniam longe se ab illo relinqui vident populari gratia, nec metus aberat, ne rerum potitus sacra suos ad usus verteret, obstruere quaerunt eius claritati nominis maioris fulgore.

72 In locum demortui Maximiliani patris Rudolphum imperatorem Germania subrogaverat; eius tunc illi fratrem Mathiam, multa pollicitando, aula excivere, nullo palam imperatoris assensu, ne Hispanum offenderet. Iidem, quod armis et validis (**51**) urbibus praeerant, facile se effecturos putarant, ut perductum ad se iuvenem, et sibi cuncta debentem, haberent in potestate, eiusque nomen iussibus suis praescriberent: quae providens Arausionensis nonnullos consciorum ab eo consilio summovit, persuasitque ut iustam potius auctoritatem in legitimo Ordinum imperio, quam partem in paucorum potentia sperarent.

73 Et forte eodem tempore accidit, ut Arscotius, princeps Nassaviis pridem aemulae domus, spe vana elatior plebem Gandavensem insolenti dicto offenderet: quae natio Flandrorum mobilissima, et nobilitatibus adversa, ipsum cum omni comitatu in custodiam pertraxit. Sed Arausionensis quanquam Mathias ab inimicis vocatus, nec ipsius sponte advenerat, Belgaeque caeteri iam tum Galliam magis respectabant, pudori illius consulens, auctor Ordinibus fuit, ut adolescentem clarum fraterna maiestate et regis propinquum, causae suae admoverent. Quod eousque placuit ut Mathiae regimen Belgicae, Arausionensi vicarium imperium imponeretur, idque velut recusanti; quo aucta illorum ira est, qui spe duntaxat eius dignitatis gratiam partis quaesiverant. Mathiae praefectura mandatis et additis adsessoribus circumscripta est; nec ipsi libido quicquam eius fastigii, praeter vitae splendorem habitumque usurpare. (**52**)

70 By those means the greater part of Brabant was saved, while the soldiers not only handed over the garrisons into the power of the States, but their commanders as well. The name 'States' is used by the delegates of the provinces to their common assembly, in whose hands most of the public business ended up after the power of the king's Council of State had been broken. For the time being there was even no war; but the States charged Don Juan before the king and other princes with openly violating the Pacification; the latter conversely accused Orange of consolidating, against the rules of the treaty, the new faith in the cities which he had added to his realm by concluding the Pacification.

71 Orange however enjoyed great fame in all towns and villages in the Low Countries as the founder of liberty,[78] and, being an expert in the personal conduct which incites people's support, he strengthened his power by the goodwill he won by pretending to reject it. Given moreover his mildness and prudence, and the fact that his keen-witted investigations and intercepted letters had shown that he and his family would be the first target of Don Juan's scheming, then all the others, when the ties of the treaty would be resolved, he achieved such popularity that the people of Brabant summoned him to the dignity of the stadtholderate. This however was more than Aarschot, (who was stadtholder of Flanders at the time) Lalaing, Champagny and several others could bear, that is, that the supreme power was moving in Orange's way, who was seen as having only a few equals in birth, and none in experience and authority. Therefore, as they were aware that he far surpassed them in popularity, and because they feared that once in power he would use the faith for his own purposes, they looked for ways to obscure his fame by the glittering of an even greater name.

72 In Germany Rudolph had been installed as Emperor in the place of his father Maximilian, who had died. The nobles just mentioned now lured his brother Mathias[79] away from that court with a great many promises, without the open assent of the Emperor, to avoid offending Spain. They also thought, because they had armies and strong (**51**) cities under their command, that once the young man would have arrived with them, and would be owing his entire position to them, they would easily secure their hold over him and sign their own orders with his name. Orange however saw through their plans, separated several participants from the conspiracy, and persuaded them to hope for power founded upon the legitimate supremacy of the States rather than a small share in the domination of a few.

73 Incidentally it happened in the same time that Aarschot, the leader of a house with a long history of competition with that of Orange, and reckless from ill-founded expectations, offended the populace of Ghent with insolent words. Of all tribes in Flanders those of Ghent are the most lightly susceptible to uproar, and hostile to nobility; they put Aarschot and his entire entourage behind bars. Although Mathias had been called in by Orange's enemies, had not come of his own accord, and the other Lowlanders were already looking more to France for support, Orange, from respect for Mathias' modesty, ensured that the States associated him with their cause, as the young man possessed greatness because of his brother's throne and was a close relative of the king. This was accepted insofar that Mathias was put at the head of the Low Countries' government, and Orange was given deputy powers, although he pretended to reject them. This aggravated the wrath of those who had only sought favour with the rebel side in the hope of obtaining this dignity. Mathias' stadtholderate was hedged in by delegating tasks to others and added co-governors; in fact there was no desire in him to derive more from the position than a life of splendour and personal greatness.

Liber Tertius

1 **(53)** Rebus eum in modum constitutis Iohanni bellum denuntiatur; quo tempore reditus menstrui ad sexcenta millia florenorum publico aerario inferebantur, quorum liberrimam dispensationem delectusque et belli consilia, quo melius laterent, senatui Ordines permiserant. Tum demum regina Angliae dignas Belgarum vires iudicavit, quibus faveretur: proprio etiam metu, quia Iohannes cum Scota coniugium, et per eam suaque arma Britanniae regnum animo agitabat; idque magnis indiciis compertum. Quapropter pecunias et auxilia promisit, interpositis restituendi cautionibus, et hoc titulo inscriptis, ut Belgicae gentes in Philippi obsequio continerentur: atque ita se reipublicae immiscuit, ut nihil magni pateretur, sine sua voluntate, decerni: dansque operam, ut res novae concordia fulcirentur, frustra a Belgarum nonnullis in Arausionensem incitata, atque alios vicissim monens, ne veterem Romanae religionis possessionem temere moverent, intendit opem quantum pericula gliscebant. Cumque haec ageret, literas ad Regem mittebat, suadentes veram pacem, et regimen iuxta leges; sin ad arma subditos adigeret, intentis iamdudum Gallis; ne moleste ferret ipsam inimicae genti Belgarum societatem praevertere, anxie interim suspiciones purgans affectatae ex alieno potentiae. Nec minus Henricum Galliarum regem, Sebastianum Lusitaniae, ipsumque imperatorem rogarant Ordines, ut Philippum sibi mitigarent; hunc etiam ut causam auxilio dignaretur, quod tum frustra fuit.

2 (1578) Valescebant interea simultates et odia regentium: multi adeo castris, ad Lucemburgum sitis, diffluebant, varia obtendentes, sed tacite honores alienos in suam iniuriam interpretabantur. At Iohannes receptis Hispanis, ingentibusque copiis auctus, quas illi Parmensis, Belgicae quondam rectricis filius, ex Italia adduxerat, exercitum Belgarum, qui ducum **(54)** discessu in dies minuebatur, introrsus recedentem in Brabantiam ad Gembliniacum praelio cecidit: nec parva victoriae praemia; Lovanium quod ex ea parte Brabantiam aperit; Limburgum ducatu insigne et cognominis ditionis caput, in Germaniae subdita excurrens; et Philippopolis, quam urbem novo validoque opere Arausionensis, regii quondam exercitus ductor, Gallis obiecerat, cum tantum externa metuerentur: sed et alia circum oppida cesserunt.

3 Victos spe pacis tentare regi placuit, Barone Sellesio conditiones ferente ex Hispania diversas a pactis Gandavensibus, et quibus Iohannis praefectura non mutabatur: quod tunc satis visum cur recusari deberent. Nosse enim se Belgae tum primum coeperant, et augebant fiduciam principes certatim operam et militem offerendo. Hinc Franciscus Valesius, Andium dux, regis Galliarum frater,

Book 3

1 **(53)** When affairs had been arranged in this way, war was declared on Don Juan. In this period the public treasury's monthly revenues ran to six hundred thousand florins, the allocation of which, as well as the levies of troops and the organisation of the war, the States left entirely to the Council of State, in order to facilitate secrecy. Now at last the Queen of England deemed the efforts of the Lowlanders worthy of her support, from fear for her own position too. For Don Juan was brooding on plans to marry the queen of Scots[1], and (using her and his own military power) to make an attempt at the British crown, which was understood from no minor indications. For these reasons the queen promised money and troops, stipulating specific conditions regarding her reimbursement, and under the prescription that the provinces of the Low Countries would preserve their obedience to Philip. She also reserved such a role in the government for herself that she would let no major decision be taken without her consent, while she also made an effort to have the young state supported by greater unity. She remained deaf to the attempts by some Netherlanders to set her against William of Orange, warning others in her turn not to inconsiderately start re-arranging the former possessions of the Roman church, and promised her help to such heights as the danger would rise. While doing so she also sent a letter to the king, pleading for a true peace, and government in accordance with the law; adding 'but in case you would induce your subjects to armed resistance, while the French have so long been looking for their chance, do not censure my person for entering into an alliance with the Lowlanders first, before that hated nation.' At the same time she was anxious to cleanse herself of any suspicion of desiring another man's sovereignty. The States on their part put no less energy in imploring Henry king of France, Sebastian of Portugal, and the Emperor himself to try and bring Philip to a milder attitude towards them; and the Emperor for actual support for their cause—which was asked in vain however at that time.

2 Meanwhile the machinations and internal hatred among the leadership grew worse and worse; with the consequence that many disappeared from the camp near Luxemburg under all kinds of pretexts, but in silence they perceived the preferment of others as violation of their own rights. On the other side Don Juan received new Spanish troops, and huge numbers at that, which had been brought to him from Italy by the duke of Parma, son of the former governess of the Low Countries. They destroyed the Netherlands army, which shrunk from day to day by the departure of its commanders **(54)** and was retreating backwards towards Brabant, in a battle near Gembloux.[2] The fruits of this victory were large: Louvain, which opens the way into Brabant from that side; Limburg, crowned by a ducal title and the centre of a region of the same name with branches far into Germany, and Philippeville, a town which Orange, once commander of a royal army, had fitted out with new strong bulwarks against the French, at a time when there were only foreign enemies to reckon with. Some other towns in the region came into Spanish hands as well.

3 Now the king decided to seduce the vanquished with hopes of peace. The baron of Selles[3] came from Spain presenting conditions different from the agreements of Ghent, including the one that Don Juan would remain in his governorship: which alone seemed sufficient reason at the time why the proposal should be refused. For by now the Lowlanders for the first time began to be aware of themselves, while princes boosted their self-confidence by vying in offers of troops and support. As a result the Low Countries leadership, even before

FRANCOIS VAN VALOIS,
HARTOGH VAN ANJOU, BRABANT EN LOTRYK,
GRAEF VAN VLAENDEREN ETC.

3.4. *Portrait of Francis of Valois, Duke of Anjou* (no signature)

3.23. *Portrait of Alexander Farnese, Duke of Parma* (no signature)

iam ante pacem Gandavensem et postea saepe ambitus Belgarum primoribus: inde Casimirus, qui Palatinatum Germaniae administrabat: domi postpositus uterque nascendi ordine, atque eo avidi increscere alienis.

4 Franciscus haud contemnendo ingenio, sed animi inquies, belli se ducem dederat, quod ad restituendam contra aulae iniurias Galliae libertatem, et pro quiete religionum sumi tum dicebatur: quod seu fratris odio fecit vita imbelli et infoecunda regnum detinentis, sive ad vim partium avertendam maternae calliditatis instrumentum fuit, famam sane sibi popularem eius causae tutela, et pace facta amplissimas possessiones paraverat. Sed famam brevi foedavit in socios versis armis, aliorum saevitiae minister.

5 Quo tempore Margarita Valesia, Navarri uxor, quo se mariti fratrumque bellis eximeret, absentiae desiderium ad aquas Spadanas itinere velans, cum Cameraco Montibusque transiret, usa occasione potissimis illic locis, moribus, lingua Galliae propioribus, nec religione diversis, Andinum valde commendaverat. At Casimirus eodem tempore, ingens Navarri partibus auxilium, quae sibi privatim pepigerat, concordiae remittens, aequi religiosique animi praebuerat argumentum.

6 Undique confusa hoc tempore Respublica fuit, velut indigesta moles, et partibus discors: dum quasi vacuum regimen rapiunt singuli, diversa via. Et contra regnum quidem armis certabatur: sed aliis laudata, principatus et leges: alii vires suas prae Venetis atque Helvetiis admirati, nec considerata dissimilitudine, optimatium **(55)** nomine imperium distrahebant: aut etiam, quod dignitate ab aliis vincebantur; plebeiae potentiae imminentes vulgus, qua turbidissimum, ductu, voce concitabant, inclementes suspicionibus, nec ullam probantes cum exceptione libertatem.

7 Intus et palam partes et seditiones erant: nec eo minus bellum; lentum tamen, nec satis intentum tempori, quia pro studiis copiae distinebantur. Amstelodamum, quam maximam Hollandicarum urbium libertati defuisse diximus, Iohanni tunc etiam fovebatur. Sed quia Nassaviani urbem circumvenerant, nec ulla spes auxiliorum e tam longinquo erat, ventum ad pactiones: quae religionis causa extorres patriae reddebant; nisi extra moenia, prohibitis eorum ritibus. Sed cum Romanae sectae homines, ambiguae fidei, interdum et in hostem reflecti crederentur, exsules pulsis magistratibus, et his qui sacris praeerant, publico potiti sunt. Idem diversis temporibus similibus ferme de causis Traiecti et Harlemi, et aliis Hollandiae in oppidis accidit, quaesito adversus fidem datam colore, ex magistratibus in hoc institutis, ut quod ipsi probarent, id invita civitate fieri non videretur; quod ibi quidem haud inutile concordiae, at sociorum animos offendit, qui Romano pontifici addicti, in se vires quaeri suspicabantur.

the Pacification of Ghent and many times since, had been seeking the favour of Francis of Valois, duke of Anjou, the French king's brother;[4] and subsequently that of Casimir, who controlled the Palatinate in Germany.[5] Both men were not first in line for succession at home, and therefore eager for promotion abroad.

4 Francis was certainly a clever man, but also restless. He had accepted the leadership of a war which people said at the time was fought for the restoration of France's freedom against offences committed by the court, and for religious peace as well. Whether he did this from aversion for his brother, who was keeping the throne occupied with his warless and barren life, or perhaps as an instrument of his mother's shrewdness in preventing a faction war, his protectorship of that cause brought him a great popularity, and when peace was concluded, virtually unlimited possessions. He managed however to spoil this fame by attacking his allies, thus making himself the executor of someone else's cruelty.

5 Around the same time Margaret of Valois, the king of Navarre's wife, wished to withdraw herself from the wars between her husband and her brothers, and dressed her desire to get away in a visit to the spas of Spa. Passing through Mons and Cambrai she used the occasion to recommend Anjou in the most positive terms to these very important cities, which are near-French in language and culture and identical in religion. While this happened Casimir, a strong pillar of support for Navarre's side, presented proof of his decent and religious nature by giving up all that he had stipulated for himself for the sake of harmony.

6 In this period the Low Countries commonwealth was in a state of general confusion, like the primal Chaos,[6] and split by internal conflict, while individuals tried in various ways to seize the supreme power which was lying more or less unoccupied. Although there was an armed struggle going on against royal power, some extolled the qualities of a monarchy bound by laws; others esteemed their own abilities even over those of Venice and the Swiss, comfortably disregarding the differences, and attempted under the name of 'aristocracy' **(55)** to pull the supreme power apart. Still others saw that other men surpassed them in dignity and set their eyes on populist power, speaking and driving to agitate the populace where it was most easily aroused: suspicion made them merciless and they only approved of liberty without any restrictions.

7 Faction strife and mutinies existed visibly and invisibly. This did not detract from the war that was going on; it only made it slow, and less alert to the possibilities of the moment, because resources were divided according to where they were most pressingly demanded. Amsterdam, the largest city in Holland, which as we have related had so far been absent from the cause of liberty was being kept friendly to Don Juan even by this time. But because the Nassau men had encircled the city and there was no hope of receiving support over such a distance, a peace was negotiated. This peace restored access to their home town to those who had fled for the sake of the faith, albeit with their worship allowed only outside the walls. Since however there were people among the Roman sect[7] whose loyalty was not beyond doubt, and who were sometimes even believed to be drawn back to the enemy, the refugees drove out the magistrate and the holy ministers and seized power. The same happened at different moments, but for roughly the same reasons, in Haarlem and Utrecht and some other towns in Holland: an excuse for breaking existing agreements was sought in the idea that magistrates were appointed in order that their decisions should not seem to go against the will of the citizenship. For the time being this strengthened unity within the commonwealth, but insulted those allies who were loyal to the Pontiff of Rome and began to suspect that violence was being prepared against them.

8 Geldriae regimen Iohannes Nassavius ordinavit, cui Arausionensis eam praefecturam mandari curaverat, quo pluribus munimentis insisteret. At in Frisia, cui tum datus Rennebergius rector, vetera Groningae urbis et agri circumiecti ob mercium evectionem certamina, velut alta pace, exarserant: dubium an sponte praefecti, ut certius imperaret. Legatos ad se partis adversae plebs urbana vinxerat: eadem, postquam privato utrinque ausu arma tentaverant, superior evasit. Et captis quidem restituta libertas: odia, quanquam Mathias et Arausionensis intercedebant, mansere, donec publicis dissidiis haec quoque miscerentur. Etiam Frisiae quosdam senatores, qui Hispanorum victoriae faverant, suffectis aliis asservari iussit Rennebergius, unaque Leovardiae pontificem. Haec ob merita proprius regendae et perdomandae Transisalanae dux eligitur: nam Campos et Daventriam Germanus a Iohanne emtus miles tenebat. Utraque urbs dedita est. Sed ad Daventriam longius haerenti recens auxilium Casimirus cum peditatu octo millium, equitatu paulo minore, advenerat: copias adducens maiores imperatis.

9 Nam Angliae regina, (**56**) promissae pecuniae loco, militem adiunxerat; et ipse ultro auxerat numerum, officii specie: quod Romanae religionis primores sinistrius interpretabantur, atque eo promptius Franciscum Valesium suae sectae principem acciendum, orandumque curaverunt, patiente Arausionensi aliisque, ne suspiciones in se onerarent. Nominatur igitur decreto Ordinum Franciscus vindex Belgicae libertatis, et super quod de restitutione impendiorum cautum erat, addicuntur illi, in praemium societatis, oppida quaecunque trans Mosam hostis possidebat.

10 Dum haec geruntur, et inferiores pietatis studiis, maximus quisque ob potentiam dissident, innovatae religionis sectatores rem impetravere egregiam sibi, ancipitem reipublicae: quia ius imperii penes multos, nulla potestas celsior partium odia coërcebat. Postulata dederant ad Mathiam et Arausionensem, nec ante ignarum: quibus demonstrabant, se ipsos[30] esse nunquam administros dominationis, sed materiam semper saevitiae Hispanicae, cui destinatum parte optima civium orbatam rempublicam opprimere. Ne nunc quidem hostibus aliunde plus invidiae: et pignus suae fidei certissimum, quod unam spem in salute publica haberent: quippe si vetera redeant, inopiam ceteris et servitutem, sibi mortes, cruciatus, flammas parari: deinde quod primi sumptis armis dominationem afflixerint, omnem sibi veniam praeclusisse. Merito igitur, quos pessima regni maneant, partem aequam precari ex libertate. Opima sacerdotia, amplissimos proventus aliis se relinquere; tantum ne velut profani templis et curia arcerentur. Non se in Deum pietate, non in patriam fide cessuros.

11 Dubitatum aliquamdiu: et tandem laudantes Germaniae Polonorumque exemplum, et vetera permulta persuasere, quorum haec consilio petebantur, concordiae interesse ne reiicerentur aequae preces. Nam in exercitu quod roboris erat,

[30] ipsos *scripsimus* illos *1657, 1658* solos *Muller*

8 The administration of Guelders was in the hands of John of Nassau,[8] whom William of Orange had had invested with this office, in order for his own power to have more pillars of support. In Friesland however, which was governed by Rennenberg,[9] the age-old struggle between the town of Groningen and the district over trade and export resumed as if it was the height of peacetime—we are not even certain that this wasn't the governor's doing, to strengthen his rule. Delegates from the opponent side were thrown into prison by the city populace: which eventually gained the upper hand in the conflict, after both sides had used violence in private deeds of bravery. Now those held in captivity were given back their freedom, but although Mathias and Orange intervened, the hatred would remain for a long time to come, until this too was absorbed in the wider political conflict.[10] Rennenberg also had a number of councillors in Friesland, who had favoured a Spanish victory, put in custody and others installed in their place, and the bishop of Leeuwarden as well. Because of these laudable actions he was elected as the right commander to rule and to tame Overijssel; for Kampen and Deventer were held by German soldiery hired by Don Juan. Both cities were surrendered, although at Deventer, where he needed more time, Casimir arrived to bring him eight thousand infantry and just slightly less cavalry, fresh auxiliaries, in greater number than demanded.

9 This was possible because the Queen of England **(56)** had sent troops instead of the money she had promised; and of his own accord Casimir had raised the number, presenting it as his duty. The Catholic leadership interpreted this as a dangerous sign, and sent messengers to Anjou to implore him urgently, with the approval of Orange and others, to avoid raising suspicions against themselves. As a result Francis of Anjou was appointed by a decision of the States as defender of the freedom of the Low Countries, and on top of the agreements about the restitution of his expenses, all towns on the other side of the Meuse currently held by the enemy, were awarded to him as a premium on the alliance.

10 In the meantime, while the ordinary people quarreled about religion, and the elite about power, the adherents of the new religion succeeded in achieving something extremely advantageous for them, but critically dangerous for the commonwealth, for the supreme power was divided over many and no overarching authority kept party-strife in check. They presented their demands to Mathias and Orange, who no doubt was already informed. In this text they argued: 'Never have we been serviceable to tyranny. No, to the contrary, we have always been the object of Spanish cruelty, which was deadly resolved to rob our commonwealth of its best citizens and suppress it. Even now our enemies' wrath has no more opulent source than this: it is a secure pledge of our loyalty that our only hope is in the survival of this commonwealth. For were the past to return, it would have poverty and slavery in store for all others, but death, torture and the pyre for us. Moreover, since we were the first to attack the tyranny by force of arms, we have precluded every possibility of pardon. Therefore we, who can only expect the worst from the monarchy, justly request a fair share in the results of the battle for freedom. We gladly leave wealthy parishes and big benefits for others, as long as we won't be dismissed like pagans from the church and the government. And we will not waver in piety towards God or in our loyalty to the fatherland.'

11 This request was kept in consideration for some time. Eventually, by praising German and Polish examples and many similar cases in the past, the instigators of this request persuaded the others that it serves unity to not dismiss reasonable requests; for it is on unity that all force of the army depends, and experience teaches that the care for the commonwealth

inde stare: compertumque experimentis, rerum curam non aliis tutius credi. His accedebat, quod Romanae sectae nonnulli, praecipue qui se Iesuitarum nomine iactitabant, in iuramentum contra Iohannem adigi non poterant, et pars haud exigua, cui plus spei in regiis partibus, sponte discesserant: multique magistratus, ita edocti, seu quod eius partis auctoritatem providebant, Nassavianae religionis studium amplectebantur. His de causis communicati illis honores, et quibuscunque in locis (**57**) familiae non minus centum postularent, iussae illorum sacris distribui aedes: hac lege, ut Latinorum caeremonias praeferentibus per Hollandiam et Zelandiam tantundem concederetur; quod tamen non evenit.

12 Post haec quae sequuntur, non sine miseratione aut ingenti exemplo transeunda, tanti motus, tanta odia, et turbae turbis obtentui. Nam et Romanenses alteris nihil prorsus concedere, et illi non iam impunitate aut arcano suo laeti, adversus contumaciores magistratus legis munus privatis viribus rapere, et postquam praevaluerant, respicere ultionem.

13 Ita qui vota iam dudum; opes et consilia contra Hispanos nuper admodum iunxerant, cives contra cives ipsis in urbibus armati stetere; dum adversarios pellerent hostium securi: ne militis quidem multo ad bellum usu, cuius praesidio pax interna continebatur. Ac sicut morborum exitiales remedia aspernantur, ita qui tum concordiae sectatores erant, eos concurrentia e diverso odia premebant, signiferis ad seditionem his, quos patientiae doctores esse oportuerat; per quos communis huius saeculi pestis in utrasque partes vulgata est; inversa rerum nomina, ut caeca dissidendi libido pius ardor, modestia et animi temperies ignavia, aut etiam proditio vocaretur.

14 Gandavenses igitur eo iam provecti licentiae, ut impunitatem nisi ex audaciae magnitudine non sperarent, concitore Imbisio, qui per tritum quondam Arteveldis iter ad potentiam grassabatur, palam satis imperium detrectant. Negabant ultra se visuros Romanas superstitiones, saevitiae et tot scelerum repertrices: non quod auctores seditionis multum sua referre existimarent, utrius religionis specie tumultuarentur: sed veteribus nova, receptis propria praeferebant; et forte convictis nefariae libidinis aliquot monachis, flagrantem recenti odio atque invidia ordinem, deinde sacerdotes exegerant. Tum conscii quantum coeptarent, urbem operibus munire instituunt: quae ingenti ambitu par maximis urbium, caeterum non tota habitatur: nam obsessi saepe, et ex moribus suis eadem in posterum metuentes, moenibus arva incluserant. Quo magis munitio procedebat, hoc minus Ordinum et Mathiae mandata audiebantur, vanissimis in illos criminibus iactatis, et ex his, quae in se irritaverant, retro quaesito colore. Nec ulla Arausionensis gratia, quanquam eo suasore avitas leges, rebellione quondam in Carolum amissas, Gandavenses (**58**) receperant. Quin et in vicinas Flandriae urbes promotum est malum.

is nowhere safer. Moreover several adherents of the Roman sect, and especially those that prided themselves on the name of Jesuits, could not be brought to swearing an oath against Don Juan; and a considerable number, who had better prospects on the king's side, had left of their own accord. When this news had spread, or because they foresaw a Nassau rule in the future, many magistrates embraced the cause of the Nassau faith. Consequently they were given public offices, and orders were issued that in all places **(57)** where at least one hundred families requested this, buildings would be made available for their worship; under the converse condition that in Holland and Zeeland the same number would be accorded to those preferring the Latin rite—a clause however which was never actually carried out.

12 The events that followed cannot be passed over without feeling great sadness or recognising a major *exemplum* in it: such chaos, so much hatred, and rebellion for the sake of masking other rebellions. For the supporters of the Roman faith were unwilling to grant even the smallest concession, and the others, no longer satisfied with just impunity or having their secret worship, took their rights from unwilling magistrates by self-organised force and after they had gained the upper hand, looked for revenge.

13 Thus people who had had shared purposes for a long time, and had only recently joined their means and plans against the Spanish, now faced each other in arms, citizens against citizens, in the heart of their towns, not worrying about the enemy as long as they could dispel their adversaries. Even the army was of little use for the war, now that its support was needed to maintain peace at home. Like sometimes the remedies against fatal diseases are spurned, so now the supporters of concord were hard-pressed by the hatred that faced them from all sides: and precisely the ones who should have been the teachers of patience, in reality became the captains of dissension. Through them the common plague of our century was spread over both camps and the names of things were turned upside down: so that blind desire for strife was called pious ardour, and modesty and moderation cowardice, or even treason.

14 At Ghent, were the anarchy had reached such a point that punishment could only be avoided by deeds of great daring, official authority was rejected more or less openly. The agitator of this was a man called Hembyze,[11] who was making his way towards power via the path once trodden by Jacob van Artevelde.[12] The people of Ghent declared they would no longer tolerate the sight of Roman idolatry, architect of cruelty and of so many crimes: not because the instigators of the mutiny considered it would matter a great deal to them which religion provided the banner for their rebellion, but they preferred new over old, home-grown over imported. When it happened that a handful of monks were convicted of heinous acts of lechery, they drove out their entire order, which had become the object of burning hatred and hostility, then the priests as well. Next they realised what they had started and began reinforcing the city walls. Ghent equals the biggest cities on earth by its gigantic circumference, but not all of it is built up. For after many sieges, and from fear that their behaviour would cause more in the future, the inhabitants enclosed fields within their defences. The more these defence works proceeded, the less the States' and Mathias' orders were heeded. Meanwhile the latter were accused of the most nonsensical offenses, and the people of Ghent retrospectively derived excuses for their conduct from the difficulties created by themselves. Moreover there wasn't the slightest gratitude towards Orange, although it had been at his pleading that the city had been given back its ancient rights, **(58)** which it had once lost in a rebellion against the Emperor Charles. The evil even propagated itself to other cities in Flanders.

15 Contra vero Atrebates et Haenovii Romanae religionis tenaciores, quod ita plerique sentirent, praeterea proceres civili obtrectatione Arausionensi adversarentur, novam legem et ipsi recusarunt. Foedere enim contineri, ne quid manente bello in religionibus mutaretur. Contendebant ad hoc, manifestam perfidiae Gandavensium civitatem bello coërcendam esse: quod Arausionensis et alii Belgarum principes commissuri non erant, ut, Hispano scilicet mediam fere Belgicam validissimis cum legionibus insidente, in cives, utcumque meritos, arma verterentur: et, quod hostium prudentissimis praedictum, sua ipsi discordia interirent. Sed dum vi cogere periculosum est, iussus, consilia, preces, ut apud destinatam malitiam, spernebantur.

16 Maximi eo tempore Belgarum exercitus dux erat Bossuvius, quem Frisio in pelago, cum Hollandiae reliquias sub Albano regeret, captum fuisse memoravimus. Lalaenio Ordines id munus abrogaverant, quod ipsorum iniussu castra reliquisset, cum ad Gembliniacum male pugnatum est. Magister equitum erat vicecomes Gandavi Melodunea domo: praefectus castrorum Lanovius, egregiam famam civilibus Gallorum bellis consecutus. Castra, non procul Machlinia ad Riminandum vicum sita, Iohannes adortus est, tantumque depulsus. Erratum in eo plerique tradiderunt, quod non institum est discedentibus: quippe illa die Hispanorum copias debellari potuisse. Sed et urbes obsidendo annus iste occupari potuit, si ducum provisu fossores atque id genus operae castrenses adfuissent.

17 Non omissa inter haec pacis colloquia: rogati enim exteri principes rationem inire concordiae suadebant Iohanni, ut quando Belgarum vires multo praepollebant, integra adhuc fama exiret, et spes alias secundiores aggrederetur. Regem quoque rectius facturum, si gentem validam et armatam sibi conciliaret; nec tantum imperium temere proiiceret, iam paratis qui exceptarent: hoc autem obtineri non posse, nisi, probato Gandavensi foedere, religiones ipsorum arbitrio permitterentur: aequissimum autem esse ut captivis omnibus et inter eos Arausionensis filio redderetur libertas. In has leges facta pace comprehendi debere qui cum Belgis societatem iniissent, ut et horum quieti consuleretur.

18 Ad haec Iohannes, nisi Arausionensi in Hollandiam relegato spem nullam (**59**) facere pacis: nec de religione quicquam concedere; tantum inducias non recusaturus videbatur. Pax scilicet validiorum fere arbitrio constitui solet: infirmis belli dilatio omnis in lucrum cedit. Sed cum novis auctus copiis triginta peditatus millia, sexies mille equites obtineret, nec iam multo se Belgis imparem crederet, praesertim discordibus, in Bonga monte, qui Namurco imminet, metatus castra, colloquium abrupit, omni pacificatione ad imperatorem reiecta. Casimirus interea diutius in Geldria moratus, aere non satis parato, quod militi solvendum erat, magnum

15 On the other hand, in Artois and Hainaut, provinces which hàd been steadfast[13] in their adhesion to the Roman faith because a majority wished it so (and further because the nobility had turned against Orange out of political jealousy), the new settlement was refused by the population. Their argument was that the Pacification itself prescribed that for the duration of the war nothing was to be changed in the religious situation. On top of this they also urged for a military operation to stop the undeniable faithlessness of the citizenship of Ghent. With that respect however, Orange and the other chief Netherlands noblemen, as long as the Spaniard occupied roughly the heart of the Low Countries with his strongest legions, were not going to allow that arms be used against fellow citizens, however much they deserved it, and the Low Countries be destroyed by its own internal conflict, as the wisest minds on the enemy side had predicted. However, while compelling by force is dangerous, commands, advice, requests were spurned, as usual in the case of willful malice.

16 The commander of the largest Netherlands army of the time was Bossu, whom as we have related had been captured in the battle on the Frisian sea[14], when he governed what remained of Holland under Alva's rule.[15] The States had taken this task away from Lalaing[16] because he had left the army camp against their orders at the time of the unsuccessful fight at Gembloux. The command of the cavalry was held by the Viscount of Ghent, from the house of Melun;[17] in charge of the army camp was De la Noue,[18] who had obtained an outstanding reputation in the civil wars in France. Don Juan attacked this camp, situated not far from Mechelen at a village called Rijmenam, and was summarily repulsed. Many have written that a mistake was made by not chasing after the retreating men; for on that day the Spanish forces could have been completely defeated. But that year could also have been filled by besieging towns, if at least the foresight of the leadership had ensured the availability of sappers and similar military workmen.

17 During these events the peace negotiations were not discontinued; for the foreign princes whom Don Juan asked for advice, recommended that he accept the plan for reconciliation, in order to leave the stage with an unstained reputation, as the Lowlanders' forces were now much stronger, and pursue other, more successful ambitions. They added that the king too would do better to make peace with this nation, who were armed and valiant, and not inconsiderately throw away such an important part of his power, given the fact that several others were ready to carry it off; but that this could only be achieved by accepting the Pacification and leaving the religious issue to their own decision. That however the fairest thing of all would be if all prisoners would be given their freedom, including Orange's son; and a peace concluded under these conditions should be extended to include those who had entered into alliances with the Lowlanders, in order to provide for their peace as well.

18 Don Juan's response to this was that he offered no hope of peace **(59)** if Orange wasn't removed towards Holland, and that there would be no concessions with respect to religion. Only a temporary truce he did not seem to be going to refuse. In most cases peace is concluded at the stronger party's decision; the weaker side will benefit from every lengthening of the war. However after his army was reinforced, and he commanded thirty thousand footmen and six thousand cavalry, Don Juan did not believe he was much weaker than the Lowlanders, especially in their state of internal conflict. He placed a new army camp on mount Bonge[19] which overlooks Namur and broke off the negotiations, leaving the entire peace process to the Emperor. Meanwhile Casimir lingered too long in Guelders because the money which was due to his soldiers was insufficiently forthcoming, and he could move

agmen tarde moliebatur. Eius adventu Belgarum exercitus quadraginta peditum, viginti equitum millia habuit: quibus cum copiis Francisci auxilia opperiri, deinde Iohannem circumsidere lentum nimis consilium erat, satis certae tamen spei, si incipi potuisset. Sed illa longi temporis peccata, honorumque nimia et divitiarum aviditas, et utrisque abutendi libido, quae Belgas antea Hispanis in servitutem mancipaverant, eadem propinquam tunc et in conspectu libertatem avertere.

19 Haenoviorum enim et Atrebatum cum Flandris contentiones eousque exarserant, ut exuta publici cura singulae gentes tributa in proprios usus retinerent. Manante latius exemplo, cohortes aliquae iam dudum otio lascivientes, cum stipendio fraudarentur, a republica secesserunt, arcano ducum instinctu, qui non satis sibi in dignitatibus profecisse videbantur. Hic igitur miles occupato Menenio[31] (Flandriae id municipium est) circumiacentem agrum rapinis incursat. Adhuc intra privatam audentiam vis statura sperabatur, cum subito praecipuae inter tribunos auctoritatis Montiniacus suscepit regimen, et in Atrebatum factionem transtulit. Adversus eorum iniurias Gandavenses proprias cohortes conscripsere: sed in hoc milite domi feroci,[32] bellorum rudi, non satis praesidii ad prohibendas inimicorum populationes erat. Ita autem illi aiebant, sacerdotes Gandavo per vim et seditionem expulsos apud se exsulare: nec potuisse negari propter sanctimoniam ordinis, aut fortunae ipsorum indignitatem, supplici turbae alimenta, quae, cum iuri locus non esset, a bonorum ereptoribus armis se reposcere. Hoc belli obtentu (nam in apertam hostilitatem dissensiones transiere) praedae quotidie ingentes agebantur: donec Casimiro Flandri accito militem ab eo accepere, stipendium de suo polliciti, (**60**) cuius tunc magna ubique penuria erat. Ipse principatum sperasse et vanitate gentis, atque rerum eventu elusus creditur.

20 Sed Franciscum ea tempestate Haenoviae oppida attinebant. Id ille Lalaenio eius regionis praefecto gratificabatur, gnarus quorum sponte venisset. Equites paulo plures octingentis, peditatus sex millia adduxerat, Gallicorum tumultuum eiectamenta: quos post inclemens iter, et violata passim hospitia captis aliquot castellis, et autumno iam procedente, apud Binckium oppidum deposuit. Id obsidio et oppugnatione in potestatem venit, pretium temporis vile. Ipse Monte Haenoviae urbe plerumque morabatur, non sine indignatione, quod attributa praesidiis loca oppidani non traderent: oratusque ut ad Belgarum exercitum accederet, prius se venturum negavit, quam idem faceret Casimirus: cuius Gandavensi profectione non mediocriter offendebatur amicus iam ante, et tunc competitor, exardentibus ad contumelias usque odiis. Nec demotus est sententia, demonstrante quamvis Mathia et Arausionensi, ipsaque Angliae regina, Flandrorum et Casimiri factum sibi non probari: quin ultro passus dilabi militem suum ad Montiniaci cohortes.

[31] Menenio *1658* Menenio, *1657*

[32] feroci, *scripsimus* feroce, *1657, 1658*

his large train forward only very slowly. At his arrival the Netherlands army comprised forty thousand infantry, twenty thousand cavalry. With these troops the plan was to wait for Anjou's auxiliaries, then close in Don Juan, a plan which would take too long, but still gave sufficient hope of success, if it could at least have been put in motion. However it was the same well-known faults again which had kept the Netherlanders in Spanish slavery before, excessive eagerness for office and wealth, and a lust for abusing both, which now prevented the arrival of freedom although it was near and ready in sight.

19 The tensions between Hainaut and Artois on the one hand, and Flanders on the other had escalated to such a point that individual provinces shed their responsibility for the common cause and retained their tax revenues for their own purposes. When this example found wider imitation, a number of regiments which had for some time been spending their days in joyful idleness, defected from the common cause when they were robbed of their wages. They were led in this by the covert instigation of their commanders who felt they were not making sufficient progress in rank. These soldiers occupied Meenen (a free town in Flanders) and fell upon the countryside, robbing and plundering. However hope was still alive that the violence would stay within this private adventure, when suddenly the count of Montigny, a man of particular authority among the officers, seized command and transferred these troops to the Artois faction. As a means against these wrongdoings the people of Ghent began levying their own regiments, which troops however, full of bravery at home but without experience on the battlefield, provided no sufficient defence to stop the robberies of their enemies. And thus the other side again claimed that the clergy expelled from Ghent with violence and mutiny were staying in exile with them; that this host of supplicants could not be refused provisions, given the sanctity of their order or the unfairness of what had been done to them; and that they reclaimed these goods, since the law could not be applied, by force of arms from those who had robbed them. Under this pretext for war (for the disagreement proceeded to forthright hostility) huge amounts of booty were taken on a daily basis until the Flemish called Casimir in and received troops from him, promising to pay the wages from their own resources **(60)**, of which at that time there was great scarcity everywhere. It is believed that the boastfulness of that nation together with the course of events misled Casimir into hoping for supreme power.

20 Around this time Anjou stuck around in towns in Hainaut. By doing so he rendered a service to Lalaing, that province's governor, because he was well aware at whose initiative he had come.[20] He had brought a little over eight hundred cavalry men, and six thousand footmen, scum cast out from the troubles in France. After a merciless journey, with violation of their quarters and seizure of a few castles, he parked these men, while autumn was already approaching, near the town of Binche. By siege and storm he got this place in his possession, a worthless reward for his time. Anjou himself resided in Mons in Hainaut for most of the time, airing his indignation at the fact that the townspeople did not hand over the spaces assigned to the garrisons. When he was requested to join the Netherlands army, he declared he would not come before Casimir had done so. Casimir's departure for Ghent had deeply offended his former friend, now a competitor: mutual loathing spilled over into open insults. Nor did these statements change his mind, which showed how much Mathias and Orange, and even the Queen of England herself, disapproved of the behaviour of Casimir and the Flemish. He even let it happen that his own soldiers leaked away to Montigny's regiments.

21 Ita duces duo, commune Belgis auxilium polliciti, accessere partibus in exitium eius enatis: nec multo post dux Andium in Galliam, Casimirus in Angliam digressus, alienae reipublicae bona malaque reliquerunt. Sed discedenti Gallo Belgae, quos ille et illius nomine alii principes ingrati animi reos agebant, si pax cum Philippo confieret, decreta, et statuas, et honorum inania pollicentur: quod si ad alia veniretur consilia, ipsius ante caeteros eam rationem habitum iri, quam dignitas ipsius et summo reipublicae tempore impensum beneficium postularent.

22 Is fuit rerum status, cum Iohannem Austriacum rapuit vis morbi subita, quam facile receptabat aeger animus, et fortunae iratus. Quippe cum egregiam sibi, non ex vitiis hostium, victoriam vellet, impediri gloriam suam ab inimicis, quos in Hispaniae regia plurimos habebat, supra quam valetudo ferret, indignabatur. In literis certe interceptis contumax desperatio apparuit: et paulo ante Scovedonem, intima eius curare solitum, in Hispania Philippus clam occidi iusserat, ut apud magnanimi iuvenis cogitationes periculose solertem. Nam supra natalium sortem Tunetense quondam regnum, tunc et Angliam (**61**) sperasse manifestus, et cum Lotharingis in Gallia aula praepotentibus, clam Philippum, sociasse consilia, facile et res Belgicas in se versurus timebatur. Unde nec veneni suspicio abfuit, incertum tamen unde dati, quippe inventis sacerdotibus Romanae professionis, qui suam in hoc operam patriae imputarent. Anglos alii suspectabant, non ita dudum supplicio affectis, qui inde immissi in ipsum percussores dicebantur.

23 Regendum militem residuasque urbes Parmensis accepit, ipsius primum Iohannis ac militum voluntate, postea et regis imperio; ingenii tectior, et ex Italia afferens fidei usum, et peritiam simulandi. Terrere norat, et ignoscere, veras artes quibus Belgae caperentur. Itaque cum nullius armis tantum debeat Hispania, plus tamen hominum studio consecutus est: perfecitque rem difficillimam, post libertatem ut dominationi faveretur. Huius occultis suscitationibus dissidia gentium vehementius etiam exarsere, maxime posteaquam de civibus aliquot sumtum supplicium est, qui, ut Atrebatum urbem ad concordiam reducerent, coitionem ausi erant intestinam.

24 Nec tamen Arausionensis destitit omnia malorum remedia experiri; acrior iis coërcendis, quorum crimina ipsius ad invidiam redundabant: et iam Gandavensibus persuaserat, ut restitutis sacerdotibus in foederis leges redirent: deinde ad Montiniaci milites, et Atrebates conciliandos diligentiam vertebat. Sed patuit primores amplecti ultro causas secessionis, eoque implacabiles, quod Flandrorum animos iterum efferavit, Imbisio summum Gandavi magistratum per vim adepto, et caetera honorum vocabula, quibus vellet, largiente. Casimiri interea equitatum tutum

21 In this way two commanders, who had promised to come to the aid of the Lowlanders together, proceeded towards a conflict capable of causing that country's destruction. Not long after, Anjou left for France, Casimir for England, leaving their good and evil to a commonwealth which was no longer theirs. While Anjou upon his departure, and other princes in his name, accused the Lowlanders of ingratitude, the latter promised him declarations of honour, statues, and the vanity of titles if he could establish peace with Philip; promising moreover that if other plans were to be developed, his interests would be looked after before all others in the way required by his rank and his services to the commonwealth at the moment when it mattered most.

22 Such was the situation when Don Juan of Habsburg was carried off by a sudden death, to which he was very receptive because of his raving mind obsessed with his bad fortune. For his desire was to have a splendid military victory written to his name which was not the result of the enemy's failure. Consequently he was more enraged than his health could bear by the obstruction by his enemies, of which he had very many at the Spanish court. From intercepted letters which are certainly his, there rises a stubborn despair; a while before Philip in Spain had secretly ordered the murder of Escobedo,[21] who administered his most personal affairs, as he was someone of dangerous shrewdness so near to the ambitious youngster. For since it was clear that he had once hoped, above the rank of his birth, to inherit the kingdom of Tunis, and subsequently to obtain England **(61)** as well; and because it was also known that he had made designs together with the Lorrainers (who were very influential at the French court), designs that were secret to Philip, it was soon feared that he would use the Low Countries' war for his own ambitions. As a result of all this, there was even a suspicion of poison, although it was unclear whom it would have come from, because Catholic priests were found who claimed to have served the fatherland by doing this deed. Others suspected the English because shortly before men had been executed who said they had been sent from there to make an attempt upon his life.

23 The command of the army and the remaining towns was transferred to the duke of Parma, first because this had been Don Juan's and the soldiers' wish, but later at the king's command as well. Parma was more secretive in nature; Italy had taught him the uses of trust and skills in dissimulation. He knew how to threaten and how to forgive—the right techniques to tackle the Dutch. Thus, although Spain does not owe as much to anyone else's arms, he achieved even more by concentrating on men; and secured that most difficult of things, that after liberty, domination is preferred. Because of his covert agitation the conflicts between the provinces flared up even more vehemently, especially after the death penalty had been inflicted on a handful of citizens who had convened internal meetings with the aim of re-uniting the city of Artois with the others.

24 Nevertheless Orange did not stop trying out every remedy against the problems, but with the more energy to stop those groups whose crimes were adding to the hatred against his person. He had already persuaded the people of Ghent to restore the clergy in their position and return to the terms of the alliance;[22] next he turned his attention to Montigny's army, and the reconciliation with the town of Arras. But it became clear that their leaders were only too happy to have grounds for defection, and were therefore irreconcilable: which fact in turn enraged the Flemish, in the situation that Hembyze had obtained the supreme power in Ghent by force and was handing out the titles of the other civic offices to whomever wished to have one. Meanwhile Parma granted safe departure to Casimir's

iter orantem Parmensis emisit: inde securus hoste nusquam obvio Traiectum ad Mosam praesidio invalidum circumvenit, et oppugnationem aggreditur.

25 (1579) Manente eius urbis obsidio imperator, ad quem relegatam fuisse pacificationem diximus, Coloniam Agrippinensem legatos miserat: eodem Hispanus dux Terraenovae cum regiis mandatis, et a Belgis Arschotius aliique convenerant. At Arausionensis, qui nunquam dubitarat omnem cum Rege pacem in suum periculum fore, divulsa tunc Belgica, tot inter partes medius ipse, atque eo cunctis invisus, ne pariter hostibus et inimicis dederetur, haud temere metuebat. Sed aversari colloquia et iudices Germanos, durum atque infame. (**62**) Occultius, quo eadem evenirent, curabat postulatis de religione insisti, quaeque alia Regem concessurum nemo sperabat. Caeterum potuisse eo tempore satis aequas conditiones obtineri, credibile est, nisi privatis pactionibus nonnulli pacem publicam corrupissent.

26 Et Parmensis, quanquam bello intentus, monere non desinebat novorum cupientes, ut celeri poenitentia gratiam occuparent. Ante alios Lamota Philippo conciliatus Gravelingam Flandriae oppidum, cui praeerat, eo traduxit, acceptaque paciscendi potestate, illexit alios, clementiae regiae laudator et exemplum. Suas deinde copias (octo eae millium erant) non exiguum partibus robur, Montiniacus addidit, aeris penuria, et quod ex merito in Belgas poenam metuebat, Lanovio imminente. Atrebates et Haenovii aliquamdiu nutavere: tandem perscriptis conditionibus ad caeteros Belgas, ut si vellent iisdem uterentur, cum Parmensi transegerunt: simulque Insula, Duacum, et Orciacum, Flandriae illius, quae a Gallis diu possessa, et postquam ad suos principes rediit sermonem inde retinet, civitates; quibus haec privatim a Belgis dissidendi causa erat, quod in concilio proprium ius suffragii non impetrarent. Pacis leges cultum Latinae religionis, solitum in principem obsequium, Gandavensis foederis comprobationem continebant: et ut intra sesquimensem dimisso milite peregrino, regia ex pecunia, in quam contribuerent nationes imperio redditae, civium exercitus, ad ea quae convenerant propugnanda, conduceretur: de praefecto rex dispiceret: interea Parmensi cuncta obedirent.

27 Ita maximum militiae robur regiis partibus Walones accessere, gens laeta bello, et cuius tuto periculis Hispanus uteretur. Isque iam finis omnino concordiae Belgarum adversus externam dominationem fuit. Ea nimirum firma demum societas est, quae spes easdem, aut vincula plura quam dissentiendi causas habet. Commune Belgis vix quicquam extra odium Hispanorum: quo impulsi pacem fecerant Gandavensem, praecipuis ad suadendum sacerdotibus. Mox potentiam sibi quisque et contrarias per vias certabant. Arausionensis, et qui cum illo conscii erant eadem quae Egmondus et Hornanus meruisse, regi diffidebant. Hinc omne

cavalry when they begged him for it; next, in safety because there were no more enemies around, he surrounded the city of Maastricht, which only had a weak garrison, and made a start with its conquest.

25 While this siege continued, the Emperor, to whom as we said the attempt to arrange peace was entrusted, had sent delegates to Cologne. The Spanish duke of Terranova, and from the Netherlands side, Aarschot and others arrived at that place too. Orange however, who had never doubted that any peace with the king would result in danger to him, since the Low Countries were then divided and he himself was right in the middle between all these parties, and was therefore hated, feared not without reason that he would be surrendered to foreign and domestic enemies alike. On the other hand, to turn away from the negotiations and the German referees was difficult and damaging to his reputation. **(62)** More in the dark, to achieve the same, he made sure the religious issue would be insisted upon, and other things which no one expected the king to agree with. Otherwise it is credible that fairly reasonable peace conditions could have been obtained at that time, if some individuals had not with private agreements subverted the public peace.

26 Although Parma too focused on war, he also did not stop urging the rebels to obtain pardon by a swift repentance. The first of all to make peace with Philip was De la Motte, governor of the town of Grevelingen in Flanders,[23] which he handed over to the king. He then received powers to conclude treaties, and seduced others, being the living praise and proof of the king's clemency. Next, Montigny joined his troops (there were eight thousand of them), no mean force for that side. He did this for lack of money and because he feared punishment for his contribution to the Netherlands cause, given the threat posed by De la Noue. Artois and Hainaut were pending for some time which way they would go; in the end they sent their peace conditions to the other Lowlanders, so that they could use the same ones if they wanted, and closed an agreement with Parma. The same was done by Lille, Douai and Orchies, cities in that part of Flanders which had long been in French possession and keeps that language now that it has returned to its own princes. For themselves they had grounds for dissociating themselves from the Low Countries in that in the general assembly they did not have their own right to vote. Among the peace conditions were observance of the Roman faith, the traditional obedience to the king, ratification of the Pacification of Ghent; as well as the condition that the foreign soldiers would be sent off within six months, and an army of domestic soldiers to defend the recent agreements would be hired from the king's pockets (to which the provinces now returned to his realm would make a contribution). The king would look into the question of a stadtholder, and meanwhile all would obey the duke of Parma.

27 Thus the royal side was joined by the great military force which the Walloons are, a people at home in war, from whose peril the Spanish could benefit without danger to themselves. This was already the end altogether of the unity among the Low Countries against foreign domination. For only that alliance is truly strong in which the same hopes are shared, and which contains more ties that bind than causes of disagreement. The Low Countries on the other hand don't have much more in common than their shared hatred of the Spanish, which had driven them to closing the Pacification of Ghent, at the special insistence of the clergy. Soon however they were each, and in conflicting ways, fighting for power for themselves. Orange distrusted the king, and so did the men who were aware they had deserved the same treatment as Egmond and Horne. Hence their plan to build a strong

consilium se suaeque religionis sectam firmare, quam ad rem gratiae peregrinae quaerebantur. Pars altera, cuius crimen non erant belli primordia, fidem principi servare, (**63**) fidem Romanae religioni, veriti maxime ne aliorum impetu longius raperentur. Sic illos temere cohaerentes promptum divellere Philippo fuit, si, hoc unum satagentibus, Hispanicum terrorem amoliretur. Ubi horum votis satisfactum, caeteri ultra tendebant; cuncta inter Belgas suspecta diu, deinde hostilia fuere: nec unquam postea religiones coaluerunt.

28 Tandem res accidit haud sane insolens, ubi semel in partes itum est, ut qui civibus noluerant cedere, violatis pactionibus sub externa imperia adigerentur. Verum, omnium animis in pacem inclinantibus, facile Arausionensis intelligebat singulorum imprudentia dissolvi rempublicam, ni in tempore obviam iretur. Idcirco, solita usus diligentia, Traiectum Batavorum se contulit, et saluberrimo ad res suas consilio evocatos Ordines eius nationis, tum Geldriae, Hollandiae, Zelandiae, Frisiae eius, quae citra Lavicum flumen, et eius, quae inter id flumen et Amasium est, arctiori omnes foedere illigavit. Summa haec erat: indivulsos nexosque inter se, haud alia republica, quam si una gens essent, pacem, inducias, nova bella, tributa, non habituros, nisi quae universi iussissent. In societatibus contrahendis, et caeteris consultationibus valitura maioris partis suffragia, et si qua dissidia orirentur, de iis concilii, aut praefectorum iudicium fore. Obiecta hostibus munirentur, neu quis praesidium recusaret: darentque operam singuli, ut in tributis, et nummi pretio aequalitas servaretur. Hollandis Zelandisque sua et una in publicum religio, caeteris nationibus eandem, an alteram, an utramque mallent, ipsarum arbitrio permittebatur. Adacti in haec verba rectores, magistratus, consilium cuiusque urbis, et sodalitates.

29 Nam veteri instituto praecipui oppidanorum, quibus idonea armis aetas, in certa corpora, velut manipulos, adscribebantur. Id praesidium bello, pace munimentum, cum nondum principatus ars fuit fidere externis: manet mos et desuetae virtutis insigne; sed usu per hos motus reddito, fidelis saepe illorum opera adversus hostem et seditiones fuit. Hoc modo, quas dixi gentes, in leges foederis Traiectini sacramentum dixere: et nequid ipsas suarum virium lateret, numerus iniri iussus est, oppidanorum simul et agrestium, qui intra decimum octavum, et sexagesimum aetatis annum agerent.

30 At per illas nationes, quae non adfuerant foederi, quantae non alias turbae et certamina; dum pars communis religionis, (**64**) aut patriae cura adscisci volunt; alios spes pacis propinquae et dissidendi libido diversos trahit. Silvamducis tenuit secta Romanensis, alterius partis vano metu desertam: cum Parmensi qui permanserant egere; hoc proprium pacti, ne unquam inviti praesidio gravarentur. Antverpiae contra cecidit, mansitque superior plebs adversae factionis, suppliciorum solennibus

position of their own and for their religious sect, for which purpose they went to look for favour abroad. Another group, with no share in the guilt for the origins of the war, remained loyal to the king **(63)**, and to the Roman faith, from an acute fear of being dragged too far by the fury of the others. Thus it was within easy reach for Philip to drive these random sets apart, if at least he could dispel the fear of Spain from those who had this as their sole [remaining] worry. When the wishes of these people were met, the others strove to go a step further. For all dealings between the Lowlanders had long been governed by distrust, which soon became hostility; the confessions never grew together again.

28 In the end something happened which is quite frequent once a society has split into conflicting parties: unwilling to accept their own countrymen as superiors, they broke the existing agreements and drifted off into the arms for foreign sovereigns. However, in a situation in which everybody was inclining towards peace, Orange was quick to realise that the lack of foresight of a few would break up the commonwealth if no measures against it were taken in time. Thus, acting from his habitual carefulness, he went to Utrecht, convened the States of that province, as well as those of Guelders, Holland, Zeeland, the part of Friesland on this side of the Lauwerszee, and that between the Lauwerszee and the river Ems,[24] and bound them together by a closer alliance, a plan most advantageous for his own interests. The essential agreements were the following: they would be inseparably connected to each other in a political constellation not different from if they had been one nation, and would engage only in peace and truce treaties, new wars, and taxation which were endorsed by all. As to closing alliances and the other political deliberations, the majority vote would prevail, and if any conflicts [between provinces] should arise, it was up to the general assembly or the stadtholder to pass judgment. The defences in the regions towards the front were to be reinforced, and no one would refuse garrisons. The provinces would each make their own efforts to preserve equality in taxation and monetary value. Holland and Zeeland obtained permission to make their religion the sole permitted one in the public space; the other provinces were allowed to decide for themselves whether they preferred the one, or the other, or both. The oath on this alliance was sworn by the stadtholders, the magistrate, each town's council, and the civic guards.

29 For by an ancient custom, the prominent citizens of a town, when of suitable age to carry arms, were allocated to specific groups, as it were to squadrons. This provided a defence force in war and a pillar of support in peacetime, at a time when reliance on foreign troops was not yet part of a prince's toolkit. The custom persisted, as well as the distinction included in this faded heroism, but the tradition was revived in the present disturbances and in many cases they provided loyal efforts against the enemy and rebellions. In this way the nations which I mentioned vowed to uphold the conditions of the Union of Utrecht. In order that none of their own forces would be unknown to them, a census was ordered of all townspeople and farmers of between eighteen and sixty years of age.

30 But how much chaos and strife there was elsewhere, among the provinces which had not been present at the conclusion of the treaty: while some people desired to join it, from commitment to the common faith **(64)** or to the fatherland, others were drawn in the opposite direction, from hopes of peace and lust for dissension. Den Bosch was held by the Roman sect, after it had been abandoned by the other side because of idle fears; those who stayed struck a deal with Parma, including the special stipulation that they were never to be burdened with a garrison against their will. Antwerp however fell to the other side, and

operatos adorta minaci concursu. Nec Arausionensis inhibere potuit vulgus suum, quo minus per vim eiicerentur sacrifici; sed inimici eius ita interpretati sunt quasi sponte eius accidisset, quod vetare non potuerat: nam erat ille ab omni truculentia alienus, sed qui dato casu sapienter uteretur, aptandisque sibi hominum studiis in longum iaceret olim profutura. Coegit id tamen multos e populo orbatos sacris, contraria reipublicae vota facere, cum mitius sub rege servitium sperarent; nonnulli etiam nobiles desciscendi ad Hispanos hanc occasionem rapuere.

31 Fuit inter hos Carolus Egmundi filius, quem, dum capere Bruxellam conatur, gnaro, ut fertur, Mathia, conscia cum manu Latinam religionem sectantium, caeteri in foro obsessum inclusere; ubi illi suum facinus, et paternae mortis imago manesque inulti in supplicium verterent. Nam erant qui obiicerent, eo in loco, et (quod mire congruebat) eodem undecim ante annis die, patrem carnificis gladio percussum, eius gentis acerbitate, cui tunc filius patriam proditum iret. Ad extremum, oppidanorum misericordia incolumis, in Nienovam irruit, Flandriae oppidum; quo a Belgis recepto, captivus ipse in popularium suorum, ut dicemus, pervenit potestatem.

32 Brugis asper et anceps tumultus, capta arma, nec procul caede res erat: et partes utraeque suae sectae militem advocarant; priores advenere Foederatorum cohortes, magistratuum accitu; isque finis certandi fuit: aliarum urbium tumultus praesidia praevenerunt. Accessit foederi sponte Ipra, sponte et Gandavum, venitque in urbem aliquanto post Arausionensis, secunda multitudinis voluntate. Tanta illi vulgo animorum diversitas inerat, et ad honesta pravaque levitas eadem. Ibi demotis qui se ingesserant, honores aliis mandavit. Plerique, quos captivos ibi detineri diximus, negligentius custoditi, eruperant; caeteros Arausionensis dimisit: accessitque honori eius, et invidiae, quod Flandriae praefectura superingesta est recusanti.

33 At Agrippinensi legatione nihil actum, nisi quod maxime Hispanus (**65**) voluerat, ut in spem pacis distractae mentes minus in commune consulerent. Oratores partium, solicitatos privatis pactionibus socios, novis contra foederibus turbatam concordiam, non ex colloquii fide, mutuo querebantur. Sed Belgae praesentis periculi causa, quod Parmensis adversus Traiectum Mosae, urbem partim Brabantici, partim Leodici iuris, quippe in ipso confinio sitam, plurimum profecerat, nec inferendi militem aut copias occasio dabatur, eximi bello paciscandi tempora rogabant: inque eo sperabant imperatoris legatos sibi auxilio fore. Sed Terranovanus negabat eius se rei potestatem ullam accepisse. Dum induciae petuntur, et negantur, dum

the populace of the other sect retained the upper hand. A threatening mob rose against the clergy who were in the midst of the sacred adorations. Even Orange could not stop this plebs of his from violently throwing the priesthood out of the city gates; his enemies however interpreted this as if things had happened at his instigation which he had only been unable to forbid. For every kind of cruelty was alien to him, but at the same time he knew how to use an occasion prudently, and, with the objective of bringing other people's efforts in line with those of himself, he sowed early in order to pluck the benefits in the long term. But however this be, the events in Antwerp brought a good part of the population, who had now lost their regular worship, to turning their prayers against the new commonwealth, because they expected a milder slavery from the king's rule; a handful of noblemen even jumped upon this occasion to defect to the Spanish.

31 One of them was Charles, son of the count of Egmond.[25] Making an attempt to seize Brussels with his band of complicit Catholics (with the foreknowledge of Mathias as some say) he was closed in on the market square and besieged by the others, who set out to turn his own infraction, the image of his father's death and his unavenged spirit into a heavy punishment. For some confronted him with his father's death by the headsman's sword in the same place and (by amazing coincidence) on the very same day eleven years earlier: which resulted from that same nation's cruelty for whom the son now set out to betray his fatherland. In the end, having first been spared by the citizen's compassion, he stormed Nienhove, a town in Flanders. When this town was captured back by the Lowlanders, he was taken prisoner and fell into the power of his own people, as we will relate.[26]

32 An uproar at Bruges was violent and undecided for a long time. There were confiscations of weaponry, it came close to bloodshed, and both parties had called in military aid from their co-religionists. The regiments of the united provinces[27] got there first, having been called in by the magistrate. This was the end of the fighting; in other towns the garrisons forestalled uprisings. Ypres joined the Union of its own accord, as did Ghent. Not much later Orange arrived in that city, with the approval of the populace: such variety of moods lived within that population, and the same lightheartedness towards good and evil deeds alike. Orange removed the administrators who had installed themselves and gave their offices to others. Many who were held prisoner in that city, as we have related, had already escaped due to careless surveillance; the others were released by Orange. The fact that he refused the stadtholderate of Flanders which was offered to him, increased the esteem in which he was held as well as the jealousy towards him.

33 The delegates to Cologne achieved nothing else than that which the Spaniard **(65)** had ardently wished for, that is, that ours were distracted by hopes of peace and put less effort in their common cause. The speakers of the delegations from both sides complained that their allies were being lured away with separate agreements, that the prospect of a settlement was disturbed by new treaties that went against it, in contravention of the trust required for negotiations. However, under pressure of the present dangerous developments—since Parma was making rapid progress against Maastricht, a town partly under jurisdiction from Brabant, partly from Liège, as it lies precisely on the border, and there were no chances to bring soldiers or provisions into the city—the Lowlanders asked for the war to be lifted for the duration of the negotiations. They hoped that the Emperor's delegates would be on their side in this. Terranova however declared that he had not received any powers for such a thing. While this truce was being requested, and rejected, while conditions for a peace

conditiones pacis ferri incipiunt, dum Belgarum mandata refelluntur, ut non satis libera, sed adstricta novis iussibus, Parmensis iam ipsis Traiecti moenibus irrepserat: inde, quanquam viribus modicis, fortiter defensam urbem post quadrimestre obsidium impetu cepit.

34 Sub hyemem vero Germanos, Hispanos, Italosque milites dimisit fere omnes, retentis tantum ducibus et ala equitum Italica, serius quam Atrebaticis pactionibus convenerat: sed tamen id illi Machliniam cum Valentianis et Insula urbe conciliavit. Praesidia idoneis locis Walonum imposuit. Horum ut quisque graviter offensus, aut ultro vicinos offenderat, ita tutissimus habebatur. Pro eo beneficio Parmensi praefecturam confirmarunt, haud satis intelligentes, si quando placitum esset armato duci, fore ut exterum militem ipsi revocarent.

35 At foederati Belgae, quanquam tot iam gentium urbiumque iactura spem pacis amiserant, ne tamen odisse magis concordiam, quam desperare viderentur, oblatas a Philippo leges compositionis in singula oppida dimiserunt, ut publico consilio expenderentur. Quae ut iniqua aut fallacia incusabantur haec erant: acta Mathiae non aliter rata essent, nisi quatenus ad principis supremam potestatem, aut alterius iniuriam non pertinebant: quem Belgis rectorem daturus erat Philippus, ei urbes, castella, machinae continuo traderentur: is cum senatu cuncta cognosceret: Ordinum nulla mentio: restituerentur eiecti sacerdotes, et quicunque honores aut magistratus gesserant: utrinque dimissis exercitibus ab armis discederetur: nec tributa manerent, nisi principis voluntate.

36 Quae cuncta eo spectare visa, ut in speciem redditae leges, studio illorum, qui Reipublicae potirentur, brevi (**66**) corruerent, atque ipsi exarmati in servitutem retraherentur: nec enim ad tutandam libertatem infirmius ullum esse munimentum regio iureiurando. De religionibus, quae controversia plurimum habebat difficultatis, ita regi placebat: unam per omnem Belgicam retineri, quae Romani pontificis auctoritate firmabatur; nisi quibus in locis alii ritus fuissent eo tempore, quo foedus Gandavense approbatum fuerat: extra eos fines diversa sentientibus tempus praestitueretur, intra quod ordinarent res suas, post Belgica egrederentur, salvis bonis, dum procurationem eorum Romanae religionis sectatoribus relinquerent.

37 Id vero omnibus durum, nec publicae quieti conveniens videbatur, statum praesentem tot urbium inverti, tot hominum millia expelli, nec saltem liberum credere quod animus testaretur. Quam autem regionem fore tantis exsiliis tutam, aut capacem? ubi quieturos quos patria eiecisset? sed nec sine summo scelere posse rectores quam veram didicissent religionem, quoquo modo inductam, per metum prodere. Ne Hollandi quidem et Zelandi satis sibi consultum putabant

were brought into the discussion, while the Netherlands demands were being rejected, as being to stringently formulated, but were burdened with new counter-demands, Parma had advanced within the very walls of Maastricht. Next, after a siege of four months, he took the city by storm which had been fiercely defended in spite of its limited forces.

34 By the time winter arrived however he dismissed nearly all of his soldiers (Germans, Spaniards, Italians), keeping only the officers and a squadron of Italian cavalry. Although this happened at a later time than agreed in the Union of Arras, it still brought him reconciliation with Mechelen, Valenciennes, and the city of Rijssel. He installed garrisons consisting of Walloons in suitable places: as each of these had either been seriously harmed, or had itself harmed others, they felt safest this way. In exchange for this generosity they confirmed Parma in his office as stadtholder, not sufficiently realising that when at some point this commander in arms would decide, it would come to pass that they would call back the foreign troops themselves.

35 Although the loss of so many provinces and cities had robbed them of the hope of peace, the Lowlanders in the Union nevertheless sent the conditions for a settlement which Philip presented, around among the individual towns, in order to avoid the impression that they had come to loathe the idea of a reconciliation more than that they saw no possibility for it; the aim being to evaluate them in a general meeting. The conditions which were censured as being unfair or deceitful were the following: decisions by Mathias would only be valid insofar as they did not conflict with the king's supreme power or somebody else's; to the person whom Philip would make governor of the Low countries, towns, fortifications, and war equipment had to be handed over immediately; this governor would discuss all affairs with the Council of State; there was no mentioning of the States; the clergy who had been driven out, would be restored in their positions, as well as all those who had held offices and magistracies; both sides would disband their armies and refrain from warfare; there would be no other taxes than those desired by the king.

36 It was felt that the aim of all these proposals was merely to ensure that the constitution, restored in appearance, would soon **(66)** be broken to pieces by the effort of the men who had grabbed hold of the commonwealth, and the Lowlanders be disarmed and brought back under the yoke of slavery; for there was no bulwark for the defence of liberty weaker than a royal oath. With respect to religion (the issue which involved the greatest difficulties), the king decided as follows: the Low Countries would keep only one religion, the one which the Roman Pontiff supports, except for the places where a different worship existed at the time of the Pacification of Ghent. Outside these areas a period would be stated for dissenters, within which they would have to arrange settlements for their possessions, then leave the Low Countries, while staying in possession of their goods, as long as they would leave the administration to followers of the Catholic faith.

37 However all considered that it would hardly be possible, nor beneficial to the public quiet, to put the status quo in so many cities upside down again, expel so many thousands of people, and not even be at liberty to believe the dictates of one's own mind. For which region would be safe for so many exiles, or capable of receiving them? Where would these people thrown out of their fatherland finally find a place to settle? Moreover, there was no way for the governors without committing the greatest of crimes, to betray the faith of which they had come to understand the truth, whichever way it had been introduced, just because they were afraid. Not even Holland and Zeeland considered their interests

usu religionis ad ea tempora revocato, quibus validae urbes a republica dissidebant: unde par novos tumultus metui; et, quod sua causa a caeteris segregaretur, suspecta benignitas. Cum Arausionensi seorsim actum: atque eminus filio libertas et paternae praefecturae ostentabantur, ipsi tantundem bonorum, quantum unquam possederat, ut relicta Belgica Germaniam destinaret tranquillae senectuti. Sed praeter causas dissidendi, animus divitiarum contemtor, eoque integer et incorruptus, satis habuit scire, quanto Hispanus redimeret sui metum.

38 Finito Agrippinensi colloquio, Arscotius et sacerdotes aliquot ab illis partibus, unde legati venerant, defecere, Regi, cui se alioquin hostes futuros in posterum intelligebant, per literas conciliati, iisdem quibus Atrebates legibus. At quae perscripserant pacis bellique consilia Hispanis fastidita, et genti nihil externum probanti ludibrio fuere. Patuit eo colloquio, quam procul inter se principis et populi studia dissiderent. Olim sanabile id malum, cum primum alienae dominationis metu nobilitas surrexit: at postquam pertinacius pressa plebem religionis specie adduxerat in partes, didicitque vulgus se esse, quos reges timerent, aut propter quos timerentur, nec posse nisi credendo capi, primum libertatis gradum putaverunt veniae desperationem. Inde ausi nihil mediocre, aut (**67**) quod poenitentiam admitteret, eo provecti sunt, ut pacis commoda, incerta belli nequicquam postea dissererent. Itum est ultra solitum armis civilibus modum, dum inde imperii et ultionis cupiditas sine fine producitur; hinc ipsa pericula delectant, et nonnulla in miseriis gloria est.

39 At tunc quidem non unus exercitus, sed exiguis copiis bellum spargebatur, et fere singulis nationibus suus miles. Id statim vitium Reipublicae[33] apparuit, quod non, ut in priscis Graecorum et Romanorum, aut hodie etiam florentibus imperiis, in una urbe summa potestas erat; sed inter plurimas civitates aequata vis, unde fit ut propria cuique curae, ex ingenio gentis ad quaerendas retinendasque divitias exercitae, falso publici nomine bonum commune pervertant. Pecuniae quoque vix conferebantur: et male cum Belgis agi potuit, nisi hostis eodem malo laborasset, dum Regis aurum Lusitania occupat, parandis procerum studiis pariter et bello. Nam desiderato Sebastiano in Africana clade, et mortuo Henrico successore, Antonium regia stirpe editum populus ad regnum vocaverat, quippe infestus Castellanis more finitimarum gentium. Sed Philippus propinquitatem sanguinis inter alios et ipse adferens, Albanum cum exercitu misit, qui recusantes armis subigeret: eius denique opera Regi Lusitania accessit, per quem Batavos amiserat: tanto facilius regna quaeruntur.

[33] Reipublicae *1657* reipublicae *1658*

sufficiently served by a return to the religious situation of the time when several important towns were outside the present commonwealth. In all likelihood this would cause new disturbances; and in any case the offer to separate their cause from that of the others was suspected generosity. With Orange a separate agreement was proposed; his son was given the distant prospect of liberty and his father's governorships; to Orange himself as many lands as he had ever possessed, on the condition that he would leave the Low Countries and depart for Germany for a quiet retirement. Apart from having his own reasons for the revolt, Orange was a man without interest in wealth, and upright and incorruptible as a result, and was already satisfied with the knowledge how much the Spaniard was willing to pay to buy off the fear of his person.

38 After the end of the negotiations at Cologne Aarschot and a handful of clergymen defected from the cause as which' representatives they had come. By letter they had made peace with the king under the same conditions as those of Arras, as they realised he would otherwise remain their enemy. But the counsel they had sent over regarding war and peace was looked down upon by the Spanish, and became the object of mockery to a people in whose eyes nothing foreign will find approval. During these negotiations,[28] it had became clear how far the desires of the king and the people were apart. It had once been possible to heal this evil, at a time when the nobility had only recently been stirred by the fear of foreign domination. But by this time it was more hard-pressed and had drawn the populace into the conflict under pretexts of religion, and the populace had come to realise that it was them who were feared by kings, or because of whom kings were feared, and that they could not be outwitted if it weren't because of their own credulity, they considered the loss of hope of a pardon as the first step towards freedom. Hence they feared that moderate action would be unsafe, or **(67)** action that would leave a possibility to repent, and reached such a point that with them any talk of the advantages of peace or the uncertainties of wars became pointless. The conflict went further than the usual in civil wars; from the one side the lust for power and revenge was unleashed without limit; from the other pleasure was in the danger as such, and even some glory in misery.

39 At this time however there wasn't one big army, but the war was spread out by small bands of men, and almost every province had its own army. Right at the outset, this defect of the Republic became clear that unlike ancient Greece or Rome, or even thriving empires today, it did not have its supreme power located in one city, but there is equality of power among a great many cities. The result is that the particular interests of each (which, given the nature of this nation, are geared towards the acquisition and preservation of wealth), undermine the common good under the guise of care for the public interest. Also, virtually no money was contributed, and there might have been an unhappy ending for the Lowlanders if their opponents hadn't suffered from the same evil, so long as the king's gold was demanded by Portugal, to win her nobility's favour as well as a war. For after Sebastian had gone missing in the lost battle in Africa, and the death of his successor Henry, the people called Anthony, born of royal blood, onto the throne, as he was hostile to Castile, in the way you often find this between neighbours. Philip however, being one of several who presented their own claims of consanguinity, sent Alva with an army in order to submit the unwilling by force of arms. Thus in the end Portugal joined his realm by the efforts of the same man by whom he had lost the Low Countries: so much easier is it to acquire a crown.

40 Nec sane quicquam Philippo felicius accidit, non modo, quod omnis Hispania unius imperio continuata est, sed quia Lusitani, plurima terrarum circumvecti navigationibus, maximas Oceani Atlantici insulas, Aethiopumque et Indorum littora imperio aut commerciis tenuere. Hoc eventu Batavi, qui e bello Lusitanico suam quietem sperare potuerant, auctis hostium viribus, aliud insuper incommodum sensere, infracto mercatu Hispaniensi, in quo tum facultates civium fere omnes consistebant. Quanquam enim portus regni Castellani hactenus illis non praecludebantur, velut armorum causa nihil extra Belgicam spectante; attamen et a sacerdotibus periculum, et solitae regibus, etiam in hospites, iniuriae, detentionesque navium fatigabant: quae Lusitani apud se abfore promiserant, etiam proviso ne suspectos ad iudices aut longas lites vadarentur. Sed postquam regna in unum coiere, nec alterius commercii usu alterius necessitas levabatur, idem utrobique dominus, variis rapinarum nominibus, maiorem (**68**) quaestus partem nautis exprimere, non quidem continua vexatione, sed talibus intervallis, et spiramentis, ut spe meliorum, et venali ad lucrum quodlibet mercatorum aviditate, nova semper praeda succederet.

41 (1580) Interim, quanquam, ob aeris penuriam, in Belgica utrinque seditiones erant, hoc tamen Hispani facilius mitigabantur, quia, stipendiorum loco, rerum omnium impunitas dabatur. Sed Parmensis exigua aliquot Haenoviae oppida recepit, quae foederatarum gentium praesidiis tenebantur, deinde Cortracum in Flandria astu militari. (1581) Bredam quoque illi Altipenna addidit, arcem improviso, inde subiecta adortus. Lanovius vero, cui summa belli iis in regionibus permissa erat, Nienova et aliis Flandriae locis exegit hostem. Inciderant in idem tempus illustrium virorum captivitates: Egmondi et Sellesii[34] superatis in oppidis: et contra ipsius Lanovii, qui a castelli cuiusdam obsidione infelici praelio detractus est, plurisque ab hoste ipso aestimatus, quam ut cum alteris duobus permutaretur. Machliniam Angli, qui Belgis militabant, impetu cepere, tam profana per victoriam avaritia, ut nec sepulchris parcerent; queis detracta saxa palam in Anglia vendiderunt. Multa alia consilia expugnationis subitae validior iterum hostis evertit, paucis victoriae praemiis penes Belgas manentibus, inopia defensantium.

42 Namurcum ea tempestate ad filium venit mater Parmensis, excipere missa notum regimen, ut sexu gratior, et usu aetatis callida pacis moderatrix. Sed ille, qui iuventae vitia abiecerat, ut gloriae indulgeret, demonstrare contra, armis et viro opus: conciliandis quin etiam studiis populi, aut militum, industriam suam sufficere. Utrumque verum erat: itaque, remissa muliere, sublatum est impium certamen.

[34] Sellesii *scripsimus* Sillesii *1657, 1658 (vide* Sellesius *3.3, Baron de Selles).*

40 And surely nothing more advantageous happened to Philip, not just because all of the Iberian peninsula became connected under the power of one man, but also because the Portuguese had covered most of the globe on their maritime expeditions, and had the biggest islands in the Atlantic Ocean, as well the Ethiopian and Indian coastlines under their commercial or political control. This course of events meant for the Dutch[29] (who could have hoped the Portuguese war would mean relief for them) that they came to feel another disadvantage on top of the growth of their enemy's powers, i.e. the collapse of their trade on the Iberian peninsula, on which until then almost the entire financial power of the citizenry depended. For although up to that time the ports of the kingdom of Castile had not been closed to them—as if outside the Low Countries their armed struggle was of no significance—there was danger to them coming from the clergy and they suffered from the usual wrongdoings from kings, even against visitors, and from confiscations of ships. The Portuguese on the other hand had promised that all those things would not happen with them, including even a provision that they would not be summoned before suspected judges or detained by bail to appear in protracted lawsuits. But when the two kingdoms had merged into one, and the needs of the one were no longer satisfied by the commercial activity of the other, that single lord of both places wrenched the bigger part of their profits from the hands of the sailors, **(68)** using various labels for this robbery. And he did not do so through continuous pestering, but with such intervals and periods of relief that the hope of improvement and the greed of the merchants (which is for sale to any prospect of profit) ensured that new booty was always arriving.

41 Meanwhile in the Low Countries, although shortage of funds led to mutinies on both sides of the front, the Spanish succeeded in more easily in putting them to rest because they handed out impunity for any offence in lieu of the wages. Nevertheless Parma obtained a few small towns in Hainaut which were kept by garrisons of the United Provinces, and subsequently Kortrijk in Flanders by military cunning. In addition to these Hautepenne fetched Breda for him as well, by making an unexpected attack on the castle, followed by one on the lower parts of the town.[30] De la Noue however, who was charged with the supreme military command in this area, drove the enemy out of Nienhove and other places in Flanders. It happened that in this time a number of eminent men were taken prisoner: Egmond[31] and Selles, in town conquests; and on the other side none less than De La Noue, who was drawn away from the siege of a particular castle[32] by an unsuccessful battle, and was considered too precious by the enemy himself to be exchanged for the two others. Mechelen was taken by storm by English troops fighting for the Lowlanders, their behaviour in victory being so barbaric[33] that even graves were not spared: gravestones removed from them were sold openly in England. Many other plans for surprise conquests were thwarted by the restoration of the enemy's strength, and few of the prizes won remained in the Lowlanders' hands, due to a lack of defenders.

42 Around the same time Parma was visited in Namur by his mother, who was sent to take up the governorship already well known to her, for as a woman she enjoyed greater sympathy, and her age and experience made her a shrewd organiser of peace. Parma however, in whom the defects of youth had given way to the ambitious pursuit of glory, argued against this that the situation called for arms and a man; and even that in order to win back the support of the citizens and the military his efforts sufficed. Both of which were true: and thus the lady was called back and the disrespectful competition terminated.

43 At in Frisia, adsitisque regionibus, velut proprium exarsit bellum, Renebergii inconstantia. Is fideliter et intrepide diu sectatus optimatium partes, cum gente omni Frisiorum Traiectino foederi subscripserat, et detrectantes Groninganos, odio maxime accolarum, qui praevenerant, obsidio coegerat in easdem leges iurare. Sed permotus postea cognatorum auctoritate, qui omnes ad Hispanum defecerant, quo dissidii principia strueret, agrestibus, qui circum colebant, permisit militum suorum iniurias propulsare. Hoc dato signo, magna rusticorum manus in ultionem prorupit, diu crudeliter vexata, egitque eo ferocius, quod fortunarum suarum **(69)** ultima defenderet. Sed rudem belli, et incompositam multitudinem missus ab Arausionensi Hohenloius, commissis aliquot praeliis, disiecit. Frisii quoque, suspecta praefecti fide, arces, quae remanserant, aggressi, in tempore solo aequavere: et Transisalanorum gentem ad defectionem sollicitatam, nutantemque discordiis, missis praesidiis restituit Arausionensis.

44 Tum ille, omissa dissimulatione, Groningam, cuius potiebatur, regio adiecit imperio. Inde transducta Rhenum arma clades mutuas, et continuam annorum quindecim miseriam invexere. Primum iubetur urbem copiis modicis circumvenire Bartolus Entesius, Markii olim sodalis; quem, post ingentes praedas terra marique partas, nimium magna sperantem ex turbidis, mors ea in obsidione intercepit. Ad urbem liberandam Parmensis Scenkium misit, Batavicarum quondam partium militem; ad quas postea reversus est, cum sperata transitionis praemia non consequeretur. Sed tunc fortem duci suo operam navavit: nam illius virtute, quod duces maiores iam desperaverant, soluta est obsidio, et caesa Hohenloii manus: quem deinde victarum partium fortunam divisis copiis retentantem, perculit iterum Rennebergius; et, fuso hoste, pleraque itinerum aut amnium munimenta irrupit; sed cum in Stenovicum, urbem Transisalanorum, vim omnem belli quinque totis mensibus converteret, a Nassavianis ducibus depulsus, victusque, inter miserabiles cogitationes, quanta cum famae iactura integras opes ad incerta redegisset, morbo finiit.

45 Successit ei Verdugo Hispanus, et commissa adversus Norisium pugna superior, caeterum nihil profecit, campis per autumnum madentibus. Hinc fames et morbi militem abegere. Patebat Parmensi magna satis et digna curari possessio, si tot in ea parte victoriis uti libuisset: dum alibi arma occupantur, dilati diu, qui tum opprimi potuerant, ambiguam fortunam meliora in tempora traxere.

46 Tumultus interea nonnulli, et non procul seditione res fuit, ut in Brabantiae, ita in Transisalanis urbibus, studio in Regem eius multitudinis, quae Latinos ritus sectabantur; quo factum ut imaginibus, sicubi permanserant, sublatis e publico, ne privata quidem sacra illis permitterentur, metu coitionis. Circumfuso undique

43 In Friesland however and the neighbouring regions a separate war of its own, so to speak, broke out, due to Rennenberg's wavering policies. He had long been a faithful and unflinching follower of the States' party, he had joined the Union of Utrecht together with all of Friesland, and had forced the Groningers (who were recalcitrating mostly from hatred of the Ommelanders,[34] who had joined it first) to swear loyalty to the same alliance. However, subsequent persuasion from his relatives, who had all defected to the Spanish side, moved him to allow the farmers in the surrounding areas to take measures against the wrongdoings of his own troops, with the intention of building the basis of a conflict. At this sign a large band of farmers, who had suffered protracted and cruel molestation, broke forth in revenge, and acted with the more brutality as they defended the last means **(69)** of subsistence left to them. This untrained and unorganised mob however was dispersed in a handful of battles by Hohenlohe,[35] who was sent by Orange. The Frisians too, from distrust of their stadtholder's loyalty, attacked the castles which remained in his control and levelled them to the ground. By sending garrisons Orange restored the loyalty of the people of Overijssel, who had been tempted to defect and were close to doing so due to an internal conflict.

44 Next Rennenberg dropped the mask and attached Groningen, which he had in his power, to the king's realm. The war that followed was fought as far as the other side of the Rhine and brought heavy losses on both sides as well as fifteen years of unbroken misery. First Bartold Entes, once a comrade-in-arms of Lumey's,[36] was given orders to surround the city with a modest force. This man generated enormous amounts of booty on land and sea and based excessive hopes and ambitions on the troubles, but was stopped in his plans by death during the siege. To relieve the town Parma sent Schenck, once a soldier on the Dutch side—to which he later returned, when he wasn't given the rewards expected for his transfer. At this time however he delivered solid work to his commander, for because of his courage the siege was lifted, an outcome already despaired of by more senior officers, and Hohenlohe's force hacked to pieces. Hohenlohe was then defeated a second time by Rennenberg when he tried the luck of the defeated side once more with his troops dispersed over the area. Now that the enemy was dispelled, Rennenberg also took most of the strongholds guarding over roads and rivers. But when he had concentrated the full force of his war effort on Steenwijk, a town in Overijssel, for five months, he was driven off by the Nassau commanders and defeated. He fell ill and died, in disconsolate consideration of how he had destroyed his good name while reducing his state of prosperity to a set of mere uncertainties.

45 His successor was the Spaniard Verdugo, who, in spite of gaining the upper hand in a battle against John Norris,[37] made no further progress as the fields were too wet because of the autumn. And soon dearth and disease dispelled the soldiers. There was a chance here for Parma to obtain a fairly large area and one worth keeping, if he wished to put all those victories achieved in that region to use. But his armies were occupied elsewhere, and as he postponed for too long turning to these people whom he could then have subjected, they drew out their uncertain chances until better times.

46 Meanwhile there were several disturbances, and the situation developed to a near revolt, in cities both in Brabant and in Overijssel, due to the efforts in support of the king by the multitude of followers of the Roman worship. As a result the images, whichever were left, were removed from public spaces, and Catholics were even forbidden to hold private services, for fear of rallies. Now that the war had to be fought everywhere around, the States

bello augebatur apud Ordines defensorum numerus, quantum tributa minuebantur: quodque difficillimum erat, verso milite ad uberiores stipendiis **(70)** rapinas, nec ager liberari sine pecuniis, nec agro insesso expediri pecuniae poterant. Iam et urbes praesidia formidare: nec duces castris imperio aut disciplina praeesse, sed vitiorum similitudine, dum luxum et omnem licentiam militaria decora existimant.

47 Has ob difficultates, inviso civibus plurium imperio, Arausionensis cum multa super iuredicundo et tributis, et milite, ad praesentem rerum statum necessaria, tum illud quoque Ordinum consilio suasit, ut propter subita belli, et tarda conventuum auxilia, senatum legerent, qui de re summa secum consultaret.

48 Rebus ita constitutis, ut cuncta sibi prona vidit damnatae Philippo religionis vinculo, et dissentientium validissimos alias in partes iisse, aperire incipit usurpatum hactenus regium nomen, dum spes maneret pacis: nunc quando ille implacabilis, tanquam rebellibus, compertumque sit, ut quis in Belgas acerbus fuisset, et crudelis, ita in Hispania inclitum et florentem conspici, quid ultra errare populum sacramenti veteris inani religione paterentur? unde enim tot turbas et dissidia, nisi quod fides inter patriam et principem ambigua penderet? At sapientibus haud ignotum, populi ex consensu, populi gratia institutas esse potestates, ut superiores singulis, ita infra universos; quae si publici curam privatos ad usus verterent, populo, hoc est Ordinibus rite coactis, iudicium et vindictam relinqui. Nec alio iure pleraque regna praesentibus sub dominis esse, nisi quod ea populi, priorum iniurias aut socordiam pertaesi, ad alios transtulissent. Quanto haec magis in Belgis valitura, quibus regium nomen ignotum, talisque obsequii modus, ut non dicerent solenne sacramentum, nisi ante principem in sua et legum verba adegissent? Gentium ius esse, alterius perfidia solvi mutuos nexus.

49 Philippo autem repudiato, alium quaerendum principem: nec enim eas res esse, quae contra Hispaniae potentiam suis opibus facile sustinerentur; et aliena nemini, ut sua, curae. Praesenti opus duce, quique Belgas, ubi mala desaeviere, salutis suae negligentes, legitimo imperio excitaret. Germanicas spes se ex animo proiecisse. Unum restare, ut Francisco Valesio principatus deferretur, quem certa iamdudum indicia dedisse non recusaturi. Nec parum referre, si iuvenis summae fortunae proximus hinc crescere inceperit. Interim non fraternam illi Galliam, non studia Angliae defutura: in quam et classem nuper paratam **(71)** habuisset Hispanus, quam partim tempestas, partim Lusitanicum bellum avertisset; et Hibernos rebellantes,

were confronted with their number of defence forces growing as fast as their revenues decreased; and the worst problem was that the soldiers turned to plundering, more profitable **(70)** than their wages, while the countryside could not be liberated without more money, nor the money be procured while the countryside was occupied. Cities were now starting to fear their garrisons: the officers were not obeyed by their men because of authority and discipline, but for equality in vice, as luxury and licentiousness in everything became regarded as tokens of military honour.

47 Because these difficulties had made the government by many unpopular with the citizens, Orange argued in a meeting of the States for the introduction of a whole range of measures regarding jurisdiction, taxes, and the army, which were necessary in the present circumstances, as well as (given the fast developments in the war and the slow allocation of support by the meetings), the election of a council for consultation with him about the affairs of the commonwealth as a whole.[38]

48 With matters arranged in this way, Orange saw that things were turning in his favour everywhere due to the ties of the faith which Philip had accursed, and that the most powerful people of the other confession were moving elsewhere. For this reason he began to divulge the view that the title of king had been kept in use until then only for so long as hopes of peace with the king remained. "But now that he is showing himself irreconcilable, as if he were dealing with rebels, and we have found out that whoever has been harsh and cruel to the Lowlanders, is held in great state and esteem in Spain, wherefore do we leave this people err around in pointless loyalty to an oath of the past? What else is the cause of all these troubles and revolts, than that their faithfulness is torn between their fatherland and their prince? No, all men in their right minds understand very well that power is instituted from the consent of the people and for the sake of the people, and that those in power are as senior to the individual, as they are junior to all. Moreover, if they turn their responsibility for the public cause to their private advantage, nothing else awaits them than judgment and punishment by the people, that is, by the States properly convened. For most lords in the present hold their kingdoms on the basis of no other right than that the people, having tired of the offences or stupidity of earlier rulers, have handed them over to others. How much more true then is this for the Lowlanders, to whom royal titles used to be unknown, and with whom the condition of obedience was such that they did not swear any solemn oath before they had made the prince swear he would obey their terms as well the laws? The very law of nations holds that faithlessness of one side dissolves mutually binding agreements."

49 "Then, after we have deposed Philip, we must find another prince. The state of our country however is not such that it can easily defend itself against the power of Spain by its own means; and no one cares as much about another's interests as he cares about his own. What we need is a prominent leader, with the ability, when our evils have subsided, by legitimate rule to re-awaken the Lowlanders, who are now neglecting their own well-being. I have abandoned the hope of finding someone in Germany. One option remains, that is: to transfer the princely dignity to Francis of Valois,[39] who has already given clear indication that he will not refuse. There will be great effects if this young man, who is very close to the highest state, will have started his rise from here. During this rise to power, his brother's France will be on his side as well as England's support—the same England against which the Spaniard recently had a fleet ready **(71)** the use of which was however averted partly by a storm and

nunc idem auxiliis concitaret: nec minora belli semina tentatus Anglis novus orbis, et in patriam perlatae, quas eripuerant Hispanis, opes.

50 Post longam dubitationem, probatum consilium, metu magis Hispani, quam ullo in Franciscum studio: et ab Ordinibus Belgarum Philippo, ob violatas leges, imperium abrogatum est: lataque in illum sententia, cum quo, si verum fatemur, novem iam per annos bellatum erat: sed tunc primum desitum nomen eius et insignia usurpari, mutataque verba solennis iurisiurandi, ut qui princeps hactenus erat, hostis vocaretur. Hoc consilium vicinas apud gentes necessitate, et tot irritis ante precibus excusatum, haud desiere Hispani ut scelus insectari, parum memores, pulsum a maioribus suis regno invisae crudelitatis regem, eique praelatam stirpem non ex legibus genitam ut iam taceantur vetera apud Francos, minus vetera apud Anglos, recentiora apud Danos ac Sueonas deiectorum regum exempla. Mathias cum gratia muneribusque dimissus. Hispanum nec rei magnitudo, nec autor latuit, unde cum iudicaret unius hominis vitam obstare felicitati suae, illum, in quem arma habebat, proscripsit, invitavitque percussorem honoribus, divitiis, impunitate etiam ante peccatorum.

51 Adversus novi moris edictum Arausionensis apud Ordines Belgicos et Christianos principes libello se defendit, adiuvante Petro Villerio, homine Gallo, qui subactum rebus forensibus ingenium, ad religionem docendam, et hinc ad intima Arausionensis consilia transtulerat. Exstat scriptum utrumque pari acerbitate, qua post crimina ad causam pertinentia, hinc animum ingratum et perduellem, inde saevam ac perfidam dominationem, veris falsisque narrationibus permixtis, porro ad alia, rixantium more, prolabebantur. Nam, quia Arausionensis, facto discidio ab uxore Saxonica, ob causas ipsius gentilibus approbatas, Mompenserii filiam, inter Deo sacras virgines educatam, in matrimonio habebat, utroque nomine incusatus; Philippo vicissim magna adulteria obiectavit, respersosque uxoris et filii sanguine penates novae dominae avunculi ad amplexus venienti patuisse: nam coniunx tunc regia Maximiliani imperatoris erat filia, e regis sorore, quod foedus Pontifex suis, ut multi iudicabant, divinis quoque legibus abrogans, autoritate (**72**) firmaverat. Sed et ipsum Maximilianum agnatum, et tunc socerum, olim ministro Granvella veneno petitum non tacebatur. Ordines, contemtis Philippi artibus, qui omnem defectionis culpam uni assignabat, Arausionensis innocentiam publico testimonio honestarunt, addita super vetus satellitium equitum turma saluti eius custodiendae.

52 Gratissima Francisco Belgarum legatio fuit, qua ad imperium vocabatur; amica et matri, cui provisum filios summae spei nimium imminentes, externis honoribus demulcere. Sed antequam conveniret, opis regiae astipulatio petebatur, quae voto quidem non respondit: tantum enim rex perscripserat, faventem se fraternae magnitudini, et ipsi et Belgis, qui sub eius ditione forent, auxilio ac subsidio fore; quod quo rectius posset, optare regni sui pacem, et fratri prospera omnia. Praesens

partly by the war in Portugal. The Irish rebels too are being stirred into action with assistance from Francois, and no less powerful seeds of war are the English challenge to the New World and their transportation back home of wealth grabbed from the Spanish."[40]

50 After a long hesitation this plan was approved, more from fear of the Spaniard than from any enthusiasm for Anjou. Philip was deposed from his power by the States General of the Low Countries because of his violation of the laws of the realm, and judgment was passed upon the man with whom, if we want to confess the truth, war was already going on for nine years.[41] Now for the first time however the use of his title and ornaments of power was abolished, and the wording of the official oath was changed in such a way that who had until then been prince, was now called enemy. This decision was excused in the eyes of neighbouring people by necessity and the huge number of spurned petitions; the Spanish never stopped prosecuting it as a crime. In so doing however they forgot that their own ancestors had driven a king from his throne who was hated for his cruelty and preferred in his place a royal house rising from illegitimate origins—not to speak of ancient examples of deposed kings in France, less old ones in England, and recent ones in Denmark and Sweden.[42] Mathias was relieved from his duties with many thanks and presents. The Spaniard did not miss the enormity of this act, nor who inspired it. Thus, since in his judgment one man's life was the obstacle to his prosperity, he published a proscription[43] against his opponent, and invited a murderer by promising wealth and impunity even for crimes committed in the past.

51 Orange defended himself against this new type of placard before the States General and all princes of Christianity by means of a pamphlet, written with the help of the Frenchman Pierre de Villiers[44] who had put his wit, first trained in judicial pleading, then applied to preaching, in the service of Orange's most secret deliberations. Both texts[45] stand out equally for the bitterness by which, after adducing wrongdoings which are relevant to the case (ingratitude and hostility from the one side, cruelty and faithless tyranny from the other), they blend together true and false accounts, then slip further away into other accusations, as quarrelling people do. For after the divorce from his Saxon spouse, for reasons approved by her own family, Orange had taken the daughter of the duke of Montpensier in marriage, who had been raised in a nunnery, and both facts were now held against him as crimes. From his side Orange accused Philip of serious acts of incest and adultery, that is, staining his home with the blood of his wife and son, then opening the door to a new mistress, who arrived into her own uncle's embrace. For the royal consort at the time was a daughter of the Emperor Maximilian, born from the king's sister, a union which the pope had endorsed with his authority **(72)** in violation of his own laws and, in the eyes of many, of divine law as well. Nor was it passed over in silence that Maximilian, a relative and his father-in-law at that time, had been the aim of poison to be administered by Granvelle. The States however ignored Philip's manipulations, who put all the blame for the revolt on one person, and honoured Orange's innocence with a public declaration. To protect his safety they added a cavalry squadron to his existing guards.

52 Anjou was very pleased with the delegation from the Low Countries which invited him to accept the sovereignty; it was also liked by his mother, whose plan it was to placate those of her sons who were too obsessed with supreme power by means of high office abroad. But before the agreement was closed, a confirmation of the king's assistance was asked for. This however did not agree with the promises: for the king had only written that he was well

necessitas Belgas, verbis contentos, caetera sperare tantum coegit: subitoque Valesius, ut amplius Belgarum studiis se commendaret, intellecto Cameracum hostilibus copiis, castrisque cinctum, extrema tolerare, profectus eo cum exercitu, ad quem alendum magnam illi pecuniam Elisabetha suppeditaverat, perrupit obsidium, statimque princeps liberatae urbis salutatus est. Neque tum ultra pertendit, quia potissima pars virium erat in clientium manu, et qui spes eius sponte, nec diu mansuri sequebantur. Situm est Cameracum in finibus Belgarum, propria antistitis sedes, sed utrius sub regni fiducia haberetur, Germaniae imperatores et Gallorum reges bello saepe contenderant. Sed bello Gallico Carolus imperator detinuerat, imposita arce, cuius praesidiarii, vincto praefecto, foederi Gandavensi accesserant. At Tornacum Flandriae oppidum circumsessum aliquamdiu, absente praefecto principe Spinoio, cuius obsessa uxor singulare edidit constantiae muliebris exemplum, tandem in Parmensis venit potestatem. (**73**)

disposed towards his brother's greatness, and that he would help and support him as well as the Lowlanders who were under his jurisdiction; and that in order to be better able to do so, he wished for peace in his own realm and success in everything for his brother. The necessity of the moment forced the Lowlanders to be satisfied with these words and only hope for the rest. Straight away, in order to further prove his worth for the Lowlands cause, Anjou departed for Cambrai, which he had heard was surrounded by enemy troops and encampments, and pressed to the limit of what it could endure. The army he was bringing was paid from a large subsidy supplied to him by Elizabeth. He broke the siege and was given a royal entry into the liberated city. He did not continue the campaign at that time however because his main basis of strength was only a crowd of clients who were following his ambitions of their own accord, and would not do so for very long. Cambrai is on the borders of the Low Countries, it constitutes a bishopric of its own, and the kings of France and the German Emperors had often been at war about the question in whose realm the city would consider itself safe. In the war against France the emperor Charles had held on to it and built a citadel, of which the garrison had put their commander in chains and joined the Pacification of Ghent. On the other hand Tournai[46], a town in Flanders which had been under siege for some time in absence of its commander, the prince of Espinoy (whose wife presented a singular example of female constancy under siege), in the end came into Parma's power.

3.52. *Lifting of the siege of Cambrai* by Jan Luyken (E&K 60)

4.12. *French attack on Antwerp 1583* by Jan Luyken (E&K 61)

LIBER QUARTUS

1 (1582) FRANCISCUS in Angliam transvectus, ubi futuro principatui amicitiam firmaret, ita Reginae placuit, aut ipse, aut spes in illo maioris fortunae, ut certis conditionibus de matrimonio ageretur, utcumque religio dissidebat. Laetus is Belgis rumor, sed frustra fuit, seu (**74**) dolo instituta simulatio, seu fraternae offensiones impedimento fuerunt; deinde ipsius infelix temeritas, quae cuncta maluit armis debere. Reversus in Belgicam, solenni ritu et magnifico cum apparatu, in Brabantia ducis, in Flandria comitis vocabulo imperium suscipit.

2 Leges principatui, praeter veteres, novae datae, ex foedere inito Burdegalae: semel ut anno foederatarum gentium convocarentur Ordines, sine quorum consensu foedus iniri cum Hispano, dux bello imponi nequiret: queisque postulantibus miles peregrinus ablegaretur. In ordinanda religione, locandis externis praesidiis, gentes singulae auctores fierent: eaedem ternos nominarent, unde singuli ipsis rectores darentur: tum si quid inter se dissiderent, ea de re ducis esset arbitrium: senatus Gallos admitteret duos: caeteri in praesens Ordinibus, in posterum duci, sed e nominatis legerentur: etiam aulae praecipua munera Belgae obtinerent. Promissa, extra patrimonium principale, ad bellum annua quater et vicies centena florenorum millia, ut his quod restaret, id privatis ducis ipsius, aut fratris opibus sarciretur. Spes aliqua erat utriusque religionis homines mansuros in fide; tum qui cum Arausionensi sentirent, tum Romana sacra sectantes propter Valesium: quippe his Antverpiae permissum, nec ultra, redire ad suos ritus, dum commune Belgarum sacramentum pro novo imperio dicerent.

3 Omnia publice gaudii signa, et ipse non absurdus vultu comitatem, sermone gratiam praeferre: sed nobilium qui supererant tacite indignabantur, respicere coacti in Burgundionum solio principem gentis diu inimicae: mutatum scilicet dominum, ut illi Belgis miscerentur, cum quibus nunquam tuta pax, infestis toties signis concursum; et iam in alterum saeculum odia durabant. Etiam vulgi animis fas illud iurisiurandi prioris, et qualiscumque principis respectus haud facile evellebatur. At contra erant, qui novam religionem animis obiicerent, ne causa pietatis auxilio dissentientium contaminaretur. Sapientiores ex discordia periculum, inde et Gallicam inclementiam formidabant.

4 At ubi patuit secreto convenisse, ut Franciscus, quamquam accepto Belgicae principatu, in Hollandos Zelandosque nullum, nisi nominis ius temporarium, usurparet, iam Arausionensis quoque consilii auctor damnabatur, ut particeps dominationis, et qui ab initio motuum munitissimas gentes sibi seponeret. Certe praescriptum (**75**) eius nomen legibus et actis publicis: neque tunc praefectura, sed

Book 4

1 **(73)** Anjou sailed over to England, to strengthen his future principate with ties of friendship. The queen liked him so much (either his person or the prospect he embodied of greater glory) that under specific conditions negotiations were opened about a marriage, in spite of the gap between their confessions.[1] This rumour was very welcome to the Lowlanders but proved vain, either **(74)** because the misinformation was intentional, or his brother's offences formed an obstacle. And lastly there was his own ill-guided rashness too, which preferred to achieve its aims by force of arms. Upon his return in the Low Countries Anjou assumed supreme power in a display with all the required ceremony and magnificent pomp; in Brabant under the title of duke, in Flanders that of count.

2 This princely power was submitted, apart from the existing conditions, to a few new ones grounded in the treaty of Bordeaux.[2] The States-General would be convened once every year, and without their consent no treaty could be concluded with Spain, nor a supreme military commander appointed. At their request foreign troops were to be disbanded. With respect to religious policy and the employment of foreign mercenaries, each province would make its own decisions; they would also nominate three men, one of whom would be appointed as its stadtholder; and if any disagreement between the provinces arose, Anjou would pass judgment. Two Frenchmen were to become members of the Council of State, while the other members would for now be appointed by the States, in the future by the duke, but only from a nominated group. Lowlanders were even given prominent positions at the court. On top of the princely possessions, a subsidy every year of two million and four hundred thousand florins was promised for the war, under the condition that the remaining amount would be covered from the duke's own or his brother's pockets. Some hopes existed that the followers of both confessions would adhere to these agreements, both those of Orange's conviction, and the followers of the Roman faith in Anjou's entourage; for the latter were granted permission to return to their worship in Antwerp, and not beyond, if at least they swore the Lowlanders' common oath of loyalty to the new government.

3 In public there was every expression of joy, and Anjou did indeed present a fair image, bearing kindness on the face and elegance in speech. Those who remained of the nobility however were secretly displeased that they were forced to behold a prince on Burgundy's throne born from the nation that had so long been their enemy: because the change of lordship meant that a people was now paired with the Lowlanders with whom there had never been a reliable peace, and so many vicious battles fought; the loathing went back more than a century. Even from the heads of the populace the sense of duty towards their former oath and the reverence for their lord, whichever kind of one he was, was not easily dispelled. On the other hand there were people who perceived an obstacle in the new religion, and warned not to compromise the cause of the faith by accepting support from followers of a different creed. The more sensible feared the danger caused by discord as well as the French brutality that might follow from it.

4 When it transpired however that a secret agreement existed that Anjou, although he had been given the lordship of the Low Countries, obtained no rights with respect to Holland and Zeeland except to use the title temporarily, William of Orange too, as instigator of the plan, was denounced as partner in this tyranny, and as having from the start of the troubles reserved the two best protected provinces for himself. It is certain **(75)** that laws and public

summum imperium penes illum fuit. Quin et comitis nomen per eas regiones a plerisque delatum; quo minus reciperet, pauca suffragia restabant, cum ad longi laboris praemia properantem inferius narranda mors intercepit. At alii hoc potius indignari, quod Gallicae potentiae seorsim manciparentur, Arausionensisque imperium et ipsi malle, qui cunctis defensandis impar, haud immerito socium adsciverat. Multitudinis sane quanta in illum studia fuerint, morbo eius compertum est. Nam cum ex vulnere, quod percussor regius inflixerat, graviter Antverpiae aegrotaret, tota civitas moestitiam et fletus suos templis affudit, ut Dei pacem exposceret, veluti in publici parentis periculo. Tunc quidem valetudo restituta: sed reliqua vitae pars infesta latrociniis Hispanicis fuit: iterumque et saepius deprehensi, qui ipsius et Francisci vitae insidiarentur.

5 Dum Ducis copiae paulatim adventant, Parmensis exercitum in Flandriam duxit, ubi Aldenardam, urbem a veteribus Nerviis appellatam, qui Scaldi adsita olim tenuere, trimestri obsidio, et telorum impetu cepit; eo facilius, quia praesidium, quod satis esset, oppidani recusarant. Inde, cum Bruxellae circumsita castris insideret, res arctas urbi facturus, consumtis per agros frugibus, et mox hyemis asperitate attritus, recessit. Multum subita quoque valuere: et inter alia oppida improviso superantur a Valesio Alostum, quam hostis tenebat; a Parmensis milite Lira, proditione aliquot praesidiariorum. Is locus magnam ad bellum oportunitatem habebat, ob propinquam Antverpiam: interim et leves pugnae aequo certamine; et Anglorum non pauci perfugae ab Hispanis contemtim habiti, aliis ad servandam partibus fidem documento fuere. Mox Lochemum, modicum Geldriae oppidum prope Zutphaniam, Verdugo circumventum, ut fame tentaret, deserere coactus est, ter invecto commeatu. At Stenovicum, de quo graviter ante certatum fuerat, labore nullo, per tenebras et inscitiam oppidanorum, idem occupavit.

6 Interim Philippus, obiecto sibi Valesio, maiore quam antehac vi et cura agendum ratus, Hispanum Italumque militem Parmensi remiserat; nec cuiquam tantum in Atrebaticis pactionibus et iure fiduciae fuit, ut contradicere auderet: ipse obtendit spectatum in ea sponsione Belgicae totius obsequium, qua spe irrita, **(76)** cum causa et obligationis vinculum concidisse. Summa recensitu comperta pedites sexagies mille, quatuor millia eorum qui equo merebant: manentque numeri, aut augentur ad haec usque tempora: quorum menstrua stipendia septies centena millia florenorum excedere putantur; atque eius dimidio non minus caetera belli impendia. Igitur, super tributa domestica, missum a Philippo quotannis non minus vicies centenis millibus. Tantum Hispano in Belgas perit: et, ne plus pecuniae traiiceretur, obstitisse crediti, qui, rebus in Belgica male gestis, alienos successus formidabant.

declarations were signed with his name; and at this time it was not the stadtholderate, but the highest power itself which was held by him. Even the title of count in these provinces was entrusted to him by most people; he was only a few voting sessions away from receiving it, when his death (to be related below) stopped him in his tracks, in sight of the rewards for his protracted struggle. Others again were primarily annoyed at being handed over into French power under separate conditions, and would rather have obtained Orange's supremacy for themselves—while Orange had only enlisted an ally for very good reasons, it being beyond his powers to provide protection to all. In any case it became clear during his illness to what extent he enjoyed the support of the populace. For when he was lying in heavy illness in Antwerp, caused by the wound which a royal murderer had inflicted upon him,[3] the entire citizenship poured their tears and sadness into the churches, in order to beg God for peace, as if the very father of the nation was in danger. At that time however his health was restored; but the remainder of his life was turned into a nightmare by Spanish entrapments. With mounting frequency men were caught who were laying ambushes to Orange's and Anjou's lives.

5 While Anjou's troops were drawing closer, step by step, Parma led an army into Flanders, where he captured the city of Oudenaarde (so named after the ancient Nervi, who once lived on the shores of the Scheldt), after a siege of three months, forcing the decision by a cannonade. This was made easier by the fact that the citizens had refused to accept a garrison of sufficient size. His next step was to occupy Brussels' surroundings with encampments, in order to prepare the city a spell of scarcity. There was no harvest left on the fields, and soon he had to retreat himself, worn out by the severity of the winter. A few sudden events had great effects: Anjou unexpectedly conquered Aalst, which was held by the enemy, together with a few other towns; Parma's soldiery Lier, using treason of a couple of its townspeople. This place had a great strategic significance, because of its proximity to Antwerp. Meanwhile there were minor skirmishes with equal chances; and a considerable number of Englishmen, who had fled to the Spanish but were treated badly, served as reminder to the others to remain loyal to their own side. Verdugo,[4] who had surrounded Lochem (a small town in Guelders, near Zutphen) with the intention of submitting it to the test of starvation, was soon forced to abandon it after three deliveries of food had succeeded. On the other hand he took Steenwijk with no trouble, although it had been the object of heavy fighting before, employing the night and the blundering of the townspeople.

6 Meanwhile Philip had concluded, now that he was confronting Anjou, that he had to act with greater force and foresight than before, and sent the Spanish and Italian troops back to Parma. No one had such confidence in the rights stated in the agreements of Arras that he dared protest; the king claimed that those vows pertained to the obedience of the Low Countries as a whole, and that since that expectation had collapsed, **(76)** together with the grounds the obligation binding him had disappeared as well. A head count of the total showed that there were sixty thousand infantry and four thousand warriors on horseback. These numbers have remained the same, or even grown until the present day. It is believed that their monthly wages are in excess of seven hundred thousand florins, and the remaining costs of the war not less than half of that. It follows from this that, on top of the domestic taxation, Philip sent no less than two million every year: so much money the Spaniard lost in the Low Countries.[5] And the story is told that squandering even more was blocked by individuals whose exploits had been unsuccessful and who feared successes by others.

7 Ordines contra, ut egregiis initiis novo imperio famam circumdarent, vicies quater annuum quod fuerat in praesens, ad quadragies centena millia extulere, qua pecunia Francisci sub signis praeter Belgas Galli, Germani, Angli, Scoti militabant. Validae utrinque copiae, sed quarum pars magna praesidiis attinebatur: quippe indiscretis finibus, et, ut belli casus tulerant, inserti oppidis, alter alteri ex proximo imminebant.

8 Hactenus sperabat Valesius fraterna subsidia ad eas opes evertendas, cum quibus varia ducentorum annorum fortuna conflictati Gallorum reges, per bellum penuria et sanguine, iterumque pacis conditionibus hostem sibi aequaverant. Sed quanquam Medicaea mater Lusitanici maris possessionem attentabat, rex ipse nec bellum palam indicere animatus, nec clam quidem suspectas vires accidere. Nam Philippus ultro praevenerat, emercatus dissidia, quibus tranquillum Galliae statum turbaret; quod ipsi facile, cui multa largiendi facultas; et Galli vix gratuito quiescant. Pars igitur validior palam Regem absterrere, ne alio quam in Romanae religionis hostes arma verteret: pars, specie altioris consilii, callide fallaces, negabant utile aut aequum esse, Regem, cui nec promissa successio, in alienos usus aerarium profundere; quin relinquendos Belgas ipsumque ducem suae paupertati, donec exhausti, et de summa rei periclitantes ad accipiendas leges venirent: satis enim mature ex affini regno vinci Hispanum posse, cum non aliis vinceretur. Et erat rex sponte etiam sua fratri iniquior, non quod offensus, sed quod offenderat: memor ob suspiciones magis quam crimina duris custodiis nec semel septum.

9 (1583) Ea res praecipitem egit Ducem in consilium atrox et plenum desperationis, sibique pariter et Belgis exitiosum. Nam cum prospiceret facile se illis contemtui fore, quibus **(77)** promissa auxilia non praestaret, tantum inutili principatu gravis, nec immemor precario se imperare: deinde (quod in regno educatos moleste habet) legibus et aliorum auctoritate retineri, orata aliquoties mutatione, nec obtenta, singularem potentiam vi statuit munire; et fidissimis ducum Flandriae oppida praesidiis occupanda delegat: ipse Antverpiam sibi sumit, ut maximam urbium, et ubi Arausionensis validior gratia, cui tacito foedere partem deberi sciret potentiae, et Ordinum legati dominationis impedimenta.

10 Credibile est huius temeritatis concitores fuisse, non modo quibus occulta cum hoste consiliorum societas, et fides pretio corrupta, qui certum duci imperium ex matrimonio Hispanico ostentabant, sed Gallos, qui urbium direptionem, aut, maiorem praedam, honores sibi proposuerant, unde legibus arcebantur, cuius cupiditatis totidem gentes compertae sunt, quot Belgae socias habuere.

7 The States on the other side, in order to dress their newly founded government in the glory resulting from an excellent start, raised the amount which was two million and four hundred thousand in the present, to four million. From this money, in addition to Lowlanders, Frenchmen, Germans, Englishmen and Scots served under Anjou's banner. Both sides possessed strong forces, but large parts of them were detained in garrisons; for there was no clear frontier, and both parties brought danger to one another from close by, from the towns where martial chance had placed them.

8 So far Anjou was hoping for his brother's support in demolishing the superpower against which the French kings, with fluctuating success, had been fighting a war of two hundred years which had brought them poverty and bloodshed: against an enemy which in the end they had made their equal by a peace treaty. But although their mother, Catharine de' Medici attempted to gain possession of the Portuguese sea,[6] the king himself was neither disposed to openly declare war, nor even to cut back in secret forces which he distrusted. For Philip had forestalled him by investing money in disturbances in order to upset France's state of tranquillity. With his powers to donate this was easy to achieve, while the French will hardly stay quiet anyway even for free. Thus the stronger faction openly deterred the king from directing his forces anywhere else than against the enemies of the Roman faith. A different group, cunning deceivers as they were, presented it as counsel of even greater shrewdness that it would be neither profitable nor fair if the king emptied his coffers for another people's benefit without being promised succession to their throne; and that moreover the Lowlanders with this leader of theirs should be left to their own poverty until from exhaustion and the imminent loss of their state they would come to him to accept his conditions. For there was still time enough to defeat the Spaniard from a neighbouring realm, if he wasn't already being defeated by others. Also the king was not completely well-disposed towards his brother, not because his brother had harmed him, but he had harmed his brother: he had not forgotten how he had put him in severe custody more than once because of suspicions rather than actual offences.

9 This situation drove Anjou head over heels into a wild and desperate plan, fateful to himself and the Lowlanders alike. For he realised he could easily lose the respect **(77)** of people to whom he failed to deliver the assistance he had promised and was only a burden, sitting on his useless throne. He was well aware that he ruled only by permission, which meant that his hands were tied by laws and the powers of others—a thing most hurtful to men raised for the throne. He had requested a change in this situation several times, but not obtained it, and now decided to use force to secure unrestricted power for himself. He assigned the towns in Flanders to his most loyal commanders, to occupy them with garrisons. He took Antwerp for himself, as this was the biggest city and the place where Orange's popularity made him strongest (and he knew that by tacit agreement he owed him a share of the power), as well as the place where the States' delegates were present as obstacles to his regime.

10 In all likelihood this heedless adventure had been instigated not only by men with secret intentions in common with the enemy, and bribed loyalties, who guaranteed the sovereignty to Anjou, based on marriage with a daughter of Spain: no, there were also Frenchmen who had promised themselves chaos in the cities or (an even greater reward) offices which the law denied them a desire which as many nations were caught having as the Lowlanders have had as allies.

11 Adfuit successus ubi Gallorum praesidia praevalebant, capiunturque Vilvorda, Tenerimunda, Dicasmuda, et Dunkerca, maritimum Flandriae oppidum, commodo situ ob Galliae commeatus. Brugis et qui ante praesidebant, et qui recens advenerant, egregia magistratuum arte elusi sunt; qui ductos in curiam tribunos, consultandi specie, coegere, ut egressum militi per literas imperarent: et hic metu armatae plebis haud gravatim paruit. Antverpiae maius periculum, cruenti exitus; eruperant quanquam indicia, et occursum ab Arausionensi urbisque rectoribus, quantum poterat dissimulata suspicione. Exercitus eo Helvetiorum Gallorumque convenerat, ut, capto tum forte munimento, cui Endovia nomen, et fuga hostium, Brabantici agri possessio retineretur.

12 Ad eos, velut agendo censui, sub ipsa moenia Dux egressus, cum familiari comitatu, obtruncari repente vigiles, invadi portas iubet, ut caeteris pateret aditus. Et iam centuriae septendecim per urbis vias, quasi victrices, volitabant, missam, Romanae religionis sacrum, inclamantes (id conspirationis signum erat,) cum oppidani relictis mensis (prandebant enim) ad subitum tumultum corripiunt arma: qui primi processerant Valesianos, transire in ulteriora conantes, obiectu corporum prohibuere. Paulatim plures manus coortae, undique egregia virtute, et concordia, (suos nimirum penates, suas fortunas tuebantur) cunctos qui urbem ingressi erant, in portam, qua (**78**) intratum, repellunt. Ibi alta strages, atque inter angustias fugientes adventantibus, mortui vivis impedimento erant. At Franciscus, ubi insaniam coepti eventu didicit, pudore et conscientia vecors, rerumque omnium egens, quantis potuit cum copiis, inter magna vitae pericula et gravem suorum iacturam, per humida camporum trans amnem Dilam profugit. Haec tam insignis iniuria multorum animos, ne ante quidem satis aequos Gallico nomini, vehementius offendit.

13 Nec omittebat Parmensis, et qui Belgarum apud illum erant, infaustam defectionem, et novi dominatus graviora, quam fugiebantur, scelera literis incessere. Ferenda scilicet superiorum ingenia, nec ulli populo tutum inter tot regna rebellare. Quodsi vel nunc tristi experimento ad obsequium rediretur, aequas leges, et Regis clementiam offerebat.

14 Senserat Arausionensis nimis oportunum rebus Hispanicis tempus pacificationis invadi: et quanquam consilium semel improspere cesserat, quo maximam potentiae suae partem amiserat, vulgi favorem, rogatus sententiam, multa cum invidiae deprecatione exposuit. Si concorditer regi respublica potuisset, et suis opibus administrari, dubitandum non fuisse, quin merito unius et externo imperio abstineretur. neque nunc illud quaeri, an ius sit eum deserere, qui prior publica iura violasset, quod satis cautum pactionibus: sed vires respiciendas; modicum sibi

11 The attempt was successful wherever the French garrisons were the stronger force; Vilvoorde, Dendermonde, Diksmuide were taken, as well as Dunkirk, a naval town in Flanders conveniently situated for trade with France. At Bruges both the garrison soldiers who were there already, and the newly arrived troops were sidelined by superior scheming of the magistrates: they summoned the officers to the town hall, under the guise of consultation, and forced them to send letters to the soldiers ordering them to make their way out; for fear of the armed populace the soldiers obeyed without objection. In Antwerp there was more danger and the outcome bloodier, although some indications had leaked out and Orange and the other governors had acted against the plans as much as they could without uncovering their suspicions. An army of Swiss and French troops had assembled near Antwerp to secure possession of the Brabantine countryside; while they were at it they captured the fortification named Eindhoven and chased off the enemy.

12 Anjou came out [of Antwerp] to meet them with his familiar entourage, as if for an inspection right under the city walls. Suddenly he gave orders to slaughter the watchmen and occupy the gates in order to open the entrances for the others. Straight away seventeen companies ran through the streets of the city, as victors after a siege, shouting "Mass, the Mass", the Roman ritual of worship (this was the sign of their conspiracy), while the citizens at the sudden noise rushed from their tables (they were having lunch) to grab their weapons. Those who came out first blocked the way for the French soldiers, who were trying to pass to the inner parts of the city, by literally throwing themselves before them. Gradually more groups appeared on the streets, and fighting on all sides with outstanding courage and unity (for they were defending their own homes and futures), they drove all the intruders back to the gate by which they had entered. **(78)** There a murderous tangle grew up, and in the narrow space men escaping and going in, the living and the dead obstructed each other's way. Now Anjou understood the madness of his venture from the outcome; out of his mind with shame and guilt, and robbed of everything, he fled with as many troops as he could, amidst serious danger to his life and heavy losses among his men, over the soggy fields to the other side of the river Dijle. Such a conspicuous crime shocked many, while before they hadn't been overly partial to the French already.[7]

13 Parma and the Lowlanders who were on his side, did not let their chance slip to publish attacks on this doomed defection and the crimes of the new regime, as heavier than the ones that were being fled. They argued that people just had to tolerate the character of their superiors, and that no nation could safely rebel in a world with so many kingdoms. However, even now, if after this harsh lesson there would be a return to obedience, he could offer fair conditions and the king's mildness.

14 Orange had perceived that for the Spanish interests a very profitable moment for a peace was arriving. Although a plan of his had failed once, and this had cost him the chief part of his power basis, that is, the popular favour, he spoke his opinion when he was asked for it, imploring many times that no grudge be held against him. "If it had been possible to govern the assembled provinces in a harmonious way, and organise them on the basis of their own resources, no doubt would have existed that we were right in turning away from monarchy and rule by a foreigner. Nor are we dealing now with the question whether it is legally right to leave the ruler who broke the constitution first, since this right is defined explicitly enough in our legal agreements. No, we must consider our own power: I have an army of limited size, the duke of Anjou has strong cities under his control. We Lowlanders should ask

militem, et urbes validas in Ducis manu: deliberandum Belgis, suas has esse, an hostium mallent. Multum autem referre, ad Hispanum, an ad Gallum ab utroque offensi reverterentur. Nam illam potentiam, imperii vetustate coalitam, reperire semper instrumenta ad opprimendam libertatem: huic, si quid moliretur, defore qui libidini eius obsecundarent. Satius igitur Gallum experiri, cui semel deprehenso non occasionem post hac, non animum eadem audendi. Ipsi vicissim, pro uno recenti delicto, multa Ducis benefacta, et proximos per annos defensas urbes, oppressos hostium conatus ipsius opera, benigne cogitarent. Ita redituram belli concordiam, si peccasse Franciscus se meminisset, ipsi obliviscerentur.

15 Cui orationi accessit ab aliis excusatio imprudentiae iuvenilis, et animi e regio sanguine, qui nulla obsequii humilitate delinitus, forte et quorundam incensus contumacia, non tamen ad caedes et rapinas, sed ad securitatem potentiae pravis consultoribus infelix iter legisset. (**79**) Rex etiam Galliarum pollicitatione, et latentibus minis fratrem commendabat. Coeptum igitur agi cum Duce, ut, restitutis oppidis quae habebat in suam potestatem, Dunkercam secederet: eodem commeaturos qui cetera componerent. Interea, longa cunctatione, dum et ipse oppidorum restitutioni renititur, et Belgae militibus, qui cum ipso erant, alimenta non suppeditant, plebis metu, quae recentis metus tenacior, maiora et vetera minus cogitabat, vix tandem placuit, Bironem Gallici exercitus ductorem mitti, ut Parmensis conatus compesceret: qui tum, captis oppidis aliquot, Brabantiam infestabat.

16 Sed nec huic bellum satis processit, et colloquium multis difficultatibus trahebatur; ultro accusante Francisco, quod velut in vanum principis nomen accitus, tributorum rationem, et res maximas celaretur, nulla ad benefaciendum cuiquam licentia: neque mirum, si, post tot aliorum exempla, qui ad res Belgicas invocati gravia sensissent mutatae voluntatis experimenta, inventus esset ipse, qui, diu cunctatus, nollet ex alieno nutu pendere. Praecipue autem flagitabat, ne cunctis principibus permissum sibi uni negaretur, ut extra curiam domesticum haberet consilium: cuius moris usum laudabat ante alios Iohannes Bodinus libellorum praepositus, notum scriptis ingenium: contra, Belgis nihil aeque perhorrescentibus: etiam pro sacris Romanensibus aliquid Galli in speciem attulere.

17 Haec inter certamina prope inclusus Dunkercae Franciscus, cum super veterem dolorem novo taedio angeretur, et arctiore oppido multitudinem vastarent morbi, in Galliam concessit: sive ut mutata locorum facie animum recrearet, sive, quod credibile est, rediturus in gratiam cum fratre, durantibus hactenus offensis. Temporaria certe profectio fuit: neque, dum vixit, adire illum Belgae legationibus desierunt, ut Flandriae nutanti suppetias veniret: orantes maxime Regem, fraternam ut causam

ourselves if we want these to be in their own, or in enemy hands. It makes a great difference whether we return to the Spaniard or to the Frenchman, although we have been harmed by both. For in the long tradition of the Empire the Spanish power has accreted [with our institutions], and will always find the instruments to suppress freedom. French power on the other hand, if it were to attempt such a thing, would never find people to support its desires. Thus it is wiser to try the Frenchman, who has been caught in the act once and will never in the future have the occasion or the will to venture the same. We on our part would do well, instead of his one recent offence, to think of the duke's many benefactions, the cities he saved in recent years, and the enemy operations that were stopped by his intervention. In this way the unity in our war effort will return: if Anjou would keep his trespasses in mind, and we forgot them."[8]

15 This argument was supported by others with an apology for Anjou's youthful imprudence, and his character of royal birth that was never tamed by the humility of obedience, that was perhaps outraged at the stubbornness of some people, and chose this unfortunate course because of the wrong counsellors, not however with a view to rape and murder, but with a view to securing his own power. **(79)** Also the French king recommended his brother by sending promises and implicit threats. Thus negotiations were opened with Anjou, with the aim that he give back the cities which he held in his possession, and retreat to Dunkirk; and that the negotiators to arrange the remaining issues would go to the same place. In the meantime, after long hesitation (while he was opposing the restitution of the towns, and the Lowlanders stopped supplying provisions to the troops under his command, for fear of the populace which was still caught by its recent fear without consideration of the earlier and greater benefits it received), after a long reluctance, that is, Anjou decided to send the seigneur de Biron,[9] marshal of the French army, to suppress Parma's attempts, since the latter had conquered a handful of towns and was ravaging Brabant.

16 However even under Biron there was no progress in the war, while the negotiations dragged from one difficulty to another. Anjou came up with the accusations that he had only been employed to fulfil an empty title of prince, that they kept him away from the allocation of tax money and major political decision-making, and that he was not at liberty to impart benefits to anyone. And that it should be no surprise, if, after so many cases of others who were called to govern the Low Countries only to end up with nasty experiences of fickleness, it became clear of him too that (having thought about it for a long time) he wasn't prepared to depend on somebody else's decisions. He insisted with particular force on his demand that one thing which was granted to every prince, not be denied to him alone, that is, to have his own private council separate from the Council of State. This practice was praised most of all by John Bodin (head of his legal affairs and a great mind famous for his writings) while on the other hand is more abhorrent to the Lowlanders. To keep up appearances the French even put forward a few demands for the sake of the Catholic faith.

17 During these struggles Anjou was more or less locked in at Dunkirk. When he got vexed by new disgust on top of his older sufferings, and diseases began exterminating the crowds living within the narrow town, he retreated to France, either to refresh his mind by the change of scene, or, which is more likely, to restore cordial relations with his brother, with whom the enmity was not yet over. There is no doubt this departure was temporary, and as long as he lived delegations from the Low Countries kept visiting him to ask him to come to the aid of the Low Countries in their critical situation. They made a special appeal to

aperte amplecteretur: id si minus posset, ut milite et pecuniis iuvaret, omnesque e Gallia commeatus in hosticum intercluderet: quae si impetrarent, non verebantur Regi successionem imperii legibus eisdem addicere, ita ut iure Francico in corpus regni multis post saeculis rediretur.

18 Sed sequentium temporum malis, et Francisci morte diremta colloquia. Superstes is fuit honoris et dedecoris sui menses non amplius septendecim, confectusque aliis per libidines, aliis (**80**) veneno, plerisque animi aegrimonia creditur, communi ferme omnium exitu, quibus ante illum, vel post, infelicium populorum malis abuti libido fuit. Etiam funus habuit, nullis Belgici imperii insignibus, et rerum ibi actarum silentio, dum rex frater vitat Hispanum, quem rebus non audebat, inanibus offendere.

19 Ut primum Franciscus Dunkerca excesserat, Gallorum cohors, quae praesidio relicta erat, acceptis stipendiis dilabi et diffidere genti quam laeserant. Ita milite nudatum et navigiis oppidum minoribus ducibus obsidendum Parmensis delegat: mox ipse adest ad perficiendam oppugnationem iusto cum exercitu. Imperatum Bironi erat insequi hostem, et vires committere: sed Gandavenses veteri in Valesium odio, et reperta specie tumultuandi, transitum negarunt: iniustum enim esse aiebant, eius copiis uti, quem neque principem ultra, neque amicum agnoscerent. Hac igitur istorum hominum pertinacia Dunkerca in Hispani venit potestatem; unde nunc perpetuo intutum mare. Nam importuoso in littore vix modicis muyoparonibus subsidia habet: hinc, ubi commodum est, observato exitu, praetervectas Batavorum naves ad piscandum, aut cum mercimoniis, ubi opposita Britannia arctat oceanum, praedones aggredi solent, et facile effugium levitati apertum per mare, aut propinqua inter vada, adversus bellicas moles.

20 Nec huius quidem oppidi tam insignis iactura sanavit dissensiones: sed necesse fuit dimitti Bironem cum exercitu, quanquam obtestante Arausionensi, ne hosti animoso et felici proderent rempublicam: adeo Gallis nihil credebatur; et ipse propter illos adverso rumore erat, ita ut Antverpiae in arma concursum sit, vulgato mendacio Gallos ab Arausionensi in arcem inductos, inde urbi imminere. Ille vero, cui nihil aeque insolitum, aut triste erat, quam civibus suis formidolosum vivere, non tulit mutatos vultus, et pro festis acclamationibus suspicax silentium; sed relicta sex annorum habitatione in Zelandiam, et certiora imperii concessit, ingratis animis et imminentibus periculis exemptus. At Parmensis, vacua nactus vincendi tempora, Neoportum Dunkercae dextro littore adsitum, et interiora Dicasmudam, Furnas, et Bergas quae Winoci dicuntur, in deditionem accipit. Inde Flandris maior indies belli detestatio, et plerique in tantum proxima meminerant, ut (**81**) contra Gallos vel Hispanis faverent.

the king to openly embrace his brother's cause; but if this was not possible for him, to help him with troops and money and lock of all traffic from France to enemy territory.[10] If he would grant them this, they would not hesitate to add the succession to their throne to his crown under the same conditions, in the sense that after many centuries it would return to the main body of the realm under Frankish laws.

18 Because of the evils of the subsequent period however and Anjou's death, these negotiations were broken off. The latter survived his glory and disgrace for not more than seventeen months. Some believe he was killed by lust, some **(80)** that it was poison, but according to most chagrin was the cause: the common death of almost all who, before and after Anjou, desired to abuse the misery of suffering nations. Even his funeral was held without any coats of arms of his realm in the Low Countries, and without a word about his exploits over there: his brother the king avoided offending by futilities the Spaniard whom he did not dare provoke by deeds.[11]

19 Of course as soon as Anjou had left Dunkirk, the French regiment which he had left behind as a garrison began to fall apart and distrust the population which it had harmed. The town having thus been stripped of soldiers and ships, Parma assigned a couple of lower officers with the task of besieging it. Soon he was present himself with a proper army to finish the siege. Biron had received orders to chase the enemy and engage him in battle; but the people of Ghent, driven by an ancient loathing of Anjou, and jumping on a pretext for rioting, refused him the passage. They argued that it was wrong that troops were employed of a man whom they did not acknowledge any further as their prince, nor even as a friend. Consequently Dunkirk fell into the Spaniard's hands because of the pigheadedness of this breed, with the result that even today the sea is permanently unsafe. Situated on a coastline without harbours the town can just offer shelter to small piratical vessels: from this port, they watch the departures and whenever a profitable occasion arises, pirates attack passing Dutch fishing vessels or freight carriers in the area delimited by Britain on the other side of the sea. When confronted with heavy men-of-war, they can easily escape over the open sea or between the nearby sandbanks.

20 However, not even the loss of such an important town cured the disagreements. No, it appeared inevitable to send Biron away, with his army, in spite of all Orange's protestations not to give the commonwealth up to an enemy both motivated and successful; but this was how little the French were trusted. Even his own reputation suffered because of them, to such extent that in Antwerp people rushed to arms after a lie had been spread that Orange had brought Frenchmen into the citadel, from where they were posing a threat to the city. Orange however, who was to nothing less accustomed, or more depressed by it, than the idea of being a source of fear to his own people, could not bear this change of treatment, and to hear silence full of suspicions instead of jubilant cheers. He took his leave from the ingratitude and threats: he left the place which had been his residence for six years, moving to Zeeland, one area where his power was more secure. Parma on the other hand got an unguarded moment to win presented to him on a silver platter, and acquired the surrender of Nieuwpoort, on the coast on the right side of Dunkirk, as well as more inland of Diksmuide, Veurne en St. Winoksbergen. As a result the aversion of the war grew in Flanders every day, and the recent events had left such strong impressions on most people, **(81)** that they preferred even the Spanish over the French.

21 Per idem tempus Hollandiam hominis ignobilis audacia turbare sermonibus scriptisque aggressa est; Hogius dicebatur: sed ipse materno dedecore, et forma non dispari, vanam sanguinis gloriam affectabat; quasi Carolo Caesare genitus: inde ab Hispanis iniecta spe, fore ut illum Philippus fratrem agnosceret, homines novorum cupidos, aut quibus praesentia displicebant, in spem pacis, et obsequium gentis Austriacae retrahebat. Sed conspiratio adhuc recens auctoris supplicio extincta est.

22 Pugnari coeptum et in Agrippinensi ditione, quae tunc Ernesto Boioaro cum pontificatu delata erat, ob Truxii coniugium. Is enim, eiusdem ante loci antistes, intempestivo amore illectus illustris foeminae, festinarat exuere coelibatum, quod per Latinas leges sacerdotibus non licet, cum in promiscuis libidinibus facile conniveatur. Ille hominum scitis fas divinum opponere, et impar tantis ipse curis, per Casimirum, et Nienarium comitem Mursae, modici utrumque exercitus ducem, inhaerere urbibus, donec vi hostium et suorum perfidia plerisque praesidiis depulsus, inito cum Belgis foedere, ad Arausionensem profugit, unde populationibus se, ut potuit, ultus est: factumque est hoc bellum maioris accessio: nec id Hispano ingratum, quo speciosius limitaneas Germaniae urbes, vetera Belgarum exsulum receptacula, armis involveret.

23 Auxit hoc quoque valescentem indies Parmensis fortunam, quod Zutfaniam, quae nec iusto praesidio, nec satis concordi tenebatur, Taxis tribunus ex insidiis illi cepit, adiutus gregarii unius opera, quem habuerat apud se captivum. Hinc iam cuncta inter Isalam et Rhenum sita Hispanorum incursibus infesta erant: nec occludi saltem exitus potuere: urbs quoque frustra obsessa est. Adeo tunc maxime Belgarum vires et tempora discordiis peribant.

24 At primores haud pauci, rebus publice desperatis, privatim remedium ex venia gratiaque Regis quaerebant, quae nisi magno facinore non sperabatur. Ita Wilhelmus Herembergensis, qui, accepta in matrimonium Arausionensis sorore, primae spei periculorumque socius fuerat, levitate ingenii, Geldriam, quam tum regebat, statuit donare victoribus; sed praeventa fraude, et accepta fide dimissus, tamen transfugit, nihil partibus conferens praeter egregia filiorum robora, quos ad defectionem impulit, nec suis criminibus implicitos, nec honorum (**82**) expertes. Geldriae mox regimen Nienario datur.

25 At Flandriae miserabilis status. Ipra a Parmensi obsidebatur. Gandavenses Imbisium revocaverant, non alia gratia, quam quod cum Arausionensi et Gallis veteres inimicitias exerceret: hic summum denuo magistratum adeptus, per turbulentos aliquot concionatores, plebis animos quatiebat. Brugarum civitas, cum Flandria bello ardesceret, praefectum sibi advocaverat Carolum Cimacensem.

21 In this time a daredevil of vulgar descent started to raise trouble in Holland with rumours and pamphlets. His name was De Hooghe[12], but he appropriated a futile greatness of lineage based on his mother's disgrace and a similarity in looks,[13] pretending the emperor Charles was his father. Next some Spaniards fed him with hope that it might just happen that Philip acknowledged him as his brother; and he started to draw people eager for revolt or dissatisfied with the present government, back to hopes of peace and obedience to the house of Habsburg. However, the young conspiracy was exterminated by the murder of its instigator.

22 A new armed conflict arose in the district of Cologne, of which at that time Ernest of Bavaria held the combined secular authority and the bishopric, because of the marriage of Truchsess.[14] This was because Truchsess, formerly the archbishop of that place and seduced by the inopportune love for a noble lady, had rushed to put off his celibacy, a step not allowed to priests by the rules of the Catholic confession, although among their widespread concupiscence it is lightly turned a blind eye to. Truchsess set divine law and human precepts against one another, and incapable of handling the enormous consequences himself, he stuck to his possession of certain cities with Casimir's help and that of Adolf of Neuenahr, count of Moers,[15] both commanders of modestly sized armies. This lasted until enemy force and the faithlessness of his own people drove him from most of his bulwarks. After concluding an alliance with the Lowlanders, he sought refuge with Orange, then took revenge, as much as he could, with pillage. Thus this war became a supplement to the bigger one; which wasn't even unwelcome to the Spaniards because it presented them with a better excuse to involve the border cities in Germany, which had a long history as places of exile for the Lowlanders, in the war.

23 Parma's success rose day by day, and was further enhanced by captain Tassis's taking of Zutphen for him by a ruse, Zutphen being kept by a garrison neither sufficiently big nor unified for this task. Tassis here used the help of an ordinary soldier, which he kept with him as a captive. As a result the entire region between IJssel and Rhine became plagued by Spanish irruptions. It wasn't even possible to blockade the city's exits, and a siege of it was unsuccessful. Thus did the Lowlanders, at this time in particular, let their forces and their chances slip away by lack of unity.

24 Now that the prospects of the commonwealth were looking so grim, a large number of the nobility began looking for a solution for themselves in forgiveness and a pardon from the king, which could only be hoped for in return for a major act of treason. Thus William of 's Heerenberg (who was married to Orange's sister and had been his companion in hope and fear ever since the earliest times) decided, with the lightheartedness characteristic of his person, to donate the province of Guelders, which he governed at the time, to the winning side. The deceit was however forestalled and William removed from his post after an oath of loyalty. He defected nevertheless, bringing nothing to his new allies than a couple of very vigorous sons, whom he had driven to defection although they were neither involved in his crimes nor devoid of high office. **(82)** The government of Guelders was soon handed over to Neuenahr.

25 In Flanders the situation was wretched. Ypres was under siege by Parma. The people of Ghent had called Hembyze back in for no other reason than that he fostered inveterate hostilities with the French and with Orange. He regained the highest magistracy and whipped up popular sentiments through a handful of mutinous preachers. While the flames of war rose up in Flanders, the citizenship of Bruges appointed Charles of Chimay[16] as their head.

Arschotii is filius, mutatis aliquoties ex fortuna partibus, proxime a patre desciscens, voluntario exsilio mutatae religionis studium professus erat, eo impensius, quia simulabat: hac arte irrepens illorum animis qui sacras literas populo interpretantur, hominum minime callidorum simplicitati illudebat, et per eos vulgi affectibus commendabatur. Non minus autem Cimacensis quam Imbisius cum Romanae sectae hominibus secreta consilia agitabant, cum tamen palam illorum nonnullos uterque vinciret, aut relegaret. Interea alteram plebis partem ita sibi ficta superstitione devinxerant, ut omnium odia incurreret, si quis de illis sinisterius suspicaretur. Hi duo fuere, qui Flandriam, nobilissimam regionem, munitam adhuc tantis urbibus, hosti tradere susceperunt.

26 Iam primum ut Gallos revocandi levarent necessitatem, Casimirum, et Truxium et Germanica foedera loquebantur; non, quod spes aliqua appareret, sed ut elapso remediorum tempore, praeter deditionem nihil restaret. Ita pacis laudatores licentiam primum loquendi, mox et auctoritatem habuere. Sed ita rem instituerant, edebantque in vulgus, quasi pax daretur; non cum Parmensi et Hispanis, sed cum Belgarum civitatibus quae ad imperium reverterant. Id enim erat aliquanto popularius: addito, resipuisse Regem, contentumque obsequio quod sibi deberetur, divina Deo permittere.

27 Simul libelli et sermones iaciebantur, cum gravi Gallorum insectatione, et eorum qui tam diu inaequali certamine publicas et privatas Belgarum opes atererent: nunc quidem nullas sibi vires, nec foris spem societatis, cum potentissimi Regis arma continuis victoriis ipsos paene inclusos haberent: manifeste nimirum Deo improbante cruentari sacra, usumque religionis per vim et caedes rapi. At veteres certe Christianos profanorum etiam principum, cum maxime saevirent, imperia tolerasse, ut impositam a Deo necessitatem, quam cum demere ipsi visum, non armasse populos, (**83**) sed mutasse imperantes. Iuris bellique arbitrio semel ad principes translato, nihil subditis praeter patientiam et preces relinqui. Quin ipsam pietatem malle saepius oppressam semet colligere, quam laxitate diduci. Multos sub Carolo et Philippo suppliciis cecidisse, nunc armis quanto plures? Et illos quidem felices, qui non suo scelere perirent: at civium inter furores aeque miserabiles, qui ista facerent, et qui paterentur. Vere spectanti non haec esse belli semina, quae dicerentur, sed paucorum ambitionem, quos domesticis periculis excidium patriae opposuisse.

28 Harum rerum conscius Parmensis institit occasioni: et Ipra castellis circumsessa, quo minoribus copiis opus haberet, exercitum sub ducibus Vicecomite Gandavi et Montiniaco in septentrionalia Flandriae dimittit, ut sibi faventium animos Belgarum procerum auctoritate confirmaret, et, qui id sponte facturi non erant, interclusa spe auxiliorum, ad traditionem cogerentur. Est in ultima Flandriae parte,

This man was a son of Aarschot and had changed sides several times, depending on which way Fortune was leaning. Recently he had deserted from his father's cause and manifested his devotion to the renewed faith by voluntary exile; and all the more zealously precisely because it was feigned. By such techniques he secured an influence over the minds of those who explain Holy Scripture to the people, and deluded the simplicity of these men, who are not the brightest; and through them he obtained the affection of the populace. Just as Hembyze however, Chimay was holding secret consultations with representatives of the Roman sect—although for the public eye both men also put some members of that confession in chains or sent them in exile. Meanwhile they had tied the other party among the populace to themselves by counterfeited zealotry to such extent that it was not possible to entertain any more gloomy suspicions about them without incurring everyone's hatred. It was these two men who took it upon themselves to hand over the famous region of Flanders, adorned by its history with so many cities, to the enemy.[17]

26 To begin with, they spoke of Casimir, Truchsess and alliances in Germany, in order to eliminate the urgency to recall the French; not because any hopes were apparent on that side, but in order that the time for finding a solution would run out and nothing but surrender would remain. Consequently advocates of peace were first given free rein to speak, next endowed with authority. These however set up the plan in such a way, and brought it to the public, as if a peace was being offered; not with Parma and the Spanish but with the communities in the Low Countries which had returned to the empire, for this was slightly more welcome to the populace. They added the claim that the king had regained his senses and was satisfied by the obedience due to him; and would leave the religious question to God.

27 Simultaneously pamphlets and gossip were spread around with heavy accusations against the French and the others who for such a long time now had been squandering the Lowlanders' public and private wealth, "so that by today no resources, nor any hope of a foreign alliance are left, now that the armies of the most powerful king on earth have more or less locked us in by an unbroken chain of victories; and all this because it is obvious that God disapproves of religion being stained with blood, and the practice of worship ruined by murder and violence. It is certain that the Christians of Antiquity suffered the rule of pagan emperors, even at the height of their cruelty, as a necessity imposed by God; and when He decided to remove this plight, He did not put arms in the hands of the nations, **(83)** but changed the rulers. Now, given the fact that the choice between war and peace is the preserve of princes, nothing is left for subjects but patience and prayer. Yes, in many cases Piety herself would prefer to gather strength under oppression, than to whither by negligence. Under Charles and Philip many died on the scaffold, but how many more are now dying in the war? While in fact the former are lucky, since they died of crimes which weren't their own; but in the frenzy of civil war victims and perpetrators are equally miserable. Moreover, if you look at it, the roots of this war are not those which we are always told, but the ambitions of a few who try to repair their private problems by putting the fatherland at risk."[18]

28 Parma was well aware of all this and did not let the occasion slip. He surrounded Ypres with bulwarks in order to require fewer troops and sent the army to Ghent and the north of Flanders under the command of Montigny and the viscount of Ghent. The aim of this was to strengthen the resolve of the Netherlands noblemen who were on his side with his authority, and to force the ones who weren't there of their own accord to a capitulation by blocking their hopes of receiving assistance. In the outermost part of Flanders is the region

quam continuus adhuc Scaldis a Brabantis, scissus deinde a Bevelandia Australi Zelandorum insula dispescit, flexuque suo amplectitur, terra Wasia nomine: quam tum regebat Stelandius, eodem quo Cimacensis et Imbisius in patriam animo. Huc ubi regii duces pervenere, continuo omnem eam regionem traditione praefecti nanciscuntur, oppidaque Hulstum et Axelam, cum castello cui Rupelmunda nomen, priscis Flandrorum historiis non incelebre. Origo vocabuli a Rupella tenui amne, qui Scaldim illabitur, unde non nimium longe in altera ripa Antverpia est.

29 Interius aliquanto recedit Alostum, cuius praesidiariis (pereginus erat ex Anglia miles) mediocris ex causa stipendiorum summa debebatur, neglecta solvi a Flandris, etiam cum milites hostium viribus, penuria sua, vicinorum exemplo ad deditionem sollicitarentur, quae deinde secuta est. At Brabanti Zelandique non omiserunt disiicere aggeres, diffundere Scaldim, et ultra eum castella disponere, ut suam ripam tuerentur, hostilem incurrerent.

30 (1584) Parmensiani interea duces, quo duarum urbium maximarum seditio pluribus malis incenderetur, inter Gandavum ac Brugas castra locarunt; obsepta etiam amnium navigatione ad arcendos commeatus. Igitur utrobique Romanae religionis sectatores, quique alii per dolum, aut, quod ita sentirent, res Hispanicas pacis nomine amplectebantur, non amplius (**84**) mussitare, aut secretos quaerere conventus, sed publici et maximae auctoritatis compotes partim suadendo, alios metu, pertrahere in suam sententiam. Hi tandem discessu caeterorum Brugis praepolluere; simul Cimacensis erupit.

31 Quae postquam ad Arausionensem per fidos magistratus delata sunt, data est opera ut ille comprehenderetur per cohortis praesidiariae praepositum. Sed hunc ipsum Cimacensis donis praevenerat, et praesenti usus occasione, edocta plebe seque et urbem inimicorum insidiis peti, munera publica et honores ereptos aliis in eos contulit, qui cum ipso consilia sociaverant. Ab his igitur adiutus, urbem Romanae religioni et regis obsequio reddidit. In easdem leges oppidi Dammae deditio facta est, et liberae universitatis, quae Brugarum olim imperiis, gravioribusque agri oneribus excepta, Franconatus vocabulo appellatur: et in Flandriae conventibus par maximis urbibus dicendae sententiae ius habet. Nec Ipra communis spem pacificationis, et obsidii mala diutius toleravit, tertia principum Flandriae urbium a Gandavo Brugisque. Gandavenses et ipsi venere ad colloquia per legatos, inducias, obsides.

32 Sed urbem servavit parum dissimulata Imbisii perfidia. Nam Tenerimundam oppidum, quod Rihovius Arausionensis iussu strenue tutabatur, Hispano tradere voluerat, gratiae duplicandae, et apertius quam ut lateret. Cumque ab aliis in tam nefario consilio praepediretur, curiam et inclusos senatores comitatu militum, quos praesidio acceperat, ibat obsessum. Utrumque hoc facinus populi animos ita abalienavit, ut in convictum proditionis capitali supplicio animadverterent. Egregium

called Waasland,[19] which was separated from Brabant by the river Scheldt when it still continued to that point, and is separated from the island of Zuid-Beveland in Zeeland by the same river now that it is cut, and embraced by the river in its curve. At this point in time it was governed by Servaes van Steelandt,[20] who had the same intentions towards the fatherland as Hembyze and Chimay. When the king's officers arrived there they obtained possession of the entire region straight away by the surrender of its commander, with the towns of Axel and Hulst and the castle called Rupelmonde, a place with some fame in the early history of Flanders. The name derives from a small river named Rupel, which feeds into the Scheldt not very far from the place where Antwerp is right on the opposite side.

29 A little further inland is the town of Aalst, which' garrison (foreign soldiers from England) were still owed a moderate sum in wages, which the Flemish had neglected to pay, even when the enemy's strength, their own poverty, and the example of nearby troops tempted the soldiers to surrender—as it has eventually happened. Brabant and Zeeland however did not neglect to demolish the dykes and let the Scheldt flow in. On the opposite side of the river they placed castles in order to be able to defend their bank and occupy the other.

30 Meanwhile Parma's commanders placed an encampment between Bruges and Ghent in order to fuel rebellions in these two big cities by increasing their problems; they even blocked traffic on the rivers to prevent the import of provisions. Consequently in both places followers of the Roman faith and others who, in the name of peace, embraced the Spanish cause (either from malice or because this was their conviction) stopped **(84)** whispering and looking for opportunities to meet in secret, but drew people over to their views in broad daylight and endowed with the greatest authority; sometimes by persuasion, others by fear. Eventually they gained the upper hand in Bruges because their opponents left; and as soon as this was the case, Chimay broke out.

31 When loyal magistrates had brought this news to Orange, an attempt was made to have Chimay arrested by the head of the garrison. However Chimay had already neutralised this man by presenting him with gifts. Moreover he took advantage of the occasion by telling the people that he and the city had become the target of their opponents' machinations, and by taking urban functions and offices away from some people, and giving them to others who shared his intentions. With the help of the latter he thus brought the city back under the Catholic religion and obedience to the king. Under the same conditions he surrender of the town of Damme was realised, and that of the free conglomerate which, having in the past been exempt from obedience to Bruges and the heaviest agricultural taxation, is called the *Brugse Vrije*, and which in the States of Flanders has the right to a vote of equal weight to that of the biggest cities. Ypres too could no longer hold out merely hoping for a general peace while suffering the evils of the siege—it is the third of the main cities in Flanders after Ghent and Bruges. Even Ghent was present at these talks, via the employment of delegates, a truce, and hostages.

32 However the city was saved by Hembyze's failure to conceal his fraud properly. For he wanted to hand over Dendermonde (which by orders of Orange was anxiously guarded by Lord Ryhove[21]) to the Spaniard in order to receive twice the thanks, and did so too openly to go unnoticed. When others intervened to block this abominable plan, he came out to occupy the town hall, with the counsellors locked in, using the army unit which he had been given as a guard. By both deeds he alienated the people so much that they condemned him for treason, and dealt with it with the death penalty. This greybeard, who filled the

infaustae ambitionis documentum, functus amplissimis honoribus senex, et diu secundis usus vulgi studiis, quem eo deripuit civilis contentio, ut sceleris magnitudine etiam misericordiam consumeret. Prostrato partium duce, quanquam tumultus retardesceret, per tempus aliquod res eorum validiores fuere, qui pacificationis insidias arguebant. Sed inclusam pene urbem, et hostilibus copiis circumsessam Parmensis satis habuit fami et discordiae relinquere.

33 Maior animo spes et labor, dum ipsi florentes copiae, et quod roboris erat Foederatis gentibus irrito Zutfaniae obsidio attinetur, superare Scaldim; adsitamque ei fluvio Antverpiam, Belgicarum urbium nobilissimam, quae acceptos e Zelandia commeatus toti Brabantiae (**85**) dividit. Hac ratione urbs una bello, caeterae penuria et metu petebantur. Transposita igitur parte exercitus depellit praesidiarias Belgarum naves: utramque amnis ripam complet tormentis et milite. Sed Antverpienses, ubi obiecta Flandriae hosti cessisse intellexerant, ad navigationem muniendam, inter alia castella ex humo excitarant duo, quorum alterum infra urbem ad vicum Lilloum erat, alterum Flandrica in ora positum retro Hulstum, Wasiae oppidum, respiciebat. Hoc, quia semifacto opere erat, oppugnatum captumque est: illud multa cum Hispanorum clade Teliniacus defendit Lanovii filius, paternarum virtutum imitator.

34 At ingruentia undique pericula mors Arausionensis impulit, importunissimo tempore, si Belgas spectamus, quorum res turbidae et afflictae eius poterant unius consilio regi; sin ipsum, immature occidisse videri non potest, qui fortunae publicae, cui suam arctissime devinxerat, crescentibus malis ereptus est. Nam post illius obitum intestina seditione, et continuis hostium victoriis oppressa iacuit, donec in filio respublica et quodammodo ipse revivisceret. Delphis in Hollandia a Balthasare Gerardi, Burgundione, glande traiectus est; qui proscriptionis praemio, seu partium fervore concitus, mira animum firmitate, ut ad facinus, ita ad facinoris poenam duraverat. Nec defuere ipsi laudatores; quanquam Italus Parmensis, cum publica ob amotum hostem gaudii signa postularentur, famam et iura belli reveritus, erubuit permittere.

35 Una morientis ad Deum vox fuit, Miserere populi. Nec dubitant qui senescentem interius novere, quin varietas casuum, quos prima ab aetate quinquaginta ultra annos pertulerat, maxime, ex quo suscepta causa plena invidiae, plena difficultatis, armis et ira potentiorum, obtrectatione aequalium, saepe et vulgi offensis afflictabatur, ut tolerantiam rerum humanarum, ita seriam pietatem illi firmaverit. Quare, ut corpore nihil fracto laboribus, ita animo semper excelso egit, secundis adversisque iuxta immotus.

highest offices and profited for a long time from the enthusiastic support of the populace, shows us a signal example of fatal ambition: the civil conflict dragged him along so far that the magnitude of his crime even consumed the compassion for his person. Now that the party leader was felled, and although the chaos cooled down for a while, the side pointing at the deceit wrapped up in the peace plan were in a stronger position for some time. But since the city was almost entirely locked in and surrounded by enemy forces, Parma did not need to do much more than leaving it alone to hunger and discord.

33 Instead he had a greater challenge on his mind: to get across the Scheldt, as long as his army was in full strength and what forces the United Provinces possessed were detained in the pointless siege of Zutphen; and to subdue Antwerp, the greatest city in the Low Countries, situated on this river, and the port which all transport from Zeeland towards Brabant passes through. **(85)** In this way one city was attacked with arms, all the others with scarcity and fear. Therefore Parma put part of his army across the river and dispelled the Netherlands vessels that protected the city; then he started filling the banks on both sides with artillery and soldiers. When the people of Antwerp realised that the area of Flanders facing them had fallen into enemy hands, they acted to protect their shipping and, among others, very quickly erected two castles, one downstream from the city near the village of Lillo, the second placed on the opposite side of the water working backwards on the town of Hulst in Waasland. The latter one was attacked however and captured, because it was only half finished; the first one was defended, causing heavy losses to the Spanish, by the lord of Téligny, a son of De la Noue and emulator of his qualities.[22]

34 Then however the danger mounting from all sides received a new impulse from William's death, at a time most unfavourable for the Low Countries which in their troubled and afflicted state could only be ruled successfully by his prudence. Seen from his own perspective it is hard to maintain that his death came too early, given the rising tide of trouble among which he was snatched away from the country to which he had so intimately tied his own fortune. For after his decease, the Low Countries ran into serious trouble as a result of the internal discord and the never-ending row of enemy victories, until the day the commonwealth and in a way the Prince himself revived in the person of his son. At Delft in Holland he was shot through with a bullet by Balthasar Gerards, a Burgundian. Whether Gerards was driven to this act by the reward that was put on William's head or by fanaticism, he carried to the end his deed and the punishment for it with amazing resolve. Nor did even this man remain without praise; although Parma, an Italian nonetheless, out of fear for his own reputation and the laws of war, shrunk back from granting a public celebration of the elimination of the enemy when these were asked for.

35 While he was dying his only words were to God: "Have mercy on this people." Among the people who knew him in his final years there was no doubt that the vicissitudes of fortune which he had experienced from his earliest childhood over the fifty years of his life—especially from the time he took a cause so full of hatred and difficulties upon him, and suffered from the wrath and the violence of the mighty, the calumny of his fellow noblemen, and often even the attacks of the people—invested him with endurance in the face of human hardship as well as the deepest piety. It was this that left him as high-minded as he was physically unbroken by the burden he was carrying, equally untouched by prosperity as by adversity.

4.34. *Assassination of William of Orange* by R. de Hoge and Jan Luyken (E&K 62)

4.37. *Tomb monument for William of Orange* by Jan Luyken (E&K 63)

36 Reticendum non puto in signum abstinentiae et infelicitatis, adeo nihil Arausionensi, praeter gloriam ex bello civili, cessisse, ut rem privatam, qua ultro publicam adiuverat, reliquerit perturbatissimam quadruplicis matrimonii liberis. Prima illi nupserat Egmundo ex sanguine Burae et Lerdami comes, ex qua Philippum sustulit, quem Hispani captivum abduxere; et Mariam, (**86**) Hohenloii comitis postea coniugem. Altera ex uxore, Ducis Saxonum, Electoris Germanici, filia, natus una cum sorore Mauritius. Tertium Arausionensis matrimonium habuit Borbonii generis, et inde liberos virilis sexus nullos, filias complures, quibus per Germaniam Galliamque amplissimae conditiones obtigerunt. Ultima excepit morientem Coliniaci, maris apud Gallos quondam praefecti, et partium ducis, filia, Henrici Frederici mater.

37 Nullum unquam funus tanto populi luctu, et prope desperatione, celebratum est. Solatio fuit, quod Mauritium, qui tum decimo et octavo aetatis anno Lugduni Batavorum sapientiae studiis inhaerebat, ob indolem virtutis, et ut parentem libertatis auctorem grata memoria remunerarentur, publicae curae licuit imponere. Huic pater, in haereditatis divisione, inter ceteras possessiones, Flissingam situ invictissimam, unaque Veriam, Zelandiae oppida, assignarat; empta sibi ab his qui Marchionis titulo tenuerant, eoque nomine in Ordinum illic conventu locum principem: praeter quod, ipsa quoque illa duo oppida, ius suffragii, iuxta Middelburgum, Zirixaeam,[35] Goesam, Tolam acceperant, Abbatis, qui olim primo loco sententiam dicere solebat, iure intermortuo. Quia vero summum regimen foris petebatur, data adolescenti Hollandiae et Zelandiae praefectura. Vicariam potestatem Hohenloius accepit, qui plurimis armorum experimentis inclaruerat.

38 Frisia vero, in honorem illustris familiae, quo externis nobilitatibus respublica esset commendatior, Wilhelmo, Iohannis Nassavii filio, quem patruus eas in partes iam ante miserat, regenda conceditur; quanquam erant qui civium imperia praeferebant, intempestive avidi libertatis, cui tolerandae impares, tunc maxime in discordias ibant, dum, summam curam ad se trahentes, hinc iudicum consessus, introductum sub Burgundico principatu morem in exemplum trahens, inde Frisiorum Ordinum legati, recens institutus Arausionensis consilio et vicinorum exemplo consessus, urbium ille, hi nobilium, agros tenentium, opibus nituntur: quas ad occasiones intentus Verdugo, cum exercitu praepolleret, terrori adiungebat clementiae famam.

39 Sed Wilhelmus, iusta moderatione medius, primos, qui acerrimi, dissidentium impetus inhibuit; interim finibus se undique obiiciens, praeter populabundos excursus nihil hosti concessit. Sic (**87**) tempus datum orta certamina colloquiis et arbitriis componere: legatisque Ordinum, quae conventui iussa exsequi et quotidiana Reipublicae ordinare: iudices, de litibus post omnes iussi cognoscere, de

[35] Zirixaeam *1657* Sirixaeam *1658*

36 To demonstrate his selflessness and lack of luck I think it should not go unmentioned that Orange derived so little profit from the civil war, apart from glory, that he left his private estate (from which he had supported the public cause all of his own accord) in a state of complete disruption to his children from four marriages. First the countess of Buren and Leerdam, from the house of Egmond married him,[23] who gave him Philip, whom the Spanish abducted in captivity, and Maria, **(86)** who later married the count of Hohenlohe. From his second wife, a daughter of the duke of Saxony,[24] one of the German Electors, Maurice was born, as well as a daughter.[25] Orange's third marriage was with one of the Bourbon family,[26] from which he had no male children and several daughters, who have obtained splendid alliances in various places in Germany and France. His last spouse, who witnessed his death, was a daughter of De Coligny,[27] formerly the admiral of France and leader of the [Huguenot] party; she is the mother of Frederick Henry.

37 No funeral was ever conducted with such popular lament, and almost desperation. One source of consolation was that it was possible to install Maurice, who was just then in his eighteenth year and immersed in the study of Wisdom at Leiden,[28] at the head of the common cause, both because of his in-born courage and in order to reward his father, the founder of our freedom, by grateful commemoration. In the division of the inheritance his father had left him, among other possessions, the towns of Vlissingen, in an unconquerable place, and Veere, both in Zeeland. Orange had bought them from the former owners who possessed them under the title of Marquis, and because of that held the first position in the States of Zeeland;[29]—even apart from the fact that these two cities as well, together with Middelburg, Zierikzee, Goes and Tholen, had received the right to vote, while the abbot's rights (who used to speak his vote first) had ceased to be effective. However because a candidate to receive the supreme power was being looked for abroad, the young man was given the stadtholdership of Holland and Zeeland. As his deputy the count of Hohenlohe was appointed, who had achieved fame by a long row of military operations.

38 The government of Friesland however was assigned to William Louis,[30] a son of John of Nassau,[31] as a sign of honour to that noble family which would raise the status of the republic in the eyes of foreign nobility; his uncle had sent him to that region already before. This happened in spite of the fact that some expressed a wish for a civil government, driven by an ill-timed eagerness for freedom, which they were unable to handle, as they broke into conflicts right at that time. From one side the supreme court tried to obtain the supreme power, referring to a practice introduced under the Burgundian princes, and leaning on the resources of the cities; from the other side the delegates in the States of Friesland (the meeting that had been instituted recently on the advice of Orange and after the example of the neighbouring provinces[32]) did the same, leaning on the wealth of the nobility, that is, the landowners. Verdugo,[33] always eager for such a chance as his army put him in a dominant position, complemented the fear he inspired with a reputation of clemency.

39 William Louis however with proper restraint placed himself between the parties and stopped the first assaults of the quarrellers, which are always the most aggressive. Meanwhile he took up the defence of all the borders, giving the enemy no chances except for a few rapacious incursions. This **(87)** gave him time to employ verdicts and negotiations to settle the conflicts which had risen: to the delegates of the States the duty to execute the decisions of the meeting and look after the day-to-day government of the State; to the court the task of speaking the final verdict in legal disputes, and the exclusive decision about death

4.38. *Portrait of Count Hohenlohe* (no signature)

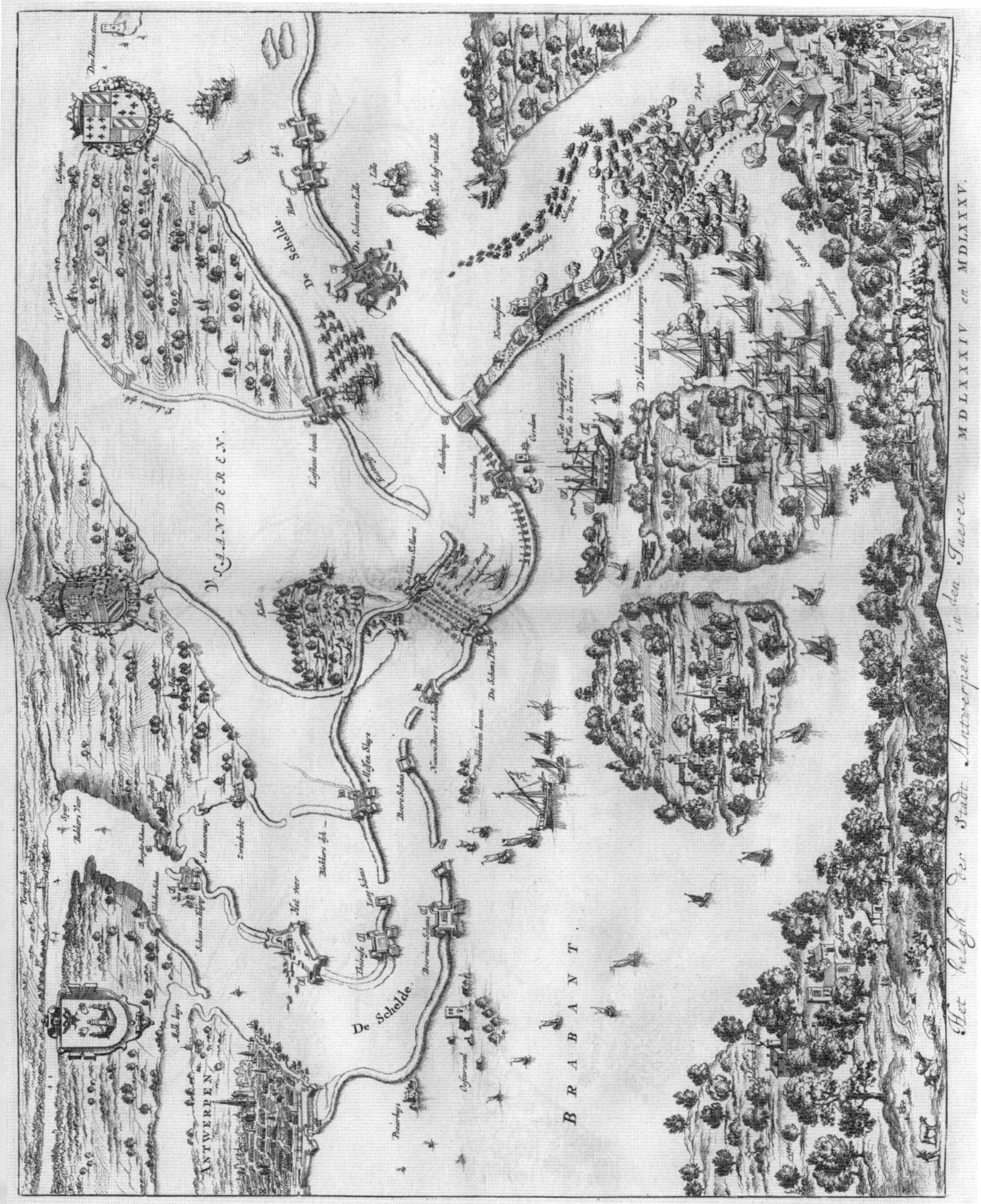

5.2. *Siege of Antwerp* by Jan Luyken (E&K 64)

capite soli, ut sub Burgundica domo: praeterea cum praefecto oppidanorum magistratuum electiones regere, ut studiis intactiores, nisi quod Leovardia et Franekera ius legendi sibi tenuere.

40 Oppida, quae olim haud aliter quam vici, in tres regiones, Ostergoam, Westergoam, Septemsilvas distributi, inter eos sententiam dixerant, aucto per bellum et usu et auctoritate, tum in conventu, tum in illo novo legatorum consessu tertiam imperii partem accepere, non tanta tamen concordiae fide, ut non pressa odia interdum erumperent; praesertim ubi de novis oneribus disceptabatur, in quibus valere maioris partis decreta vetabat hic, ut apud vicinas nationes, mos sub principatu haud imprudenter introductus, libertati periculosus, ni pro iure succedant prudentia et publici amor.

41 Quo magis admirandam ego, per omnem belli historiam, et istis maxime temporibus, arbitror Batavum fortitudinem, quos non sociorum ab omni latere defectio, non aucta continuas inter clades tributa unquam fregerunt, non illa mors ducis, ut pacem poscerent, rati eius nominis illecebra deditionem trahi.

42 At Parmensis, velut Arausionensi bellatum hactenus foret, quem defectionis ruptorumque foederum auctorem divina nunc ultio mactasset, ipsos ad poenitentiam, et vetus obsequium revocabat: quae postquam constanter vidit repudiata, coeptum Scaldis obsidium perficere proximum arbitratus, Brabantiae aggeres castellis instruit, aperitque idoneis locis, ut amnem adiacentibus superfunderet. Deinde omisso Lilloo, quod aliquamdiu frustra obsederat, subito Tenerimundam versus (haec pars est eius Flandriae, pro qua comites iam olim neutri regno fidem debuere) rapit exercitum, et aqua moenibus abacta, milites praesidio relictos deditionem facere cogit, missaque trans Scaldim parte copiarum, ut Bruxella Antverpiae commerciis abscinderetur, Vilvordam capit, quod oppidum ad Sinnam amnem interiacet.

43 Simul Gandavenses, quod Hollandorum arma alibi occupabantur, nulla spe auxilii, imminentem necessitatem festina pactione praeveniunt, conciliatore Campiniaco, qui, captivus ea in urbe, liberaque in custodia habitus, legati officium tuto fungebatur. Sed et (**88**) Ricardoti celebratur solertia, quod leges deditioni praescribens, sacrorum diversitatem repudiaturus, non ante prae se tulit, quam inclinatis ad pacem omnium animis, recedere tutum non erat; et alterum eiusdem commentum, quo sex e civibus, ad explendam ultionem, Parmensis arbitrio exceperat, magno proventui fuit, dum aequale omnibus periculum singuli pro se deprecantur. Nec omisit Parmensis, priorum gnarus et in posterum providens, arcem reponere, quae civitatis immodestiam coerceret: totiusque iam Flandriae potens (praeter oppida maritima duo, Clusam et Ostendam,) commeatus bellique copias inde adventantes adiuvit, deducta fossa ad eam ripae partem, quam castris insederat.

penalties, as it had been in the times of the House of Burgundy; furthermore together with the stadtholder they were to control the election of the urban magistrates, to keep them free of faction influences (although Leeuwarden and Franeker reserved the right to these elections for themselves).

40 Formerly the towns had a judicial arrangement among themselves, precisely like the villages, which are divided into three regions, Oostergo, Westergo and Zevenwolden. Now that the war had increased both their experience and their authority, they joined the [States] assembly as well as the above-mentioned new meeting of the delegates as a third party in power. Their unity was not so reliable however that there weren't from time to time eruptions of suppressed hatred, especially when new taxation was debated. In these matters a majority vote cannot force a decision, according to a rule that was introduced (here and in the neighbouring provinces) in the times of the princes,[34] which is a very wise rule, but also dangerous to liberty if strict legality does not give way to prudence and devotion to the public cause.

41 All the more admirable I think is the courage of the Dutch throughout the history of this war but especially in these days, as they were never broken by the defections of their allies on every side, or the rising taxation among the never-ending row of disasters, nor by the death of their leader, so as to beg for peace, as they considered that the seduction of that word carried the reality of surrender.

42 Now Parma made a call to them to repent and to return to their former obedience, as if up to this point the war had been against William of Orange, and now divine revenge had slain him as the instigator of defection and the breaking of alliances. When he saw that this was steadfastly refused, he decided that his next step was to complete the occupation of the Scheldt which he had begun; he built castles on the river dikes on the Brabant side and opened the dykes in suitable locations to let the river flow over the adjacent fields. Next, leaving Lillo aside, which he had besieged in vain for some time, he suddenly pulled his army towards Dendermonde (in that part of Flanders for which, already in the distant past, the counts owed obedience neither to the French nor the German monarch). There he drove the water out of the defence moat and forced the soldiers who had been left as a garrison to surrender the town. Next he put part of his troops across the Scheldt, to cut off trade between Brussels and Antwerp; and seized Vilvoorde, a town between these cities on the river Sinne.

43 Straight away the people of Ghent forestalled the imminent emergency (because the forces of Holland were occupied elsewhere and there was no hope of receiving support) by accepting a hastily prepared peace. The intermediary here was Champagny[35] who was held in captivity in that city but enjoyed a degree of freedom, and could act as an envoy in safety. Many have also **(88)** remarked about the skills of Richardot,[36] who was drafting the conditions for surrender and wasn't going to make religious freedom one of them, but did not make this known until all were inclined to accept peace and there was no safe way back. Another trick found by him was to have Parma pick six citizens out of the total number, to fulfil his revenge on; which was of great use as everyone tried individually to avert the danger that threatened them all equally. Neither did Parma neglect, as he was aware of the past and prepared for the future, to rebuild the castle, to restrain the intemperateness of the citizens. Now he was in control of all of Flanders (except only two towns on the coast, Sluis and Ostend) and boosted the flow of goods and military provisions coming from that direction by digging a canal to that part of the river bank where he had put up his camp.

44 Inter haec, ad quos Antverpiae cura pertinebat, sociorum opem implorare, nova instituere tributa, per Belgicam et Angliam conscribere militem; nec certe ullius rei obsessis maior copia fuit. Nam praeter classiarios centuriae fere octoginta, sedecim turmae Brabantiam tuebantur. Sed incertum urbis imperium senatores, magistratus, centuriones plebis, praepositi militares distrahebant, nimia regentium turba: eoque perniciosius id vitium, quia inundationes, et alia publice profutura, privati commodi ratione, avertebantur. Vicini, quos altricis omnium urbis periculum spectabat, alii alium respicientes, auxiliandi tempora, dum nondum hosti firmatae sedes, praetermisere: sero, cum ultima urgerent, opes et vitam profundere libuit, nemini profutura. Maxime autem consilia Belgarum frustrata est accitae foris potentiae exspectatio: nam eo angustiarum deventum erat, ut vellent regnis accrescere, nec admitterentur.

45 Regis quidem Hispaniarum vires brevi immensum adauctae, si Belgas recuperaret, et labore armorum levaretur, iuxta positis formidabiles erant: nec ullus iam Arausionensis, qui sub onere fatiscentes, et tot cladibus afflictos sua fortitudine in spem meliorum erigeret. Nam ille quidem ita comis fuerat et popularis, ut nunquam libertatem aut dignitatem suam cuiquam gratificaretur, neque detegendis vitiis parceret, supra omnes positus avaritiae suspiciones: quo nomine admirabilem, simul aetate, genere, experientia gratum, plerique iudicio, alii assuetudine venerabantur. Hoc collapso, etiam obsequium concidit, ut sine externae potestatis firmamento restitui non posset: nec enim plebs tantum nullo fulgore eminentem, et tot nuper infortuniis concussam procerum (**89**) auctoritatem coeperat contemnere: sed et miles imparatus obsequio: et contra imperiis vetus prudentia aberat.

46 Inter quae via patebat Parmensis artibus, servitium amicis nominibus velantis. Quare visum occurrere desperationi, simulque rex Gallorum et Angliae regina misere, qui luctum ducis, et caeterorum casuum moestitiam solarentur, notabili argumento, vicinos principes, ut suis Batavos opibus et constantiae interdum relinquere, ita periculis non defuturos.

47 Sed dubitatum fuit utrius regimen praeoptaretur: nam invisa Gallorum imperia per Italiam, Anglorum per Galliam Hiberniamque memorabantur: apud hos, populo consuli, parco usu tributorum: illic plus leges valere, nec infinitam regni potestatem. Apud Gallos, mores pretio corruptos, magnoque emi ut patriae serviatur; Anglis dura dilectus, dura in pupillos iura: quae mala ut primum pactis caveantur, paulatim exemplo serpere. Sed religio cum Anglia communis, quam per Gallias atteri aut evelli odiis crudelibus et perfidiis: hinc contra, spes Borboniorum, qui

44 Meanwhile the men charged with the protection of Antwerp begged their allies for help, instituted new taxes, and enlisted troops throughout the Low Countries and England; with certainty nothing was available in greater abundance in the besieged city. For apart from the sailors Brabant was protected by eight thousand cavalry and sixteen squadrons of cavalry. However supreme authority in the city was uncertain, as it was torn asunder by the council, the magistrate, the commanders of the civic guard, and the military leadership: too big a crowd of captains, and an evil which was all the more dangerous as it meant that inundations and other measures which would have helped the public cause were prevented for the sake of private interests. The neighbours, who were equally threatened by the danger to the city that fed all, let the time pass in which they could have sent assistance, while the enemy's positions were not yet firmly settled, by waiting for each other. Only when it was too late, and the end was near, did people feel ready to sacrifice life and goods, when no one would benefit any more. But the greatest obstacle to a strategy on the Low Countries side was the expectation to be joining a foreign power: for the emergency had reached such heights that they wanted to be absorbed by a kingdom, but found all doors locked.

45 The powers of the king of Spain had increased enormously in short order and were, if he would recover the Low Countries and be relieved of the burden of the war, a source of fear to his royal equals. Moreover there was no one left like Orange, with his ability to restore people who were bending under the burden and wounded by so many disasters, to new hopes by his own strength and courage. For Orange was friendly and open to everyone, but in such a way that he never sacrificed his independence or dignity for the sake of a particular person, or turned a blind eye to reprehensible lapses, being placed as he was above any suspicions of greed. Because of this he was admired, and loved at the same time because of his age, birth, experience: honoured by most for their judgement of him, out of habit by others. When he fell, obedience collapsed as well, even to such a degree as to be irreparable without the support of a foreign power. For not only did the populace begin to despise the authority of the elite, **(89)** which had lost every brilliance to recommend it and was shaken by so many recent setbacks; but the military was refusing obedience as well, while on the other hand those in charge lacked the wisdom they had of old.

46 In this situation the way was open to machinations by Parma, who was offering servitude in a cover of friendship. For this reason it was decided to respond to their desperation, and both the king of France and the English queen sent envoys to bring solace to these people grieving over their leader's death and their other misfortunes; an unmistakable proof that the neighbouring princes, while they had left the Dutch to their own resources and endurance for some time, would also not leave them alone in their hour of danger.

47 There was a debate however as to which government had to be opted for first; for the stories went round of how the French had made their rule hated in Italy, and the English in France and Ireland. With the latter, the people's interests are important, and taxation is kept within limits; with the first, the laws carry great weight, and the power of the king is not unlimited. In France, culture and character have been spoilt by the desire for profit, and one needs to pay a high price to serve the fatherland. In England levying is a harsh practice and they have harsh laws with respect to orphans; evils which, although at first it was tried to ban them by means of covenants, later crept back in following bad examples. However, religion was shared with the English, while cruel hatred and faithlessness put it under pressure of prosecution and extermination throughout France; then again, there was the prospect

eadem sacra propugnabant; inde, ambigua successio, et inter inhiantes Scotorum regina, Romae et Hispanis devincta, prospiciebatur. Ita certabant res praesentes et ratio venturi. Ingens Gallis et propemodum par hostili potentia: minores Britanniae, sed maritimae vires. Praelata est Gallia, Anglis ultro suadentibus, qui se fassi infirmiores, subsidia duntaxat, et acceptis pignoribus, offerebant. Ita veteres et renovatas Francisci facto inimicitias temporum necessitudo evicit: arcanumque ingens patefactum est, posse Belgas sub domino esse, non posse sub Hispano.

48 Nam minora multo postulabantur quam quae Francisco praescripta fuerant, et quae secretiora habebant legati mandata, metu offensae, statim aperuere: ex his etiam circumcisa quae invisae erant libertatis, puta, ut Ordinibus iniussu Regis convenire liceret, senatus e Belgis esset, praefecti et magistratus e nominatis legerentur, inque omnibus honoribus, eius religionis, quae tum sola per istas partes recepta erat, ratio haberetur: quanquam erant nationes quae ad ista remittenda non consenserant. Quibus agitatis diu, lentiore colloquio quam praesentes necessitates ferebant, invito non minus Rege quam Belga, accidit, ne iuncti adversus Hispanum imminentem, alter alterius ope rem[36] statumque firmarent. Laetari se honore, et uti voluisse, sed impediri intestino tumultu Henricus imputavit.

49 Nam, (**90**) Lotharingorum familiam, invidiosae iam olim per Galliam potentiae, Philippus eo maxime tempore, imminutionem[37] virium suarum metuens, arcanis opibus in spes magnas erexerat; qui, facta coniuratione, Romanae religionis tutelam, dissentientium poenas, tributorum levamenta, et alia captandae plebi iactantes, Regem timoris manifestum, quantum ipsis plura largiebatur, tanto insolentius contempsere: ac postquam orbitas ipsius, mortuus frater, e propinquo Carolus Borbonius senectute et sacerdotio invalidus, caeteri a Romano pontifice devoti, successionem fecerant incertam, tandem apertius innuebant, venire suum a Carolo Magno genus, cuius stirpe deiecta, occupatam a Capeto regiam sex per secula detineri. Horum libidine Henricus, spem pacis socordiae praetendens, agi se diu ferrique passus est; donec, erumpentibus in rebellionem dissidiis, sero didicit irritatam cedendo audaciam. Igitur, ea per impedimenta Rege absterrito, ne id quidem obtentum, ut, matre aut Navarreno nomen praebente, Regis beneficium dissimularetur, clausique limitum Gallicanorum transitus penuriam hostibus facerent.

[36] ope rem *1658* operem 1657 (*fortasse* operam?)
[37] imminutionem *1658* immunitionem *1657*

of the Bourbon succession, who were fighting for the same religion; while in England the succession was uncertain and among the eager candidates one could see the queen of the Scots, subservient to Rome and the Spaniards. And thus there was a conflict between the present and a calculation of the future. The power of the French was enormous and more or less equal to that of the enemy; those of Britain were smaller, but counted at sea. In the end France carried the day, at the advice of the English themselves, who acknowledged that they were weaker, and in any case offered auxiliary forces, after taking pledges. In this way the urgency of the circumstances overcame ancient enmities renewed by Anjou's actions, and a big secret came to light: that the Lowlanders can live under a monarchy, only not the Spanish monarchy.

48 For the demands were much smaller than those once presented to Anjou, and the envoys revealed the more secret instructions which they had right at the beginning, for fear of giving offence. Moreover the demands that marked our loathed mentality of freedom were cut, that is, that the States would be allowed to meet without being convened by the king, that the Council of State was to consist of Lowlanders, that stadtholders and magistrates were to be appointed from a pre-selected group, and that in all appointments the religion would be taken into account that was then the sole accepted one in these areas, in spite of the fact that some provinces had not agreed with the withdrawal of these demands. After these negotiations had been carried on for a considerable time, in slower consultations than the urgent necessity allowed, the outcome was—as much to the king's chagrin as to the Lowlanders'—that they would not join forces against the Spanish threat and strengthen each other's realm and position with mutual assistance. Henry explained this by saying that he was delighted by the honour shown to him, and would readily accept the proposals, but was unable to do so because of domestic troubles.

49 Now **(90)** the cause of these was Philip, who feared a loss of influence. By this time especially he had, by secret subsidies, roused the house of Lorraine (which had long been suspect in France because of its power) to great expectations for the future. When this conspiracy was a fact, Lorraine began ostentatiously to protect the Catholic faith, to punish heretics, reduce taxation and other things to please the populace, and to ignore the king, whose fear of them was manifest—and ignore him more insolently the more he granted them. Then, after the succession had become uncertain because of the king's childlessness, the death of his brother, and the fact that of his relatives, Charles of Bourbon was disqualified because of his age and priesthood, and the others were condemned by the pope, those of Lorraine eventually began producing more open intimations that they were descendant of Charlemagne, whose offspring had been unseated, and the throne usurped and occupied by the house of Capet for six centuries. Henry, who dressed up his sloth as commitment to peace, let himself be plundered and manipulated by their lust for power for a long time: until disagreement turned into rebellion, and he realised too late that by making concessions he had stimulated their boldness. And therefore, because the king was deterred by these obstacles, it could not even be obtained that the king's favour would be veiled (his mother or Navarre lending their name) and closure of the French border passages would lead to scarcity among the enemy.

LIBER QUINTUS

1 **(91)** POST longi temporis, et quidem tanta ferentis momenta, factam in Gallia iacturam, ad Elisabetham recursum est, asperiorem hoc ipso, quod secunda rogabatur: tractaeque et illic foederis pactiones, donec validae civitates, auxiliis destitutae, a republica **(92)** desciverunt.

2 Adhuc inter arma et machinas Hispanorum, onustae commeatu ab Hollandia Zelandiaque naves, ubi ventus ferret, Scaldim subvehebantur, tanta certe copia, ut intempestiva magistratuum frugalitate, dum rebus necessariis pretium minuunt, relatum sit frumentum quantovis tempori suffecturum. Et Parmensis, manu multo impar obsessis, nisi per famem, praecluso hoc itinere, victoriam non sperabat: sed ingens amnis latitudo infra urbem, qua ostiis advolvitur, et profundi aestus, quos hucusque Oceanus impellit, terrebant vani laboris metu. Quia tamen una haec ratio obsidendi videbatur, adhibere diligentiam statuit, et aliquid credere fortunae; quam non alias secundiorem expertus est. Nam dum natura obstare operi creditur, neglectae a Batavis diruendi occasiones: ita factum est facillimum, quia difficillimum putabatur.

3 Ab utraque ripa proiectis molibus arctatum flumen, qua minimum patebat, Ordamum Calloumque inter: media eius completa navigiis, quae anchoris, et inter se vinculis continebantur; ac constrata deinde, in usum pontis et speciem. Addita ripis munimenta, et praesidio operis bellicae naves, infraque et supra in flumine ratium compages tignis prominentibus, ut, siquid turbandi operis causa esset immissum, hoc impedimento detineretur. Nemo dubitat, contra imperfectum opus multa utiliter excogitari potuisse, si Belgarum in evertendo studia aedificatorum diligentiam adaequassent: sed hyems tota Parmensi condonata est: cuius diligentiam excitabat novum Philippi beneficium, arce Placentina ipsi reddita, quae Hispanorum praesidio hactenus tenebatur. Vere primo mirari magis licuit consummatam molem, quam exscindere; cum densissimae per utramque ripam machinae arcerent. Naves quin etiam coacto intus tormentario pulvere et saxis fulminantes, et alia, sero usurpata incertis tempestatum et significationum, quibus socios obsessi admonebant, partim et pravo ministrorum obsequio, eventum perdidere. Nec contabulato Scalde aliud restabat, quam per campos, quos amnis inundaverat, inferre commeatus, cui navigationi Caudesteinius agger intercedebat, quem, humentibus Brabantiae pascuis eminentem, quod Belgas fecisse oportebat, munimentis aliquot hostis praeceperat. Hunc missi Antverpia Zelandiaque pariter oppugnavere: et iam tenebant, sed fortissime dimicantes tormentis eminus **(93)** discerpebantur, donec loco cederent.

Book 5

1 After this protracted waste of time in France, and time which so much depended on at that, recourse was sought to Elizabeth, who was all the more intractable because she was now second to be asked. And here too the alliance negotiations dragged on, until the commonwealth **(92)** lost a number of strong cities which could not be given assistance.

2 Even now ships from Holland and Zeeland, heavy with provisions, sailed down the Scheldt, when the winds allowed, right between the Spanish armies and siege engines: in such quantities indeed that the magistrate, in ill-timed parsimony (since the provisions lowered the prices of daily necessities), sent back loads of wheat which would have seen them through indefinitely. And Parma, numerically far inferior to the besieged, saw starvation as his only means to achieve victory, for which he would have to close off this road. However the huge width of the river downstream from the city, where it approaches its mouth, and the deep waves which the sea drives forth up to this point, gave him nightmares of a wasted effort. But because this seemed the only way to besiege the city, he decided to proceed with the greatest commitment, and to rely in part on his good fortune, which he has nowhere found more on his side. For while nature herself seemed to oppose the operation, the Dutch neglected their chances to demolish it: and thus it became a very easy one, precisely because it was considered to be very difficult.

3 From both banks the stream was narrowed by throwing large masses in the water where it was narrowest, between Oordam and Kallo. The middle of the stream was bridged with boats, which were kept in place with anchors and chains between them, then given a layer on top, to provide both the use of a bridge and the sight of it. More bulwarks were added on the banks, and warships in defence of the construction; and upstream as well as downstream, interconnected rafts on the river with protruding beams, so that, if anything were to be sent down in order to upset the construction, this hindrance would stop it. There is no doubt that against the unfinished project many measures could have been employed with success, if the efforts on the Lowlands side had equalled the commitment of the builders. But no, the entire winter was presented to Parma on a tray, and his commitment prompted a new benefice from Philip, that is, that he was given back the castle of Piacenza which Philip had kept with him until then to support the Spanish.[1] When spring came the finished giant could be gaped at rather than eliminated, since a host of defence works on both sides of the river prevented it. Even exploding ships packed full with gunpowder and stones, as well as other means, which were all tried too late, missed their effect because of the uncertainties of the weather and the message traffic by which their allies aimed to notify the besieged, and partly even as a result of disobedience among the executing agents.[2] Now that the Scheldt was covered, nothing else remained than to carry supplies over the fields inundated by the river. These shipments however were prevented by the dyke of Kauwenstein which stood out high over the flooded pastures of Brabant, which the enemy had equipped with a handful of bulwarks—while obviously the Lowlanders should have done this. This dyke was attacked simultaneously by men sent from Zeeland and from Antwerp; and they actually obtained possession of it; but in spite of their heroic combat, they were shot to pieces by cannon from afar **(93)** until they gave up their positions.

4 (1585) Ea clades spes ultimas infregit; tandemque interseptis auxiliis imminentes rei frumentariae angustias sueta commerciis civitas non toleravit, cum aliquanto ante Bruxellam et Machliniam necessitas eadem, et annixi turbatores in Parmensis potestatem redegissent: quarum conditio durior, quia, rescissis legibus, modus servitutis a Rege petebatur. Ideo quod temporis Antverpiae ad suprema restabat, hoc victoris clementia redempta est; qui et ipse occupandae gloriae properus, utque alias deditiones exemplo incitaret, pleraque indulsit, nisi quod alieni a Romanis sacris quatuor intra[38] annos, constituta re familiari, excedere iubebantur. In ipso ponte, memorabili ad omnem posteritatem opere, Parmensis, victoriae decus, concessum a Rege vellus aureum induit. Mox et arcem, qua urbem respicit, studio libertatis pridem deiectam, firmando imperio restituit.

5 Multum famae, multum et virium urbs tam clara Hispanicis partibus attulit; non tamen, ut plerique tunc iudicabant, res caeteras in se tractura: quod eventu adeo revictum est, ut Batavi, maximo ad liberandam urbem sumptu ac labore, suspiciones tamen non vitaverint proditae fidei socialis, velut aliorum mala suas in utilitates verterent. At contra, ipsi Aldegondium (namque is urbem rexerat) culpae subdiderunt, qui ad Zelandos reversus, cum primos accusantium impetus et custodiam pertulisset, post honorate habitus, in nulla tamen reipublicae parte, ingenium paci quam bello aptius intra artes privatas et tranquilla studiorum tradidit senectuti.

6 Fracta tot malis et militum virtus, qui, dum spes adhuc erat hostem Antverpia avocandi, Silvam ducis, Hohenloio praeeunte, feliciter ingressi, continuo profugere, per metum et imprudentiam, dum porta et hostibus omissis in praedam ruunt. At Noviomagum, urbem Geldriae cum Dosiburgo oppido, Romanae religionis sectatores adiuti partium fortuna victori adiecere. Eandemque circa regionem passim clades, ducum temeritate, aut gregariorum ignavia. Moerorem publicum auxit miserabilis exsulum populus, Brabanti et Flandri, religionis ergo, aut quia pactionibus diffidebant, propter iniquos interpretes, commerciorum denique inopia, in Hollandiam insulasque diffusi, qui exhaustas bello urbes viresque in maius extulere, ingens mox fortunae melioris auspicium.

7 Vix interim Anglicani foederis exspectatio animos sustinebat. Delatum Elisabethae imperium (**94**) diximus. Sed prudens foemina detrectavit invidiam interversae dominationis: neque tam arcta societate, rebus ambiguis, famam fortunasque suas implicuit. Consultius visum, secreta habere per Belgicam potentiae munimenta: et modicis ibi viribus, et missis iterum qui Americae oras popularentur, Hispanum fatigare, donec flexis in pacem animis amoliretur suspectos exercitus. Auxilia autem promisit, id se iure facere scripto testata, quo morem

[38] intra *Boot* ultra *1657, 1658*

4 This defeat broke the last hope that remained; for now that military support was finally cut off, the citizenship, accustomed to having the benefits of trade, could not bear the prospect of bread shortages, since only a little earlier the same emergency, and troublemakers taking advantage of it, had driven Brussels and Mechelen back in Parma's hands. Their situation was very harsh because their privileges had been cut back and they had had to implore the king for a moderation of their servitude. For precisely this reason what little time remained for Antwerp until the end was sold for clemency from her conqueror, who granted most of the demands, out of a haste to get hold of his triumph, and stimulate other surrenders by this example. The only exception was that non-Catholics were commanded to leave within four years, but with the possibility to re-arrange their possessions. On the aforementioned bridge, a monument for all future generations, Parma donned the Golden Fleece, awarded by the king as a decoration for his victory. Soon, in order to strengthen his rule, he re-erected the citadel which had been taken down in zeal for liberty, in an orientation which overlooks the city.

5 To the Spanish side the famous city of Antwerp contributed much renown and a great deal of power; but she would not, as many thought at the time, draw all the rest with her—a prediction which the facts refuted so much in the end that the Northerners, in spite of their enormous efforts and spending to release the city, did not escape the suspicion of having betrayed the loyalty to their allies, as if they would turn the misfortunes of others to their own profit.[3] No, to the contrary, they burdened Marnix van Saint-Aldegonde (who had governed the city during the siege) with the guilt; Marnix returned to Zeeland and first had to suffer custody and attacks from accusers. Later he was held in high esteem, but never assumed another political role; he dedicated his mind, more at home in peacetime than war, in his final years to private pursuits and the quietness of his study.

6 A setback of such magnitude also dealt a blow to the courage of the soldiers. When there was still hope of drawing the enemy away from Antwerp, they had made good use of a chance to enter Den Bosch under the command of Hohenlohe, but now turned to flight straight away for fear and ignorance, chasing after booty oblivious of the city gates and the enemy. Nijmegen however, a city in Guelders, as well as the town of Doesburg, were adjoined to the victor by adherents of the Roman faith riding on the wave of good fortune for their side. All over the same region defeats were suffered, caused either by rashness of the officers or cowardice of their subordinates. The general sadness was increased further by the miserable host of refugees from Brabant and Flanders, who had fled for the sake of their faith, from distrust of the peace treaty, or an unfair interpretation of it, or finally because of a lack of possibilities for commerce. They spread out over Holland and the islands[4] and lifted the forces of the cities, exhausted by the war, to a higher level, and soon proved to be an unmistakeable omen of better times.

7 Meanwhile however the prospect of an alliance with England was barely enough to keep up morale. We have already mentioned that sovereignty **(94)** had been offered to Elizabeth. But the wise woman foresaw the accusation of having pilfered someone else's dominion: and avoided the involvement of her own fame and fortune by such a close tie in doubtful circumstances. It seemed wiser to have secret bases of support spread over the Low Countries, and, while keeping moderate forces there, and sending forces over every now and then to destroy the American colonies, to exhaust the Spaniard, until he would turn his thoughts to peace and remove the hated troops. However, she promised help, testifying her

5.4. *Explosion of the ship-bridge at Antwerp* by E. Decker

PHILIPS VAN MARNIX,
HEER VAN SANT ALDEGONDE,
BURGERMEESTER DER STADT ANTWERPEN.

5.5. *Portrait of Marnix van St. Aldegonde* (no signature)

principum oppressos sublevandi, pactas olim Britanniae et Belgarum amicitias, cum Hispanicorum scelerum insectatione, memorabat. Simul religio praetendebatur, cuius securitatem sibi nulla alieni cupidine commendatam, Galliae et Scotiae rebus probabat.

8 Perscriptae foederis leges, pleraeque in eandem formam qua prima societas convenerat, et ut quinque millia peditum, equites mille in Belgis Reginae stipendiis militarent: legatus, qui eius copiis praeficeretur, cum Anglis praeterea duobus, receptus in senatum publicis bellique consiliis interesset: classem struenti Reginae Belgae parem navium numerum adiicerent. Pro restituendis impensis, ubi bellum desiisset, obligatae pignori maritimae urbes Brila et Flissinga, nihil immutato earum regimine, cum Zeburgo Walachriae castello, Anglorum praesidiis traduntur, non sine metu in posterum, quem tunc praesens necessitas averterat.

9 Auxilii Anglicani imperium Robertus comes Licestrius accepit, egregius virtutum simulator, et qui invisos atque infelices Dudleiae gentis spiritus haud ingrata comitate velaret. Origo illi fortunae (nam claritudo generis inter adversa fuerat) a carcere coepit, quo inclusam simul Elisabetham sororis Reginae suspicionibus, non pro rerum praesentium conditione coluerat: unde, per obsequia consortiumque infortunii, conciliatis affectibus (quibus illa muliebriter indulgebat, non tamen ut viriles curas omitteret),[39] ita animum eius erudito luxu permulsit, ut iam regnantis coniugio electus crederetur: quod aemulantium metu quanquam non obtinuit, ad maxima tamen evectus, et, ambiente invidia, valentes inter inimicos illaesus egit.

10 (1586) Advenienti in Batavos obvia populi studia, et procerum assentatio. Nam inerat et vultui sermonique amoena quaedam maiestas, et quasi collapsae fortunae restitutor conspiciebatur: nec liberalitas aberat in literis aut armis eminentes: tantaque festinatio fuit, ut homini extero, et apud suos morum minime inculpato (nam, sublato (**95**) Essexio, domum sibi vacuam nuptiis fecisse dicebatur) ante ullla ingenii experimenta, praefectura totius Belgicae, qualis Caroli temporibus fuerat, et omne terra marique regimen permitteretur, cum pecuniae publicae administratione.

11 Senatus ita illi additus, ut adsessuros e nominatis ipse legeret, et quodammodo omnium suffragiis unus aequaretur. Praecipue grata pietatis species a rerum divinarum ordinatione imperium auspicantis: et recens Valesii ob contraria odium, illum favorabilem fecerat. Erant et qui Arausionensi ante haberent, sperantes minus gratiae datum iri, quanto domesticis opibus et egregiae principis amicitia florenti pro recto tendere expeditius foret. Sed decernebant honores immodicos, alii ambitione, simpliciores demerendae Reginae; quod tamen contra cecidit, ut excusandum

[39] affectibus, (quibus... omitteret,) *1658* affectibus, quibus... omitteret, *1657*

promise in writing, in which she referred to the custom of princes to relieve the oppressed, to the old friendly alliances between Britain and the Low Countries, together with a condemnation of Spanish crimes. At the same time, she pretended to act for the sake of religion, the security of which she demonstrated, by referring to the events in France and Scotland, to be entrusted to her without any desire for another one's possessions.[5]

8 The conditions for the treaty were drafted, most of them in similar vein to those under which the first alliance had been concluded; that is, that five thousand footmen and a thousand cavalry would serve in the Low Countries on wages paid by the queen; that the envoy who would be put at the head of these troops, plus two further Englishmen, would join the Council of State and take part in political and military deliberations; and that the Lowlanders would contribute an equal number of ships to the fleet the queen was building. As a pawn for the restitution of the expenses[6] when the war would be over, the harbour towns of Den Briel and Vlissingen (without changes in their government) were handed over to English garrisons, together with Zeeburg castle on the island of Walcheren,[7] not without fear for the future, which was then suppressed by the necessity of the moment.

9 The command of the English force was given to Robert, Earl of Leicester,[8] an outstanding forger of virtues, who hid the unpopular and unfortunate arrogance of the house of Dudley under very friendly manners. The origin of his success (for his high birth had also worked against him) had been his time in prison, where he had adored Elizabeth, who had been locked up simultaneously because of the suspicions of her sister the queen,[9] without regard for her present circumstances. Dutifulness and shared misfortunes produced mutual feelings—to which she gave herself up, as women do, but not to the extent of abandoning her masculine concerns; and so much did he flatter her mind with sophisticated exuberance that it was believed she had chosen him as her consort now that she had obtained he throne. Although this did not happen because of the fears of his competitors, he was given the highest offices, and in spite of the jealousy waiting in every corner, he moved among powerful enemies without ever getting hurt.

10 At his arrival in the United Provinces he was greeted by the people's enthusiasm and flattery by the elites. For his words and appearance had an air of amicable greatness, and he was looked upon as the saviour of the country's ruined condition.[10] He was generous towards the great men in the fields of literature and warfare; and such haste was made that the governorship of all the Low Countries, as it had been in the times of the Emperor Charles, including the military command on land and sea and the government of the public finances, was granted, before they had obtained any experience of his talent and character, to a foreigner who wasn't of unreproached behaviour at home—for people said that by the elimination of Essex **(95)** he had opened that house to himself for marriage.[11]

11 The Council of State was attached to him in this way that he would appoint the members from a nominated group, and his vote was more or less equal to all the others together. They were particularly pleased with his type of religion, in which the secular power derives from the religious institutions; and his recent quarrel with Anjou[12] because of their differences made him all the more beloved. There were even people who rated him higher than William of Orange, in the expectation that from now on so many fewer individual favours would be granted as it would be easier for Leicester to keep a straight course, given his family wealth and the fact that he enjoyed the friendship of an important crowned head. However they lost the right measure in the offices awarded to him, some driven by ambition, the more

5.9. *Portrait of Robert Dudley, Earl of Leicester* (no signature)

5.20. *Siege of Grave* by Jan Luyken (E&K 65)

illi haberent, quae videri voluit timere, ne recusatum sibi imperium per Licestrii personam ingererent nisi forte gnaram illius ingenii altior suspicio incesserat.

12 Statim, imminens omni potentiae malum, adulatores accessere, quibus impellentibus et ipse delinitus (ut est humani ingenii natura) occasione dominationis, cum iam ab Ordinibus in verba solennis sacramenti et reipublicae insignia adsisceretur, beneficium eorum in ipsos vertit: et, quasi in provinciam missus, occulta cum Anglis maxime hominibus consilia init, qua ratione muniret imperium.

13 Plurimum autem differunt harum nationum ingenia et mores: nam Angli, ut addicte serviunt, ita evecti ad dignitates priorem humilitatem insolentia rependunt: Belgarum est parere et imperare cum modo, nec gens ulla fidelius amat eminentes, aut iisdem, si contemtus adsit, implacabilius irascitur. Quae non expendens Licestrius, ignarus etiam dignitatis suae auctoribus poenitentiam restare, (tantum in Anglo milite, et praesenti fastigio fiduciae erat) indulgere pertinaciae coepit: idque eo periculosius, quia rerum Batavicarum intima nec ipse norat, nec peritioribus auscultabat.

14 Assumti sunt et Belgae in partes, sed quorum alii, rebus domi afflictis per bellum aut luxum, qualicunque servitio paupertatem, ut summum malorum, fugiebant; alii, patria capta, assueti honoribus, et privatae vitae impatientes, non alium videbant insurgendi gradum: caeteri, novorum propter ipsa avidi: quibus deinde, ut sit rebus turbatis, perfidi et hostibus venales miscebantur.

15 Talis Belgarum praesidem cohors obsederat, quae primo in Ordines obliqua convitia iacere, et, (**96**) ubi haec pronis auribus excipiebantur, apertas criminationes a paucorum culpa in cunctos intendere, quasi nihil hosti arcanum, nihil impervium esset apud suis commodis distentam multitudinem. Arausionensis etiam exemplo ad spem dictaturae praeproperam hortabantur, ipso ad omnia credulo, ut cui longa felicitate corruptum iudicium, nec satis discerneret, quanto aliis artibus muliebris gratia, et in libero populo principatus quaererentur. At plebi in Ordines concitandae, quae sponte etiam rectores odit, sub quibus fortunam adversiorem experta est, aerarii patrocinium, res maxime popularis, usurpatur; cum tamen, in eo tractando, tam verum sit, ministris Licestrii fidem, quam ipsi perspicaciam defuisse.

16 Offendit statim plurimos edicto, quo non modo cum subactis Belgarum gentibus et Hispanis negotiationem rescindebat, quae nisi ob certas temporum occasiones hactenus tolerabatur, sed ne in Galliam quidem, aut maritima Germaniae

simple-minded by a desire to please the queen: which however came out precisely wrong, and they had to apologise to her, for she was anxious to be perceived as not wishing that, via Leicester's person, they would land her with the authority she had refused; unless perhaps, conscious of Leicester's character, she had begun to harbour even greater suspicions.[13]

12 Right from the start he was surrounded by flatterers, the evil threatening everyone in power. Driven partly by their admonitions, and partly giving in (as human nature does) to an opportunity for domination, he took the solemn oath before the States and accepted the symbols of supreme power—only to turn to their generosity against them. Like a governor sent to his province he started secret deliberations, mostly with Englishmen, as to the means by which he might consolidate his power.

13 However, the characters and customs of the two nations are very different. For so willingly as the English resign themselves to obedience, in such a way they recompense their earlier humility with brutality once they arrive among the higher ranks. The Lowlanders on the other hand obey and command with measure, and there is no nation which cherishes its superiors with greater loyalty, or becomes more implacably enraged once they lose their respect. Leicester however did not take these differences into account and was unaware that those who had given him his power had left a way open to revoke it (so much confidence did he have in the English soldiery, and in his elevation of the moment); and gave free reign to his obstinacy. This was all the more dangerous because neither did he have any intimate knowledge of Dutch politics himself, nor did he consult people better informed.

14 There were also Lowlanders who joined his side. Some of them had suffered damage to their private wealth from the war or luxurious living and were looking to escape poverty, as if this was the worst of evils, via servitude to whomever. Others had seen their region of origin captured by the enemy and, being accustomed to high office or unwilling to become private citizens, saw no other road to ascendancy. All the others were out for revolt for its own sake; among whom finally, as always in troubled times, there were traitors and mercenaries even available to the enemy.[14]

15 Such was the regiment surrounding the governor of the Low Countries. They began by spreading indirect incriminations against the States, **(96)** and when these were willingly received, they pronounced open accusations against all States members based on the errors of a few, as if there existed no secrets for an enemy, nor any closed doors in a multitude so focused on their individual profit. They even adduced Orange's example to encourage a speedy takeover, while Dudley himself was willing to believe anything, as does a man who had his judgment spoilt by too much success and who doesn't discern how far apart are the techniques by which the favours of a woman are procured, and those by which the kingship of a free people. In any case, in order to pit the people against the States (while even of their own accord the people will develop a loathing of their governors when they have experienced adversity under their rule), he put the treasury, a thing most precious to everyone, under his own personal protection. Unfortunately however in the execution of this plan his ministers displayed a lack of integrity no smaller than Leicester's own failure in sharp-sightedness.

16 Straight away he angered a majority by imposing a law which forbade trade not only with the areas of the Lowlands living in subjection and with the Spaniards (which had so far been allowed except in cases dictated by particular circumstances), but he even wanted that traffic stopped towards France and the coastal regions of Germany, as he claimed that a

transferri merces volebat, quod obtenderet rerum penuria debellari hostem posse, si nec ex Britannia nec ex Belgica ullis copiis iuvaretur: incogitato, merces esse multas, nec hosti necessarias, et Batavis superfluentes. Sapientiores iudicabant assentantium avaritiae obtemperatum, qui venalem apud se exportandi licentiam, aut ex delationibus lucra animo antecepissent; auctaque fides, cum Ringaltius, sub Albano quondam et Requesenio quaesturis exercitus, mox peculatus crimine aspersus, tunc vero flagrantissima apud Licestrium gratia, ius ex edicto inquirendi in tabulas mercatorum et litteras accepit, contra vetera instituta, quae maximam partem habent libertatis, amovere a cuiusque re privata speculatorem.

17 Ergo cum aliae gentes, ad quos bellum non pertinebat, arceri Oceano et hostium commerciis non possent, compendio duntaxat a Batavis averso, quo uno res hactenus steterat, magna mercatorum multitudo patriis urbibus emigrabant. Nam Angli quidem facilius mercaturae damnum patiebantur, gens praedis laetior, et tunc, egregia belli specie immissi oceano, parentes Hispano insulas navesque infestabant. Nec interea Batavis abstinebatur, si qui forte, emissi custodum dissimulatione, per fretum tentabant in occidentem erumpere: unde repertum postea, Britanniam insulam retro vehi, quo vasto et vix usurpato mari praedonum insidiae effugerentur. Vetitam evectionem vicissim, eorum quae peregre solita (**97**) peti, penuria sequebatur, ita quidem ut non aliud remedium Ordines invenirent, quam frumentum omne decreto publico coercere: qua lege iidem incognitae hactenus necessitatis auctores, et maligni interpretes, famem Angliae quaeri calumniabantur.

18 Simile erat, quod hostiles agros, qui stipendium pendebant, Licestrius solitudini et excidio damnabat, praeter ultionis metum, saevum in eos, qui vi aut dolis avulsi a patriae corpore quandoque redituri sperabantur. Commotus et miles, quod aliarum nationum cohortibus Angli duces insererentur: aditusque Hohenloius, qui cunctantes ante in Licestrii verba adegerat, ut impermixtos ordines et armorum praemia tueretur, suscepit causam: odioque tam gentis quam ducis interritus, ut pollicitationibus incorruptus, apertissime defendit optimatium partes, generosa simplicitate simulandi impatiens, et per vinolentiam tegendi quoque ignarus.

19 Sopivit nascentem dissensionem nonnihil cura belli recrudescentis. Nam Parmensis per praelia aliquot, et castellorum utrinque ereptiones circa Rhenum hyeme extracta, ad nuncium Anglicani foederis pecunia a rege auctus et milite, ut reliqua Brabantiae perficeret, Graviam, oppidum in sinistra Mosae ripa, obsidio premebat, supra infraque clauso amne, quod ad commeatus arcendos toties sibi prosperum rursus experiebatur. Sed missus a Licestrio Hohenloius cum delecto militum comitatu hostilia munimenta vincendo perrupit, et, adiutus verno fluminis incremento, liberavit oppidanos famis et reliquae penuriae metu.

dearth of goods could defeat the enemy if they received no provisions from either the Low Countries or Britain. He did not realise however that much of the merchandise is not essential to the enemy and available in great quantities in Holland. Wiser people concluded that he had submitted to the avarice of his flatterers, who in their minds already saw themselves selling export licences, or profiting from denunciations. This reading achieved greater credibility when an ordinance was issued which authorised Jacques Reingout (who had served the treasury under Alva and Requesens, subsequently became tainted with suspicions of embezzlement, but was now outrageously popular with Leicester)[15] to inspect the accounts and correspondences of merchants; this went against established rights (which are an important carrier of liberty) prescribing that everyone's private affairs be kept free of spying.

17 And thus, since other nations which had nothing to do with this war could not be kept away from the sea and trade with [our] enemy, and precisely those profits were led away from Holland which had so far been the sole basis of the common cause, a great host of merchants began to emigrate from their ancestral cities. For the English at least accepted the loss of their trade more easily, being a more rapacious nation; so next they set out to sea with an excellent pretext for war and started disturbing islands and ships obedient to Spain. And while doing so they didn't even keep their hands off Dutch merchants, that is, the few who had escaped due to the connivance of the guards and tried to break out over the sea towards the west. Later this problem was solved by sailing round the back of the island of Britain, in order to escape the pirates' ambushes via the vast and virtually shipless sea. The export ban was followed in turn by a scarcity of goods which used to be brought in from abroad **(97)**, and even such scarcity that the States found no other remedy than a decree which placed the entire supply of corn under their supervision. This law however led the very instigators of the emergency, which had not been seen before, to ascribe an evil intention to it and falsely accuse the States of seeking to cause famine in England.

18 A comparable case was that Leicester condemned farmlands in enemy territory, for which imposts were paid, to abandonment and demolition without having to fear revenge; a cruel act towards to people who were driven from their ancestral communities by violence or evil intent and hoping to return at some point. There was also upheaval among the soldiers because English commanders were put in charge of regiments from other countries. The count of Hohenlohe, who had induced men who couldn't decide to swear loyalty to Leicester before, was approached to restore order in the ranks and secure the payment of the wages, and accepted the task. Being as unafraid of hatred from that nation or its commander, as unsusceptible to corruption, he defended the side of the elites[16] without reserve, while his in-born straightforwardness made him intolerant of deceit, and his penchant for drinking incapable of secrecy.

19 Worries about the re-brutalising war calmed the rising disagreement down somewhat. For Parma had spent the winter fighting a couple of sieges and picking castles on both sides of the Rhine. At the news of the English alliance he had received reinforcements in money and troops from the king, to enable him to finish his job in Brabant, and he had laid siege to Grave, a town on the left bank of the Meuse. For this purpose he had locked the river both upstream and downstream from the town; a system which had so often given him success in blocking supplies was tried here once again. However, Leicester sent Hohenlohe with a company of elite soldiers, who gained the upper hand and broke through the enemy defences. Aided by the rising waters of spring, he set the townspeople free of the fear of famine and other deprivation.

20 Nec eo minus perstitit hostis maiore cum exercitu oppugnationem moliri; quam imminentem Hemerta vir nobilis Belga (hunc Hohenloius praefectum reliquerat,) cum iam auxilia adventarent, festinata nimium deditione praevenit; blandiciis, ut creditur, pellicis emollitus, cuius flagitii crimine a Licestrio capite plexus est. Disciplinam vocabant aequiores, alii gentis odium, quia Rolandus Eboracensis Imbisianis quondam consiliis permixtus, Anglique plures nihilo tutioris fidei, aut manifesti ignaviae, non modo securi, sed primarum admissionum compotes, agerent. Secuta Graviam Venloa, Geldriae oppidum superius, et in dextra ripa situm, prodente plebe egregia militum studia. Dimissae interea manus agrum hostilem praedabantur; posuitque Mauritius rudimenta Axelae expugnator, quam Ternusio egressus (id Flandricae orae munimentum Foederati (**98**) tenuere) nocturno scalarum ascensu invasit.

21 At Agrippinense bellum, de quo ante retuli, non tam partium viribus, quam ducum virtute flagrabat. Scenkius, relicto Parmensi, transgressus ad Truxium, occupatis passim praesidiis, cuncta antistitis ditioni subiecta ferro et igni populabatur: deinde iussu Licestrii insulam muniit; quae ad ipsum Rheni divortium laevo Bataviae lateri praeiacet, Gravewartae[40] nomen: idque nunc maximum imperii istius propugnaculum est. At Nienarius, earundem partium ductor, Novesium, veteri celebritate oppidum, furto ceperat: quo contendit Parmensis, oratus a Boioaro, et cupiditate cum felicissimis ducum gloria certandi. Nam Carolo Burgundo secundissimam prius fortunam is locus retudit, vertitque.

22 At ipsi prospera oppugnatio, et superba victoria: collucentem incendiis ingressus urbem; mox Alpa, Cracovio, Mursa in deditionem acceptis; ad Bercam haesit, spem praeter defensam a Scenkio: tandemque detrahitur, Licestrio post captum Dosiburgum Zutfaniae imminente. Sed huic, dum aditus claudere et castra praemunire ignavum putat, invecto commeatu reversus hostis experiendarum virium occasionem dedit. Eius pugnae felicem alioqui Anglis eventum mors Philippi Sidnei funestavit, iuvenis ad maxima quaeque nati, ut qui claris natalibus opibusque rarum decus literas adiunxisset; hoc maior avunculo Licestrio, cui et fortunae, quantacunque ea futura erat, successor destinabatur.

23 Mox venit in potestatem castellum contra Zutfaniam in altera ripa, quae cisisalana est, coeptum olim Belgis, et, cum incremento fluminis fugarentur, ab hoste perfectum. Huius curam cum omni terra Velavia Licestrius Rolando Eboracensi; Daventriam, quam defectionis suspectam praesidio Hiberni militis ab omni humanitate alienissimi ultro irritaverat, Wilhelmo Stanleio credidit: utrumque adversa Ordinum voluntate, qui satis gravibus de causis, quas exitus comprobavit,

[40] Gravewartae *1657* Gravewardae *1658*

20 This however was no reason for the enemy to give up preparing an attempt to conquer the town by storm. The lord of Hemert, a Netherlands nobleman, whom Hohenlohe had left as head of the garrison, forestalled this attack by a premature surrender while the auxiliaries were on their way. It is believed that he was softened to take this step by the caresses of his concubine, and Leicester made him pay with his head for this disgraceful infraction. Those with the more equitable view called this a measure of discipline, others an act of hatred towards the nation, because Roland York, who had once been involved in Hembyze's plans,[17] as well a few other Englishmen of no greater truthfulness, or even manifest worthlessness, were not only walking about in perfect safety, but even did so in the highest circles. Grave was followed by Venlo, a town in upper Guelders on the right-hand bank of the Meuse, because the townspeople betrayed the special efforts made by the garrison. Meanwhile the enemy countryside was looted by unconnected bands of soldiers, and Maurice planted his first proof of competence by conquering Axel. Starting his operation from Terneuzen (a stronghold which the United Provinces **(98)** had preserved on the Flemish shore) he invaded the town in a nightly ascent with ladders.

21 The Cologne war, on which I reported earlier,[18] kept raging on, not so much because of the strength of the parties as for the valour of the commanders. Maarten Schenck deserted from Parma and defected to Truchsess.[19] He captured a handful of garrison towns and destroyed the entire district under the bishop's authority by fire and sword; next, at Leicester's orders, he built a fortification on the island called 's-Gravenwaard which is situated right at the fork of the Rhine on the left side of the Betuwe region;[20] the same is currently the most important bulwark in that part of the country. The count of Neuenahr however, another commander on that side, took Neuss, a town of age-old renown, by crafty deceit. Parma hasted towards that place, spurred on to do so by the count of Bavaria and a desire to compete for glory with the most successful commanders. For this town had been the first to break Charles the Bold's continuous row of victories and turn it around.

22 Parma's siege on the other hand was rewarded with success and a proud victory; his entry into the town was illuminated by the fire he set to it. This was soon followed by the surrender of Alpen, Cracau and Moers, but at Rheinberg[21] his progress halted, which was defended by Schenck beyond expectation, and finally he withdrew, when Leicester first took Doesburg then began to threaten Zutphen. However, while the latter frowned upon laying a blockade to the city and securing his positions, [Parma], returning from a supply mission to the town, gave him an opportunity to test his enemy's strength. And although in all other respects the outcome of the battle was a success for the English,[22] it turned out a disaster after all because of the death of Philip Sidney, a youth capable of every greatness imaginable, given the conjunction he embodied of magnificent birth and wealth, and a rare distinction in literature. In this last respect he surpassed his uncle Leicester, his mother's brother, whose position (whichever that would be) he was destined to inherit.

23 Soon the castle opposite Zutphen on the other bank fell into their hands, on the [West] side of the river IJssel, the beginnings of which had once been built by the Lowlanders, but which, after they had been chased by the rising waters, had been completed by the enemy. Leicester left Roland York in charge of this castle and the entire region of the Veluwe; the town of Deventer, which he suspected of imminent defection, having made them rebellious himself by billeting Irish soldiers (who are strangers to every kind of humanity), he trusted to William Stanley. Both decisions went against the wishes of the States, who had

illorum hominum perfidiam metuebant. Nec ullum hac in re Licestrii dolum arguerim, sed quod in caeteros contumax, et tantum adulantibus patens, inexploratis amicitiis turpiter fidebat. Nam et aliorum, quos ad consilia praecipuos habebat, factiosi conatus eruperant: quos inter conspicuus etiam in reatu Ringaltius cuncta iudicum tribunalia eiurabat, donec ad extremum transfuga vitam infamem inter hostes inopia finivit.

24 Regressum (**99**) igitur a bello ducem innumerae simul querelae premebant, quod non sine civium iniuria bellum et praesidia agitarentur, contra quam expediret imperium sponte populi obtinentibus: addebatur, traditam alienigenis quaesturam malis artibus geri, turbatum nummi pretium, nec milites et caetera reipublicae onera cum aerario comparari: exhaustis rei navalis obventionibus prodi maris arbitrium: labare commercia: male meritis mandatos honores: at secundae ab ipso praefecturae vim omnem destrui, et ius in praesidia eripi multis annis servatum. Nec tacebatur, quod conductus eo tempore e Germania miles non adventasset (suspicio erat, Anglorum dolo factum, qui suum robur et proprias vires mallent inducere) tenuitate copiarum, quando et auxiliares numeros ducum aut quaestorum avaritia exhauserat, cessum hosti, neque eius victoriis obsisti quivisse.

25 Perlata haec Ordinum verbis tum foederatorum, quorum eo primum tempore crebri conventus haberi coepere, ut agi extra senatum possent ea, quae Anglorum conscientiam formidabant; tum Hollandorum, qui pro se et Mauritio privatim multa questi etiam communia pleraque ad suam curam retrahebant. Quae Licestrius impatienter tulit: eos scilicet ex officinis et tabernis in curiam evadere, quo praeter sordidas artes venalemque animum nihil afferrent: se eo genere, ea dignitate, accepturum leges ab rudi plebe, et alieno imperio militaturum.

26 His ille accensus, a republica, si posset, amovere plebem, quae fere dominantibus infestior est, et acris depeculatorum observatrix, optimum factu iudicavit: idque eo facilius processurum, quia exteri et civium multitudo longe maxima regiminis exsors laeto animo acceptura videbatur aequalitatem. At mihi sapientum praecepta et veteres civitatum species animo repetenti, videntur magnifica dictu verius, quam factu sequenda excogitasse, quotquot partem eam populi, cuius ad communem utilitatem quaestus maxime redundat, honoribus exuunt. Nam, ut maritimas taceam gentes, apud quas vulgus plurimum pollebat, etiam Spartiatae dilectos e plebe, tanquam adulandi nescios, regibus aequavere; Romaeque haud ante pax

sufficiently serious reasons to fear the disloyalty of both men—which the outcome has confirmed. However I do not want to accuse Leicester of any evil intent in this affair, only of stubbornness towards others, and, given his tendency to listen to flatterers only, of a disgraceful reliance on untried friendships. For several others who figured among his most important advisors turned out to be making dissident assaults as well. The most conspicuous of these was Reingout, who even when charges were brought against him did not recognise any judicial court, until finally he defected to the enemy and spent his last days in poverty and disrepute.

24 Thus right at this return **(99)** from the war the commander was buried under a mountain of complaints, that the war and the billeting were handled with too much damage to the citizens, in contravention of the interests of those who held the supreme power at the initiative of the people. On top of this, that the financial management had been handed over to foreigners and that it was executed with evil artifice, that the value of the currency was disturbed, that the armies and the other public spending were in disbalance with the contents of the treasury; that since the maritime profits had dried out, power over the sea was getting lost; that trade was dwindling, that high offices had been given to unworthy people, but that the power of the stadtholderate, now second in rank after him, was going completely to pieces, while the control of the garrisons, which had been preserved for so many years, was being taken away. Nor was it passed over in silence that the soldiers which at this time had been hired in Germany, had never arrived (there was a suspicion that this had been done on purpose by the English who preferred to bring their own strength and forces into the country); and that, as the avarice of the officers and tax-receivers had also thinned the ranks of the auxiliary forces, the dearth of troops had led to retreats on the ground, and that it was no longer possible to stop his row of victories.[23]

25 These complaints reached Leicester in two ways, in the words of the States-General (who at this very time had begun to have frequent meetings, so that they could discuss outside the Council of State such matters as shunned awareness by the English); and in those of the members of the States of Holland, who, by submitting many private complaints on their own behalf and that of Maurice, had brought most political affairs, and even some of the Union, back under their own control. Leicester had great difficulty accepting this, and complained that these were men escaping from shops and inns to the council chamber, bringing nothing to the task except their proletarian tactics and a mercenary spirit; while he, in spite of his high birth and dignity, would have to have the rules laid down to him by the basest populace, and to conduct a war under another man's command.

26 In his anger about the situation he decided that the best thing to do was to remove this plebs from the government, as in general it has a loathing for autocratic rulers and keeps a very sharp eye on whom it suspects of peculation. He thought it would be all the more easy to proceed in this because it seemed that the foreigners and the overwhelming majority of the citizens, who do not take part in the government, would be delighted to see everybody having the same amount of power. However when I rehearse the teachings of the philosophers and the examples of ancient societies in my mind, they appear to have designed whichever brilliant schemes that bar those parts of the population from public office whose profits are the chief flow of resources towards the commonwealth, really more for the debate than for execution in reality. For (leaving aside the maritime peoples, with whom the lower ranks of the people had very great power), even the Spartans put a number

ordinum fuit, quam plebs in imperii partem vocata est; quin et hodie florentissimis in urbibus, quas optimates regunt, negotiatores patriciorum nomine plebis officia exercent: nedum ab ista republica, quae cuncta mari et amnibus debet, is ordo (**100**) arceatur, maiore multo, quam olim fuit, mercaturae dignitate, ex quo orbem totum navigationes aperuerunt: et nunc divitiae fere penes illos sunt; quarum in mandandis honoribus haberi rationem priscis quoque ac severis legum latoribus placitum est: minusque suspectae esse debent ullius opes aut avaritia, ubi potentia nec perpetua est, et fere mandatis includitur.

27 Sed haec atque alia semper servata mutare Licestrius parabat, non tam vano novandi studio, quam ut nobilitatem et clara ingenia a caeteris segregando partes proliceret. Interpretes primum sacrarum literarum (qui soli multitudinis aures et affectus hoc seculo possident) adiungebat sibi specie pietatis, et aliorum dissimilitudine. Nam primis in republica religio minus tum cordi quam par erat, hanc unam armorum causam vulgantibus: et olim contra supplicii metum acrius cupita, per impunitatem neglectui erant: non sacris salva reverentia: non administris honos. Erant et qui omne ius ecclesiasticae censurae eriperent: acerbam scilicet sacerdotum dominationem infestis animis meminerant, veterumque odio cuncta novabantur.

28 Quae contra Licestrius, autoritatem atque alia commoda Angliae exemplo ostentans, concionantium voces, et per illos populi studia sibi conciliabat: pleraque reipublicae non magistratibus credens, sed his, qui in aliqua sacrorum parte, aut plebeio centuriatu versabantur, quibus etiam optima volentibus rerum notitia et usus aberant. Iam vero multi, quorum fortia pro patria consilia exstabant, palam demoti honoribus, quia cum Romana Ecclesia aut per omnia, aut ex parte sentiebant, parum proviso, quam non pacifici exempli res foret, si semel evulgaretur, eam induci religionem, quae consortes reipublicae alios non admitteret.

29 Brevi apud Frisios, Traiectique Batavorum, ubi ereptum civibus imperium incolae occupaverant, aliasque per urbes quae turbidae etiam olim ac nimia vi multitudinis regebantur, Ordinum nomen magna in invidia esse coepit: ille unus religionis vindex, ille et hostium et intestini ambitus avaritiaeque expugnator coli. Praeter haec, munimenta, insulas ad mare sitas, et alios limites Anglicano milite tenebat: nec minus in Sonoio praesidii, qui ob egregia facta Westfrisiae regimen sub Arausionensi meritus, intendere vim suae praefecturae sperabat, favente Licestrio ut proximas suo fastigio potestates imminueret, atque avido hanc regionem, (**101**) aliaque praesidia ab Hollandiae imperio et Mauritii cura divellere, qui magnam

of elected men from the populace at equal rank with their kings, as being alien to flattery. In Rome there was no peace within the orders of society before the populace was given a share in power. Yes even today in the most prosperous cities, which are ruled by their elites, the representatives of the upper classes hold their offices in the name of the populace; all the more reason for this arrangement **(100)** to belong to the commonwealth we are talking about here, which owes everything to the sea and the rivers, given that the importance of trade is far greater than it was ever before, now that shipping expeditions have opened up the entire world. Currently the groups just mentioned are where almost all the wealth resides, which also the stern law-makers of Antiquity decided should be an important criterium for appointment in public office. And someone's wealth and greed must necessarily be less suspect when his power is neither lasting and hedged in by additional conditions.

27 But although these and related circumstances have always remained so throughout the ages, Leicester set out to change them, not so much from a vain desire for novelty, as in order to stir up factional strife by creating a division between the nobility and people with outstanding capacities, and the others. First, for the sake of the appearance of piety and in order to set himself clearly apart from others, he allied himself with the interpreters of Scripture, the only ones in our age to which the masses pay heed. For the political leadership in this period took less care of religion than was right, while they spread the view that religion alone was the cause of the war. That which was once vehemently desired in spite of the fear of execution, was now neglected because of the absence of punishment: the esteem for sacred ritual was broken, respect for the ministers gone. There were even people who wanted to rob ecclesiastical supervision of all its powers; full of hatred they remembered the cruel domination by the priests, and from aversion of the past they desired to change everything.

28 Against this Leicester posed his authority and the other advantages of the English alliance to serve as example. Thus he brought the views of the preachers over to his side, and through them the support of the population. He assigned most of the business of government not to the magistracy but to people with some kind of religious function, or to popular officers[24] who, even when they acted from the best of intentions, lacked the relevant knowledge and experience. On the other hand many men who had served the country with excellent policies were openly deposed from office because their views were partly or entirely those of the Roman church. He did not realise how little this example would contribute to the public peace once it would become widely recognised that here a confession was introduced of a nature which did not allow others to have a share in the secular government.

29 Soon the name of the States became the object of hatred in Friesland and Utrecht where the political power had been seized from the citizens and usurped by immigrants, as well as in other towns where disturbances had occurred before and which were ruled by the mob in violence and excess. And Leicester himself acquired esteem as the sole defender of the faith and the only victor over the enemy, domestic competition for office, and greed. Moreover he kept the defence works, the islands on the side of the North Sea and the other borders regions occupied with English soldiers. No smaller was his reliance on Diederik Sonoy,[25] whose outstanding achievements had earned him the government of West-Friesland under William of Orange, and who now hoped to extend the force of his governorship. These intentions had Leicester's full support, as it was his aim to weaken the powers that came closest to his, and given his eagerness to tear West-Friesland, **(101)** and other buffer areas away from Holland's control and the care of Maurice, who was so far

indolem pertinaci silentio dissimulabat, cum eodem tempore et falsissimis criminibus et per amicitiae speciem tentaretur.

30 His praestructus Licestrius cum suorum e numero multos evexisset, et vulgus ubique discordiis ambiguum, pars maior in ipsum vergeret, non multum sibi ad liberam potestatem restare credidit, si veteri apud Elisabetham gratia niteretur. Ergo ne longae absentiae tempora largiretur inimicis, peritus eius regiae, domum proficiscitur. Apud Ordines, evocatum se ad Angliae concilium praeferebat, ibi quoque res Belgicas acturum; apud plebem, Ordinum contumeliis irritatum excedere, et nisi alio rerum vultu haud rediturum minabatur: quod plurimos incendit, sparsis et in vulgus literis, quibus aut Ordinum acerbitas, aut Licestrii merita et in populum studia differrentur; additoque insuper rumore, Reginam principatum Belgicae non detrectaturam, nisi terrerent primae societatis experimenta, et innumerae leges, quibus iustissima quamvis imperia eluderentur: per quae eo deventum est, ut Traiecti novi magistratus, et in Frisia privati publico nomine legatos ad Reginam mittere auderent, qui principatus conditiones non tam ferrent, quam acciperent.

31 At illa, quanquam Anglorum concilio collationes, si vellet, eam ad rem pollicente, pernegavit: nec tamen quorundam effugit suspiciones, quasi consensu publico delatum honorem et recusatum, plebis ac militum seditionibus debere mallet. Discedens autem Licestrius senatui permisit rempublicam: sed non multo post scriptura prolata est, qua ius in praesidiarios et praecipua imperii sibi exceperat. Missi hac de causa in Angliam, qui mutilum regimen, et si subita ingruerent, nulla in potestate praesens subsidium conquererentur. Sed inauditos Britannia diu detinuit, suis ipsa motibus involuta: nam regina Scotiae, a suae gentis Ordinibus exacta, supplex ad Elisabetham profugerat, cui, praeter similitudinem summi nominis, propinquo sanguine connectebatur: ibi, magnis suffulta clientelis Romanas caeremonias sectantium, spem recepisse prioris fortunae, et Elisabethae saluti, regnoque imminere credita, custodiis primum, deinde, ne sic quidem infra metum, morti tradita est.

32 (1587) Apud Batavos saevi interim tumultus, et, ut quaeque partium praevaluerat, exsilia aut vincula decernebantur. Sed ubi Wilhelmus (**102**) Stanleius Daventriam, Rolandus Eboracensis oppositum Zutfaniae munimentum Taxi Hispano, accipienti perfidiam et tamen aversanti, tradiderunt, gratiosus apud Licestrium uterque, e plebe multi efferre Ordinum prudentiam, sua studia damnare: etiam Anglorum nonnulli, eluendae gentis infamiae, procerum iussibus applicabantur. Inventus tamen ex eadem gente Alanus, Cardinalis postea factus, qui libello in id edito religionis obtentu defenderet facinus, ut pessimi exempli, ita autoribus quoque suis

hiding his enormous talents under a persistent silence, although he was simultaneously put under pressure with the most ludicrous incriminations ànd a show of friendship.

30 Thus Leicester found himself in a secure position, as he had advanced advanced many of his own men to high positions, and the majority of the populace leaned over to his side (though in their state of conflict everywhere there could be no certainty about this): and he believed he had come close to having absolute power, if at least he could rely on the queen's favour, as of old. Therefore he left for home, in order not to give his enemies too much time in his absence, as he had ample experience of that court. In front of the States he claimed to have been summoned to the Parliament of England, and stated that from there he would also administer the affairs of the Low Countries. To the populace he said he was leaving vexed by the insults from the side of the States, and threatened he might not return unless this situation changed. This enraged many people and several writings were circulated among the populace in which either the States' rigor, or Leicester's achievement and efforts for the people were spelled out. On top of this a rumour went round that the queen would not refuse the throne of the Low Countries, if she wasn't deterred by her first experiences with the alliance and the countless laws which paralysed even the most righteous of empires. As a result of these it even happened that the new magistrates of Utrecht and private individuals in Friesland dared to send delegates in an official capacity to the queen in order not so much to bring the conditions for a transfer of sovereignty, as to receive them.[26]

31 Although the Parliament of England promised negotiations to that end, if the queen should wish them, her refusal was adamant. Nevertheless she did not escape suspicions by some as that she preferred to owe this dignity (offered by public consent and refused) to a popular and military revolt. At his departure Leicester left the Council of State in charge of the commonwealth; a little later however a document surfaced in which he reserved the command of the garrisons and the chief political decisions for himself. On that account an embassy was sent to England to complain about the incomplete government and the fact that if an emergency should arise, no might would be available to provide help. Britain however kept them waiting for a long time without even giving them a hearing, as it was deeply immersed in its own upheavals: for the queen of Scotland, expelled by the States of her own people, had humbly sought refuge with Elizabeth, with whom she was connected not only by similar royal title, but also by immediate family ties. When however it came to be believed in England that she, who enjoyed the support of powerful networks of dependents loyal to the religion of Rome, had been given hope of a restoration to her former position, and was therefore a danger to Elizabeth's life and to the kingdom, she was taken into prison and subsequently executed—even in prison not harmless enough to be unfeared.[27]

32 Meanwhile in the United Provinces there were violent disturbances, and according to which side gained the upper hand, exile and imprisonment were meted out. But when two men who enjoyed great favour with Leicester, William Stanley **(102)** and Roland York handed over Deventer and the bulwark opposite Zutphen to the Spaniard Taxis, who accepted this act of treason while denouncing it at the same time, many among the populace praised the prudence of the States, and condemned their own efforts.[28] Even several Englishmen now submitted themselves to the commands of the States, in order to wash off the dishonour of their nation. However among that nation a man was found called Allen[29], who was later made a cardinal, who saw fit to defend this crime in a pamphlet published for the purpose using religion as a pretext, thus not only setting a very bad example but

infelix. Nam postquam ipsi inter se odiis commissi, Eboracensem, hominem formidandae in quidvis audaciae, veneno sublatum fama est: Stanleius Daventria demotus, cohorte, quam secum traduxerat, subductis stipendiis diffluente, in Hispaniam profectus, neque praemia ibi sperata, neque consiliis fidem reperit.

33 At foederati Ordines accepta voluntatum tam vulgi quam militis pro se inclinatione, ut quamvis magna reipublicae calamitas in bonum verteret, paternum in Mauritio favorem excitarunt, mandato per summi ducis absentiam armorum imperio. Quin et praetermissum hactenus sacramentum a militibus in nomen Ordinum, et cuiusque nationis praefectorum postulabant, quod proditores et seditiosissimus quisque hoc colore scelera velaret, simpliciores etiam Licestrii honorem, quasi dictum Reginae iusiurandum, interpretarentur. Edictum de evectionibus ita temperatum est, ut in pacatas gentes cuncta, praeter quae bello idonea ad hostiles Belgas locaque his finitima, excepto super haec frumento, caetera exportarentur: quae lex pro usu sequentium temporum contracta saepius, aut laxata est.

34 Itaque ea tempestate diversissima fortuna per Belgicam agebatur. Nam Brabanti Flandrique, raro commeatu et perpetuis agrorum populationibus exhausti, extrema penuria conflictabantur; ditesque olim homines ad famem et mendicitatem redactos constat: vix populorum defectiones metus, atque obsessi dominantium viribus limites, arcebant. Contra prolatis pomoeriis crescere videres oppida Batavorum, et utrumque in latus classes oceano dispergi: ut unam gentium hanc arbitrer, quae bello etiam magis quam pace commerciis profecerit; habendamque merito felicissimam, si non, qui senescentibus fere imperiis et consumptae fortunae finis est, ipsa magnitudinis suae primordia, valido adhuc hoste, intestinis discordiis attrivisset. (**103**)

35 Tribunus Hispanicarum partium Altipenna postea quam oppidum Geldram, unde Geldriae regioni nomen est, cum praefecto pactus in se traduxerat, apud Silvam ducis ab Hohenloio caesus, occupandum illi castellum reliquit non longe ab urbe, cui ex ea clade vocabulum Crepicordii factum est. At Clusam, in ultima Flandrici maris ora, quae Zelandiam spectat, a tergo insulaque adiacente (Catzandia dicitur) circumventam Parmensis incredibili machinarum violentia labefactabat. Quod simul comperit Licestrius, nihil tardato reditu, frustra de portu irrumpendo cogitationem instituit. Sed cum ad alteram versus rationem, Ostendam profectus, hostem propter castra posuisset, incogniti exercitus numerum augente fama, constat utrumque alterius vires supra verum formidasse. Digressus tandem prior Licestrius iacturam oppidi apud cunctos graviter acceptam, non hostium virtuti, non partium studiis ob suspiciones male adhuc coalescentibus, imputavit: persequi

also bringing bad luck to his principals. For Stanley and York entered into a feud between them, and there is a rumour that York, a man of frightful audacity ready to do anything, was cleared out of the way by poison; while Stanley was kicked out of Deventer, and the regiment which had switched sides with him fell apart when their wages were withdrawn. He left for Spain but found neither the rewards he hoped for there nor reliance on his counsel.

33 However the States-General now found the sympathies of the people and the army on their side, and in Maurice they rewoke the favour in which his father had held them, so that he would turn whichever adversity that threatened the commonwealth, for the good; and in the absence of the supreme commander they charged him with the military command. They even demanded an oath of loyalty to the States, by the soldiers and the stadtholder of every province, which had been omitted so far because traitors and rebels of every kind were hiding their crimes under this cover and the more simple-minded even interpreted it as an oath in honour of Leicester, as if it was taken to the queen. The decree on the exportation of goods was mitigated insofar that to nations with whom there was peace, all goods could be exported; to the enemy side of the Low Countries and neighbouring regions, only goods not useful in war, and also no wheat. According to the needs of the subsequent periods, this law has often been relaxed or tightened since.

34 Thus, in this period, the various parts of the Low Countries were in very different states of prosperity. For Brabant and Flanders, sapped by the virtual disappearance of trade and the never-ending devastation of the countryside, were afflicted by the direst poverty. It is a known fact that people who had once been wealthy were reduced to starvation and mendicity. Fear plus intensive border control by the regime's forces were hardly enough to keep large crowds of people from making their way out. On the other hand you could almost see the towns in Holland grow by the constant expansion of their outlines, and fleets spread out towards East and West over the ocean: so that to my knowledge this nation is the only one in the world which' trade made even more progress in wartime than in peace. And it would justly be considered the most fortunate of all, if she hadn't herself crippled the very beginnings of her greatness, while the enemy was still strong, by internal discord—and end usually reserved for ageing empires which have used up their credit with Fortune. **(103)**

35 The Spanish officer Hautepenne struck a deal with the commander of the town of Geldern (from which the region of Guelders derives its name) and brought the town over to his side.[30] Next however he was killed near Den Bosch by Hohenlohe, and left the latter a bulwark ready for occupation not far from the city, which was given the name of Crevecoeur[31] in commemoration of this defeat. On the other hand the town of Sluys, on the outermost part of the Flemish coast, facing Zeeland, was surrounded by Parma from the back and the adjacent island (called Cadzand), and brought to ruin under incredible violence of gunfire. The moment Leicester became aware of this, he did not postpone his return any longer, and began developing a plan, in vain, to invade the port. Then however he opted for a different course, moved in the direction of Ostend, and placed his camp near that of the enemy. As rumour amplified the size of the unknown army, it is certain that both parties feared the other side's forces more than was justified by the facts. In the end Leicester retreated first and blamed the loss of the town, which news was received nowhere without protest, not on the quality of the enemy, nor on any internal divisions still growing because

iam pene obductas dissensiones, et Ordines culpae subdere, libido erat: cupienti sibi hostem depellere, militem, pecuniam, et caetera maligne subministrari ait: vix praesidiis sufficere quae tribuebantur, ne dum exercitu contra certaretur: aut si tanta esset paupertas, quid desperatam rempublicam infelici bello detinerent?

36 Quippe tunc solitas post victoriam artes iterante Hispano, et ipsa Regina in pacem nutare videbatur: quanquam missa nuper sub Dracone classis, vastatis Hispaniae littoribus, ostenderat quam infirmum domi, quod alibi adeo metueretur, imperium; et sub Cavendisio alia aversam Americae oram et Moluccas cum lucro perspexerat. Sed ingravescente aetate foeminam multa terrebant; Hiberni saepe rebellando, et per Belgica arma in iustam militiam exerciti; et praeter hostem Hispanum suspecta Scotia, infesta Gallia; nec pauci in Anglia motuum avidi. At Ordines, gnari quantum id rebus suis alias nocuisset, colloquii mentione, ut poterant, discussa, si ex fide administraretur aerarium, negabant annuum tricies florenorum (id praeter Angliae auxilia et maritimas proprie opes erat virium) quasi magnam tenuitatem contemni debere, cum Arausionensis minori copia res magnas saepe gessisset. Attentos et parvo uti nosse: ubi pecuniae negligenter habeantur, etiam cum nimium datur, non satis dari.

37 Deinde repertis Licestrii ad amicos literis, quibus ipsi dedidicisse (**104**) obsequium, et iniquitate adversus eminentes rerum ad se non pertinentium satagere accusabantur, edicto ostendunt, olim in se populi ius, nuper et principis translatum: utrumque delata praefectura detinuisse: aliaque de conventu suo magnifica, et quibus ambitionis crimen purgarent.

38 Spes Licestrii directius iam petebantur, quam ut intellectis tardisque artibus insisteret. Indignatus igitur plebis iram adversus magistratus adhuc intra voces stare, festinata audacia urbes interius sitas, et unde terror in caetera, factione et praesidiis opprimere parat, haud satis proviso Valesii exemplo, quem tentata vis pacto iam principatu extruserat. Sed ante periculum Lugduni detecta coniuratio incolarum, qui pravae in alienam remp. curiositatis poenas capite luerunt: et quanquam errore nonnulli quam malitia peccaverant, salutaris ea saevitia fuit, ac coeptantes tunc maxime motus compescuit.

39 Et ille infaustae iam affectationis manifestus in Angliam concessit; ibique eum Regina, postquam non omnino amicum ipsi Buchorstium ad res Belgicas explorandas miserat, quo minus causam in consilio diceret potestate regia texit; attamen in Belgas imperium eiurare coegit. Sed cum adhuc veteres partes litteris sustentaret,

of mutual suspicions. No, he fell for the temptation to revive the almost forgotten dissension and put the blame on the States. He claimed that when he wished to dispel the enemy, he had been ill-served with men, money and the other necessities; that the supplies he had been sent were hardly enough for the garrisons, let alone when an actual battle would have to be fought; or why, if poverty was so a great, did they want to detain a commonwealth with such hopeless prospects in a hapless war any longer in the first place?

36 For at that time the Spaniard was repeating his usual trickery after a victory, and the queen herself seemed to be leaning towards a peace—although by sending a fleet under the command of Francis Drake laying waste to some of the shores of Spain, she had also shown how weak this empire was at home which was elsewhere feared so much; and another fleet under Cavendish had explored the west coast of America as well as the Moluccas and returned with profit. Given her advancing age however there was much that gave this lady reasons for fear: the repeated rise of rebels in Ireland, which had got organised into a proper army through the campaigns in the Low Countries; also, apart from the Spanish enemy, her suspicions towards Scotland and hatred of France; and the sizeable groups in England who were looking for a revolt. The States however, although fully aware how much this might have damaged their interests at a different time, kept the idea of negotiations at bay as much as they could and stated that, provided the treasury was managed in good faith, a yearly income of three million guilders[32] (this was their financial power, apart from the English support and the overseas returns as such), was not to be looked down upon as magnificent poverty, since William of Orange had often achieved great things with fewer resources. The vigilant know how to make use of little; and where money is handled carelessly, you don't provide enough even when you provide too much.

37 Next letters were discovered by Leicester to his friends in which they were accused of having unlearned obedience, **(104)** and of, in offence to people of higher rank, having their hands full with business that wasn't theirs. In reaction the States demonstrated in a treatise that in the past the political rights of the people, and recently those of the prince, had been transferred to them; that they retained ownership of both sets of rights even if the executive was delegated to someone else; and finally a number of other high-spirited claims about their own assembly in order to cleanse themselves of the offence of lusting after power.[33]

38 However, Leicester was already pursuing his ambitions too directly to confine himself to well-considered and slow-working artifice. Thus, in his indignation about the populace's anger towards the magistrate still not going any further than words, precipitous audacity led him to make preparations to overwhelm a number of inland cities with his partisans and garrisons. The example was supposed to inspire fear in all others: but Leicester failed to give due consideration to the example of Anjou, whose attempt to use force had robbed himself of a crown already agreed upon. Before the situation became dangerous however, in Leiden a conspiracy of immigrants was discovered, who paid with their heads for their crooked interference with other people's commonwealth.[34] And although several of them had trespassed in error rather than out of malice, this cruelty had a beneficial effect in that it served to put down upheavals which were beginning right at that time.

39 Leicester himself disappeared to England now that his unwanted ambitions had become manifest. The queen sent Lord Buckhurst,[35] not exactly a good friend of Leicester's, to the Low Countries to investigate the situation, and next she used her royal power to shield him from having to defend himself in her council[36]—although at the same time she forced him

bello quoque per Angliam mox impositus, annum non integrum explevit: incertum, uxoris dolo, quae impari post eius mortem coniugio prius adulterium fassa sit, an fatali, aut sumpta morte: quae Reginae luctum ac lachrymas, Batavis gaudium et salutem tulit, exemptis periculo, quo[41] par nullum res istae adierant.

40 Bonnam interea, Germanici imperii cisrhenanam urbem, a Boioaro ad id tempus possessam, Scenkius clandestino introitu ceperat. Caeterum quieta per Belgicam arma: nec Parmensis, ut solebat, intentus discordes bello irrumpere: maiores animo conatus, omnisque Britannia, gloriosum et minus difficile certamen, obversabatur. Plerisque ducum, qui regi Hispaniae bellaverant, ea insula cumulus meriti, aut laboris praemium placuit, utque Galliae et Germaniae adsita per occasionem armorum, ita transmarinum regnum bello complecti consilium fuerat. Sed illis sua cuiusque fortuna, aut morte praepeditis, hac tempestate, velut iustae ultioni post initum foedus palamque missa rebellibus auxilia, classis in proximam aestatem per Hispaniam struebatur. Ei tum praesidia Parmensis apparabat, dignumque finem **(105)** decem annorum victoriis, ut spes ferebant, vetera imperatorum nomina Britannica expeditione aequaturus.

41 Sed imminentis periculi rumorem Hispanus sopivit ostentata pace: cui componendae etiam Danus leges praescribere aggressus est, misso ad Parmensem Caio Ransovio; quem in hostili comitatu proficiscentem, et inter pugnantes ignoratum, Batavus miles intercepit: sed rex violata legationis sacra, maxime quia literae reclusae erant, interpretatus, adeo arripuit ultionem, ut septingentis navibus, quae frumento Cimbricum fretum pervehebantur, detentis, subito ingens periculum famis intulerit populis in diem viventibus, et nullo antehac exemplo talium securis. Sed penuriae subventum consilio necessario, ut Gallicae Anglicaeque naves, mari eodem venientes, ad portus Batavos et mercatum pertraherentur. Ita vitatum discrimen sola pecuniae a Danis expressae iactura: quod ipsum tamen, et quia rex missos ad se legatos audire dedignabatur, haesit altius multorum animis iudicantium minora regna maiorum opibus obnoxia teneri.

42 Interim et cum Anglis actum Philippi nomine, quoniam Regina Belgicarum iam rerum arbitram ageret, discedi ab armis et metu posse, si gentes, quae rebellaverant, veteri obsequio redderentur: quomodo Anglicanos ritus sibi extra curam, ita per Belgicam sacra Hispani iussibus permitterentur: nec perniciosum instituerent exemplum; religionis iudicium penes alios, quam principes esse. Neque vero minori calliditate accipiebat Elisabetha pacificationem quam offerebatur, id maxime cupiens, ut per speciem compositionis, quando de classe iam inaudiverat, periculi tempora extraheret. Sed, dissimulato metu, pia concordiae vota, et

[41] quo *1657, 1658* cui *Muller*

to resign his authority over the Lowlanders. However, while he kept supporting his former party from a distance, and was also charged with the supreme command of a war in England, he died unexpectedly before another year was over. It is unclear whether this was his wife's design, who confessed her former adultery by a marriage outside her class after his death, or Fate, or a self-chosen death. In any case it brought the queen tears and sadness, the Dutch joy and safety, as they were freed from a danger bigger than any other which had threatened their commonwealth.

40 Meanwhile Bonn, a city in the German empire on the west bank of the Rhine held by Bavaria at the time, was captured by Schenck after an incursion by stealth. Apart from this the fighting in the Low Countries had come to a halt; nor was Parma, as he usually did, looking for an opportunity to assault the divided Lowlanders with an attack. His thoughts were fixed on a bigger endeavour: that is, all of Britain was hovering before his mind's eye, a glorious and less difficult struggle. For most of the commanders who had led wars for the king of Spain, that island had attracted them as the summit of achievement, or the prize for their labours, and precisely as they had planned to seize the regions neighbouring on France and Germany when their campaigns would create an occasion, they had made plans to obtain the kingdom on the other side of the sea by force of arms. Although they had all been stopped by their respective circumstances or by death, this time, as if for deserved revenge after the alliance had been made and support sent to the rebels openly, a fleet was built throughout Spain for use in the following summer. For this fleet Parma was organising the protecting regiments, a worthy conclusion **(105)** of ten years of victories, as his expectations went: seeing himself on the verge of emulating the memory of the Roman emperors by an expedition to Britain.

41 But the Spaniard suppressed the rumour of this danger by holding out the prospect of a peace. For the negotiations even the king of Denmark set out to draft conditions, and to this end Gaius Rantzau was delegated to Parma. Rantzau travelled in enemy company and wasn't recognised among the warriors: so Dutch soldiers arrested him.[37] The Danish king however interpreted this as a violation of the immunity of envoys, especially since his letters were opened. His revenge went so far that by detaining seven hundred ships which were sailing through the Sound carrying wheat, he caused a sudden major threat of famine to several nations which lived from one day to the next and were counting on these supplies, having no previous example of such interruptions. This scarcity however was obviated with an emergency plan, which meant that French and English ships, coming over the same sea, were drawn towards the Dutch ports and markets. Thus a crisis was averted at the cost of only the money that had been seized by the Danish. Nevertheless, and also because the king disdained to give the envoys that were sent to him a hearing, this incident has stuck deep in the memories of many who conclude that smaller realms are kept subordinate to the wealth and power of the bigger ones.

42 Meanwhile negotiations in Philip's name were opened with the English as well, because the queen had acted as mediator in the Low Countries affairs before. It was proposed that the war and fear might be withdrawn, provided that the rebellious provinces returned to their former obedience; and just as the Anglican faith was not his business, just so the religion in the Low Countries would be left to the Spaniard's orders; nor would this set a destructive example, for the decision about religion belongs to others than the prince. Elizabeth received this peace proposal with no smaller cunning than it was proposed with, for her chief desire

gentium commeatus praetexebat: missique talibus verbis ex Anglia qui Batavos iuberent alto silentio pacis rationes invenire, et ne semet ipsi tanta invidia onerarent, quasi perpetuas caedes et sanguinem, crudeli obstinatione, elegissent.

43 At illi repetere infida Hispanorum blandimenta: quid enim Requesenii colloquio captatum aliud, quam ut correptis munitionibus intimae urbes obsiderentur? An non Agrippinensi pacificatione spem verae pacis corruptam, sollicitatis ad defectionem tot gentibus? Ita et Flandriam non nisi per sermones eiusmodi proditoribus patuisse: tandemque hostem, pollicendo fallaciter religionis usum, eo virium venisse, ut iam abnuere auderet. Nunc (**106**) tantis civium discordiis, si mentio pacis incideret, excuti manibus arma: aliis alios legibus, ut cuique commodum, deditionem praefestinaturos. Et si maxime res aequis conditionibus componeretur, non Gandavense foedus, non Iohannis perfidiam excidisse: regibus, quos Romanus pontifex iurisiurandi religione exsolveret, omnem cum subditis pactionem pro victoria esse: nec defuturos qui honores sibi et opes cum patriae servitio pararent.

44 Sed haec apud se quisque palam: quia suadebat pacem quae cogere poterat, velut dubitando tempus terebatur; aut quoties cunctantes Regina impulerat, illi obsecrare, ne Dei hominumque causam, et sexaginta urbes paratamque gentem, si praesentia non sufficerent, privatis opibus publicas augere, proiiceret praedam perfidiae Hispanorum. Consenserant civitates (nam ad singulas relata erat consultatio) non esse mittendos ad hostem legatos. Sola Regina adulta iam hyeme in Flandriam misit, alienam si posset pacem factura.

45 Dum de conventus loco deque mandatis quaeritur, et Angli inducias rogant, Parmensis negat, tres menses abiere. Elisabetha Belgis veniam priscasque leges et civium imperia, sibi antiqua foedera, sumptus salvos, et quae firmandae securitati, ablegato utrinque milite, postulabat: caeterum de sacris, ritibusque per Belgicam tam remisse, ut nonnihil cessura videretur, et iam eo descenderat, ut ferri ea in biennium tantum postularet: oppida vero, quae Angli ex pacto aut occasione tenebant, reddere non abnuebat, dum impensas servaret. Hispani, dum de religione pernegant, resque Belgicas Philippi clementiae permitti iubent, Anglorum impendiis sua per Anglos aucta obiiciunt, alia vero prolatant, iam manifesti erant colloquium voluisse, pacem nolle; donec argumenta in dies clariora hostilis conatus erupere, ac tandem in conspectu formidata diu classis spem et fraudes diremit.

was, now that she had perceived rumours about the fleet, through an appearance of conciliation to draw out time until the arrival of danger. However she hid her fears and presented an image of sincere wishes for peace and traffic between the nations; and then messengers came from England with similar messages, to tell the Dutch to keep their mouths shut and find arguments for closing a peace, and not burden themselves with such wrath that it looked as if in blood-stained obstinacy they preferred neverending slaughter and bloodshed.

43 But the Dutch repeated that the Spanish flatteries were faithless: "For what else has been achieved by negotiating with Requesens than the dismantling of the defence works followed by sieges of the most central cities? Have the peace negotiations at Cologne not actually undermined the prospect of a real peace, since they induced so many provinces to desert? And has Flanders not been laid open in this way, by the talk of this type of traitors? And last but not least, by treacherously promising a religious arrangement, the enemy has achieved such strength that he can now afford the boldness to reject any settlement. And **(106)** right in the middle of such civil disturbances, now that the word 'peace' is mentioned once, we should all drop our weapons and throw ourselves into a hasty surrender, each [province] under their own conditions, whichever ones suit them best? No indeed, even if a peace were to be arranged with the fairest possible conditions, the Pacification of Ghent and Don Juan's faithlessness would not suddenly be erased from history: to kings from whom the pope has lifted the obligation to honour the oaths they have sworn,[38] any treaty with their subjects is equal to a victory: and there will be no shortage of men to extract office and wealth for themselves from the downfall of the fatherland."

44 They all kept words like these among themselves however: because the lady who could impose a peace was only advising it, they filled time as if they couldn't decide; and every time the queen urged them to finish their hesitations, they implored her not to throw the cause of God and men, sixty cities and a people willing, if the current means were not enough, to supplement the public funds from their private pockets, to the teeth of Spanish faithlessness. All cities agreed (for this question had been relegated back to them individually) not to sent envoys to the enemy. Only the queen sent some, when the winter was almost over, to Flanders, to negotiate other people's peace if she could.

45 While the location for the meeting and the mandates for the delegates were being discussed, the English requested a truce, and Parma rejected this, three months passed by. For the Lowlanders Elizabeth demanded a general pardon, restoration of the privileges, and government positions for citizens; for herself, renewal of former agreements, reimbursement of her costs, and a few points to improve her sense of safety, including the withdrawal of forces on both sides. For the rest, with respect to the issue of the faith and worship in the Low Countries, her stance was so tame that she seemed about to make several concessions, and it even came to a point where she demanded not more than that the religion in question would be tolerated for another two years; and in fact she did not refuse to return the towns which were held by the English (either by treaty or circumstance), if only to avoid the expenses. On their part the Spanish rejected any concessions with respect to religion, they insisted that the matter of the Low Countries had to be left to Philip's clemency, and against the English expenses they placed the rise of their own costs because of the English' doing. Their other demands they postponed to a future occasion and soon it was clear that they wanted negotiations, not peace: until the signs of their hostile efforts became more manifest every day, and finally the appearance of the long-dreaded fleet dispersed the hope as well as their fraud.

46 (1588) At non cum Licestrio dissidia et nomina partium Batavis excesserant: quin passim hoc obtentu a praesidiariis urbium castellorumque in turbas et raptus ibatur; maxime, quibus stipendia ob pravam aerarii administrationem insoluta, pacis metu properabant militiae commoda rapere. Placuit et hic quibusdam color, ut partem stipendii tertiam, quae moribus Belgarum penes aerarium manet, melioribus olim rebus exsolvenda, repraesentari iuberent. Quod cum obtineri non posset, quia et multorum annorum (**107**) reliqua, et a multis flagitabantur, quem vellent licentiae modum sibi quisque statuebant: defensi interim a nonnullis quos Regina allegaverat, quasi Anglorum nomini haec flagitia gratificarentur. Habitus Gertrudisbergae miles, accepta ingenti pecuniae summa velut sedatus; in quam deinde licentiam et perfidiam proruperit, in tempore expediam.

47 Sonoium in urbe Medemelaca, quae in Frisii sinus occidentali est littore, ubi rebellante in ipsum suo milite negati rectoribus obsequii poenas luebat, Mauritius obsessum suis et Ordinum imperiis subegit. Flissingani praesidii moderatorem Russelium, sperata praefectura Zelandici militis, tractisque in partes Vera et Arnemuda, oppidis Walachriae insulae, imperium affectantem, tandem Reginae iussus, edoctae meliora, cohibuerunt, et sero nuntiata Licestrii abdicatio. Alibi seditiones minore periculo, sed magna pecuniae iactura sanabantur. Haec in sequentem annum exeuntia, quia cohaerent, annexui.

48 Sed priusquam turbidis digressus iustiori operi me componam, haud iniucundum fore legentibus arbitror, maxime si quae nobis super domesticis rebus laborata in aliarum gentium notitiam pervenient, breviter inspicere, quale id certamen fuerit, cum littore exiguo inclusae nationes, multisque cladibus perculsae contra tantam se magnitudinem rursus erexere. Igitur qui medio tempore fines, quis reipublicae status, quae virium copia, qui habitus animorum, inter partes utrasque comparabo.

49 Post firmatam Gandavensi foedere libertatem, Namurcum, Lucemburgumque ac Limburgum Iohannes Austriacus, Atrebates et Haenovios propriis pactionibus Parmensis, Flandriam fraude proditorum, Brabantios et Machliniam fame subegerat: nisi quod e Flandriae oppidis, Ostenda, Brabantiae, Bergae ad Zomam, dictumque ab Arausionensi Wilhelmostadium, simul castella aliquot, cuncta in maris aut amnium margine resederant. Frisia ac Transisalana penes Foederatos: sed illi Groninga aberat: haec amissis Stenovico, Daventria, totque aliis munimentis cum hoste divisa: et ne Geldriae quidem praeter Arnhemum multa oppida restabant, Geldram, Noviomagum, Zutfaniam principes urbes, et minora praesidio tenente Hispano. Hollandiam et Zelandiam integras Mauritius regebat: post caetera eius

46 With Leicester's departure however the conflicts and the names of the factions had not disappeared from the northern Netherlands; in many places the garrisons of cities and strongholds even used this pretext to start riots and plundering; especially the men whose wages were unpaid because of maladministration of the treasury lost no time, for fear of peace, in seizing the benefits of military service. Some also invoked the excuse that they wanted to be paid in cash the third part of their salary, which, according to a Dutch custom, remains in the treasury, having to be paid out at some point in better times. When it appeared impossible to obtain this money, because the remaining sum of many years **(107)** was being demanded, and by many men at the same time, they decided that each man would decide about the limits of his own licentiousness. They were even defended for a while by a handful of envoys sent by the queen, as if such disgraceful behaviour was a service to the reputation of England. The soldiers encamped in Geertruidenberg seemed to be kept in check by the payment of a huge sum of money; the wantonness and fraud this situation developed to subsequently I shall describe in due course.

47 Maurice besieged Sonoy in the city of Medemblik (on the western shores of the Zuiderzee), where a rebellion by his own men punished the latter for refusing to obey the government, and made him submit to the government of the States and himself. Russell, the commander of the garrison of Flushing, who before had held hopes to obtain the military command in Zeeland, who had drawn Veere and Arnemuiden (towns on the island of Walcheren) over to his side, and was now striving for the supreme military command, was at last held back by orders from the queen, who had become better informed, and by the late news of Leicester's abdication. In some other places rebellions were remedied with less danger but against great financial losses. This account however I have attached to the narration of the following year because that is what it is connected with.

48 Now before I leave these troubled times behind and get myself ready to embark on a more proper work of history, I think it will not be unwelcome to my readers—especially since the exposition above of our domestic affairs will come to the knowledge of readers in other countries—to have a quick look what kind of struggle it was when these nations, contained within such a small stretch of coast and beaten down by a long succession of disasters, raised themselves up again despite of the greatness of the power against them. Therefore I shall now compare between both parties, where the borders were during this time, which the situation of their commonwealths was, as well as the sizes of their forces and their mental disposition.[39]

49 After the confirmation of liberty by the Pacification of Ghent, Don Juan brought Namur, Luxemburg and Limburg back under the king's authority; the duke of Parma did the same with Artois and Hainaut via individual treaties; with Flanders by means of fraud by traitors, Mechelen and Brabant by starvation; except that in Flanders the town of Ostend, in Brabant those of Bergen op Zoom and Willemstad (named after Orange), had stayed with the other side, as well as a handful of castles, all situated on the banks of rivers or the sea. Friesland and Overijssel were on the side of the United Provinces, but from Friesland the city of Groningen was missing, and the province of Overijssel was shared with the enemy after the loss of Steenwijk, Deventer, and a great many other fortified places. Even of Guelders not many towns remained other than Arnhem, since the Spaniard held the principal cities of Geldern, Nijmegen and Zutphen, and a number of smaller ones with his garrisons. Maurice ruled over Holland and Zeeland in their entirety; later the other provinces came under his

praefecturae, extra Frisios, accessere et maritimum una imperium, quaeque hostili in solo Foederatos penes manebant; magna (**108**) exempla proprios urbibus praefectos, nisi in ultimis finibus sustulerant.

50 Nec de vicinis omiserim trans Amasium comitem Frisiae Orientalis, quae Emdana regio vulgo dicitur; ad Mosam, Rhenumque Agrippinensium et Leodici praesulem Boioarum, Philippo propinquum, qui totam Belgicam fere ambiens, nominibus sacerdotiorum diversis, latissimas ditiones possidebat; aulamque Cliviae et Iuliaci principis, quanquam bello abstinebant, ad Hispanos tamen vergere, maiori inde formidine, et Burgundicorum foederum obtentu: tum si quas urbes Batavis similitudo religionis conciliabat, his imminere hostem, et suos non minus implacabiles. At Cameracum, quam post affinium civitatum defectionem praesidio suo insessam, Valesius supremis tabulis regno Galliae commendaverat, Baligniacus, a Regum matre Catharina impositus, post utriusque mortem detinuit: ac Lotharingicae mox factioni se quoque immiscens, dum gaudet Parmensis dilatione belli agrorum raptus redimere, nec regi Henrico, suis ex urbibus profugo, circa extrema otium est, invasit haud diuturnam dominationem.

51 Ea limitum species; nunc interna videamus. Foederati, ex quo Arausionensis diu regio, dein suo nomine summam rerum complexa, mox et Licestrii ad principatum utraque accedens potestas cessaverat, edocti usu, vim imperii in plures sparsere, quod ut libertati tutius, ita, si paulum remittat hostis, concordiae periculosum. At praefecturae, quantum de vi detractum erat, tantum benevolentiae accreverat: quippe et venia et honores inde,[42] onera atque indictiones aliunde accipiebantur, atque ea praeterea vulgi natura est, ut casuum adversa his imputet vulgus, apud quos plurimum e republica est, victorias uni debeat.

52 Vetere instituto agros vicosque nobilium primores, ut cuique haereditaria ditio est, oppida civium delecti regunt: quia plebi negotiosae non concio, non comitia placuere: illi quadraginta aut pauciores numero (Sapientibus nomen est) convocati de republica deliberant: et si quem mors aut exsilium demit, adoptant sibi alios, divitiis et prudentia insignes, adeoque eius ordinis decreta pro civitatis totius consensu valent, ut vix unquam plebs obsequium defugerit, quin et armis saepe tutata sit regentium auctoritatem. Iidem nominant quotannis complures, ex queis praefectus (id olim principis munus) seligat quietis publicae (**109**) defensores, quos populi Magistros vocant, summum quatuor: et alios septem admodum, qui privata ac criminum iudicia exerceant Scabinorum appellatione. Hae functiones nullo aut

[42] honores inde, *1658, 1657a* honores, inde *1657b*

stadtholderate too (exept Friesland), together with the supreme command of the maritime forces, and the places in enemy territory which remained in the hands of the Provinces:[40] his great achievements **(108)** had given courage to the proper governors of these cities, except in the most far-removed areas.

50 Of the neighbours I should not omit mention of the count of East-Friesland, across the Ems, which is usually called Emden; then, along Meuse and Rhine, the prince-bishop of Cologne and Liège, [Ernest] of Bavaria,[41] one of Philip's relatives, who possessed large territories, surrounding the entire Low Countries with a collection of ecclesiastical titles; nor finally [omit to mention] that the court of the prince of Jülich and Cleves (although they were neutral in this war) had their sympathies on the Spanish side, given that they had more to fear from that side, and the excuse of having once closed treaties with Burgundy. Nor [should I omit] that in the cases where a similarity in religion connected cities [in these areas] with the United Provinces, the enemy became a threat to these as well, or otherwise their own people did, who were no less implacable. Cambrai however was guarded by a garrison of its own after the defection of the neighbouring cities; Anjou had trusted the place to the protection of the kingdom of France in his last will, and the Lord of Baligny, put at its head by the queen-mother Catherine [de' Medici], remained in command after the death of mother and son.[42] Soon afterwards De Baligny joined the side of Lorraine;[43] and while Parma was glad that this suspension of the war enabled him to avert despoliation of the countryside and king Henry, chased from his own cities, did not get the occasion to look after his borders, De Baligny seized a supremacy which would escape him again soon.

51 Such was the situation at the borders; let us now take a look at the inland territories. Ever since the central power holding sovereignty had disappeared (that of William of Orange, who had exercised it for a long time in the king's name, then in his own; followed by that of Leicester, and both came very close to royal power) the United Provinces, having learned from experience, divided the force of government power over many institutions. As beneficial as this is to freedom, it is dangerous to coherence, when the threat of the enemy slackens a little. However the stadtholderate gained in goodwill what it had lost in force—which happens because pardon and offices are granted from one side, taxes and prohibitions imposed from another; and moreover it is in the nature of the populace to attribute adversity to the men who have the greatest share in the government, but victories to one man.

52 Following ancient custom the countryside and its villages are governed by the most prominent of the nobility, according to where their hereditary lands are, and the towns are ruled by men chosen from the citizenship. This because the populace, busy with their trade, has no interest in meetings and assemblies. Of the citizens just mentioned, forty or fewer assemble (their meeting, *vroedschap,* carrying the name of Wisdom herself[44]) to discuss public business. When one of the members falls away because of death or emigration, they choose a replacement themselves, someone of outstanding wealth and prudence. And indeed do the decisions of this group count so well as consensus of the entire citizenship, that the populace has almost never withheld her obedience; yes it has even in many cases defended the authority of the regents by force of arms. The same council each year nominate a selection of men, from which group the stadtholder (for this was once the prince's task) chooses the defenders of public order **(109)**, whom they call the People's Masters (*Burgomasters*), in a total number of four. And in addition to these he chooses seven others, who conduct private and criminal proceedings, carrying the title of *Schepenen* (Aldermen).

exiguo praemio, ut debitum patriae praestantur. Atque horum omnium potestate, et consilio adsessorum, qui ius civile didicerunt, res oppidanae administrantur, concesso iure, etiam leges et modica vectigalia intra suum statuendi.

53 Hinc velut in fastigium coeunte imperio, qui singuli partibus, universae nationi coniunctim praesident. Nam ter, quaterve anno, aut quoties digna incidunt, concilium advocatur, cui Ordinum nomen, ex utraque populi parte. Sed nobilitas, quia diversis e sedibus haud facile coeat, curam sui in paucos contulit, qui genere et possessionibus praestantes in commune consulerent. Iis primum loco, sed unum omnibus suffragium est.

54 Ubi ergo cuiusque oppidi concilium[43] de rebus propositis domi deliberavit, mittuntur ad conventum magistratus et adsessores, qui illi visa enuntient, permissis, quae repentina obveniunt, ipsorum prudentiae et fidei. Hoc igitur in coetu cum alia tractantur omnia, quae principum fuere, tum tributa quotannis edici necesse est, quibus belli onera in singulas gentes dispensata pro viribus sustinentur. Sed quoniam conventus hic rursum dissolvitur, delegant nobilitas et qui primariis urbibus praesunt homines ex se idoneos, ut apud imperii sedem rerum quotidianarum disposita Ordinibus placita exsequantur: simul mederi subitis, et perscripto, si quid curam maiorem flagitat, conventum indicere permissum: is honor ad tempus fere sumitur.

55 Sed perpetua est dignitas Hollandiae Advocati. Is principum temporibus vox erat publicae libertatis, utque tunc periculis, ita mutata republica auctoritate praecipuus, in conventu Ordinum et delegatorum consessu exquirit sententias, praeit suadendo, componit dissidentes. Hoc munus a Paulo Busio, ab initiis belli, cum laude administratum, excepit mox Iohannes Oldenbarneveldius, auxitque virtutibus propriis, quarum insigne documentum dedit adversus Licestrii minas artesque, ut fidus consilii, ita animi invictus.

56 Haec fere Hollandiae regendae est facies: unde mos aliarum nationum haud longe discrepat. Habent et quaeque rei fiscalis curatores, et iudices legum peritos, ad quos ab oppidanis tribunalibus provocatio est, qui omnes perpetuas obtinent dignitates, (**110**) legente praefecto eorum ex numero, quos ipsi Ordines nominavere.

[43] concilium *errata 1657a (vide Intr. § 11.4)* consilium *1657, 1658*

These offices are fulfilled against little or no payment, as a debt one has to one's community. The cities are governed by the might of all these men and the advice of pensionaries, who have a training in law; and they have even been granted the right to issue laws and impose smaller taxation within their own territory.

53 From this level, as if the realm gathers for a summit, the gentlemen who each direct a part of the nation, direct the whole together. That is, three or four times a year, or as often as a worthy matter arises, this meeting is convened, which carries the name of States[45], and represents both classes in society. The nobility however, because from their dispersed residences they cannot easily assemble, have conferred the care of their business onto a small group of men, pre-eminent in birth and wealth, who look after their common interest. Their vote is the first in the row, but all together they have only one.

54 Thus, when the council of each town have debated the current issues at home, they send magistrates and pensionaries to the assembly to pronounce their town's decisions, who also have permission to deal with unexpected matters guided by their own prudence and faithfulness. Now in this meeting all other issues are dealt with which used to be among the princes' tasks, and they must pronounce the yearly tax levies as well, by which the costs of the war (distributed over the individual provinces in proportion to their financial powers) are supported. But since this meeting is dissolved again, the nobility and the leadership of the most important towns choose capable men from their midst who stay at the seat of the Generalty and look after the execution of the daily business settled by the decisions of the States [General]. Their tasks also include solving urgent business, and writing out convocations for a meeting if some matter requires the attention of a wider circle. This office can generally be held for a limited time only.

55 However the office of Advocate of Holland is given for a lifetime. In the times of the princes this man was the voice of the freedom of all; and just as he was on a pedestal because of the danger involved in his position, so he is in the new form of government because of his personal authority. In the assemblies of the States[46] and the meetings of the Gecommiteerde Raden[47] he investigates the various viewpoints, leads the process of arguing, and creates consensus among the dissenting delegates. This task was fulfilled with excellent result by Paulus Buys[48] from the early days of the war, and subsequently taken over by Johan van Oldenbarnevelt.[49] The latter has added to the weight of the office by his personal qualities, of which he provided memorable proof by his resistance against Leicester's threats and machinations, as a man as trustworthy in judgment as he is undaunted in spirit.

56 This is roughly the way Holland is governed; it is not much different in the other provinces. They all have their administrators of the public finances, and judges well-trained in law, to whom appeal can be made against the judiciaries of the towns. These men all hold their offices for life, **(110)** and they are appointed by the stadtholder from a group nominated by the States.

57 Iam vero communia foederis et quae bello necessaria, Senatus providet: in quem qui veniunt, iurant nullo eorum, ex quibus mittuntur, respectu (mittunt enim singulae nationes, sed tres Hollandi, binos Zelandi, item Frisii, singulos caeterae,) quod universae rei optimum, se consulturos: acciuntur huc, ubi gravis deliberatio est, praefecti nationum. Sed quia res maiores antiquitus nisi gentium singularum consensu non expediebantur, mole negotiorum et periculo cunctationis repertum est, legatos mittere cum liberis mandatis, qui supremae curae imminerent, et, ubi quid gravius obveniret moraque dignum, suae quisque patriae Ordines consulerent.

58 Nationibus, quae modo e primariis urbibus aliquam[44] apud foedera habent, ius aequum suffragii; vicibus praesident. Hae tum erant, Geldria, Hollandia, Zelandia, Traiectina, Frisia intra Flevum et Lavicam, et Transisalana. Haec legatio sensim in perpetui consessus speciem transiit, Ordines foederatos referens, eoque nomine utitur. Et huc, et in senatum missis, praefinito tempore potestas inclusa, non nisi voluntate mandantium prorogatur. Similiter inferiores alii maritimas in urbes delegantur, qui res navales iudiciis et consiliis defendant.

59 Talis in summa reipublicae[45] habetur status: neque enim congruens sit exigua persequi: unde clarum, nec paucas intra familias conclusum, nec rursus ita populare imperium, ut apud multitudinem sit. Sed nobilibus suam auctoritatem, potestatis plurimum penes cives praecipuos clariorum oppidorum relinqui: hinc velut per gradus designari qui nationibus singulis, quique cunctis imperitent; non ut in vulgi potentia, promiscua et fortuita dignatione, sed nomina maiorum, partas opes, ingenii decora spectando: nec pessime provisum libertati, dum praecipua rerum inter plurimos tractantur, semperque in alios transeunt maximae potestates, ut multi citra spem continuandae licentiae iustis regendi artibus assuescant. Sane olim video, et cum in Romanos bellatum est, Galliae, Germaniae, Britanniaeque populis placuisse per gentis proceres et civitatum legationes res maximas disceptari, ac manere eius moris reliquias ab ultima libertate, etiam ubi nunc regna sunt. Quod si vetera repetimus per Graeciam, Amphictyones haud discrepant, quorum consensus Medorum potentiae restitit; aut (**III**) Achaia, cuius res alioqui exiguae sola concordia valuere.

60 Caeterum sua cuique urbs regioni caput. Commune nunc imperii domicilium apud Hollandos, qui ut opibus longe ante socios, ita auctoritate non parum pollent, Haga est vicus, eademque Mauritii sedes, nemore et vicino littore imprimis amoena. Haud multo diversus regia in parte reipublicae status, nisi quod eius Belgicae Ordines, extra tributorum causam, vix convocantur. Privatis cuiusque

44 aliquam *1657, 1658* aliquem *Boot*
45 *reipublicae* 1657 *Reipublicae* 1658

57 Then the Council of State, which looks after the common politics of the Union and the demands of the war. The men sent to this council swear an oath that they will advice what is best for the common cause, and not be guided by the interests of the region they come from (for they are sent by the individual provinces, but Holland sends three, Zeeland two, Friesland two, and the other provinces one each). When there is a serious matter to discuss, the stadtholders of the provinces are summoned to this council. But since by old custom the most important questions are only settled with the approval of the individual provinces, given the mass of business this produces and the danger of delays, the practice has been invented to send delegates with a so-called free mandate to oversee the eventual fulfilment of the decisions, and, whenever a more serious complication arises which justifies the delay, to go consult the States of their respective home regions.

58 The provinces which have at least one of their main cities in the area of the United Provinces, possess the full voting rights, and take turns as president of the meeting. These were then Guelders, Holland, Zeeland, Utrecht, Friesland between Zuiderzee and Lauwerszee,[50] and Overijssel. Gradually this delegation assumed the form of a permanent gathering, which represents the States-General and acts in their name. The men sent to this council and to the Council of State have powers only for a pre-defined period, which is not extended without the approval of their superiors. In the same way office-holders of lower rank are delegated to the maritime cities to support the maritime business with their advice and decisions.

59 This is broadly the organisation of the republic, for it wouldn't be fitting to pursue it into detail here. But the above makes clear that power is not reserved for a small number of families, while on the other hand it is not of such popular nature that it is held by the crowd. No, the nobility retain their authority, and the main share of power is in the hands of the foremost citizens of the more important towns. Departing from them, as it were in progressive order, people are appointed to assume command of the individual provinces and of the whole. And this is not done, as where the crowd rules, by hot-headed and fortuitous exaltation, but under consideration of rank of birth, wealth acquired, and intellectual achievements. And for the protection of freedom it is an excellent practice to discuss the chief political issues with the majority, and pass the major executive powers on to new men continuously, so that many administrators, not having any expectation of seeing their freedom to act become permanent, acquire the habit of ruling in a fair and proper manner. For I see clearly in the ancient histories of France, Germany and Britain (including the times when they were at war with Rome) that it was the wish of these peoples to have the main political issues dealt with by the most prominent men of the nation and delegations from the towns, and that traces of this habit have remained ever since their original liberty, even where there are now kingdoms. And if we take a closer look at the ancient history of Greece, it appears that the Amphictyonic league, which' coherence withstood the power of the Medes, was nothing different; nor Achaia, **(111)** which was small by itself but derived strength from unity.

60 For the rest, each region has its own capital town. In Holland the seat of the common government is the village of The Hague; and since Holland by far surpasses its allies in wealth, it has no mean share of influence over the union. The Hague is also Maurice's residence; because of its situation with a forest and the coast nearby it is a place of first-rank pleasantness. In the royal part of the Low Countries the form of government is not much different, except that their States-General are hardly ever convoked, except for the sake of taxation. Of the men who were elected to administer each province's own business, only

nationis rebus delecti pauci supersunt: regimen omne cum praefecto senatus obtinet, et qui adsunt senatui consessus fiscalis et iuridicus. Adscriptis semel is honor manet.

61 Foederatorum reditus ante qui fuerint memoravimus; mox liberalius, amoto omni terrore dominatus, pro republica quasi sua tribuere coeperunt, et postquam auctis commerciis per Brabantiae excidium cum opibus animi crevere, aderantque successus, maiora audendo sumptus et onera duplicabantur. Agri, aedes, annona, vestis, capita, nihil immune, nec subeundo foenori temperatum: certissimum vectigal, apertum mare, nec, ut alia, bello obnoxium: quanquam mercaturae prae caeteris parcebatur regentium studiis; tum ne maximum atque instabile commodum alio pelleretur.

62 At Belgicae Hispaniensis opes, quanquam tributis difficulter certantibus, regiae pecuniae accessione immenso anteibant, nisi multitudine tractantium, et largiendi facilitate, dum partim singuli retentant ut suas, partim profundunt ut alienas, ante veros usus interceptae perirent.

63 Miles Batavis conductus, civis, socius, peregrinus, praeter Anglicana auxilia, ad decies et octies mille pedites sub haec tempora non excrescebat, modico cum equite: pars maior detenta praesidiis: et hostium multitudini impares, antequam illorum vires Gallia distraheret. Sed Licestrii incuria, et tot seditiones docuerant parvis potius se copiis tueri, quam supra aerarii vires militis nomine hostem conscribere. Disciplinae indies acrior ratio, ne cives et vicinae gentes, quique agri ipsos inter et hostem siti raptus tributo redimunt, per iniurias vexarentur: et cum hybernatum ducitur miles, nulla privatim impendia; quicquid praestitum est, respublica persolvit: ea aequalitate effecta est res mira, ut ultro expeterentur armati hospites.

64 Peditatus omnis in cohortes distributus, ita enim vocabimus, constat decem vexillis, raro pluribus. Vexilla centum homines continent: sunt et (**112**) maiora: sed, in universum si inspicias, per mortes et fugas et ducum furta ad hunc ferme numerum devenitur. Totidem equites habent turmae, quarum tres, velut ala, communi imperio reguntur. Quo paratius expedirentur stipendia, certas cohortes turmasque nationes singulae in se receperunt, quibus aera de suo numerant. Coeptum et hoc usurpari, ut tribunos ordinumque ductores ipsi designarent; minora belli munera mandant ductores ipsi; maiora, qui summae reipublicae praesunt, ex virtute, aut gratia. Hostium copiae plus quam altero superabant, quibus suspecta cuncta lateque diffusos fines coercerent. Aequale utrinque gregario stipendium:

a few remain; their Council State holds all the reigns of government together with the stadtholder[51] and the financial and judicial committees which assist the Council of State. Once appointed to these committees, their members remain in office for life.

61 The United Provinces' sources of income before the revolt have been discussed already;[52] after it they soon began to contribute more liberally, now that the fear of tyranny was gone, for the sake of the commonwealth as if it was their own home. Their trade increased because Brabant had dropped out, so that with wealth, their confidence rose as well. When subsequently the first successes arrived, spending and levies were doubled to enable even greater pursuits. Land, building, food, cloth, people, nothing was exempted and not even the need to take a loan could give you a reduction. The surest source of income however was the wide sea, which was not, like everything else, liable to the effects of the war: although the efforts of the regents made sure that trade was spared more than all other activities, also in order to prevent this enormous but fleeting profit from being forced to move elsewhere.

62 Although their tax collection was struggling heavily, the resources of the Spanish Netherlands were far greater [than those of the North] because they were augmented enormously by royal money—if these resources wouldn't disappear again before reaching their proper destination as a result of the many hands that they go through and an easiness in donating; while the receiving individuals partly cling to the money as if it was their own, partly spend it lavishly as that of somebody else.

63 The army of the Republic included mercenary troops, citizens, allies, foreigners, and by this time (apart from the English auxiliary troops) did not exceed the number of eighteen thousand footmen, plus a modestly sized cavalry. The majority of these were detained in city garrisons, and numerically inferior to the masses of the enemy before France started to occupy their forces.[53] However Leicester's negligence and the great number of [military] rebellions taught the Dutch to defend themselves with a small army rather than, at a cost beyond their treasury, to hire their own enemy under the label of soldiers. The disciplining system became stricter day by day to keep the citizenship and neighbouring nations, as well as the countryside between our soldiers and the enemy (which buys off plundering by paying a tribute), from suffering offences. When the soldiers are marched off for the winter, no one is left with the costs privately; and whatever is provided to the army is paid for by the commonwealth. By this equal division of costs an astonishing thing is achieved: that citizens of their own accord invite these armed guests for accommodation.

64 The infantry is subdived into regiments (for this is what we will call them), and one regiment consists of ten squads,[54] rarely **(112)** of more. A squad contains a hundred men, but bigger ones exist. However, if you look at the whole, including death, desertion, and fraud by the officers, it amounts to roughly this number.[55] The same number of horsemen makes up a cavalry squadron, which are grouped in units of three under one command, like a wing. To stimulate the timely payment of the wages, particular regiments and squadrons are adopted by individual provinces, who provide the money from their own funds. In addition the practice has been introduced that these provinces appoint the higher officers and the commanders of the ranks, and that the said commanders distribute the lower military appointments. The highest positions in the army are handed out by the leaders of the commonwealth on the basis of merit or favour.[56] The forces of the enemy exceeded even the double number of ours, which he used to control everything that might be suspect in his widely dispersed territory. A common soldier earned the same wages in both armies, but

sed penes Hispanum maiora extra ordinem praemia, et ingens duplarium turba; nec eo minus oppidis agrisque per castra aut praesidia graves, bis aerario nocebant. Regimen quoque armorum aemulatu dissidebat.

65 Contra Mauritius, ex quo primum belli curae admotus est, nihil eorum praetermisit, quae vetus aetas, aut recentior usus invenerant: impiger suas accelerare, et res hostium attendere: etiam supremo imperio inferiora non extra suam sollicitudinem pati. Ergo, admirandum, militiae doctor, cuius doctorem non viderat, firmare cuncta belli meditamentis, ut intentae essent vigiliae, munitae urbes; castra docte metari, oppugnandi machinationes in promptu habere: tum milites, ignari operum ac praeliorum, equos regere, servare ordines, ferre cibum, ferre aggerem iubentur, non in huius saeculi morem.

66 Ea diu ludibrio, ob eorum inscitiam, qui quae ignorant discere erbubescunt, post eventus aliquot miraculo fuere: quippe ubi multis cladibus fugaces ausi iterum consistere, et oppida velut impetu rapta: plane ut iam omnes faterentur, quemadmodum affectandis populorum studiis, ac fundandae reipublicae, neminem patre priorem, ita ad tuendas res augendasque coelesti munere filium obtigisse. At, quantum belli ratio ab usu priori discesserit, in ipso sequentis operis contextu intelligetur. Navium haud contemnenda vis ad maritimas hostium urbes, aut amnium commeatus excubat: partim piscationi mercatoribusque praesidio eunt, aut, ad proturbandos praedones, oceanum pervagantur. Non dubie hostis hac parte inferior, cui portus haud multi, nec sane utiles, et naves paucae, quae pro urbibus speculantur.

67 Nobilitas utrinque segni otio aut tranquillis honoribus (**113**) imminebat; frigore in partes, ob invidiam, hic plebis, illic Hispanorum: an et inveterata inertia, quia callidi quondam principes militarium officiorum gratiam illis fecerant, translata in possessiones functione: pauci, amore laudis, aut per familiares angustias, arma et dignas genere suo curas capessebant. E vulgo memores peiorum, et iuniores, quia pacem non viderant, contenti qualicumque rerum statu, bellum nisi per rumores et tributa non sentiebant: et multi, quibus religio sine affectu publice recepta, non ob aliud, sequebantur.

68 At Romanis caeremoniis innutritos, post tot coitionum exempla, leges Batavorum, mulctae non admodum gravis sanctione, privatis quoque sacris prohibebant. Iidem praecipuis honoribus usu tacito arcebantur. Reliquias sacerdotum utriusque sexus, quia publicatae possessiones plerisque in locis erant, dum tranquilli degerent, alimentis Ordines solabantur. Aliarum sectarum conventus placebat dissimulando transmittere. Ministri publicae religionis nulla in parte consiliorum: ne

in the Spanish army the extraordinary bonuses were higher and there is a huge crowd of double-earners. Nevertheless they were a source of problems for the towns and the countryside, whether they were in garrisons or in the camp, doing double harm to the treasury. And among their military leadership competition led to strife.

65 On the other side, Maurice, as soon as he was put in charge of the war, did not neglect to introduce any of the improvements which ancient or modern practice had invented. With great energy he pursued his own agenda and kept a close eye on the enemy's plans; even from his position at the top he let no detail escape his vigilant care. The astonishing result was that this teacher of warfare, who had had no teacher himself, secured every imaginable success by relying on planning and preparation, so that the watchmen were awake, the cities fortified; army camps were built skilfully, the siege machines were ready; while the soldiers who were inexperienced in battle and field labour were being commanded to steer horses, keep their ranks, carry their food, and build ramparts, as was no longer customary in our century.

66 For a long time these exercises were the object of ridicule, because of the stupidity of people who shy away from learning things they don't know already. But after the first handful of successes they became an object of marvel: because where many defeats had made the soldiers prone to flight, they dared hold their ground again, and towns were taken as by storm. With the clear result that everyone declared that, just as no one had been better than his father at getting groups of people behind his efforts, and laying the groundwork for a commonwealth, just so the son was a gift from heaven to protect and extend it. How much Maurice's approach to the war was different from the earlier practice will become clear in the pages of the subsequent work.[57] It is no mean force of ships that keeps an eye on the enemy's ports or their river traffic; in part they also provide protection to fishing and trade, or patrol the sea to dispel pirates. There is no doubt the enemy is the weaker party in this respect, as he has only a small number of ports, and not very useful ones; and few ships that keep watch in front of his cities.

67 The nobility on both sides of the divide was primarily intent on having undemanding lives free of business, and quiet administrative positions **(113)** because of a coldness towards the parties, caused by wrath against the populace on the one side and the Spaniards on the other. Or perhaps by an inveterate laziness, created by cunning princes in the past who excused them from military duties, so that their tasks concentrated on the management of their possessions. Only a few, driven by love of glory, or family poverty, pursued military service or other occupations worthy of their birth. Among the populace all who remembered worse times, as well as the younger generation because they had never seen peace, accepted whichever political situation. They felt the war only through rumours and taxation, and many followed suit, adhering without passion to whichever religion was the received public one (and for no other reason).

68 Now after many meetings of people brought up in the Roman worship had been discovered, the Dutch[58] issued a law that forbade them even in private services, although the punishment was not a very heavy one. At the same time a tacit practice kept these people out of the most important public offices. Because in most places their possessions had been declared public property, the remains of the clergy (of both sexes) were soothed by the States with a pension so long as they kept quiet. It was preferred to ignore the gatherings of other sects and leave them unaddressed. The ministers of the public church had no

ecclesiastici quidem coetus citra inspectionem magistratuum. Omnino, si proximi motus consedissent, haud facile novi timebantur.

69 Parte quoque alia Belgarum, longa peritia turbarum causis occurrerat. Species legum quae ante bellum: nec gravis cuiquam Parmensis modestia: et aliquot civitates praesidiis, cunctae vi regentium tenebantur: ac quanquam episcopi datas sub Parmensis matre, et Albano, sedes occupabant, et Iesuitarum in gratiam pleraque inclinaverant, inquisitionibus et suppliciis temperabatur, belli et hostium respectu; tum quia dissentientes pars magna profugerant, reliqui metu quam poenis didicerant parere.

70 Utrisque in partibus annonae caritatem, et caeterorum, quibus vita indiget, intenta magnis oneribus pretia [et][46] agrorum fructus parum commode, negotiatio, et operarum pariter adauctae mercedes facilius sustinebant. Florebat Batavis mercatura, inferiorum artium nutrix: unumque Amstelodamum veterum et huius saeculi maximis emporiis aequabatur.

71 Per bellum interea pacis ut bona manebant, ita mala non emoriebantur; armorum usu adeo non efferatis ingeniis, ut in contrarium vergerent: nam cultus victusque nimia et supervacua externorum contactu, qui non inops illic exsilium tolerabant, nullis legum habenis, secuti ditiores, mox neutiquam pares pudore paupertatis in eadem traxerant. Itaque tum primum prisca (**114**) Batavorum fortisque simplicitas et castae munditiae in luxum vertebant, aerario quidem vectigalem, at moribus perniciosum: quippe quo avaritia, malum vetus, in audaciam impellitur, nec sinit meminisse victas esse gentes, quae eum vivendi modum tradiderunt. Sed pro virtute erant hostium vitia, quorum intolerabilior luxus ne inopia quidem mutabatur.

ANNALIUM FINIS.

[46] pretia [et] *scripsimus*   pretia *1657, 1658*

share in the secular government; conversely not even the meetings of the church boards escaped supervision by the magistrates. In short, once the present disturbances were over, there would be little fear of new ones.

69 In the other part of the Low Countries too the experience of many years had provided the means against the causes of disturbances. Outwardly the laws were as they had been before the war, and Parma's restraint made things difficult for nobody. A handful of towns were controlled by garrisons; all by the power of their regents. Although the bishops' seats were in the places as regulated under Parma's mother and Alva,[59] and although most of the country had an inclination favouring the Jesuits, religious investigation and executions were generally avoided, in view of the fact that there was a war and an enemy. Another reason was that most of the dissenters had fled, while those remaining had learned obedience from fear rather than through punishment.

70 In both parts of the Low Countries food was expensive, the prices of the other necessities of life were high because of the taxes [and] harvesting the produce a lot of hard work: but commerce and the labour wages which had grown at equal pace sustained these without difficulty. In Holland trade, which feeds all the lower professions, flourished. Amsterdam alone was put on a par with the greatest emporia of ancient and present times.

71 Meanwhile, in spite of the war, the good things of peacetime were preserved, nor did the bad things perish. The practice of warfare had done so little to turn people into savages that in fact they leaned to the contrary. In the absence of restraining laws, the contact with foreigners sustaining an unpenniless exile in our country, inspired the rich to imitate the vanity and excesses in their dress and food. And soon, for shame of poverty, they dragged along others who couldn't afford it in any way. Thus it started in this time that the original **(114)** and steadfast simplicity and chaste elegance of the Dutch changed into luxuriousness, which, although it is a source of income to the treasury, is lethal to moral character: because it drives greed, the ancient evil, to insolence, and leaves no space for the awareness that the nations which have handed down such fashions of life, are on the losing side of history. Nevertheless they regarded as virtues the faults of an enemy, whose unsustainable luxury was not even corrected by the experience of poverty.

Andries Vaillant Sculp.
JOHAN VAN OLDENBARNEVELT,
RIDDER, HEER VANDEN TEMPEL, BERKEL, RODENRYS etc.
ADVOCAAT VAN HOLLANDT EN WESTVRIESLANDT.etc.

5.55. *Portrait of Johan van Oldenbarnevelt* by Andries Vaillant

Notes to *Annals* Book I

1 A reference to the war between Rome and its Italic allies, 90–88 BC, also called *Bellum Italicum* or *Bellum Marsicum*, after the largest group that revolted against Rome.

2 The words *Belga, Belgica* and *Belgicus* refer to the Low Countries as a whole, so all seventeen provinces together; the name derives from that of the Roman province *Gallica Belgica*, the northernmost one of the three provinces that Roman Gaul was divided into. In Grotius' time, the usual way to refer to the province of Holland and its population in Latin is *Batavia* and *Batavi*, after the inhabitants of the central river area during the Roman era. Grotius himself wrote about these (perceived) ancestors in *De Antiquitate Reipublicae Batavicae* (see bibliography). Sometimes Batavia and Batavi are used to refer to the Dutch Republic as a whole.

3 That is, reason of state; see Introduction § 4–6.

4 On the image of the ancient Batavians in Grotius' time see primarily Grotius, *De Antiquitate* and Hadrianus Junius, *Batavia*.

5 As in: 'the emperor's companion'; Latin *comes* (pl. *comites*), Dutch 'graaf'. In *De Antiquitate* 5.2 Grotius suggests another historical explanation for *comes*, one that could point to mutual equality of (local) *comites*. (The Dutch word *graaf* has a different origin that probably goes back to a legal title ('judge') in the Frankish empire.

6 *Munimenta libertatis*, similar to *Praesidium libertatis* ('bulwark of freedom', also the motto of Leiden university where Grotius studied); but phrased differently because no reference to the university is intended here.

7 i.e. the princes.

8 The States' meeting is that of the three above-mentioned Estates in medieval society. Originally (representatives of) the medieval Estates were convened by the prince (e.g. count or duke) of a province to give policy advice. Over the course of the Middle Ages the States as a deliberative, representative body extended their own position of power by attaching political conditions to support granted to the prince (e.g. permitting taxation, '*bedes*'). The rights (*privileges*) resulting from these conditions, together with the privileges awarded to specific noble families and towns were collected in charters which a new prince had to take an oath to uphold upon his accession. At these moments the charters were often revised and sometimes extended, adding up to milestone general Privileges such as the Joyous Entry of Brabant (1356) and the Great Privilege of Mary of Burgundy (1477) which bound new princes to far-going limitations on their power. On the basis of this logic the Estates eventually came to claim a share in the actual sovereignty. Grotius defended this view of the division of power between States and princes, arguing that a prince's acceptance in power depended on the permission of the States; that the States could meet and make decisions at their own initiative; and ultimately that a prince held power only by delegation from the States.

9 Tacitus, *Histories* 4.12.3, a direct reference to the ancient Batavians; see also Grotius, *De Antiquitate* 3.5.

10 i.e. the Viking invasions.

11 Hadrian VI (1459–1523), Adriaan Florensz., pope from 9-1-1522 to 14-9-1523. He came originally from Utrecht, and had been teacher to both Erasmus and Charles V; he was regent for Charles V in Spain for some time and bishop of Tortosa afterwards. He imposed limits on papal court culture and acted against nepotism and the sale of offices. In Germany he tried to have the imperial ban against Luther actually enforced. Next to this he tried to put an end to the conflict between Habsburg and France in order to free forces for an emergency operation against the Turkish advances in Europe. When these attempts failed, he tried to mobilise an army himself, which forced him to alleviate the aforementioned disciplinary measures. In the end he was forced to enter into an alliance with Charles V against France. He was impopular in the Vatican, and rumours of poisoning surround his death.

12 William II of Croy (1458–1521), lord of Chièvres, duke of Soria, marquis of Aarschot and count of Beaumont; a close confidant of Philip the Fair and Charles V. In Spain he was accused of abusing his

position for personal profit and other varieties of corruption and avarice; see *Historische* WP ad loc. and Caspar Burman, *Hadrianus VI sive analecta historica de Hadriano Sexto*, Utrecht 1728, p. 45).

13 In the Italian or Four-Years' War (1521–1526) between Venice and France, and an alliance of Habsburg, England and the Vatican. At an early stage in this war France invaded Navarre and the Low Countries but both operations were countered. The main confrontation took place in Italy; France suffered a crushing defeat in 1525 in the battle of Pavia where king Francis I was taken captive.

14 Possibly a reference to the actions of the lords of Croy and others mentioned in 1.12.

15 The Council of State, the Secret Council and the Financial Council respectively; together these are called the *Collaterale Raden*, and were instituted by Charles V in 1531. Under Philip II the Council of State lost influence; in order to reduce the influence of the higher nobility, the governess, Margaret, consulted mostly with three men from the Council of State, i.e. Granvelle, Viglius and Berlaymont (the *Consulta*); see also note to 1.37.

16 'Netherlanders' or 'Lowlanders' in this translation.

17 A rendition of *De Zwijger, le Taciturne*, 'the silent'.

18 In 1558, during the last phase of the French-Habsburg war of 1557–1559.

19 Lamoraal, count of Egmond (1522–1568). Successful commander in the Spanish army, stadtholder of Flanders and Artois, and member of the Council of State where together with Orange and Horne (see below) he would lead the high nobility's resistance against Granvelle. After Granvelle's departure they continued the resistance against Spanish policies, leading to the arrest and execution of Egmond and Horne.

20 Philip of Montmorency, count of Horne (1518 or 1524–1568). Admiral of the Low Countries and member of the Council of State since 1561. For a biography, see P. Geurts, *De graaf van Horne: Filips van Montmorency, 1524–1568*. Zaltbommel 1968.

21 A passage of comparable spirit in *Meletius* c. 2 (Grotius, *Meletius sive de iis quar inter Christianos conveniunt Epistola*, ed. G.H.M Posthumus Meyes, Leiden Brill 1988; see p. 75, 103, and Intr. p. 23).

22 A *Staatsgezind* statement of principle; see Intr. § 2.4.

23 Until the end of the 12th century the Church rarely used violence to discipline believers. The Albigensian heresy in France, which threatened the social and ecclesiastical order in the first half of the 13th century, brought secular governments to act against disobedience within the Church. Roman law provided the principle that insurrection agains the Church be treated as lèse-majesté. Pope Lucius III and Frederick Barbarossa issued the edict *Ad dolendam*, which excommunicated persistent heretics and delivered them to secular jurisdiction. The inquiry into heresy pertained to the Church; the Inquisition became am important tool to root out heresies.

24 In 1521.

25 Two quotations adapted from Tacitus *Annals* 1.6 and 1.12, suggesting a parallel between Habsburg rule and the beginning of Tiberius' tyranny.

26 Mary of Hungary (1505–1558), younger sister of Charles V. She was expected to become queen of Hungary by marriage to Louis II of Hungary. However the death of her husband in the battle of Mohács in 1526 against the Turks meant the end of this position. Charles appointed her in 1530 as governess of the Low Countries, which she remained until his abdication in 1555.

27 Margaret of Parma (1522–1586) was an illegitimate daughter of Charles V and Janneke van der Gheynst. From 1559 to 1567 she was governess of the Low Countries. Originally she leant on the cardinal Granvelle's support, until differences of opinion drove them apart. At Alva's arrival Margaret resigned from her post. See also note to 5.3.

28 Antoine Perrenot de Granvelle (1517–1586), son of Nicolas (1484–1550, advisor and seal-keeper of Charles V). Antoine was first bishop of Arras and inherited his father's position after the emperor's death. In 1561 he became cardinal-archbishop of Mechelen. After Philip's departure from the Low Countries he was Margaret's most important advisor for some time and became the face of Spanish policy in the Low Countries. He was known for his avarice, was regarded as the architect of the reorganisation of the bishoprics and incurred the hatred of many, which led Philip to dismiss him. After his departure from the Low Countries in 1564 he was envoy in Rome and viceroy of Naples

from 1571–1575. From 1579 he served as royal counsellor in Madrid, among others on the affairs of the Low Countries, which again brought him hatred and a conflict with the king.

29 Philip I the Magnanimous, Landgraf of Hessen (1504–1567), one of the leaders of the protestant, anti-imperial and anti-catholic Schmalkaldic League. He was captured by Charles V's army in the Schmalkaldic War (1546–1547), and remained prisoner until Maurice of Saxony forced the emperor to release him and Johann Frederick of Saxony in 1552.

30 In 1546–1547, after Charles V had made peace with France, a war was fought between the emperor and the Schmalkaldic League (see above), ending in the (unexpected) defeat of the League in the battle of Mühlberg.

31 Margaret of Parma was married to Ottavio Farnese (1521–1586). The Farnese family carried the title of dukes of Parma and Piacenza. In 1512 both cities had become part of the Vatican state. Pope Paul III united them to one duchy and gave this to his son, Pier Luigi Farnese in 1545. After Pier's violent death in 1547, Charles V claimed the duchy as a punishment for the fact that the Farnese had sided with the French. Luigi's son Ottavio received his Italian possessions back from Philip II in 1556 in exchange for siding with Habsburg in the future. As collateral, Piacenza kept a Spanish garrison and Ottavio's son Alessandro (who would serve in the Low Countries from 1578) was raised at the court in Madrid. Ottavio and Margareta kept urging Philip for a long time to return Piacenza, which was partly responsible for the troublesome relationship between Margaret and Philip. See also 5.3.

32 In May 1560 a naval battle took place near the island Djerba in the Gulf of Gabes (Tunesia) between an Ottoman fleet and that of a Christian alliance under Spanish command. The occasion was the conquest of the island by the Christian alliance, which however suffered a crushing defeat in this battle.

33 Antoine de Lalaing (ca. 1535–1568), count of Hoogstraten, took part in the opposition against Philip II since 1556; he was married to Eleonora de Montmorency (ca. 1530–1600).

34 Charles de Berlaymont (1510–1578) was president of the Financial Council as re-instituted by Charles V. Viglius of Aytta (1507–1577) was president of the Secret Council since 1549 and the most senior public servant in the Habsburg administrative organisation in the Low Countries. He enjoyed the favour of Mary of Hungary and Charles V; Granvelle was his patron and a personal friend. In the religious controversy his principles were an Erasmian humanism and the integrity of Catholicism. He supported only limited persecution of heretics, but did not succeed in changing the approach of the Inquisition. See Postma, F. Postma, *Viglius van Aytta als humanist en diplomaat 1507–1549*, Zutphen 1983 and id., *Viglius van Aytta. De jaren met Granvelle 1549–1564*, Zutphen 2000.

35 The 'Geheime Raad' (Secret Council), instituted to handle the most important administrative and juridical matters; for these Councils see also 1.14 and note.

36 The city of Reims was an episcopal seat since the third century, and later archi-episcopal seat. Since the Diocletian re-organisation of the Roman Empire (296 BC) it was the capital of the province *Belgica II*.

37 Terwaan, Terenburg.

38 i.e. archbishoprics.

39 Kamerijk, Camerick.

40 Traditionally (i.e. up to 1559) the northern Low Countries, except the province of Groningen, belonged to the bishopric of Utrecht which (together with that of Liège) fell under the archbishopric of Cologne. Flanders, Artois and Hainaut fell under the archbishopric of Reims. The new episcopal organisation created three archbishoprics in the Low Countries: Utrecht, Mechelen and Cambrai (only Liège remained under Cologne). These three were sub-divided into 18 bishoprics. The bishops now had to be graduated theologians and were no longer appointed by the clergy from the bishopric, but by the pope at the king's recommendation. Over the whole, the archbishop of Mechelen would preside, i.e. Granvelle, who was raised to the rank of cardinal by the pope.

41 For the episode, see Postma, *Viglius, jaren met Granvelle* 243–258, esp. p. 249.

42 13 March 1564

43 In Tacitus this type of behaviour is characteristic for Tiberius, who is portrayed as a tyrant; see e.g. *Annals* 1.11, 3.11–12, 3.44.
44 i.e. the members of the Council of State and esp. Orange, Egmond and Horne.
45 January to April 1565.
46 A group of monks (including Casiodoro de Reina, 1520–1594) in the monastery of San Isidoro del Campo (near Sevilla) had access to writings from the Lutheran world and worked on a Spanish translation of Scripture (building on the work of a.o. Francisco de Enzinas and Juan Pérez de Pineda). They came under suspicion by the Inquisition and fled in 1557 first to Geneva then to London, Antwerp and Frankfurt. Their Bible translation was published in 1569. See a.o. Onnekink, 'Casiodoro de Reina'; for Spanish protestants in the Low Countries in the 1540s see Enzinas, *Bericht over de Toestand in de Nederlanden*.
47 The long tour that Catharine made with her son Charles IX to present him to the kingdom included a meeting with Alva in Bayonne in 1565. This encounter of the Iron Duke with the woman who was held responsible for the St Bartholomew Massacre has often been seen as heralding the oppression that would follow. In fact Catharine was looking for Spanish spouses for her children, and Alva for guarantees regarding the prosecution of heretics in France; while neither party granted anything to the other. With respect to religious question, Catharine was looking more for possibilities for co-existence and toleration (Garrison, *History of sixteenth-century France* p. 259–260).
48 A reference to the famous conversation between Orange and Henry II in the Bois de Vincennes, described in Orange's *Apology* (see ed. Lacroix p. 88–89; ed. Mees-Verwey p. 60–61; English. ed. Wansink p. 61–62; for the hunting party, see Mees p. 62).
49 May 1565.
50 See also 2.11–12.
51 The *Council of Brabant* was the highest court and highest court of appeal in the province of Brabant, instituted by Philip the Good at the administrative reforms in 1430.
52 Georg Cassander (1513–1566) from Bruges (Cologne from 1549) shared much of Erasmus' thinking. His approach was to arrive at a precise understanding of the theological differences between the confessions in order to enable a reconciliation, with a general re-unification of Christianity as the ultimate aim. Like Erasmus he agreed with many criticisms of the Catholic church brought forward by the Protestants, but did not leave the Catholic church. Orange and Horne attempted in vain to have Cassander appointed as a moderate force in the Secret Council. Later in his life Grotius worked for a similar re-unification of the confessions and produced an edition of one of Cassander's works in 1642 (www.dutchrevolt.leiden.edu).
53 François Baudouin (1520–1573) came from Artesian nobility and worked as a lawyer. In 1542 he was prosecuted for heresy and sent in exile. He subsequently lived in Geneva, Bourges, Strasbourg and Heidelberg; in the last three of these he held professorial posts. In 1561 he was a mediator in the Colloquy of Poissy in the French wars of religion. William of Orange was considering organising a similar attempt at reconciliation in the Low Countries, and at his initiative Baudouin's sentence was reversed in 1563. Baudouin now accepted a post as professor in Douai; however the plan to have in appointed to the Secret Council failed. By now Baudouin was voicing stronlgly Catholic opinions but fled to France to avoid having to sit on Alva's Council of Troubles (www.dutchrevolt.leiden.edu; zie ook Klink, *Opstand, politiek, religie* p. 175).
54 i.e. after the death of Mary in 1558.
55 Anna of Saxony, 1544–1577; the marriage was concluded in 1561 and dissolved in 1571. Horne married Walburgis von Neuenahr-Moers (1522–1600), a protestant, in 1546; see also 4.22.
56 29 July 1565.
57 The League of Nobles (*Verbond der Edelen*), first concluded 1 or 2 December 1565 in Culemborg House in Brussels and soon extended by the accession of more (and higher-ranking) nobles.
58 Willem (IV) count of Den Bergh (1537–1586); brother-in-law of Orange and co-signatory of the Compromise of Nobles (see below). Like Orange he fled to Germany and captured a number of towns for the Revolt during Orange's invasion in 1572. After the Pacitication of 1576 he hoped for

an appointment as stadtholder of Guelders; and when this did not happen he made contact with Don Juan and Parma. In 1581 the obtained the appointment after all and took oaths of allegiance to both Parma and the Union of Utrecht. After this act of treason he was taken prisoner, and chose the Spanish side after his release.

59 Floris van Pallandt (1537–1598) initially enjoyed the favour of Charles V and Philip II. In 1566 however he converted to Protestantism and joined the resistance against Granvelle. He played a central role in the Compromise of Nobles. He evaded a summons before Alva's Council of Troubles by moving to his possessions in Germany, and was sentenced to exile and confiscation of his possessions. In 1574 he returned to Culemborg, and was considered one of the leading men of the Revolt in Guelders and a respected administrator.

60 Hendrik of Brederode (1531–1568), Lord of Brederode and Vianen, and Viscount of Utrecht. He was a member of the Compromise of Nobles, and part of the delegation that offered the Petition to Margaret in 1566. He negotiated with her after the Iconoclastic Fury, a.o. greater religious freedom. Hij resorted to armed resistance against the government at an early stage and atempted to have anti-Spanish city-governments appointed, without success in Utrecht and Amsterdam but successfully in 's Hertogenbosch. An army organised by him was defeated near Antwerp while Orange prevented assistence being sent from the town (see 1.59). In 1567, like Orange, he fled to Germany. In 1568 Alva's Council of Troubles convicted him in absentia, but he had already died by this time.

61 Compromise of Nobles (*Smeekschrift der Edelen*).

62 'Beggars'; transformed to *Geuzen* in Dutch.

63 These *turmae populares* are probably the same as the *cunei* and *turmae* from the population which Grotius refers to in *De Antiquitate* 2.8 as stemming from Batavian times, which are said to consist of neighbours and relatives. Is Grotius thinking of the *schutterijen* (civil guards) of the Dutch towns of his own time? Goris translates '*benden van Ordonnantie*' which however are regulier troops in paid government service, which is not what seems to be meant here.

64 Floris de Montmorency, baron of Montigny (1528–1570; Grotius has *Iohannes*); and John IV of Glymes, marquis of Bergen, stadtholder of Hainaut and governor of Valenciennes, Cambrai and Binche (1528–1567), were sent on an embassy to Philip II in 1566 by the Council of State in order to explain the Compromise of Nobles and try change his approach, which they did not achieve. Bergen died in Spain of an illness, Montigny was killed in prison in 1570.

65 The Confession of Augsburg is the Lutheran creed, written by Philipp Melanchton and presented to Charles V at the Diet of Augsburg in 1530.

66 May–July 1566.

67 *Beeldenstorm*, Iconoclastic Fury, August-October 1566.

68 Viglius of Aytta (1507–1577), humanist, lawyer and prominent administrator from the Habsburg government apparatus. He was patronised by Granvelle, but had a difficult relationship with Alva as he advocated moderation in the persecution of heretics and opposed the 10th Penny. For his life see Postma, 'Viglius van Aytta als humanist', and id., 'Viglius, jaren met Granvelle'.

69 23 August 1566.

70 A small Calvinist army, assembled by Henry of Brederode and led by Jan van Marnix threathened to take the city. It was destroyed by Egmond (battle of Oosterweel, 13 March 1567), while Orange prevented assistence being sent from the city. For Brederode see also 1.50. Grotius' account is very short and euphemistic, and concentrates on Orange's efforts for freedom of religion.

71 Dutch *burggraaf*. Although the title had become mostly ceremonious in the later Middle Ages, in Antwerp Orange had returned real significance to it by his government as the king's governor in the 1560s. See G. Marnef, *Antwerpen in de tijd van de Reformatie,* Amsterdam and Antwerp 1996, p. 43.

72 February-March 1567. Grotius avoids mentioning the battle of Oosterweel, see note above.

73 This bother being the count of Montigny, see above. The intercepted letters are said to be forgeries, see Geurts, *De graaf van Horne* p. 28.

74 3 October 1566.

75 For the early-modern (and older) notion that climate and national character are connected, see e.g. Grotius himself in *De Antiquitate*, or John Barclay in *Icon Animorum* 2.11, 10.1 and passim; for further literature, L. Jensen, 'Introduction' in *Roots of Nationalism* p. 9 and note 3.

76 Early in 1567.

77 Philip of Croy (1526–1595; Grotius has *Carolus*); duke of Aarschot and prince of Chimay. Originally Aarschot was a loyal Catholic and sat on the Council of State, but became more critical in Requesens' time and came to favour negotiations. After the 'coup' in the Council in 1576 (see 2.62) he ended up on the rebel side and negotiated with Don Juan. He was one of the moderate leaders of the revolt who brought Mathias of Austria to the Low countries. He was appointed stadtholder of Flanders by the States-General in 1577, but the appointment was sank by the resistance of the passionately Calvinist city of Ghent, where Aarschot was taken prisoner. After his release Aarschot made his peace with the king.

78 These events happened from March to May 1567.

79 See also 2.8 and note.

80 April 1567.

81 Maximilian of Hénin-Liétard, count of Bossu (or Boussu, 1542–1578), South-Netherlands nobleman and friend of Granvelle. After Orange's departure in 1567 he acted as stadtholder of Holland, Zeeland and Utrecht. In 1572 he attempted re-conquer Den Briel, and supported Don Fadrique's (Alva's son) expedition against the rebel towns. In the naval battle on the Zuiderzee (October 1573), part of an operation to restore royal authority in the North of Holland, Bossu was defeated and taken prisoner. In captivity he was persuaded to choose Orange's side. After the Pacification of 1576 he was released and has served the States' cause until his death (see also 2.45, 3.16).

NOTES TO *ANNALS* BOOK 2

1 On the rationale behind Philip's appointments of governors in the Low Countries, see V. Soen, 'Philip II's Quest. The Appointment of Governors-General during the Dutch Revolt (1559–1598)' in: *Bijdragen en Mededelingen betreffende de geschiedenis der Nederlanden*, vol 126-1 (2011), p. 3–29 and further literature suggested there; for Grotius' view of Philip's realm as an agglomerate polity, see Waszink, 'Hugo Grotius on the agglomerate polity of Philip II', in: *History of European Ideas*, Volume 46-3, 2020, p. 276–291.

2 *Dux* has the double meaning of 'duke' and 'military commander'.

3 A dinner, 9 Sept. 1567.

4 The sentence echoes the ominous opening sentence of Tacitus *Annals* 1.6, which foreshadows Tiberius' tyranny. For other echoes of classical Latin examples in this passage, see Intr. § 7.1.

5 i.e. after the peace between Habsburg and France in 1559.

6 The so-called *Bloedraad* (Blood Council); the first meeting was on 20 Sept. 1567.

7 A Spanish proverb; see Motley, *Rise of the Dutch Republic* vol. 1 p. 150 (also De Thou, V. 300; Bor, IV. 219, Hooft, IV. 154; Bentivoglio. IV. 58).

8 Filips Willem (1554–1618), oldest son of William of Orange and Anna of Egmond.

9 *Bosgeuzen*, 'woodland-*geuzen*', as distinct from 'watergeuzen'; see note to 1.51 above.

10 1.52.

11 Don Carlos (1545–1568, son of Philip and Mary of Portugal) is often portrayed in the literature as a cruel and power-hungry psychopath, whose anger was aggreviated by being kept away from power. He would have aspired to the governorship of the Low Countries, would have been been enraged by seeing given to Alva and would have attempted to escape to the Low Countries. This notion provided the basis for many myths connected with his person; noble motives would have prompted him to try protect the Lowlanders. Elizabeth of Valois (1545–1568) had been chosen by Philip for Carlos, but when his (second) wife, Mary Tudor died, Philip married her himself. There was much talk about a (fictitious) romance with Carlos after her wedding to Philip, who was later accused of having poisoned her (see 2.24 below). The story that Philip had Don Carlos killed originated in Orange's *Apology* (*Apologie of Prince William of Orange*, ed. Wansink, p. 45–45; or *Apologie ofte Verantwoordinge*, ed. M. Mees-Verwey, p. 47), became part of the Spanish 'Black Legend' and has circulated for centuries (e.g. Schiller, Verdi); see also Motley, *Dutch Republic* II 195–206 for other anecdotes and versions of the story; see also Swart, *Willem van Oranje* p. 191; Rodríques Perez, *De Tachtigjarige Oorlog in Spaanse ogen*, p. 176, 199–202; and 1.65 and Intr. § 7.1 above.

12 The battles of Heiligerlee and Jemmingen.

13 The *Verantwoordinge* of 1568 and other pamphlets collected in M. Schenk, & A. van Schelven (eds.), *Geschriften van 1568. Verantwoordinge, verklaringhe ende waerschowinghe mitsgaders eene hertgrondighe begheerte des edelen, lancmoedighen ende hooghgeboren Princen van Oraengien*, Amsterdam 1933.

14 Orange converted to Lutheranism in 1566–1567 (Klink, *Opstand, politiek, religie* p. 245–246) and would officially join the Calvinist church in 1573 (Swart, *Willem van Oranje* p. 46–47).

15 Probably a paraphrase of the key thoughts in 'Waerschowinge' also included in Oranje, *Geschriften van 1568* (p. 117–128). NB *tamen*: Grotius means that not the religious issue is Orange's motivation for rebellion, but the political issue, 'to drive servitude from the country'.

16 The Joyous Entry of Brabant of 1356, the charter that played a central role in the constitutional justification of the Revolt.

17 cp. 1.46 and the argument in *De Antiquitate* chapter 5 (focusing mostly on Holland).

18 Note the phrasing: Charles was not emperor or king in any province in the Low Countries; see also 2.59, 4.40.

19 In the night of 5 to 6 October 1568.

20 The French king Henry II intervened with an army in the (Habsburg) politics in Italy in 1556–1557. However his commander, François de Lorraine, 2nd duke de Guise did not achieve much due to Alva's clever defence tactics.

21 Part of the literal text of the inscription on the statue, see the engraving on p. 184
22 In a pamphlet at the time it was claimed that a death sentence was passed against the entire population of the Low Countries, which Alva then issued an edict to deny. Already during the revolt the reality of the original accusation was called into doubt, but it was only finally debunked in the 19th century (see Geurts, *Opstand in de pamfletten* p. 35–38 and Blok, 'Advies der Spaanse Inquisitie').
23 *Universitates*; for the word, cp. Grotius, *De Iure Praedae,* ed. Hamaker p. 106. Corporations are for example guilds, schools, universities, monasteries, chapters and charities for care for the sick and the poor; see Mehr, *Römischrechtliche Institute,* p. 216.
24 *Pignorationes*; for the word, cp. Grotius, *De Iure Praedae*, ed. Hamaker p. 107.
25 Mary I, queen of Scots (1542–1587); sole surviving child of James V of Scotland. She was first married to François II of France who died young (1560). She returned to Scotland as Mary I, but was forced to abdicate in favour of her one-year old son after her second husband was killed and she had married one of the suspects. She then fled to her cousin Elizabeth I but was kept under close watch since she had also once claimed the English throne and had been supported in this by English Catholics. In 1586 she was said to have been involved in a conspiracy against Elizabeth (see also 5.31 and note) and condemned to death.
26 His brother.
27 i.e. *Watergeuzen*, or 'Sea-Beggars', see 1.51 and note.
28 On Grotius' view of Providence, see Intr. § 7.3.
29 Note here that Grotius inludes no mention of the Synod of Emden in October 1571, the meeting which has since been regarded as the founding meeting of the Dutch Reformed church.
30 Urban legend in Rotterdam has it that some people stained their doors and doorposts with cattle blood, to make the roaming Spaniards think that the inhabitants had already been killed, and succeeded. The story was particularly connected with one house on the Grote Markt, carrying the name *In duizend vreezen* ('In a thousand fears'); this house however was built only in 1594 (but might have had a predecessor). See P. Haverkorn van Rijsewijk, 'Het huis "In duizend vreezen"', in: *Rotterdamsch Jaarboekje* vol. 2 (1890), p. 129–132.
31 A similar line of thought as in *De Iure Belli ac Pacis*.
32 i.e. the *Watergeuzen* mentioned above, e.g. 1.51, 2.25.
33 The placement of this subject break here emphasis the image of Holland and Zeeland as the original basis and core of the Revolt.
34 Dutch: *Maas.*
35 i.e. West-Friesland or North-Holland west of the Zuiderzee, and Friesland on the east side of the Zuiderzee.
36 i.e. the North Sea.
37 i.e. seen in the flow direction of the river.
38 i.e. *Betuwe*, derived from *Batavi(a).*
39 To distinguish Friesland from West-Friesland, see above.
40 Holland from *Holt-land*, i.e. wood-land.
41 See note to 1.3.
42 Resumes the story of the Revolt where it was left off, in 1572.
43 i.e. the Tenth Penny, see 2.20, 2.22 above.
44 But cp. 2.60, 4.6 and Waszink, 'Grotius on the agglomerate polity of Philip II', esp. p. 11.
45 Battle on the Zuiderzee, 11 October 1573, See also 1.66, 3.16. As to "cause of the war": the resistance against the Inquisition related no only to the religious issue, but also the political issue at the basis of the Revolt, since the imposition of this special court was seen as infringement of the towns' political and judicial privileges.
46 The Echinades (or Curzolari) are a group of islands in Western Greece, near the western exit of the Corinthian gulf (which was then called the gulf of Lepanto in Italian, Naupaktos in Greek). In 1571 a great naval battle against the Turks took place here, in which Requesens participated (see also 2.67).
47 The battle on the Mookerheide, 14 April 1574.

48 Mutinies occurred frequently in the Spanish army and knew a returning pattern and organisation, similar to that in civil uprisings. See e.g., G. Parker, 'Mutiny and Discontent in the Spanish Army of Flanders 1572–1607', in: *Past & Present* 58 (1973), p. 38–52; L. Kattenberg, 'Military rebellion and reason of state. Pacification in the Habsburg Army of Flanders, 1599–1601', in: *Bijdragen en Mededelingen betreffende de geschiedenis der Nederlanden* 131-2 (2016), p. 3–21.

49 Frédéric Perrenot, lord of Champagny (1536–1602), brother of the cardinal Granvelle and governor of Antwerp at the time.

50 Günther von Schwarzburg (1529–1583) was married to Orange's sister Catharina. In 1560 he had negotiated on behalf of Orange with Anna of Saxony's family regarding her intended marriage to Orange, to which the difference in religion was a major obstacle; Orange insisted on keeping his promise to Philip and Granvelle that his spouse would live as a Catholic, while Anna insisted on her Lutheranism.

51 According to the principle of *cuius regio, eius religio* as established in the German empire by the Peace of Augsburg of 1555, and which gave the regional princes in the empire the power to decide which religion would be imposed in their realm.

52 Pliny the Elder, *Naturalis Historia* 10.110.3: during the siege of Modena by Mark Anthony in 44 BC, the general Decimus Brutus sent messages to the Roman consuls by means of pigeons.

53 See also 2.49–50 above.

54 Another description in Carnero, *Historias de las Guerras Civiles en los Estados de Flandes,* Brussels 1625, book 3, ch. 9–11; a Dutch translation is available in J. Brouwer, *Kronieken van Spaansche soldaten,* p. 238–251, esp. 240–241.

55 While on the north side, the conquest of Haarlem (2.45) had cut the connection between Holland's centre and the *Noorderkwartier.*

56 *Nassaviani* here seems to denote Calvinists; after more than two centuries in English possession, Calais returned to France in 1558 and, being very close to the Spanish-held Low Countries, soon became a place where Calvinist refugees assembled in relative freedom to exercise their faith (esp. at the castle of Guines).

57 i.e. an insurance; see J. van Niekerk, *The Development of the Principles of Insurance Law in the Netherlands 1500–1800*, Cape Town 1998, p. 191 and n. 75, where this formulation is referred to as Grotius' "best description of the insurance contract"; cp. Grotius, *Inleidinge tot the Hollandse Rechtsgeleerdheid* III.24.1: "*Verzekering is een overeenkoming, waer door iemand op hem neemt het onzeecker gevaer dat een ander had te verwachten: den welcke wederom hem daer voor gehouden is loon te geven*" (Insurance is an agreement, by which someone takes upon him the undetermined risk that waits another; who in turn is obliged to pay him for it").

58 5 March 1576.

59 Joachim Hoppers (1523–1575), of Frisian birth and a confidant of Viglius (see 1.57); professor of Law in Louvain, member of the Great Council of Mechelen, the Secret Council and the Council of State. In 1561 he established a university at Douai. He was a very popular professor, but made a weak impression as a councillor (Granvelle and his entourage called him "councillor yes-madam"), en this reputation has stuck with him (see e.g. Motley, *Rise of the Dutch Republic* I p. 381–382 en III p. 2–3). With respect to the religious issue his ideas were Erasmian and oriented towards reunification, and he stood in contact with François Baudouin (see 1.47). See also Postma, *Viglius, Jaren met Granvelle* esp. p. 130–134.

60 Grotius strictly observes the terminological difference between 'king' and 'prince', which is presented more elaborately in *De Antiquitate* chapter 1: the rule of a prince is subject to laws, conditions and limited by the power of others. See also 2.13, 4.40 and notes.

61 This refers to the Spanish bankruptcy of 1575. During the Franco-Spanish war in 1557 an earlier bankruptcy had occurred. However cp. 2.45 *sub opulentissimo rege* and Waszink, 'Agglomerate polity', esp. p. 11.

62 *Novae tabulae:* 'an abolition of all debts whether wholly or in part' (W. Smith, *A Dictionary of Greek and Roman Antiquities*, London 1875); see Suetonius *Julius* 42, Cicero, *De Officiis* 2.23.

63 This rebellion, which would indeed become a turning point, started in the first days of July 1576. See also Parker, 'Mutiny and Discontent' p. 48–49.
64 26 July 1576.
65 See 2.49.
66 4 September 1576; see also Motley, *Dutch Republic* III p. 30 sq. Grotius' chronology is not entirely correct; see also 2.63 below on Geronimo de Roda.
67 Geronimo de Roda (ca. 1525–1580) originally came to the Low Countries as assistant to Alva, and later became an important pillar of support for Requesens, who relied on him in many matters. After Requesen's death in 1576 Roda formed a provisional government with Berlaymont and Mansfeld. However he was generally hated in the Low Countries because of his cruelty and greed, and in July 1576 objections were even uttered against him in the Council of State. By the end of that month he was arrested by the people of Brussels, but escaped to the Antwerp citadel on 1 August, where he had soldiers at his command. Roda, Vargas and Romero then proclaimed themselves *Conseil de Gouvernement* and ruled by proclamation. This move irritated both friends and foes; on 11 September Philip called Roda back to Spain, which the latter refused. Meanwhile on 4 September the members of the Council of State were arrested in Brussels (see 2.62), which prompted Roda to proclaim himself governor-general and commander of the Low Countries. By this he destroyed his authority, but it was only after Don Juan's arrival that he agreed to leave for Spain.
68 20 October1576.
69 The notorious Spanish Fury, 4 November 1576.
70 The Pacification of Ghent, 8 november 1576.
71 Caspar de Robles (1527–1585), stadtholder of Friesland from 1568–1576, achieved some successes in the suppression of the revolt in Friesland and the reorganisation of the waterworks after the All Saints' Flood of 1570 (see also note to 4.28). Gradually however he made himself hated, even by his own troops, partly by delays with their payments. The Spanish bankruptcy of 1575 (see 2.60) destroyed his authority. Robles died in the explosion during the siege of Antwerp in 1585 (see 5.3).
72 The Union of Brussels, early January 1577.
73 Compare Grotius' regret at the loss of Flanders in 4.25 and that of Antwerp in 5.1–6.
74 This decision had been taken much earlier, i.e. directly after Requesen's death.
75 The battle of Lepanto, 7 October 1571 (see 2.47), against the Ottoman advances in the Adriatic sea and the Eastern Mediterranean. Don Juan had the supreme command of the united fleets of the Spain, the Vatican, Venice, Genova and Malta.
76 i.e. his half-brother.
77 The 'Eternal Edict' of 12 February 1577, concluded in Marche-en-Famenne.
78 Orange's triumphant entry in Brussels was in September 1577.
79 Mathias of Austria (1557–1619), third son of emperor Maximilian II. A group of moderate Catholics siding with the revolt (including Aarschot) brought him to the Low Countries in 1577, to take Orange's place as leader of the revolt. After the States-General had made an agreement with Francis of Anjou, the French king's brother, to fulfill this role (see 3.3 sqq) Mathias left (1581). Later he was stadtholder of Upper and Lower Austria. Via a power struggle with his brother, the emperor Rudolph II, he became king of Hungary and Bohemia, and finally the latter's successor in 1612. In this position he did not succeed in controlling the conflicts that would develop into the 30-years War after his death.

Notes to *Annals* Book 3

1 The Scottish queen Mary I; see 2.23 and note.

2 31 January 1578.

3 John of Noircarmes of Saint-Aldegonde, baron of Selles (?-1585), an important courtier at Philip's court in his role as lieutenant (but commander in fact) of the royal guard. In 1568 he was sent on an embassy to France and the Low Countries, and Philip consulted him about Low Countries affairs since then. He asked permission to travel to the Low Countries to arrange personal business, which was granted in 1578 together with a mission to negotiate about peace. A covered aim of this mission was to override the Pacification of Ghent. At his arrival he was distrusted by both parties. After a number of failed proposals and attempts he organised a conference with the States-General in Mechelen in April, which however failed as well. In 1579 he negotiated again on behalf of the king, this time about the conditions of the Union of Arras, and, against his instructions, granted a ratification of the Pacification by the king. In 1580 he was ambushed by rebels near Bouchain and taken prisoner. Hij died in captivity (see www.dutchrevolt.leiden.edu).

4 François-Hercule de Valois, duke of Anjou (1556–1584), fourth son of king Henry II of France.

5 Johann Casimir, count palatinate on the Rhine (1543–1592), fourth son of Frederick II Elector Palatine. An ardent Calvinist who had fought on the Huguenot side in the French wars of religion. He came to the Netherlands in 1578 as commander of military aid contributed by Elizabeth. Soon he ended up in a quarrel with Orange, and in October 1578 he occupied Ghent to support the Calvinists in the town. Orange's arrival forced him to leave, and he moved out of the Low Countries in 1579. In 1583 he intervened in the Cologne war on Truchsess' side, and appropriated power in the Palatinate by ruling as guardian of Frederick IV.

6 *indigesta moles*, see Ovid, Met. 1.7, where it is said of the original Chaos from which the world arose.

7 Grotius frequently uses the word *secta* for branches of Protestantism (e.g. John Bucholt's group in Münster, 1.24), as well as for Catholicism. The negative connotations of the word were clearly felt at the time, as appears from the Vatican Index's report on the *Annales et Historiae* from 1659, where this use of the word is objected to; see App. 2 below p. 387 and Waszink, 'New Documents', p. 118–119.

8 William of Orange's oldest brother.

9 George de Lalaing, baron of Ville and count of Rennenberg (ca. 1540–1581) chose the side of the revolt in 1576, fought against Spanish mutinies and became stadtholder of Friesland, Groningen, Drenthe and Overijssel in 1577. However he remained Catholic, attempted to maintain freedom of religion for Catholics in his provinces and gradually began countering the growth of Protestantism. This caused suspicions against his person and cost him his position in Friesland in 1580. In the same year, and with overwhelming support among the citizenship and the town government, he brought the city of Groningen back under Spanish rule, and succeeded in including parts of the Groningen *Ommelanden* ('surrounding district') and Drenthe in the move. Re-conquest by the revolt party happened after 1589; the city of Groningen itself returned to the republic in 1594 (the *Reductie* of Groningen). Rennenberg himself had died of illness in 1581.

10 This probably refers to the Truce Conflicts (see Intr. § 2.4).

11 John of Hembyze (1513–1584) deposed the Catholic city government of Ghent in 1577 and subsequently presided, together with Francis of Ryhove (see 4.32), over the Calvinist republic in the town until 1584 (with interruptions; see also 4.25–32). Other parts of Flanders were also brought under the authority of this government. Their uncompromising Calvinist politics interfered with Orange's conciliatory and co-existential approach. An open conflict ensued; in 1579 Ryhove chose Orange's side. Hembyze was removed from the city government by Orange and went in exile to the Palatinate. He returned in 1583, during the siege by Parma's army. After the discovey of his secret correspondence with Parma Hembyze was arrested on 12 March 1584 and executed for treason. This outcome led to an image of Hembyze on the Catholic side as a warrior for Catholicism; the Vatican censor of the AH identified the paragraph above as a reason for the prohibition of the AH; see Waszink, 'New Documents' p. 113 n. 4).

12 Jacob of Artevelde (ca. 1290–1345), local hero in Ghent from the time of the Hundred Years war, who resisted the French ban on trade with England, and stood in close contact with the English king Edward III.
13 i.e. unlike the others (*tenaciores*).
14 Battle on the Zuiderzee, 11 October 1573; see also 2.45.
15 See 1.66.
16 Philip, count of Lalaing (1537–1582), stadtholder of Hainaut, chose the side of the revolt in 1576. As commander of the revolutionary army, he was blamed for the defeat at Gemblours, although (or because) he had not taken part in the battle. He opposed the spread of Calvinism, seemed jealous of Orange, and tried to build his own independent relationship with Anjou. He became of the leaders of the group of *Malcontents* with Orange's policies and turned away from the revolt when Orange blocked the establishment of Anjou's authority in Hainaut (see note to 3.20). He attached Hainaut to the Union of Arras in 1579. See also 2.71 and 3.20.
17 Robert de Melun (ca. 1550–1585).
18 François de la Noue (1531–1591), famous Huguenot military commander in the French wars of religion. He settled his reputation with the conquest of Orléans in 1567. In the years 1570–1572 and 1578–1580 he fought in the Low countries on the side of the revolt. Both times he was taken prisoner. In 1570 he lost an arm, for which a metal prothesis was made which gave him the nickname *bras de fer*. During his imprisonment of 1580–1585 he wrote his *Discours politiques et militaires*, which would become widely known and was translated into several languages. From 1589 onwards he supported Henry de Navarre (later Henry IV); he died from wounds in 1591.
19 Currently Bouge, north-east of Namur, on the river Meuse.
20 Philip de Lalaing (see also 3.16); Motley, *Dutch Republic* III, p. 146 presents a story based on the memoirs of Marguerite de Valois (Anjou's sister) relating how her visit to Hainaut in 1577 had laid the basis for an understanding between Lalaing and Anjou that Hainaut and Flanders would eventually come under French authority.
21 Juan de Escobedo (1530–1578), Don Juan's secretary.
22 i.e. the Pacification
23 Now: Gravelines.
24 i.e. Groningen
25 Who had been executed in 1568, see 2.6.
26 In 1579 (see 3.41).
27 i.e. those of the Union of Utrecht.
28 i.e. those at Cologne.
29 Note the appearance of the word *Batavi* here (rather than *Belgae*); the reference must be to the provinces joined by the Union of Utrecht. I have therefore translated Dutch (elsewhere the word usually refers to the province of Holland, or Holland and Zeeland together; see Waszink, 'The Low Countries: constitution, nationhood and character', Conclusion).
30 Also known as 'Houtepen's Fury', in the night of 26 to 27 July 1581.
31 See 3.31.
32 Ingelmunster (West-Flanders), May 1580.
33 Possibly a foreshadowing of the difficulties of the Leicester period (?); see also Intr. § 8.3.
34 See note to 3.8.
35 Philip of Hohenlohe-Neuenstein, count of Hohenlohe zu Langenburg (1550–1606) served William of Orange since 1575 And married his daughter Maria in 1595. Because of his military experience the States of Holland asked him after Orange's death to continue as lieutenant-general. Hohenlohe was a courageous but reckless commander, and an alcoholic to boot; Maurice found him unreliable and unable to keep secrets. Disagreement about Orange's estate also contributed to their bad relationship; as the oldest child (after Filips Willem's abduction, see 2.6), Maria managed the possessions after her father's death. This would make Hohenlohe the chief administrator of the estate, to Maurice's displeasure. In 1591 the States-General split the possessions, allocating a relatively small portion

to Maria. Years of litigation resulted in very few changes. In 1600 Maurice discharged Hohenlohe as lieutenant-general of Holland en Zeeland. Grotius' father Jan was advisor to Hohenlohe and administrator of his possessions since ca. 1600.

36 See 2.25.

37 The battle of Noordhorn, 30 September 1581. The operation to remove Rennenberg (see 3.8) from the province of Groningen, which is the topic here, was executed under the command of William Louis (1560–1620, son of Orange's brother John of Nassau, see 4.38). The States sent him English and Scottish auxiliaries under the command of Sir John Norris. At first Norris had defeated Rennenberg's successor Verdugo, who then moved his camp to Noordhorn, on a strategically important road to Groningen. Norris and William Louis attacked him there again, but suffered a crushing defeat; William Louis was wounded himself.

38 This seems to be the oration contained in the pamphlet Knuttel 524: *Vertooch aen myne heeren de ghedeputeerde van de Staten generael by mijn heere den Prince van Orangien*, 9 January 1580. For an English translation, see Kossmann-Mellink, *Texts concerning the Revolt of the Netherlands* p. 200–203 no. 45: 'Remonstrance made to the deputies of the States General at Antwerp, by the prince of Orange, 9 January 1580'.

39 i.e. Anjou

40 This oration, spoken on 15 January 1580, is published as pamphlet Knuttel 526: *Corte vermaeninghe aende naerdere geunieerde Provincien ende Steden der Nederlanden* etc. See Geurts, *Opstand in de pamfletten* p. 109, and for its content, Nuyens, *Geschiedenis der Nederlandsche Beroerten* vol.2, p. 50–54.

41 By the *Plakkaat van Verlatinge*, 'Act of Abjuration', 26 July 1581.

42 The *Corte Vermaeninghe* (see note above) is probably Grotius' source for this argument here.

43 This text too was published as a pamphlet, and dated 15 June 1580: *Ban ende edict by vorme van proscriptie, vuytggaen ende ghedecreteerd by ... de Coninck, tegens Wilhelm van Oraignyen* etc., pamphlet Knuttel 527. See Geurts, *Opstand in de pamfletten*, p. 103–105. Proscription is confiscation of one's possessions, while outlawing the person.

44 Orange's *Apology* van 1580 (written) or 1581 (published); pamphlet Knuttel 557; see also Intr. § 7.1 and 10. Pierre L'Oyseleur, Lord of Villiers (ca. 1530–1590) was Orange's court preacher.

45 i.e. Philip's *Ban* and Orange's *Apologie*.

46 Doornik

1 Talks about a possible marriage were conducted at least since 1572, see the letters collected in L. Marcus, J. Mueller, M. Rose (eds.), *Elizabeth. Collected Works,* Chicago 2000, p. 205 sqq. A 12-line love poem is extant under Elizabeth's name, *On Monsieur's Departure*, couched in the language and imagery of the Petrarchan love poetry and that of the English 'Metaphysical poets'; see ibid., p. 302–303.

2 In 1580 the States-General concluded a treaty with the Duke of Anjou, that was ratified as the Treaty of Bordeaux, installing the duke as 'prince et seigneur' of the Low countries. However the notion that this would include the undivided sovereignty over the provinces was explicitly denied by the States; see Kossman, 'Volkssouvereiniteit' p. 12–15.

3 Orange incurred a critical headwounded from the assault on him by Jean Jaureguy in Antwerp on 18 March 1582. Although he survived, his wife Charlotte de Bourbon exerted herself so much in his care that she died (5 May 1582).

4 Francisco Verdugo (1536–1595) was the king's stadtholder in Friesland, Groningen, Drenthe and Overijssel, and Rennenberg's successor (1581, see 3.8, 3.44). In 1581 the rebels appointed first William of Orange, then William Louis to take Rennenberg's place, and thus from 1581–1594 there were two competing stadtholders in these provinces. After the loss of Groningen in 1594 Verdugo left the Low Countries. The Spanish lost the remaining areas in Drenthe only in 1597. See also 4.38.

5 For other comments on Philip's financial position, see 2.45 and note, 2.60.

6 In the Portugese succession conflict of 1580, after the death of Henry I, Catharine de' Medici had also advanced a (weak) claim to that throne.

7 Given several correspondences Grotius' source for his discussion of the French Fury seems to be the *Corte Verclaering gedaen by Burgemeesteren, Schepenen* etc. (Antwerp, Plantin 1583) which was also used by Bor and others; see Motley, *Rise of the Dutch Republic* III p. 429.

8 This content was also published in the pamphlet *Advis du Prince d'Orange sur la partie à prendre* etc., see Geurts, *Opstand in de Pamfletten* p. 117–118.

9 Armand de Gontaut, seigneur de Biron (1524–1592) was a gifted marshal with a long record of service in the French king's army. Anjou had already worked with him during the siege of La Rochelle in 1573.

10 The issue of trade with the enemy returns in the Leicester period, see 5.16–17 (and see 3.40).

11 Anjou's reputation in the Dutch Republic was to remain like this; see e.g. the scathing inscription on the portrait by Pieter van Gunst of ca. 1700 (Rijksmuseum Amsterdam, RP-P-OB-55.742): FRANCOIS DUC D'ALENÇON. *Elisabeth et la fortune / Me trompant tour à tour se moquerent de moi/ Et j'achevai mon infortune / En trompant les Flamans, et leur manquant de foi.* Masks and snakes as accessories above and under the portrait complete the impression of Machivellism and unreliability.

12 Dutch *hoog* = high.

13 A 'Habsburg jaw'?

14 Gebhard Truchsess von Waldburg (1547–1601), Archbischop and Elector of Cologne. After his election to the office (1577) he fell in love with Agnes von Mansfeld-Eisleben, a Calvinist, and converted to Calvinism. The institution of freedom of religion for Calvinists in the district of Cologne in 1582 led to resistance from the Catholic side. In 1583 Truchsess married Agnes, and set out to transform the Electorate-and-archbishopric of Cologne into an hereditary principality. This led to the Cologne war (1583–1588) in which both parties were supported by foreign allies, i.e. Spain and the protestant Netherlands respectively, and in 1583 the Catholic side brought Ernest of Bavaria onto the throne. Truchsess was expelled in 1584 and left for the Low Countries, from where he continued the struggle until 1588. In 1589 he moved to Strasbourg where he became dean of the cathedral and died in 1601.

15 Adolf, count of Neuenahr and Moers (ca. 1545–1589), military commander. In 1570 he married his cousin Walburgis, widow of the count of Horne (see 1.48). He served in Truchsess' army and from there to the revolutionary forces in the Low Countries. In 1584 he was appointed stadtholder of

Guelders as successor to William van de Bergh who had defected to the king's side. After the assassination of Orange, Neuanahr succeeded him as stadtholder of Overijssel, and in the next year of Utrecht as well. He lost his life in an accident with new artillery in Arnhem in 1589.

16 Charles of Croy, duke of Aarschot and prince of Chimay (1560–1612), son of Philip (see note to 1.62). In 1577 he entered the service of Don Juan, but fled after the latter's attack on Namur. In 1580 he married the Calvinist Marie de Brimeu, and called himself prince of Chimay since. He joined the revolutionary side and became stadtholder of Flanders in 1583 at the instigation of Bruges, Ypres and Ghent. However he ended up disappointed in the leadership of the revolt and came to work for reconciliation with the king and an end to the troubles. In 1584 he re-converted to Catholicism.

17 See also Grotius' regret at the loss of the unity of all the provinces in 2.66, and his implied irritation at the blundering which led to the loss of Antwerp in 5.1; see Intr. § 9.3.

18 For the pamphlets referred to here, see e.g. Geurts, *Opstand in de Pamfletten*, p. 118–127.

19 Waasland or Land of Waas is situated in the north-east of the present-day Belgian province of East-Flanders; the main town is Sint-Niklaas. The 'Drowned land of Saeftinge' lies to the north of Waasland, on the Westerschelde. The All-Saints' flood of 1570 (see also note to 2.65) immersed this area almost entirely. For strategic purposes, soldiers of the revolt broke the last remaining dikes in 1584 leaving Saeftinge to disappear again under the water.

20 Servaes of Steelandt II (?-1607), bailiff of Waasland, handed the Waasland over to Parma on 30 October 1583.

21 Francis of Kethulle, Lord of Ryhove (1531–1585), Calvinist bailiff of Dendermonde. In 1578 he ruled, together with John of Hembyze (see 3.14), the city of Ghent, which aspired to establish a Calvinist republic in Flanders. Originally he opposed Orange's policy of religious reconciliation but became more moderate over time. Consequently he had to leave Ghent, but was restored in his position by Orange, while Hembyze was removed from the city government. After Hembyze's return in 1583 Ryhove was expelled again; after the city's surrender to Parma he fled to England, and come to Utrecht with the Earl of Leicester in 1585 (see book 5).

22 Odet de la Noue, lord of Téligny (1565–1618); oldest son of Francis de la Noue (see 3.16) and Marguérite de Téligny. He served in the States army under the command of his father and besieged by Parma in 1584 in the fortress of Lillo, which he defended successfully. Late in 1584 he was wounded in an operation on the dike of Kauwenstein (see 5.3) and taken prisoner by Parma, which he remained until 1591. Afterwards he served the French king Henry IV and played an important role among the Huguenots, a.o. in the creation of the Edict of Nantes. In the years 1600–1605 he served again in Maurice's States army, including during the battle of Newport, and came to The Hague in 1617 on a diplomatic mission in support of Oldenbarnevelt.

23 Anna of Egmond, countess of Buren, 1533–1558. They maried in 1551.

24 Anna of Saxony, 1544–1577. They married in 1561 and divorced in 1571.

25 Maurice (2), 1567–1625 and Emilia, 1569–1629. Two older children died young, Anna en Maurice (1).

26 Charlotte de Bourbon, 1546–1582. They married in 1575. On her death, see note to 4.4.

27 Louise de Coligny, 1555–1620.

28 The goddess of wisdom, Minerva, allegorically represents the university at Leiden.

29 This happened in 1581.

30 William Louis (1560–1620), son of John of Nassau, stadtholder of Friesland, later also Groningen and Drenthe, see also 3.45. Together with Maurice he led the far-reaching re-organisation and modernisation of the States army after 1588, which was a crucial factor in the success of the Republic after 1590.

31 John of Nassau (1536–1606, Jan de Oude), younger brother of William of Orange.

32 In 1577 Orange initiated the institution of a Delegated council from the States of Friesland as a day-to-day government, after the model of the arrangement in the other provinces, a move opposed by the full States. Their instruction was renewed in 1591 and 1611. See Israel, *Dutch Republic* p. 201 and R. Fruin, *Geschiedenis der staatsinstellingen in Nederland tot den val der Republiek*, 2nd edition, The Hague 1922, p. 248, 250–251.

33 Francisco Verdugo, see 4.5 and note.
34 i.e. the counts and dukes of the high and late Middle Ages; see on Grotius' use of the term *princeps* (as opposed to *rex*) 2.13, 2.59 and notes.
35 See 2.51.
36 John Richardot, 1540–1609, lawyer, councillor, president of the Secret Council. Appointed under the patronage of Granvelle, Richardot joined the rebel side in the aftermath of Requesen's death in 1576, but ended up in an intermediate position when Don Juan appointed him in the Secret Council, and the appointment was confirmed by Mathias. After Parma's arrival he returned more unambiguously to the Spanish side. He played an important role in the complicated negotiations with formerly rebel towns and territories (like Ghent) in the process of Parma's re-conquest campaign. See further https://dutchrevolt.leiden.edu/dutch/personen/R/Pages/richardotjean.aspx.

Notes to Annals *Book* 5

1 See also 1.33.

2 Grotius' treatment of the legendary siege is extremely concise once again. During the siege of Antwerp (from July 1584 to August 1585, i.e. 13 months) a long series of occupations and inundations of neighbouring polders, attacks with exploding ships on the Scheldt blockade, sieges of fortresses, counterinvasions from Zeeland, etc took place. The most famous and spectaculair episode is probably the attack on Parma's floating bridge on the Scheldt with ships loaded with explosives by the Italian engineer Giannibelli on 5 April 1585, which would indeed have broken the blockade if the northern auxiliary fleet, which was waiting in Zeeland, would have been better prepared for the effects of the explosion; see the account by the Spanish officer Alonso Vazquez (see Brouwer, *Kronieken*, p. 322–325).

3 This debate on the merits of the northern effort for Antwerp began already during the siege itself. Grotius has already indicated that it was too little and too late, and too careless to make a difference; a view which is qualified here, albeit in order to refute the claim that the north let its allies down. Vazquez (see Brouwer, *Kronieken*, p. 314 sq.) refers to this debate too and rejects a lack of effort on the revolutionary side as well, though obviously with a parallel interest in not belittling the Spanish effort.

4 i.e. the islands of Holland's south and Zeeland.

5 Among Grotius' papers kept in Amsterdam UL, IIIC2 no. 96 there is *Articles du Traitte et accord....entre les deputez de la Ma.te de la Reine d'Angleterre et ceux des estats generaux pour le secours de la ville d'Anvers;* dated 2.8.1585 (old style); see Intr. § 10 and note 213.

6 *Obligatae pignori maritimae urbes Anglorum praesidiis traduntur* seems to invoke *pignus obligatum* from Roman law (= pawn not actually handed over, as opposed to *pignus datum*); however *obligatae* goes with *urbes* not the *pignus,* so it seems Grotius considers the admission of the English garrisons as expression of the obligation rather than an actual transfer of possession. For the term see e.g. Spruit, *Cunabula Juris* § 359.

7 Also known as the fortress Rammekens. In 1616 it returned under Dutch authority.

8 Robert Dudley, Earl of Leicester (1532–1588).

9 Mary Tudor (1516–1558). Both Mary and Elizabeth (1533–1603) were daughters of Henry VIII; born from his first marriage with Catharine of Aragon, she married Philip II in 1554 and during her reign (1553–1558) Catholicism was restored. Religious prosecutions gave her the epithet Bloody Mary. Elizabeth, daughter of Anne Boleyn, succeeded after her death, and government and country reverted to Protestantism.

10 See e.g. the correspondence of Justus Lipsius, who speaks of Leicester and the English actually in such terms: *Iusti Lipsi Epistolae* vol. 2 nos. 85 10 06, 86 00 00D1, 86 02 26, 86 08 24, 86 07 22; see also Lipsius Politica, ed. Waszink, Intr. p. 25.

11 After the death of Walter Devereux, 1st Earl of Essex (1541–1576) from dysentery there were suspicions of poisoning administered at Leicester's instigation. Post-mortem investigation produced insufficient evidence of a crime. Two years later Leicester married Essex's widow. Leicester was also godfather to Essex's son Robert (was was eventually executed in 1601 on charges of attempted coup d'état).

12 Since both men had sought Elizabeth's hand in marriage.

13 The queen was strongly opposed to Leicester formally accepting the governor-generalship of the Low Countries, first because she wanted to avoid a direct controntation with Spain, and secondly since is said to have feared that Leicester would use his rise to power abroad to obtain supreme power at home (a particularly sensitive issue with respect to Elizabeth who had no heir of her own). See MacCaffrey, *Queen Elizabeth 1572–1588*, 351, 357–359 and Waszink, 'Savile's Tacitus'.

14 Grotius' negative judgment of Leicester is no doubt partly inspired by Leicester's puritan sympathies and their influence on the rise of the tensions which had resulted in the Truce conflicts in Grotius' time; see Intr. § 6 and § 8.3.

15 Jacques Reingout (Ringault; 1530–1595), Lord of Couwenberg, from Bruges. Merchant and (after a bankruptcy) secretary to Egmond; subsequently registrar in the Financial Council (see 1.14 and note), Until 1580 his career path there was regular, then accusations of malversation meant the end of it. Reingout returned to trade, but also turned to politics and obtained a role as advisor to Leicester in the northern provinces. In 1586, and in spite of resistance from the Council of State and the States of Holland, Leicester instituted an equivalent to the Financial Council in the northern provinces, whose main purpose was to make Leicester less dependent on the States-General, to uphold the ban on trade with enemy territory, and to detect tax evasion by merchants from Holland. The States of Holland started a trial in which Reingout was accused of, among others, collaboration with the Spanish government, undermining of the priviliges of Holland and financial malversation. A conviction did not follow; but attempts by Reingout to escape to England with Leicester failed as well. After Leicester's return Reingout lived in Brussels as a private citizen. (www.historici.nl/Onderzoek/Projecten/BWN/lemmata/bwn3/reingout; Oosterhoff, *Leicester and the Netherlands*, p. 93–97).

16 i.e. the Dutch nobility and town regents represented in the States.

17 See 3.14; on Roland York, see also 5.23, 5.32.

18 See 4.22.

19 Maarten Schenck of Nydeck (1549–1589), military commander. Until the battle of Gembloux (1578, see 4.2) he served on the side of the States-General, but then on Parma's side until 1585. He defeated Hohenlohe in 1580, broke the States' siege of Groningen and captured Oldenzaal and Breda for the Spanish. In 1585 he was taken prisoner and returned to the States side. In 1586 he constructed the *Schenkenschans* in the eastern Betuwe (see next note), a contested fortress between Frederick Henry and the Spanish in 1635–1636. Schenck drowned in 1589 during an attempted surprise attack on Nijmegen.

20 The *Schenkenschans* ('Schenck's rampart'), situated on an island in the river Rhine near Lobith, where the Rhine splits into the rivers Waal towards Nijmegen and Nederrijn towards Arnhem (the course of the rivers has changed since the 16th century; today the fortress is no longer on an island, but the village Schenkenschanz near Cleves).

21 Dutch *Rijnberk*, currently Rheinberg (Westphalia, Germany)

22 The battle near Zutphen (village of Warnsveld) on 22 september 1586, which however was won by the Spanish. Philip Sidney (1554–1586), the courtier, poet, diplomat and soldier died in Arnhem on 17 oktober of the wounds sustained in the battle.

23 For the accusation of financial mismanagement, see e.g. MacCaffrey, *Queen Elizabeth 1572–1588*, 362–67.

24 Dutch *burger-hoplieden* (in Goris' translation); these are heads of city neighbourhoods, e.g. in Amsterdam: 'The first administrative division of Amsterdam into districts was carried out in 1529 to organise the support for the poor. In 1579 this division was changed and 11 neighbourhoods were created. Each of these had a burger-hopman or captain at its head, who was also charged with the control of fires and uprisings. In 1630 these officers carried out the first census in Amsterdam', see *www.os.amsterdam.nl/pdf/2006_gebiedsindeling_historie.pdf.*

25 Diederik Sonoy (1529–1597) was one of the signatories of the Compromise of Nobles (see 1.50ff). He was a successful fundraiser for William of Orange, and took a commanding position among the *Watergeuzen* (see 1.51, 2.25) on Orange's behalf. In 1572 Orange made him governor of the town of Enkhuizen in North-Holland, from where he conquered several other places. As governor of North-Holland (1572–1588) Sonoy acted with cruelty against Catholics. During the Leicester period he chose the latter's side against the States of Holland, even after Leicester's departure, which led to him being besieged in the town of Medemblik by Maurice (februari-april 1588). Because of his merits he nevertheless received a pension from the States of Holland.

26 This does not seem to be entirely true; an offer of sovereignty *sonder eenighe conditie* ('without any restriction') is recorded to have been made to Elizabeth, via Leicester, by pressure groups of private citizens from the province of Utrecht in June 1586. The movement was backed by some city councils but not by the magistrate, who, in reaction, sent a polite letter to Elizabeth reaffirming

their 'conformiteyt en de goede affectie' while avoiding the word sovereignty (see Pieter Bor, *Nederlantsche oorloghen, beroerten, ende borgerlijcke oneenicheyden*, vol. 3.1, Amsterdam [1626], book 21, fol. 31 r-v).

27 In 1586 a scheme, supported by Philip II, was directed from France to kill Elizabeth and put Mary Stuart on the throne (see 2.23 & note). This 'Babington Plot' was found out in time and the participants arrested: it was named after the Catholic nobleman Anthony Babington (1561–1586), who carried a coded letter by Mary, although she persisted in denying her authorship.

28 January 1587. It seems Stanley did not act purely on his own; the loyalty of the magistrate of Deventer to the revolt had been in doubt for some time. Among the papers of Jean Hotman (Leicester's secretary) is an anonymous report from October 1586 on the unrelability of the magistrate and their covert opposition to the States, apparently written as a call to Leicester to take measures; see R. Broersma en G. Busken Huet, 'Brieven over het Leycestersche tijdvak uit de papieren van Jean Hotman', in: *Bijdragen en Mededeelingen van het Historische Genootschap*, vol. 34 (1913), p. 1–271, esp. 59–64.

29 A text printed in Antwerp in 1587 and again in Paris in 1588; see the edition in Th. Heywood (ed.), *Cardinal Allen's defence of sir William Stanley's Surrender of Deventer, January 29, 1586–1587,* Manchester 1851 (Chetham Society).

30 On the ‚impregnable' fortress of Geldern: '*Geldern hatte im Laufe seiner Geschichte eine Anzahl von Belagerungen auszuhalten. Erst 1587 hatte eine Belagerung Erfolg, wenn auch nur durch den Verrat des im Dienste der Generalstaaten stehenden Schotten Patton. Wegen einer Ohrfeige, die er während eines Trinkgelages von dem Offizier der Generalstaaten Martin Schenk von Nideggen erhalten hatte, öffnete der Gouverneur Ariston Patton den Spaniern unter Oberst von Hautepenne in der Nacht vom 4. zum 5. Juli 1587 die Tore.*' (http://www.adel-genealogie.de/1703.html).

31 Creve-coeur = 'heartbreak'; one explanation for the name of the fortress is that Hautepenne died from a wound in the heart, and it enables the Dutch wordplay *Hartepijn* on *Hautepenne*; however the name probably has a different explanation since the name Crevecoeur appears more often for fortresses, and for this one only after 1601.

32 This translation of *tricies florenorum* is based on a.o. Martialis 4.37.4; Goris translates 'dartigh tonnen schats jaerlijx' (=30.000/year); but cp. 3.1 (1579) where 'the public treasury's monthly revenues ran to six hundred thousand florins', or 7,2 million yearly. Although the revolt had lost a great deal of territory since 1579, still a ratio of 2,4 between the amounts of 1579 and 1588 seems more likely than 240.

33 François Vranck's *Corte Vertoonighe* (1587), written in response to a *Remonstrantie* bij Thomas Wilkes, Leicesterś spokesman; Grotius' *De Antiquitate* can be read as a continuation of Vranck's argument, see *De Antiquitate,* Intr. p. 4, and Kossmann, 'Bodin, Althusius Parker'; a translation of the text is available in *The Dutch Revolt,* ed. M. van Gelderen, Cambridge texts in the history of political thought, Cambridge 1993.

34 Led by the Italian nobleman and colonel Cosmo de Pescarengis. Other participants or suspects included John Cabbeljau (also recorded as governing member of a refugee church at Maidstone around the years 1572–1576), captain Nicolas de Maulde, commander of the squadron which would enforce the coup, Adrianus Saravia, professor of Theology in the university of Leiden, and Adolf van Meetkercke, a prominent administrator originally from the Southern Netherlands. Cabbeljau, Saravia and Meetkercke managed to escape in time and were condemned *in absentia* to decapitation and quartering; Meetkercke and Saravia fled to England. De Pescarengis and De Maulde were executed. See https://www.genealogieonline.nl/stamboom-van-rooy/I10163.php.

35 Thomas Sackville, Lord Buckhurst (1536–1608) came over early in 1587, partly in order to improve relations after the English surrender of Deventer and the Zutphen fortresses. Once in the Low Countries he chose the side of Leicester's opponents (Oosterhoff, *Leicester and the Netherlands,* ch. 11).

36 The Privy Council.

37 Cai Rantzau or Von Rantzau (1562–1591) came to the peace negoatiations in 1587 as the Danish king Frederick II's envoy, but was taken prisoner during the journey and brought to The Hague. He was eventually released, but without compensation. Frederick retaliated by locking 600 ships in the Sont, which were only released after excuses and a financial compensation (*Dansk Biografisk Lexikon,*

ed. C. Bricka, Kopenhagen 1887–1905, vol. 13, p. 404–405). The arrest is also discussed in Justus Lipsius' correspondence with Cai's father Heinrich von Rantzau, an important royal counsellor and scholar; see *Iusti Lipsi Epistolae* vol. 2, no. 87 06 01 R.

38 The question whether breach of oaths and treaties was permissible towards pagans and heretics was central to the reception of Machiavelli's thought in the Low Countries, see A. Clerici, 'Trust, Heresy and Rebellion'.

39 Grotius' *De Antiquitate* ends in a similar way with an overview of the current form of government in the United Provinces; see DA 7.8 sqq.

40 Such as Ostend, which remained in republic's hands until 1604.

41 Ernest of Bavaria (1554–1612), prince-bishop of Cologne and Liège, bishop of Münster, Hildesheim, and Freising; Abbot of Stablo-Malmédy.

42 Jean de Monluc, lord of Baligny (1560–1603); Maréchal de France and governor of Cambrai under Henry IV.

43 See also 4.49 above.

44 The old Dutch adjective '*vroed-*' means wise, venerable.

45 i.e. States-General.

46 i.e. the (provincial) States of Holland, not the States-General.

47 Since the States meetings cannot be assembled permanently, there are a number of executive councils for the various aspects of government (e.g. finance, army, etc), which run the business on a day-to-day basis according to the decisions by the States.

48 Paulus Buys (1531–1594) was councillor in Leiden, counsellor to William of Orange and public prosecutor of Holland since 1577. He played an important role in the negotiations for the treaty with England in 1585, but turned against Leicester in 1586 and was imprisoned by him. After his release in 1587 he played no political role.

49 Johan van Oldenbarnevelt (154–-1619) was first a lawyer in Delft and The Hague, pensionary (=paid counsellor) to Rotterdam from 1577 onwards and representative of this city in the States of Holland. In 1586 he became Paulus Buys' successor as public prosecutor of Holland; in this role he led the opposition against Leicester. After Leicester's departure he developed into the leader of the government of the province of Holland.

50 i.e. Friesland proper, as distinct from West-Friesland (North-Holland) and East-Friesland (in modern Germany). The addition "then" refers to the situation of the United Provinces in 1588, without for example Groningen (which came back in Spanish hands in 1580 (see 3.44) and was only re-conquered in 1594.

51 i.e. the king's place-holder, the Archdukes Albert and Isabella.

52 See 3.1 and 5.36

53 i.e. until ca. 1589.

54 Dutch: *vendel*

55 See also M. de Jong, *Jong,* 'De bewapening van het Staatse Leger 1590–1621', *Armamentaria* 32, Jaarboek Legermuseum 1997–1998, p. 7–21. As to 'fraud by the officers': in order to stimulate the recruitment of troops, there was a financial bonus system which rewarded recruitment, but was liable to fraud, so that often the number of actually recruited troops was lower than the reported number.

56 For *tribunus* (senior officer) Goris' Dutch has *Kornel;* for *ductor ordinis* Goris has *hopman*.

57 i.e. in the *Historiae*, which are not included in this edition.

58 *Batavi* or 'the Dutch' as in: the northern provinces, see Intr. § 9.3. This probably refers to the decision by the States meeting in Leiden in 1573 (which was also adopted by Zeeland at the administrative union of Holland and Zeeland in 1575) which is mentioned by Orange in the *Apology*; zie ed. Wansink p. 85 and ed. Mees-Verweij p. 80; see also Israel, *Dutch Republic*, p. 362.

59 The much-resented re-organisation of the bishoprics in 1559, see 1.38 and notes.

SUMMARIES OF *ANNALES* 1–5

Book 1: *Previous history of the Conflict* (–1567)

Preface: A sensational war and the importance of historiography. The Low Countries in Antiquity and the Middle Ages. Origins and growth of their administrative tradition. Changes in this under the houses of Burgundy and Habsburg Spain; the deterioration of political relations. Comparison of the Spanish and Dutch national characters. Charles V understood the Lowlanders and took care of their interests. Philip II's lust for power. His attack on the laws that limit his power and departure for Spain. Orange, Egmond and Horne are the first among the nobility. Internal strife and focus on self-interest among the Dutch nobility paves the way for Spanish domination. The population avoids involvement but does protest against the religious prosecutions. Causes and brief history of the Reformation. Religious prosecutions and the Inquisition are introduced in the Low Countries under Charles V. Religion always stimulates hatred and intransigence in people. Philip resumes and intensifies the prosecutions and uses the Church's authority for his political aims. At his departure Margareth of Parma is appointed as governess. The States' insult to Philip. Margareth rules in name, Granvelle in reality. Granvelle is hated by the nobility, and Orange becomes the chief voice of the resistance against him. The new ecclesiastical districts. Part of the nobility request a meeting of the States-General to solve the deadlock concerning Granvelle, but the request itself causes further disagreement. Orange, Egmond and Horne obtain Granvelle's dismissal from Philip; after which they draw power to themselves (in the Council of State) and ease the prosecutions. Philip however searches precisely for harsher measures. Decrees by the Council of Trent. Resistance against the Inquisition by the States of Brabant and other provinces; growing discontent among the population. The nobility institute a (somewhat clumsy) League for religious peace, which presents a petition to the governess, requesting reduction of the prosecutions and meeting of the States-General. The governess makes only few promises; the King makes fewer concessions than the circumstances require. Both sides threaten a military intervention. Three groups of non-catholics in the Low Countries: Anabaptists, Lutherans and Calvinists. Rapid increase in the number of protestant gatherings, which lead to insurrections among the lower populace and the Iconoclastic Fury. Margareth forced to grant amnesty to the nobility and suspension of the prosecutions. Intercepted letters from Spain however speak of the death penalty for Orange and other prominent nobles. Orange sends a letter of advice to the King and withdraws from his public offices, as does Horne. Margareth revokes her concessions and attempts to break the alliance between the nobility and the population. The nobles in the League abandon their cause. The Spaniards seize this occasion to restore their power, but also to take revenge. Philip does not come to the Low Countries himself, but sends the Duke of Alva instead, man known for his ruthless approach. Orange goes in exile to Germany; many refugees leave the country. Thus order is seemingly restored.

Book 2: *Tyranny and War.* From Alva's arrival to Don Juan's (1567–1577)
Alva's reign of terror. Execution of Egmond and Horne. First armed resistance; Orange is operating very cautiously. He publishes a justification, based on the 'disobedience clause' in the Privileges. The German emperor tries to act as mediator. Orange assembles an army which however falls apart soon. Alva and the Spaniards rule victoriously. Introduction of the 10th and 20th Penny, suppression of resistance. Anger produces greater unity among the Lowlanders. Orange takes new courage and starts searching for a foreign alliance, which he finds in France. The 'Sea-Beggars' act as his naval force. Capture of Den Briel. Plundering of Rotterdam by Spanish troops. which causes the defection of several cities in Holland and Zeeland to the revolutionaries. First free meeting of the States of Holland in Dordrecht. Fighting in North and South. The support from France does not appear – to the contrary, De Coligny is murdered in the St Bartholomew Massacre. Orange disbands his army. Cruel tyranny by the Spanish wherever they can. *Digression: short history of Holland and Zeeland since Roman times; Philip is the 13th Count of Holland.* Orange arrives in the break-away territory and organises the government. The number of towns represented in the States is extended. In name loyalty to Philip is maintained, although catholicism comes under pressure. Calvinism becomes the public religion, but there is religious freedom at the same time. Monasteries and royal property revert to the treasury. New taxes. The war is conducted in chaos and bloodshed because of lack of experience on both sides. Sieges of Haarlem and Alkmaar. Alva called back, succeed by Requesens. A Dutch army defeated on the Mookerheide as a result of a mutiny among Orange's troops. Mutiny on the Spanish at the same time, which causes suffering among the population which tends more towards Orange's side as a result. Failed attempt at negotiations. The fighting continued; siege and liberation of Leiden. Failure of a Spanish naval operation, but a success for them in Zeeland which cuts Holland off from Zeeland. On top of this, it appears impossible to find a foreign ally for the revolt, except from some secret financial assistance from France. The sudden death of Requesens. Flanders and Brabant join the resistance. The pressure of Turkish advances leads to financial crisis on the Spanish side, which causes new mutinies among their troops. Brussels by its own citizens saved from plundering. The Council of State arrested by prominent nobles from Brabant who take power in their own hands. Maastricht and Antwerpen pillaged by break-away Spanish troops. This strengthens concord among the Lowlanders, who unite behind Orange. Peace talks between the loyal and the revolutionary provinces results in the Pacification of Ghent, which is also

endorsed by the Council of State. A rare moment of unity in the Netherlands, which are now all united against Spain. Philip decides to accept the situation for the time being, waiting for an opportunity to drive the alliance apart. He sends Don Juan over as governor; in name with the task of enforcing the Pacification, but his true motives are soon seen through. Orange advocates armed resistance against Don Juan before he gets a chance to settle in, but this idea finds no support among the high nobility. Installation of Don Juan as governor and departure of the Spanish soldiers, the latter of which is show not reality. The agreements appear difficult to enforce on both sides, with Don Juan continuing attempts to win back towns, and Orange being accused by the king of spreading protestantism. Orange's popularity and calls for appointing him as governor. This in turn leads to jealousy among the other nobles who propose Mathias (the German emperor's brother). Appointment of Mathias with Orange as his lieutenant.

Book 3: *Struggle and Experiment.* Shifting tides of battle, the Pacification of 1576, weakness of the Dutch unity; political experiments (1577–1581).
Declaration of war to Don Juan. The threat of Spanish intervention in England moves Elizabeth to send support, mostly financial. Because of division among the Dutch nobility many defect to Don Juan. Don Juan assembles a strong army and defeats a Netherlands army at Gembloux; he captures Louvain and rules in Brabant and Limburg. Growing self-awareness among the Netherlanders, who reject peace negotiations now that they can choose between several foreign alliances. The Duke of Anjou, the French king's brother, rises as a possible successor in the Low Countries. The search for a form of government and/or a new prince. Returned protestant exiles bring Amsterdam, Utrecht and Haarlem over to the revolutionary side. They do not uphold agreements about religious co-existence. Gelderland is ruled by Jan van Nassau. Internal conflicts break out in Groningen and Friesland which are ruled by the count of Rennenberg. The latter restores order and captures Spanish cities in Overijssel (Deventer, Kampen), due in part to English support with that of Casimir of the Palatinate. His support leads catholics on the revolutionary side to press for a fast appointment of Anjou (who is a catholic). The protestants request a fixed share in the government of church and state. Many magistrates convert to protestantism. After lengthy deliberations it is decided that in places in catholic areas where at least one hundred families request this, some churches must be handed over to protestants, and vice versa in protestant areas (only the latter rule was never effectuated). This arrangement causes many painful local conflicts which undermine the unity of the Netherlands. Chaos in Ghent; refusal of the new arrangement in Artois and Hainaut. Unexpected victory over Don Juan at Rijmenam. Continuation of peace negotiations. Don Juan appears unwilling to make concessions, but he considers himself the weaker military party and thus seeks to protract the talks. When his army is reinforced, he returns to the armed approach and leaves the peace talks to the German emperor. A Dutch

counteroffensive fails because of private ambitions of its commanders. Tensions between Flanders and Artois/Hainaut also cause defections of other provinces from the common cause and focus on their own interests, which in turn leads to chaos, desertion among the troops and the danger of civil war in the South. Casimir attempts to benefit from the situation for his own ambitions. Meanwhile Anjou lingers in the South, angry about the competition from Casimir. The deadlock leads to the departure of both. Death of Don Juan, not without suspicions of obstruction or even murder on behalf of Philip. The Duke of Parma, a man of great political skill, is appointed as his successor. Parma stirs the quarrel in the South back up; Orange tries to calm it down, but with little success. Parma's siege of Maastricht. The peace negotiations in Cologne fail because Orange, with that purpose in mind, insists on religious demands which the king would certainly reject. Parma resumes the military operations, but also holds out clemency for those who repent and reconcile themselves with the king. Several Walloon nobles, commanders and towns accept these terms; once again showing the lack of unity among the Netherlanders. In order to keep provinces in the North from making the same step, Orange proposes a closer alliance of six rebellious provinces, which results in the Union of Utrecht. Chaos rules in the remaining provinces. Antwerp, Bruges and Ghent join the union; Den Bosch chooses the other side. During new peace negotiations the revolutionaries request a truce; but Parma plays for time in order to make further conquests. Capture of Maastricht by the Spanish. Next Parma dismisses the troops, which brings him great popularity with the Walloons. Philip makes an offer of peace, which the rebels reject because it amounts to a return under Spanish domination. Separate proposals are made to Orange. Thus the negotiations fail; the only result is that after this time, the nobility are no longer interested in talking about peace but only about continuing the war. The rebels' position is weak because of their lack of central authority and armed forces. Alva's conquest of Portugal for Philip, which increases his income enormously because of the Portuguese global trade. This conquest also damages Dutch trade with Southern Europe. Internal war in Groningen and Friesland, during which Rennenberg hands over Groningen to the Spaniards, causing war and misery in the North for fifteen years to come. Parma is too busy elsewhere to secure these gains. The rebels are unsuccessful in keeping their troops from looting. Orange reorganising the government. Formal deposition of Philip as king; Orange proposes appointing Anjou as successor. Orange banished by Philip; his publication of a defence. Anjou accepts the authority offered to him and comes over immediately with an army. Vague promises of support by the French king.

Book 4: *The Revolt hard-pressed.* Failure of the Anjou experiment. Parma's advances from the south. Assassination of William the Silent. Search for a new ally (1581–1584). Anjou's departure for England, for negotiations about a marriage to Elizabeth, but this prospect fails. His inauguration in the Netherlands and the conditions to which his rule is submitted. Discontent among the nobility about these close ties with France. Changes in the military situation. Anjou's arrival puts pressure on Spain to improve their operations. The armies are called back, in contravention of the agreements of Arras. The funding for the war. Lack of funding from France puts Anjou into trouble, who now makes a desperate attempt to seize power by force. In some places this attempt succeeds, but it leads to disaster in others, especially Antwerp. Anjou has discredited himself completely, Orange's plan with him has become impossible and Orange's own reputation suffers as well. Parma makes a new attempt to seduce the Netherlands to return to obedience to the king, while Orange argues nevertheless for a new attempt with Anjou, with whom new negotiations are conducted. Anjou demands more power. The negotiations do not lead to a result and Anjou returns to France, where he dies not long after. Parma captures Dunkirk because the people of Ghent will admit a French relief army. The hatred of the French is so great in Flanders that it damages Orange's popularity. Orange moves to Zeeland; Parma uses the occasion to seize a range of towns in West-Flanders. The Cologne war (the Truchsess case) as occasion for the Spaniards to start operations in the eastern border area as well. Spanish incursion into the Ijssel region and sieges in Flanders. Hembyze and Chimay, prominent men in Ghent and Bruges, devise strategies of cunning and deceit to deliver these towns back to the Spanish. Their plan supported by Parma. Waasland and the town of Aalst are handed over to Parma, followed by Bruges, Damme, the *Brugse Vrije* and Ypres. Ghent is saved for the time being however because Hembyze, blinded by ambition, overplays his hand. Parma starts the operation towards the reconquest of Antwerp. The murder of William of Orange, which causes further trouble for the Netherlands because of the internal divisions and Parma's successes. Obituary and funeral. His 18-year old son Maurice becomes Stadtholder of Holland Zeeland, his cousin William Louis of Friesland. The latter makes good progress there against the Spaniards and against discord, and carries out some administrative reforms. Parma makes a new offer of peace, but this is rejected. Parma now directs all his attention towards the operation against Antwerp; for Ghent this becomes a reason to surrender. As a result Parma rules in almost all of Flanders. Antwerpen tries to arm itself against the approaching siege, but makes little progress because many private interests are prioritised. Thus Spain's position gets stronger, that of the rebels weaker, all results of the loss of William of Orange. The remaining government members do not enjoy the same degree of trust and obedience among the population. However that now the danger becomes so acute, France and England start sending further support. This creates a debate as to which of them should be the preferred ally. Partly on English advice, France is chosen, even with fewer conditions than previously requested from Anjou. In the end however the king of France shies away from the alliance.

Book 5: *The rebuff of the monarchical quest.* England as new ally. Loss of Antwerp. Leicester and his prolonged struggle with the States. Parma's further advances. Maurice's first successes. (1584–1588).
Now that the prospect of an alliance with France has failed, the rebels turn to Elizabeth. Parma's siege of Antwerp is beginning and again he is making sure he is very well prepared; but without experiencing any countermeasures by the Dutch. The bridge on the Scheldt. Surrender of the city; the effects on morale on the Dutch side. All hope is vested on the English alliance. The agreement with Elizabeth and the arrival of the Earl of Leicester. His dishonest character. There is great enthusiasm at his arrival, but soon his tyrannical attitude becomes clear. His lack of knowledge of Dutch politics and the gap between Dutch and British characters. Leicester is surrounded by flatterers, agitators and careerists. Their attempts to discredit the States. Leicester's ruinous ban on trade with the enemy, that produces no useful effects but reduces the income which keeps the warfare going. Philip sends additional support to Parma. The loss of Grave through treason, and of Venlo. Maurice takes Axel. Spanish and Dutch successes in the Cologne war. Sir Philip Sidney killed in a battle near Zutphen. The States' distrust of some of the English commanders. Leicester confronted by complaints about abuses from the States-General and the States of Holland. Leicester's contempt for them, and his search for ways to reduce their power. Digression: the need to give those involved in trade and commerce a share in the government. Leicester forges an alliance with the reformed ministers and gives them influence on government business. Many non-Calvinists lose their positions. Leicester's popularity among the lower populace produces a kind of popular tyranny in Utrecht and Friesland. Leicester supported by the mob. His (temporary) return to England, allegedly because of his treatment by the States. Calls for transfer of the sovereignty to Elizabeth, but she refuses. Chaos in the Netherlands; treason by the English commanders Stanley and York, who hand over Deventer and Zutphen to the Spanish. This finally turns general opinion against Leicester. Moderation of the ban on trade with the enemy. Poverty in Flanders and Brabant, economic recovery in the North. New conquests by Parma. Confused countermeasures by Leicester, who blames the States and openly questions the usefulness of this war. Elizabeth considering peace with Spain, in spite of the successes of English fleets against Spanish shores, near the Americas and in the Moluccas. The States refuse to join these negotiations. Frustration moving Leicester towards imitation of Anjou's coup, but the plan is discovered in time. Leicester departs for England, and tries to prolong his influence on the troubles in the Netherlands, but dies soon after. Parma does not continue the operations in the Netherlands straight away, but works on a plan to take England as well. In Spain a very large fleet is built against England and the Netherlands. In order to hide this plan, Spanish ambassadors arrive in the North to talk about peace. An incident with the Danish intermediary. Elizabeth playing along with the fake negotiations game in order to buy time, and asking the

Dutch to do the same. The Dutch refuse because negotiations have so far only brought misery. Elizabeth negotiates with Parma, also about the Netherlands, but does not really stand up for Dutch interests. The negotiations end in failure; and finally the aforementioned fleet appears. In the Netherlands tensions keep rising, because of mutinies in Leicester's armies and other events. Maurice defeats Sonoy in Medemblik.

Digression: brief overview of the geography of the Netherlands, bordering countries, and the organisation of the government in the North: administrative levels, public offices, magistracies, the working of the Union. The distribution of power, the role of the province of Holland; finances, the military organisation, Maurice's army reforms. The lack of interest in the common cause among the traditional nobility. Relationships between Church and secular government. The flourishing of Dutch trade; and the dangers of the increasing luxury and greed

APPENDIX I
THE EXTANT MANUSCRIPTS OF THE *HISTORIAE* (SEE ALSO § II.I ABOVE)

Apparently the original working title of the entire work was *Hugonis Grotii Commentarii de rebus Belgicis,* which was subsequently changed to *Annales* and *Historiae*. The changes in the book titles and their arrangement can be followed in the manuscripts. It should be noted that up to and including *Historiae* book 5 the numbers of the *Commentariorum* books are 2 ahead of the eventual *Historiae* numbering (suggesting that the part now entitled *Annales* was then conceived of as 2 books of *Commentarii*)[1]; while from Hist. 6 onwards the *Commentariorum* numbers are 5 ahead of the eventual *Historiae* numbers, suggesting that from roughly the time of composition of Hist. 6 onwards the subdivision of the *Annales* was changed from 2 into 5 books, and that the change to *Annales et Historiae* followed later.

I.
Leiden University Library, ms. Papenbroeck 9.1: *Historiae* 1-4

The manuscript has a soft vellum cover which might well be original and which seems to have been made and preserved as a whole. The text and make-up look like a fair copy, with later additions and deletions.

The manuscript has apparently been interleaved at some point after its original completion[2] so as to add one additional white sheet for every sheet with text, sometimes more (e.g. fol. 40–41 and 45–48 are added). Many of these have been used for notes and additional sections of text. The extra pages are not included in the original folio numbering (top left of the pages). There is a new numbering at the top right of the pages, which includes all folia, which is probably also in Grotius' hand. The numbers below are of the later numbering.

[1] When exactly the change to a division into 5 books was made remains unclear. It might be noted that the printed edition of Casaubonus' letter of April 1613 (see note 246) mentions '21 books of *Historiae*' which is wrong in any count, for the number was probably 18+5=23, or (in case the re-arrangement of the earlier part had not yet been carried out) 18+2=20.

[2] See § II.I.

Remarks per book

Book 1 (fol. 1–16): 1588–1589
Original title: *Hvgonis Grotii Comme<n>tariorum de Rebus Belgicis Liber Tertius*
first changed to: ... *Annalium... Liber Tertius* or *Sextus,* then to ... *Annalium Liber Sextus*
then changed to .... *Historiarum ... Liber Primus*

Book 2 (fol. 17–32): 1590–1592
Original title: *Hvgonis Grotii Commentariorum de Rebus Belgicis Liber Quartus*
changed to: ...*Commentariorum* or *Historiarum... Liber Septimus*
then to: ...*Historiarum... Liber Secundus*

Book 3 (fol. 33–48): 1593–1594
Original title: *Hvgonis Grotii Commentariorum ~~Liber~~ de Rebus Belgicis Liber Quintus*
changed to: ...*Commentariorum* or *Historiarum... Liber Octavus*
then to: ...*Historiarum... Liber Tertius*

Book 4 (fol. 49–64): 1595 (The arrangement of one year, one book starts here)
Original title: *Hvgonis Grotii Commentariorum de Rebus Belgicis Liber Sextus*
changed to: ...*Commentariorum* or *Historiarum... Liber Nonus*
then to: ...*Historiarum... Liber Quartus*

fol. 65–[71] empty (except for a few notes in Grotius' hand on fol. 71v).

Watermarks:[3] type 1–4 throughout the manuscript; type 5 only once:

1. Eagle A: tail piece with 3 little balls in triangular arrangement, 'D' above them
   a.o. on fols. 25, 43, 45, [71]
2. Eagle B: very similar to A, but with small differences (e.g. form of wings)
   a.o. on fols. [27], 47
   A or B (not yet identified): 5[4], 57, 61, **65**
   Very similar (but not identical) eagles in:
   – Autograph of letter Grotius to Heinsius, 19 dec. 1606 (Briefw. I no. 90); Eagle B in ARA, Suppl. I f. 392 (letter Grotius to Heinsius, 28-7-1612
   – BPL 917 *De Iure Praedae*, fol. 31, 44, 45, 49, 51-53
   – W. Tschudin, *Paper Mills of Basle*, no. 261, 262, 266, 267 (manufacturer: Düring; dating: *c.* 1600)

[3] I thank Martine van Ittersum and Peter Borschberg for their assistance with the identification of these watermarks and for sharing their knowledge on this topic. On watermarks and the dating of the *Historiae* ms., see also M. van Ittersum, *The Working Papers of Hugo Grotius* (forthcoming).

[4] Page numbers printed in bold carry no writing and therefore show the watermark most clearly.

3. Dragon; similar to Tschudin 299 (of 1591) but different; manufacturer Dürr, Basle

Fols. 17, 23, 48

4. Round emblem with house with harlequin on chimney and letters 'N.C.H.'

Fols. 51, 53, 55, **66**

Identical watermark in: -Tschudin no. 381 (Niklaus Heusler, Basle, 1603); Autograph of letter Grotius to Heinsius, November 1606 (*Brfw.* I ep. 87; ep. 35 in UB Leiden, BPG 77).

5. One watermark appears only once: eagle with coat of arms (instead of staff): fol. 70

There is a note by Gerard van Papenbroeck on an additional inlaid folded sheet, addressing the question of the whereabouts of the parts not in Papenbroeck's possession ('... three books, i.e. 5, 6 and 7, are missing and were lost in Blaeu's printing shops, or in the fire in that place, or by some other incident, together with the books of the *Annals*').[5]

[5] The sheet is not permanently attached to the manuscript. It consists of two sheets of paper glued together, then folded once so as to make 4 pages. Only the first page caries text (maybe Papenbroeck expected to add further observations on the ms.?). Papenbroeck's signature appears in the top right-hand corner of the page. The full text of Papenbroeck's note is: *Hugonis Grotii/Historiarum/De Rebus Belgicis Libri/ ab anno MDLXXXVIII ad annum /MDCIX./*

Hi omnes scripti sunt ipsa Grotii manu:/ Tres autem libri, nempe V.VI et VII hic deside-/rantur, qui in Tijpographia Blauiana, vel eius/ incendio, vel alio quodam fato, perierunt/ una cum Annalium Libris. /

Hoc Illustrissimi Scriptoris autographum mihi comparavi ex Bibliotheca Eminentissimi Cardinalis Duboisii, III. Octobris MDCCXXV. ('Hugo Grotius' *Histories of the War in the Low Countries*, from the year 1588 to 1609. All these books are written in Grotius' own hand; however three books, i.e. 5, 6 and 7, are missing and were lost in Blaeu's printing shops, or in the fire in that place, or by some other incident, together with the books of the *Annals*. I bought this autograph of the famous writer for my collection from the library of the Eminent Cardinal Dubois, 3 October 1725').

2.
Paris, Bibliothèque Nationale, Fonds Latin, no. 17796[6]

Volume in a vellum cover which might well be original. Title on spine: *Grotius. Manuscriptum*
There are many changes and additions to the text, especially in book 5-6. Additions are either placed in the margins or on separate inserted sheets.

Ownership marks and (former) shelfmarks

On the inside of vellum front cover:
upper left-hand corner: Ms. mark *'mm:905'* in red ink
below this, in the middle: label with '*latin 17,796*'
central: ex-libris of a coat of armes (without name, but appears to belong to François-Michel de Verthamon (1657–1738)[7]

On the flyleaves:
first flyleaf, recto (fol. 1r):
Upper left: worn round label with *W*? and *A*? and '*96 5*' (?) in black
Upper right: ms. note '*Nouv. acq. lat. 1024*' (probably 17th or 18th century hand).
– notes in Grotius' hand
– ms. note '*Volume de 72 Feuillets. Plus les Feuillets 14bis. 16bis. 18bis. Les Feuillets 2.3.70.71 sont blancs. 1er Juin 1870.*'

Fol. 4r (opening of book 5), left margin, from top to bottom:
– round stamp in red: *MSS. BIBLIOTHEQUE IMPERIALE* and eagle
  same stamp on fol. 14bis, 16bis (both are insertions) and fol. 69r (last page with text)
– small oval stamp in black: *EMPIRE FRANCAIS DIRECTION GENERALE DES ARCHIVES*
  same stamp on fol. 25 (opening of book 6); fol. 69r fol. 72r (inserted note)
– small square stamp with bevelled edges in red: *Arrêté du 19e Avril 1862 ÉCHANGE*
  same stamp on fol. 25; 69r; 72r

[6] See also L. Delisle, *Inventaire des manuscrits de Notre-Dame* etc., p. 68, no. 17796: "Hugonis Grotii de rebus belgicis libri V et VI—Venu des Arch. de l'Empereur." —implying that book 7 is missing from the Paris ms, which is however not the case.

[7] See https://numelyo.bm-lyon.fr/BML:BML_06PRV01000395519l008, which states 'François-Michel de Verthamon was counsellor to the King in the Parlement, elected first president of the Grand Conseil in 1697, then *Greffier commandeur des Ordres du roi* in 1716. He was a bibliophile, and founded the so-called library of the Grand-Conseil, both by donating his own books, and by bequathing a fund to enlarge it. The library burnt down in the fire of the Palais in the middle of the 18th century.' With great thanks to Guus van Breugel of the Dutch *CBG Centrum voor familiegeschiedenis* for this identification.

Page numberings

There is one old page numbering (upper left of the pages), starting on the first page of the actual text, which does not count empty pages and does not include the inserted folia (—although some inserts have been given a number under this numbering, so that e.g. page numbers 13, 15, 55 appear twice, 26 three times etc; however the double p. 27 and the double pp. 6–7 in book 7 look like mistakes).

There is another old folio numbering (upper right), starting on the second flyleaf, which does include the inserted sheets and shows changes and irregularities, e.g. '24 bis' as older number on fol. 25.

Fol. 1v–3 are empty. Folio numbering continues until 73. Fol. 69v–71v are empty. Fol 72r–v are a bound-in sheet with notes in Grotius' hand.

Remarks per book

Book 5 (page 1–28 and fol. 4r–24v; see above for some irregularities) 1596
Original title: *Hugonis Grotii Commentariorum de rebus Belgicis liber Septimus* changed to … *Decimus*; later changed to: *Historiarum de rebus Belgicis Liber Quintus.*
The text displays many changes and insertions (added in the margins).
Paper size slightly narrower than in books 6–7.
Dark brown ink.
Inserted folia: 9, 11, 13, 14bis, 16, 16bis, 18bis, 21, 22 (new numbering, see above)

Book 6 (page 29–56 and fol. 25r–40v) 1597
Original title: *Hugonis Grotii Commentariorum de rebus Belgicis liber XI* changed to: *Historiarum de rebus Belgicis Liber Sextus* (NB without intermediate stage '… Octavus')
Dark brown ink. Page and folio numberings continue from book 5.
Inserted folia: 38,39

Book 7 (page 1–7 then 6–56 (i.e. 6 and 7 appear twice); and fol. 41r–44v then 44r–69r (i.e. 44 appears twice) 1598
Original title: *Hugonis Grotii Commentariorum de rebus Belgicis liber XII* changed to: *Historiarum de rebus Belgicis Liber Septimus.*
Yellow-brown ink.
Inserted folia: none, except fol. 72 with loose notes. After fol. 73 there is another sheet with notes.

Watermarks

fol. 2,71,73 (flyleaves): Eagle with Basle staff;
fol. 7, 8,14, 15, 19, 20, 23, 24 /25, 32, 33, 34, 35, 36, 37 (i.e. book 5 and 6): crest of armour with bend sinister and B at lower end
fol. 11, 13, 21, 22 (inserted sheets): shield with vertical pale and tower on the right, 'golden fleece' type sheep at the lower end
fol. 16 (insert): Basle staff on shield
fol. 42, 43, 48, 49, 52, 56, 57, 58, 60, 61, 64, 65, 66, 67 (i.e. book 7): Basle staff with little tower underneath; fol. 70 (flyleaf): the same but slightly smaller

3.
Leiden University Libary, ms. Papenbroeck 9.2: *Historiae* 8–18

The make-up of Papenbroeck 9.2 is markedly different from 9.1. In Papenbroeck 9.2, the individual books can be recognised as individual quires or units bound together in one cover. Each book/quire has a slightly different paper size; only 10–11 and 17–18 are unities. The manuscript has a soft vellum cover.

The text and make-up look like that of a fair copy, with later additions and deletions. There is a modern folio numbering in pencil in the upper right-hand corner of the pages. There are old folio numberings per book in most of the books. The numbers below are of the modern numbering. Two different hands are discernible; the handwriting in book 16 appears to be that of Grotius' father Jan de Groot, the other books are in Grotius' own hand.

Book 10 and 11 originally had only very brief titles, 'XV' and 'XVI' respectively, which belong in the numbering of when the working title was still *Commentarii*. These are then changed to directly to the final form with *Historiarum* etc. Book 12 has an original title with *Commentariorum* again.

The range of watermarks is as varied as the paper sizes; a watermark in book 13 (type 'Wittelsbach coat-of-arms') is identical to one in the manuscript of Grotius' *De Iure Praedae* (Leiden UL, BPL 917). i.e. on an insert probably datable to Nov./Dec. 1608. The inserted pages in book 15 (fol. 92bis-ter) carry a French watermark (grapes) and thus seem to have been inserted while Grotius lived in Paris, i.e. around 1622 or in 1635–1637 (see § 11.1-2 above). The *bis-ter* numbering indicates that the main folio numbering was in place before this sheet was inserted. The cahier with book 17–18 is a composite one: it consists of two quires and two inserts from different moments. The precise order of events here provides an interesting puzzle.

Remarks per book

Book 8 (fol. 1–16) 1599
Original title: *Hvgonis Grotii Commentariorum de Rebus Belgicis Liber XIII*
changed to: ...*Historiarum*... *Liber Octavus*
Watermark: Dragon on fol. 3, 6, 15

Book 9 (fol. 17–30) 1600
Original title: *Hvgonis Grotii Commentariorum de Rebus Belgicis Liber XIIII*
changed to: ...*Historiarum*... *Liber Nonus*
Paper much darker than in book 8.
Watermark: Post horn suspended from cord hanging in triangular shape, lily on top of triangle. letters 'Hob' or 'H.O.C' (?) written underneath; fol 17. Not found in G. Piccard, *Wasserzeichen Horn*

Book 10 (fol. 31–38; unity with book 11) 1601
Original title: *XV*
changed to: *Hvgonis Grotii Historiarum de Rebus Belgicis Liber Decimus*
Different paper again, thinner
Watermark: coat of arms with crown on top, and smaller coat of arms on it; suspended lamb underneath (as in 'Golden Fleece').

Book 11 (fol. 39–48) 1602
Original title: *XVI*
changed to: *Hvgonis Grotii Historiarum de Rebus Belgicis Liber Undecimus*
Paper and watermark as in book 10

Book 12 (fol. 49–57) [—fol. 57v–58 empty except for a note on fol. 58v] 1603
Original title: *Hvgonis Grotii Commentariorum de Rebus Belgicis Liber ~~X.~~ XVII*
changed to: ...*Historiarum*... *Liber ~~Vndecimus~~*[8] *Duodecimus*
Watermark: Basle staff on scutcheon, similar to Tschudin 233 (Dürr, Basle) [or perhaps to Tschudin 224, i.e. Heusler, Basle, *c.*1603?]; fol. **58**

Book 13 (fol. 59–64): possibly written *c.*1608 (see below); [fol. 65–66 empty] 1604
Original title: *Hugonis Grotii Commentariorum de Rebus Belgicis Liber XVIII*
changed to: ... *Historiarum de Rebus Belgicis Liber ~~Duodecimus~~ Tertius Decimus*
Watermark: Wittelsbach coat of arms divided into 4 fields with crown on top and H underneath (similar to Churchill, *Watermarks in Paper,* no. 275). Identical watermark in *De Iure Praedae* fol. 118 (an insert, probably of Nov./Dec. 1608).

[8] The mistake seems caused by the fact that book 10–11 are a physical unity that can easily be mistaken for one book.

Book 14: (Fol. 67–79) [fol. 80–82 empty] 1605
Original title: *Hugonis Grotii Commentariorum de Rebus Belgicis Liber XIX*
first changed to: ... *Historiarum... Liber ~~De~~ Decimus ~~Tert~~ Tertius ~~<et> Decimus~~*
then to .... *Historiarum ... Liber Decimus Quartus*
The handwriting is very neat and formal and spacious
Watermark: Coat of arms with inward-curved sides, divided into 4 fields (upper left: lion, upper right and lower left: diagonal bar; lower left: ?); fol. 80
similar to Tschudin 400 (Blum, Rötteln, 1587)

Book 15 (fol. 83–98); inserted pages (fol. 92bis–ter); [fol. 99–100 empty] 1606
Original title: *Hvgonis Grotii Commentariorum de Rebus Belgicis Liber XX*
changed to: ...*Historiarum... Liber ~~Quartus~~ Quintus Decimus*
Watermark as in book 13, on fol. **100**
Insert fol. 92 bis–ter: '*Sed ut intelligatur... pervectus huc esset, Angli rursum*', on pp. 492–494 in ed. 1657. Watermark: French, bundle of grapes with crown and lily, with a rough resemblance to R. Gaudriault, *Filigranes*, no. 954.

Book 16 (fol. 101–127); [128–132 empty]. In the hand of Jan de Groot.[9] 1607
Original title: *Liber XXI*
changed to: *Hvgonis Grotii Historiarum de Rebus Belgicis Liber Sextus Decimus*
Very few changes and additions to the text.
Watermark as in book 13 on fol. 108, 109, 113, 114, 115, 119, 121, 123, 124, 125, 127, 128, 131.

Book 17 (fol. 133–151); [152 empty] 1608
Original title: *Hvgonis Grotii Commentariorum de Rebus Belgicis Liber XXII*
changed to: ...*Historiarum... Liber Septimus ~~et~~ Decimus*
Messy and mixed structure. The book consists basically of two quires with two inserts in the second quire. Insert 1 seems to have been added later, insert 2 seems to have been present almost *ab origine* (since fol. 146v has been left partly empty, while the text continues on 147r).
Watermarks: quire 1) fol. 133–140: watermark Dragon (cp. Papenbroeck 9.1); e.g. fol. 139
quire 2) fol. 141-15: watermark Basle staff on shield, as in book 12; fol. 146, **148**, **152**

[9] In *Briefwisseling* vol.1, ep. 141 of 6 August 1608, it appears that by that time there were copies of the (parts of the) text in other hands than Hugo's. Writing from Zeeland to his father in Delft, Hugo asks him to look into the chest near his (Hugo's) bed, in which there are a number of *capsae* (boxes) with papers relating to his *Historiae*: in one of them he will find the beginning of the *Historiae* in his own (Jan's) hand, and also the fifth book, which is the last book of the first part [of the entire work: this would have to be book 5 of the *Annales*], once in Hugo's own hand and once in that of [the servant] Johannes.

insert 1: fol. 144–145: *Constat his queis… labefactare aggressi sunt*, on pp. 553–554 in ed. 1657. Watermark: Grapes (similar to book 15, but bigger)
insert 2: fol. 147 + 150: *Exierat patria… ab aliis regibus literae,* on pp. 555–561 in ed. 1657. Watermark: Xanten city crest

Folio structure of quire 2: folio	141 – 152	
	142 – 151	
	143 – 146	
	144 – 145	(insert 1)
	145 – 144	"
	146 – 143	
	147 – 150	(insert 2)
	148 – 149	"
	150 – 147	"
	151 – 142	
	152 – 141	

Book 18 (*1609*; fol. 153–155); [156–157 empty] ….); Bishop's staff as in book 12 and 17.
Original title: *Hvgonis Grotii Commentariorum de Rebus Belgicis Liber XXIII*
changed to: …*Historiarum… Liber Octavus ~~et~~ Decimus*

APPENDIX 2
THE VATICAN INDEX REPORTS
(SEE § 11.5 ABOVE)[1]

Sigla

[ ]: Additions and completions by the editor are put between [ ].
< >: Corrections by the editor are put between < >.
{ }: Deletions are put between { }.
†: Doubtful or illegible characters are put between †...†.
Quotations from the AH are put in *italics*.
|: The insertion mark | in Gradić's text, or in the quoted passages from the AH in the footnotes, marks places where Gradić or Grotius have fewer words than the other. Words or lines in Grotius which are left out by Gradić are printed in *italics* in the footnote. The passages from the AH are supplied from the quarto edition by Blaeu, Amsterdam, 1658, to the page-numbering of which the footnotes refer.
| |: The double insertion mark is used for other insertions.
Division into paragraphs follows that of the manuscripts; paragraph numbers were added by the editor.
Gradić or his copyist underlined most quotations; they are here (all) given in italics.

[1] For the full editions, introduction and notes, see Waszink, 'New documents'.

Stefano Gradić's report
(Roma, Indice, Protocolli KK 226r–231r, formerly 236–241)

The *Histories and Annals* of Grotius

1 We bring to your judgement, most eminent Fathers, Hugo Grotius, an author known to this holy court, a man famously loaded with condemnations from many sides, though also of outstanding merit to the world of learning, and a man who should be considered second to very few men his contemporaries because of that, had he not from immoderate self-esteem exalted himself above all others. Among other writings of this author – which, for the most part, are more outstanding for the talent expressed in them than their piety – there appeared in the preceding year, in a posthumous edition, his commentaries on the wars in the Low Countries between the Spanish and the Dutch, the first five books of which he entitled *Annales*, the other eighteen *Histories*. In the argumentation of this book he sets out to equal the renown for novelty achieved by other authors by the merit of his eloquence, studiously and quite successfully emulating the greatness of Sallust's style, and the brevity and tense dignity of Cornelius Tacitus. However, he did not attain to the fuit he hoped his laborious effort would bear: for indeed, since the sparkling expression is kept up neither evenly nor in all parts, he seems more to have affected, than to have actually achieved it, and he either unwisely postponed or proudly negelected to relieve, by work of the file, the aspired brevity from the usual trouble of obscurity.

2 Since this man possessed a heatedly talented nature, which was also well-versed in stirring up controversy on divine and human law, he could not keep his pen from occasionally straying from the course of his project, and mixed in various discussions of ecclesiastical and divine matters, and thus from betraying that he is seeped in and nourished with views at odds with those of Catholic orthodoxy.

3 This happens first in matters relating to the Church of Rome and its authority. For after the opening of his work, when he discusses the causes of the Low Countries' revolt, Grotius begins an elaborate account of the origins and progress of the Inquisition against the evil of heresy, and after he has obliquely pointed at the various doings of this holy tribunal, he unreservedly condemns the policy of punishing religious crimes with the ultimate punishment, as being full of cruelty, and totally alien to the original Christian gentleness. Next, seizing the opportunity to object to the primacy of the Church of Rome, he asserts that its pride of place was by no means instituted by the Lord Christ, but was established †in later times† by various tricks of the Roman pontiffs. This is a commonplace and daily repeated chant of the heretics of this age, some of whom proclaim that the Holy See was given supremacy over all churches from the general councils, some from Constantine, and some from subsequent Roman Emperors.

4 The old Church policy to keep the more subtle mysteries of the Faith from the knowledge of the populace, and that of not freely permitting translations of the

Scripture into whichever languages from all around, he turns into a false charge of cunning and dexterity, and he smears the entire institution of Canon Law and its use with slanderous accusations of ambition and greed, among others in the following words: 'Meanwhile the Roman pontiffs, who always retained the highest authority, after the cities of Asia and Egypt, and the rival power of Constantinopel had disappeared from the scene, had established a kind of religious empire, and for themselves the highest authority in it, as well as cardinals as co-governors, and in connection with that a long line of ecclesiastical authorities etc. | As a consequence, worship was everywhere conducted in Latin, and Latin the language of religion. However, the Roman pontiffs, after they had brought all relating to religion under their jurisdiction, issued new laws, interpreted the existing ones, and knocked the books of Scripture out of the hands of the populace; | Thus they could easily put everything into the service of their own authority and profit.'

5 In these words, most distinguished fathers, you recognise indeed the familiar phrases from Calvin and his followers which they usually employ in order to disgrace the customs of the Catholic Church and to provoke enmity against the Popes of Rome in the minds of the faithful.

6 In another place he chastises in appearance the temporal authority of the Pope over secular princes, which every Catholic knows to be a mere indirect influence, and one directed at a better application of spiritual power. He censures most of all, however, the use of this power to the benefit of the Church as a whole, to free subjects from the ties of oaths which bind them to bad and ruinous princes. He inveighs so much against the theory underlying this use of power, which is founded on age-old practice of the Holy See and a special decree of the general council, that he does not shrink from asserting 'that no opinion more destructive to the political order was ever uttered.'

7 A similar verbal extravagance worth noting is that which Grotius employs when he comes to speak of the castigations hurled at Elizabeth the renewer of the Anglican defection. For in the first book of the *Histories* he writes thus: 'The Pope (the one called Sixtus) tried to use the Spaniard to bring England under his laws, which had once been made subordinate to that priesthood by the simplicity of its kings. Thus, emulating the examples of the popes of Antiquity, who used the conflicts of princes, first to obtain jurisdiction over their realms, then over the kings themselves, he offered England to a conqueror.' After these words however, which are full of malice and detraction against the Holy See, when he has related, with great bitterness, Sixtus' call to the faithful to kill the queen, he finally finishes his account with the following formula: Pope Sixtus 'added as a prize to this crime immunity from punishment for all crimes, || even before God, || and other ridiculous things of that sort, which certainly worked in a cruder age, but are now only given in appearance and taken in appearance.'

8 Of this same kind is also the following, which he says when referring to the ban of Pope Paul V against Venice, where he relates that the Venetians were enraged with the Pope *for good reasons*; it cannot be said, however, that the Venetians' cause

in that conflict was just without damaging the dignity of the Holy See or without prize-winning affront to the Church's immunity.

9 To these utterances inspired by self-confidence and injustice towards the Holy See, I add a passage full of unfounded insult against the sacrosanct ordinances of the Council of Trent, which runs as follows: 'In that meeting nothing of their doctrine or customs was corrected, as a result of which entire nations withdrew from the Church of Rome; only the priests were submitted to censure.' What Grotius' intentions are in saying this I do not understand, unless it is that he considers the fathers of the Council blameworthy because they did not follow Luther's blaspehemies for the sake of preserving Germany.

10 However, the pen of this author does not insult the power of the Church alone, he also betrays his loathing of the sacred rituals of the Catholics in many places in this work. For in the first book of the *Histories*, when he discusses the war movement in the district of Cologne provoked by the marriage of Truchsess [von Waldburg], archbishop of Cologne, who attempted to preserve his spiritual marriage to his church together with a carnal wife, Grotius writes on this matter as follows: 'The Archbishop of that place, prompted by an inopportune love for a noble lady, hastened to lay off his celibacy, which by the laws of the Latin Church is not allowed to priests, though in their ubiquitous wantonness it is easily turned a blind eye to. This man put divine right before the decrees of men' etc.; which way of speaking, especially from the mouth of an heretic, is a clear denunciation of the beneficial doctrine of the chastity of the clergy as being irrational and contrary to divine right.

11 In the eighth book he insolently scorns the ritual by which desecrated churches are restored, and the ceremonies which by ancient and praiseworthy custom are employed for that purpose; as if these purifications and atonements directed at floors and walls are foolish as well as superfluous, since of course these are inanimate objects and incapable of doing evil.

12 In another place he seems to be judging the prayers and rituals by which he relates that Alexander of Parma implored Divine assistance for the Spanish expedition against England, as if his doing so demonstrates the unfoundedness of the expectations and the deficiencies in the planning, rather than his piety and his praiseworthy trust in God; for he speaks as follows: 'The Spanish awaited the Duke of Parma and with him more mobile ships, | while in the meantime Parma himself ran about in churches and said prayers, as those with absurd hopes but without a proper plan tend to do.'

13 But nowhere does this kind of impiety appear more clearly than where he says, when the occasion arises, and with the intention to describe the transition from the Catholic faith to the madness of Lutheranism: 'The Prince of the Protestants entered the town and restored religion after having kicked out the images', where he uses the odious word *images* to refer to Catholic ritual as a whole, and thus taints it with the heinous crime of idolatry and superstition.

14 The author here conspicuously, from a particular fixation in his mind, attacks that part of our doctrine which includes the worship of holy images and the invocation of saints, i.e as someone who does not hesitate to self-confidently assert that the entire Church errs in this matter and was put on the wrong track by the second Council of Nicea (i.e. in his work on the power of secular authorities in religious matters, recently condemned by this Holy tribunal).

15 Such opinions lead him to accuse Justus Lipsius' pious and tasteful treatise on the venerable statue of the Blessed Virgin of Halle of superficiality, as if the famous author had greatly diminished the credit built up by other, more serious works by publishing that study. In order to demonstrate beyond doubt that the views Grotius expresses here are genuinely his own (although he expresses himself cautiously and does not posit his own view without qualifications, but presents it indirectly, as if it was just someone else's), I shall here quote his own words, which he writes elsewhere [in the AH] on this same statue and its miracles, where he discusses Archduke Albert's putting down of the insignia of the cardinalate. His words are thus: 'He dedicated his cardinal's hat and robe at the altar of the Blessed Virgin which is worshipped in Halle, a town of Hainault. This sanctuary is famous because of its long history as an attraction and its portents, which were used to convince the nearby populace that the presence of the godhead was proven etc. | Justus Lipsius wrote a great many stories in elegant Latin, by which pledge he once sealed his adherence to the faith of Rome and his belief in the images, in spite of the fact that other authors publicly discussed well-known acts of fraud by the priests, and other such things designed to yield profit, [and argued that] many things which were called miracles, in fact happened by chance or the laws of nature, while on the other hand the magicians of Antiquity, especially those of Egypt, Tyanaeus, and other teachers of damnable religion, since they strenghtened their sayings with stunning devices, serve as proof to us that we should only believe those things, which spur on our souls towards the one God, which do not bring in protection from other sources, and do not corrupt our piety by the forbidden worship of images.'

16 Here Grotius even puts his words into the mouths of others, that is, of Lipsius and of the authors who wrote against Lipsius. But this cannot excuse him, just as the ancient Church too did not excuse Pelagius who used this same artifice, and the less so [in this case] since by calling into doubt a thing not at all doubtful, he began an inappropriate debate. Now someone who calls the faith into doubt is no less an heretic than someone who denies the faith, although Grotius' position on this matter is not one of doubt, since he puts the worse opinion last, and thus seems to support that opinion; and in the treatise which we mentioned above on the power of secular authorities in religious matters, he pronounces similar views explicitly.

17 No less pernicious is what is written at the end of book fourteen, where he relates the conspiracy against King James of Britain, begun by a group of Catholics,

who endeavoured to eliminate the king himself and all the leading nobles of the realm by a fire from gunpowder. For he unduly inveighs against the Jesuits, as if they were the instigators of this deed, because they had not betrayed repentant conspirators, from whom they had heard about it during the sacrament of confession. Grotius eloquently censures the Catholic doctrine which forbids betrayal and which demands inviolability of the secret of the confession, even if the safety of the Prince or the people is at stake, and calls it a *ruinous precept*. This is an ungodly statement and infected with manifest error indeed, since it conflicts with the doctrine established by the sacrosanct Council of Trent, whose explicit instruction (since, departing from divine right, it stresses the obligation to speak out to the confessor all deeds and every deed which are considered sins), accepts the security and indemnity of the faithful, when the principle in question is put into practice, to be necessarily protected by that same [=divine] right. Consequently, it prescribes that all human points of view, however important and urgent in other respects, must be put second, an opinion shared by all theologists and scholars of canon law.[2]

18 In another place he openly seems to be disparaging this Society in order to increase hostility towards the Catholic faith. Most of all, however, this appears where he amply and carefully describes the origins and organisation of the Society. He says: 'The founder of the organisation was Ignatius of Loyola, who, being physically weak after being wounded at Pamplona during the war in Navarre, turned his still courageous and combative mind to more tranquil occupations. This spirit was accompanied by the ambition to found an organisation of followers which, in the expectation of future greatness, he named not after some outstanding person, as was usual at the time, but after Jesus himself. Having allied themselves with men who desired change, the members of the Society cultivated two things especially: the power of the Pope and the wealth of Spain; they were the first of all to provide excellent support to a cause which was already dwindling, and to things which were up to then neglected, that is, innocent conduct, and the Arts' etc. | 'They inhabit the palaces of kings, because keeping the middle, by a praiseworthy

[2] This objection is interesting because it illustrates Gradić's critical attitude. The passage in question, Grotius' relation of the Gunpowder Plot at the very end of *Historiae* bk. 14, throws a particular negative light on the role of the Jesuits, not just in preserving the secrecy of the plot, but also, and more importantly, 1) in justifying beforehand the unavoidable 'collateral damage' (innocent members of Parliament who would also die in the explosion); 2) in trying to provoke a general rebellion after the plot was discovered; 3) in advocating deception under interrogation in order to mislead the authorities; 4) in their preaching activity to strengthen the morale of the accompanying Catholic insurgence; 5) in preserving the secret of the confession even if it concerns the safety of the state. To four of these points of accusation however, Gradić does not object, though in fact these are far more damaging to the Society and the Church than his theological point concerning the secrecy of the confession. It demonstrates that Gradić does not 'blindly' attack any passage that disparages any element of the Church, but takes a perspective beyond party sympathies and censures passages which might damage the authority of Catholic faith and doctrine as such.

balance, between depressing haughtiness and shameful docility, they neither adopt the vices of men, nor flee from them.'

19 Two utterances in this passage I find worthy of a stricter censure. The first is the one by which Grotius ascribes to ambition and a lust for novelty, rather than to love for God and for the people most closely around them, the things which we hear St Ignatius and his first followers, when founding their Society, have done with great piety towards God and with great profit to the well-being of the faithful. This view seems to be sacrilegious in every respect and to conflict with the most authoritative opinions on the holy man within the Church. The second is the claim that no one in the Catholic Church approved the use of the Arts to refute the Lutherans before the Jesuits took the near-lost cause of the Faith upon them; which is as laudatory towards the Society (which indeed it is), as it is insulting and full of infamy towards all other parts of the Church.

20 Near the end of the work Grotius makes an extensive and accurate reference to that famous controversy on the help of Divine Grace,[3] and he does not conspicuously seem to depart from the view held by the Catholic Church, since he acknowledges both the liberty of human choice, in as extensive a form as suffices for the fairness of rewards and punishments and, on the other hand, attributes as much to Divine Grace, as the weakness of our fallen nature, and the size of our perils and temptations requires. Still however, his words cannot be said to be entirely wiped clean from the soot of heresy, since they are wrongful and offensive towards St Augustine, who is by far the greatest and most outstanding of all Church teachers, both in every other field of theology, as especially in this field dealing with Divine Grace. For Grotius' words are thus: 'Augustine was the first, in the heat of the debate from the time his dispute with Pelagius and Pelagius' followers began, | to put the word freedom on paper in such a way that he put certain Divine decisions before it, which seemed to destroy its very force.'

21 Here Grotius seems to be criticising the opinion of the holy teacher on the reasoning to explain the working of Divine assistance and on the absolute principle of predestination, as appears from the similar but much more modest argument on the same question by Johannes Gerardus Vossius, an author from the same sect.[4] In his history of the Pelagian controversy, Vossius makes St Augustine the instigator of change and of useless controversy within the Church, but does not dare to call him an heretic, as Grotius here seems to do, as he tries to infix upon the holy man the abominable stamp of Manicheism with respect to the question of the bondage of the human will, which cannot be tolerated in any way. However this might be, whether Augustine's doctrine on Divine Grace was accepted by the

[3] i.e. the debate on free will which played a crucial role in the theologies of the Reformation period: the question whether man can of his own accord (his own free will) accept God's help to strive for the good and thus deserve his salvation, or that he is predestined to accept or not accept this help, and to be saved or damned accordingly.

[4] i.e. the Arminian or Remonstrant Church in the Netherlands.

entire Church, even to the degree of being considered an indispensable part of the Faith, [or not], it is testified by a | |some of the| | letter(s) of Pope Coelestinus to the bishops of Gaul that it is certain that Augustine was not even tainted with the rumour of an unfavourable suspicion; nor does the *communis opinio* among the scholastics with respect to the latter's views allow doubts on this, of which fact the same Grotius is a sufficiently equipped witness against himself.

22 Grotius' rashness is even increased a little further down by the fact that he does not hesitate to compare the holy man with the impious Luther. For he writes: 'The Prince of Protestants, Luther, came from a monastery which, as it had adopted Augustine's name, followed his views; he took hold of a part of Augustine and began to destroy what Augustine himself had, in name, left intact of freedom', as if he was saying that there is only a difference of terminology between Augustine's teachings and the blasphemies of Luther, which is the most foolhardy and absurd proposition imaginable.

23 These, most eminent Fathers, are the points which in the *Annals and History of the Low Countries* of Hugo Grotius occurred to me as worthy of deletion, which doubtlessly are things which must be kept away from the devoted ears of the faithful.

However, since these are not so great in number, and not so deeply embedded in the work as a whole, that they cannot easily be isolated; and since the work itself, because of the quality of its argument, and the elegance of its style, will be difficult to remove from the hands of the learned, my judgement would be that the work should by no means be condemned absolutely, but should be expurgated and suspended until this is done.

This is my judgement; I, Stefano Gradić

Giovanni Arata's censure
(Roma, Indice, Protocolli KK 232r–234v formerly 242–244)

1 Of Hugo Grotius' *Annals and Histories of the Low Countries Wars*, most eminent Lords, I read only the title with an unoffended mind. In all the rest of the work my eyes to my sorrow found not histories, but insults against the Spanish, cunning of the Italians and blasphemies against the Catholics, scribbled down with an abusive pen in some kind of raging madness. If Plutarch indeed considers Herodotus a slanderous historian who deserves no trust because of his malice, this author on p. 6 et seq. inveighs vehemently against the Spanish; on p. 28 presents the Duke of Alba as a man of tyrannous cruelty; on p. 75 he calls the Spanish robbers; on p. 241 he accuses their nobles of precisely the same heinous behaviour; he flogs Philip, he derides Albert, he scorns Requesens, he offends the Spinola brothers,[5]

[5] Ambrogio Spinola (1569–1630) and Federico Spinola (1571–1603), Italian commanders in Habsburg service in the Netherlands.

he smears Parma and his mother Margaret; he seems to be composing satires and recantations, but not a History, which, according to Cicero, *De Oratore* book 2 is the herald of truth; Cornelius Agrippa, in *On the Truth of Science*, calls it as it were a living and truthful picture of life, and according to the well-known book one of the *Geography* of Strabo, it must be distinguished from myth in more or less this very respect.

2 But let us leave aside the atoms and proceed to the mountains. We have heard Tubalcain the Hammerer against the Catholics, let us now hear Tubal playing the herald of heretics.[6] Grotius praises the piety of the dead William of Orange on p. 85; he calls the Count of Herenberg Teacher of Virtue on p. 151; he extols the funeral of Elizabeth with an extraordinary panegyric on p. 432; he wears out his pen praising Heny IV of England [sic] on p. 474. These are without doubt hallmarks of a great heretic; just as according to Theodoretus in the *Historia Tripartita* chapter <40>, the well-known Arianus of Alexandria praised luxury instead of the honourable and extolled impiety over piety, and just as the heretic sect of the Rhetoriani exalt the Cuneti who were separated from the faith of Peter by their leader Rhetorius.

3 From here Grotius even transcends his own foolhardiness with his thoroughly shameless pen; on p. 18 he recommends Luther's creed as supported by an appearance of justice, and he shows that Zwingli's confession was lightened up by the light of Calvin's mind: 'which confession was accepted by part of the Swiss, and a certain part of Germany, and by Geneva, magnificent in this only.' Do you hear the blasphemies? They are precisely the same as those that were rashly spewed out by Luther, when he called his followers the true evangelicals, as mentioned by Hosius, book one of *The Heresies of our Time.* He honours Calvin, whom the Lutherans did not dare to praise; they passionately inveigh against him in Gretser's work against Goldast, book one in the following words: `The Calvinists are fanatics, a viperous brood, Soul-slaughterers, infernal monster-dogs, German Turks, baptized Muslims, the deeply satanised, the over-satanised, the super-satanised'. And finally he praises Geneva, which is called an `appalling abomination' by Lindanus in his dialogue *Dubitantius*, book 2 and by Hosius, book one of *The Heresies*, and which David foresaw on a holy site, i.e. the Church of God.

4 Nor is approving of heretics sufficient for this author, no, he even goes so far as defending them against the Roman Church, which he does ingeniously, it is true, but very deceitfully.[7] So on p. 433 he sides with Elizabeth against the Pope; on p. 458 he deems Franciscus Rhedanus' book against St Peter's successors, and

[6] Tubal and Tubalcain appear in Gen. 4:19–22. Ancient and medieval mythography further developed the story of these brothers (see the internet site of K. Verduin at http://www.leidenuniv.nl/fsw/verduin/ghio/sourchro.htm), but the allusion here remains obscure.

[7] The use of *Nec satis, quin* + subjunctive with the repeated *non* in the sub-clause is contrived but not necessarily incorrect; see Leumann-Hofmann-Szantyr, *Lateinische Grammatik*, bd. 2 Syntax und Stilistik, München 1965, no. 374, p. 677.

against the Spanish and Catholic creed, worthy of praise. On p. 496 he calls Paulus Servita's works which call for support of the Republic of Venice highly useful. On p. 553 it is claimed that the creed of the Arminians is in harmony with that of the ancient Christians. On p. 434 he gives great praise to the oration of the United [Provinces] to the king of Scotland to persuade him to dissociate himself from the Roman shepherd. On p. 82 he calls Hembyze and Chimay, popular leaders of our faith, rebels against the Low Countries.[8] In this way this heretic, working on behalf of heretics, 'departs from the true faith with them who, giving heed to seducing spirits, and doctrines of devils, speak lies in hypocrisy, and have their conscience seared with a hot iron', as Canon Law and the prophesy in the first letter to Timotheus say. For to defend heretics and to approve of their writings, is an heretic act. On the basis of this principle the orthodox Faith forbade the writings of heretics, and even more those favouring them; see the judgement of Clement [V] in the first book of the [*Clementine*] *Constitutiones*, Eusebius book 7 chapter 6, Socrates, *Ecclesiastical History*, book 6 chapter 9 and Hadrian IV. But even superstitious heathendom itself punished those who weakened its religion, and forbade their concoctions, such as Greece did with Pitagoras the Athenian's books, as testified by Philostratus in *Lives of the Sophists*, as Athens did with other books, see Cicero book 10 [sic], and Rome with many books, as demonstrated by Augustine, *The City of God*, book 7 chapter 34-35. Likewise, vilifying preachers of the Gospel was Herman of Rijswijk's crime, whom Pope Alexander VI condemned in the time of the Emperor Maximilian in Bernard of Luxemburg's catalogue of heretics.

5 However, so far we have seen Grotius wearing a mask and appearing in disguise. From here onwards, we shall have to watch him in a more insolent role, busy shaking off the yoke of the Faith, and slandering with such rashness the true Faith itself, the Councils, the Pope, the Saints, and the Holy Virgin herself. On p. 19 he calls the measures taken by the council of Trent a *Latin superstition*: to say this, however, is spurning the General Councils, together with the Ruthenians whom Strabo calls Rosani, as noted by Pius II in his *Description of Europe*. And it means joining Luther who, as Lindanus says, imagined that the Oecumenical Councils could potentially be wrong. On p. 21 he censures Philip's zeal and very strict observance of the laws by calling it obstinacy. On p. 66 he considers it difficult to achieve unity of religion in the Low Countries, and altogether undesirable from the point of view of public peace. On p. 100 Leicester is reproached for persecuting the Roman religion. On page 187 he presents the Christian faith as

[8] A fascinating mixture of careless reading and divergent perception (cp. Grotius' words): Jan van Hembyze (1513–1584) was a Calvinist and ardently anti-Spanish nobleman and popular leader, who indeed in 1583, from disappointment with Orange's policies, entered into a private understanding with Parma and was later beheaded for it; Charles of Croy, Prince of Chimay (1560–1612; son of Philip, duke of Aarschot) was married to a Calvinist noblewoman and first sided with the revolt, but, also from disappointment with Orange's policies, returned to obedience to the king and handed over Bruges in 1584.

not accepted by all nations for this alleged reason, that *just as it disunited minds, it dissolved government*. On p. 358 he dips his pen in venom against Mendosa because he decreed that Catholic worship had to be restored. On p. 443 he rebukes a decree by the Archduke in which he forbids all worship other than Catholic worship. On p. 479 he reproves Bellarmine and Baronius, most ardent defenders of the orthodox Faith. Thus, because anyone who presumes to have an opinion in conflict with the Faith is considered an heretic – see *Corpus Iuris Canonici*, introductory chapter of the *Sixth Book of Decretals*; because a blasphemer is he who proclaims foul words about good things – see St Augustine in book 2 chapter 11 of *The Morals of the Manicheans*; and because he who rashly denies the universal cogency of the Roman church (outside which no one whomever obtains salvation) incurs the accusation of apostasy – see the Lateran Council under Innocent III, I am deeply afraid I must call the author himself of this book `an autumn tree rooted out from the vineyard of Christ, twice dead, foaming out its own shame.'

6 Because however, just as in David's experience, `flood follows flood', I shall demonstrate that the blaspehemies that follow are worse than the ones so far made. On p. 56 he calls Francis of Valois leader of the Roman sect. On p. 64 he observes that 's Hertogenbosch is held by a sect of the Romans. On p. 302 he shows that Calatagironi of the Franciscan sect controlled a king. On p. 195 he calls all religious communities of the Catholic church by the term *sects*. So be it, for the word *sect* might refer to all adherents of any institution; since however the condemned author uses this word as a synonym for schism and apostasy, he must, according to the gloss in the Clementine Constitutions to the chapter 'Ad nostram' in the *Clementine Constitutions*, and Thomas Aquinas in note 3 to *Summa Theologiae*, 2. 2ae, art. 11, be seen as someone from the bad camp. And into this same blasphemy Wiclif threw himself (against whom Thomas Valdensis argued) as well as the sacrilegious sectarians who, following Frederic Staphylus in his *Apology*, rashly called all religious communities of the Catholic Church sects. Nor must we overlook here the injustice to the Pope, who is the source of all these religious institutions. And all Saints and illustrious men who, inspired by the Holy Spirit, created those, practically deserve the name of Patriarchs, as Benedictus Capra noted to the chapter 'Cum rationi' in the *Clementine Constitutions*, De Electione, no. 33 in the Commentary to Canon Law.

7 Having thrown, with raging arrogance, these darts at the common denomination of all clerical people, he chooses first the Fathers and then the Jesuits for his target, and on p. 194 strikes them with [the mark of] the most cruel cleverness. He deems it a matter of no weight at all to call them *politiques*, robbers, usurpers of royal power, conspirators against kingdoms, disturbers of public peace, plotters of the murder of the king of France, assailers of Elizabeth's life, priers into the secrets of kings, and the most pestilent contamination of the entire earth. But he presents Loyola as the leader of such an eminent institution, who from enormous ambition, and a desire for the control of many things, did not, *as was usual at the time, name*

his already established society after some outstanding person, but after Jesus himself, in the expectation of future greatness. It is superfluous to adduce the Popes, who praise and approve of this society as beneficial to the whole world, as witnesses against the heretical seriousness of this author, who through his own way of speaking makes it clear that he is a derisor of Saints.

8 Next on p. 285 he bestows great praise on Anna van den Hove, who underwent an insane execution because she dismissed a Catholic law and spurned the Gospel of Jesus, he censures her sisters who returned to right reason, and denounces the stubbornness of Albert, who punished her. In this he follows the Montanists and the Marcionists, who boasted that their members who where burnt in punishment by the Holy Inquisition, were martyrs -see Nicephorus and Apolinarius of Hierapolis.

9 Next on p. 121 he ridicules Parma running about in temples and saying prayers, as exerting himself in an absurd labour. On p. 222 he produces some gossip about the Spanish, who believe St James' day to be a lucky day for them, and by believing so often make themselves lucky. On p. 330 he relates the miracles of the Holy Virgin of Halle, but calls them into doubt by putting them on one level with Egyptian tales. Behold what enormous crimes in one seeming trespass! Here the following heresies are bundled: first that of the Lampetians, who dismiss prayers, as we learn from Calvin in the *Institutions of the Christian Religion* – and Franciscus Horantius of Spain has spiritedly refuted them in his book of Catholic Commonplaces; secondly, that of Wicliff, who mistakenly held the idea that addressing prayers to saints has no effect, see Johannes Nider, book 3; thirdly that of Eustatius of Sebaste, who, according to Socrates, book two of the *Ecclesiastical History*, irreligiously decreed that there should be no invocation of saints; tainted with the same pitch are the Bohemians, the southern Saxons, the Hussites, the Adamites, the Orphani, Zysca and Procopius, all of whom were condemned with public notification and approval in the great council of Constanz as described by Aenea Silvio Piccolomini in the *Description of Europe*; fourthly the heresy of Karlstadt and the Iconoclasts that was favoured by the [Byzantine] Emperor Leo IV against the will of Pope Stephan III, but with the approval of the Council of Constantinople, who all perversely decreed that images should not be worshipped. Against them first the Council of Nicea was held, and finally under Gregory III, another Council in Rome, according to the writings of Sabellius and Platina: which ignored the emperor Leo and called in Charles Martel from France to provide timely support. Fifthly, the heresy of the Antidikomarionists, who ceaselessly raged against the worship of the Holy Virgin, as related by Epiphanius; and finally that of Eunomianus, Eustatius and Vigilantius who, under the flags of Luther, Zwingli and Calvin, with raging spirits tried to destroy the miracles carried out by saints, as if they were quackery peformed by demons, as Lindanus tells us in the second book of his dialogue *Dubitantius*.

10 Next on p. 496, he praises the oeuvre of Justus Lipsius, but regrets with stubborn cleverness that Lipsius' fame was diminished by the fact that he wrote about the miracles of the Holy Virgin of Halle and Scherpenheuvel. O true brood of vipers, together with Julian the Apostate! Who, according to Nicephorus book 10 chapter 32, and Rufinus *Ecclesiastical History* book 10 chapter 38-9, scoffing the writings of Christians, spew out the following opinion of his: 'I read them, I got to know them, I condemned them'. Upon which the great Basilius from Cappadocia replied: 'you have read them, but did not get to know them, for if you had, you would not condemn them.'

11 However, most eminent gentlemen, since a war then becomes especially big, when enmities take root in people's heads, we must have some fears about Hugo Grotius; and since, after the storm is sent to Peter's little ship, he launches an attack against the Pope himself, he wields his arms and fights [us] with all his might as an embittered and deeply wicked enemy. And thus on p. 12 he presents Philip as a threat to heretics, who lavishly donates many cities to the Pope for the sake of the latter's greatness. On p. 117 he rebukes Sixtus V and other Popes for being usurpers of kingdoms. Next on p. 231 he calls the fact that she escaped being submitted to the Pope's power, the greatest fruit of the war for Elizabeth, Queen in England. And on p. 454 he condemns, in an account full of artifice, the priests exiled from England by king James, because they extolled the papal power above that of kings. This however amounts to expressing doubts regarding the sacred power of Rome, which Jacobus Zochus thought was a great sacrilege, in the chapter 'Omnis utriusque sexus' in De poenitententiis en remissionibus, no. 406. And since the Pope is the head of the entire world, he is, as superior to the Emperor and without anyone above him in this world, called the Highest because of his pre-eminence and the fulness of his power, as Stephanus de Gaeta notes on the chapter 'Ad limina' 30, quest. 1 no. 8. And since all are subjected to him, see Stephanus Aufrerius on the chapter 'Ut Clericorum' in De officio [iudicis] ordinarii no. 55, his own power gives him the right to depose kings and emperors and give their kingdoms to others, albeit for very serious reasons only. Such is the opinion of the Cardinal Alexander on the chapter 'Lex', distinction 2, and of our own Father Delbene in section 25 of *On Parliaments* under the first and second corollary; so that to claim the opposite is the abominable sacrilege of the Armenians, as testified by Guido the Carmelite in his book *On Heresies*, and that of the Fraticelli with their leader Hermannus Italus, who was burnt to the last crumb of his ashes by Pope Bonifacius VIII in 1297.

12 What other poisonous bites from this serpent? Let them listen I pray, though we have not yet reached the end of this author's filth. On p. 15 he claims that the Popes undertook to enlarge the number of bishoprics of the Church; and on p. 113 he insists that very many bishops occupied their seats because of the favour of Rome – and thus he 'sets his mouth against Heaven', blessed with the rashness of sectarians, nor does the fact of his huge heresy excuse him: for since the Pope

has the entire world for his jurisdiction, as Louis Gomesius explains to the chapter 'licet' in De Constitutione in the *Sixth Book of the Decretals*, no. 4, he does possess the power to appoint bishops wherever the field is clear to do so, except on agricultural estates, see Peter of Ancarano on the chapter 'Canonum Statuta' in De Constitutione, no. 37.

13 Next on p. 157 he says that the German Empire was split as a result of the machinations of the popes. On p. 160 he batters the popes as *Politiques*, and on p. 479 he demonstrates his ignorance of Canon Law by presenting a negative picture of Paul V in his fight against the Venetians. For – as Abbas notes to the chapter 'Querelarum' in De Electione, no. 1 – since the pope cannot be refused anything on the grounds of suspicions against him, it also cannot be presumed of him that he wants to cause any serious detriment to anyone, as Ioannes Calderinus adds in the note to the chapter 'Mandatum' in De Rescriptis, no.9; it is his duty to defend his right up to the point of actual bloodshed; and he is allowed to conduct a war even by cunning. Thus is argued by Anthony of Burgos on the chapter 'Quae in ecclesiarum' in De Constitutione, no. 221 and by Gamma in the note on 'Iulii 2' in De Simoniaca Papae Electione in the *Extravagantes Decretales*, no. 201.

14 To conclude, then, Grotius mixes abuse with injury: on p. 34 where he asserts that the Pope dismissed Elizabeth of England, though she was loyal to him, which is simply not true: she, who had beforehand received admonitions from her father, was publicly placed under a ban by Pope Pius V.[9] And on p. 404 [he does so by saying] that the Pope did well in granting Henry of France a divorce from Margaret of Valois on the grounds of infertility. He does remember the divorce, but forgets the reasons for it, in order to deceitfully incriminate papal authority. For the Pope cannot undo the bonds of marriage, even if the wife is a queen and infertile, as this is forbidden by that Divine law which says 'What God has united, man shall not divide' – see Baldus on the chapter 'Lator' and Ioannes Crotus on the chapter 'Super eo' in De Usuris, no. 5.

15 These, most eminent gentlemen, are the lies in the Histories of the Low Countries, the abuse from this gossip-monger, the injuries against the Roman Pontiffs, the orthodox religion, the Saints and God himself; these are the ravings of Hugo Grotius. It is yours to judge. I, however, following the advice and example of the Apostles in their Acts chapter 19, most firmly believe that such a work, in order that it be illuminated by the light it deserves, should be thrown into the fire.

Joannes Baptista Arata, gentleman, Royal Councillor

[9] On 25 February 1570.

APPENDIX 3
BIOGRAPHICAL EPILOGUES ON PHILIP II BY GROTIUS AND BY VAN METEREN

GROTIUS, *HISTORIAE* 7, PP. 331–332

Italics: information also in Van Meteren's biographical epilogue (see below)

Is finis Christianorum potentissimi fuit, et principum quotquot nascuntur ditissimi, annum agentis primum aetatis et septuagesimum, imperandi tertium et quadragesimum. *Corporis habitus mediocris*, nisi quod *frons celsior, tum labia in modum Austriacis gentilem prominebant; vultusque tanto Belgae propior*, quanto moribus in Hispanum concesserat. *Mitem ingenio* libenter crederes: quippe et accessu comis, nec temere saeviebat; sed quoties dominationi expediret, famam clementiae haud multum morabatur. *Solertiam, quae non perinde ut parenti adfuisse creditur*, perfecit aetas et *diligentia, cum parcus otii somnique maiora* ipse, non per ministros, *tractaret*. Quae in maius tollentes Hispani aequant eum Solomonis laudibus. Pecuniae usuum gnarus, Imperatores, Pontifices, ferme quos vellet renuntiabat, arcana regnorum scrutabatur: adversus prospera et ruentia vultu, an et animo aequabili, *sed conditus in dissimulationem, odiis et suspicionibus* indulgebat: spei improbior, et regnandi libidine cuivis veterum conferendus: *religionis*, quae quidem in externis actibus versatur, *servantissimus*: circa imperii artes principum exemplo excusatus, et in his, quae ut privatus peccabat, laudatae verecundiae.

Bella illi prima aetate fuere, sed praeter Gallicum, quod iuvenis vidit tantum, caetera per legatos administravit. De *maioribus* et posteris varie meritus, *quorum imperium, ut Americanis proventibus auxit, et Lusitaniae accessione*, ita amissis Goleta,[1] *Tuneto et Batavis* dehonestavit. *Et tamen in tempora paternis diversa incidisse notabatur, en eo saeculo, quo penes eosdem homines summa virtus et fortuna fuit, sed cum foeminas puerosque et imbelles aemulos, aut hostes haberet.*

[1] Goleta (Golette) is a strategic fortress on the Bay of Tunis, near the site of ancient Carthage. Spain lost Tunis and Goleta in 1574 to the Ottoman ruler Selim II; a 'second front' that was hampered by Spain's involvement in the Netherlands, while conversely this struggle reduced pressure on the Dutch. Via Charles IX of France William of Orange maintained contact with Selim II for some time; see G. Parker, *The General Crisis of the 17th Century*, London 1978, p. 61.

Haec ferme prudentiorum de eo iudicia fuere. Alii ob partes infensi suscepta temere bella, perfide gesta, nec minus cruentam pacem[2] per Hispaniam Belgicamque, in idem saevitiae concitas Gallias, pluraque mala publica et domestica exprobrabant; ipsam exitus foeditatem in argumentum trahentes: innoxias scilicet filii, uxoris Isabellae umbras has patri, has marito poenas irrogare, quomodo olim Herodes, (quicum pleraque morum et fortunae comparabatur) et regina Cyrenaeorum Pheretime parricidia luissent: aut hostem verae religionis, omnium qui unquam fuissent acerrimum, Antiochi illustris et Herodis alterius Caesarisque Maximini, aut Tyrannum Cassandri et Sullae libertatis oppressorum exemplis merito periisse: quanquam claros sapientiae, et iuris, et carminum auctores, aliosque eodem morbo absumptos memoriae proditum novimus.

'This was the end of the most powerful prince of Christendom, and one who was as rich as princes can be, in his seventy-first year of age, the forty-third year of his reign. His was of average looks, except that his forehead was higher, and his lips more prominent, in the Habsburg way; his face being that of a Lowlander as much as his conduct was Spanish. You would easily believe that he had a mild character, because he was kind in company, and did not display anger without reason. But whenever it involved his supremacy, he showed little concern for a reputation of clemency. His intelligence, which was believed to be inferior to that of his father, was compensated by experience and dedication, as he dealt with all the major affairs himself, not through intermediaries, allowing himself little rest and sleep. In Spain they are extolling this highly, raising his praise to the level of Salomon. He knew how to use money, disposing emperors, popes, and almost whomever he wanted; and had a deep understanding of reason of state. Outwardly, and inwardly perhaps, he was unmoved by success and misfortune alike, but, being well-versed in dissimulation, he cherished enmities and suspicions. Excessive in his expectations, he was second to no one in Antiquity in his lust for power; and extremely servile to the Faith, at least with respect to its outward performance. His princely power stratagems are excused by the practices of others, and in his trespasses as a private person, he showed a modesty which has been praised.

He has been involved in wars from his childhood onwards, but except for the war in France which, as a young man, he merely saw, he conducted all others via intermediaries. He delivered both services and disservices to his predecessors and descendants; while he enlarged their realm by the American proceeds and the accession of Portugal, he marred it by the loss of Tunis, Goleta, and Holland. However it was noted that he happened to live in an age different from that of

[2] A classic Tacitist turn-of-phrase, though not actually from Tacitus but based on a phrase in Lipsius' dedication of his 1574 edition of Tacitus: '.... et pacem quovis bello saeviorem'. Cp. however Tac. Ann. 3.44 'miseram pacem vel bello bene mutari'; and Agr. 30' ... solitudinem faciant, pacem appellant'; and perhaps Ann. 2.46 'adversum Romanos bellum an pacem incruentam malint.' Cp. also Juv. Sat. 6.292–3 'saeuior armis luxuria incubuit' and Ann. 14.61 'ea in pace ausi quae vix bello evenirent.'

his father: not at a time when the highest virtue and the greatest power met in the same men, but at a time in which he had children and cowards for his competitors and enemies. Such as these were the judgments about him from the wiser people among his observers. Others, speaking from partisan hatred charged him with wars begun without cause and conducted dishonourably, with the establishment of a peace in Spain and the Netherlands that was no less cruel, with similar cruelty being provoked in France, and a whole series of evils at home and abroad. They adduced the filthiness of his deathbed as proof, as showing that the innocent deaths of his son and his spouse Isabella invoked these punishments upon their father and husband: just as once Herodes (with whom his character and position were compared in several ways) and Pheretime queen of Cyrene had paid the price for their parricide;[3] or as showing that this enemy of true religion, and the most vicious one that ever lived to boot, had justly perished after the example of the famous Antiochus[4], Herodes II[5] and the emperor Maximinus[6], or that of the tyrants Cassander[7] and Sulla,[8] oppressors of liberty – although the memory of humankind preserves the knowledge that famous philosophers, lawyers, poets, and others have been carried away by the same illness.'

[3] Pheretima was a cruel queen of Cyrene (a Greek city in modern Libya) who died of a disgusting skin disease; Herodotus book 4.

[4] Probably Antiochus IV Epiphanes, ruler of the Hellenistic kingdom in Syria from 175–164 BC, and a cruel persecutor and suppressor of Judaism.

[5] Marcus Iulius Agrippa, or Herodes II Agrippa (AD 27–92); vassal king of parts of Palestine and Lebanon under Roman supremacy. He sided with the Romans during the Jewish War.

[6] Here seems to be meant Maximinus II Daia, Roman emperor AD 308–313, who organized one of the last persecutions of Christians and died of a disease described by Lactantius and Eusebius (possibly Graves' disease).

[7] King of Macedon 305–297 BC; one of Alexander the Great's successors (Diadochi) who showed himself particularly aggressive and faithless in his pursuit of power.

[8] Lucius Cornelius Sulla, dictator of the Roman Republic 82–79 BC. During the first Civil War he led an army against Rome in 88, subjected the city, and carried out constitutional reforms which strengthened the influence of the *optimates* at the cost of that of the *populares* and which helped lay the foundations for the later Principate. He had a mixed press in subsequent historiography, but that he was the first to carry out proscriptions has given him a reputation for cruelty.

Emanuel van Meteren, *Memorien* (1599a) p. 430r–v

Sigla:
1599a = *Memorien* etc., 1599
1599b = *Historie* etc., 1599 (see the discussion in § 2.3).
The textual notes below describe differences in content, not orthographical differences.
Italics: information adapted in Grotius' biographical epilogue (see above)

Marg. Den Coninc van Spaegnien sterft den xiii. September / Anno 1598

[p. 430r] *Hy heeft geleeft Lxxi.* [=71] *jaer* en omtrent vier Maenden /redelijk gesont: Hy was van goeder ghedaente en maeksel/ *eer middelbaer dan cort van persoone/* wel gemaect van alle leden / wit van coleure ende van hayr/ ende van Baert /gheel[9] *geen Spaensch maer een Nederlantsch aensien hebbende/ hooch van voorhoofde / minnelic van wesen / de lippen wat hooge/ also alle syn gheslachte hadde /* ende wat gapende / van complexie swaermoedich/ stille ende statich van manieren / *van vernuftheyt oft verstande en was hy by synen Vader ofte voorouders niet te ghelijcken /* dan was *neerstich / arbeydich / gheerne bisoignjerende /* tzy schrijven ofte andersins doende/*dicmael diep inde nacht*: hy was geneycht tot melancolie / *afgonstich / nijdich / seer diep geveynst* / straf ende strenge / niet licht vergetende / contrarie syn wesen ende aensien / hy was eer liberael dan gierich / manierich ende ghestadich ghenoech/ maer hoochmoedich / ambitieus / veel aenslagende / meer dan hy wel conde wtvoeren: syn principale familiaren waren Don Ruygomes de Silva[10] / Prince de Eboli / Don Johan Idiaques/ ende den voorsz. Don Christophoro di Mora / met andere / van synen humeure synde.

Oorloghen heeft hy meest alle synen tijdt gevoert / maer selve niet / dan was int winnen van sint Quintijn / ende den naesten jaere MDLviii [1558]. *leyde hy synen grooten Legher tegen den Coninck Heyndrick van Vranckrijck* in Piccardijen ende Artoys / daer den vrede wt volchde: *alle andere oorlogen heeft hy door syn Veldoversten* van verscheyden Natien *gevoert* / ende menige schoone victorien gehadt / oock altemet schade / *het Conincrijk van Thunus* / de heerlicheyt van Siena in Italien hem by den Vader gelaten / heeft hy *ende de principale Nederlanden verloren / ende Portugael gewonnen /* mette conquesten van Indien die groot zijn. *Hy is een wtermaten grootmachtich ende vermoghende Heere gheweest* / als syn *Voorsaten passerende in machte* / van middelen / van ghelde / van volcke / van dappere vermaerde Krijchsoverste ende Capiteynen / ende wijtstreckende Heerschappije / als nu in beyde de *Indien dominerende met so grooten schatten* / nochtans soo luttel[11] notabels wtrechtende / *hebbende in synen tijden niet gevonden ofte teghen gehadt eenen strijtbaren Soltan Soliman / noch grooten*

[9] 1599a & 1599b: gheel/
[10] i.e. Ruy Gómez de Silva
[11] 1599a: lutter

Coninck Francoys van Vranckrijck / noch eenen Hendrick de VIII. van Enghelandt / met andere dappere Vorsten / noch cloecke Pausen / als synen Vader den Keyser Karel in synen tijde ontmoete / maer heeft ghevonden verwijfde Torcken / kinderen in Vrancrijc[12]*/ ende onder haer selven verdeylt / een Vrouwe in Engelandt / ende Pausen meest van syn maecksel.* [430v]

Hy heeft vier huysvrouwen ghehadt / ten eersten Anno MDxliiii. [1544] troude hy Mariam / de Dochter van Coninck Johan van Portugael / die baerde Anno MDxlv. [1545] int xviii. Jaer syns ouderdoms eenen Prince Carel / sy stervende int kinderbedde / qualijck bewaert zijnde / alsoo wy verhaelt hebben. Den Sone Prince Carel is ghestorven als hij sevenentwintich Jaer out was / in ghevanghenisse syns Vaders: op wiens graf een Epitaphium gevonden wert / *Aqui iaze, quien para dezir verdad, morio sin enfermidad.* Dat is / hier leyt die/ begheerende de waerheyt te seggen / sterf sonder sieck zijn.

Hy troude Anno MDLiiii. [1554] syn tweede huysvrouwe Maria / de Coninghinne van Enghelandt / syn Grootmoeder Susters Dochter / die sonder kinderen nae vijf Jaren sterf.

Daer na troude hy Anno MDLx. [1560] Isabella / de outste Dochter vanden Coninck Hendrick van Vranckrijck / daer by heeft hy ghewonnen de Infante Isabella Eugenia Clara/ gheboren Anno MDLxvi. [1566] den xxii. Augusti op Sinte Clara dach / dien hy de Nederlanden tot Erfgoet ende ten Houwelijck gegeven heeft: noch een ander Dochter was de Hertoghinne van Savoyen[13]/ die veel kinderen ghebaert ende nagelaten heeft / ende is ghestorven.[14]

Syn vierde huysvrouwe was Anna van Oostenrijck / Keyser Maximiliaens Dochter / ende den Eertshertoch Albertus Suster / ende eygen[15] Susters Dochter / die hy troude by des Paus dispensatie / Anno MDLxx. [1570] ende hem baerde drie Sonen ende een Dochter / die alle vroech ghestorven zijn / behalven den teghenwoordighen Prince Philips den derden / die nu Coninc van Spaengien is / ende gheboren is in Junio MDLxxviii. [1578] Van syn onechte kinderen / die hy ghehadt heeft by sijn bywijven / is noch gheen groote wetenschappe.

Hy was seer Religieus ende scrupuleus / de Jesuyten voorstaende / maer verstont Religie nochtans alsoo / dat sy moeste wijcken ende plaetse geven heerschappije ofte regeeringe[16] / na den te veel generalen reghel onder veel Princen / slachtende de Spaengiaerden in Indien[17]/ die de verdienste meer achten van eenighe Indianen tot Christendom te brengen / haer leerende den Latijnschen Ave Maria

[12] 1599b *has an extra line here*: /wtgheseyt den Coninc Hendrick den IIII. dien hy oock meest vreesde/

[13] was de Hertoghinne van Savoyen 1599adie hylickte aenden Hartoge van Savoyen 1599b

[14] ende is ghestorven. 1599aende is ghestorven al voor haer vader. 1599b

[15] ende eygen 1599aende sijn eygen 1599b

[16] Rendered as a different reason-of-state-coloured thought by Grotius; focus on outward religion.

[17] na den te veel generalen reghel onder veel Princen / slachtende de Spaengiaerden in Indien 1599a na den generalen regel van veel Princen / die welcke slachten de Spaengiaerden in Indien 1599b

te segghen / ende de geleerste den Pater noster / ende also ghedwongen wt vreese haer laten doopen / dan de sonde is van veel[18] honderden ende duysenden te vermoorden / om vande reste meester te worden. Welcke[19] Religie genoech eylacen in Nederlant gebleken heeft / ende noch int Lant van Cleve ende Westphalen op dit pas blijct[20] byde handelinge vanden Admirante aldaer / als volcomelijck gheparsuadeert[21] / dat breken van eeden / beloften / vryheden ende Privilegien / verjagen / vernielen ende moorden / cleyn sonde zy / naedemale[22] het tot een goede meyninge ende eynde gheschiet / om nae vercreghen victorie[23] tot haer voornemen te comen van de[24] de Landen van Ketters ende Ketterijen te suyveren ende so Gode de zielen te gewinnen / ende haer de heerschappije.

Aldus den Coninck Philips de tweede van Spaengien gestorven zijnde/ sullen wij nu oock dese Memorien eynden / die meest syn regieringhe in Nederlant verhaelt hebben.[25] [Philips III etc.]

[18] ende also ghedwongen wt vreese haer laten doopen / dan de sonde is van veel 1599adie sy also dwingen wt vreese haer te laten dopen / dan sy achten de sonde van veel 1599b

[19] Welcke 1599aVan welcke 1599b

[20] blijct 1599ablijckende is 1599b

[21] aldaer / als volcomelijck gheparsuadeert 1599aende van syne Spaengiaerden aldaer / als met daet in alle hare actien betoonende 1599b

[22] naedemale 1599aals 1599b

[23] nae vercreghen victorie 1599adaer na 1599b

[24] van de 1599aende de 1599b

[25] Aldus den Coninck ... gestorven zijnde/ sullen wij nu oock dese Memorien eynden / die meest syn regieringhe in Nederlant verhaelt hebben 1599aAldus is Coninck... ghestorven / met wiens doodt wy oock dese Memorien sullen eyndighen/ als alleen voorgenomen ghehadt hebbende / sijne regieringhe in Nederlant te verhaelen.1599b

APPENDIX 4
THE NIJMEGEN COPY OF POMPEIO GIUSTINIANI'S *BELLUM BELGICUM*

Radboud University Nijmegen, University Library, sign. 80 C37
Pompeius Iustinianus, *Bellum Belgicum sive Belgicarum rerum e commentariis Pompei Iustiniani libri VI*, Coloniae 1611
Manuscript notes on back flyleaf, almost certainly in Grotius' hand. The notes below correspond with underlinings in the text at the given page numbers. See Introduction § 10.

Fredericus Spinola. 11.
eius mors. 26.
Ante Ostendam 140000 hominum occubuere. 73.
Marchio della Laguna succedit don Balthasari de Zuniga. 76
Spinola proficiscitur in Hispanias 109
Spondit pro octingenta millibus aureorum 110
Idem pro 260 millibus coronatorum 116
Carafa in locum Frangipani nuntius. 153.
Rex quotannis sex milliorum impendia in militiam. 181.

BELLVM BELGICVM,
siue
BELGICARVM
RERVM, E COMMEN-
TARIIS POMPEI IVSTINIANI PEDI-
TATVS ITALICI TRIBVNI, ET A CON-
silijs Bellicis Regis Catholici
LIBRI SEX,
supplemento Auctoris aucti.
EDENTE IOSEPHO GAMVRINO,
Nobili Aretino.
Ex Italicâ Latinitate donati. Cum tabulis aliquot æneis.

COLONIAE AGRIPPINAE,
Apud Joannem Kinckium sub Monocerote.
ANNO M. DC. XI.

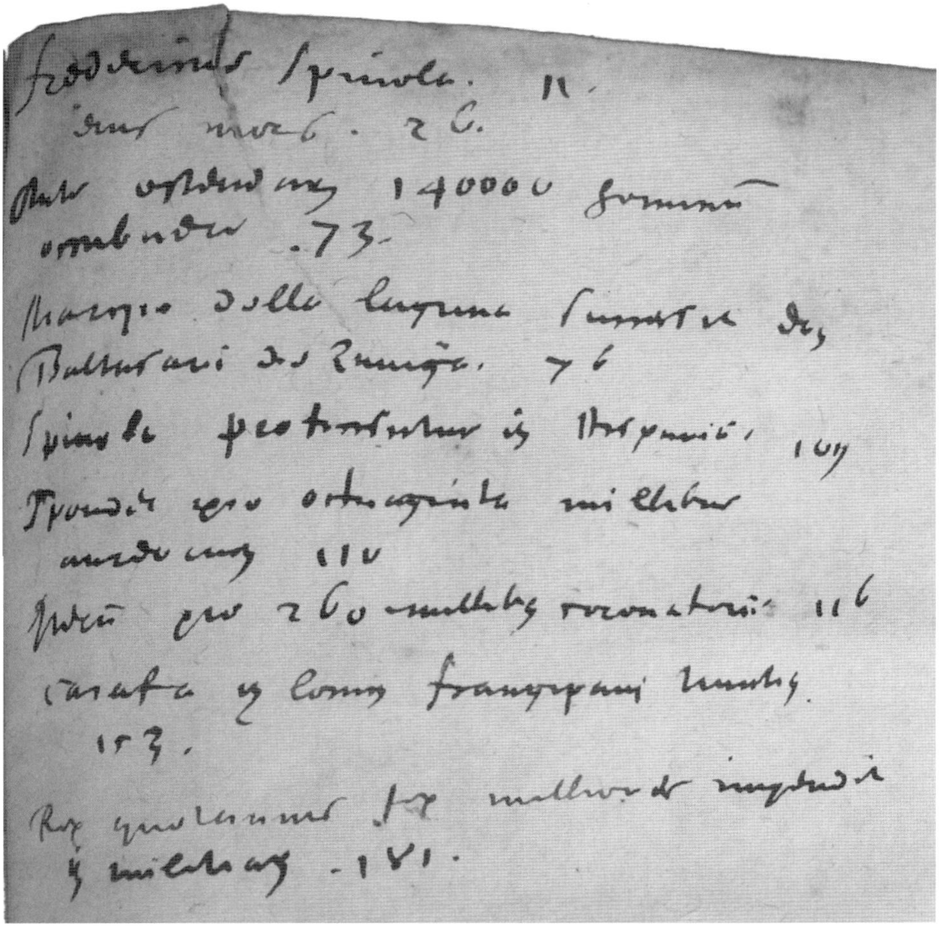

Frontispiece and flyleaves of the Nijmegen copy of Pompeio Giustiniani's *Bellum Belgicum*

APPENDIX 5
PIETER FEDDES VAN HARLINGEN'S 'MONSTER' PRINT OF 1619[1]

Rijksmuseum Amsterdam, RP-P-OB-67.665

Satirical print on Johan van Oldenbarnevelt by Pieter Feddes van Harlingen, 1619, etching and engraving, coll. Rijksmuseum Amsterdam

[1] See Intr. p. 32-33 and further J. Waszink, 'Oldenbarnevelt and Fishes. Satirical Prints from the 12-Years Truce', in: *History of European Ideas* vol. 46.7 (2020), pp. 903–915 https://doi.org/10.1080/01916599.2020.1756894.

Paraphrase of the poem on the Feddes print:

[No Title]
Big fish eat small fish, as is well known. The little fish Oldenbarnevelt, originally appointed to watch over the waters of Holland and protect their safety from interference by foreigners, grew big through political shrewdness and cunning. He moved among the great fish of Europe and thus learned the secrets of state and politics. Over time he ate many smaller fishes [= *subjected them to his will, made them his instruments*], obtained a position of power over them and became vainglorious. He controlled all foreign contacts, both outgoing and incoming. He also swallowed the Spanish fish, with all the money sticking to it, [*see the scene in the middle of the engraving*] but this fish then sat inside him and controlled him instead of being subdued. Consequently Oldenbarnevelt brought Maurice and the army in great danger, especially during the Flanders campaign [*1600–1604*]. Maurice, the Admiral protected by God, was expelling all the Spaniards. Oldenbarnevelt saw the Spanish fishes being locked out of Dutch waters and feared the loss of his Spanish profits. So he coughed up the Spanish fish from his bowels and sent it to Spain to get help, in order to conclude a false peace after which, he promised, he would by a secret plan bring the Netherlands back under Spanish domination. Thus, the Truce was concluded, and the reward received from Spain made Oldenbarnevelt so rich and proud he could barely behave himself. Now he began developing his plan; what he needed was discord. So he sent for his chief helpers; Grotius from Rotterdam, Ledenberg and Moersberg from Utrecht, and Hoogerbeets from Leiden, and promised them supremacy and the admiral's subordination. Grotius objected: 'We cannot achieve this by peaceful means, the unity of the fishes is too strong.' Oldenbarnevelt the Old Fish replied: 'Do I not possess all right and might? Am I not all in all? I know all secrets of state, I have force and deceit at my disposal. All depends on me, no one dares to resist me. I will seduce them to fall into discord: and just as the faith has been the origin of their freedom, it will now be its destruction. I will bring Vorstius from Steynfurt, who will introduce a new doctrine, which some of the fishes will accept, and some will resist with force. Meanwhile I will bring in Wtenbogaert, that most hypocritical preacher of the elite, whose deceitful eloquence will cover our purpose, in ways that even the Devil can't.' Oh what evil times in which the teachers of God's word fall into such evil and pride. They care more about secular government [*politie*] than about the faith. They even use the faith as an instrument to achieve power, and as a cover for their purposes. Oldenbarnevelt: 'Van Toor, you go out and spread the new doctrine; and when you have a nice group of adherents I will add a great many new fishes of our sort that will make our party invincible. We will use the semblance of devotion to the faith and to freedom to bring the governments on our side so that we can deprive the Admiral of his power.' The fishes applauded this plan. Oldenbarnevelt swam to Utrecht and set loose a great number of his followers.

With the use of *Waardgelders* [*mercenary civic guards*] he began a purgation of the city government, shitting out an endless number of men of his party. Soon they covered all of the country, and many burghers, as well as the preachers, had a fish in their bodies, and you could hear it in their sermons. Now Oldenbarnevelt and his party were all that was spoken of; he had completely eclipsed Maurice. However when Vorstius tried to take up a chair at [*the university of*] Leiden he failed; he settled in Gouda from where he spread his doctrine. Many accepted it and the Netherlands looked like a desert. Oldenbarnevelt had played it in such a way that the secular government also endorsed this doctrine, o double evil! However the Frisians resisted it: Sybrand Lubbertus skinned Vorstius, and the States of Friesland did not subject to Oldenbarnevelt. Vorstius was driven out. Oldenbarnevelt now turned to Grotius, and told him to stop Lubbertus. 'Lubbertus keeps us from acquiring more adherents, this must be banned.' Then Vorstius resumed his teaching, and the old doctrine was forbidden. Many preachers were forced from office. Tyranny, discord and envy were everywhere.

The Spanish fish had been quiet for a while, but rose to the occasion and began capturing cities on the Rhine [*in Germany*]. The Admiral intervened to save the country: 'The Spaniard has recently concluded peace and acknowledged our liberty; now he is advancing towards our border with secret force in a semblance of peace. I will fight him as long as I live.' He advanced and stopped him by taking Rees and Emmerich; the Spaniard withdrew immediately like a snail into its shell. Maurice came back to Holland like a conqueror, but remained anxious of Oldenbarnevelt whose attacks he was not equal to, but whose misuse of religion he saw through. He also saw how much strife and chaos the Old Fish was causing in order to carve out a path to supremacy. Maurice turned to the government of the free fishes [*States General*] and after thorough consideration set out a net, and cleverly captured the Old Fish plus a number of men of his party. Oldenbarnevelt's cunning, splendor, wisdom and artfulness lay prostrate. Behold this *exemplum*, all you who glorify in worldly pride: slippery are the steps to supremacy. All wealth and state and fame which they had, equality with princes; – the sea was not enough for the Old Fish, he wanted to follow Neptune's son[2] onto land, but was caught when the water retreated. Oldenbarnevelt, you should have stayed in your element; the whale that stranded not far from The Hague three years earlier was the herald of your downfall. All four of you should have stayed were you were appointed to be. However the two Pastores [*to be explained*] were more clever and escaped. Moersberg, the fifth fish, lives in Westphalia. Time will learn how it will all end, but for sure when they open this fish there will be many Spanish, Brabantine and Italian fishes inside, as well as others. But I do not wish for their

[2] A cryptic allusion: when Neptune desired to wed the sea-nymph Thetis there was a portent that Thetis' son would eclipse his father. Neptune then married Amphitrite instead; she gave him a son called Triton, with whom no stories are connected that fit this situation. Neptune's illegitimate children however include the Cyclops Polyphemos, who might perhaps be referenced here?

fall; the Lord wants that everything ends well, and so I wish that they are all innocent of the above.

* To the reader
This verse was written 3 months before it was published. Meanwhile the Old Fish has been killed.[3] I cannot find what was found in his bowels, but I will tell you if I ever find out. Meanwhile I shall take classes from a pagan prophet or priest and learn about soothsaying from animal intestines.

* Explanation of the image: a, b, c, etc. [see image].

[3] This remark shows that the text was composed in late winter or spring 1619.

APPENDIX 6
SENTENTIAE AND EPIGRAMS IN ANNALES 1 AND 2
(See definitions in C. Damon, commentary to Tacitus *Histories* book 1, pp. 15–16)

Book 1

1.3 unde una cura belli et libertatis
1.4 metu aut gratia
1.5 imperitandi libido, antiquissimum malum
1.6 cum boni principes essent, ne malis fieri liceret
1.8 cuncta eo vergere ubi poena et merces erant
1.9 potentiam temperando auxere, qua arte libertas, magis etiam quam vi, expugnatur.
1.9 in cogentes resistendo crescit ferocia, comititati et mansuetudini ultro subitur.
1.9 corruptis licentia moribus concedi solita imperantur; ex obsequio servitium fit.
1.11 nec Belgae gratia superiorem ferre quenquam poterant, nec Hispani parem.
1.18 animus ingens et celans sui (= '*the Silent*')
1.19 victoriis laudem et gratiam meritus nisi numium imputasset
1.20 multi publica mala suis remedium aut obtegumentum quarebant (*cp. Tac. Ann. 5.3 and Hist. 1.53.2*)
1.20 [turba] ut cuique plurimum spei aut desperationis erat, in partes transgressura
1.21 ut quaererent pecuniam prodigerentque
1.25 facta arguebantur, cogitata impune erant
1.25 [saevire] episcopis inhumanum, nec principibus tutum videbatur
1.26 [suppliciorum] saevitia velut pietate certabant
1.27 neminem esse tam innocentem, qui illis invitis posset salutem et dignitatem tueri.
1.29 vis religionis [...], dissentientis impatiens
1.29 unum reipublicae corpus una religione velut spiritu contineri (*cp. Tac. Ann. 1.12.11*)
1.29 optime constare rationem si multitudini non reddatur (*cp. Tac. Ann. 1.6*)
1.29 effecto ut perirent multi, plures succrescerent
1.31 in quantam stragem processissent illa quae remedia dicebantur
1.35 Nec plus in sua prudentia subsidii, quam in aliorum ignavia fuit
1.44 alimenta morbi facta, quae remedia crederentur
1.45 consilia se metuisse quae celabantur
1.48 pars poenae metu, alii rerum novarum cupientes

1.52 ne poenae metus in spem belli transiret
1.55 sed mox iudicium principi, subditis obsequium relinqui *(cp. Tac. Ann. 6.8.6)*
1.55 nisi in religionibus compertum foret, esse omnia pertinaciae quam concordiae proniora
1.56 licentia firmat audaciam
1.57 [eos] cum ratione insaniisse
1.60 quae fraus plurimum valet, specie simplicitatis
1.65 cum pleraque non tam vis praesens quam metus contineret
1.66 spe vivendi inducti ut perirent *(cp. Tac. Ann. 2.52.5)*

Book 2

2.4 id maximum potentiae praesidium, iudiciorum potiri
2.4 [laesa maiestas] tam suspecta bonis principibus quam tyrannis oportuna *(cp. Sall. Cat. 7.3 & Lipsius praef. to Tac. ed. 1574, line 42)*
2.5 quaesitique honores et recusati *(cp. Tac. Hist. 1.2.6)*
2.5 pauca salmonum piscium capita multis ranunculorum millibus praestare *(cp. Tac. 4.19.2)*
2.5 [sententia quae docet] sublatis e republica primoribus munire regnum
2.7 quibus nec exsilium egestas sua concesserat
2.8 similem exitum oportuna morte praevenit *(cp. Tac. Ann. 4.21.5)*
2.8 patris ira in filii necem durasset *(cp. Tac. Ann. 1.6)*
2.10 alterno hostium et suo sanguine bellum imbuerunt
2.11 eius erroribus principatus obsequium non deberi
2.14, *set of four accumulating sententiae:*
- sua sibi curae
- cui nota ut clementiae, ita severitatis tempora
- in eos qui spreto Deo mox et principem spernere didicissent
- ipsos facturos rectius tutiusque si rerum alienarum arbitrio abstinerent

2.15 pleraque polliciti in eventum distulere
2.16 praesenti aere inescata, futuri improvida
2.16 egregio usus victoriae genere non pugnando
2.17 pace mox inita deceptus fuit, et in deceptos pars insidiarum
2.18 parato qui cogeret, velut sponte recipiebantur
2.21 certa pecuniae summa infinitum onus redimere conabantur
2.22 nullam essa tam firmam concordiam quam quae privatae rei vinculo continetur
2.24 Gallicis ingeniis bello opus, ut pacem servarent
2.25 ita humanam fiduciam et consilia illudere ut numquam simul essent spes magna et bonus eventus
2.28 minore casu praeventum se [esse]
2.29 ne tanto rerum discrimine alieno se dedecori immisceret
2.29 parcere sanguini in summam belli nihil profuturo

2.32 homines re nulla magis quam clementia vinci assuefeceris
2.32 graviora pacis mala, quam belli metuebant
2.39 mala quae domi fugerant, alienis in armis ulciscebantur
2.43 neminem volentem errare, aut nolentem credere
2.43 nec grata [Deo] pietas, quae non sponte procederet
2.44 omnia dabant ne decimam darent
2.44 vetitus saepe, semper retentus *(cp. Tac. Hist. 1.22.2 (Boot))*
2.45 vinci posse qui tam lente vicerant
2.49 ubi bellum semel omnia permisit, nihil tutius est paupertate
2.52 [non recte facere quod] defensionem prae poenitentia elegissent
2.55 dubium audacia maiore an felicitate
2.59 nemo est ita sapiens ut eum nunquam Fortuna fallat
2.59 ne olim quidem principum satis patiens, cum tantum principes essent
2.59 quo magis necessario exigebantur, hoc confidentius negaverant
2.60 ut eadem defensae patriae praemia quam proditae mallent
2.66 instrumenta in libertatem
2.69 erat illis promta perfidia, sed iners animus
2.71 potentiam quasi remitteret, gratia muniebat

APPENDIX 7
BOOK SUMMARIES BY THE EDITORS OF 1657

Book 1

Belgicae situs et regimen. Belli Belgici primae causae. Inquisitionis origo, administratio, infaustus apud Belgas eventus. Philippus in Hispaniam discedens Margaritam Parmensem Belgicae praeficit. Implacabile eius in Belgas odium, Belgicae regimen vocabulo penes Margaritam, vi penes Granvellam. Graves inter illum et proceres inimicitiae. Philippus novos per Belgicam constituit antistites. Quibus Belgae aliique se opponunt. Arausionensis, Egmondi, atque Hornani literis impulsus Granvellam e Belgica discedere iubet. Egmondus in Hispaniam missus spem vanam inde adfert. Rex in religionis diversos immisericorditer animadverti, ac Synodi Tridentinae placita publicari iubet. Hinc magni ubique motus. Proceres pacem religionum procurare instituunt. Contra inquisitionem foedus pangunt. Foederatorum ad Margaritam, ut edicta super religione mutentur, preces. Gueusiorum nominis origo. Montiniacus et marchio Bergensis ad Regem mittuntur. Transmissa a Senatu Belgico moderandarum legum forma Regi displicet. Pontificis Romani imperia abnuentium tria per Belgicam genera. E vulgo erumpunt qui sacra novo ritu peragunt. Templa per totam Belgicam violantur. Margarita veniam gestorum nobilibus promittit, conciones plebi concedit. Arausionensis, Hornanus aliique offensam eius incurrunt. interceptis ex Hispania ad eam literis omnes exitio destinantur. In medium consulentes frustra in Egmondum oculos vertunt. Arausionensis missionem a republica urget. Consilium suum ad Regem scripto complectitur. Hornanus suos se in penates abdit. Foederati nobiles rem communem produnt. Praefecta conscripto milite duces iurare cogit, hostes futuros quoscunque Rex designasset. Soli Arausionensis et Hooghstratanus detrectant. Regis praesentia comprimendarum partium optimum habetur remedium. Rex moras nectit. Tandem constat Albanum cum exercitu mitti. Abit ad fratrem in Germaniam Arausionensis.

Book 2

Intranti in Belgicam Albano nemo obsistit. Egmondum et Hornanum capitis supplicio afficit. Exarmatis urbibus arces imponit. Novum tribunal erigit. Arausionensis aliorumque bona in fiscum vertuntur. Arausionensem ad arma impellunt exules. Caeditur a Ludovico Nassavio in Frisia Arembergius, mox ipse ab Albano fugatur. Arausionensis iustitiam causae suae libris evulgat. Maximiliano Caesari pro Belgis apud Philippum intercedenti acerbe respondetur. Conscriptus ab Arausionense exercitus ab Albano debellatur. Donatur a Pontifice sacrato ense. Sibi statuam ponit. Leges iuraque Belgarum omnia regis servat arbitrio. Inaudita Belgis tributa pendi iubet. Se armis in libertatem vindicare statuunt. Belli aleam iterum experiri constituit Arausionensis. Brilam Belgae exules capiunt. Roterodamum a Bossuvio direptum exules iuvat. Flissinga aliaeque urbes ab Hispanis desciscunt. Albanus Hollandis ac Zelandis coalescendi dat spatium. Arausionensis spei irritus dimisso exercitu in Hollandiam abit. Mons deditur. In Zutphaniam et Nardam turpiter saevit Fridericus Albani filius. Foederatarum provinciarum descriptio. Arausionensis adventu turbata omnia composita. Omnia cum Ordinibus administrat. Rebus omnibus contra Regis mandata Regis praetenditur nomen. Romanae caeremoniae templis eiiciuntur. Genevensis disciplina publice recipitur. Agri et vectigalia principis aliaque in publicos vertuntur usus. Tunc quoque inventa tot tributorum nomina. Albani error. Harlemum Hispani expugnant, quorum impetum prima frangit Alcmaria. Nassaviani Geertrudisbergam et ipsa cum classe Bossuvium capiunt. Albanus cum filio revocatur in Hispaniam. Succedit Requesenius. Statuam Albani statim amolitur. Middelburgum Zelandis accedit. Ludovicus Nassavius cum Henrico fratre et Christophoro Palatino caeditur. Tumultuantes Hispani quadringenta florenorum millia Antverpiae extorquent. Frustra Bredae de concordia agitur. Lugduni obsidio, eiusque incredibilis solutio. Petri Melendis infelix in Foederatos maritima expeditio. Bommenedae portum et Zyrixaeam expugnant Hispani. Angliae regina oblatum a Batavis summum imperium respuit. Carolus Galliae rex eos clam fovet. Extincto Requesenio ad senatum regiarum partium administratio delata. Iura Ordinum et leges celebrari incipiunt. Bruxella rapinae destinatur. Miles Hispanus hostis patriae iudicatur: Alostum irrumpit. Primores Brabanti aliquot foedus in Hispanos cum aliis pangunt. Roda Traiectum ad Mosam et post Antverpiam diripit. Belgae Arausionensem in auxilium vocant. pax Gandavensis. Deiectis arcibus exuitur servitus. Philippus tempori cedens pacta (**28**) confirmat. Iohannes Austriacus Belgicae rector mittitur. Namurcum occupat. Apud Regem violatae pacis accusatur. Ad praefecti dignitatem vocatur Arausionensis; intercedente Arscotio summum Belgicae regimen Mathiae Austriaco datur, vicarium tamen Arausionensis accipit.

Book 3

Iohanni bellum indicitur. Regina Angliae Belgis favere incipit; Regi pacem illis suadet. Belgarum exercitum caedit Iohannes. Victi spe pacis tentantur, conditiones repudiantur. Franciscus Valesius et Casimirus Belgis operam offerunt. Respublica undique confusa. Nassaviani Amstelodami atque alibi Romanae sectae magistratus authoritate exuentes socios offendunt. Iohannes Nassavius Gelriae, Rennebergius Frisiae rector; huic Campi et Daventria deduntur. Casimirus cum copiis advenit. Valesius ordinum decreto Belgicae libertatis vindex. Reformatorum postulata ab Ordinibus admittuntur, dissidia inter illos et Romanenses. Gandavenses ordinum imperium detrectant. Romanas caeremonias urbe exigunt, eamque muniunt.

Atrebates et Haenovii illos bello coercendos contendunt, obsistunt Arausionensis et alii. Castra irrito conatu adortus Iohannes. De pace instituuntur colloquia. Eius conditiones. Iohannes copiis auctus ei renunciat. Belgarum inter se dissidia, propinquam quae libertatem avertunt. Montiniacus Atrebatum factionem amplectitur. Gandavenses militem adversus eos conscribunt. Belli obtentus. Flandri a Casimiro militem accipiunt. Franciscus Binckium expugnat. Militem suum ad Montiniacum dilabi patitur: Belgas ingratitudinis reos agens in Galliam digreditur. Iohannes subito moritur non sine veneni suspicione. Parmensis illi succedit; eius indoles et artes. Belgarum dissidia magis exardescere facit, quibus frustra remedia quaerit Arausionensis. Parmensis Traiectam ad Mosam obsidet. Legati interim ad faciendam pacem conveniunt, cui occulte obsistit Arausionensis. Belgas ad Regis gratiam invitat Parmensis. Illi reconciliatur primus Lamota, quem alii sequuntur. Pacis conditiones. Plures dissidentium Belgarum nationes Philippus iterum sub imperium redigit: caeteras arctiori foedere Traiecti Batavorum illigat Arausionensis. Foederis Traiectini summa. Per alias Belgicae nationes maximae turbae. Secta Romanensis Sylvaeducis praevalet, Reformati Antverpiae. Multi hinc ad Hispanos desciscendi occasionem rapiunt. Ipra et Gandavum foederi accedunt. Arausionensi Flandriae praefectura confertur. Parmensis Traiectum ad Mosam expugnat. Machliniam aliasque urbes sibi conciliat. Foederis oblatae a Rege pacis leges displicent. Cum Arausionensi seorsim agitur. Foederatae reipublicae vitium. Philippus per Albanum Lusitaniam subigit, hinc magna Batavis incommoda. Parmensis aliquot oppida recipit. Machlinia ab Anglis diripitur. Parmensis mater ad regendos Belgas revocata remittitur. Bellum in Frisia exardet. Groninga ad Regem desciscit. Entesius eam obsidet. Schenckii opera solvitur obsidio. Rennebergius a Stenovici obsidione depulsus moritur. **(53)** Romanensibus in Brabantia et Transisalana privata quoque sacra interdicuntur. Arausionensis Ordinibus novi senatus autor. Ut Philippum repudient suadet, ac Francisco Valesio principatum deferant. Philippo imperium abrogatur: Hostis vocatur. Mathias honorifice dimittitur. Hispanus in proscriptum Arausionensem percussorem invitat: Hic libello se defendit. Eius innocentiam Ordines testantur. Franciscus ad imperium vocatur, cum exercitu adveniens obsessum Cameracum liberat. Tornacum Parmensi deditur.

Book 4

Franciscus ambitu frustra Elisabethae matrimonio Belgicae imperium suscipit. Leges illi praescriptae. Belgarum nobilium indignatio; eius causae. Flagrans Arausionensis apud multitudinem gratia: latrociniis Hispanicis petitur. Parmensis interim Aldenardam capit, Alostum Valesius, Liram Parmensis miles, Verdugo Stenovicum. Externus miles Parmensi remittitur. Ordinum validae quoque copiae. Valesius frustra exspectatis fraternis auxiliis atrox consilium capit; varias vi occupat Foederatorum urbes; eius miles Brugis eiicitur: omnium infelicissime tentat Antverpiam; cum suis aufugit: offensis illius incoepto Belgis Regis offertur clementia: Valesium tamen non esse repudiandum censet Arausionensis; quod et

Galliarum regi cordi: Dunkercae cum illo agitur, multa causatus in Galliam concedit. Belgarum ad Gallum preces. Valesii mors. Dunkerca in Parmensis venit potestatem, cuius iactura nondum sopiuntur dissensiones. Arausionensis in Zelandiam abit. Parmensis multas interea expugnat urbes. Hogii mendacio Hollandiam turbantis supplicium. Truxii coniugium novi belli causa: ab hostibus pulsus ad Arausionensem profugit. A Taxi Zutphania capitur. Herembergius ad Hispanos cum filiis transfugit. Imbisius et Cimacensis Flandriam Hispanis tradere suscipiunt. Parmensis oblata occasione utitur; illi Wasia variaque deduntur oppida. Brugas Regis obsequio reddit Cimacensis, quas aliae urbes sequuntur. Gandavenses capitali supplicio plectunt Imbisium. Parmensis Scaldim obsidet. Antverpienses duo excitant castella. Arausionensis Delphis occiditur: illius perturbatus rei privatae status; quadruplex matrimonium: funus maximo luctu celebratum. Mauritius filius illi succedit. Hohenloius vicariam sub illo accipit potestatem. Wilhelmus Nassavius Frisiae rector Frisiorum discordias prudenter componit. Constans Batavorum fortitudo. Scaldis coeptum obsidium urget Parmensis, Tenerimundam capit et Vilvordam: Gandavenses se ei dedunt. Ricardoti solertia. Arx Gandavi reponitur. Antverpienses sociorum opem implorant. Vicini auxiliandi tempora praetermittunt. Calamitosus Foederatorum status; Gallus et Angla illos consolantur: dubitant utri velint accrescere: a praelato Gallo non recipiuntur.

Book 5

Foederati ad Elisabetham recurrunt. Parmensis Antverpiam obsidet, eaque post Bruxellam et Machliniam potitur: arcem restituit; tentata ab Hohenloio irrito eventu Sylvaducis, Noviomagum et Dosiburgum Hispanis deduntur. Belgarum imperium recusans Elisabetha auxilia promittit; illorum imperator Licestrius; nimii ipsi a Foederatis concessi honores Reginae non probantur. Imperium in Belgas affectans Ordines criminatur, et plebem in illos concitare studet: negotiationis libertatem circumscribit, hostiles quoque agros excidio damnat. Gravia Parmensi ab Hemerta deditur: eam sequitur Venloa. Axelam Mauritius expugnat. Gravewartam munit Scenkius. A Nienario captum Novesium cum aliis urbibus iterum in Parmensis venit potestatem. Licestrius magnis premitur querelis, Ordines pleraque ad suam curam trahere aegre fert: sacrarum literarum interpretes simul et populi studia sibi conciliat; in Anglicano milite et Sonoio multum praesidii ponit. Mauritii prudens dissimulatio. Licestrius in Angliam proficiscitur. Elisabethae frustra iterum imperium offertur. Belgas querentes diu in Anglia Licestrius detinet. Daventria et oppositum Zutfaniae munimentum Anglorum perfidia traduntur Hispano. Absente Licestrio summum Mauritio armorum mandatur imperium. Edictum de evectionibus temperatur. Ex miseria Brabantorum ac Flandrorum Batavi incrementa sumunt. Hohenloius caeso Altipenna Crepicordium occupat. Clusam expugnat Parmensis, quod Ordinibus a Licestrio, in Belgicam reverso, imputatur. Elisabetha in pacem propensa. Licestrii criminationibus Ordines respondent; hic urbes vi opprimere parat; eius coniuratis Lugduni capite plexis in Angliam abit; ubi eiurato in Belgas imperio moritur. Scenkius Bonnam capit. Ingens ad subiugandam Angliam in Hispania classis struitur, quod Philippus ostentata pace dissimulat; pari arte cum illo agit Elisabetha. Classis adventans fraudes dirimit. Militum propter insoluta stipendia apud Belgas turbae. Brevis inspectio, quo pacto se contra Hispanicam potentiam perculsi erexerint Batavi. Finium, reipublicae status, virium, ac habitus animorum inter partes comparatio.

BIBLIOGRAPHY

Primary Material

Manuscript sources

Hugo Grotius, *De Iure Praedae*, Leiden UL, BPL 917

——, *De Bello ob libertatem eligendo*, Leiden UL, BPL 922.I.c

——, *Historiae* 1-4 and 8-18, Leiden UL, Papenbroek 9.1 and 9.2

——, *Historiae* 5-7, Paris, Bibliothèque Nationale, Fonds Latin 17796

——, state papers foreign, Amsterdam UL, special collections, ms. IIIC2 and IIIC3

[——], ms annotations in printed copy of: Pompeius Iustinianus, *Bellum Belgicum sive Belgicarum rerum e commentariis Pompei Iustiniani libri VI*, Coloniae 1611, Radboud University Nijmegen, University Library, 80 C37

Inventaris van het archief van de Staten van Holland en West-Friesland, 1572–1795: *Resolutien 1601–1605*, The Hague, National Archive, 3.01.04.01

Anon., *Apologia Remonstrant*[ium] *verbis praecipue Taciti conscripta. Juny 1620,* Municipal Library Rotterdam, mss. Remonstrants-Gereformeerde Gemeente, 417a

Anon., *Pro Contraremonstrantibus Apologia verbis Taciti praecipue conscripta,* Municipal Library Rotterdam, mss. Remonstrants-Gereformeerde Gemeente, 417b

Anon., ms annotations in printed copy of Grotius, *Annales et Historiae* 1658 (120, TMD 744); Nijmegen UL, shelfmark 9 d 16

Petrus Burmannus, ms annotations in printed copy of *Annales et Historiae* 1657 (folio, TMD 742); Amsterdam University Library, ms. UBA, OTM KF62-4241

—— & M. Romswinckel, *Aantekeningen*, Tilburg University library, ms. KHS D91

Petrus Hofman Peerlkamp, ms annotations in printed copy of: Grotius, *Annales et Historiae* 1658 (80, TMD 743); Leiden UL, collection Maatschappij Nederlandsche Letterkunde, 1499 D 34

Printed sources

Grotius

Hugo Grotius (ed.), *Minei Felicis Capellae Carthaginiensis viri proconsularis Satyricon, in quo de nuptiis Philologiae et Mercurii libri duo, et De septem artibus liberalibus libri singulares,* Leiden (Raphelengius) 1599

—— (ed.), *Syntagma Arateorum: Opus poeticæ et astronomiae studiosis vtilissimum,* Leiden (Raphelengius) 1600

——, *Parallelon rerumpublicarum liber tertius: De moribus ingenioque populorum Atheniensium, Romanorum, Batavorum. Vergelijking der gemeenebesten door Hugo de Groot. Derde boek: Over*

de zeden en den inborst der Athenienseren, Romeinen en Hollanderen, Haarlem (Loosjes) 1801–1803
——, *Sacra in quibus Adamus Exul tragoedia* etc., The Hague (Albert Henrici) 1601
——, *De Iure Praedae*
- Final state of the text in ms. BPL 917: ed. G. Hamaker, The Hague (Nijhoff) 1868
- Translation: M. van Ittersum (ed.), *Commentary on the Law of Prize and Booty*, Indianapolis (Liberty Fund) 2006
- Critical edition of the ms. BPL 917, ed. J. Waszink: http://arkyves.org/view/DeIurePraedae

——, *Tragoedia Christus Patiens,* Leiden (Basson) 1608
——, *The Antiquity of the Batavian Republic*, ed. J. Waszink et al., Assen 2000 (Bibliotheca Latinitatis Novae)
——, *Meletius sive de iis quae inter Christianos conveniunt Epistola*, ed. G. Posthumus Meyjes, Leiden (Brill) 1988
——, *Annales et Historiae de rebus Belgicis*
editions: Amsterdam (Blaeu) 1657 (small folio), TMD 741
Amsterdam (Blaeu) 1657 (small folio), TMD 742
Amsterdam (Blaeu) 1658 (in quarto), TMD 743
Amsterdam (Blaeu) 1658 (in duodecimo), TMD 744
——, *Ordinum Pietas*, ed. E. Rabbie, Leiden (Brill) 1995
——, *Remonstrantie nopende de ordre dije in de landen van Hollandt ende Westvrieslandt dijent gestelt op de Joden,* ed. J. Meijer, Amsterdam 1949
——, *Remonstrantie nopende de ordre dije in de landen van Hollandt ende Westvrieslandt dijent gestelt op de Joden*, ed. by D. Kromhout and A. Offenberg, Hugo Grotius' Remonstrantie of 1615. Facsimile, Transliteration, Modern Translations and Analysis, written by David Kromhout and Adri Offenberg, Leiden (Brill) 2019
——, *Oratie vanden hoogh-gheleerden voortreffelycken Meester Hugo de Groot, Raet ende pensionaris der Stadt Rotterdam ghedaen inde vergaderinghe der 36. Raden der Stadt Amsterdam* (Enkhuizen 1622); Knuttel 2250
——, *De Imperio summarum potestatum circa sacra*, ed. H.J. van Dam, Leiden (Brill) 2001
——, *Inleidinge tot the Hollandsche Rechts-Geleerdheid,* ed. H. Fischer, 2nd edition, Leiden (Universitaire pers) 1965
——, *The Rights of War and Peace* ed. with intr. by Richard Tuck, 3 vols., Indianapolis (Liberty Fund) 2005
——, *De Origine Gentium Americanarum,* s.l. 1642
——, *De Origine Gentium Americanarum dissertatio altera,* Paris (Cramoisy) 1643
——, *Briefwisseling van Hugo Grotius*, edd. P. Molhuysen, B. Meulenbroek, P. Witkam, H. Nellen en C. Ridderikhoff, The Hague 1928–2001 (17 vols., in: Rijks Geschiedkundige Publicatiën)
Online edition of the *Briefwisseling*: http://grotius.huygens.knaw.nl/years
——, *De dichtwerken van Hugo Grotius*, ed. B.L. Meulenbroek e.a., Grotius Instituut Amsterdam, & Koninklijke Nederlandse Akademie van Wetenschappen, Assen (Van Gorcum) 1970 and later

Other

Aggaeus van Albada, *Acten van den vredehandel, gheschiet te Colen*, Leiden (Silvius) 1580

François van Aerssen, *Provisioneele Openinghe van verscheyden saecken*, s.l. 1618, pamphlet Knuttel 2634

Antoine Arnauld, *Difficultees proposees a M. Steyaert*, Cologne (Le Grand) 1692

——, *Oeuvres de Messire Antoine Arnauld*, vol. 9, Paris (D'Arnay) 1777

L. Aubery du Maurier & Amelot de La Houssaye, *Mémoires pour servir à l'histoire de la République des Provinces-Unies et des Pays-Bas: Contenant les vies des Princes d'Orange, de Barneveld, d'Aersens & de Grotius, London 1754*

Ban ende edict by vorme van proscriptie, vuytggaen ende ghedecreteerd by … de Coninck, tegens Wilhelm van Oraignyen etc., 's Hertogenbosch (Schoeffer) 1580, Pamphlet Knuttel 527

John Barclay, *Icon Animorum or the Mirror of Minds. Translated by Thomas May (1631)*, ed. M. Riley, Leuven 2013, Bibliotheca Latinitatis Novae

Dominicus Baudius, *Libri tres de Induciis belli Belgici*, Leiden (Elzevir) 1613

——, *Van 't bestant des Nederlantschen Oorlogs drie boecken*, Amsterdam (Pers) 1616

Pierre Bayle, *Dictionnaire historique et critique*, Rotterdam (Leers) 1697

Georgius Benedicti Werteloo, *De rebus gestis illustrissimi principis Guilielmi* (Leiden: J. Paets, 1586; modern edition in: G. Benedicti, *De Krijgsdaden van Willem van Oranje*, ed. Collegium Classicum c.n. E.D.E.P.O.L., Leiden (Dimensie) 1990

Guido Bentivoglio, *Della Guerra di Fiandra*, vol. 3, Livorno 1831

Bibliothèque Choisie de M. Colomies La Rochelle (Pierre Savouret) 1682

Giovanni Botero, *Della Ragion di Stato libri dieci* (first edition), Venezia (Gioliti) 1589

Caspar Brandt & A. van Cattenburgh, *Historie van het leven des heeren Huig de Groot: Beschreven tot den aanvang van zyn gezantschap wegens de koninginne en kroone van Zweden aan 't Hof van Vrankryk*, Dordrecht & Amsterdam (Van Braam & Onder de Linden) 1727 [and 2nd ed. 1732]

Geeraert Brandt, *Historie der Reformatie en andere kerkelyke geschiedenissen in en omtrent de Nederlanden* vol. 1, Amsterdam 1671

Joannes Boeckler, *In Hugonis Grotii ius belli et pacis Commentatio*, Strassbourg (Dulssecker) 1704

Pieter Bor, *Vande Nederlantsche oorloghen, beroerten ende borgerlijcke oneenicheyden, gheduerende den gouvernemente vanden hertoghe van Alba inde selve landen*, Utrecht (S. de Roy) 1601

——, *Nederlantsche oorloghen, beroerten, ende borgerlijcke oneenicheyde*, vol. 2, Leiden and Amsterdam 1621

——, *Nederlantsche oorloghen, beroerten, ende borgerlijcke oneenicheyden*, vol. 3.1 Leiden and Amsterdam (Basson and Colyn) [1626]

Caspar Burman, *Hadrianus VI sive analecta historica de Hadriano Sexto*, Utrecht 1728

Petrus Burmannus, *Nicolai Heinsii Dan. Fil. Adversariorvm libri IV: In quibus plurima veterum auctorum … eiusdem notae ad Catullum et Propertium nunc primum productae […] praefationem & commentarium de vita Nicolai Heinsii adjecit*, Harlingen (Van der Plaats) 1742

——, *Sylloges epistolarum. Tomus III. Quo Nicolai Heinsii, J.Fr. Gronovii, Isaaci Vossii, Jani Vlitii, Arnoldi Slichtenhorstii, Vincentii Fabricii, Ezechielis Spanhemii, et Hadriani Wallii epistolae maximam partem mutuae exhibentur*, Leiden (Luchtmans) 1725

Dudley Carlton, *The speech of Sir Dudley Carlton* [...] *Touching the discord and troubles of the church and policie, caused by the schismatic doctrine of Arminius*, London 1618

Isaac Casaubonus, *Isaaci Causauboni Epistolae, quotquot reperiri potuerunt* etc., The Hague (Theodorus Maire) 1638

——, *Polibio*, ed. G.F. Brussich, Palermo (Salerno editore) 1991

Jean Chapelain, *Les Lettres authentiques à Nicolas Heinsius (1649–1672). Une amitié érudite entre France et Hollande*, ed. B. Bray, Paris (Champion) 2005

Hermann Conring, *Thesaurus Rerumpublicarum Pars 1,* Geneva (De Tournes) 1675

—— (ed.), *Gasparis Scioppii Paedia Politices et Gabrielis Naudaei Bibliographia Politica ut et ejusdem argumenti alia. Nova editio reliquis omnibus multum emendatior*, Helmstedt (Muller) 1663

Corte Verclaering gedaen by Burgemeesteren, Schepenen etc., Antwerp (Plantin) 1583

Corte vermaeninghe aende naerdere geunieerde Provincien ende Steden der Nederlanden etc., pamphlet Knuttel 526

Jean Denis, *Recoeuil des Mémoires et conferences sur les arts & les sciences, presentées à Monseigneur Le Dauphin pendant l'Année M.DC. LXXII par Jean Baptiste Denis conseiller, et Medecin ordinaire du Roy, qui y continuë Le journal des Sçavans* Amsterdam (Le Grand) 1673

Janus Dousa, *Iani Duzae Nordovicis Nova poemata (...). Item Hadriani Iuni Carminum Lugdunensium Sylva,* Leiden (Academia) 1575

Jacob Duym, *Het Moordadich Stuck van Balthasar Gerards begaen aen den Doorluchtigen Prince van Oraignen* 1584, 1606

Elizabeth I, 'On Monsieur's Departure', in: L. Marcus, J. Mueller, M. Rose (eds.), *Elizabeth. Collected Works*, Chicago 2000

Caspar Ens, *Princeps Auriacus, sive Libertas defensa (1599) = (De prins van Oranje of de verdediging van de vrijheid)*, edd. J. Bloemendal & J. Steenbeek, Voorthuizen (Florivallis) 1998

Pompeio Giustiniani, *Delle guerre di Fiandra libri VI*, Antwerp (Trognese) 1609

——, *Bellum Belgicum sive Belgicarum rerum e commentariis Pompei Iustiniani libri VI*, Cologne (Kinckius) 1611

Marquardus Gudius, C. Sarravius, P. Burmannus, *Marquardi Gudii et doctorum virorum ad eum epistolae: Quibus accedunt ex Bibliotheca Gudiana clarissimorum et doctissimorum virorum, qui superiore et nostro saeculo floruerunt: Et Claudii Sarravii epistolae ex eadem Bibliotheca auctiores, Utrecht (Halma & Van de Water) 1697*

Franciscus Haraeus, *Annales Ducum seu Principum Brabantiae totusque Belgii*, Antwerpen (Plantin) 1623

Daniel Heinsius, *Danieli Heinsii Orationum Editio Nova*, Leiden (Elzevir) 1627

——, *Auriacus, sive Libertas saucia (1602)*, ed. J. Bloemendal, Voorthuizen (Florivallis) 1997

——, *Peplus Graecorum Epigrammatum,* Leiden (Elzevir) 1613.

Heywood, Th. (ed.), *Cardinal Allen's defence of sir William Stanley's Surrender of Deventer, January 29, 1586-7*, Manchester (Chetham Society) 1851

Pieter Cornelisz. Hooft, *Nederlandsche historien, seedert de ooverdraght der heerschappye van Kaizar Kaarel den Vyfden op kooning Philips zynen zoon, tot de doodt des prinsen van Oranje*, Amsterdam (Van Someren) 1677

Edward Hyde (Lord Clarendon), *A Collection of Several Tracts,* London (Woodward & Peele) 1727

Hadrianus Junius, *Batavia*, Leiden (Plantin-Raphelengius) 1588

Joannes de Laet, *Ioannis de Laet Antuerpiani, Notae ad dissertationem Hugonis Grotii De Origine Gentium Americanarum: et Observationes aliquot ad meliorem indaginem difficillimae illius Quaestionis*, Amsterdam (Elzevier) 1643

Justus Lipsius, *Iusti Lipsi Epistolae* (ILE)
 vol. 1, edd. A. Gerlo, M.A. Nauwelaerts and H.D.L. Vervliet, Brussels 1978
 vol. 2, edd. M.A. Nauwelaerts and S. Sué, Brussels 1983

——, *Politica. Six books of Politics or Political Instruction*, ed. J. Waszink, Bibliotheca Latinitatis Novae, Assen (Van Gorcum) 2004

Hubert Loyens, *Brevis et succincta synopsis rerum maxime memorabilium bello et pace gestarum ab serenissimis Lotharingiae, Brabantiae, et Limburgi Ducibus* etc., Brussels (Fricx) 1672

Niccolò Macchiavelli, *The Prince*, translated by L. Ricci, revised by E. Vincent, Oxford (Clarendon Press) 1934

Adrianus van Meerbeeck, *Chroniicke van de gantsche werelt, ende sonderlinghe van de seventhien Nederlanden,* Antwerpen (Verdussen) 1620

Emanuel van Meteren, *Memorien der Belgische ofte Nederlantsche Historie, van onse tijden. Inhoudende hoe de Nederlanden aenden anderen gehecht, ende aen Spaengien ghecomen zijn* [etc] Delft (Vennecool) 1599

——, *Belgische ofte Nederlantsche historie, van onsen tijden. Inhoudende hoe de Nederlanden aenden anderen ghehecht, ende aen Spaengien ghecomen zijn...* [etc], Delft (Vennecool) 1599

Johannes Meursius, *Rerum Belgicarum liber unus, in quo Induciarum historia*, Leiden (Elzevir) 1612

——, *Rerum Belgicarum libri quatuor in quibus Ferdinandi Albani sexennium belli Belgici principium*, Leiden (Elzevir) 1614

Frans van Mieris, *Verhandeling over het zaamenstellen en beoevenen der Historien inzonderheid de geschiedenissen van Holland*, Leiden 1757 and Amsterdam 1790

M. de la Neuville, *Histoire de Hollande depuis la treve de 1609, ou finit Grotius jusqu'a notre tems*, Paris (De Grieck) 1702 (2 vols.)

William of Orange, *The Apologie of Prince William of Orange against the proclamation of the king of Spaine*, ed. H. Wansink, Leiden (Brill) 1969

——, *Apologie ofte Verantwoordinge van den Prince van Orangien*, ed. M. Mees-Verwey, Santpoort 1942

——, *Apologie, ofte verantwoordinghe des doerluchtighen ende hooghgeborenen vorsts ende heeren, heeren Wilhelms* [...] *teghen den ban* [...] *ghepubliceert by den coningh van Spaegnien,* Leiden (Silvius) 1581, pamphlet Knuttel 557

——, *Geschriften van 1568*, ed. M. Schenk, Amsterdam (Wereldbibliotheek) 1933

Guy Patin, *Correspondance complète et autres écrits de Guy Patin*, online edition by L. Capron, https://www.biusante.parisdescartes.fr/patin/

Plakkaat van Verlatinge, edd. G. Janssen and M. Mout, *in: Bijdragen En Mededelingen Betreffende De Geschiedenis Der Nederlanden*, vol 124 (2009)

Pracktyke van den Spaenschen Raedt, dat is: clare vertooninghe dat den Raedt door I. Lipsium, Er. Puteanum ende F. Campanellam gegeven om de vereenighde Nederlanden wederom te brengen onder t gebiet van den Coninck van Spaengjen etc, s.l. 1618, pamphlet Knuttel 2622

Resolutien van de Heeren Staten van Holland en Westvriesland 1601, 1603, 1612 [via Google books]

Everard van Reyd, *Historie der Nederlandtscher Oorlogen ende Voortganck tot den Jaere 1601*, Leeuwarden (Sybes) 1650

——, *Trouhertige vermaninge aen het vereenichde Nederlandt, om niet te luysteren na eenighe versierde vreed-articulen, nu onlangs wtgegaan ende ghestroyt*, s.l., 1605 (pamphlet Knuttel 1300–1302, Tiele 544–546)

Toussaint Sailly, 'Nassovius' in: *Panagii Salii Audomarensis Varia Poemata*, Paris (Dionysius a Prato) 1589

Claudius Sarravius, *Claudii Saravii senatoris Parisiensis epistolae,* Orange 1654

Simon Stevin, *Het Burgherlick Leven* 1590, ed. by P. den Boer and A. Fleurkens, Utrecht 2001

Famiano Strada, *De Bello Belgico decas prima*, Rome 1632

——, *De Bello Belgico decas secunda,* Rome 1648

Jean Swart and Pierre de Hondt, *Bibliotheca Duboisiana, ou catalogue de la bibliothèque de … le Cardinal Du Bois, recueillie ci devant par … l'abbé Bignon: La vent publique se fera le 27 Aoust 1725 par Jean Swart et Pierre de Hondt, The Hague* (Swart & De Hondt) 1725

Vertooch aen myne heeren de ghedeputeerde van de Staten generael by mijn heere den Prince van Orangien, 9 January 1580, pamphlet Knuttel 524

Gisbertus Voetius, *Gisberti Voetii theologiae in Academia Ultrajectensi professoris Politicae Ecclesiasticae pars secunda*, Amsterdam (Waesberge) 1669

Joost van den Vondel, *De werken van Vondel* vol. II, ed. C. de Vooys, Amsterdam 1929

Jan Wagenaar, *Vaderlandsche Historie,* vol. 6, Amsterdam (J. Allart) 1792

——, *Vaderlandsche Historie vervattende de geschiedenissen der nu vereenigde Nederlanden* etc., vol. 6, Amsterdam 1792

Cicero, *De Officiis*, ed. W. Miller, Cambridge Ma. 1921

Pliny the Elder, *C. Plini Secundi Naturalis historia,* ed. D. Detlefsen, Berlin 1866

Quintilian, *Institutio Oratoria*, ed. H. Butler, Cambridge MA: Harvard UP, 1920–22 Loeb Classical Library

Suetonius, *De Vita Caesarum libri VIII*, ed. M. Ihm, Leipzig, 1908

Tacitus, *C. Cornelii Taciti opera quae exstant. Ex recognitione Iani Gruteri,* Francofurti, E collegio Paltheniano, sumtibus Ionae Rhodii, 1607

——, *Opera quae exstant, a Iusto Lipsio postremum recensita,* etc…, *item C. Velleius Paterculus* etc…, Antwerp (Plantin) 1648

——, *The Annals of Tacitus*, ed. H. Furneaux, 2nd edn, Oxford 1896–1907, 2 vols.

——, *De origine et situ Germanorum*, ed. J. Anderson, Oxford 1922/39

——, *Historiarum libri*, ed. C. Fisher, Oxford 1924/1967

——, *Histories* 1, ed. & comm. by Cynthia Damon, Cambridge UP, 2003

Secondary literature

'Cai Rantzau' in: *Dansk Biografisk Lexikon*, ed. C. Bricka, Kopenhagen 1887–1905, vol. 13, pp. 404–405

Abbing, C., *Hugonis Grotii et Famiani Stradae Latinititas. Loca selecta e Grotii Annalibus et Stradae, De Bello Belgico, Decadibus*, Hoorn 1843

Baldini, U., 'Una fonte poco utilizzata per la storia intellettuale: le "censurae librorum" e "opinionum" nell' antica Compagnia di Jesu' in: *Jahrbuch des italienisch-deutschen Instituts in Trient* 11 (1985), pp. 19–68

Bass, M., *Insect Artifice. Nature and Art in the Dutch Revolt,* Princeton UP 2019

BeDuhn, J., 'The historical assessment of Speech Acts: Clarifications of Austin and Skinner for the study of religions', in: *Method and Theory in the Study of Religion*, vol. 14 no. 1 (2002), pp. 84–113

Bell, J., *Hugo Grotius Historian*, Ph.D. diss., Columbia 1973

Blok, P., *Het Advies der Spaanse Inquisitie*, s.l. 1907

Boot, J.C.G., 'Hugo Grotius et Cornelius Tacitus', in: *Verslagen & Mededelingen van de Koninklijke Academie van Wetenschappen afd. Letterkunde*, 2e reeks, 12 (1883), pp. 333–362

Borschberg, P., ' "Commentarius in Theses XI". Ein unveröffentlichtes Kurzwerk von Hugo Grotius' in: *Zeitschrift der Savigny-Stiftung für Rechtsgeschichte* vol. 109 (1992), pp. 450–474

——, "Grotius, the Social Contract and Political Resistance. A study of the Unpublished Theses LVI' in: *IILJ Working Paper* 2006/7

Bremmer, R., 'Het beleg en ontzet van Leiden (1574): een venster op de opstand', *Nederlands Archief voor Kerkgeschiedenis* 47 (1965) pp. 166–183

Broersma, R., en G. Busken Huet, 'Brieven over het Leycestersche tijdvak uit de papieren van Jean Hotman', in: *Bijdragen en Mededeelingen van het Historische Genootschap*, vol. 34 (1913), pp. 1–271

Brooke, C., 'Grotius, Stoicism and 'Oikeiosis', in: *Grotiana* vol. 29-1 (2008), pp. 25–50

Brouwer, J., *Kronieken van Spaansche soldaten uit het begin van den Tachtigjarigen Oorlog*, Zutphen 1933; repr. Zutphen 1980

Brummel, L., *Twee ballingen 's lands tijdens onze opstand tegen Spanje; Hugo Blotius (1534–1608) Emanuel van Meteren (1535–1612)*, The Hague 1972

Burke, P., 'Tacitism, Scepticism and Reason of State' in: J. Burns & M. Goldie (eds.), *The Cambridge History of Political Thought 1450–1700*, Cambridge UP, 1991, pp. 479–498

——, 'Tacitism' in: T. Dorey (ed.), *Tacitus*, London (Routledge) 1969, pp. 149–171

——, 'The Politics of Reformation History: Burnet and Brandt', in: A.C. Duke and C.A. Tamse (eds.), *Clio's Mirror, Historiography in Britain and the Netherlands*, Zutphen 1985, pp. 73–85.

Cifres, A., ‚Das historische Archiv der Kongregation für die Glaubenslehre in Rom', in: *Historische Zeitschrift* 268 (1999), pp. 97–106

Churchill, W., *Watermarks in paper in Holland, England, France, etc. in the XVII and XVIII centuries and their interconnection*, Amsterdam (Hertzberger) 1935

Clarke, J., 'Abbe Jean-Paul Bignon "Moderator of the Academies" and Royal Librarian', in: *French Historical Studies*, Vol. 8, No. 2 (1973), pp. 213–235

Clerici, A., 'Trust, Heresy and Rebellion: Reactions to Machiavelli in the early Dutch Revolt' in: L. Kontler and M. Somos (eds), *Trust and Happiness in the History of European Political Thought*, Leiden (Brill) 2018, pp. 257–280

Cools, H., and H. de Valk, *Institutum Neerlandicum MCMIV-MMIV. Honderd jaar Nederlands Instituut te Rome*, Hilversum 2004

Cornelissen, J., 'Hugo de Groot's Annales et Historiae op den Index', in: *Mededelingen Nederlands Historisch Instituut Rome* 8 (1928), pp. 161–172

——, 'Hugo de Groot op den Index', in: *Miscellanea historica in honorem Leonis van der Essen*, 2 vols., Brussels 1947, vol. II, pp. 757–768

——, *Hooft en Tacitus. Bijdrage tot de kennis van de vaderlandsche geschiedenis in de eerste helft der 17de eeuw*, Utrecht/Nijmegen 1938; reprint in: J.D.M. Cornelissen, *De Eendracht van het Land. Cultuurhistorische studies over Nederland in de zestiende en zeventiende eeuw*. Met een essay over leven en werk door E.O.G. Haitsma Mulier en A.E.M. Janssen, Amsterdam (De Batafse Leeuw) 1987, pp. 53–102

Craig, P., 'Chronology of Colonial Swedes on the Delaware 1638–1713' in: *Swedish Colonial News*, Volume 2, Number 5 (2001).

Damon, C., '"Tritus in eo lector": Grotius' emendations to the text of Tacitus', in: *Grotiana* vol. 29 (2008), pp. 133–148

Delisle, L., *Inventaire des manuscrits de Notre-Dame et d'autres fonds conservés à la Bibliotheque Nationale sous les numeros 16719–18613 du Fonds Latin*, Paris 1871

Deneire, T., 'The Philology of Justus Lipsius' Prose Style', *Wiener Studien* vol. 125 (2012), pp. 189–262

Den Tex, J., *Oldenbarnevelt vol. II Oorlog 1588–1609*, Haarlem 1962

Descendre, R., 'Ragion di Stato', in: *Enciclopedia machiavelliana*, vol. II, Istituto della Enciclopedia italiana fondata da Giovanni Treccani, 2014, pp. 382–384

Draeger, A., *Syntax und Stil des Tacitus*, Leipzig 1882; repr. Amsterdam 1967

Droetto, A., 'Il Tacitismo nella storiografia Groziana' in: id., *Studi Groziani*, Torino 1968, pp. 101–151 (Pubblicazioni dell' Istituto di scienze politiche dell' Università di Torino, vol. 18)

Eeghen, P. van & J. van der Kellen, *Het werk van Jan en Casper Luyken*, Amsterdam (Frederik Muller) 1905

Enzinas, F. de, *Bericht over de Toestand in de Nederlanden en de godsdienst bij de Spanjaarden*, ed. by C. Heesakkers en T. Osinga, Hilversum 2002

Everts, P., *De Tacitea historiae conscribendae ratione*, Ph.D. diss. Utrecht; publ. Kerkrade 1926

Eyffinger, A., 'Het Parallelon Rerumpublicarum van Hugo de Groot' in: Z. von Martels, P. Steenbakkers & A. Vanderjagt, *Limae Labor et Mora. Opstellen voor Fokke Akkerman ter gelegenheid van zijn zeventigste verjaardag*, Leende 2000

——, 'Amoena gravitate morum spectabilis – Justus Lipsius and Hugo Grotius' in: *The world of Justus Lipsius: A contribution towards his intellectual biography*, ed. by M. Laureys, Proceedings of a colloquium in the Belgian Historical Institute in Rome, 22-24 May 1997, Brussels (Belgisch Historisch Instituut te Rome), 1998, pp. 297–328

——, 'Justus Lipsius and Hugo Grotius: Two views on Society' in: *Lipsius in Leiden*, ed. by K. Enenkel and C. Heesakers, Voorthuizen (Florivallis) 1997

——, P. de Boer, J. Schmidt and L. van Holk, 'De Republica Emendanda: a juvenile tract by Hugo Grotius on the emendation of the Dutch polity' in: *Grotiana* NS vol. 5 (1984)

Eysinga, W. van, 'Eene onuitgegeven Nota van De Groot', in: *Mededelingen van de K.N.A.W. afd Letterkunde, Nieuwe Reeks* vol. 18 (1955), pp. 235–252

——, *Sparsa Collecta*, Leiden (Sijthof) 1958

——, 'De Groots Jodenreglement' in: *Mededelingen der Koninklijke Nederlandse Academie van Wetenschappen afd. Letterkunde* NR vol. 13.1 (1950)

Friedeburg, R. von, and J. Morrill (eds), *Monarchy Transformed. Princes and their Elites in early modern Western Europe*, Cambridge UP 2017

Fruin, R., 'Meursius' geschiedenis van het bestand', in: idem, *Verspreide Geschriften* vol. VII, The Hague 1903

——, *Geschiedenis der staatsinstellingen in Nederland tot den val der Republiek*, 2nd edition, The Hague 1922

——, *Verspreide Geschriften* vol. iii, ed. P. Blok, P. Muller and S. Muller Fz., The Hague 1901

Fruytier, J. 'Hubert Loyens' in: *Nieuw Nederlandsch Biografisch Woordenboek* vol. 6 (1924), p. 971

Fumaroli, M., *L'âge de l'éloquence: rhétorique et "res literaria" de la Renaissance au seuil de l'époque classique*, Geneva 1980

Fueter, E., *Geschichte der Neueren Historiographie*, München & Berlin 1911

Garrison, J., *A History of Sixteenth Century France, 1483–1598: Renaissance, Reformation and Rebellion,* London 1995

Gaudriault, R., *Filigranes et autres caractéristiques des papiers fabriqués en France aux XVIIe et XVIIIe siècles*, Paris 1995

Gelderen, M. van (ed.), *The Dutch Revolt*, Cambridge 1993, Cambridge Texts in the history of political thought

Geurts, P., *De graaf van Horne: Filips van Montmorency, 1524–1568,* Zaltbommel 1968

——, *De Nederlandse Opstand in de Pamfletten 1566–1584*, 1956 / Repr. Utrecht (HES) 1978

Godman, P., *The Saint as Censor. Robert Bellarmine between Inquisition and Index*, Leiden (Brill) 2000

Graaf, B. de, 'Grotius' Annales et Historiae de rebus Belgicis. De beide uitgaven van 1657 nader beschouwd' in: *Van pen tot laser. Opstellen aangeboden aan Ernst Braches*, Amsterdam 1996

Grafton, A., *What was History? The Art of History in Early Modern Europe*, Cambridge UP, 2007

——, *Athenae Batavae. The Research Imperative at Leiden, 1575–1650*, Leiden (Primavera Pers) 2003, Scaliger Lectures 1

Grendler, P., ' Printing and Censorship', in: C. Schmitt & Q. Skinner (eds.), *The Cambridge History of Renaissance Philosophy*, Cambridge UP 1988, pp. 25–54

Groenveld, S., *Evidente factiën in den staet: Sociaal-politieke verhoudingen in de 17e-eeuwse Republiek der Verenigde Nederlanden*, Hilversum (Verloren) 1990, *Zeven Provinciën* series vol. 1

——, *Hooft als historieschrijver. Twee Studies*, Weesp (Eureka) 1981

Grootens, P.L.M., *Dominicus Baudius. Een levensschets uit het Leidse humanistenmilieu 1561–1613*, Nijmegen and Utrecht 1942

Haak, S., *Paullus Merula 1558–1607*, Zutphen 1901

Haitsma Mulier, E., 'Grotius, Hooft and the Writing of History in the Dutch Republic' in: A.C. Duke and C.A. Tamse eds., *Clio's Mirror* (Britain and the Netherlands 8, 1985), pp. 55–72

——,'Willem van Oranje in de historiografie van de zeventiende eeuw' in: id. & A. Jansen (eds), *Willem van Oranje in de historie 1584–1984. Vier eeuwen beeldvorming en geschiedschrijving*, Utrecht 1984

——, G. van der Lem and P. Knevel, *Repertorium van Geschiedschrijvers in Nederland 1500–1800*, The Hague 1990

——, *Het Nederlandse gezicht van Machiavelli*, Hilversum 1989

Haverkorn van Rijsewijk, P., 'Het huis "In duizend vreezen"', in: *Rotterdamsch Jaarboekje* vol. 2 (1890), pp. 129–132

Heesakkers, C., 'Grotius als geschiedsschrijver' in: *Het Delfts Orakel. Hugo de Groot*, Delft, 1983, pp. 103–110

Helmers, H., 'Foreign News in Times of Domestic Crisis: the Truce Conflicts, the Thirty Years' War and the Rise of the Dutch Newspaper' in: A. Wilkinson and G. Kemp (eds.), *Negotiating Conflict and Controversy in the Early Modern Book World*, Leiden 2019, pp. 253–268

——, 'Angstcultuur en complotdenken tijdens het Bestand', *Tijdschrift voor Geschiedenis*, vol. 134-2 (2021), pp. 230–253

Hengst, D. den., 'Naturalis sermonis pulchritudo?' in: *Grotiana* vol. 29 (2008), pp. 77–84

Hollstein, F., *Dutch and Flemisch Etchings and Engravings* vol. 11, Roosendaal 1994

Irish, B., 'The Literary Afterlife of the Essex Circle: Fulke Greville, Tacitus, and BL Additional MS 18638' in: *Modern Philology* 112 (2014), pp. 271–285

Israel, J., *The Dutch Republic: Its rise, greatness, and fall, 1477–1806*, Oxford (Clarendon Press) 1995

Ittersum, M. van., *Profit and Principle: Hugo Grotius, Natural Rights Theories and the Rise of Dutch Power in the East Indies, 1595–1615*, Leiden 2006

——,'The Working Methods of Hugo Grotius: Which Sources Did He Use and How Did He Use Them In His Early Writings on Natural Law Theory', in: P. du Plessis & J. Cairns (eds.), *Reassessing Legal Humanism and its Claims*, Edinburgh UP 2016, pp. 154–193

——, 'Confiscated Manuscripts And Books: What Happened to the Personal Library and Archive of Hugo Grotius Following His Arrest on Charges of High Treason in August 1618?' in: Flavia Bruni & Andrew Pettegree (eds.), *Lost Books: Reconstructing the Print World of Pre-Industrial Europe*, Leiden (Brill) 2016, pp. 362–385, Library of the Written Word – The Handpress World 46

——, *The Working Papers of Hugo Grotius: How a Process of Transmission, Dispersal and Loss Shaped a Jurist's Legacy to the Modern World, 1604–1864* Leiden (Brill); forthcoming)

Janssen, A., `A `Trias Historica' on the Revolt of the Netherlands: Emanuel van Meteren, Pieter Bor and Everhard van Reyd as Exponents of Contemporary Historiography' in: A.C. Duke and C.A. Tamse (eds.), *Clio's Mirror, Historiography in Britain and the Netherlands*, Zutphen 1985, pp. 9–30

——,'Prins Willem van Oranje in het oordeel van tijdgenoten' in: id. & E. Haitsma Mulier (eds), *Willem van Oranje in de historie, 1584–1984. Vier eeuwen beeldvorming en geschiedschrijving*, Utrecht 1984

——, 'Grotius als Geschichtsschreiber', in: *The World of Hugo Grotius*, Amsterdam 1984, pp. 161–178

Jansen, J., *Brevitas. Beschouwingen over de beknoptheid van vorm en stijl in de renaissance*, Hilversum (Verloren) 1995, 2 vols.

——, *Imitatio. Literaire navolging* (imitatio auctorum) *in de Europese letterkunde van de renaissance (1500–1700)*, Hilversum (Verloren) 2008

Janssen, L., *Hugo Grotius, antiquarianism and the Gothic myth. A critical study of the ideological dimension and methodological foundation of the Historia Gotthorum (1655)*, Ph.D. diss. Louvain 2016

Jensen, L., (ed), *The Roots of Nationalism. National Identity Formation in Early Modern Europe, 1600–1815*, Amsterdam 2016

Jong, M.A.G. de, 'De bewapening van het Staatse Leger 1590–1621', *Armamentaria* 32, Jaarboek Legermuseum 1997-8, pp. 7–21

Jonge, H.J. de, 'The Study of the New Testament' in: *Leiden University in the Seventeenth Century*, Leiden (Brill) 1975, pp. 65–110

Jorink, E., *Reading the Book of Nature in the Dutch Golden Age, 1575–1715*, Leiden 2010

Kalff, G., *Geschiedenis der Nederlandse Letterkunde* vol. III, Groningen 1907

Kaplan, B., *Calvinists and Libertines: Confession and Community in Utrecht, 1578–1620,* Oxford (Clarendon Press) 1995

Kattenberg, L., 'Military rebellion and reason of state. Pacification in the Habsburg Army of Flanders, 1599–1601', in: *Bijdragen en Mededelingen betreffende de geschiedenis der Nederlanden* 131-2 (2016), pp. 3–21

Kerviler, R., 'Les Bignons: Grand Maitres de la Bibliothèque du Roi', in: *Le bibliophile français* 6 (1872), pp. 275–283, 300–312, 322–342

Klink, H., *Opstand, politiek en religie bij Willem van Oranje, 1559–1568. Een thematische biografie*, Heerenveen 1997

Klönne, B., 'Leonardus Marius en Hugo de Groot' in: *De Katholiek. Godsdienstig, geschied- en letterkundig maandschrift*, no. 95 (1889), pp. 337–350

——, 'Nogmaals Leonardus Marius en Hugo de Groot' in: *De Katholiek. Godsdienstig, geschied- en letterkundig maandschrift*, no. 96 (1889), pp. 220–225

Kossmann, E., 'Volkssouvereiniteit aan het begin van het Nederlandse ancien régime', in: *Bijdragen en Mededelingen Betreffende de Geschiedenis der Nederlanden*, 95-1, (1980), pp. 1–34

——, 'Bodin, Althusius en Parker, of: over de moderniteit van de Nederlandse opstand' (1958); repr. in: id., *Politieke Theorie en Geschiedenis*, Amsterdam 1987, pp. 93–111

——, & A. Mellink, *Texts concerning the Revolt of the Netherlands*, Cambridge UP 1975

Kramm, C., *De levens en werken der Hollandsche en Vlaamsche kunstschilders, beeldhouwers, graveurs en bouwmeesters van den vroegsten tot op onzen tijd*, deel 5, Amsterdam 1861

Kuyk, J. van., 'Lijst van Nederlanders, studenten te Orléans (1441–1602)', in: *Bijdragen en Mededeelingen van het Historisch Genootschap* vol. 34 (1913), pp. 293–349

Laes, C., and T. Van Houdt, 'Over Goten Germanen en Indianen: de controverse Grotius-De Laet', in: *De Zeventiende Eeuw* vol. 25:1 (2009) pp. 120–136

Lagatz, T., & S. Schratz (eds), *Censor Censorum. Gesammelte Aufsätze von Herman H. Schwedt. Festschrift zum 70. Geburtstag*, Paderborn 2006

Laureys, M., 'Sine amore, sine odio partium': Nicolaus Burgundius' Historia Belgica (1629) and his Tacitean quest for an Appropriate past' in: K. Enenkel and K. Ottenhey (eds.),

The Quest for an Appropriate Past in Literature, Art and Architecture, Leiden (Brill) 2018, Intersections vol 60, pp. 397–417

Leeman, A., 'De functie van de dramatisering bij Tacitus', *Lampas*, 7 (1974), pp. 368–377

Lenarduzzi, C., 'De oude geusen teghen de nieuwe geusen' in: *Holland, Historisch Tijdschrift* 43 (2011), pp. 65–81

——, *Katholiek in de Republiek: De belevingswereld van een religieuze minderheid 1570–1750,* Nijmegen (Vantilt) 2019

Lesaffer, R., & J. Nijman (eds.), *The Cambridge Companion to Hugo Grotius,* Cambridge UP 2021

Leumann-Hofmann-Szantyr, *Lateinische Grammatik*, bd. 2 Syntax und Stilistik, München 1965

Löfstedt, E., 'Stilgeschichtliche Gesichtspunkte' in: id., *Syntactica.* Studien und Beiträge zur historischen Syntax des Lateins, 2 vols, Lund 1933–1942

——, 'The Style of Tacitus', in: id., *Roman Literary Portraits*, Oxford 1958

MacCaffrey, W., *Queen Elizabeth and the Making of Policy, 1572–1588,* Princeton UP 1981

Marnef, G., *Antwerpen in de tijd van de Reformatie,* Amsterdam and Antwerp 1996

Martin, R., *Tacitus*, London 1981

Meinecke, F., *Die Idee der Staatsräson in der Neueren Geschichte*, Munich and Berlin (R. Oldenbourg) 1925

Mellor, R., *Tacitus,* New York (Routledge) 1994

Menge, H., *Repetitorium der lateinischen Syntax und Stilistik*, 17. Auflage, Darmstadt 1979

Meulen, J. ter & P. Diermanse, *Bibliographie des écrits sur Hugo Grotius imprimés au XVIIe siècle,* The Hague (Nijhoff) 1961

Miert, D. van & H. Nellen, 'Media en tolerantie in de Republiek der Letteren. De discussie over Isaac de la Peyrère (ca. 1596–1676) en zijn pre-Adamitae' in: *De Zeventiende Eeuw* 30 (2014), pp. 3–19

Miller, P., *Peiresc's Europe. Learning and Virtue in the Seventeenth Century*, New Haven and London, (Yale UP) 2000

Momigliano, A., 'The first political commentary on Tacitus' in: *The Journal of Roman Studies* Vol. 37 (1947), pp. 91–101, 92.

Morrill, J., 'Dynasties, Realms, Peoples and State Formation 1500–1720', in: id. & R. von Friedeburg (eds), *Monarchy Transformed. Princes and their Elites in early modern Western Europe*, Cambridge UP 2017

Motley, J., *History of the United Netherlands from the death of William the Silent to the Twelve Years' Truce-1609*, (4 vols), The Hague 1867

——, *The Rise of the Dutch Republic. A History,* London (Routledge), no year, 3 vols. [first printed 1856]

Mout, N., 'Justus Lipsius between war and peace. His public letter on Spanish foreign policy and the respective merits of war, peace or truce (1595)', in: J. Pollmann & A. Spicer (eds.), *Public Opinion and Changing Identities in the Early Modern Netherlands*, Leiden – Boston, 2007, pp. 142–162

Muller, H., *Hugo de Groot's Annales et Historiae,* Ph.D. Utrecht, 1919

Müller, L., *Geschichte der klassischen Philologie in den Niederlanden,* Leipzig 1869

Nellen, H., 'The significance of *Grollae Obsidio* in the development of Grotius' relations with the fatherland', in: *LIAS* 11 (1984) pp. 1–17

——, ' "Het Leidse haylichje". Hugo Grotius in de twintigste eeuw', in: *Jaarboek van de Maatschappij der Nederlandse Letterkunde* 1995, pp. 37–58 (originally presented as a public lecture at the *dies* celebration of the Leiden Classics students' society E.D.E.P.O.L., 28-10-1995)

——, *Hugo Grotius. A Lifelong Struggle for Peace in Church and State,* Leiden (Brill) 2015

——, *Geen vredestichter is zonder tegensprekers. Hugo de Groot; geleerde, staatsman, verguisd verzoener,* Amsterdam (Polak & Van Gennep) 2021

—— and J. Trapman (eds.), *De Hollandse jaren van Hugo de Groot (1583–1621): Lezingen van het colloquium ter gelegenheid van de 350-ste sterfdag van Hugo de Groot ('s-Gravenhage, 31 augustus–1 september 1995),* Hilversum (Verloren) 1996

Niekerk, J.P. van, *The Development of the Principles of Insurance Law in the Netherlands 1500–1800,* Cape Town 1998

Nierop, H. van., 'De troon van Alva. Over de interpretatie van de Nederlandse Opstand' in: *Bijdragen en Mededelingen betreffende de Geschiedenis der Nederlanden* 110 (1995), pp. 205–223

Nuyens, W., *Geschiedenis der Nederlandsche Beroerten in de XVIe eeuw* vol. 2, Amsterdam (Van Langenhuysen) 1868

Onnekink, D., 'Casiodoro de Reina' in: "*Een pilaar in de tempel mijns Gods". Geloofsvervolgingen in Spanje,* Middelburg 2009, see http://www.theologienet.nl/documenten/Haamstede-Martelaren%20in%20Spanje.pdf

Oosterhoff, F., *Leicester and the Netherlands 1586–1587,* Utrecht 1988, Hes studia historica 16

Oosterhout, M. van, *Hugo Grotius' Occasional Poetry (1609–1645),* PhD Nijmegen 2009

Otterspeer, W., *Het bolwerk van de vrijheid. De Leidse universiteit 1575–1672,* Amsterdam 2000

Papy, J., 'Lipsius' (Neo-) Stoicism: constancy between Christian faith and Stoic virtue', in: H. Blom and L. Winkel (eds.), *Grotius and the Stoa,* Assen (Van Gorcum) 2004 (= *Grotiana* vol. 22/23)

Parker, G., 'Mutiny and Discontent in the Spanish Army of Flanders 1572–1607', in: *Past & Present* 58 (1973), pp. 38–52

——, *The General Crisis of the 17th Century,* London 1978

——, *The Imprudent King. A new life of Philip II,* New Haven (Yale UP) 2014

Philo, J.-M., 'Elizabeth I's Translation of Tacitus: Lambeth Palace Library, MS 683' in: *Review of English Studies, New Series* (2019), pp. 1–30

Piccard, G., *Wasserzeichen Horn,* Stuttgart (Kohlhammer) 1979

Pintard, R., *La Mothe le Vayer, Gassendi, Guy Patin. Études de bibliographie et de critique suivies de textes inédits de Guy Patin,* Paris (Boivin) 1943

Poel, M. van der, and J. Waszink, ‚Tacitismus' in: *Historisches Wörterbuch der Rhetorik,* ed. G. Ueding, vol. 9, Tübingen (Max Niemeyer Verlag) 2009, col. 1113–1123

——, 'Tacitean Elements in Grotius' narrative of the Capture of Breda (1590) by Stadtholder Maurice, Count of Nassau (Historiae, book 2)', in: *Grotiana* vol. 30 (2009), pp. 207–246

Poelhekke, J., *Het verraad van de pistoletten?,* Amsterdam and London 1975

Pollmann, J., *Religious choice in the Dutch Republic. The reformation of Arnoldus Buchelius (1565–1641),* Manchester UP 1999

——, *Herdenken, herinneren, vergeten. Het beleg en ontzet van Leiden in de Gouden Eeuw*, Leiden 2008

——, 'Hij had geen oog op zijn tijd'. Robert Fruins gebruik van egodocumenten als bron voor de cultuurgeschiedenis' In: P. Herman & H. te Velde (eds.) *Het vaderlandse verleden. Robert Fruin en de Nederlandse geschiedschrijving,* Amsterdam (Bert Bakker) 2010, pp. 60–81

——, 'Met grootvaders bloed bezegeld. Over religie en herinneringscultuur in de zeventiende-eeuwse Nederlanden' in: *De Zeventiende Eeuw* 29 (2013), pp. 154–175

——, ' "Brabanters do fairly resemble Spaniards after all." Memory, Propaganda and Identity in the Twelve Years' Truce', in: J. Pollmann & Andrew Spicer (eds.), *Public Opinion and Changing Identities in the Early Modern Netherlands.* Essays in Honour of Alastair Duke, Leiden (Brill) 2007, pp. 211–228

Postma, F., *Viglius van Aytta als humanist en diplomaat 1507–1549*, Zutphen 1983

——, *Viglius van Aytta. De jaren met Granvelle 1549–1564*, Zutphen 2000

Rabbie, E., 'An Illegal Manuscript Copy of Hugo Grotius' Ordinum Hollandiae Ac Westfrisiae Pietas (1613)', in: *Nederlands Archief voor Kerkgeschiedenis*, vol. 74.2, (1994), pp. 162–172

——, 'Grotius' denken over kerk en staat', in: H.J.M. Nellen and J. Trapman (eds.), *De Hollandse jaren van Hugo de Groot (1583–1621): Lezingen van het colloquium ter gelegenheid van de 350-ste sterfdag van Hugo de Groot ('s-Gravenhage, 31 augustus–1 september 1995),* Hilversum (Verloren) 1996, pp. 193–206

——, 'Grotius, James I and the Ius Circa Sacra' in: *Grotiana* vol. 24–26 (2003–4), pp. 25–39

Ridderikhoff, C., 'Een aristocratische geschiedenis van de Opstand: Grotius "Annales et Historiae de rebus Belgicis". *De Zeventiende Eeuw,* 10-2 (1994), pp. 277–291

Rodríques Perez, Y., *De tachtigjarige oorlog in Spaanse ogen de Nederlanden in Spaanse historische en literaire teksten (circa 1548–1673)*, Nijmegen (Vantilt) 2003

Rogier, L., *Eenheid en Scheiding,* Utrecht 1968

——, *Geschiedenis van het Katholicisme in Noord-Nederland in de 16e en de 17e eeuw* Amsterdam (Urbi et Orbi), 1947

Sandys, J., *History of Classical Scholarship*, Cambridge 1908

Santoro L'Hoir, F., *Tragedy, Rhetoric, and the Historiography of Tacitus' Annales,* Ann Arbor (University of Michigan Press) 2006

Schenk, M., & A. van Schelven (eds.), *Geschriften van 1568. Verantwoordinge, verklaringhe ende waerschowinghe mitsgaders eene hertgrondighe begheerte des edelen, lancmoedighen ende hooghgeboren Princen van Oraengien,* Amsterdam 1933

Schmidt, B., 'Space, time, travel: Hugo de Groot, Johannes de Laet, and the advancement of geographic learning', in: *Lias* 25 (1998), pp. 177–199

Schwedt, H., *Die römische Inquisition. Kardinäle und Konsultoren1601 bis 1700*, Freiburg 2017

Seaward, P., 'Clarendon, Tacitism, and the Civil Wars of Europe', in: *Huntington Library Quarterly* 68 (2005), pp. 289–311

Shirley, R., *The Mapping of the World. Early Printed World Maps 1472–1700*, London 1983, Holland Press Cartographica series vol. 9

Sicking, C., 'Inleiding', in: *Bataafs Athene. Een bloemlezing van klassiek Griekse poëzie van de hand van Leidse humanisten van de zestiende tot en met de twintigste eeuw*, ed. Collegium Classicum cui nomen M.F., Leiden 1993

Sierhuis, F., *The Literature of the Arminian Controversy. Religion, Politics and the Stage in the Dutch Republic*, Oxford UP 2015

Sinclair, P., *Tacitus the Sententious Historian. A sociology of rhetoric in Annales 1-6*, Pennsylvania State UP 1995

Smith, W., *A Dictionary of Greek and Roman Antiquities*, London 1875

Soen, V., 'Philip II's Quest. The Appointment of Governors-General during the Dutch Revolt (1559–1598)' in: *Bijdragen en Mededelingen betreffende de geschiedenis der Nederlanden*, vol 126-1 (2011), pp. 3–29

——, *Vredehandel. Adellijke en Habsburgse verzoeningspogingen tijdens de Nederlandse Opstand (1564–1581)*, Amsterdam UP 2012

Soll, J., 'The reception of The Prince 1513–1700, or why we understand Machiavelli the way we do', in: *Social Research: An International Quarterly*, Vol. 81/1 (2014), pp. 31–60

Somos, M., 'Enter Secularisation: Heinsius's De Tragoediae constitutione' in: *History of European Ideas*, vol. 36-1 (2010), pp. 19–38

——, 'Secularization in De iure praedae: from Bible Criticism to International Law', in: *Grotiana* vol. 26–28 (2005–2007), pp. 147–191

——, *Secularisation and the Leiden Circle,* Leiden (Brill) 2011

Spaans, J., 'Public opinion or cultural celebration of concord? Politics, religion and society in competition between the chambers of rhetoric at Vlaardingen in 1616', in: J. Pollmann & Andrew Spicer (eds.), *Public Opinion and Changing Identities in the Early Modern Netherlands*. Essays in Honour of Alastair Duke, Leiden (Brill) 2007, pp. 188–209

——, Review of *Remonstrantie... Joden*, edd. Kromhout & Offenberg in: *Grotiana* vol. 41-1 (2020), pp. 246–250

Spruit, J., *Cunabula Juris: elementen van het Romeinse privaatrecht*, Deventer 2001 (and later)

Steen, J. van der, *Memory Wars in the Low Countries 1566–1700*, Leiden (Brill) 2015

Stevin, S., *Het burgherlick leven & anhangh*, ed. by Pim den Boer; transl. [into modern Dutch] by A. Fleurkens, Amsterdam 2001

Stolleis, M., *Arcana imperii und Ratio status: Bemerkungen zur politischen Theorie des frühen 17. Jahrhunderts*, Göttingen (Vandenhoeck & Ruprecht), 1980

Storoni-Mazzolani, L., *Empire without End*, New York (Harcourt) 1976

Strauman, B., 'Appetitus Societatis and Oikeiosis. Hugo Grotius' Ciceronian argument in favour of natural law and just war', in: *Grotiana* vol. 24/25 (2003–2004), pp. 41–66.

Swart, K., *Willem van Oranje en de Nederlandse Opstand 1572–1584*, ingel. door A. Duke & J. Israel, bezorgd door R. Fagel, M. Mout & H. van Nierop, The Hague 1994

Syme, R., *Tacitus*, Oxford 1958, 2 vols.

Tex, J. Den, Oldenbarnevelt vol. II, *Oorlog 1588–1609*, Haarlem 1962

——, *Oldenbarnevelt* vol. III, *Het bestand 1609–1619*, Haarlem 1966

Toffanin, G., *Machiavelli e il 'Tacitismo'. La Politica storica al tempo della Controriforma*, Padova, (Angelo Draghi) 1921; repr. Napoli (Guida Editori) 1972

Tschudin, W., *The ancient paper-mills of Basle and their marks*, Hilversum (Paper publications society) 1958

Tuck, R., *Philosophy and Government 1572–1651*, Cambridge UP 1993, Ideas in Context 26

Tully, J., 'The pen is a mighty sword. Quentin Skinner's analysis of politics', in: *British Journal of Political Science*, vol. 13 no. 4 (1983), pp. 489–509

Vermaseren, B., 'Humanistische drama's over de moord op de vader des vaderlands', in: *Tijdschrift voor Nederlandse Taal- en Letterkunde,* vol. 68 (1951), pp. 31–67

——, *De katholieke Nederlandse geschiedschrijving in de 16e en 17e eeuw over de opstand,* Leeuwarden 1981

Viroli, M., *From Politics to Reason of State. The Acquisition and Transformation of the Language of Politics 1250–1600*, Cambridge UP 1992, Ideas in Context 22

Voss, B.-R., *Die pointierte Stil des Tacitus*, Münster 1963

Vroomen, I., *De Taal van de Republiek. Het gebruik van vaderlandretoriek in Nederlandse pamfletten, 1618–1672*, PhD Erasmus University Rotterdam 2012

Vugt, Y. van, and J. Waszink, 'Politiek in Hoofts Baeto: De middenweg als uitweg?' in: *Tijdschrift Voor Nederlandsche Taal- en Letterkunde,* 116-1(2000) pp. 2–22

Waard, J. de, *De portretten van Marnix van St. Aldegonde: Een ikonografische verkenning*, Deventer (Sub Rosa) 1988, Deventer Studiën 4

Wansink, H., and C. Wels (eds.), *Zeven pijlen, negen pennen. Negen Nederlandse historici over de vaderlandsche geschiedenis,* Zeist (W. de Haan) 1963

Wansink, H., *Politieke Wetenschappen aan de Leidse Universiteit*, Utrecht 1981

Waszink, J. 'Hugo Grotius on the agglomerate polity of Philip II', in: *History of European Ideas*, Volume 46-3 (2020), pp. 276–291

——, 'A nouveau agenda de recherche: Origins of Secularisation, Tacitism', in: C. Secretan and D. Antoine-Mahut (eds.), *Les Pays-Bas aux XVIIe et XVIIIe siècles. Nouveaux regards*, Paris 2015, pp. 217–238

——, 'Grotius as Historian' in: R. Lesaffer & J. Nijman (eds.), *The Cambridge Companion to Hugo Grotius,* Cambridge UP 2021

——, 'Henry Savile's Tacitus and the English role on the Continent: Leicester, Hotman, Lipsius', in: *History of European Ideas*, vol. 42-3 (2016), pp. 303–319

——, 'Lipsius and Grotius: Tacitism' in: *History of European Ideas,* vol. 39-2 (2013), pp. 151–168

——, 'Oldenbarnevelt and Fishes. Satirical Prints from the 12-Years Truce', in: *History of European Ideas* vol. 46.7 (2020), pp. 903–915

——, 'Shifting Tacitisms. Style and Composition in Grotius' Annales' in: *Grotiana* vol. 29 (2008), pp. 85–132

——, 'The Low Countries: constitution, nationhood and character according to Hugo Grotius', in: L. Jensen (ed.), *The Roots of Nationalism. National Identity Formation in Early Modern Europe 1600–1815,* Amsterdam UP 2016, pp. 135–152

——, 'University and Court: the case of Leiden, 1572–1618' in: B. Lindberg (ed.), *Early Modern Academic Culture*, Stockholm 2019 (Kungl. vitterhets historie och antikvitets akademien, Konferenser 97)

——, 'Hugo Grotius' Annales et Historiae de rebus Belgicis from the Evidence in his Correspondence, 1604–1644', in: *LIAS* 31-2 (2004), pp. 249–267

——, 'New documents on the prohibition of Grotius' Annales et Historiae by the Roman Index' in: *Grotiana* vol. 24-25, (2003–2004), pp. 77–139

——,'Tacitism in Holland: Hugo Grotius' Annales et Historiae de rebus Belgicis' in: Rhoda Schnur (ed.), *Acta Conventus Neo-Latini Bonnensis: Proceedings of the 12th International Congress of Neo-Latin Studies* (Bonn 2003). Medieval & Renaissance Texts & Studies vol. 315, 2006

Wells, G., 'The unlikely Machiavellian: William of Orange and the Princely Virtues' in: Ph. Mack & M., Jacob, (eds), *Politics and Culture in Early Modern Europe. Essays in honour of H. G. Koenigsberger*, Cambridge 1987

Womersley, D., 'Sir Henry Savile's Translation of Tacitus and the Political Interpretation of Elizabethan Texts', in: The Review of English Studies, 42, no. 167 (1991), p. 313–342

ILLUSTRATION CREDITS

We thank the following institutions for the permission to reproduce the images from their collections:

Leiden University Library
Radboud University Library, Nijmegen
Rijksmuseum Amsterdam

The Latin editions of 1657–58 contain no images except a portrait by Grotius in the front matter. The portrait reproduced in this book (p. viii) is that from the 1658 edition.

The image of the Antwerp statue of Alva (p. 184) is reproduced from P.C. Hooft, *Nederlandsche Historien* vol. 1 (ed. Amsterdam 1703), p. 223 (courtesy of University Library Nijmegen).

The following images are taken from Joan Goris' Dutch translation of 1681 (see § 11.6, p. 105).

page number in 1681:		page number current edition:
p. 13	no. 1. *Portrait of Margareth of Parma*	141
p. 23	no. 2. *Iconoclastic fury*, Jan Luyken invenit et fecit (E&K 51)	166
p. 37	no. 3. *Portrait of the Duke of Alva*	167
p. 39	no. 4. *Capture of Den Briel* (perhaps by Jan Luyken?; E&K 52)	185
p. 41	no. 5. *Massacre at Naerden 1573*, Jan Luyken invenit et fecit (E&K54)	196
p. 46	no. 6. *Siege of Haarlem*, E. Decker fecit et invenit	197
p. 47	no. 7. *Portrait of Don Luis de Requesens*	206
p. 47	no. 8. *Siege of Alkmaar*, no sign., probably not by Jan Luyken	207
p. 49	no. 9. *Lifting of the siege of Leiden*, no sign., probably not by Jan Luyken	212

p. 55 no. 10. *Portrait of Mathias of Austria* 213

p. 65 no. 11. *Portrait of Alexander Farnese, Duke of Parma* 227

p. 77 no. 12. *Portrait of Francis of Valois, Duke of Anjou* 226

p. 77 no. 13. *Lifting of the siege of Cambrai*, Jan Luyken invenit et fecit (E&K 60) 260

p. 83 no. 14. *French attack on Antwerp*, Jan Luyken invenit et fecit (E&K 61) 261

p. 91 no. 15. *Portrait of William of Orange* 140

p. 91 no. 16. *Assassination of William of Orange*, R. de Hoge invenit Ian Luyken fecit (E&K 62) 282

p. 91 no. 17. *Tomb monument for William of Orange* (sign. 'I.L.'= Ian Luyken) (E&K 63) 283

p. 92 no. 18. *Portrait of Count Hohenlohe* 286

p. 98 no. 19. *Explosion of the ship-bridge at Antwerp*, E. Decker invenit et fecit 298

p. 99 no. 20. *Portrait of Marnix van St. Aldegonde* 299

p. 99 no. 21. *Siege of Antwerp*, I. Luyken fecit (E&K 64) 287

p. 101 no. 22. *Portrait of Robert Dudley, Earl of Leicester* 302

p. 104 no. 23. *Siege of Grave*, Jan Luyken invenit et fecit (E&K 65) 303

p. 117 no. 24. *Portrait of Johan van Oldenbarnevelt,* Andries Vaillant schulpsit 338

E&K = Eeghen, P. van & J.Ph. van der Kellen, *Het werk van Jan en Casper Luyken*, deel 1, Amsterdam 1905

The images in Appendix 4 (p. 398-399) are reproduced from the frontispiece and flyleaves of the Nijmegen copy of Pompeio Giustiniani's *Bellum Belgicum*.

The image in Appendix 5 (p. 401) is a satirical print on Johan van Oldenbarnevelt by Pieter Feddes van Harlingen, 1619, etching and engraving, coll. Rijksmuseum Amsterdam.

INDEX TO THE INTRODUCTION

Aarschot, Duke of 30, 59
Abbor, Robert 31
Abbing, C. 113
Act of Abjuration 2, 64, 84
Aethiopia 77
agglomerate polity 64, 65
Albert (Archduke of the Southern Netherlands, *see also there*) 65, 68
Alciatus, Andreas 38
Alva, Duke of 52
Amelot de la Houssaie, Abraham 39, 110
America, American 30, 68–70, 77–79
Amsterdam 3, 19, 42, 59, 85, 93, 99, 104, 105, 111
  Admiralty 16
  Athenaeum Illustre 111
ancient constitution, *see* constitutionalism
Anjou, Duke of 52
Antarctica 77
antiquarianism 75, 77, 79, 80
Antwerp 43, 52, 60, 84, 86
  Corte Verclaeringe 84
Arabia, Arab 93
Arata, Giovanni Battista 102–104, 384–390
Aristotle, Aristotelian 14, 73
Armada 54
Arminius, Jacobus; Arminianism (*see also* Remonstrants) 9, 11, 13, 16
Arnauld, Antoine 109
ars historica, *see* history
Asian trade (*see also* VOC) 4, 16, 17, 19, 67–70, 85, 89, 93, 121
astrology 54–56
Athens 73
Aubery du Maurier, Louis
  Mémoires 110
Augsburg (*see also* Lutheranism) 24
autocracy 59
Barclay, John 81–82
Bas, Diederick 3, 4
Batavi, Batavia, Batavian myth 73–75, 81
Baudartius, Willem 62
Baudius, Dominicus 8, 23, 73
Bayle, Pierre 23, 94, 109
Begriffsgeschichte, *see* Conceptual history
Belgium 81
Bentivoglio, Guido
  Della Guerra di Fiandra 86–88
Beroaldus, Philippus 21
Bestandstwisten, *see* Truce Conflicts
Bible, *see* Scripture
Bignon, Jean-Paul 97, 98
Bignon, Jérôme 23, 94, 97, 98, 109, 112
Bignon, Marie Anne Françoise 98
Bignon, Thierry 98
biographical epilogue 30, 60, 63, 65, 84, 391
Blaeu (publishing house) 93, 96, 98–101, 104, 119, 124, 369, 377
Boccalini, Trajano 38, 39
Boeckler, Johann Heinrich 94, 109
Bohemia 34
Boot, Johan Cornelis 101, 113, 116, 117, 123, 125
Bor, Pieter 26, 44, 83–87, 105, 106, 113
Boreel, Johan 7, 70
Botero, Giovanni 39
Brabant 59, 81, 108, 113, 121
Brandt, Caspar 93, 95, 98, 111
Brandt, Geeraert
  History of the Reformation 110, 111
Breda 35, 84
Breugel, Pieter 32
brevitas (*see also* style) 44–46, 56, 109
Britain, British, *see* England, Scotland
Bromsebrö, Treaty of 79
Burgundius, Nicolaus
  Historia Belgica 87, 107
Burmannus, Petrus II 111, 112, 116, 125
Caesar, Gaius Julius 106
Calais 43
Calvinism, Calvinist (*see also* Counter-Remonstrants, Reformed Church, Protestantism) 8, 11, 19, 24, 27, 30, 31, 58, 60, 62, 65, 69, 119
Carlos, Don (son of Philip II) 43, 64
Carlton, Dudley 81
Carneades 76
Carthage 63
Casaubonus, Isaac 5, 39, 93, 112
Catholicism, Catholic, Catholic Church, Vatican 10, 27, 58, 70, 86, 87, 102–104, 108, 109, 119, 120

Certamen Hoeufftianum 113
Chapelain, Jean 96, 106, 107, 109
Charles IX (King of France) 43, 63
China, Chinese 93
Christian IV (King of Denmark) 8
Christina (Queen of Sweden) 95, 100, 111
Cicero, Ciceronian 27, 36, 39, 71, 106
Clarendon, Earl of (Edward Hyde) 108
Coligny, Gaspar de 48
Cologne 30, 57
Conceptual history 35
Conestaggio, Ieronimo
Istoria delle guerre della Germania Inferiore 87
Conring, Hermann 107, 108
constitutionalism (*see also* Grotius, *De Antiquitate*) 75, 81, 120
Coornhert, Dirck Volkertszoon 5
Cornelissen, J.D.M. 102–103, 112–114
Counter-Remonstrants (*see also* Calvinism, Reformed Church, Protestantism) 12, 13, 18, 33, 78
De Keyser, Hendrick 62
De Laet, Johannes 78
De Thou, Jacques-Auguste 5, 27–29, 93, 113
Decker, Coenraat 105
Delaware 79
Delff, Willem 100
Delft 6, 7, 13, 14, 42, 59, 62, 92, 105
Délisle, Leopold 98, 99
Den Briel 24, 53
Denmark, Danish 8, 48
Denys, Jean-Baptiste 108
Deventer 67, 89, 100
Athenaeum Illustre 98
Domitius Afer 46
Dordt, Dordrecht 13, 42, 59
Dousa, Janus 1, 3, 14
dramatic structuring 49–56, 119
Droetto, Antonio 114
Dubois, Guillaume 97, 98
Dudley, Robert, *see* Leicester
Dupuys, Jean 87
Duym, Jacob 51
East India Company, *see* VOC
Egmond, Count of 58, 108
Elisabeth of Valois 43, 64
Elizabeth I (Queen of England) 24, 29, 30, 31, 32, 38, 40, 42, 44, 65–66, 86, 95
Engineering School, *see Nederduytsche Mathematique*
Ens, Caspar 51
England, English 5, 6, 13, 19, 30, 31, 43, 48, 51, 52, 54, 65–68, 85, 100, 105, 119, 121
Episcopius, Simon 9
Erasmus, Desiderius; Erasmian 11, 62
Essex, Robert Devereux Earl of 38
ethics 15
exemplarity 15, 26, 79, 118
Farnese, Alexander, *see* Parma, Duke of
Feddes, Pieter F. van Harlingen 32, 33, 401–403
Ferretus, Aemilius 38
finances 63–66, 89
Flanders, Flemish 3, 27, 81, 121
foreshadowing 49
France, French 15, 30, 43, 48, 54, 63, 68, 71, 85, 92, 94–96, 98, 100, 104, 119, 121
Francis of Valois, *see* Anjou
Free will, *see* Predestination
French Fury, *see* Antwerp
Friesland, Frisian 89
Fruin, Robert 80, 112, 113, 115
Fueter, Edward 114
Gamurini, Giuseppe 88
Gelre, Guelders, Guelderland 88, 89
Germany, German Empire, German Emperor 8, 30, 34, 42, 43, 64, 68, 75, 121
Ghent 84
Giustiniani, Pompeio
Bellum Belgicum 87–89, 397–399
Golette 63
Gomarus, Franciscus; Gomarist 9, 11, 13
Goris, Joan 105, 114
Gothic Myth, *see* Sweden
Gouda 42, 59
Gradić, Stefano 23, 103–104, 110, 377–384
Graswinckel, Dirk 108
Greenland 77
Greville, Fulke 38
Groenlo (Grol) 88
Gronovius, Johannes 98–100, 106–107
Groot, Cornelis de (son) 2, 99, 100, 409–413, 119
Groot, Cornelis de (uncle) 14
Groot, Jan de (father) 13, 37, 82, 91, 92
Groot, Pieter de (son) 2, 93, 98–100, 107, 409–413, 119

Groot, Willem de (brother) 87, 98
Grotius, works:
Adamus Exul 37, 51, 90
Apologus 72
Christus Patiens 51
De Antiquitate Reipublicae Batavicae 2, 7, 16, 73–75, 80, 81, 91, 95, 105, 117, 120
De Bello ob Libertatem Eligendo 70–72
De Imperio Summarum Potestatum 3, 19
De Iure Belli ac Pacis 16, 73–76, 79, 83, 109, 113, 120
De Iure Praedae 2, 4, 16, 17, 70, 73–76, 83, 85, 120, 124
De Mari Libero 4, 17, 19, 70, 74, 105
De Origine Gentium Americanarum 77–80
De Republica Emendanda 74
Grollae Obsidio 88, 105
Historia Gotthorum 73, 76–77
Meletius 17
Memorie van Oldenbarnevelt 71
Memorandum VOC 70
Observationes Iuridicae 70, 72
Ode pro Induciis 72
Onuitgegeven Nota 70
Ordinum Pietas 3, 4, 8, 18, 19, 29
Parallelon Rerumpublicarum 2, 73, 90, 91
Poemata Collecta 72
Remonstrance regarding .. the Jews (draft) 17
Syntagma Arateorum 37
Theses LVI 74
Theses XI 74
Tolerance Resolution (draft) 18
Gruterus, Janus 23
Guiccardini, Francesco 20
Gustavus II (King of Sweden) 95
Haarlem 42, 59
Habsburg 1, 2, 9, 40, 65, 71, 121
Hamburg 98
Hannibal 36
Haraeus, Franciscus 86, 87, 108
Harderwijk 14
Heidelberg 27
Heinsius, Daniel 14, 25, 38, 40, 42, 44, 51, 93, 94
Heinsius, Nicolas 96, 9, 100, 106–107, 111, 112
Hembyze, John of 24
Henry III (King of France) 43
Henry IV (King of France) 15
History, historian, historiography, *ars historica* 4, 6, 15, 25–29, 40, 63, 76, 79–80, 82, 83, 106–115, 117–119
Hoeufft, Jacob Hendrik 113
Hofman Peerlkamp, Petrus 101, 114, 116–117, 123, 125
Hohenlohe, Count 6, 46
Holland 2, 15, 17, 45, 63, 81, 82, 98, 113, 121
Hooft, Pieter Corneliszoon 4, 5, 12, 30, 39, 40, 87, 95, 106, 111–114
Hoogerbeets, Rombout 33
Hooghe, Romein de 105, 106
Hoorn 113
Horatius, Horace 48, 116
Horne, Count of 58, 108
Hotman, Jean H. de Villiers 27, 85
humanism 14, 15, 26, 27, 80, 100, 113, 115, 117, 120
Hyde, Edward, *see* Clarendon
Index, Vatican I. of forbidden books, *see Sancta Congregatio Indicis*
Isabella (Archduchess of the Southern Netherlands, *see also there*) 65, 68
Italy, Italian 87, 95, 111, 113, 114
iudicium 28, 32, 37, 40, 41, 56, 84, 107–113, 119, 120
James I (King of England and Scotland) 13, 67
Jena 22
Judaism, Jews 17, 18
Johannes (servant of Grotius family) 92
Johnson, Ben 51
Juan, Don 52, 59, 85
judgment, *see iudicium*
Julio-Claudian (emperors, period) 3, 49
Julius Vindex 61
Junius, Franciscus 14
Klönne, B.H. 88, 103
Knuyt, Johan de 68
late humanism 1, 14, 15, 61, 117, 120
Lassonius, Jacobus 14
Le Clerc, Jean 106, 110
Leicester, Robert Dudley earl of 24, 27, 34, 52, 54, 60, 65–67, 85, 120
Leiden, Leiden University 5, 7, 8, 11, 12, 14, 15, 18, 23, 37, 42, 45, 59, 71, 73, 88, 92, 96, 98, 114, 117, 367–369, 372–375
Law Faculty 7, 8, 14

Libertatis ergo or *Religionis ergo*-controversy 9, 12, 34, 58, 118
Lingelsheim, Georg 27, 28, 31, 35, 91
Lipsius, Justus 5, 14, 15, 22, 23, 36–38, 40, 42, 44, 47, 49, 55, 56, 69, 71, 72, 94, 102, 103, 108, 109, 118
literary criticsm 36–40, 56, 119
Livius, Livy 36, 106, 108
Loevestein Castle 11, 13
Loyens, Hubert
Synopsis 108
Lucretia 36
Lund UL 7, 83
Luther, Lutheranism 24
Luxemburg 81, 121
luxuria 53
Luyken, Jan 105, 106
Maastricht 30
Machiavelli, Niccolo; Machiavellism, Machiavellian 20, 21, 22, 24, 31–34, 39, 57, 61, 64, 66, 72, 73, 86, 119, 352
Madrid 104
Malacca 16
Manley, Thomas 105
Marius, Leonardus 88, 103
Mary Stuart 67
Maurice, Prince 3, 6, 10, 12, 13, 14, 34, 51, 52, 54, 62, 89, 95, 111, 114
Maximilian, German emperor 42
Medici, Cosimo de' 38
Meerman, Johan 73
Mellor, Ronald 40
Memory Culture, memory 9, 25, 34, 82, 118
Merula, Paullus 6, 7, 8, 85
Meursius, Johannes 8, 14, 62
Mexico 77
Middegaels, Matthaeus 108
Middelburg 7
Mierop 4, 91
Modena 45
Mokerhei 45
Monteverdi 51
Montigny, Count of 64, 116
Motley, John Lothrop 89, 113
Muller, H.C.A. 102, 114, 116, 125
narrative structure, n. technique, n. development 35–37, 40, 49–56, 67, 119, 120
Nassau (family, party) 43
Nassau, Justinus of 15
nationalism, *see* nationhood
nationhood 80–82, 121
natural law, naturalism (*see also* realism) 74, 79, 117, 120
Naudé, Gabriel
Bibliographie Politique 107
Nederduytsche Mathematique 14
Neo-Stoicism, Stoicism 56, 63
Nero 39, 51, 106
Nieuwpoort, battle of 3, 110
Nijmegen 88–89, 102–103, 108, 112, 115
Norway, Norwegian 77–79
novel 50
Nürnberg 105
obscurity 48
Oldenbarnevelt, *see* Van Oldenbarnevelt
opposition 10, 25
Orléans 14, 15
Overijssel 46, 88, 89
Pacheco, Don Pedro 110, 193
Pacification of Ghent 41, 52, 84
Paris 11, 77, 88, 92, 96, 98, 106, 107
Paris, *Bibliothèque Nationale* 96–99, 370–372
Parma, Duke of 52, 64, 67, 88, 120
Patin, Guy 34, 37, 94, 96–99, 107
patriotism 23
Pauw, Adriaen 17
peace negotiations
at Cologne 1579 30–31, 57, 86–87
of 1607–1609 8, 10, 67–72, 89, 111, 117, 121
other negotiations 6, 19, 67
Peregrinus, Laelius 102
peripeteia 51–53
Perizonius, Jacobus 110
Persia, Persian 93
Petilius, Marcus 102
Petition of Nobles 64
Philip II (King of Spain) 2, 23, 24, 30, 40, 42, 43, 45, 47, 48, 58, 62–66, 75, 84, 113, 120, 391–396
Philip III (King of Spain) 67
philology 22, 35, 51, 80, 113, 116–117
Plato 18
Plinius, Pliny 48
politique 32, 119, 387, 390
Polybius 39, 108, 111
polygenetism 78

Pope (*see also* Catholicism) 24, 44, 70
Poppaea 51
Portugal, Portuguese 4, 16, 67, 70, 74, 89, 93, 121
pre-emptive strike 76
predestination 9, 10, 11, 13, 93
Prinsgezind 12
Protestantism, Protestants (*see also* Reformed Church, Calvinism, Counter-Remonstrants) 53, 58, 64, 69, 86, 109, 119, 120
providence 50–56
prudentia (*see also iudicium*) 28, 37, 108
Puritan, Puritans 65–67
querelle des anciens et des modernes 78, 80
Quintilian 46–48
Ranke, Leopold von 80, 112
realism 22, 35, 54–56, 74, 79, 118, 120
realpolitik, *see* reason of state
reason of state 15, 20–25, 29–34, 35, 39, 42, 47, 50, 55, 56, 59, 63, 74, 76, 79, 86, 108, 113, 115, 118–120
Reformed Chruch (*see also* Calvinism, Counter-Remonstrants, Protestantism) 8, 10, 12
religious policy 8, 18, 29–34, 44, 47, 63, 64, 77, 66, 86, 103, 118, 119
Remonstrants, Remonstrantism, (*see also* Arminius) 9, 11, 16, 19, 33
Requesens, Louis de R. y Zuniga 41
Rijnberk 108–109
Rome, Romans, Roman (period, law, etc) 17, 18, 27, 36, 73, 75
Romswinckel, M. 112
Rospigliosi, Giacomo 108
Rotterdam 11, 18
Sallustius, Sallust 50, 108, 110
Sancta Congregatio Indicis 102–104, 109, 114, 119, 377–390
Santa Catarina (ship) 4, 16, 74
Sarravius, Claudius 96, 97
Savile, Henry 61
Scaliger, Joseph 14, 15
scepticism, skeptical 15, 20–22, 73, 75, 79, 115, 118, 120
Schenkenschans 89, 356
Scherpe Resolutie 13
Schoppius, Gaspar
Paedia Politices 107
schuilkerken 13
Scotland, Scottish 30
Scripture, Bible 25, 66, 74, 77–79
Scriverius, Petrus 7, 80
Sea-Beggars (*Watergeuzen*) 24, 53
secularisation, secularism 9, 11, 15, 17, 22, 25, 55, 79, 114, 117
Selim II (Ottoman ruler) 63
Seneca 51
sententiae 21, 35, 37, 40, 46–47, 49, 56, 118, 405–407
's Hertogenbosch 87
Sluis 67
Snellius, Willebrord 18
sociability 72, 76
Socinus, Faustus; Socinianism, Socinian 13
Sorø 8
South-America 77–79
Southern Netherlands 9, 67–72, 80–82, 108
Southland 77–79
sovereignty 10
Sozzini, Fausto, *see* Socinus
Spain, Spanish 3, 9, 23, 24, 30, 33, 40, 41, 43, 45, 54, 60–65, 67–70, 74, 81, 86–89, 95, 100, 114, 118, 121
Spinola, Ambrogio 68, 88
Spinola, Federico 89, 397–399
Spon, Charles 96, 98, 107
Springer, Leendert 116
Staatsgezind 11–13, 25, 27, 29, 33, 34, 55, 56, 62, 118
Stadtholderless era 100
Stanley, William 67
States of Holland and West-Friesland 1–4, 6, 8, 9, 13, 17, 18, 19, 25, 29, 31–33, 42, 47, 52, 65–67, 75, 90, 92, 95, 100, 107, 117–119
States-General, Generalty, United Provinces 2, 3, 6, 7, 8, 25, 33, 64, 75, 85, 106, 107, 118
Statesman-historian, *see* history
Steenwijk 81
Steinfurt, Burg 13
Stevin, Simon 12, 14, 29
Stoicism, *see* Neo-Stoicism
Strada, Famiano
De Bello Belgico 86–88, 107, 113
Strait Magelhaes, Magellanica 77–79
style 20–25, 34 sqq, 56, 100, 106–115, 117, 119, 120
Sweden, Swedish 48, 76–77, 79, 95, 107

Synod of Dordt 13, 78, 81
Synod, others 6
Tacitus, Tacitism, Tacitist, Tacitean 1, 3, 5, 20–25, 26, 28, 29, 31–34, 34–57, 63, 75, 87, 94, 95, 97, 100, 104–119
Ten Grotenhuys, Jan 16, 91–93
Terranova, Duke of 30
The Hague 7, 8, 13, 16, 27, 70, 97
Thucydides 111
Tiberius 39, 43, 106, 111
Tidore 93
Tilburg UL 112
Toffanin, Giuseppe 34, 114
toleration 17, 18
tragedy 49–56
Trent, Council of 48
Truce Conflicts (*see also* Twelve Years' Truce) 3, 8, 9, 10, 17, 29, 32, 55, 62, 65, 68, 94, 110, 115
Truce period, *see* Twelve Years' Truce
Tunis 63
Turfschip van Breda 84
Turkey, Turks 54
Tuscany 38
Twelve Years' Truce (*see also* Truce Conflicts) 9, 10, 16, 25, 32, 34, 54, 67–72, 93, 115, 117, 121
Ughello, Ferdinando 104
Union of Utrecht, *see* Utrecht
United Provinces, *see* States-General
Utrecht 66, 81, 84, 86
Uytteneng, Geertruyd 14
Vailliant, Andries 105
Van Albada, Aggaeus
  Acten van den Vredehandel geschiet te Colen 86
Van Asperen, Paulus 3, 4
Van Cattenburg, Adriaan 93, 95, 97, 98, 111
Van den Vondel, Joost 12, 87
Van der Haer, Florentius
  De Initiis Tumultuum Belgicorum 87
Van der Linden, J. Antonides 107
Van der Myle, Cornelis 85
Van der Wenne, A. 105
Van Eysinga, Willem 70, 71
Van Kerckhoven, Johannes Polyander 9, 13
Van Leedenberg, Gilles 33
Van Meerbeeck, Adriaan
  Chronycke van de gantsche wereld 86
Van Meteren, Emanuel 6, 7, 26, 45, 83, 84, 86–88, 113, 391–396
Van Mierevelt, Michiel 105
Van Mieris, Frans 111
Van Moersbergen, Adolph 33
Van Oldenbarnevelt, Johan 3, 11, 13, 15, 16, 29, 32–34, 54, 68–72, 92, 117–121, 402–404
Van Papenbroeck, Gerard 97–99
Van Reigersberch, Maria (wife) 96–98
Van Reigersberch, Nicolas 92
Van Reyd, Everhard 26, 83
Vatican Library 103
Vatican, *see* Catholicism
Vennecool, Jacobus (printer) 6
Verbond der Edelen, see Petition of Nobles
Verthamon, François-Michel de 98, 99
Vlacq, Adriaan 96–99
VOC (*see also* Asian trade) 4, 16, 68–70, 85, 121
Voetius, Gisbertus 108
Vorstius, Conradus 9, 13
Vossius, Gerardus Johannes 31, 38, 40, 44, 47
Vulcanius, Bonaventura 14, 55
Waardgelders 13
Wagenaar, Jan 111
Wallonia, Walloon 81, 121
Watergeuzen, see Sea-beggars
Werteloo, Georgius Benedicti 51
West India Company (WIC) 78
West-Phalia, peace of 68
William of Orange 3, 8, 12, 24, 29, 30–32, 40–42, 51–53, 55, 57–64, 84, 86, 88, 106, 113, 118, 120
  written works: *Apology* 43, 59, 84, 342, 345, 351, 358
    Waerschowinghe 84, 345
Wilson, Thomas 39
Wtenbogaert, Johannes 7, 16, 33, 102
York, Roland 67
Yucatan 77
Zeeland 67, 81, 121
Zutphen 67
Zwingli

INDEX OF NAMES TO THE TRANSLATION AND NOTES

Aalst 217, 265, 279, 363
Aarschot, Charles of (*see also* Chimay *and* Croy) 125, 171, 275, 277
Aarschot, Philip of (*see also* Croy) 125, 30, 59, 223, 241, 249, 277
Adriaan Florenszoon, pope Hadrian IV 137
Africa, African 217, 249
Aldegonde, Marnix of St. 209, 297, 299, 349
Alkmaar 203, 205, 207
Allen, Cardinal 315, 357
Alps 177
Alva, Fernando Alvares de Toledo, duke of 151, 159, 167, 173, 177, 179, 181, 183, 187, 189, 191, 193, 195, 201, 203, 205, 209, 217, 235, 249, 307, 337, 340, 342, 343, 345, 346, 348
America, American 137, 139, 173, 191, 211, 297, 319
Amphictyonian League 331
Amsterdam 173, 201, 205, 229, 337, 343, 345, 352, 355, 356, 357
Anabaptists 165, 359
Angles 199
Anglican faith 321
Anjou, Francis of Valois, duke of 226, 229, 231, 237, 239, 257, 259, 263, 265, 267, 269, 271, 273, 293, 301, 319, 327, 348-352
Anna of Egmond 285, 353
Anna of Saxony 285, 353
Anthony of Portugal 249
Antiquity 131, 133, 137, 149, 159, 179, 187, 191-195, 199, 249, 265, 277, 311, 313, 331, 335, 337, 339
Antwerp 149, 153, 155, 169, 184, 187, 209, 211, 217, 219, 243, 245, 261-269, 273, 279, 281, 287, 291, 295, 297, 298, 343, 347, 348, 351-357
Aquitania 201
Aremberg 171, 177, 181
army (of the Republic) 5.63-5.66
Arnemuiden 325
Arnhem 325, 353, 356
Arras 151, 155, 159, 239, 247, 249, 265, 340, 350
Artevelde 233, 350
Artois 137, 143, 169, 219, 235-241, 325, 340-342
Asia 145
Atlantic Ocean 137, 191, 251
Augsburg (Diet of, peace of) 165, 343, 347
Augsburg confession (*see also* Luther) 165, 173, 343
Austria see Habsburg
Axel 279, 309
Baligny, Jean de Monluc, lord of 327, 358
Batavians 199, 339, 343
Baudouin, François 159, 342, 347
Bavaria, Bavarian 201, 321
Bavaria, Ernest of 275, 309, 327, 352, 358
Bayonne 159, 342
Bergen [op Zoom], John IV of Glymes, Marquis of 163, 171, 179, 343
Bergen op Zoom 325
Berlaymont, Charles of 153, 171, 340, 341, 348
Betuwe 309, 346, 356
Bible, Scripture 145, 277, 313, 342
Binche 237
Biron, Armand de Gontaut, seigneur de Biron 271, 273, 352
Bodin, Jean 271, 357
Bommelerwaard 201
Bommenee 215
Bonge see Bouge
Bonn 321
Bordeaux, treaty of 263, 352
Bosch, den 155, 243, 297, 317, 343
Bossu, Maximilian de Henin, count of 173, 191, 193, 205, 235, 344
Bouge, Bonge 235, 350
Bourbon, Charlotte de 285, 352, 353
Brabant 143, 155, 159, 177, 181, 199, 205, 209, 215-219, 223, 225, 245, 253, 263, 269, 271, 279, 281, 289, 291, 295, 297, 307, 317, 325, 333, 339, 342, 345
Breda 209, 219, 251, 356
Brederode, Henry of 161, 173, 343
Britain, British (*see also* England, Scotland) 145, 161, 191, 225, 273, 293, 301, 307, 315, 321, 331,
Bruges 155, 245, 269, 275, 279, 342, 353, 356

Brugse Vrije 279
Brunswick, Erik of 171
Brussels 161, 179, 189, 217, 219, 245, 265, 289, 297, 342, 347, 348, 356
Bucholt, John 145, 349
Buckhurst, Thomas Sackville, Lord 319, 357
Buren, *see* Anna of Egmond
burgomasters 327
Burgundy, Burgundian, House of Burgundy 133, 154, 157, 177, 187, 201, 263, 285, 289, 327, 339
Burgundy, Mary of 181, 339
Byzantium 145
Cadzand 317
Calais 201, 215
Calvin, Calvinism 165, 343-350, 352, 353 (*for more reff. see index to intr.*)
Cambrai (Camerick) 153, 229, 259, 260, 327, 341, 343, 358
Capet 293
Carlos, Don, son of Philip II 173, 179, 345
Casimir of the Palatinate 229, 231, 235-239, 275, 277
Caspar de Robles 219, 348
Cassander, Georg 159, 342
Castile, Castilian 137, 249, 251
Cateau-Cambrésis, peace of 159
Catholicism, Catholic; Roman church, religion etc. (*see also* Vatican, Pope) 137, 145, 147, 149, 152, 155-161, 165, 169, 173, 179, 181, 183, 189, 201, 203, 225, 229-235, 239, 241-247, 253, 263, 267-271, 275-279, 293, 297, 313, 315, 323, 335, 339-342, 344, 346, 347, 349, 352, 353, 355-357
Cavendish 319
Channel 131
Champagny, governor of Antwerp (*see also* Granvelle) 223, 289, 347
Charlemagne 293
Charles IX, king of France 159, 177, 191, 195, 215, 342, 391
Charles the Bold 309
Charles V 137, 139, 143, 147-151, 155, 165, 181, 191, 199, 203, 221, 233, 259, 275, 277, 301, 339-341, 343
Chatti 199
Chièvres (*see also* William II of Croy) 137, 339
Chimay, *see* Charles of Croy
Christianity, Christian, Christ 133, 137, 143-149, 187, 217, 257, 277, 341-342
Christina, wife of Francis of Lorraine 151
Christoph of the Palatinate 209
Claudius Civilis 199
Cleves 183, 327, 356
Coligny, Caspar de 191, 195
Coligny, Louise de 285, 353
Cologne 153, 241, 245, 249, 275, 309, 323, 327, 341, 342, 349, 350, 352, 358
Council of Brabant 159, 342
Council of State 139, 151, 153, 157, 161, 163, 177, 215-219, 223, 225, 247, 263, 271, 293, 301, 311, 315, 331, 333, 340, 342-4, 348, 356
Cracau (castle in Krefeld, Germany) 309
Crevecoeur 317, 357
Croy, Charles of (*see also* Aarschot, Charles of) 125, 275, 277, 353, 386
Croy, Philip of (*see also* Aarschot, Philip of) 125, 171, 344
Croy, William II of 137, 339
Croy, William of 137
Croy 137, 340
Culemborg, Floris of Pallandt, count of 161, 342, 343
Curzolari, *see* Echinades
Damme 279
David of Delft 145
De Hooghe 275
De la Motte 241
Delft 145, 201, 281, 358
Den Briel 185, 191, 211, 301, 344
Dendermonde 169, 269, 279, 289, 353
Denmark, Danish 161, 201, 257, 321, 357
Deventer 155, 231, 309, 315, 317, 325, 357
Diet of Worms 147, 340
Dijle, river 269
Diksmuide 269, 273
Djerba 153, 341
Doesburg 297, 309
Dordrecht 1923, 201
Douai 241, 342, 347
Drake, Francis 319
Dunkirk 269, 271, 273
East-Friesland 327, 358
Echinades 209, 346
Edam 203
Ems, river 131, 183, 199, 243, 327

Egmond, Anne of Egmond of Buren 285, 353
Egmond, Charles of 245
Egmond, Lamoraal count of 143, 151, 153, 157, 159, 169, 171, 173, 177, 241, 251, 340, 342, 343, 345, 356
Egypt 145
Elisabeth of Valois 159, 179, 189
Elizabeth I, Queen of England 189, 225, 231, 237, 259, 263, 291, 295, 297, 301, 315-325, 345, 346, 349, 352, 355-357
England, English (*see also* Britain, British) 165, 175, 189, 193, 211, 215, 225, 231, 237, 239, 251, 255, 257, 263, 279, 291, 293, 297, 307, 315, 319-325, 340, 350, 353, 356-358
Enkhuizen 203, 356
Entes, Bartold 253
Escobedo, Juan de 239, 350
Espinoy, prince of 259
Essex 301, 355
Europe 145, 339, 345, 362, 386
Farnese, Alexander, *see* Parma
Farnese, Ottavio 151, 341
Ferdinand I, Emperor of the Holy Roman Empire 173,
Feria, Gomez Figueroa, count of 151
Filips Willem (son of William of Oranje) 179, 249, 285, 345, 350
Flanders, Flemish 137, 143, 155, 171, 199, 217, 219, 223, 233, 237-241, 245, 251, 259, 263-269, 273, 275-281, 289, 297, 309, 317, 323, 325, 340, 341, 344, 347-350, 353
Florida 191, 211
Flushing, *see* Vlissingen
France, French, 133-139, 143, 145, 151, 159, 161, 165, 171, 173, 177, 183, 189, 191-195, 201, 203, 211, 215, 217, 223, 225, 229, 235-241, 255-277, 285, 289, 291-295, 301, 305, 319, 321, 327, 331, 333, 339, 340-342, 345-350, 352, 353, 357, 358
Franks 133, 199
Frederick Henry 285, 356
Friesland 165, 181, 191-195, 199, 205, 211, 231, 243, 253, 285, 313, 315, 325, 327, 331, 346, 348, 349, 352, 353, 358
Galicia, Galician 153
Gallia Belgica 153
Gaul 191, 199, 339, 356
Gecommitteerde Raden 329, 358
Geertruidenberg 205, 325
Geldern 317, 325, 357
Gelre, Gelderland, *see* Guelders
Gembloux 225, 235, 350, 356
Geneva 165, 203, 342
Genlis 195
Genova, Genovese 189, 348
Gerards, Balthasar 280
Germany, German 133, 137, 143-151, 161-165, 169-175, 181, 183, 195, 201, 203, 211, 217, 221-225, 229, 231, 241, 247, 249, 255, 259, 267, 275, 277, 285, 289, 305, 311, 321, 339, 342, 343, 356, 358
Germania Inferior 153, 183
Germania (ancient) 199, 331
Geronimo de Roda 217, 221, 348
Ghent 155, 171, 219, 223, 225, 229, 233-241, 245, 247, 259, 273-279, 289, 323, 325, 344, 348-350, 353, 354
Goes 285
Golden Fleece (order of the) 135, 153, 177, 297
Gorinchem 203
Goths, Gothic 137
Gouda 201
governess, *see* Margareth of Parma
Granada 209
Granvelle, Antoine Perrenot de 151, 157, 209, 257, 340, 343, 347, 354
Granvelle, Frédéric Perrenot de, Lord of Champagny 209
Granvelle, Nicolaus of 151, 340
Grave 303, 307, 309
Gravelines, *see* Grevelingen
Gravenwaard, *see* 's Gravenwaard
Greece, Greek (*see also* Achaea) 143, 249, 331, 346, 347
Grevelingen 143, 241, 350
Groningen 155, 231, 253, 325, 341, 349-353, 356, 358
Guelders, Gelre, Gelderland 153, 155, 171, 193, 199, 201, 205, 231, 235, 243, 265, 275, 297, 309, 317, 325, 331, 343, 353,
Guise, de 183, 195, 345
Haarlem 155, 197, 201, 205, 229, 347
Habsburg 135, 143, 155, 181, 201, 213, 221, 239, 275, 339-347, 352
Hadrian IV, pope, *see* Adriaan Florenszoon
Hague, the 331, 353, 357, 358

Hainaut 169, 171, 195, 201, 219, 235, 237, 241, 251, 325, 341, 343, 350
Hautepenne 251, 317, 357
Heerenberg, *see* 's Heerenberg
Hembyze, Jan of 233, 239, 275, 277, 279, 309, 349, 353
Hemert 309
Henry II, King of France 159, 342, 345, 349
Henry III, King of France 215, 225, 255, 263, 267, 271, 273, 291, 293, 327
Henry of Portugal 249
Hesdin 153
Hessen, Philip the Magnanimous, landgrave of 151, 341
Hohenlohe, Philip of Hohenlohe-Neuenstein 6, 46, 253, 285, 286, 297, 307, 309, 317, 350, 351, 356
Holland, Hollanders 143, 145, 155, 161, 181, 189, 191-195, 199, 201, 205, 209, 211, 215-221, 229, 233, 235, 243, 247, 263, 275, 281, 285, 289, 295, 297, 307, 311, 313, 317, 325, 329, 331, 337, 339, 344-347, 350, 351, 355, 356, 358
Holy Roman Emperor (*see also* Germany) 133, 137, 145, 181, 201, 221, 223, 225, 235, 241, 245, 257, 259
Hoogstraten, *see* Lalaing
Hoorn 203
Hoppers, Joachim 215, 347
Horne, Montmorency count of 143, 153, 161, 163, 169, 171, 177179, 241, 340, 342, 343, 352
Hulst 279, 281
Hungary 149, 340, 341
Iconoclastic Fury 165-169
Ieper, *see* Ypres
IJssel, river 195, 199, 275, 309
Ingelmunster 350
Inquisition, Inquisitors 147, 149, 157, 159, 161, 163, 187, 203, 205, 209, 337, 340-342, 346
insurance 215
Ireland, Irish 291, 319
Italy, Italian, Italic 247, 265, 281, 339, 340, 341, 346, 355, 357
Jesuits 233, 337
Jews 143, 159, 165
John II, count of Brabant 181
John of Nassau 231, 285
Joyous Entry of Brabant ('Brabant's law') 339, 345, 351, 353
Juan, Don 221-225, 229-239, 323, 325, 343, 344, 348, 350, 352-354
Jülich 327
Kallo 295
Kampen 231
Kauwenstein 295, 353
Kleve, *see* Cleves
Kortrijk 251
Krimpen 211
Lalaing, Philippe, count of 223, 235, 237, 341, 350
Lalaing, Antoine de, count of Hoogstraten 153, 341
Lalaing, George de, *see* Rennenberg
Lauwerszee 243, 331
League of Nobles 161-171, 342
Leerdam 285
Leeuwarden 231, 289
Leicester, Robert Dudley, Earl of 301, 302, 305-319, 325-329, 333, 350, 352, 353, 355-358
Leiden 145, 199, 201, 211, 212, 285, 319, 339, 340, 342, 349, 353, 354, 357, 358
Lek, river 199, 211
Lepanto, battle of (Echinades) 209, 221, 346, 348
Liège 153, 155, 183, 245, 327, 341, 358
Lier 265
Liguria, Ligurian 173
Lille 241
Lillo 281, 289, 353
Limburg 225, 325
Lochem 265
Lorraine 151, 239, 293, 327, 345
Lorraine, Francis of 151, 345
Louvain 149, 179, 225, 347
Lumey, Willem, count of Marck, 191, 201, 253
Luther, Lutheran, Lutheranism (*see also* Augsburg) 143, 147, 165, 173, 335, 339, 342, 343, 345, 347
Luxemburg 169, 171, 177, 219, 221, 225, 325
Maastricht 219, 241, 245, 247
Marche (Marche-en-Famenne, Luxemburg) 221, 348
Maria, daughter of Willem of Orange 285, 350, 351

Mary Queen of Scots 293
Mathias, archduke of Austria 213, 223, 231, 233, 237, 245, 247, 257, 348, 354
Maximilian I, Emperor of the Holy Roman Empire 181
Maximilian II, Emperor of the Holy Roman Empire 173, 183, 223, 247, 348
Mechelen 135, 153, 155, 195, 235, 247, 251, 297, 325, 340, 341, 347, 349
Medemblik 203, 325, 356,
Meden 331
Medici, Alessandro de' 151
Medici, Catharine de' 159, 267, 327, 352
Medina Coeli, Juan de la Cerda, Duke of 193
Meenen 237
Megemus, stadtholder of Guelders 171
Melendez, Pedro 211
Melun, Robert de 235, 350
Moers 275, 309, 352
Meuse, river (Maas) 179, 183, 191, 199, 201, 203, 211, 231, 307, 309, 327, 346, 350
Middelburg 155, 201, 209, 285
Milan 173, 221
Modena 211, 347
Moluccas 319
Monnikendam 203
Mons (Dutch: *Bergen*): 195, 229, 237, 325
Montigny, Emmanuel-Filibert of Lalaing, Baron of 237-241, 277
Montigny, Floris of Montmorency, baron of 123, 125, 179, 163
Montigny, Johannes of, *see* Floris of Montigny
Montpensier 257
Münster 145, 153, 349, 358
Muslims 147
Naarden 195, 205
Namur 155, 221, 235, 251, 325, 350, 353
Nassau, Adolf of
Nassau, party, house of etc. (*see also* William of Orange) 143, 173, 183, 193, 203, 205, 215, 219, 229, 233, 253
Nassau, Henry of 209
Nassau, John of 231, 351, 353
Nassau, Louis of 161, 181, 195, 209
Nassau, William Louis of 285, 353
Navarre 191, 195, 229, 293, 340, 350
Nederwormter 193
Nervi 265
Neuenahr, Adolf of, count of Moers, 275, 309, 352
Neuenahr, Walburgis von Neuenahr-Moers 161, 342
Neuss 309
Nienhove 245, 251
Nijmegen 209, 297, 325, 356
Noircarmes 171, 349
Normans 133, 137
Norris, Sir John 253, 351
Noue, François de la ('La Noue') 235, 241, 251, 281, 350, 353
Oldenbarnevelt, Johan van 329, 338, 353, 358
Ommelanden 349
Oordam 295
Oostergo 289
Orange, William of books 1-4 *passim*; 301, 305, 313, 319, 325, 327, 340, 342-345, 347-353, 356, 358
Orange, principality 143, 157
Orchies 241
Osnabrück 153
Ostend 289, 317, 325, 358
Ottoman Empire (Turks, Turkish) 139, 153, 159, 189, 217, 221, 339-341, 346, 348
Oudenaarde 265
Oudewater 211
Overijssel 155, 193, 199, 231, 253, 325, 331, 349, 352, 353
Pacheco, Don Pedro 110, 193
Pacification of Gent 219-223, 229, 235, 241, 247, 259, 323, 325, 344, 347-350
Paderborn 153
Palatinate 203, 209, 229, 349
Parma, Alexander Farnese, Duke of 225, 227, 239, 241-247, 251, 253, 259, 265, 269, 271-281, 289, 291, 295, 297, 307, 309, 317, 321-327, 337, 340, 341, 343, 349, 353, 354, 355, 356
Parma, Margaret of Austria, Duchess of 141, 151, 153, 157, 161, 163, 169, 173, 177, 225, 340
Paul IV, pope 152
Pavia, battle of 137
Peter of Mansfeld, stadtholder of Luxemburg 171, 348
Philip II, king of Spain, Count of Holland etc 139, 149-159, 165, 169, 173, 177, 181, 183,

189, 195, 201–205, 209, 217, 221, 225, 239–243, 247–251, 255, 257, 265, 267, 275, 277, 293, 295, 321, 323, 327, 340–353, 355–357
Philip the Fair 339
Philip William, *see* Filips Willem
Philippeville 225
Piacenza 295, 341
Pole, Polish 231
pope, papal 137, 147–155, 159, 163, 165, 173, 187, 221, 257, 293, 323, 339–341
Portugal, Portuguese, 205, 219, 225, 249, 251, 257, 267, 345, 352
Purmerend 203
Raad van State, *see* Council of State
Rammekens, *see* Zeeburg
Rantzau, Gaius 321, 357, 358
Reims 153, 341
Reingout, Jacques 307, 311, 356
Rennenberg, George de Lalaing, count of 231, 253, 349, 351, 352
Requesens, Don Louis de Requesens y Zúñiga 206, 209, 211, 215, 217, 307, 323, 346, 348
Rhine, river 131, 179, 183, 191, 199, 253, 275, 307, 309, 321, 327, 349, 356
Richardot 289, 354
Rijmenam 235
Rochelle, La 191, 352
Roermond 155
Romans, Rome, Roman Empire, law, etc. 131, 133, 199, 248, 321, 330, 339–341, 347, 355
Roman as in 'Catholic', *see* Catholicism
Rotterdam 193, 203, 346, 358
Rudolph II, Holy Roman Emperor 223, 348
Rupel, river 279
Rupelmonde 279
Russell 325
Ryhove, François of de Kethulle, lord of 279, 349, 353
Sardinia 173
Savoy 177, 193
Saxony, Anna of 161, 257, 285, 342, 347, 353
Saxony, August Elector of 173
Saxony, Maurice, Elector of 285, 341
Scheldt, river 199, 215, 256, 279, 281, 289, 295, 355
Schenck, Martin Schenck van Nydeck 253, 309, 321, 356
schepenen 327, 352
Schiedam 203
Schmalkaldian League 203, 341
Schoonhoven 203
Scotland, Scots, Scottish 189, 225, 267, 293, 301, 315, 319, 346, 349, 351
Schouwen 215
Schouwenburg 193
Schwarzburg 347
Scripture, *see* Bible
Sebastian of Portugal 225, 249
Selles, Jan of Noircarmes of St-Aldegonde, baron of 225, 250, 251, 349
's Gravenwaard 89, 309
's Heerenberg, Willem count of 193, 275
's Hertogenbosch, *see* Bosch, den
Sicily 173
Sidney, Philip 309, 356
Sinne, river 289
slavery 137, 231, 237, 245, 247
Slavs, Slavonic 199
Sluis 289
Sonoy, Diederik 313, 325, 356
Sont, estuary 357
Spa 229
Spain, Spanish 131, 135–139, 143, 147, 151, 157–163, 171, 173, 177, 179–183, 187, 189–195, 203, 205, 209, 211, 215–225, 231–245, 249–257, 263–281, 285, 291, 293, 295, 297, 301, 307, 317–323, 327, 333, 335, 339, 340–343, 345, 347–349, 352, 354–356, 358
Spartans 311
St Isidore 159
St Omar 155
St Quentin 143
St Winoksbergen 273
stadtholder, stadtholderate 143, 169, 171, 173, 177, 191, 193, 215, 219, 223, 241–247, 253, 263, 265, 285, 289, 293, 311, 317, 327–333, 340, 343, 344, 348–350, 352. 353
Stanley, William 317, 357
States (provincial States, States-General) 133, 135, 139, 151, 155, 161–165, 169, 181, 193, 201, 209, 211, 217, 223, 225, 231–235, 243, 247, 253–257, 263, 267, 279, 285, 289, 293, 305–319, 325, 329, 331, 335, 339, 344, 348–353, 356–358

Steelandt, Servaes of 279, 353
Steenwijk 253, 265, 325
Stuart, Mary, Queen of Scots (2.23) 189, 225, 293, 301, 315, 346, 349
Sweden, Swedish 161, 257
Switzerland, Swiss 165, 177, 229, 269
Taxis 274, 315
Téligny, Odet de la Noue, lord of 281, 353
Tenth Penny 187, 189, 205, 209, 217, 343, 346
Terneuzen 309
Terranova, duke of 241, 245
Terwaan 341
Tholen 285
Tournai 155, 259, 351
Trent, Council of 159, 187, 189, 359
Truchsess, Gebhard Truchsess von Waldburg 275, 277, 309, 349, 352
Truel 153
Tudor, Mary 301, 345, 355
Tunis 217, 239
Turks, *see* Ottoman Empire
Tyrrhenian Sea 137
Union of Utrecht 243, 253, 343,
Union of Atrecht (Arras) 247, 249, 265, 349, 350
United Provinces (States-General, Republic, Union) 245, 247, 251, 262, 281, 285, 309, 311, 317, 325, 327, 331, 333
Utrecht 211, 229, 243, 253, 313, 315, 331, 339, 341, 343, 344, 350, 353, 356
Valdes, Francisco de, 211
Valenciennes 171, 195, 247, 343
Valois, Elisabeth of, *see* Elisabeth of Valois
Valois, Francis of, *see* Anjou
Valois, Margaret of 191, 229
Veere 285, 325
Venice 229, 340, 348
Venlo 309
Verbond der Edelen, *see* League of Nobles
Verdugo 253, 265, 285, 351, 352, 354
Vespasian 199
Veurne 273
Viglius van Aytta 153, 159, 169, 171, 340, 341, 343, 347
Villiers, Pierre de 257, 351
Vilvoorde 269, 289
Vlie, estuary 199
Vlissingen 193, 285, 301
Voorne 191
vroedschap (town council) 243, 291, 311, 327, 329, 358
Waal, river 199, 201, 356
Waasland, Land of Waas 279, 281, 353
Walcheren 301, 325
Wallonia, Walloon 171, 241, 247
Warni 199
West-Friesland 191, 199, 205, 211, 313, 346, 358
Westergo 289
Wiclef 144
Willemstad 325
William Louis, *see* Nassau
York, Roland 309, 315, 317
Ypres 155, 245, 275, 277, 279, 353
Zeeburg 301, 355, 356
Zeeland, Zeelanders 143, 155, 173, 193, 195, 199, 201, 205, 215, 219, 233, 243, 247, 263, 273, 279, 281, 285, 295, 297, 317, 325, 331, 344, 346, 350, 351, 355, 358
Zevenwolden 289
Zierikzee 215, 285
Zuid-Beveland 279
Zuiderzee 325, 331, 344, 346, 350
Zutphen 195, 265, 275, 281, 309, 315, 325, 341, 356, 357, 364,
Zwingli 165